MW00805920

Benjamin Harrison · *Hoosier Statesman*

Benjamin Harrison

Hoosier Statesman

By

HARRY J. SIEVERS

Published by American Political Biography Press

Newtown, CT

Reprinted with the permission of the
Arthur Jordan Foundation

Published by
AMERICAN POLITICAL BIOGRAPHY PRESS

Library of Congress Catalog Card Number 96-78888
ISBN Number 978-0-945707-17-2

The Special Contents of this Edition
are Copyright © 1996, 2007, and 2018

by

AMERICAN POLITICAL BIOGRAPHY PRESS
39 Boggs Hill
Newtown, Connecticut
06470-1971
Tel: (203) 270-9777 ✧
E-Mail: APBPress@EarthLink.Net

WWW.APBPRESS.COM

This is the third printing of the first edition.

All publications of
AMERICAN POLITICAL BIOGRAPHY PRESS
Are dedicated to my wife
Ellen and our two children
Katherine and William II

This particular book is
Dedicated to:

Robinson Risner 09/16/65
James N Rowe 10/29/63
Robert Harper Shumaker 02/11/65

And all the others.

Acknowledgments

BIOGRAPHERS need and use the helping hands of hundreds who render the toil of research and writing an incomparably pleasant experience. Only in their prefaces can authors attempt the impossible task of adequately acknowledging the myriad obligations thus incurred.

The preface to the first volume of this series, *Benjamin Harrison: Hoosier Warrior,* catalogued my indebtedness between 1949 and 1952. In presenting this second volume, *Hoosier Statesman,* I feel impelled to discharge another salvo of thanks to those same friends and colleagues who have continued their interest and support during the past six years. To relist their names is unnecessary; each knows his contribution, and each has my gratitude.

The marked courtesy of James Blaine Walker and of his son and daughter, Benjamin Harrison Walker and Dr. Jane Harrison Walker, grandchildren of the former President, has served me well. They permitted me to examine numerous family papers which have given perspective to the Harrison story. Similar cooperation by the President's two other grandchildren, Marthena Harrison Williams and former Congressman William Henry Harrison, enabled me to interpret the papers of Russell B. Harrison, the President's only son. This collection, salvaged by the Vigo County Historical Society of Terre Haute, Indiana, proved a rich mine of information. To the alert members of this Society I publicly acknowledge my gratitude.

My warmest thanks go to Mrs. Clarence W. Messinger of Houghton, Michigan, for putting at my disposal innumerable personal letters which Harrison had sent her grandmother, Margaret Shelby Peltz. Addressed to his "Cousin Mag" and handwritten by the Hoosier statesman, these letters were a biographer's boon.

ACKNOWLEDGMENTS

In these recent years, the courteous cooperation extended to me at the Library of Congress has continued undiminished. To John de Porry, Division of Manuscripts, and to Milton Kaplan, Photographs and Prints Division, I owe sizeable debts for assistance and advice. Also in Washington, at the Riggs Library of Georgetown University, Peter J. Laux, Chief of Public Services, Joseph E. Jeffs, Associate Librarian, and Carol Evans, Reference Librarian, have rendered me invaluable service.

The New York State Library at Albany and the libraries of Princeton University and The Catholic University of America in Washington have also extended courtesies beyond the call of duty.

In the Empire State, new helping hands took up the Harrison cause: A. B. Carlson, Director of the Map and Print Room of the New York Historical Society; Amy LaFollette Jensen, and Howard C. Jensen, art editor; Mildred Bellah, Charles McAdam, and Frank Jay Markey of the McNaught Syndicate; Sister Mary Lucille, G.N.S.H.: Freeman Cleaves of the *Financial World;* and Eleanor Sherman Fitch. Neighboring Connecticut yielded two firm allies and friends in the field of authorship: Leonard M. Fanning and Charles O'Neill. The latter, with his charming wife, Connie O'Neill, offered me not only hospitality but also an introduction to the rich resources of the Pequot Library, whose genial staff aided me considerably. Among the gallant folk in the Garden State, I thank most sincerely the Reverend Thomas T. Barry and Eileen Butler for support and friendship at every bend in both the Parkway and Turnpike.

Northern New York is the home of Bellarmine College, where Jesuit faculty colleagues and young Jesuit students have supported my efforts in ways too numerous to mention. The Reverend William J. Gleason, S.J., President of Bellarmine, has consistently shown a spirit of accommodation, interest, and encouragement. Acknowledgments to him, the staff (including our once portly librarian), and all other confreres of the cloth, would take this listing far beyond its limits. Let it simply be known that they are warmly appreciated.

Since Georgetown University has been a second home for Benjamin Harrison and the author, I wish to express my heartfelt gratitude to her President, the Reverend Edward B. Bunn, S.J., to her Academic Vice-President, the Reverend Brian A. McGrath, S.J., and to her Physical Plant Administrators, the Reverend T.

Byron Collins, S.J., and Brother Francis Weiss, S.J., who have afforded me room, office space, and the facilities of the University for many years. Likewise, her Department of History has contributed sound professional advice. My debt to Georgetown can scarcely be estimated.

The Hoosier State again justified its reputation for friendliness. The host of personal acquaintances in Indianapolis who assisted me greatly during the writing of the first volume, has now been re-enforced by the following citizens of Indianapolis: the Donadio family, Alan T. Nolan, the Stimming and Wilmeth clans, Marian Batty, Anna Pich, Ed and Rosemary Sovola, Harvey Elam, Irving M. Fauvre, Dave and Jane Klausmeyer, the J. B. Lanagans, and the James McNutt family. In Evansville, Roy Ryan and in Greencastle, William Unsworth both contributed time and encouragement.

With profound regret and a sense of loss, I here pay humble tribute to the memory of Bernard R. Batty, Hilton U. Brown, and H. Foster Clippinger, recently deceased members of the Board of the Arthur Jordan Foundation in Indianapolis. Their unfailing interest and untiring efforts on the writer's behalf have been taken up and continued, however, by Emsley W. Johnson, Jr., and his fellow trustees, who have not wavered in their support or deviated from their self-imposed rule of no censorship. Indeed, without the financial backing of the Foundation, this story of Benjamin Harrison would still remain hidden beneath a massive pile of undigested documents. Perhaps only the genial and efficient auditor, Gerald V. Carrier, can estimate the full extent of this debt.

As this biography evolved from written drafts and typescript and reached an editor's desk, I became extremely conscious of how much I owed to Professors Emeritus Charles Callan Tansill and Louis Marin Sears (who still do literary battle within the confines of the Cosmos Club, the National Archives, the Library of Congress, and the State Department). Also, the skilled and patient assistance of the editorial staff of University Publishers has served me well.

I also wish to express my sincere appreciation to the Very Reverend Thomas E. Henneberry, S.J., Provincial of the New York Province of the Society of Jesus. Without his encouragement, this second volume might never have seen the light of day.

An acme of praise and gratitude goes to Margaret Mary duFief, secretary extraordinary, research assistant, uncanny typist, and junior editor. She belongs to the nobility of those willing workers who habitually eliminate the word "overtime" from their vocabularies. My scrawl she deciphered and my dictation she understood.

Finally, for the simple but powerful prayers of a queenlike mother I am eternally indebted.

HARRY J. SIEVERS, S.J.

Bellarmine College
Plattsburgh, New York
December 8, 1958

Contents

xi

List of Illustrations

(between pages 202 and 203)

Prologue

THIS VOLUME narrates General Benjamin Harrison's life from the end of the Civil War until his election in 1888 as twenty-third President of the United States. During these twenty-three years, the period of his maturity, Harrison served his White House apprenticeship. Lincoln had brevetted him brigadier general, citing his "ability . . . manifest energy and gallantry." Three years in uniform had taught him self-mastery. Now the Hoosier warrior returned to face the challenges of post-bellum America.

Similar patterns of war, victory, and political reconstruction had influenced the lives of two distinguished ancestors. In the formative period of our national life, his great-grandfather, Benjamin Harrison, "the Signer," played an important rôle in establishing the State, War, and Navy Departments. As statesman of the Revolution and war governor of Virginia, he had also presided over the momentous debates that culminated in the Declaration of Independence. Later he gave the Constitution and the new federal government his hearty support.

In the days of the Northwest Territory and of severe skirmishes with the Indians and the British, the "Signer's" son, William Henry Harrison, acquitted himself well first as a general, then as governor of the Indiana Territory. After victory in the celebrated Battle of the Thames, he went on to become Congressman, Senator, and Minister to Colombia. In 1840 the enthusiastic "log cabin and hard cider" campaign swept "Tippecanoe" Harrison to Washington as ninth President of the United States.

Young Benjamin Harrison, William Henry's grandson, had himself traveled the highway of success rather tranquilly until the great civil conflict of 1861. Born August 20, 1833, on his grandfather's estate near Cincinnati, he experienced a pioneer boyhood. Private tutors until he was fourteen, three years of the liberal arts at Farmers' College just outside the Queen City, and two years of intense study at Miami University, Oxford, Ohio, earned for Harrison his bachelor's and master's degrees. After graduation and while still reading law in Cincinnati, he married Caroline Lavinia Scott, his campus sweetheart. In the spring of 1854 the Harrisons settled in Indianapolis, then just a growing Western town with a population of less than 16,000.

By indefatigable industry in the law and by an active interest in politics, young Harrison soon forged to the front. When the struggle over slavery reached the stage of crisis, he pledged his unswerving allegiance to the new Republican party despite the fact that his father, John Scott Harrison, then represented the Whig party in Congress. Campaigning for Frémont and winning top rating as a speaker, Benjamin prepared for a political career of his own. In 1857 he won election as city attorney and the following year became secretary to the Indiana Republican Central Committee. Two years later he had won the lucrative post of Reporter of the State Supreme Court, but his growing family—Russell, six, and Mary, two—helped to consume the royalties that accrued from his compilation and sale of the *Indiana Reports*. When war broke out between the states, Harrison had just about reached sure financial ground.

In 1862 as a second lieutenant he mustered the 70th Indiana Volunteer Infantry into Union service. Within a month Harrison was made first captain, then colonel. Although still a novice in military drill and discipline, he hurried his regiment to Bowling Green, Kentucky, to check the marauding cavalry band of Confederate Colonel John H. Morgan. Ignorant of the art of war and in command of a rank and file who knew even less, Colonel Harrison studied the manual while tirelessly drilling and disciplining his raw recruits. After four moderately successful encounters with the enemy, the 70th Indiana did guard duty along the tracks of the Louisville and Nashville Railroad. Harrison used this prosaic period to study tactics and emerged a severe but respected disciplinarian. In 1864, when his command joined Sherman's army, Harrison's troops were already a fighting unit. During the Atlanta campaign, the 70th Indiana's colonel frequently commanded a brigade which contributed heavily to the Union victories at Resaca, Cassville, Golgotha, New Hope Church, and elsewhere until the fall of Atlanta.

At Peach Tree Creek, Harrison won his brigadier's star with cold steel, for "Fighting Joe" Hooker quickly followed up a battlefield promise with a letter of commendation to the Secretary of War. After the Atlanta campaign, Harrison's furlough enabled him to return home, where he took an active part in the political campaign of 1864 and easily won his re-election as Supreme Court Reporter. Meanwhile, Sherman had marched through Georgia, and Harrison, temporarily separated from his command, won distinction in the Union victory at Nashville. Rejoining his own troops in the Carolinas, he led them in the grand review in Washington. The war had ended. General Harrison, as well as the whole country, looked for the dawn of a new era.

Although the conflict had been waged for the preservation of the Union, Harrison and countless others began to realize that this had not been its sole objective. Gunsmoke, bayonet wounds, and death underscored other goals equally as vital as national unity. The victorious nation, "conceived in liberty," as Lincoln phrased it, "and dedicated to the proposition that all men are created equal," desired slavery abolished and a "government of the people, by the people and for the people." Whatever else would characterize the new era, these three ideals, union, freedom and democracy, would become the principal concern of the reunited States during the final decades of the nineteenth century. The ensuing struggle to attain these goals paralleled Harrison's period of maturity.

Benjamin Harrison

☆　☆

CHAPTER I

The Challenge of Change

AT ABOUT 11 P.M. on April 9, 1865, the electrifying news of Lee's surrender aroused a sleeping Indianapolis to a night of unrestrained joy, punctuated by artillery fire, bells, parades, and bonfires. The Civil War had ended and men could at last turn their thoughts to peace.

Indiana's governor, Oliver P. Morton, appointed April 20 as a day of thanksgiving. On April 15, however, the news of Lincoln's assassination transformed the day into one of "mourning, humiliation and prayer." Flags edged in black hung at half-mast in the stunned Hoosier town; all business was suspended; and men and women wore mourning. For eighteen hours, on the gloomiest Sunday Indianapolis ever knew, Lincoln's body rested in the corridor of the old State House and throngs trudged through a "shoe-top depth of sloppy mud" [1] to pay their last respects. Cox's oil painting [2] rested near the closed casket of the martyred President. It portrayed Lincoln wearing a rather short beard, gray mingled with black, framing a face that Hoosiers would not soon forget. In the streets, patrolled by soldiers,[3] there swarmed uncounted acres of men, women, and children. This was April and the immediate end of the war.

May promised better things. While the Union legions tramped in grand review along Washington's Pennsylvania Avenue on May 23–24, 1865, Indianapolis readied itself to receive its own returning sons. In the State House yard an artistic speakers' stand [4]

---

[1] Hilton U. Brown, *A Book of Memories*, pp. 15–16. Also Kenneth Stampp, *Indiana Politics During the Civil War*, pp. 259–60.

[2] Jacob Cox was the painter; Mrs. Vajen Collins presented the portrait to the Benjamin Harrison Memorial Home in Indianapolis, where it now hangs in the library.

[3] Jacob P. Dunn, *History of Greater Indianapolis*, I, 237.

[4] Indianapolis *Daily Sentinel*, June 3, 1865. (Hereafter this paper and the Indianapolis *Journal* will be cited as the *Sentinel* and *Journal*, respectively.)

was raised from which the governor and other dignitaries would address the veterans. Since welcoming festivities would be official, and repeated frequently during the summer, a routine was worked out: a delegation would meet troop trains at the Union Depot; a cannon salute would alert the ladies of the city to prepare refreshments at the Soldiers' Home; and a parade of triumph would precede Governor Morton's welcome at the State House. The patriotic harangues which followed were interspersed with "original songs" rendered by their author, Chaplain Lozier, who possessed what contemporary journalism termed "a fatal facility for rhyme, with lungs of steel and a voice like a thunderstorm." [5]

Scheduled for Friday afternoon, June 16, was an extraordinary reception. On this day the "sun-browned veterans" of the 70th Indiana Volunteer Infantry were coming home, with Brigadier General Benjamin Harrison in command. These troops claimed the environs of the Hoosier capital as their home. Here, in the shadow of the State House, young Lieutenant Harrison had recruited them three years before. In mid-August of 1862 they had marched to war, 1,021 strong. In Kentucky, Tennessee, Alabama, and Georgia they had earned a reputation as fighters. They had marched with Sherman to the sea, and their commander, Ben Harrison, had been brevetted brigadier general. The price paid in blood and human sacrifice had been high: dead—188, nearly 20%; wounded in action—194, another 20% of the original band of volunteers. Now the survivors, fresh from their triumphant review in Washington, were coming home with their leader to families, friends, and neighbors. Together they would resume civilian life, remembering the challenge of Sherman's farewell message: "As in war you have been good soldiers, so in peace you will make good citizens." [6]

Shortly before three o'clock that afternoon, the cannon on the State House grounds roared once again, this time signaling that the famed Seventieth had arrived.[7] The jubilant veterans were soon cheering Governor Morton through another of his "homecoming" addresses, replete with flowery exaggerations and embarrassing comparisons.[8] The governor, in top form, exhibited on this special

[5] William D. Foulke, *Life of Oliver P. Morton,* I, 445.

[6] *Journal,* June 1, 1865.

[7] The shot shook the Capitol Building until loosened plaster littered the floors, and "in the law library room considerable part of the ceiling" fell. *Sentinel,* June 17, 1865.

[8] Harry J. Sievers, *Benjamin Harrison: Hoosier Warrior,* pp. 313 ff.

occasion a "remarkable fertility of resources." [9] General Alvin P. Hovey followed Morton, who then introduced the man of the hour, General Harrison.

Benjamin Harrison was well known in Indianapolis. Before the interruption of war, he had already won a moderate success in both law and political life. At the moment a war hero, his true forte was not that of a soldier. Awaiting him in civilian life was a new era—the era of his maturity. Three years of battle had changed him little externally. Still somewhat stocky—his one hundred and forty-five pounds were borne by a five foot seven-and-a-half inch frame—Harrison at thirty-two was quick-moving, dapper, affectionate, with smiling blue eyes, light hair, fair complexion, and a reddish beard.[10]

The scene before him was a familiar one. Under these same shady trees he had made several recruiting appeals to the men of Marion County. Now, called upon for a hero's speech, he humorously observed that his regiment "had been too long engaged in speaking with the muzzles of their rifles to listen to speeches." He admitted, however, that the occasion did demand a word or two. Briefly, he recapitulated the events in the field, rising to eloquence in "a touching tribute to the memory of the men fallen in conflict." [11] He was convinced, he said, that the heroic dead had "lived to accomplish more for the good of their country than most men who go down silvered to the grave." Alluding to his own part at the Battle of Resaca, he declared that he "would rather lie within that little mound at the foot of the hill, than to have had no participation in this struggle." [12]

In his praise of the valorous dead, Harrison was at one with his audience. But he also sensed the hidden fears of some who anticipated riot and bloodshed from the returning veterans.[13] This fear he tried to allay. Soldiers, he assured his listeners, would expect no special consideration either in the market place or the political arena. They had shown that they could take care of themselves in

[9] *Journal*, June 17, 1865.

[10] William A. White, *Masks In A Pageant*, pp. 69–72, measures Harrison at barely five feet six inches, while the General's official discharge papers credit him with an additional inch and a half. Harrison MSS (Library of Congress), Vol. 6. (Hereafter the Harrison MSS in the Library of Congress will be cited as [L.C.].)

[11] *Sentinel*, June 17, 1865.

[12] Sievers, *op. cit.*, pp. 314–15.

[13] During June and July, 1865, the *Sentinel* voiced this foreboding, shared by many Democrats.

war, and this same ability and energy would now be turned to peaceful pursuits. If you intend to outstrip the soldier, the General argued, "you will have to brighten your wits and quicken your pace," for "we mean to be felt in politics as well as business." [14]

The General's remarks were cheered by his audience and received in good part by the press of the city, the *Daily Sentinel* characterizing the speech as "graceful and dignified, becoming alike to the soldier and the gentleman." [15]

When the fanfare of homecoming had subsided, Harrison returned to his old law office. On this first stroll as a civilian he must have been amazed at the changes he noted. In October, 1864, while home on furlough, he had admitted that "he found himself almost a stranger in his native town, lost in a labyrinth of new and eloquent buildings, and the busy world of commerce." [16] Now, at war's end, Indianapolis was even busier. Several new buildings were going up; choice downtown property was selling at $800 a foot; almost twice as many people were crowding the unpaved streets; four new national banks were ready for business; the Union Depot, constructed in 1853, had been whitewashed and expanded some 200 feet with "offices . . . and an eating house added." Altogether prospects for trade "were never better in Indianapolis." [17]

Harrison's old law office on the northeast corner of Washington and Meridian Streets also displayed the new look. A freshly-painted shingle, *Porter, Harrison and Fishback, Attorneys and Counsellors at Law,* greeted the General after his leave of absence. It advised clients that the firm would give "special attention . . . to business in the Federal Courts and in the Supreme Court of the United States." [18] The new face in the office was that of Albert Gallatin Porter, who had just declined the presidency of the Gosport Railroad Company in order to devote full time to the law partnership.[19]

---

[14] *Journal,* June 17, 1865.

[15] June 17, 1865.

[16] Sievers, *op. cit.,* pp. 268–70.

[17] Dunn, *op. cit.,* pp. 153 ff.; *Sentinel,* June 26, 1865. *Ninth Census,* Vol. I, *The Statistics of the Population of the United States* (June 1, 1870), p. 127. Logan's *History of Indianapolis from 1818,* p. 92, estimated a population of 80,000 in March of 1865. Likewise, John D. Barnhart and Donald F. Carmony, *Indiana: From Frontier to Industrial Commonwealth,* II, 207–307, describe the forces that helped make Indianapolis a city.

[18] *Journal,* July and August, 1865.

[19] *Sentinel,* June 26, 1865. Albert Gallatin Porter, later Governor of Indiana

Both Porter and William Pinckney Fishback, Harrison's original partner, welcomed the General back warmly. Despite the fact that in October, 1864, Harrison had been elected to a four-year term as State Supreme Court Reporter, a time-consuming task, the two older partners felt that with his excellent memory and serious habits of research, Harrison could ably shoulder his share of the legal load.[20]

The lines of Harrison's character had deepened during the course of the Civil War.[21] On the battlefield and in camp he had had time to reflect on his married life. Devotion to his profession and to political life had been repaid in terms of income, but in the hours he might have spent with his wife and children it had cost heavily. He resolved to change this after the war. In numerous letters from the front he promised the understanding Carrie that he would settle down to "a life of quiet usefulness" in a "home brighter and happier for you and the children." This prospect, he wrote, ". . . has been on my mind on the march, on my cot, and even in my dreams." [22]

His son Russell was ten, almost eleven, and his daughter Mary— affectionately known as "Mamie"—had just turned eight. Both were important in their father's plans for a "brighter, happier" home. Before he left Camp Sherman in South Carolina, he had counseled them

. . . to help Ma fix up the yard, and keep . . . all nice and clean. The grape vines will need to be tied up and trimmed and the strawberry bed weeded and thinned. . . . You know that I am to come home from the army to stay at home with you . . . and I want to see our little house and everything about it as neat and trim as an old maid.

What a good time we will have when we all get together again at home, and Pa does not have to go away to war any more. We will make everything about the dear cottage shine like a new dollar, and will try to keep things as bright inside the house as they are outside. We will have

---

(1881–1885), had during Harrison's absence in the field, associated himself in a law partnership with William P. Fishback.

[20] Fishback recalled that Harrison "was able upon re-entering the law office to share its labors with his partners to their satisfaction." Lew Wallace, *Life of Gen. Ben Harrison*, p. 89.

[21] White, *op. cit.,* p. 7.

[22] Harrison to his wife, May 21, 1865, (L.C.), Vol. 6.

the stable fixed up and bring our horse . . . home and maybe get a nice little buggy to ride in. . . .[23]

The General now strove to realize his dream, and to a certain extent he was successful. During his first summer at home he took his family on regular buggy rides along the White River. Sometimes father and son tried to lure a few bass to their hooks, while at home Mamie and her mother concentrated on painting and piano lessons.[24] On many evenings Ben worked for a half-hour or so in the garden before returning to the desk in his study.

Nor did he and Carrie neglect the social life of Indianapolis. Church-sponsored strawberry festivals and dinners often brought them together with neighboring friends, and there were occasional evenings at the opera or theater. Perhaps the most notable event was the ball given on June 29 in honor of the gallant 70th Regiment. The *Daily Sentinel* described it as a "round of revelry; brave women and fair men; music; gaslight, and other things in proportion." [25] All of this, of course, was in contrast to the strict Sabbath observed by the Harrisons, who spent that day in prayer and in giving Bible instructions at the First Presbyterian Church. Mrs. Harrison cared for the small fry, while the General, a church elder, taught the young men.

Former soldiers found economic readjustment much more difficult than resumption of domestic and social obligations. Some veterans claimed that the government owed them a living in return for three or more years of military service. Harrison, while admitting the loss of three productive years, felt differently. He acknowledged the warmth of public plaudits, but wryly warned homecoming comrades that gratitude alone could not support them and their families. "They would find it a thin drink and no meat at all." Striking out against profit-seeking merchants, he further warned the veterans that "if they were not sharp, they

[23] Benjamin Harrison to Russell and Mary, March 31, 1865, Harrison Home MSS. This letter was found tucked away in a small drawer of Harrison's desk after his death.

[24] Music instruction cost only seventy-five cents a lesson. In Personal Bills, Notes, Checks . . . 1865–1869, (L.C.).

[25] June 26, 29, 1865.

would have to pay about fifty cents more." [26] Harrison himself was on guard. He had two sources from which he could reduce the debts he had accumulated while away: earnings from his growing law firm would supplement his steady income as Supreme Court Reporter. On this latter task of editing, publishing, and selling the *Reports*, he concentrated his efforts. Many men failed to recognize opportunity, he felt, because it often came disguised as hard work. This Reporter's job was his own opportunity and he knew it.

Six months had elapsed between Harrison's election as Reporter in 1864 and his military discharge. During this period he had employed an enterprising attorney, John Dye, to collect and edit the Supreme Court decisions for the term ending November, 1864. Dye had executed his task with commendable care and in late June had turned over to Harrison some 700 page-proofs. By the end of the first week in August, the bulky tome, Volume 23 of the Indiana Supreme Court *Reports,* was on the market. Particularly rich in decisions upon state constitutional law, the publication won editorial praise from the Indianapolis *Journal,* which commended the General and his assistant for a work destined to be a "great convenience to the profession, especially in the progress of trials." [27] Harrison capitalized on this good publicity by running a front-page notice in the morning papers for a week, offering "to send the Reports to any express office in the state, free of charge, on receipt of price, $4.50." Content, format, and the handy method of distribution greatly pleased the legal fraternity, including state officials and lawyers in towns far distant from Indianapolis.

Within five days of publication Harrison had banked $925, and at the end of two months had deposited another $2,500.[28] Before winter set in, the first edition of over 1,200 copies had been exhausted. After Dye's salary, printing costs, and other expenses had been met, Harrison realized about $1,500 net profit. This, in addition to his share of the law firm's earnings, gave him a more solid financial footing. He was able to settle with creditors, help some less fortunate members of his family, and gratify a desire to beautify his home on the corner of Alabama and North Streets by put-

[26] *Journal,* August 12, 1865. Barnhart and Carmony, *op. cit.,* p. 189, describe the inflation which had prevailed since 1862.

[27] August 8, 1865.

[28] Harrison Cash Book and Ledger, August 5–25, 1865, August 26–October 19, 1865, (L.C.).

ting "some additions and improvements upon his property." [29]
Russell and Mamie were enrolled in private academies for the fall
term of 1865, and the domestic picture looked bright.

Before Volume 24 of the *Reports* could be published in the
spring of 1866, Harrison had his troubles. He now worked alone,
although with the same pertinacity that had characterized his pre-
war efforts. In court a good part of the day, he turned more and
more to night work in his study, preparing abstracts of Supreme
Court cases. When he was in court, it was difficult to tell whether
he was appearing as Reporter or attorney. He had developed the
habit of carrying a roll of proof sheets in his pocket when he went
to the courthouse—reading them at favorable intervals. Carrie
soon came to realize that he was working more than he was living,
and often reminded him of his pledge to avoid overwork. One
night she prevailed upon him to take her to a concert. Her joy
was short-lived, however; he came downstairs dressed for the concert—carrying proof sheets in his pocket.[30]

As Supreme Court Reporter, Harrison was often a difficult person to work with. He hated stupidity, expecting of subordinates
the same high level of workmanship of which he himself was capable. Small talk and unnecessary intrusions annoyed him most;
more than once his anger fell on the typesetters in the book rooms
of the *Journal*, where copy for the *Reports* was set. Every day,
sometimes hourly, some printer would approach Harrison at his
desk in the Clerk's office for help in reading *Reports* copy, handwritten by the judges in almost indecipherable scrawls. One of
them recalls such a moment:

Without a word or sign of recognition the paper was almost jerked from
your hand when you presented it to him and asked what a certain word
was. If he had no trouble in deciphering it, you were told in a harsh,
unpleasant voice what it was, but if he had trouble in making it out,
it seemed to anger him. It always appeared to us that he considered
our coming and asking an intrusion, and that a printer ought to be
able to read any kind of hieroglyphics a Supreme Court Judge might
make.[31]

[29] Wallace, *op. cit.,* p. 89.
[30] *Ibid.*
[31] These details, related at the time of Harrison's death in 1901, appeared in an
undated clipping from the Topeka (Kansas) *Mail* in Russell B. Harrison Scrapbooks,
Vol. 3, (Indiana State Library).

Harrison's quick temper underwent further trial in October, 1865, when a collector for the Bureau of Internal Revenue, J. J. Wright, notified him that he would have to procure a license "to carry on the business or occupation of manufacturer at No. 2 East Washington St." Wright also insisted that Harrison pay a tax as publisher of the *Indiana Reports*,[32] contending that as a "book manufacturer" Harrison was pursuing a trade subject to federal taxation. The General hotly objected. As an elected officer of the State of Indiana, he questioned the right of the federal government to tax his official state work. Hence he sought an injunction, but without apparent success. Harrison's position was understandable. He held an elective office whose emoluments were obtained solely by the sale and distribution of the *Reports*. He drew no other salary.

There ensued a legal tussle as to the right of the United States to tax a state officer of Indiana. Harrison confidently presented his case, but the decision was adverse. Pride, as well as the money involved, prompted an appeal to the federal Circuit Court, which ultimately vindicated the Supreme Court Reporter.[33] It was a fruitful victory and the General, even as President, never tired of telling how he "received something like $1,200 back for taxes which had been taken from me." [34]

This controversy in no way delayed Harrison's publication of Volume 24 in May, 1866, or of Volume 25 early in January, 1867. Both netted a substantial profit, and the workmanship of the latter volume was especially praised because Reporter Harrison had "prefaced each case with a concise syllabus, and furnished a compendious index, whereby every point decided can be readily found by the legal practitioner." [35] In addition to augmenting his in-

[32] Benjamin Harrison to Hon. John Hanna, October 14, 1865, John Hanna MSS (Indiana University Library, Bloomington, Indiana). In this letter Harrison writes that the U. S. Collector and he agreed to submit the question to Judge McDonald on a motion for an injunction. Hanna was U. S. Attorney at the time. On January 4, 1886, Harrison procured the license. Personal Bills, Notes, Checks . . . 1865–1869, (L.C.).

[33] Emsley W. Johnson, Jr., Indianapolis attorney, and his staff, after intensive research, were unable to find any record of the case in question. Emsley Johnson to the author, May 27, 1957.

[34] Boston *Sunday Herald*, February 22, 1891. Harrison, then President, granted a special interview to correspondent George Alfred Townsend. All details available on the outcome of the case come from Harrison's own recollection.

[35] *Journal*, January 15, 1867.

come, Harrison was fast gaining a sound reputation in Indiana legal circles while becoming steeped in legal precedents.

Carrie gradually learned to tolerate her husband's long working hours. He was good to her, banked their profits, and both enjoyed public esteem. He had promised to make himself felt in business, and by New Year's Day, 1867, it would seem that he had succeeded. Carrie was wearing a newly-mounted diamond pin and ring, while the General sported a new "cassimere coat, pants, & vest" costing $65.[36]

Ambivalence best describes Harrison's political attitude between 1865 and 1867. On the eve of his discharge from the Army, he had told Carrie: "I could go to Congress for our district at the next election, but positively I would not accept the office, for the reason that it would take me away from home so much." [37] A month later, in his first public address at home, Harrison gave fair warning that as a former soldier he meant to make himself felt in politics. The General had fashioned a political philosophy for which he had fought, and, for him, reconstruction controversies made silence impossible. Finally, during the summer of 1865, several events placed Harrison in the midst of political controversy.

During July and August Governor Morton was ill, and Harrison found himself on the rostrum in the State House yard where, in place of Morton, he and other local heroes greeted the still returning regiments. The *Journal* reported that "General Ben Harrison's earnest and impassioned oratory secured the profoundest attention of his auditors, whose upturned, sunburned faces reflected the sympathetic working of emotions conjured by the General's vivid delineation." [38] The Democratic *Sentinel* also applauded Harrison, but noted that "the General slid on to political questions before he concluded." [39]

Scarcely any American could divorce himself from the perplexing problems that agitated the postwar Union. This was true of Hoosiers in general and of Harrison in particular. Indiana had furnished over 200,000 men, nearly 75 per cent of the male popu-

[36] Bills and Checks, 1867, (L.C.).
[37] Harrison to his wife, May 21, 1865, (L.C.), Vol. 6.
[38] July 21, 1865.
[39] July 21, 1865.

lation capable of bearing arms. Close to 25,000 had been war fatalities.[40] No citizen of Indiana could be indifferent to the returns on so precious an investment in a reunited nation. Many veterans, however, were deeply embittered. They had returned from war to find their little homesteads seized, as Harrison phrased it, "by hardhearted grasping men." The men who stayed home, many of whom had procured substitutes, were apparently filling the better jobs. Harrison recognized this feeling of resentment and, while he sympathized with his comrades, in his speeches he appealed to their nobler selves. Again and again the General asked which one of them "would exchange today the proud consciousness of having periled his life in defense of his country for all the gain piled up by those who stayed at home? It is better than bank stocks, houses or lands . . . how much more worthy of esteem is he who has assisted in saving a nation, in whose destiny are wrapped up the hopes of a world." [41]

Towards the defeated Confederates in the south and the Democratic Copperheads in the north, Harrison showed no sympathy. In his strongest language the General warned homecoming Hoosier regiments against placing traitorous Democrats in political power. He urged them to stand guard against the "mean, impudent and devilish" wartime traitors who, "if they can, will sneak in upon you while you sleep, and steal away the fruits of this bloody contest." He characterized "Southern politicians" as the "wiliest in the world," for

. . . beaten by the sword, they will now fall back on the "resources of statesmanship." Satan himself, when hurled from the battlements of heaven into the seething hell below, had not a more realizing sense of the power of the Almighty than the Southern politician has of the all-conquering power of the Yankee.[42]

He also warned against "northern allies, some of whom with hair cropped short, are now working for their board and clothes,

<hr>

[40] *Report of the Adjutant General of the State of Indiana* (8 vols., Indianapolis, 1865–1869), I (1869), App. 5, shows the grand total of troops furnished as 208,367. Casualties, listed at 24,416, amounted to almost 12 per cent.

[41] *Journal*, August 12, 1865.

[42] *Ibid.* Harrison's speeches as reported in the contemporary press show him clinging to a war mentality even after the surrender, but it was a period when "war shibboleths became political slogans, and 'loyalty' was stamped with the party die." See James G. Randall, *The Civil War and Reconstruction*, p. 689. It is difficult, if not impossible, to substantiate the finding of Wallace, *op. cit.*, p. 255, "that in treating of the Confederate soldier, he [Harrison] was respectful and forgiving."

at Columbus." [43] Southern sympathizers in Indiana, cautioned the General, "will meet you with professions of joy at your safe return, but don't believe them. They would rather you had been buried beneath four feet of rebel soil." Harrison's vindictive attitude had been forged in the fires of war. When the North suffered a series of reverses in the field and gloom enveloped the White House and War Department, Hoosier Democrats "did not weep with us," thundered an angry Harrison,

. . . they said it was not their funeral. Now when we are rejoicing in victory, tell them that this is not their day. Let it be branded upon them as an enduring mark that in our hour of trial they struck no blow for our common victory and had no word of cheer for the soldier.[44]

By the middle of summer, 1865, Harrison had entered the camp of the radical reconstructionists.[45] The record shows him opposed to Lincoln's plan of conciliatory reconstruction.[46] He made it clear that he himself felt "there should be no forgiveness without repentance" and that he saw "no genuine effort at self-repentance either among Northern or Southern rebels." [47] Such impassioned statements brought cheers from the Boys in Blue. Despite the Sentinel's editorial objections, Harrison refused to soften his doctrine. At the very moment that "those of the South are pardoned, their treason breaks out afresh," he insisted. He continued to urge Union veterans to "keep them and their Northern allies out of power. If you don't, they will steal away, in the halls of Congress, the fruits won from them at the glistening point of the bayonet." [48] Here Harrison approached the position of Thaddeus Stevens, who held that the logical outcome of any war

[43] The reference was to Copperheads who were convicted of "treason" before military tribunals and who were serving prison sentences at Columbus, Ohio.

[44] Journal and Sentinel, August 12, 1865. The Democratic paper charged Harrison editorially with "cant and hypocrisy."

[45] Randall, op. cit., pp. 689–717, treats the social background of the battle within the Republican party on sundry questions of Reconstruction. His relatively objective treatment of the politicians and statesmen connected with the complex issues is both enlightening and refreshing. For a popular and more recent summary, see Malcom Moos, The Republicans: A History of Their Party, pp. 122–36.

[46] Randall, op. cit., p. 699, and Paul L. Haworth, Reconstruction and Union, 1865–1912, pp. 7–39. The reference is to Lincoln's "ten per cent" plan of executive recognition of state governments which abolished slavery.

[47] Journal and Sentinel, August 12, 1865. The latter said Harrison didn't believe in forgiving "a sinner who persisted in sinning."

[48] Journal, August 12, 1865.

between two governments was that "the conqueror rules; the conquered is ruled." [49]

Among the chief challenges produced by the change from war to peace was the question of Negro suffrage. On his return to civilian life, Harrison discovered that this problem had reached a crisis, not only within the state but also within his own party. Influential Republican leaders were trying to stave off an immediate decision on equal voting rights for the freed Negro in the South, while the Julian wing of the party manifested "a dogged determination to force it on the people, even at the expense of a split in the party, resulting in the triumph of the Democracy." [50] Governor Morton, spokesman for Hoosier Republicanism, pleaded for a period of probation and preparation for the "four million slaves just freed from bondage . . . before they are brought to the exercise of political power." His was a realistic position, for, as he argued, "perhaps not one in a thousand can read, and perhaps not one in five hundred is worth five dollars in property of any kind." [51] To the Indiana Democracy this position was only an uneasy straddle. The *Sentinel* found no difficulty in expressing itself editorially:

We are against Negro suffrage and Negro equality in all its forms. In a word, we are for the supremacy of the White race. Where does our neighbor stand? [52]

Harrison's own views on Negro suffrage had been shaped primarily by his military experience. Early in the conflict he had opposed the use of Negro soldiers in the Union Army, but in 1864, in the heat of the fight at Nashville, he exclaimed his admiration for "these black men who had charged the rebel works," and declared that they "were better than all of the traitors who had fought against the flag." [53] In the summer of 1865, however, he was neither for nor against immediate Negro suffrage. His stand

[49] Moos, *op. cit.*, pp. 123–24.

[50] *Sentinel*, June 26, 1865. See also Grace Julian Clarke, *George W. Julian*, pp. 273–97, for Julian's rôle.

[51] Foulke, *op. cit.*, pp. 448–50.

[52] August 17, 1865.

[53] *Journal*, August 12, 1865.

was that he did not favor "letting the Negro vote just yet, if the rebels were also kept from voting. If, in the course of two or three years, you can't get a loyal white population down there, then take a black one." [54] Neither three nor twenty-three years solved the problem in Harrison's mind. During his presidency he would still wrestle with the question of the South in a vigorous but ineffective fashion.[55]

Equally thorny in 1865, and for several years to come, was the political debate on the civil disabilities to be imposed on ex-Confederates. Here the General was outspoken. Declaring that "officials of doubtful loyalty in Southern States" should not be permitted to hold office in the reconstructed governments, Harrison adopted an extreme radical position. Conservative Republicans were alienated by his statement that "if necessary, he would send to the South governors from Massachusetts or Indiana." All in all, in 1865 and 1866 Harrison opposed at every turn any reconstruction proposition based on harmonious compromise. He was still too close to gunpowder, smoke, and military hardship. There had been too little time for his vindictive spirit to cool. He further believed "in eternally disfranchising every man who had fought against the flag. Adopt this rule, and there will be but little voting in Dixie. Then it will not matter whether the Negroes vote or not." [56] This was radical Republicanism.

Harrison must have realized that his veteran's status and military title were as valuable politically as the name he bore. There was a certain magic connected with the old blue uniform. Twice within his first summer at home the General participated in affairs which dramatized the power and glory with which the veterans of the Grand Army had been endowed. In July he planned and headed the rousing reception given by Indianapolis to Major Gen-

[54] *Ibid.* Also *Sentinel,* August 12, 1865.

[55] Vincent P. De Santis, "Benjamin Harrison and the Republican Party in the South, 1889–1893," *Indiana Magazine of History,* 51 (1955), 279–302.

[56] *Journal,* August 12, 1865. Randall, *op. cit.,* p. 739, gives a detailed ramification on the proposed constitutional amendment submitted by Congress. A year later, on the floor of Congress, another future President of the United States would advocate the same policy. James A. Garfield of Ohio, also a man with the smoke of civil conflict in his nostrils, urged that the "disfranchisement of ex-Confederates be made perpetual." Garfield's stand is drawn from the *Congressional Globe* (39th Cong., 1st Sess.), p. 2463.

eral William T. Sherman.[57] Two months later, on horseback again, he welcomed General Grant to the heart of Hoosierdom.[58]

Preparations for "Old Cump" Sherman's arrival had been flurried but extensive. Local army officers and veterans chose Harrison to handle reception and banquet details, and three days of feverish activity put all in readiness.

Sherman arrived on July 25 and was immediately submerged in "a sea of blue." Soldiers who had followed him back and forth across the land of Dixie clustered about their old commander. After an informal reception in the governor's room at the State House, Sherman, flanked solidly by an honorary escort, toured the city, greeted by enthusiastic applause at every street corner. Shortly after two o'clock, Harrison's reception committee accompanied their guest to the stand in the State House yard to the prolonged cheers of a boisterous assembly.

From the dais, Harrison heard Sherman pay handsome compliments to Indiana, her governor, her hard-fighting soldiers and military leaders, after which he expressed his conviction that when the bitterness of the contest had worn away, the South would thank the North for having "saved the nation from the danger of disintegration and death." Harrison shared this belief of Sherman's, and it became the partial basis for his political philosophy and the keynote of many a campaign speech during the next quarter of a century.[59]

General Grant's visit to Indianapolis took place on September 26, 1865, with Harrison again on the welcoming committee. After greeting Grant at the depot, he dined with him at Bates House and acted as a mounted escort during the afternoon parade.[60] Much to Harrison's pleasure, the celebration was executed without formal speeches or long toasts. Grant enjoyed the Hoosier hospitality, and Harrison's own prestige was enhanced by this close association with one of the country's most celebrated military leaders. From that day his active interest in veterans' affairs grew. Few future encampments of the Grand Army of the Republic would find the "Hoosier Warrior" absent.

[57] *Journal,* July 21, 24, 1865.
[58] *Sentinel,* September 27, 1865.
[59] *Journal,* July 21, 24, 25, 26; *Sentinel,* July 26, 1865. These issues carried accounts of the preparations for Sherman's visit, and of the events and speeches that dignified the occasion.
[60] *Sentinel,* September 26, 27, 1865.

For Harrison, two years of double labor as lawyer and Supreme Court Reporter had ended in both financial and professional triumph, but he had failed to calculate the cost. In April, 1867, hard on the heels of a notable court victory, he suffered a physical collapse from overwork. While Carrie was nursing him back to health, he had time to plan a less arduous future.

When his health broke in 1867, Harrison had been earning well over $10,000 a year,[61] of which he had saved little. In addition to providing needed assistance for his father, brothers, and married sisters,[62] he had contributed generously to civic and religious groups. Furthermore, he was living well at home. His family enjoyed the luxury of a second horse, and the General had paid $485 for a sporty new carriage "with revolving seat, full finished and guaranteed for twelve months." Carrie now possessed many things that a General's pay had not been able to provide, and Russell and Mamie were still in private schools.

In view of his impaired health and favorable financial status, Harrison decided to relinquish his Reporter's post. He therefore announced that he would not stand for re-election in the fall of 1868. To complete his convalescence, he then proceeded to enjoy his first vacation in three years, hunting and fishing in and around the beautiful lakes of Minnesota. In the fall of 1867, he returned greatly rejuvenated to Indianapolis, his law practice, and the last few months of his Reporter's term.

[61] Included here is a federal income tax receipt for $502.80. Personal Bills, Notes and Checks, 1865–1868, (L.C.).

[62] John Scott Harrison was a poor manager and, like his father, General William Henry Harrison, seemed to draw more than his share of bad luck both in farming and property speculations. Some twenty letters from father to son (1865–1868) plainly indicate the older man's financial plight. Also Bettie Eaton to Benjamin Harrison, May 14, November 1, December 11, 1866; Jennie Morris to Benjamin Harrison, May 10, June 6, July 8; and Anna Harrison to Benjamin Harrison, June 6, 1867, (L.C.), Vol. 6.

CHAPTER II

The Emergence
of a Prosecutor

URING HIS FIRST POSTWAR VACATION, Harrison had had time to evaluate himself and his situation. At thirty-four, by dogged industry at the desk rather than by courtroom brilliance, he had earned a high place at the Indiana bar and an adequate income. So much for the credit side. On the debit side he placed his first twenty months' Reportership with its overwork and his consequent breakdown. This, he reasoned, had prevented him from keeping pace with his older, more experienced partners, who had been handling most of the firm's lucrative practice. To them had come the lion's share of prestige, while Harrison remained the plodding, meticulous student of law with little opportunity for growth.

He now realized that his health had broken because he had failed to use the administrator's primary tool: the delegation of routine work to subordinates. He needed no further lesson; immediately upon his arrival home, he hired two clerks,[1] with whose help he was able to edit, publish, and sell without strain three additional volumes of the *Reports* before relinquishing his office.[2] In addition, he occasionally found time to hunt wild duck and go bass fishing, which kept him happy, healthy, and interested in his work.[3] Another most important dividend was his new-found time for private practice—and for political activity.

[1] Henry Scott, Harrison's brother-in-law, was one choice, and Howard Cale, a promising attorney, was the other. Cale became Harrison's life-long friend and eventually handled his business and personal affairs when he was away from Indianapolis.

[2] Volumes 26, 27, and 28 were published before Harrison relinquished his office. Volume 29, which also bore his name, came on the market after Colonel Black assumed the Reporter's office on January 15, 1869.

[3] John Scott Harrison to his son, June 1, August 28, 1868, (L.C.), Vol. 6.

Politics had been in the Harrison blood for more than two and a half centuries. Long before the General's great-grandfather, Benjamin Harrison, "the Signer," put signature to the Declaration of Independence, the family had enjoyed political prestige in colonial Virginia.[4] More recently, William Henry Harrison, President, and John Scott Harrison,[5] U. S. Congressman, had added to the family's laurels. In 1856, the General took his own first major political step by joining the new Republican party,[6] to which he had now adhered for over a decade.

In addition to an illustrious name, Harrison had the advantage of living in the heartland of American politics after the war. Indiana, always a pivotal state, bred powerful orators and crafty strategists for the political arena. Schuyler Colfax was to be first of many Hoosier Vice-Presidents,[7] but it was reserved to Benjamin Harrison to be the state's only President.

Initially, Harrison's political maneuverings were modest. In 1865, he had publicly voiced his radical reconstruction views, reiterating them during the midterm elections of 1866. Feelings ran high across the continent. In that year President Johnson traveled from Washington to Chicago in his "swing around the circle," campaigning for his more moderate policies.[8] The Radicals organized demonstrations against him, and in Indianapolis a noisy crowd prevented the President from speaking. After Johnson had retired, hecklers created more confusion, culminating in indiscriminate gunfire. "One of the bullets crashed through the President's room and narrowly missed General Grant, who was in the presidential party."[9] The near tragedy calmed only a few, and Harrison himself experienced the political emotions that surged about the stump in the Hoosier state.[10] The Radicals were ultimately victorious, carrying both Houses of Congress by large majorities. In

[4] Clifford Dowdey, "The Harrisons of Berkeley Hundred," *American Heritage*, 8 (April, 1957), 58–70.

[5] Harry J. Sievers, *Benjamin Harrison: Hoosier Warrior*, pp. 13–19, 117–21.

[6] Charles Zimmermann, "The Origin and Rise of the Republican Party in Indiana, 1854–1860," *Indiana Magazine of History*, 13 (1917), 407–8. A more recent and detailed study has been made by Roger H. Van Bolt, "The Rise of the Republican Party in Indiana," *Indiana Magazine of History*, 51 (1955), 185–220.

[7] Willard H. Smith, *Schuyler Colfax, the Changing Fortunes of a Political Idol*, pp. 269–311.

[8] Stefan Lorant, *The Presidency*, p. 279.

[9] J. D. Barnhart and D. F. Carmony, *Indiana: From Frontier to Industrial Commonwealth*, II, 195.

[10] Harrison to Hanna, September 28, 1866, Hanna MSS, (Bloomington, Indiana).

Indiana, Harrison had helped his party to an overwhelming victory.[11]

In 1867, an off-year for national elections, there began to emerge a strong reaction against radical Republicanism. Conservative victories in the California and Maine elections alarmed the Radicals, and prompted Harrison to cross over into Ohio, where he stumped vigorously for the principles of Congressional reconstruction. While the General's effectiveness as a campaigner earned him several more speaking invitations, an accumulation of business and personal matters limited his public appearances in 1867.[12]

In one sense, Harrison's law office was a better political workshop than the hustings. His politically active partners sent up many a trial balloon. "Pink" Fishback, in particular, was a valuable instructor. Able to hold an audience regardless of time, topic, or weather, he was a clever behind-the-scenes strategist and possessed the unique faculty of pleasing Senator Morton while also holding the confidence of his party's reform element. In the heat of a political campaign, Democrats feared the tactics by which "Pink" carried "the war straight into the enemy's camp." [13] From both partners—Porter was equally in demand as a party spokesman—Harrison learned the practical art of politics.

Indiana took a leading part in the intense Presidential campaign of 1868. Grant, the Republican nominee, enjoyed the support of the state machine, but it was his running mate, Schuyler Colfax of South Bend, who most stirred Hoosier enthusiasm. As Speaker of the House, Colfax had been a successful radical leader, and he was fighting hard to make the ticket a winning one. When the Democrats chose as their standard-bearers Horatio Seymour of New York and General Francis Blair of Missouri, sectional hatred loomed as the issue, and most editors predicted that the two parties would fight the war all over again,[14] from Sumter to Appomattox.

During the canvass Fishback and Porter spoke regularly, but Harrison found time for only two speeches. His major effort came

[11] Barnhart and Carmony, *op. cit.*, II, 195. The Republican majority in Indiana was 15,000 and the party elected eight of the eleven congressmen.

[12] Harrison to Gen. B. R. Gowen, September 14, 1867, in the Gates McCarrah Collection of Presidential Autographs (Library of Congress).

[13] *Journal*, September 16, 1868.

[14] Smith, *op. cit.*, pp. 259–64.

in mid-August at Kent, Indiana, in strongly Republican Jefferson County.[15] It was a strict party-line speech, in which he labeled all Democratic activity during the war "treasonable schemes." This bit of rebel-baiting, known as "waving the bloody shirt," had been provoked by Blair, who claimed that the "only real issue in this contest" was the overthrow of radical reconstruction in the South. He railed against the Reconstruction Acts as usurpations of Congress and pleaded for a President who would trample them into the dust.[16] Ultimately the Blair doctrine castigated the Acts as unconstitutional, revolutionary, and void, and this sentiment formed the main plank of the Democratic platform. At Kent, Harrison savagely attacked both Blair and his position in an impassioned rebuttal where epithet was fought with epithet. Partisan cheering rewarded Harrison's oratorical onslaught, and the Madison *Courier,* Republican in sympathy, styled the General "one of the ablest speakers in the West." [17]

In November, after a bitter contest, Grant, the "man on horseback," had won the race, and Harrison shared the glory of his party's triumph. His political apprenticeship had not been in vain. Not until the following February, however, was he to win personal fame as attorney for the prosecution in one of the most sensational trials of the day.

In the midst of the Presidential campaign—on Sunday morning, September 13, 1868, to be exact—the news report of a cold-blooded double homicide shocked Indianapolis. The twin murder, the most celebrated in the annals of Marion County,[18] had taken place at Cold Springs, several miles up the White River, late the preceding Saturday afternoon. A little after dawn, young Robert Bow-

---

[15] *Journal,* August 17, 1868. For the usual Republican preponderance in Jefferson County, see William G. Carleton, "Why Was the Democratic Party in Indiana a Radical Party, 1865–1890?" *Indiana Magazine of History,* 42 (1946), 226–27, n. 46.

[16] Lorant, *op. cit.,* p. 292. *Journal,* August 29, 1868 (the Supplement), and Smith, *op. cit.,* p. 296. Charles H. Coleman's *The Election of 1868* remains the best analysis of the issues. James G. Randall, *Civil War and Reconstruction,* p. 794, seems to be in agreement with General Blair.

[17] Cited in the *Journal,* August 17, 1868.

[18] J. P. Dunn, *History of Greater Indianapolis,* I, 59 ff. An enterprising subscription book publisher, A. C. Roach, issued in pamphlet form the history of *The Cold Springs Tragedy,* of which the first edition of 8,000 copies sold out within a week; ten days later another 20,000 copies were nearly exhausted and a third edition of 100,000 was issued. A copy of this pamphlet is still among the holdings of the Indiana State Library.

man, going after his father's cows, found the bloody corpse of Jacob Young, a respected businessman. Nearby was the half-burned body of Mrs. Young. Also discovered was a double-barreled shotgun, still half-loaded. The post-mortem examination proved, however, that Mrs. Young had been killed by a pistol shot. The Youngs' overturned buggy was found in the woods not more than fifty yards from the dreadful scene. Another finding was the distinct print of a woman's shoe—clearly not Mrs. Young's. The mystery thickened as darkness fell.

On Monday morning the press furnished avid readers with the shocking details of the death of Jacob and Nancy Young. As the Coroner's investigation dragged on, Indianapolis could talk of little else; the Presidential campaign was all but forgotten. Finally, the Coroner, after examining more than one hundred witnesses, unearthed several vital clues. On the day before his death, Jacob Young had drawn from the bank $7,500, of which no trace could be found. Also, the strange feminine footprint, "tiny and neat," led to the tracks of a second buggy, whose horse had been peculiarly shod.[19] A chain of circumstantial evidence was gradually being welded. By the end of the first week in October, three suspects, two men and a woman, had been arrested and held for questioning before the Coroner's jury.

William Abrams, a local broker and business friend of the murdered man, was the first. On the morning of the crime, Abrams had purchased at a pawnshop the old shotgun used in the slaying.[20] He denied any guilt, claiming witnesses to prove that he had been at home at the alleged time of the murder. Abrams failed to impress the Coroner's jury and was, in due course, indicted for first-degree murder.[21] Silas Hartman, identified as the driver of the second carriage, was the next arrest. He, too, claimed an alibi— that he had been out for a long drive with his cousin from St. Louis. But Hartman was also indicted for first-degree murder.[22]

[19] *Journal,* September 14, 1868; also Roach, *op. cit.,* p. 65. These tracks had been made by a "preventive shoe," used to keep the horse from hurting itself in moving about.

[20] Roach, *op. cit.,* p. 8. The identification of the gun was beyond contradiction and there was no reasonable doubt that Abrams had purchased it from the pawnshop.

[21] Subsequently Abrams was tried, convicted, and sentenced to life imprisonment. He was pardoned, however, by Governor James D. Williams on July 3, 1878. See Dunn, *op. cit.,* I, 60.

[22] Three separate grand jury indictments read that "by force of arms, unlawfully, feloniously, purposely and with premeditated malice" one Jacob Young and his wife were murdered. See *Journal,* October 24, 1868. Shortly after Mrs. Clem's

The third arrest proved the most shocking of all. This was Silas Hartman's sister, 35-year-old Nancy Clem, wife of a respectable grocer. Unknown to her husband, Mrs. Clem had been engaging in some questionable financial transactions, whether with counterfeiters or with loan-sharks still is not clear.[23] It was established that Jacob Young was one of her principal creditors, and witnesses had seen her riding with the Youngs on the afternoon of their murder. Others testified that, shortly after the hour of the crime, they had seen her riding with her brother in his carriage.[24] The tide ran swiftly against the accused. Arrested on October 7, 1868, Nancy Clem was indicted for first-degree murder on October 20.[25]

With Abrams and Hartman, Mrs. Clem entered a plea of not guilty. Separate trials were ordered, with Mrs. Clem scheduled to go first before the Criminal Court. December 1, 1868, was the date set for a trial which was to hold Indianapolis spellbound.

Named on behalf of the State of Indiana to assist in Mrs. Clem's prosecution was the law firm of Porter, Fishback and Harrison.[26] A tribute to the firm's legal standing, the appointment came at an inopportune time for General Harrison. Political engagements and the last of his Reporter's duties were already requiring more time than he had to give. In addition, two weeks before the trial was to open, the Bar Association had appointed him one of a committee of five to study the inadequacies of the Indianapolis court system. This would entail writing a report on the complete reorganization of the federal, county, and common pleas courts. Since Porter was also deep in other pursuits, the burden of the Clem case fell on Fishback's shoulders, with Harrison and Porter

---

second trial, Hartman confessed the crime in an effort to exculpate his sister. The public did not believe Hartman, and in a fit of despondency he took his own life. Dunn, *op. cit.*, I, 60.

[23] *Ibid.* "There was evidence adduced . . . tending to show that Mrs. Clem was operating a system of interchangeable loans . . . and at a certain point frightening her duped creditors into silence by threats of exposure of participation in the profits of counterfeiting, or some other illegal business."

[24] Roach, *op. cit.*, p. 12.

[25] *Journal*, March 15, 1880.

[26] *Sentinel*, December 2, 1868. In charge of the prosecution was John T. Dye, Harrison's former associate. John S. Duncan was the prosecuting attorney, assisted by Barbour and Jacobs, attorneys for Marion County. Porter, Fishback and Harrison were named to the State's staff late in October. The defense was to be conducted by W. W. Leathers, John Hanna, and General Fred Knefler.

available for consultation and as many hours in court as possible during the actual trial.

Indianapolis could talk of little else; daily features in the *Journal* and *Sentinel* [27] kept public interest at white heat. Scarcely a citizen in Marion County was ignorant of the smallest detail of the bloody affair. Indeed, many feared it might be impossible to secure an impartial jury.

On December 1, 1868, however, a jury was agreed upon, and the trial began.[28] Harrison was in court on opening day and made frequent appearances during the next seventeen days, during which more than one hundred and fifty witnesses were heard in contradictory testimony.

The jury took the case on Saturday, December 19, but on failing to reach a verdict by the following Monday afternoon they were discharged, and a new trial was scheduled for early February.

In the six-week interval between the first and second Clem trials, Harrison had issued Volume 28 of the Indiana *Reports* [29] and on January 15, 1869, relinquished his Reporter's office. Free, too, of political pressures, he began at once to study the transcripts of the first trial and within three weeks had redesigned the State's case. Countless handwritten notes, still preserved among his legal papers, remain a monument to hours of solitary, painstaking preparation.[30] Harrison was now ready to put his legal abilities to the courtroom test. A conviction won in such a case as this might well be the first step towards both legal and political prominence.

On the first day of the retrial, Harrison and his associates successfully argued against the defense motion for a change in venue.[31] The defense then moved to restrain the public prosecutor from employing Harrison and his partners as assistants. After a heated

[27] *Ibid.*, January 15, 1869. Both organs published a galaxy of rumor and fact before and during the trial. Eventually the editors were fined for contempt of court for publishing the evidence during the trial.

[28] *Sentinel*, December 2, 1868. The State, entitled to six peremptory challenges, used five, while the defense used ten of the twenty to which it was entitled.

[29] *Journal*, January 9, 1869.

[30] Legal Papers and Diaries, (L.C.).

[31] *Journal*, December 21, 1868, February 6, 1869. Harrison and Fishback argued against the motion on the score of added expense to the state. The magnitude of the crime would necessitate the maintenance and transportation of over one hundred and fifty witnesses to wherever the trial would be held. Judge Chapman, mindful of the large expense incurred during the first trial, overruled the defense motion.

exchange between the General and opposing counsel, Judge George Chapman again overruled the defense.[32] A jury was quickly chosen, followed by the swearing in of 150 witnesses for the State and 115 for the defense. The courtroom was jammed, and visiting lawyers vied with reporters and with one another for seats near the bench.

By far the most difficult task facing Harrison and his associates was the smashing of Mrs. Clem's strongly supported alibi. If she could prove she was actually at home all day on September 12, 1868, the State had no case.[33] With great care, therefore, after an incriminating exposure of Mrs. Clem's secret financial transactions, three key witnesses were introduced. Each swore to seeing Mrs. Clem in Young's buggy, with Young and his wife, headed for Cold Springs on the afternoon of the murder.[34] Next, Mrs. Clem's brother, Silas Hartman, was identified as having followed a short distance behind them in the second buggy.[35] The State then called an altogether new witness, John S. Pierson, Mrs. Clem's neighbor. Admitting that he had been bribed to leave the city during the first trial, he now bluntly declared that he had seen the accused returning home on September 12, riding in a buggy with her brother. By this time the credibility of the Clem alibi had practically vanished, and Harrison proceeded to prove to the court that Mrs. Clem had bribed her two alibi witnesses to testify that she was at home on the afternoon of the murder.

In the summations which followed, the General presented the final argument for the State, holding the jury a full eight hours. First, he hammered mercilessly at the defense's theory of murder

[32] *Ibid.*, February 10, 1869.

[33] Roach, *op. cit.*, p. 53. According to her signed statement submitted to the Coroner's jury, Mrs. Clem not only claimed her presence at home, but she also testified that Abrams came to her home at 2:30 or 3:00 P.M. and did not leave until 5:00 P.M. Moreover, she alleged that her own brother, Silas Hartman, passed her house, driving with another man, at about 4:00 P.M. To substantiate her claim Mrs. Clem said the following people saw her at home: Mr. Brown, a paper hanger, and his son; her colored girl, Jane; and her own mother. These were to be her alibi witnesses, though it appeared later in the trial that she had tried to bribe others.

[34] *Journal*, February 18, 1869.

[35] Roach, *op. cit.*, p. 19. The defense rested upon a series of closely related alibis. Hartman had his saving story; the apparent uncertainty of the witnesses who identified Mrs. Clem; and minor disagreements as to the time of the shooting and the actual seeing of the accused on the road to and from Cold Springs. If the generally feeble testimony of the State's witnesses had failed to shake the perjured alibi of Mrs. Clem during the first trial, the truth that was exposed in this trial left the defense without a real case.

and suicide as nothing more than a "remote conjecture made for the purpose of getting the jury to construe it into a reasonable doubt." [36]

Harrison then focused the jury's attention on the death scene and on the little Young girl, left parentless:

It was a scene to freeze one's blood . . . Not only dead but burned! Those bleached remains, charred until scarce a vestige of her image was left! The little orphan left at home waited in vain for their return that night. How slow . . . the moments must have passed. [37]

As he eyed each juror, Harrison bitingly added: "Whoever committed this deed has no grounds on which to base an appeal to any jury." Were Mr. Young's pockets rifled? His excessively large amount of cash gone? If so, he went on, "it gives us certain knowledge of the motive; it was sordid avarice that prompted the murder." [38] He scoffed at the defense's contention that since no one had seen the deed, no verdict of guilty could be returned. Why, he exclaimed, if this rule were to be accepted, bloodshed would run riot.

Harrison took up next the question of perjury and the original Clem alibi. Julia McCarthy, Mrs. Clem's maid, had sworn before the Grand Jury that Mrs. Clem was at home all afternoon on the day in question. She had also made several other false statements during the first trial, and this perjury had been devastatingly exposed. Why had Julia McCarthy lied, Harrison asked the jury. Simply because Mrs. Clem had requested and paid her to do so. He then cited the example of Mrs. Clem's young niece, who had confessed in this second trial that her aunt had forced her to lie. [39] Harrison turned to the jury: "I do not know," he said with deep earnestness, "which is the worst criminal, the man who takes the life of his fellow, or he who saps the foundation of childish innocence and truth." [40]

Thus, Harrison's most telling strokes were directed against Mrs. Clem's alibi and her attempts to suborn witnesses to perjury. What, he demanded, did Mrs. Clem actually do on that fatal after-

[36] *Journal,* February 27, 1869.

[37] *Ibid.*

[38] *Ibid.* Harrison maintained that no other conclusion was possible: "Was there anyone who stood in the position that in addition to getting the money, they would profit otherwise?"

[39] *Ibid.*

[40] Roach, *op. cit.,* p. 76.

noon? "She went away from her house," Harrison declared, "going through Hartman's backyard, and climbing over the back fence . . . to join Young and his wife on their way to Cold Springs." [41] He asked the jury to trace that fatal journey, forcefully reviewing for them the testimony of witnesses who had seen Mrs. Clem in Young's buggy. Harrison closed with the warning: "They appeal to you in terms setting out the shame and disgrace that would attach to the household of this woman if you should find her guilty . . . they ask you not to forget the living. I ask you not to forget the dead, and the interest of society." [42]

The defense offered a stirring six-hour summation and appeal by John Hanna, in which he argued that a reasonable doubt had been established and that, beyond that, his client was truly innocent. This effort, filled with every sentimental appeal, was received in absolute silence. Judge Chapman then delivered his charge to the jurors, who retired.

While the jury considered its verdict, all Indianapolis fell to reviewing the case. The opinion prevailed that Mrs. Clem had been proved guilty, and on the editorial page of the *Journal* the evidence against her was set forth in minute, chronological detail. [43]

After forty-eight hours of public suspense, the jury returned its verdict: "Guilty of murder in the second degree." [44] On the first vote the jury had stood nine for hanging, three for life imprisonment—not one for acquittal. [45]

[41] Roach, *op. cit.*, p. 73. Mrs. Clem admitted in later testimony that she had left the house for a short time in the morning in order to go to the post office and to the New York Store. Subsidiary witnesses were introduced to testify to Mrs. Clem's presence at these two spots. They also had been suborned and consequently broke badly under cross-examination.

[42] *Journal*, February 27, 1869.

[43] *Ibid.*, March 2, 1869. According to the editor, the gist of the matter came to this: "Mrs. Clem had mysterious money transactions with Mr. Young, which she concealed from her husband. . . . [She] needed either Mr. Young's money, or his disappearance, to prevent a development which must reach her husband. These strange transactions Mrs. Clem could have explained, if they were innocent transactions, but she would not. . . ." The editorial summation concluded: ". . . [Mrs. Clem] takes a large roll of bills to her sister's house and hides it in a hole in the chimney 'because she is afraid her house will be searched,' though she is not suspected; when Abrams is arrested and sends to her for money, she sends him nearly $5,000 without taking a receipt . . . ; she tries to bribe one woman to swear that she was home the afternoon of the murder; she frightens or cajoles her sister, her niece and her sister's servant into swearing falsely; she induces an important witness to absent himself at the first trial. . . ."

[44] This carried a sentence of confinement in the State Prison for life; hanging was the penalty for a verdict of guilty in the first degree.

[45] *Journal*, March 2, 1869. The editor noted that "no jury in Indiana will ever

Mrs. Clem heard the verdict with no evidence of grief, guilt, or surprise. On March 29, 1868, she was sentenced to life imprisonment.[46]

For Harrison, the conviction of Mrs. Clem was undoubtedly his greatest courtroom triumph. Lawyers from all over the State had witnessed his efforts as public prosecutor, and the Harrison name, already celebrated in Indiana, enjoyed fresh renown. Said the *Journal:* "No prosecution within our knowledge was ever more skillfully conducted. . . . The road was mapped out from the beginning, and followed with a patience, vigilance and energy that has added to the already high reputation of General Harrison. . . ." [47] The victory was in fact a springboard to public recognition. Friends and a few politicians were already discussing Harrison's chances for the governorship in 1872.

---

hang a woman, as long as they have another alternative, and imprisonment for life is equally the penalty for murder in the first and the second degree."

[46] *Clem v. State* in *33 Indiana*, pp. 418–34 (November Term, 1870), and *Clem v. State* in *42 Indiana*, pp. 420–49 (May Term, 1873), indicate that Harrison and the courts had not seen Nancy Clem for the last time. After the Indiana Supreme Court had reversed her conviction, Harrison, on a change of venue to Boone County, tried and convicted Nancy Clem a second time. Again the Supreme Court reversed the findings of the lower court. In 1874, when a Board of County Commissioners declared that they "would incur no further expense in the prosecution of Nancy E. Clem," the case was dropped. Mrs. Clem's liberty, however, was short-lived. In 1880, and partially through Harrison's efforts, she was convicted of perjury in another case and served a four-year sentence in Women's Prison. For details, see *Journal,* March 15–20, 1880, and Dunn, *op. cit.,* I, 60.

[47] March 2, 1869. Similar praise was voiced by the *Sentinel,* March 1, 2, 1869.

CHAPTER III

An Echo of the War

IT WAS FORTUNATE in view of Harrison's family responsibilities that he had the guarantee of a steady income,[1] for poverty, sickness, and death in Ohio and Iowa during 1869 and 1870 were to leave the General the unassisted mainstay of his father and the continued benefactor of his brothers and sisters. His chief concern was for his favorite brother, Irwin, the soldier who had contracted tuberculosis. Ben saw that he had good physicians, costly medicines, and trips to Denver and the West. Then there was Carter, struggling to make a go of it at the Point Farm in Ohio, and another brother, John Scott, Jr., the youngest, who "couldn't make a dime." [2] His clothes were bought by brother Ben, who also kept him in spending money.

So far as his immediate family was concerned, however, the picture looked bright in the spring of 1869. In the comfortable home on North Alabama Street, Carrie and the children were well and Harrison himself felt relaxed and contented. With only one profession to occupy his energies, now that he had given up the Reportership, Harrison's life had returned to the rhythm of a slow, placid stream. For the second spring in a row, he and his wife worked together to beautify their yard. Soon shade trees, small shrubs, several fruit trees, and even a little strawberry patch adorned their property.

At the same time, the General did not lose interest in G.A.R. affairs. His first public appearance after the celebrated Clem con-

[1] Though no longer Court Reporter, Harrison's legal income was steady and lucrative. Cash Book, 1870–1871, (L.C.). The *Journal*, April 20, 1870, shows that Harrison was in the upper 10 per cent bracket of taxpayers.
[2] John Scott Harrison, Jr. to Benjamin, February 14, 15, March 3, 8, 1870, (L.C.), Vol. 6.

viction was on the fifth anniversary of the Battle of Peach Tree Creek. For Hoosiers, the courageous charge of the 70th Indiana Volunteer Regiment at the Georgia creek was the action that led to "the capture of Atlanta by Sherman's Army."[3] On July 20, 1869, hundreds of veterans, with their wives and children, crowded into Martinsville, some twenty-five miles south of Indianapolis, for the reunion. The principal speakers were to be two of the chief actors in the original drama, Generals Harrison and John Coburn.

As the young veterans gathered, memories of the war gathered with them. They recounted tales of bravery under fire—and perhaps invented a few new ones. Naturally there were many stories about "Little Ben"—his heroism and his constant concern for his men. One soldier recalled how Harrison, after the Battle of New Hope Church, unable to find surgeons for his wounded and dying men, tore his own shirt and tent into strips and went about bandaging their wounds himself.[4] Other similar stories [5] made understandable the bond of devotion that existed between the former commander and his "Boys in Blue."

In his twenty-minute address, Harrison dwelt first upon the stirring scenes at Peach Tree, the theme his audience had come to hear. He then reminded them solemnly that the war had advanced the causes of human liberty and just government. He urged them to finish the work of reconstruction and to extinguish the debt of war "by the stroke of the hammer and the axe in the shop, and the toilsome work of the brain." He ended with a statesmanlike appeal to let "no stain of dishonor rest upon our country in peace, which so gloriously maintained its honor in war." Three lusty cheers greeted the General as he sat down, with three more for the regimental flags displayed on the dais. General Coburn's remarks followed and, after an interlude of band music, the crowd dispersed for a companionable dinner.[6] It was the sort of occasion Harrison liked best.

For the remainder of the summer, Harrison avoided patriotic and political meetings alike. Busy with the task of maintaining his own financial equilibrium and restoring that of his less fortunate relatives, he must also have been glad of the rare oppor-

[3] *Journal*, July 22, 1869.

[4] Lew Wallace, *Life of Gen. Ben Harrison*, pp. 204–6; Syracuse (N. Y.) *Herald*, March 17, 1901.

[5] Memphis (Tenn.) *Evening Scimitar*, March 31, 1901.

[6] *Journal*, July 22, 1869.

tunity to stay at home and tend his garden. Only half-heartedly did he consider an invitation from his sister in Iowa to visit "the boundless west for health, wealth and prosperity." [7] The peace and quiet of Indianapolis were sufficient. In addition, he and Carrie were frequently visited by relatives who chose the state's capital as their vacation spot. More and more his family had come to depend on Ben's reliability and, as often as not, these visits mixed business with pleasure. Not until November did he finally take his usual vacation of hunting and fishing in the north country. [8]

Admittedly an important factor in shaping Benjamin Harrison's destiny was his close association in peace with the men who had won the war. In the late winter of 1869, this alliance was further extended by the General's joining a newly-formed veterans' group, the Society of the Army of the Cumberland. It had come into existence in Cincinnati in February, 1868, in response to a call by General George H. Thomas, the famed "Rock of Chickamauga," who had been Harrison's commanding officer during the battle for Nashville. [9] A thousand former officers of Thomas's old unit had elected the "Rock" president at the organizational meeting, and he had presided over the first annual meeting, held in Chicago. Harrison was among the many Hoosiers who joined and closed ranks behind Thomas.

Indianapolis was selected for the Society's second annual encampment on December 15 and 16, 1869. Harrison's specific task, as one of the committee on arrangements, was to choose a dozen "toast speakers" for the convention's closing banquet in Washington Hall. He named ten generals, including himself, and one colonel to respond to the toasts. The twelfth—"To our Heroic Dead"—would be drunk in silence. The *Journal* termed the two-day meeting "one of the grandest affairs ever seen in this city" and praised Harrison's speech in particular as "one of the most appropriate and eloquent responses of the evening." The General had paid a masterful tribute to the sacrifices and loyalty of the women, who "had nerved the soldier's arm and brought victory to the country's flag," and had concluded with raised glass and the toast:

[7] Sallie Devin to Benjamin Harrison, September 14, 1869, (L.C.), Vol. 6.

[8] *Ibid.*, November 21, 1869.

[9] *Journal*, October 21, 1869. For Harrison's service under Thomas, see Harry J. Sievers, *Benjamin Harrison: Hoosier Warrior*, pp. 279–85.

"God bless the loyal women!" He had prepared no manuscript; thus Carrie for one knew that his words came from the heart.[10]

Even before the last of the veterans left the city, preparations for Christmas and the New Year were in full swing. In accordance with the custom of the times, the Harrisons held open house on the first day of January. The ladies, headed by Carrie Harrison, began receiving callers at about eleven o'clock New Year's morning; the whirl of visitors, including coquettish belles and eligible gentlemen, continued through the day.[11]

Thus pleasantly launched, the first half of 1870 was uneventful for the Harrisons, who continued to enjoy the tranquil routine of home life, in spite of the General's continued concern for his brother's welfare. John Scott, Jr., dependent as ever on Ben's purse, now contemplated a law career, which would mean money for tuition.[12] On the whole, however, family affairs improved. In the early summer, Carter moved his family from Ohio to Murfreesboro, Tennessee, where his farming income could be supplemented by employment in the Federal Assessor's office.[13] And Irwin appeared to be responding favorably to the western climate, giving Ben hope that he might eventually be cured.

In mid-June, 1870, "Pink" Fishback announced that he would soon resign his partnership in order to devote full time to his new role as editor of the Indianapolis *Journal*.[14] From this point on, Harrison assumed a still greater share of the firm's legal work. With the approach of fall and the quickening of the state's politi-

[10] *Journal*, December 17, 1869. A reporter managed to catch most of Harrison's extemporaneous address in shorthand.

[11] *Ibid.*, January 1, 1870.

[12] John Scott Harrison, Jr. to Benjamin Harrison, February 14, 1870, (L.C.), Vol. 7. Once, with rent overdue, young John Scott Harrison, Jr., drew on brother Ben for "twenty-five dollars at three days sight. My board was due today, and I could not stave it off any longer." He apologized on the following day, writing, "I sincerely hope that I have not put you to very great inconvenience. . . . But brother I need a pair of pants and a hat very badly . . ." The youngest Harrison soon emerged from such financial straits. In October, 1871, he moved to Kansas City and joined a real estate firm. Five months later, he happily reported that he was "just making a start in life" and had saved $400 in four months. *Ibid.*, February 21, 1872.

[13] Carter B. Harrison to Benjamin, February 2, June 2, July 19, 1870, (L.C.), Vol. 6.

[14] Fishback became editor of the *Journal* on June 11, 1870. A letter from Samuel M. Douglass, James C. Douglass, and A. H. Conner, addressed "To the Readers of the Journal," appeared in that paper on June 13, 1870, and states that these three gentlemen had sold their interests to Lewis W. Hasselman and William P. Fishback on June 11. See also W. P. Fishback to O. P. Morton, June 17, 1870, O. P. Morton MSS.

cal activities, there was also some pressure from fellow Republicans for help in the coming campaign. The General, having taken no active part in the State Convention of 1870, had likewise resolved to avoid the stump in the fall. This proved impossible. On his desk one morning in late August he found a desperate appeal from General Lew Wallace for just one speech. His old family friend was running for Congress.[15] "Your name is good here," Wallace wrote, "and the people would like to see and hear you, and there is no doubt you can do me . . . great good. . . . Don't fail me —come and help me." [16] Harrison yielded, and on September 13, 1870, at a great mass meeting in Marshfield in Warren County, he beat the political drums for his future campaign biographer. The election, however, proved disillusioning: Wallace lost by 393 votes out of 30,685.[17]

Almost immediately after his speech for Wallace, Harrison took his family for an extended vacation in the East. This included a trip to Niagara Falls, a tour of New England, and visits to relatives in New Jersey and Pennsylvania. It was the family's first real vacation together since the war. Sixteen-year-old Russell was his father's favorite partner in quail hunting, but they also spent time searching for an eastern college suitable for the son, who was soon to be graduated from preparatory school. As for Mamie, old enough now to be noted as one of the "bewitching, handsome, fascinating and intelligent young girls" [18] of Indianapolis, she wisely used the trip as an opportunity to understudy her mother's personal charm and social grace. It was soon reported that pretty Mamie Harrison learned easily.[19]

Returning to Indianapolis refreshed, Harrison once more plunged into his legal duties and prepared to welcome a new partner. After Fishback's resignation, the firm had continued as Porter and Harrison until New York-born Cyrus C. Hines, having stepped down from the bench of the Circuit Court, entered the office. Three years Harrison's senior, Hines had settled in Indianapolis the same year as the General. He, too, had left a flourishing law career to join the Union forces. After service in the Virginia campaign, and a major's commission, he had been made colonel

15 Irving McKee, *"Ben-Hur" Wallace*, pp. 120–1.
16 Lew Wallace to Benjamin Harrison, August 27, 1870, Harrison Home MSS.
17 McKee, *op. cit.*, p. 121.
18 *Journal*, July 31, 1869.
19 Sallie Devin to Benjamin Harrison, September 29, 1870, (L.C.), Vol. 7.

with assignment to the Army of the Cumberland. Wounded at the Battle of Stone's River, he had had to resign his commission and return to Indiana. A staunch Republican and a distinguished jurist, Hines remained associated in law with Harrison for more than a decade, becoming his close personal friend and ardent political supporter.[20]

During the first weeks of the new partnership, Harrison remained free of family worries. Encouraging news from the West [21] assured him that Irwin had gained some temporary relief in the mountain air, though not a complete cure.

On the other hand, the climate had restored his ailing wife, Bettie, to complete health. What optimism Harrison may have permitted himself to feel was short-lived. Irwin died in December, 1870, after returning to Indianapolis, and his brother's grief was intense. Irwin was only thirty-eight, a year older than Benjamin. Both before and during the war, his military career had marked him as a man of competence.[22] He and Ben had been close. Together they had farmed, fished, and gone to school, and the bonds of war had strengthened the bonds of blood.[23] For Benjamin Harrison, the year 1870 ended sorrowfully indeed.

More than ever, the law now claimed his primary attention, and 1871 crowned his redoubled efforts with another major courtroom triumph—the decision in the Milligan case.

Six-foot-four, light-complexioned, blue-eyed, Irish-born Lambdin P. Milligan was a northern Indiana lawyer, onetime president of the Chicago and Atlantic (now Erie) Railroad, a scientific farmer, and promoter, who kept a stable of fine race horses. He had read law in Ohio with Secretary of War Stanton and soon became a close student of the teachings of Jefferson and Jackson. The latter he knew personally and admired greatly. Milligan was a vigorous Catholic by faith, and in politics always a Democrat. Twenty-one years Harrison's senior, the two had met while riding the legal circuits and stumping their adopted states for opposing parties.

[20] J. P. Dunn, *History of Greater Indianapolis,* II, 849. Hines served as Marion County Civil Circuit Court judge from November 3, 1866, to November 5, 1870.

[21] Irwin Harrison to Benjamin, May 20, September 20, 24, 1870; and Bettie L. S. Harrison to Benjamin, August 12, 1870, (L.C.), Vols. 6 and 7.

[22] *Journal,* December 17, 1870.

[23] Sievers, *op. cit.,* pp. 24, 25, 29, 40–45, 128–29, 133, 168–69, 296–97.

When war came, the two men walked different roads. After Harrison had enlisted and gone to the front, Milligan still opposed the war with great energy. He advocated "a Union restored by negotiation rather than war and denounced military arrests, conscriptions, emancipation, and other war measures." [24] Newspaper stories, avidly devoured in camp, kept Harrison aware of Milligan's activities until he returned to Indianapolis on furlough in the fall of 1864.[25] Then began a conflict which lasted seven years and profoundly influenced the lives of both men. The story, with its background and finale, is worth recounting, for both the issues and the personalities have left their stamp on American constitutional and political history.[26]

Most publicized of the Indiana societies suspected of aiding and abetting the South during the war was the Knights of the Golden Circle,[27] founded on Independence Day, 1854, at Lexington, Kentucky. In reality, two younger groups, the Order of American Knights and the Order of the Sons of Liberty,[28] made the greatest impact on Indiana in 1863, 1864, and after the war. The Hoosier Council of the American Knights was organized at Terre Haute in August, 1863, temporary officers were installed the following month at Indianapolis, and by February, 1864, some sixty counties were reported organized. The old Knights of the Golden Circle furnished the nucleus of the new group, whose password was "Nu-oh-lac," Calhoun spelled backwards. Their purpose was to achieve "the independence of the individual states as secured by the Revolution of 1776." [29] Their leaders, boasting of more than 12,000 followers, opposed the liberation of four million blacks and

[24] See Florence L. Grayston, "Lambdin P. Milligan—A Knight of the Golden Circle," *Indiana Magazine of History*, 43 (1947), 379–91. The author has drawn heavily on Miss Grayston's excellent research. There is also a readable chapter on Milligan in John A. Marshall, *American Bastille*.

[25] Sievers, *op. cit.*, pp. 269 ff.

[26] James R. Randall, *The Civil War and Reconstruction*, pp. 398–99, 802 ff. Also Charles Warren, *The Supreme Court and the United States*. (2-vol. ed.), II, 427 ff.

[27] Kenneth P. Stampp, *Indiana Politics During the Civil War*, pp. 149 ff. More detailed are these scholarly articles: C. A. Bridges, "The Knights of the Golden Circle: A Filibustering Fantasy," *Southwestern Historical Quarterly*, 44 (1940–1941), 287–302; and Ollinger Crenshaw, "The Knights of the Golden Circle," *American Historical Review*, 47 (1941–1942), 23–50.

[28] Mayo Fesler, "Secret Political Societies in the North During the Civil War," *Indiana Magazine of History*, 14 (1918), 183–286.

[29] *Ibid.*, pp. 231–32.

declared that Lincoln's national government and Morton's state government were usurpations under which the people could not remain passive. Before long, the American Knights became the Sons of Liberty, adopting the initials "S. L." and the expression "Give me liberty or give me death." Indiana was divided into four districts, and in command of one was Lambdin P. Milligan, who had just failed in his quest for the Democratic gubernatorial candidacy.[30]

When the Sons of Liberty began to operate in Indiana, bitterness between Union men and the "peace-at-any-price" opponents of the administration grew intense. Unionists organized the Loyal League, a secret military organization composed chiefly of members of the Republican party, for action against "all enemies at home and abroad." Robbing, stealing, and general outlawry became so prevalent in southern Indiana that men went armed, "slept with rifles under their pillows, barricaded their houses and places of business, and in a number of cases good citizens rose in their might and without judge or jury put to death many of the outlaws."[31] It is only fair to point out that the overzealous spirit of the Loyal League led to abuses. Partisan Republicans blamed the Sons of Liberty, whom they identified with the Democratic party, for resistance to the draft, raiding bands of outlaws, and for drunken riots between "butternuts"[32] and soldiers home on furlough. Federal, state, and local authorities, in quelling disturbances, frequently inflicted upon Democrats, just because they were Democrats, "abuses and punishments which were undeserved."[33]

After the Democratic national convention, held in Chicago in late August, 1864, the victory of pro-Union War Democrats cleared the air somewhat of treason talk. Peace Democrats, and particularly the Sons of Liberty, felt less secure and less united. The latter certainly could not count on the full sympathy of the Democratic party. Harrison H. Dodd and William H. Harrison, Grand Commander and Grand Secretary, respectively, for the state, quickly

---

[30] Grayston, *loc. cit.*, p. 382; Fesler, *loc. cit.*, pp. 238, 264–65.

[31] Fesler, *loc. cit.*, p. 239.

[32] "Butternuts" were southern sympathizers. They were folks from the backwoods whose homespun garments were dyed with the juice of butternuts. Their women often wore broaches carved from the nuts. Harrison himself used the term in the sense of "Copperheads." See Grayston, *op. cit.*, p. 383. Elucidating also is Charles H. Coleman, "The Use of the Term 'Copperhead,' During the Civil War," *Mississippi Valley Historical Review*, 25 (1938), 263–64.

[33] Fesler, *loc. cit.*, pp. 239–40.

grasped this fact. When Dodd returned to Indianapolis after the convention, he immediately declared that the charges of conspiracy made against the Sons of Liberty were without foundation. He urged his fellow citizens to withhold judgment until such charges were substantiated. State Republican leaders, anxious for potent campaign material, remained belligerent and suspicious. Finally, Dodd issued a public statement that "the immediate purpose of the Sons of Liberty and the Democratic party were identical." [34]

Republican reaction to Dodd's statement was swift, and when rumor whispered that the Sons of Liberty were planning an armed uprising in Indianapolis itself,[35] action followed. The military, whose spies and detectives had long been active, moved rapidly. General Alvin P. Hovey, military commandant, arrested Dodd early in September. Within thirty days a number of arrests followed, including Indiana's four "major generals" of the Sons of Liberty, Bowles, Horsey, Humphreys, and Milligan.[36]

Meanwhile, with Atlanta in Union hands, Harrison's thoughts turned to home and to his impending campaign for re-election as Supreme Court Reporter, an office from which he had been ousted, he believed,[37] by Copperhead intrigue in November, 1862. Arriving in Indianapolis on furlough, on September 20, 1864, Harrison was quickly briefed on the state's explosive political situation. The Democrats, incensed by the "sensational and effective exposé of the Sons of Liberty or Knights of the Golden Circle," [38] were prosecuting a bitter state campaign, hotly denying Republican allegations of treason. The battle in the hustings paralleled the fight in the press.[39] Harrison had long held the fixed, partisan belief that most Indiana Democrats were guilty of treasonable designs against Union war efforts. Yet, while still in the field, his solution to the Copperhead problem was a soldier's rather than a politician's. "I think the Union papers and speakers are making too much noise and parade about . . . Copperheads," he had then confided to his wife. "It would be better to say less and *do* more." If more loud-talking Union men were fighting before Atlanta and

34 *Ibid.*, p. 257.

35 For details of the rumored revolt, see Grayston, *loc. cit.*, p. 386.

36 Fesler, *loc. cit.*, pp. 257–58.

37 Many Republicans shared Harrison's belief and renominated him for the same office at the Union State Convention on February 23, 1864. See Sievers, *op. cit.*, p. 267.

38 Dunn, *op. cit.*, I, 236, and Kenneth P. Stampp, *op. cit.*, pp. 149–50.

39 During September and October, 1864, both the *Sentinel* and *Journal* featured several vitriolic editorials.

Richmond, he wrote, "the Copperheads would be dead and no one would know who killed them." [40] Back in Indianapolis, however, he found that political strategists had more devious plans. Treason charges make excellent political fireworks, and it was at this point that the arrest of Lambdin P. Milligan was effected.

Particular care was taken in the apprehension of Milligan on October 5, 1864. A special "train had been backed from Indianapolis at night to the tracks beside his home to prevent any interference, because Milligan was a popular figure in Huntington." [41] The arrest was made without incident, and fifteen days later Milligan was placed on trial at Indianapolis before a military commission. Together with other leaders of the Sons of Liberty, he was charged specifically with 1) conspiracy against the Government of the United States, 2) affording aid and comfort to the rebels against the authority of the United States, 3) inciting insurrection, 4) disloyal practices, and 5) violations of the laws of war. [42]

While Milligan pleaded not guilty, his attorney, John R. Coffroth, advanced the special argument that the military commission had no jurisdiction to try and sentence his client. Milligan, he argued, was not a resident of one of the rebellious states, nor a prisoner of war, nor a soldier, but a citizen of Indiana, arrested at his home by a military power. On this crucial point of jurisdiction, the Judge Advocate maintained the military's right to hold court, for President Lincoln had suspended civil law in trials for conspiracy and treason, and General Hovey was acting as representative of the commander in chief of the Army of the United States. Counsel for Milligan was overruled, and the celebrated trial got under way. [43] It was still in progress when Lincoln was re-elected, and after Harrison, himself re-elected to the Reportership, had left Indianapolis to rejoin his command.

The trial, lasting until the early part of December, 1864, attracted wide public attention. Interest and surprise reached a peak

---

[40] Benjamin Harrison to his wife, August 24, 1864, (L.C.), Vol. 5. Harrison hammered at the principle of not singing "rally round the flag, but *rallying* around it and dying in its defense."

[41] Grayston, *loc. cit.*, pp. 379–91.

[42] Fesler, *loc. cit.*, pp. 183–286.

[43] Benn Pitman, *Trials for Treason at Indianapolis, 1864*, pp. 69–71.

when several of the accused, including one of the "major generals," turned state's evidence. These men, long-time associates of Milligan, gave damaging testimony against him. In his defense, Milligan's attorney could only angrily assail the government's star witness as that "mudsill of infamy, who turned informer to purchase his own release." [44] After a brief consultation, the military commission found the accused guilty of the charges preferred against them. Milligan was sentenced to be hanged on May 19, 1865, between the hours of twelve and three on the parade grounds between Camp Morton and Burnside Barracks, near Indianapolis. In the meantime, the convicted man was to be confined in the military prison at Columbus, Ohio.

Milligan's many friends exerted every effort to secure a Presidential pardon. Lincoln showed himself inclined to release Milligan,[45] but any official action was precluded by his assassination. Andrew Johnson, on the contrary, approved the findings of the military commission and ordered that the hangings take place without further delay. Confederate prisoners, then at Camp Morton, were detailed to erect the gallows. At this point Milligan himself gave up all hope and notified his family to prepare for the worst. He made his funeral arrangements, even to the selection of pallbearers.[46] Neither Mrs. Milligan nor Attorney Coffroth, however, shared his despair. His wife hastened to Washington and gained an interview with Secretary of War Stanton, with whom her husband had read law.[47] Stanton promised that he would seek a commutation of sentence from President Johnson. Simultaneously, a group of Republicans led by Governor Morton pleaded for a stay of execution. On May 18, 1865, Attorney Coffroth filed a petition for a writ of habeas corpus, a move which postponed Milligan's execution until June 2, 1865. On that very day, President Johnson finally commuted Milligan's sentence to life imprisonment at hard labor in the Columbus penitentiary.[48]

In the meantime, the wheels of justice continued their slow grind. The judges of the Indiana Circuit Court failed to agree

[44] Fesler, loc. cit., pp. 262–65.
[45] Grayston, loc. cit., p. 387.
[46] W. D. Foulke, Life of Oliver P. Morton, I, 428.
[47] Huntington (Indiana) Herald, December 22, 1899, as cited in Grayston, op. cit., p. 388.
[48] Foulke, op. cit., p. 431.

on the habeas corpus writ, and the question was certified to the Supreme Court of the United States. Thus the stage was set for a landmark decision in constitutional law. After elaborate argument and consideration, the Court held that General Hovey's military commission had no jurisdiction to try and sentence Milligan. The Court firmly stated that "the constitution of the United States is a law for rulers and people, equally in war and in peace, and covers with the shield of its protection all classes of men, at all times and under all circumstances." [49] On April 2, 1866, Milligan's discharge from prison was ordered and executed. Cannons roared their welcome to the released resident of Huntington, whom eighteen months of imprisonment had brought to the point of physical prostration.[50] Within a month, the Federal Grand Jury at Indianapolis indicted Milligan on the same charges on which he had been tried by the military commission. He was released on bail. When the case was not pressed, Lambdin P. Milligan was dismissed and many believed the episode was closed.

Two years elapsed before Milligan, restored to health, made his own move in court. In the spring of 1868, he brought suit against the members of the military commission for damages. Among the twenty-two named were General Alvin P. Hovey, Joseph Holt, Judge Advocate General of the United States Army, and former Governor Oliver P. Morton. While there was never any question of Milligan's technical right of recovery, the suit stirred deep emotions.

When Milligan opened his case in the Common Pleas Court of Huntington County, he employed former Senator Thomas A. Hendricks as counsel. This added fuel to the fire, for Hendricks was not only the leading Democrat in Indiana but had also sympa-

---

[49] The phrase "*ex parte* Milligan" keynotes the doctrine that it is unconstitutional to try civilians by military tribunals outside the theatre of war. At the time of its issuance, however, it was greeted with a virulence reminiscent of the Dred Scott decision. See C. B. Swisher, *American Constitutional Development*, pp. 287–89, 320. Also S. Klaus (ed.), *The Milligan Case*, and J. F. Rhodes, *History of the United States Since the Compromise of 1850*, VI, 11; see also IV, 248. P. Orman Ray, "The Milligan Case (1866)," *Dictionary of American History*, III, 405, writes: "The Supreme Court held that neither the President nor Congress has the power to set up military tribunals except in the actual theatre of war, where the civil courts are no longer functioning, and that elsewhere courts-martial have jurisdiction only over persons in the military or naval service of the United States."

[50] Grayston, *loc. cit.*, pp. 390 ff.

thized with Milligan and his objectives during the war.[51] When, in May, 1871, the proceedings were transferred to the United States Circuit Court for the District of Indiana, President Grant appointed General Harrison counsel for the defense. This move had a distinct political and military tinge. A soldier-President was appointing a soldier-lawyer to defend soldier-administrators and executives. At the outset, therefore, the smoldering fires of civil war hatred were rekindled. After all, people said, Harrison was defending personal friends, many of whom, like General Hovey, had been comrades in arms and in politics. Also, many Republicans believed that the plaintiff and his counsel still labored under the stigma of treason during wartime.[52] For Harrison himself, the case was fairly bursting with potential political and legal capital.

On the first day, and throughout the long trial, the courtroom was jammed with spectators. There was an enormous display of popular feeling against Milligan, although even the uninitiated knew that the law was on his side. Once the Supreme Court had spoken, Milligan's claim, amounting to $100,000 in damages for false arrest and subsequent injury,[53] rested on sure legal ground. This right of recovery Harrison recognized, and his legal sense bade him concentrate on mitigation of the damages. Harrison's real objective, however, was to get into the court record the entire story of alleged treason, as perpetrated by Milligan and sundry other Knights of the Golden Circle. If he could convince the jury that the conduct of the plaintiff and his associates was "treasonable," and if he could paint the picture "in a glaring light" and with "an overwhelming accumulation of evidence," [54] his twofold objective would be accomplished: mitigation of damages and castigation of Democrats.

[51] When Hendricks, then United States Senator, addressed a mass meeting of Democrats on May 20, 1863, in Indianapolis, the affair was broken up by a squad of blue-coated soldiers who discovered several men and women fully armed. It was the belief of the military that the meeting and the speaker were merely a cover for the then Knights of the Golden Circle. Sentinel, May 21, 22; Journal, May 21, 22, 23, 1863; and Logan Esarey, History of Indiana, Vol. 2, 78–83, as cited in Grayston, loc. cit., p. 385, n. 6.

[52] Indianapolis Evening News, May 17, 1871. (Hereafter cited as the News.)

[53] Case No. 9605, Milligan v. Hovey, Circuit Court, Indiana, May, 1871, in 17 Fed. Case Reports, pp. 380–83. This action was "of trespass, by Lambdin P. Milligan, for an alleged wrongful arrest and imprisonment."

[54] Lew Wallace, in writing Harrison's Presidential campaign biography, gives the General's full argument. Before Wallace put pen to paper, Harrison had supplied him with a written memorandum on the case. Lew Wallace, Life of Gen. Ben Harrison, p. 96.

After two weeks spent in examination of witnesses, Harrison was ready to go before the jury. The crowded courtroom was astounded by the thunder of his opening salvo. "Gentlemen of the jury," he began, "the case you have been called to try is a legacy of war. It has brought back to our minds with vividness the vicissitudes and anxieties of that protracted struggle for national life." Harrison pitched his appeal to the jury on the broad plane of patriotism and devotion to duty. More than once the General hammered home the point that Hovey and his codefendants, amid war, conspiracy, and subversion, had kept unsullied their character as public officers. "They were United States soldiers," Harrison proclaimed, "who had heard the cry of national distress, and with brave, true hearts, had forsaken all and dared all, that they might preserve us as a nation." [55] This indirect attack on both Hendricks and Milligan, neither of whom had seen military service, was not lost on the jury.

Then, in carefully chosen phrases, Harrison paraded before the jury the maimed survivors of the national struggle. To them the country owed a debt beyond calculation, for it was by "the blessing of God upon their valor" that the supremacy of the Constitution and civil law had been restored. Milligan, Harrison pointed out, was now assailing these very men "under the shield of that constitution and those laws, in a court whose continued existence is due to them and their associates in arms." Was it fair, demanded the General, that a man "who compassed the destruction of that charter of liberty and personal right," should now draw his weapons of attack from the Constitution itself?

As a piece of oratory and special pleading, Harrison's summation was masterful. Without a note in hand, he recited for the jury the history of the Sons of Liberty. He whispered their passwords, demonstrated their special grips, and revealed the stringent obligations of secrecy under which the group operated. The Sons, Harrison declared, were a military organization on Hoosier soil with "a full complement of officers . . . and a fair supply of arms and ammunition." [56] In that hour of crisis, Hovey and his men "had im-

---

[55] *Report of the Benjamin Harrison Memorial Commission* (77th Cong., 1st Sess., House Doc. No. 154), pp. 105 ff. Wallace, *op. cit.*, p. 96. Hendricks complained that Harrison frequently tried to inflame the mind of the jury. Harrison retorted that the facts of history, not his presentation of them, caused the inflammation. *Ibid.*, p. 127.

[56] *Ibid.*, p. 93.

prisoned conspirators shown to be engaged in activities dangerous to the Nation's safety." [57] Shall the law enervate the men who risked their limbs that the law itself might have life? Could General Hovey have acted otherwise? Could the military tribunal, appointed by Hovey to try Milligan, "have refused to perform that duty? The command was an imperative one, and a refusal to obey would be as grave an offense and as conspicuous a disregard of military duty as a refusal to march at the trumpet call." Here Harrison eyed each juror. "What is the duty of a soldier?" he demanded. And answered for them:

> His not to reason why,
> His not to make reply,
> His but to do or die.

It was very late on the afternoon of May 29, 1871, when Harrison launched his final appeal. He restated for the jury the defense's contention that General Hovey and his aides had acted for the public welfare in perfectly good faith. In a series of rhetorical questions he asked who could impugn the good character of the military tribunal that had tried and convicted Lambdin P. Milligan. In particular he cited the valor of defendant General Ben Spooner (now a federal marshal), who, thundered Harrison, had been "maimed for life" in the Atlanta campaign.

Yonder, on the bloody sides of Kenesaw, he gave an arm, almost a life, for the country which he, and these his comrades, loved so well. While he lay upon the field, bleeding, almost dying, here in Grand Council in the State of Indiana Milligan and his associates were plotting treason; and now they seek to rob him of the little savings from the office which a grateful country, and a President who honors his valor, have conferred upon him, in order to enrich the traitors.

Gentlemen, I feel sure that it will not be so. On the morrow when the booming gun shall salute the rising sun, and . . . maidens come to hang floral offerings upon the head-stones of our dead, may your returning feet vindicate the living.[58]

Judge Drummond immediately charged the jury in a way that satisfied Harrison.[59] The twelve took the case at six o'clock that

[57] *Report of the Benjamin Harrison Memorial Commission, op. cit.,* p. 105.
[58] Wallace. *op. cit.,* pp. 128–29.
[59] Drummond said, in part, that "all the circumstances should be regarded in weighing the acts of the defendants. If you should believe there is any evidence connecting the plaintiff with a conspiracy against the government, though it would not justify his trial by a military commission, yet it would undoubtedly affect your

Memorial Day eve, and at eleven the following morning they rendered a verdict which, though in favor of Milligan, was a paper victory. The plaintiff's claim for damages was reduced from $100,-000 to a nominal sum of five dollars.[60]

For Harrison, the verdict ranked with his victory in the Clem case. From it he was to draw legal, personal, and political prestige. Although the Republican state convention was still nine months away, friends began anew to acclaim him as Indiana's next governor. Hoosiers the state over now knew him as a good general, a relentless prosecutor, and a skillful defense attorney. His reputation soon crossed state lines, and political preferment appeared clearly on Harrison's horizon.[61]

---

conclusions upon the question of damages; so, too, if you should believe the acts of the defendants were done without sufficient excuse, and the plaintiff was an innocent man." *17 Fed. Case Reports,* pp. 382–83.

[60] Foulke, *op. cit.,* I, 431–32; Grayston, *loc. cit.,* p. 391; *News,* May 30, 1871. The *Report of the Benjamin Harrison Memorial Commission, op. cit.,* p. 105, lists the verdict as one cent and costs. The *Federal Case Reports* simply state that the jury found a verdict for the plaintiff, with nominal damages.

[61] John Scott Harrison to Benjamin, June 21, 1871, (L.C.), Vol. 7.

CHAPTER IV

A Favorite Left at the Post

ARRISON, allowing his thirty-eighth birthday to pass without ceremony on August 20, kept at legal work throughout the remainder of 1871. Court routine coupled with a quiet life at home composed for him a sufficiently agreeable pattern. Continued rumors that political friends wanted him as the party's nominee for governor in 1872 evoked from him no public sign of interest. In this he was following the advice of his father. John Scott Harrison, now a sage seventy, had counseled at least a temporary refusal to seek or even accept another public office. Writing from his own experience, he warned his son that a man must first accumulate a sufficiency of this world's goods and bank them against the day on which distaste or disgust drives him "from the crooked and devious ways of politics." [1] For Harrison, the political arena had a strong allure, but in 1871 his father's words influenced him to wait until his financial status should justify taking a partial or complete leave of his profession.

Shortly after New Year's Day, 1872, the strong tide of Indiana politics began to roll in on the capital city. The two party papers, the *Journal* and the *Daily Sentinel*, as well as the independently liberal *Evening News*, bristled with political excitement. Practically every county had a candidate for governor; Marion County boasted three, including General Benjamin Harrison. [2] Political fever also invaded the courts, where Harrison and Porter were defending their former partner, William P. Fishback, editor of the *Journal*. In an astute political move, the Democratic Attorney General, Bayless W. Hanna, had charged the Journal Company with

[1] John Scott Harrison to Benjamin, June 21, 1871, (L.C.), Vol. 7.
[2] *News*, January 3, 1872.

defrauding the State Treasury of $30,000 while under contract to do the state printing. Also named as parties to the alleged fraud were Lewis W. Hasselman and Postmaster William R. Holloway, part owner of the *Journal* and Senator Morton's brother-in-law. To add to the political significance of the suit, the State had employed a liberal Republican, W. R. Harrison, to prosecute the case in Superior Court. The action was charged with political dynamite. If these leading Republicans were found guilty, the Democracy and the reform elements within the Republican party stood an excellent chance of breaking Morton's hold on Indiana.

The case against the Journal Company came to trial during the first week of January, 1872, but the anticipated political explosion failed to materialize. The parade of witnesses for the state was thrown into confusion by General Harrison's grueling cross-examination. After two days, Harrison had proved the State's case deficient in evidence,[3] and Judge Rand dismissed the suit. Fishback, Holloway, and the Republican administration, though vindicated, were far from satisfied. There ensued a bitter, personal war between the *Daily Sentinel* and the *Journal*. It stemmed from Fishback's countercharge that Richard J. Bright, the incumbent state printer and owner of the *Sentinel*, "had unlawfully extracted from the treasury in less than three months over $27,000 of the people's money." Again the State started legal action to recover funds, but the case was dropped when Bright made restitution.[4]

Fishback, whose editorial finger had already pointed to fraud and corruption within the Grant administration,[5] continued to harry Bright, the Democrats, and the *Sentinel*. Claiming that Bright had perjured himself in swearing to false accounts, the *Journal* editor procured a Grand Jury indictment, an action which attracted wide attention and full newspaper coverage. Interest grew when Fishback employed Harrison as his counsel. The trial occupied the first two weeks of February, ending only

[3] *Sentinel*, January 4, 5, 1872.

[4] *Journal*, February 19; *Sentinel*, February 21, 1872. This practice of defrauding the State Treasury was known as "cat-skinning," a term made famous by the couplet: "When you get a good thing, save it, save it,/And when you catch a black cat, skin it to the tail."

[5] *News*, September 16, 1872. Fishback took the editorial stand that Grant was killing the Republican party, and that officeholders were killing Grant in their zeal to secure his renomination. This gave Postmaster Holloway, part owner of the *Journal*, untold anguish of mind.

five days before the Republican State Convention opened.[6] In preparing his case, Harrison had scrutinized the *Sentinel's* business books and papers closely and subjected Bright's employees to a searching examination. But the General's efforts, though vigorous, were futile. The jury quickly decided that the State had not proved perjury and brought in a verdict of not guilty.[7]

Bright's acquittal was a severe political blow to Fishback, whom the Democratic press excoriated as, among other things, "a wilful calumniator, liar and perjurer."[8] As "Pink's" counsel Harrison also felt the full lash of public criticism. Attention was drawn to the fact that in trying to show "treasury thieving," Harrison had spared neither Republican nor Democrat, nor friends nor foes. In presenting evidence to the jury, the General had uncovered shady practices for which his own party and personal friends, including Morton's brother-in-law, were responsible. This fearless course was interpreted in Bright's *Daily Sentinel* as a soulless betrayal of friendship, and Harrison himself was portrayed as "the torrid serpent that, warmed into life," strikes with "his serpent fangs through Republican ex-officials."[9] This namecalling was brushed off on the following day by the *Journal* as merely the fulmination of "Booby-Dick" Bright.[10] Such unfavorable publicity, however, coming on the eve of the Republican convention, may have hurt Harrison more than he realized.

Prior to the Republican State Convention on February 22, 1872, the political skies in Indiana and in the nation had been far from fair. Cries of corruption and jobbery filled the air, and political bossism—both local and national—was being roundly censured in Washington as well as in Indianapolis. Throughout the land a clamor arose for first-class candidates who would take a determined stand for political purity and reform.[11] In Indiana,

[6] *Sentinel*, February 19, 1872.

[7] *Journal*, February 19, 1872.

[8] *Sentinel*, February 19, 1872.

[9] *Ibid.* It took no little courage for Harrison to show that W. R. Holloway, S. M. Douglass, and A. H. Conner, his political and personal friends, had raised, scratched, and changed treasury vouchers. It was Harrison's contention that Bright had done the same thing. The Republicans, however, were protected from prosecution by the statutes of limitation.

[10] February 20, 1872.

[11] Earle Dudley Ross, *The Liberal Republican Movement*, pp. 17–20; *News*, February 21, 1872.

the younger members of the party were protesting violently against the customary squads of political "bummers" and ring-masters. Early in January these reformers issued a plea for "good men" who would attend "the primary meetings and control the nominations." [12] Closely connected with the cry for reform was the fast-developing Liberal Republican movement.[13] Some who had supported Grant in 1868 were now in full revolt against him and the cynical elements which had captured control of the party organization. Men who cherished standards of political decency felt outraged by repeated tales of administrative corruption and official fraud. Several Democrats shared this reform sentiment, among them General Harrison's father, as he was soon to affirm in an eloquent letter to his son.

Naturally enough, people's thoughts turned to the "Hoosier Warrior." During the first four weeks of January, several "Har-rison-for-Governor" letters appeared in the *Journal*.[14] These flattering notices, representing the sentiment in several counties, praised Harrison's unquestionable integrity. His candidacy, it was argued, would relieve both press and party of the labor of defending moral and political delinquencies. An enthusiastic correspondent from Bloomington, Indiana, claimed that if the "young, ambitious, and eloquent" Harrison were nominated, "his bitterest political foe will not have the audacity to charge him with a single dishonorable act, committed either in public or private life." [15] Also, the fact that Harrison was among the few who had not sought high elective office certainly enhanced his standing.

Harrison's admirers stressed his legal and military stature. They boasted that "many of the soldier boys . . . know that Gen. Ben has both the courage and the ability to meet and rout, whether on the battlefield or on the stump, and that the 'cat-skinners,' hangers-on, and 'political tricksters' . . . would find cold comfort in his presence, if elected." [16]

But political heat lightning was also flashing in the vicinity of such veteran officeholders as General Thomas McLelland Browne, United States Attorney for the district of Indiana, and

---

12 *Journal,* January 15, 16, 24, 1872.
13 Russell B. Nye, *Midwestern Progressive Politics,* pp. 44–45.
14 *Journal,* January 8, 11, 15, 16, 17, 18, 19, 20, 22, 25, 1872.
15 *Ibid.,* January 11, 1872. The letter, dated January 8, 1872, was signed "Monroe."
16 *Ibid.,* January 27, 1872.

Congressman Godlove Stein Orth, both of whom had numerous adherents throughout the state. By the middle of January, at least ten prominent names had been entered in the race for the Republican gubernatorial nomination. Although the *Journal* endorsed no single candidate, and wary Senator Morton kept his own counsel, the Democratic *Daily Sentinel,* echoing the Cincinnati *Commercial,* claimed that the contest lay "between Gen. Browne and Gen. Harrison." [17]

As the time for the county conventions approached, Harrison's supporters grew more active. An editorial in the Lebanon *Patriot,* strongly endorsing the General, summed up the Harrison case succinctly:

His undoubted purity of life, his wondrous powers as a speaker, his vigor of intellect and strength of will, together with the well known fact that he has never had the slightest connection with any of the cliques or rings of politicians, make him popular. He is a young man, yet his name is familiar in all parts of the state, although he has not spent a day in trying to secure his nomination.[18]

As the preconvention handicapping progressed, the Harrison camp felt that their candidate was at least a slight favorite in the betting. Rated a close second and third, however, were Browne and Orth. This gave rise to the story, published in the Fort Wayne *Journal,* that a combination had been formed by General Browne, General Harrison, and their friends with a view to nominating one of them for Governor and the other for Congressman-at-large. A prompt denial was made by Fishback in a *Journal* editorial that characterized the rumor as "utterly without foundation." [19] At the same time, the *Daily Sentinel* reported that the Republican State Convention had already been rigged to nominate "O. P. Morton for Governor and Ben Harrison for Lieutenant Governor." The alleged scheme was for the almost certain Republican majority of the new legislature to re-elect Morton

[17] *News,* January 2; *Journal,* January 8, 16, 17, 18, 19; and *Sentinel,* January 15, 26, 1872. Listed as "probable starters" were: R. W. Thompson, T. M. Browne, B. Harrison, A. G. Porter, T. A. Morris, G. S. Orth, N. Kimball, B. Spooner, and C. Allen.

[18] Reprinted in the *Journal,* January 27, 1872. This contradicts a common opinion that Harrison had always been a machine politician who "never expressed an independent political thought in his life." See R. C. Buley, "The Campaign of 1888 in Indiana," *Indiana Magazine of History,* 10 (1914), 35.

[19] *Ibid.* "None stands higher in the estimation of the people than General Ben Harrison."

United States Senator, thus pemitting Harrison "to slip into the Governorship" upon Morton's resignation. The *Sentinel* charged that this was part of the new Republican program, whose slogan would be "Great is Ulysses and Oliver is his prophet." [20]

While such stories tended to reduce the odds on Harrison, other Republicans were spreading the rumor that Harrison "did not wish his friends to consider him a candidate." Apparently preoccupied with the Bright-Fishback legal tussle, the General had not as yet committed himself, and his silence and political inaction appeared to bolster this report until the *Journal* spiked the story in a forthright editorial:

We presume that General Harrison feels as any other honorable and worthy candidate should feel under similar circumstances; and while there would be a manifest impropriety in personal seeking and laboring for the nomination, he would feel grateful to his Republican friends, if they should see fit to honor him by their free choice. In such an event he would doubtless accept the nomination, enter the field, and make a thorough canvass of the state.[21]

Meanwhile, behind his puzzling silence Harrison was in reality pondering the problem of his own future. Uncertain of which path to follow, Benjamin turned to his father for counsel. He first confessed the fear that, if he should accept the nomination and win the gubernatorial race, the cares and responsibilities of the office might again undermine his health. His father's reply [22] contained the jocular assurance that "auxiliaries to more perfect health can be found in the *otium cum dignitate* of the Gubernatorial Chair." Then, more seriously, he suggested that campaign travel and fatigue—liabilities for most candidates—"may be the very thing for you—and the attending excitement, like a change of tonics, may do you good."

A second deterrence, one that he himself had mentioned the previous summer, was less easily disposed of. Much of Harrison's reluctance to enter full-time politics was based on the fact that the salary of the governor of the state of Indiana did not begin

20 January 26, 1872.

21 January 27, 1872.

22 John Scott Harrison to Benjamin, January 29, 1872, Harrison Home MSS. As the years passed, General Harrison treasured this lengthy letter and kept it at his desk in his law office both before and after the Presidency. The author discovered it still secreted in the desk, which now adorns the Benjamin Harrison Memorial Home in Indianapolis.

to approach the earnings of an able lawyer.[23] His chief concern, however, was that retirement from law would lessen his ability to aid others financially. John Scott's answer was indeed that of a father: "This is an argument in favor rather than against your throwing off (for a time) your professional armor." He warned Ben that his present rapid pace as a lawyer would soon bring him to complete exhaustion, and that then his ability to serve either family or friends would be gone.

"If I were your physician," he continued, "I would recommend the relaxation of a year's travel abroad, *with your family*—leaving all business and cares behind. But this I fear you won't do. And as I am convinced that any change will be of service to you, I will be satisfied with anything that will relieve you from the constant stretch of mental labor to which you are now subjected." Moreover, the father went on, "if you can at all aid in cleansing the 'Augean Stable' of American politics, yourself and your friends should be willing to make the sacrifice." Here was ample indication of John Scott Harrison's changed attitude towards what six months earlier he had called the "disgusting and polluted political atmosphere." [24]

As to whether or not Harrison should seek the nomination before the convention, the father was himself uncertain. He knew little or nothing, he wrote, of the relative strength of the parties in Indiana, although he did have a practical suggestion: "In making up your mind as to the candidacy—I would make the chance of success a very prominent matter of consideration." Since Governor Conrad Baker, the Republican incumbent, had won the 1868 race by only 961 votes, John Scott Harrison had introduced a sobering thought. He had no doubt that his son could win the Republican nomination, but he reserved judgment as to the outcome of the race.

Both father and son recognized the fact that the General's political future might depend largely on choosing the right course of action in 1872. The elder Harrison cannily noted that "the greater the sacrifice you make, the stronger will be the claim on your party." He then revealed the deeper motive behind the outward intent of his remarkable letter. "Son, if I thought your prob-

[23] *Journal*, February 3, 1872.
[24] John Scott Harrison to Benjamin, June 21, 1871, (L.C.), Vol. 7.

able election would end with the Governorship of Indiana, I would not care to see you a candidate." John Scott Harrison's eyes were on the White House. The son of William Henry Harrison could not resist cherishing the hope that one day a son of his own would become the President of the United States.

John Scott Harrison's advice, sage in most details, was gratefully received by General Harrison in Indianapolis on February 1, 1872, just three weeks prior to the convention. The encouragement of his father, added to a favorable press and the proud approval of Carrie Harrison,[25] led him to re-evaluate his chances for the gubernatorial nomination. Nevertheless he continued to refuse any public avowal of his candidacy, choosing to trust his political future to the capable hands of friends. Heading the Harrison forces was William P. Fishback. Day after day, his *Journal* carried letters endorsing the General. The Seymour *Times* pronounced him as "beyond doubt the most available." He had won three previous political victories and was blessed with a grandfather who had "killed and scalped more Injins, drank more hard cider, and lived and died in more log cabins" than any other political warrior.[26] This "grandfather line" had been suggested by his politically astute father, who had written: "I believe that you might get hundreds of votes from the Democratic party for your namesake—if nothing else—the Old Democrats of Tippecanoe memory knew your grandfather to be honest—and they will believe that his grandson can't well be otherwise." [27]

The real problem facing Harrison, and every other Republican candidate, was Senator Oliver P. Morton. The Morton wing of the party was pretty much the whole bird,[28] and everyone believed that the senator would control the choice of candidates.

25 Carrie Harrison to Benjamin, December 1, 1871, (L.C.), Vol. 7. These letters, representing a cross section of Republican opinion, underscored Harrison's high moral and intellectual qualifications and emphasized the fact that he was not actively seeking the nomination.

26 *Journal,* February 3, 5, 7, 9, 13, 15, 1872.

27 John Scott Harrison to Benjamin Harrison, January 29, 1872, Harrison Home MSS.

28 *News,* July 13, 1872. On February 8, 1872, the Democratic *Sentinel* pointed out that Orth "will have no more show in the Republican State Convention than a stump-tail bull in fly time." The *Sentinel* concluded that Morton still held the Republican party of Indiana in the hollow of his hand, and had made up his slate without Mr. Orth's name on it.

However, Morton's policy of not showing his hand until after the nominations made it appear "that he was from the beginning the particular friend of the successful candidate." It was known in 1872 that Morton ardently desired to succeed himself in the United States Senate. With this in view, the *Sentinel* essayed an editorial conjecture: "Morton desires the nomination of General Ben Harrison rather than a sharper and more ambitious politician, who might be in the way in the event of the Republicans carrying the Legislature." [29] This conjecture seemed to square with an informal commitment on the part of Morton to favor Harrison long before the convention met. Subsequent evidence substantiates the story that "Pink" Fishback, in return for Morton's acceptance of Harrison, had promised the *Journal's* facilities in endorsement of Grant and the national administration.[30]

During the two weeks before the convention, the political tide seemed to be running as both Fishback and Morton had agreed it should run. Although Morton was out of the city, General W. H. H. Terrell, "the right hand of Morton," arrived from Washington "to work the wires for the ambitious Senator." The Harrison stock immediately rose, for Terrell kept "diligently at work to obtain the influence of the preachers and the temperance men" in behalf of the General. As the *Daily Sentinel* sharply observed, "General Harrison is an Elder in the Presbyterian Church, [and] Morton calculates largely upon the influence of that denomination to secure his nomination." [31] To all outward appearances a few days before the convention, Harrison was Morton's first choice for Governor, and when Morton created and backed a favorite, his choice usually won going away.

Fishback early spread the word about the hotels that "General Harrison would be acceptable to Morton." This made less likely the nomination of either Browne or Orth. It was known that Morton disliked and even feared Orth, and generally conceded that Browne was too light to carry much weight in the convention.[32] On February 21, the day before the convention, the Democratic press reported that General Terrell, as Morton's henchman,

29 February 21, 1872.
30 *News*, September 16, 1872. The price Fishback allegedly paid was a promised editorial about-face on Grant. He agreed to concentrate his fire on Indiana Democrats rather than on scandals in the national administration of President Grant.
31 February 21, 1872.
32 *News*, September 16, 1872.

had succeeded in lining up the following ticket: For Governor, General Ben Harrison; for Lieutenant Governor, Godlove S. Orth; for Congressman-at-large, Colonel Tom Browne.[33] This arrangement, it was alleged, satisfied Harrison, shelved Orth, and would make Browne useful in the campaign.

Candidates for the various positions on the state ticket were busy electioneering, and in some cases forming optimistic combinations. Orth and Browne in particular were "as busy as bees in a sugar hogshead." [34] General Benjamin Harrison alone was conspicuously absent. He had refused to take a room at the Bates House on the principle that it was unfitting that "a candidate should open headquarters and solicit support." Friends sent word that "if he would come down and take a room, he would be given the nomination beyond question." Harrison's persistent refusal to lobby for himself puzzled many of his supporters and angered others. As one friend ruefully put it, "some of the delegates got it into their head that he was too good to come down and shake hands with them." [35]

With Harrison absent from the bar and the smoke-filled rooms of the hotel, Tom Browne's stock rose rapidly. Most of the delegates knew him by name, and those unacquainted with him personally were quickly assured that he was a fine "orator, an able debater, a wit of high order, and able to entertain a crowd as well as any man in Indiana." Much of Browne's personal popularity stemmed from the fact that he was a "native Hoosier . . . with the bluff and hearty manners of a man of the people, and with a modesty not unlike that of the lamented Lincoln." Even General Harrison's backers were compelled to admit that Browne would make a popular and sufficiently able governor, although they insisted that he would not bring to the office "as much dignity as would General Harrison." [36] Harrison's friends felt confident that "their man would come out best," despite the rumor circulated at a late hour

33 *Sentinel,* February 21, 1872.

34 *Ibid.,* February 22, 1872. The paper carried the false report that Harrison had established headquarters. In listing such, the *Journal,* February 21, 1872, omits Harrison's name. This squares with other available evidence.

35 The testimony of W. C. Van Arsdel in an unidentified newspaper clipping in the Benjamin Harrison Scrapbooks, (L.C.), Vol. 52.

36 *Journal,* February 13, 1872. An editorial in the *News,* September 16, 1872, mentions whispering campaigns against Browne for heavy drinking.

that Browne would win the nomination and Harrison be transferred to the candidacy for Congressman-at-large.[37]

Although Harrison has left no clue as to why he absented himself from the usual political caucusing, it may be conjectured that he saw "the handwriting on the wall" as early as Saturday, February 17, 1872. On that evening three hundred Republicans of the Second Ward, the one in which Harrison lived, had met to select delegates to the State Convention. Two of the three men selected were "outspoken against Harrison for Governor" and, as the *Sentinel* coldly observed, "a candidate for Governor who cannot carry his own ward will stand a sorry chance, we should think, for a nomination." [38] This blow to Harrison's prestige came on the very day that he lost Fishback's case against Editor Bright.

On the other hand, Harrison may have been informed of Czar Morton's eleventh-hour judgment that a successful canvass by the General "would lift him into dangerous prominence." At any rate, Harrison's decision to remain aloof until the hour of the convention, though it may have cost him the nomination, nevertheless saved him from the barrage of personal abuse that filled the hotel corridors and lobby. At a late hour on the night before the convention, and before the General's supporters knew what was happening, the air became alive with stories to his detriment and a whispering campaign against him gathered momentum. Undecided and uninstructed delegates were told that Harrison was as "cold-blooded as a fish"—"a stinking little aristocrat" who "never recognized men on the street." Others sneered that "he had a big head" but was only "the grandson of his grandfather." Still others: "Men will be afraid to visit the State House with their hats on, with such a man for Governor . . . the people want a man of themselves . . . [Harrison] cannot speak to a common man as Tom Browne can" and "he is not to be seen anywhere about the hotels." [39] But more ominous was the whisper that he was unsympathetic to the Senator. "Harrison is an anti-Morton man and

[37] *Sentinel*, February 22, 1872. "Browne's stock is above par while Harrison's is quoted about sixty asked and bidding very slow. Orth has a few friends but not enough to frighten Browne's party who do not anticipate any coalition against them."

[38] In an editorial headed "Beaten in His Own Ward," the *Sentinel*, February 19, 1872, angered by Harrison's prosecution of Bright in the perjury case, highlighted the fact that Harrison's neighbors failed to back the General by selecting delegates who favored his nomination.

[39] *News*, September 16, 1872.

must be defeated." [40] This above all really weakened his chances. So, while Harrison slept, the odds on the morrow's convention race changed.

Delegates to the Republican State Convention began to assemble in the spacious Academy of Music about nine o'clock on the morning of Washington's Birthday. By ten o'clock, after much noise and bustle, all delegates were seated and Harrison took a place with his Marion County friends. How much the General had been told about the previous night's doings has not been revealed.

After the opening prayer and the routine organizational procedure, General Morton C. Hunter, president of the convention, announced that nominations for Governor were in order. At this word there arose a shout for Browne "that made Harrison grow a shade paler than usual." Immediately his supporters staged a rousing demonstration for Harrison but the volume of a second shout for Browne "swallowed it up." Yet, from the enthusiastic cheers that greeted Orth, Harrison, and Browne as they were severally placed in nomination, it was difficult to form "any estimate of their respective strength." [41] Indications for a close finish in the balloting were strong.

As the poll of the 1,582 votes got under way, with 793 votes necessary to nominate the Governor, Browne showed early speed and good staying power. The result of the first ballot gave Browne 704½, Harrison 451, and Orth 424½. It was apparent to most observers that Harrison, although an early favorite in the paddock, had gotten off to a poor start and would probably not have the speed necessary to close the gap between Browne and himself. The results of the second ballot confirmed this, as Orth lost 111 and Harrison 44½ votes. Browne's 853 put him under the wire first with plenty to spare. In short order, his nomination was made unanimous amid cheers that "seemed to raise the roof." [42] After Browne's speech of acceptance, Godlove Orth was called upon. He responded with a pledge of full support for the Republican

40 *Ibid.* Indiana had seen many governors promoted to the Senate. The name of Harrison could be a real challenge to Morton's prestige and to his ambition for the Presidency.

41 *Proceedings of the Republican State Convention, 1872*, pp. 3–5. This pamphlet was based on the report of the *Journal*, February 23, 1872. (Hereafter cited as *Proceedings.*)

42 *News*, February 22; *Sentinel*, February 23, 1872; *Proceedings*, p. 5.

ticket, and it was reported that he managed a smile that would have done credit to Schuyler Colfax himself.[43]

Loud calls were then made for "Harrison!" "Harrison!" The president of the convention looked in Harrison's direction but he had already "made for the door." "General Harrison is not on the stand," General Hunter announced, "but I understand he is in the house; if so, I hope he will come forward." [44] Continued calls and cheers accompanied Harrison on his long walk to the speaker's stand. He was outwardly calm, although a reporter for the *Daily Sentinel* was inspired to write that the General's glance "seemed to indicate a willingness to bite someone." [45] If Harrison was filled with either disappointment or envy, his speech to the convention did not reflect it. Applause greeted his personal endorsement of Browne's nomination. Then, after thanking his many supporters and friends, he added: "Those of you who have urged my name for this nomination, and all others in the Convention, will bear me witness that I have not sought it with much personal effort. . . . Indeed, my friends have most complained of me for manifesting so little personal interest in the result."

If some expected Harrison to chew the cud of disappointment in public, they were themselves disappointed. Instead, he drew rounds of laughter by expressing the regret that General Browne would not have a more "compact foe upon which to expend the force of his ardent nature. . . . Our adversaries are so scattered that I am afraid we shall have to follow them as we did the guerrillas when the rebellion ended." The General concluded with a reminder of their party's primary obligation, "to bring freedom and equal civil rights to the enslaved of the land." The Republican party's mission, he told the convention, was complete civil reconstruction in the southern states. That work would not be finished, he warned, "until the cabin of the negro, which always afforded a refuge for our soldiers, shall be safe from the midnight incursions of barbarian Democrats, and be rendered secure against the assaults of the old supporters of slavery." [46] Then, having expressed his satisfaction with the results of the convention and having promised

[43] *Sentinel,* February 23, 1872. Schuyler Colfax's ever-gracious manner had won him the rhymed sobriquet, "Smiler."
[44] *Proceedings,* p. 6.
[45] February 23, 1872.
[46] *Proceedings,* pp. 6–7; *Journal* and *Sentinel,* February 23, 1872.

to help in the campaign "so far as I can," Harrison prepared to leave the Academy of Music. The applause that followed him must have rung ironically in his ears. But there was still to be an anticlimax.

As the General made his way from the convention floor, a fervent backer nominated him as candidate for Congressman-at-large. The General stopped, turned, and walked back to the stage with a determined air. Cries of "keep still" and "you sit down" drowned his first efforts to decline politely. Calling for quiet, Harrison made his feelings clear: "Those who have favored my nomination for Governor, and at much trouble to themselves have endeavored to secure it, I shall always keep in my warm remembrance . . . but I must say to them now that under no consideration whatever can I allow my name to go before the convention for congressman-at-large." [47] With Harrison's name scratched from the ballot, Godlove S. Orth was overwhelmingly nominated for the rejected office on the first poll of the delegates. Finally, after arriving at an informal agreement to vote for Grant and Colfax "first, last, and all the time," the convention adjourned.[48] The next morning's *Daily Sentinel* headlined the convention results thus: "General Ben Harrison Mercilessly Slaughtered"—"Pink Fishback's Eye Blacked." [49]

For the next four months, Harrison devoted himself almost exclusively to trial work, attracting favorable press comment on several occasions.[50] The political wounds sustained in the February state convention seemed to heal rapidly, but he again refused a petition, received early in July, to make the race for Congressman-at-large.[51] However he did open the Republican state campaign in Mooresville, Morgan County, on July 19, 1872. There, crowds from Martinsville, Monrovia, and adjoining towns came to cheer Harrison's "able, effective and telling speech," in which he handled

[47] *Proceedings*, p. 7; *Sentinel*, February 23, 1872.
[48] *News*, February 22, 1872. Actually, the convention did endorse Grant and Colfax, but did not pledge or instruct its delegates to the National Convention. See *Sentinel*, February 23, 1872.
[49] February 23, 1872.
[50] *News*, March 18, 26, 27, June 28; *Sentinel*, March 18, June 25, 26, 29, 1872.
[51] J. R. Gray, William O'Brien, C. J. McCole, Thos. J. Kise, J. L. Evans, E. Millers, M. W. Essington, D. W. Patty, and Isaac Williams to General Ben Harrison, July 3, 1872, Harrison Home MSS. This was a week in advance of a state delegate convention that met in Indianapolis, July 10, 1872, to nominate a second candidate for Congressman-at-large. See *Sentinel*, July 11, 1872.

Greeley and the Liberal Republican movement "without gloves." [52]
Five days later, he made another speech. Indianapolis Republicans
had arranged a demonstration at their wigwam to honor Grant
and his Vice-Presidential running mate, Senator Henry Wilson of
Massachusetts. Billed as the two principal speakers were Mississippi's former Senator, Hiram Rhodes Revels, a Negro who had
been educated in Indiana,[53] and Illinois Governor Richard James
Oglesby.[54] With boundless enthusiasm, both white and Negro
Republicans cheered Senator Revels, but when Governor Oglesby
began to speak he broke down and had to be assisted from the
stage to his hotel.[55] The *Journal* reported that the "crowd lost one
splendid speech, but they were treated to another by Gen. Ben
Harrison, who was called out and made one of his best efforts." [56]

With this unscheduled speech Harrison ceased any further summer campaigning. In a sense, he had fulfilled his promise to the
February convention; yet his contribution to the state campaign
was negligible. In August, at the peak of the canvass, he left the
campaign scene for a pleasure trip along Lake Erie and down the
St. Lawrence, accompanied by his first law partner, William Wallace, and another friend, Edward King.[57] Although this vacation
came at the regular season, it may be interpreted as a silent protest
against Senator Morton and as a sign of Harrison's lingering political disappointment. During the General's absence, the liberal *Evening News* and the rabidly Democratic *Sentinel* did not allow their
readers to forget that he had been sacrificed on the altar of Morton's
political ambition, the latter declaring bitterly: "Morton does not
want brains on his side. He merely wants tools." [58]

By the time General Harrison returned from vacation, his political stock had again risen. The *Daily Sentinel*, which in February
had vilified Harrison, now blandly posed the question: "Why was
it that the State Republican Convention ignored such a man as

[52] *Journal*, July 20, 1872.
[53] *Sentinel* and *Journal*, July 24, 1872.
[54] Oglesby also served one term as United States Senator from Illinois, 1873–1879.
[55] The *Sentinel*, July 24, 1872, intimated that over-indulgence felled the speaker,
but the *Journal*, July 24, 1872, attributed Oglesby's illness to fatigue.
[56] The *Journal* and *Sentinel* reported opposing versions of Harrison's effectiveness
as a pinch-speaker.
[57] *News* and *Journal*, August 1, 1872.
[58] *Sentinel*, August 27, 1872. Also a political series, "Cat's Paws and Catpawism,"
carried in the *News*, July 9, 10, 13, 23, September 16, October 2, 1872, detailed
Morton's iron rule over Indiana and portrayed Harrison as one of his many victims.
See also W. D. Foulke, *Life of Oliver P. Morton*, II, 257, n. 1.

General Benjamin Harrison, whose private character is spotless and ability unquestioned, and nominated a man who was compelled to take the temperance pledge in order to get the nomination?" The answer, continued the editorial, was simple: "The treasury leeches said they could not approach Harrison. Honest men like Governor Baker and General Harrison are not in demand just now with the plunderers." [59]

Meanwhile Tom Browne's gubernatorial canvass had slowed down to a walk and the press tagged his rambling stump efforts "verbose and inconclusive." [60] Tom Hendricks, on the other hand, veteran Democratic nominee for the post,[61] began to prove himself a superior campaigner. This prompted the man in the street to ask questions that Morton and his followers preferred to leave unanswered: "Has the Republican party no stronger man to put in the field?" "Why was Tom Browne nominated?" The replies came on September 16, 1872. In a three-column lead editorial in the *Evening News* (which yielded only to the *Sentinel* in its hatred of Morton and Mortonism), the Senator was charged with having manipulated the state convention against Harrison. It reviewed in minute detail the alleged Morton strategy: the capture of Fishback and the silencing of his pungent pen; the defeat of Harrison, whom Morton feared as a competitor for the Senate; and the nomination of Browne. Although the *Journal* branded the *Evening News* exposé a malicious lie, the account appeared to be substantially correct.

Harrison remained in character. He neither affirmed nor denied the *Evening News* story.[62] His political future rested with the Republican party for whose principles he had fought. Morton was only a temporary roadblock, and time would settle the score between him and Harrison.

[59] *Sentinel*, August 27, 1872.

[60] *News*, September 16, 1872. Inquirers were told that Browne had been nominated over Harrison, "the ablest debater in the state, the only man in the state whose talents and private life make him in any sense a match for Mr. Hendricks."

[61] Thomas Andrews Hendricks, although Ohio-born, lived most of his life in Indiana. He had served two terms as a Democratic Congressman before the Civil War, failed to win the governorship in 1860, but was elected to the United States Senate in 1862. Renowned as an attorney in Indianapolis since 1860, he enjoyed popularity at the polls.

[62] The issues of the *News* containing the "Cat's Paws" articles (*ut supra*, n. 58) were early exhausted and the series was later published in pamphlet form. It should be noted here that Fishback was no longer editor of the *Journal*, having sold his interest in January, 1872, and moved to St. Louis.

CHAPTER V

Depression and Recovery

BENJAMIN HARRISON returned to the political wars in Indiana during the closing weeks of the bitter 1872 gubernatorial campaign between Browne and Hendricks. He made only a few speeches for Browne and Grant, but the party press hailed him for breaking his long silence. The state contest appeared extremely close and party managers felt that the power of Harrison's oratory could swing undecided voters to Browne and the Republican cause. In what was announced as "the greatest rally of the campaign," staged at Danville, Indiana, on Saturday, September 28, 1872, Harrison acted as chief spokesman for his party. Such final efforts were unavailing. On the state election day, Hendricks won over Browne by a majority of 1,148 in a total vote of more than 377,000.[1] Morton suffered a loss of prestige, but the original Harrison-for-Governor men were not altogether displeased. The Democratic victory, however, included only the offices of Governor and Superintendent of Public Instruction; the remaining state posts, including that of Lieutenant-Governor, were captured by Republicans.[2]

Despite Hendricks' gubernatorial victory in October, the Republican national ticket of Grant and Wilson carried Indiana in November, 1872, by a majority of more than 22,000 votes.[3] Grant's party also controlled the state legislature and, as anticipated, Morton was re-elected to the United States Senate.[4]

[1] *Sentinel*, September 7, 30, October 23, 1872.
[2] J. D. Barnhart and D. F. Carmony, *Indiana: From Frontier to Commonwealth*, II, 199; also *Sentinel*, October 23, 1872. For a brief summary of the economic factors in the 1872 campaign in Indiana, see William G. Carleton, "The Money Question in Indiana Politics, 1865–1890," *Indiana Magazine of History*, 42 (1946), 115–18.
[3] W. Dean Burnham, *Presidential Ballots, 1836–1892*, p. 390.
[4] *Sentinel*, November 26, 27, 1872.

All in all, Benjamin Harrison had emerged from the 1872 convention nightmare politically unscathed, although his second refusal to run for Congressman-at-large [5] had annoyed an influential group of party members, who felt it was politically unwise for him to remain in private life. But Harrison had a mind of his own. As he continued to mature during this first post-bellum decade, his temperament became more and more of the judicial order. When he reached a conclusion after thoroughly examining a question, it was generally irrevocable. As this characteristic deepened, he came to be typed as a man "of remarkably strong individuality." [6] Several contemporaries considered him reserved, even frosty, but such an impression belied Harrison's true self. While he was never what politicians term a "mixer," or one destined to enjoy the personal popularity of a Blaine, Clay, or Bryan, there remains abundant testimony that beneath his apparently cold exterior "lay a warm heart and a tender nature." [7] One of his friends described him thus:

He was a quiet, undemonstrative man, and was credited with being cold and unsympathetic by those who saw him only in his public capacity, and when acting under the stress and strain of public duty. But to those who were on terms of close personal intimacy with him . . . Harrison appears in a different light, a genial companion, a tender, great-hearted man. . . .[8]

Certain eccentricities were largely responsible for the General's reputed coldness. Even during a casual stroll down an Indianapolis street he held his head high, kept an erect military bearing, and often passed friends on the street without seeing them. Some attributed this to a mind preoccupied with business, but others charged it to an innate feeling of superiority. Anecdotes of this kind still circulate among older citizens of Indianapolis, yet no universal judgment can be formed. His political opponents capital-

[5] A group of Hamilton County (Indiana) Republicans to Benjamin Harrison, July 3, 1872, Harrison Home MSS. The appeal was intense and based on Harrison's "past services in the cause of Republicanism and your acknowledged ability to present and defend the record and principles of the Republican Party."

[6] Detroit *News*, March 14, 1901.

[7] Russell B. Harrison Scrapbooks, Vol. 1, a clipping from a Milwaukee paper, March 17, 1901 (further identification lacking), (Indiana State Library). It contains a critical summary of Harrison's career and character.

[8] This tribute by Benjamin Franklin Tracy (a leading New York lawyer and later Harrison's Secretary of the Navy) was published in *Leslie's Weekly*, March [30?], 1901.

ized on, and even invented stories about, the General's undemonstrative nature; his friends, on the other hand—many of them known from early manhood—abode with him until the end.[9]

Once the social entertainments attendant upon the New Year of 1873 were over,[10] the Harrison home again seemed lonely to the General, who missed Russell. He had enrolled his 19-year-old son as a cadet at the Pennsylvania Military Academy at Chester. While daily drill and campus confinement were none too agreeable to Russell, such a manly regime satisfied his father, who had feared that his only son was being spoiled by the women of the house. Whether the law or the military would claim Russell was as yet undecided, but the General was in accord with his son's desire to matriculate at Cornell University.[11]

In her brother's absence Mamie received her father's special attention. She had always been a favorite of his, but now the General could not do enough for his daughter in the way of clothes, books, and little vacations. There were limits to his indulgence, however, when it came to more frivolous matters. Along with many of her teen-age friends, Mamie had long wished to take dancing lessons. But she knew it would be useless to appeal to her father for permission. What could block his consent to such a seemingly harmless request? The Indianapolis historian J. P. Dunn has the answer: "There was nothing at all in the way," he writes, "except the Methodist and Presbyterian Churches."

Thanks to Mrs. Harrison, this social impasse was surmounted. By nature, Carrie had little sympathy for continual ecclesiastical restraint. Besides, she remembered having teased Ben into going to more than one dance—off the college grounds—before they were married. Quietly she plotted her social and religious revolution, in conspiracy with several other good mothers. All agreed that their daughters should be taught dancing, but privately and in their respective homes. This latter restriction created a momentary

[9] As to his generosity, an examination of Harrison's expense and account book reveals that he gave an average of $500 a year to church and charity, and an additional $700 annually to needy relatives. Harrison Cash Books, 1868–1880, (L.C.).

[10] Mrs. Harrison and her daughter were always listed as holding open house on New Year's Day. *Journal*, January 1–3, 1869–1874. Likewise, *Sentinel*, January 1, 1873.

[11] Russell Harrison to Benjamin Harrison, March 28, 1872, (L.C.), Vol. 7. Actually, Russell spent his college years at Lafayette College, Easton, Pennsylvania. What changed his mind is not recorded. (See p. 129, n. 18.)

crisis for Carrie Harrison. "But I don't know what to do," she protested, "Ben would never allow an ungodly fiddle in the house." [12] Mrs. Fred Baggs, a Methodist friend, soon snipped this social Gordian knot by offering her home for the daring experiment. A competent and likeable instructor was hired and the secret classes proceeded harmoniously. Soon young gentlemen were slyly sought out as partners, and, between terms, young Russell himself became one of the willing victims. Mrs. Harrison took great pride in her children's accomplishments; the General, if he ever did suspect what was going on, certainly interposed no objection.

The spirit of change and progress was not confined to the family circle; it was also being felt in the offices of Porter, Harrison and Hines. In the spring of 1873, the senior member, Albert G. Porter, decided to retire. His loss, by a firm that was grossing over $25,000 a year income, was felt keenly.[13] Harrison and Hines had early agreed that they would remain partners, but they felt strongly the need of a third member. Despite many applicants, almost a full year passed before the right man came along. He was William Henry Harrison Miller, of Fort Wayne, Indiana.[14] Miller, seven years Harrison's junior, was of staunch Scottish and English origin, and held an exceptionally fine legal record. His mind possessed strong dialectic powers, and his arguments showed a broad grasp of the law.[15] Harrison had noted these qualities at first hand when Miller practiced in Federal Court in Indianapolis. This chance professional acquaintanceship soon ripened into a friendship built upon mutual esteem and admiration. Consequently, when in April, 1874, Miller contemplated a change of residence, Harrison was delighted to receive his frank letter marked "Confidential." [16] In it the Fort Wayne attorney requested advice as to possible openings in an Indianapolis law firm, and assured Harrison that he could still control a large amount of business in northern Indiana. In short order, Harrison and Hines agreed that they had found a worthy successor to General Porter.

[12] J. P. Dunn, *History of Greater Indianapolis*, I, 493.

[13] During their last calendar year the firm boasted an income of $26,322.77, and Harrison's one-third share amounted to $8,777.59. Benjamin Harrison's Diary and Account Book, 1872–1873, Harrison Home MSS.

[14] Miller, a member of the Fort Wayne law firm of Combs, Miller and Bell, had specialized in collections in federal and state courts of Northern Indiana.

[15] Dunn, *op. cit.*, II, 1231–34.

[16] W. H. H. Miller to Benjamin Harrison, April 12, 1874, (L.C.), Vol. 7.

Indianapolis at once welcomed the new law firm, Harrison, Hines and Miller. From the very beginning it was successful, surpassing easily the legal output of many older firms. Its reputation grew rapidly, and soon the partnership was recognized "as one of the strongest in the state" with "business of strong scope and of important ramifications." [17] Miller became an important factor in Harrison's life, and their friendship was elastic enough to embrace all issues: political, personal, religious, and legal. Only such machine politicians as Boss Tom Platt of New York or Matt Quay of Pennsylvania were surprised when Harrison as President, some fourteen years later, invited William Henry Harrison Miller to be his Attorney General.

Back in September, 1873, the failure of the banking house of Jay Cooke and Co. and the spectacular closing of the New York Stock Exchange amounted to much more than a Black Friday for Wall Street. Financial panic bred depression; 1874 emerged as a dismal year. The entire country suffered. Industrial plants shut down, railway construction came to a standstill, workless fathers walked the streets, and in the larger cities long bread lines filled the squares and parks.[18] It was a kind Providence that kept Harrison from public office during such trying days.

Indianapolis, a city closely tied to eastern railroad magnates and financiers,[19] felt the shock of the national panic early and seriously. Natives in the Hoosier capital never remembered a more abrupt setback. "Several banks closed their doors"; [20] manufacturing slowed or stopped completely. People were not only poor, but, what was worse, they were frightened. Even so, those "hardest-hit did not realize that ten years would elapse before normal conditions were restored." [21] Harrison himself, though caught in the

17 Dunn, *op. cit.*, II, 1232.

18 J. F. Rhodes, *History of the United States*, VII (1872–1877), 43–53.

19 War Governor Morton had guided the growing city's destiny along those lines. See J. B. Martin, *Indiana: An Interpretation*, pp. 63–64. Also, Barnhart and Carmony, *op. cit.*, p. 252, observe that between 1860–1900 railroad mileage multiplied three times, and trade via rail and water (especially the Great Lakes) soared. See also pp. 257 ff. Dunn, *op. cit.*, I, 254 ff. shows the importance of eastern capital in financing railroad construction.

20 Jeannette C. Nolan, *Hoosier City: The Story of Indianapolis*, p. 201. Also Barnhart and Carmony, *op. cit.*, pp. 201–3.

21 Nolan, *op. cit.* Also Rhodes, *op. cit.*, p. 52, details how "the aftermath of the panic of 1873 was of long duration."

financial storm, was not lashed by it. Actually, it was not very long before his firm's business increased as defaults, mortgage fore-closures, and bankruptcy cases flooded the office. In 1873 Harrison grossed over $12,000 from his practice, and another $400 from rents.[22]

The city's recovery was hastened in some quarters by the ener-getic spirit of its businessmen. For example, the Belt Railroad, "the first of its sort in the country, was planned and gradually built, a fourteen-mile track, like three-quarters of an oval—east, south, and west—which partially encircled the city, facilitating transportation of freight and affording access to all other railroad lines entering Indianapolis."[23] While most property depreciated in value, Indianapolis downtown property—due to the belt plan and construction—actually increased in worth. This proved for-tunate for Harrison. In the late summer of 1874, he received a good offer for his downtown house and property. His diary reads: "A certain John F. Hill proposed to buy my residence, corner of Wash. (North) and Ala. for his daughter, Mrs. Neal" for $7,000. Harrison agreed to sell, with the specific provision that the new owners would not take possession until the Harrisons had a house of their own.[24]

The fall and winter of 1874–75 found the General and his wife carefully supervising the erection of their new home. The site had presented no problem, for at a public auction in 1867 the General had purchased a double lot with a 150-foot frontage on North Delaware Street.[25] Located in a promising section of a grow-ing city, the property "was just far enough up town to be con-venient to Harrison's Market Street law office, and at the same time be away from the hum of business."[26] Ben and Carrie de-cided on a red brick, square-built edifice, with two stories and an attic. Fronting east, it would stand well back in a 200-foot yard.

The house took almost a year to build and when fully furnished,

[22] Gilbert L. Harney, The Lives of Benjamin Harrison and Levi P. Morton, pp. 124–28. The general picture is rounded out by the account in Harrison's own note-book and diary for 1874–1875, Harrison Home MSS.

[23] Nolan, op. cit., p. 201.

[24] A memorandum of this sale is found under date of August 29, 1874, (L.C.), Vol. 7.

[25] Bidding in at a cost of $28 a front foot, the General had made a total invest-ment of $4,200 in 1867. A clipping in the Benjamin Harrison Scrapbooks, (L.C.), Vol. 52, p. 92.

[26] Harney, op. cit., p. 155.

it cost well over $20,000.[27] Friends admired the harmony of its structure, which included a beautifully decorated reception room opening off the entrance hall. The General's pride and joy, however, was his spacious library where hung a large steel engraving of his grandfather, former President William Henry Harrison, and a picture of the General and his staff. It also contained the costly bookcase made for him by a poor German cabinetmaker in appreciation for his legal assistance.[28] This was filled with books gathered through every stage of his life.

Thus was begun the dwelling that today stands in Indianapolis as the President Benjamin Harrison Memorial Home, a "comfortable, well-built brick house of sixteen rooms. Surrounded by the original large elms and oaks, it still stands on the wide tree-lined street within a few blocks of the former homes of Booth Tarkington, James Whitcomb Riley, Meredith Nicholson, Charles W. Fairbanks," [29] and many others prominent in American as well as Hoosier history.

Housebuilding, duckhunting and an unremitting law practice conspired to keep General Harrison's mind free from political calculations, especially those of a personal nature, until late in 1875. In September of that year, while still successfully avoiding the current political whirlpool, Harrison found himself swept backwards some forty years into another political controversy. In a fiery letter, his father called upon him to defend the good name of William Henry Harrison. The father had been deeply angered by the appearance of certain quotations from *The Diary of John Adams* in a critical review published in the Cincinnati *Commercial* on August 20, 1875. The aging John Scott Harrison furiously resented the fact that his distinguished father and former President had now been publicly branded a "political adventurer" whose "thirst for lucrative office" was "absolutely rabid." The diarist had also expressed his opinion that the hero of Tippe-

---

[27] According to the figures in Harrison's own handwriting, the total cost was $21,123.10. "Expenses and Assets for 1874–1875," Harrison Home MSS.

[28] Harney, *op. cit.*, p. 120. The gift meant much to the General, who had taken the German's case through several trials, at great personal expense, and finally won it in the Supreme Court.

[29] *Brochure of the History of the Harrison Home* (privately printed), Indianapolis, Indiana. The material and illustrations were prepared by Mrs. Ruth Woodworth, hostess at the Home.

canoe possessed "a lively and active but shallow mind . . . not without talents, but self-sufficient, vain and indiscreet."

Such vilification had made John Scott Harrison rise up in full anger. Writing Ben of this "infamous slander on the character of your grandfather," he declared hotly:

If I was twenty years younger to find out the miserable slanderer of my father's reputation, I would travel to Boston and wear out as many horsewhips on his back as the police would allow me to do before an arrest.

William H. Harrison—a political "Adventurer!" Is there a county in Indiana where this slanderous scoundrel could make that declaration and escape a coat of tar and feathers? I trow not. . . .[30]

The General's task of quieting his enraged father was no easy one. The old man thirsted for immediate retaliation. "Why," he wrote venomously, "the Adams family from the foundation of the Government have had the spoon of the U. S. Treasury in their mouths and took care to hold on until choked off by the voice of the people. A charge of office-seeking comes with poor grace from a member of this Adams family." [31] As far as available evidence goes, Benjamin Harrison seems somehow to have convinced his father that it would be far better to ignore so shameless an attack. Benjamin Harrison could fight when angered, but on this occasion he preferred not to dignify the slander, either by a public denial or a vituperative response. This decision of Harrison's is perhaps one of the most revealing instances of his almost stoic self-mastery.

One of the most notorious of the General's law cases had been chiefly responsible for his busy summer of 1875. Throughout the warm days of June, July, and August, his defense of the accused in the investigation of the Ida K. Fawkner case made Harrison's name public property and the case itself a popular topic of Indiana conversation. The trial came about as the result of the State's

[30] John Scott Harrison to Benjamin Harrison, September 1, 1875, (L.C.), Vol. 7.

[31] *Ibid.* John Scott Harrison had prepared some brief notes for Benjamin's use should he wish to write an article for the Cincinnati paper, pointing out that "your grandfather was appointed to two important offices by the Adams—father and son. W. H. H. was appointed Governor of the Indiana Territory by the Elder Adams and was sent to Columbia by John Quincy Adams. Why was this 'political adventurer' appointed to govern the people of Indiana—or represent at a foreign court the honor and the interest of his country—and that too when he was so shallow of mind and so 'vain or egotistic?' "

investigation into one of its own schools, the Indianapolis Deaf and Dumb Institute. Charges of mismanagement and loose morals had been directed against Dr. Thomas H. McIntire, superintendent of the school,[32] and an aroused public opinion finally prompted the trustees to launch a full-scale investigation into the affairs of the Institute, then in its thirty-second year.

What actually sparked the investigation was the alleged seduction and abortion of Ida K. Fawkner, a mute member of the school's senior class. Mystery surrounded the discovery of Miss Fawkner's condition in mid-February, 1875. In endeavoring to hide her shame, the young student had walked close to death's door. A severe hemorrhage, followed by microscopic examination, confirmed Dr. F. S. Newcomer, the school physician, in his suspicions of abortion. Dismissed as a student, the girl was confined to the hospital ward as an invalid. As her convalescence progressed, members of the hospital board questioned her closely. She at last confessed that her uncle, John E. Fawkner, had seduced her at his home in October, 1874. In a signed statement, witnessed by two doctors, Ida spelled out the lurid details of her uncle's attack and of her subsequent fright and misery. Some weeks later, she recovered sufficiently to leave the institution and live with her grandmother in neighboring Danville.[33]

On March 6, 1875, and before the facts in the case had been made public, Superintendent McIntire consulted his friend Harrison as to precisely what was his duty and responsibility in the matter. Harrison apparently advised him that the girl's statement ought to be turned over to the prosecuting attorney for submission to the Grand Jury during its regular May session. Convinced of the seriousness of his situation, McIntire retained Harrison as his counsel. Before any considered action could be taken, however, Ida Fawkner's signed statement accusing her uncle was given to the press.[34] This premature revelation of the school scan-

[32] Dr. McIntire enjoyed a national reputation as an educator of the deaf. He had instructed in institutes for the deaf in four states, and was superintendent of the Indianapolis school between 1852 and 1879. See Dunn, op. cit., II, 1209.

[33] Sentinel, March 28, 1875.

[34] Ibid. The Grand Jury was scheduled to sit in May, but by April 1 most Hoosiers were conversant with the story. Ida Fawkner had sworn that her uncle had come "into my bedroom and got into bed with me and remained about an hour. I resisted him and tried to get away from him but could not. His wife was absent from home—she had gone to Crawfordsville. A German woman was in the house. She slept in another room."

dal shocked Indianapolis. In the same news account Fawkner denied his niece's allegation, claiming an apparently airtight alibi.[85] The conflicting statements served to confuse the public, whose suspicion was now directed to the Institute itself and to the officials responsible for student morals and discipline. The *Sentinel* led the campaign for a complete investigation into the management of the Deaf and Dumb Institute,[36] and insisted on a public hearing.

Meanwhile, the Institute's Board of Governors had been conducting its own investigation, which so far had led to no definite findings. The Board now apprised the public prosecutor of Ida's sworn statement, adding the testimony of one doctor that there were strong grounds for believing John Fawkner innocent of the charge. The Grand Jury nevertheless indicted him on the double count of seduction and abortion. The Board of Trustees, anxious for its own reputation, at once employed top legal talent to assist the prosecuting attorney. Their choices were Porter, Fishback, and the firm of Harrison, Hines and Miller.[37] Fawkner's trial in criminal court was set for mid-May, but Harrison and Fishback secured a month's postponement. During the delay, Ida Fawkner retracted her original statement. She cleared her uncle and accused instead one of her teachers at the Institute, Ezra G. Valentine, academic counselor and school librarian. This new version of the sordid tale served to re-excite public indignation and to emphasize the significance of the investigation being conducted by a three-man board of inquiry at the school.

By June 8, 1875, sufficient evidence had been collected to permit a private trial within the precincts of the school itself. Defendants were Superintendent McIntire and instructor Valentine, represented by Benjamin Harrison and William P. Fishback. The prosecution was handled by William Dye and Cass Byfield on behalf of the State Board of Inquiry. Day-by-day testimony was faithfully published in the *Sentinel*, with the more lurid portions well highlighted for a curious public. Since most of the witnesses on both sides were deaf-mutes, testimony had to be taken in writ-

[85] *Ibid.* The uncle's alibi rested on his statement that he had slept with his brother George on the night of the alleged attack; he stated that he could prove this by the testimony of the German maid.

[36] *Ibid.,* June 16, 1875. A leading editorial; also an article entitled "The Fawkner Fiasco."

[37] *Ibid.*

ing, thus assuring a "long, weary and tedious" [38] trial. Within the first week Harrison and his colleagues decided to concentrate exclusively on vindicating McIntire and Valentine, as well as the entire administration of the Institute, even though this would necessitate dropping the criminal case against John Fawkner in the regular courts.[39]

As the trial at the Institute proceeded, Dye introduced prosecution witnesses who intimated that Ezra Valentine had taken more than a passing interest in Ida, who had been in the institution since she was nine-and-a-half years old. These innuendoes were destroyed by Harrison in cross-examination, and he went on to show that Ida had been a girl of easy virtue since the age of nine, when her uncle first tried to seduce her.

Ida Fawkner, an 18-year-old of some natural beauty, first took the stand on June 29, 1875. Under Dye's direct questioning she painfully wrote replies, stating that she had visited Valentine's room as early as February, 1874, and several times after that, but especially during the fall of the same year. Ida further alleged that when her pregnancy became evident, Valentine advised her to blame one of her fellow students and instructed her to take a "reddish" medicine calculated to effect an abortion. The medicine having failed, Ida in desperation permitted the use of instruments. When this resulted in discovery, she had named her uncle in order, she contended, to protect Valentine.

On July 2, 1874, General Harrison began his slow and deliberate cross-examination of Ida Fawkner. Armed with exhibits, he reviewed for the three-man jury Ida's earlier statements against her uncle, and her subsequent change of story. The latest of three confessions, he pointed out, had been written and signed by her in the home of her own lawyer. For two days Harrison questioned the mute witness unmercifully in an effort to learn why she had changed her original sickbed story. The net result was complete confusion on Ida's part. Nor could anyone else make out precisely what to believe. At this point, Ida admitted to Harrison that her uncle had "used" her since she was eleven or twelve years old.[40]

[38] *Ibid.*, June 12, 1875.

[39] Harrison advised against the two trials being held simultaneously, and the trial before the Board was well under way. The prosecuting attorney and the court agreed to *nolle* the indictment against Fawkner. The *Sentinel* censured this move on June 16, 1875.

[40] *Ibid.*, March 28, June 9, 10, 11, 12, 25–29, July 2–8, 1875.

When Harrison concluded his cross-examination, the trial adjourned until July 23, 1875, to allow time for further investigation and the taking of depositions. During the interlude, the Indiana press continued its clamor over the case. Cries of reform dotted several editorial pages, and one organ claimed that Valentine was "even more guilty than Beecher." [41]

When the trial resumed, another parade of witnesses took the stand, and the "mute misery" lasted more than a month. By mid-August, both Superintendent McIntire and Valentine had testified in their own defense. Both told stories, under Harrison's questioning, that substantiated Ida Fawkner's first confession and undermined her changed testimony.[42] Ida Fawkner returned to the stand to repeat her charges against Valentine, again exonerating her uncle. She also complained that she had been misrepresented both by her classmates and by the school officials.

Closing arguments by opposing counsel began on August 18, 1875. Cass Byfield's emotional summation for the prosecution extolled Ida's spotless purity and blamed Valentine for her predicament. Then came Fishback's "philosophic, systematic and exhaustive" [43] final argument. In reviewing the evidence, Harrison's former partner made much of the fact that neither John nor George Fawkner, nor John's German maid, had appeared on the stand.

Dye closed lengthily for the prosecution, after Harrison had spent an entire day explaining why Ida Fawkner had changed her testimony. He told the jury that Ida, in her hour of possible death —an honest one for most people—rightfully blamed her uncle. After recovering and consulting with her uncle, she took second thought. The General alleged that Ida was under the impression

[41] On July 10, 1875, in an article entitled "The State's Shame," the *Sentinel* reprinted excerpts from the *Democratic Herald*, the Seymour *Democrat*, Auburn *Courier*, Bartholomew *Democrat*, Lafayette *Dispatch*, Goshen *Democrat*, Columbus *Republican*, and other state newspapers. All comments from the Democratic press were in a vein of virtuous indignation at the Institute's officers. Republicans, led by the *Journal* and the *News*, placed the blame and shame on Ida and Uncle John. The case referred to was the Tilton-Henry Ward Beecher case of 1874, the famous trial in which the celebrated Beecher was accused of adultery.

[42] *Sentinel*, August 5, 1875. McIntire denied that he had had any improper relations with students, as he had been charged. He reviewed the entire Fawkner affair, and Dye's cross-examination failed to change his testimony. Valentine, who had been at the school since 1870, followed McIntire to the stand. He testified that students came to his room for books and tutoring, but never alone. Another teacher always was present.

[43] *Ibid.*, August 17, 19, 23, 1875.

that when a man seduced a girl, he must marry her, go to jail, or pay a heavy fine. By reversing herself and accusing Valentine, she had hoped to achieve greater protection: Valentine could marry her, her uncle could not. That there had been a conspiracy against Valentine was the gist of Harrison's argument.[44]

By a two-one vote, the Board of Inquiry acquitted Valentine of wrongdoing and McIntire of mismanagement, and the case was soon forgotten. Harrison, however, in the public eye constantly for three months, was not forgotten. His legal acumen and oratorical genius had once more enhanced his political possibilities, for few in Indiana had failed to follow the fascinating story of "A Dumb Innocent That Could Not Say Him Nay." [45]

[44] On August 23, 1875, a *Sentinel* editorial sourly summed it up: "General Harrison closed the case for the defense in the Deaf and Dumb Investigation in a very elaborate argument, in which he attempted to establish the innocence of the accused by assailing the accusers. This line of defense in investigations of this kind seems to be as popular as the plea of emotional insanity in murder cases where every other defense is out of the question.

[45] *Ibid.*, March 28, 1875.

CHAPTER VI

A Vacation from Politics

BENJAMIN HARRISON's eldership and his regular Bible classes, coupled with his wife's devotion to Sunday School teaching, soon won them new friends from among those who worshiped at the First Presbyterian Church.[1] After services, and often during the week, the Harrisons used their new and spacious home to entertain the Elijah B. Martindales,[2] the William H. H. Millers, and the Thomas H. McIntires. The McIntires in particular, always good friends, had now grown closer to Ben and Carrie since the General had justified McIntire's superintendency of the state institute for the deaf.

From among the older families in the neighborhood the Thomas H. Sharpes visited most frequently. Sharpe, also a church elder, enjoyed telling the General about the "old days" in politics, boasting that in 1840 he had voted for "Tippecanoe and Tyler too"; his wife Elizabeth, greatly attracted by Carrie Harrison, helped her conduct mothers' meetings for the church.[3]

John and Evaline Holliday, it seems, always received a special welcome. As thirty-year-old owner-editor of the independent *Evening News*,[4] Holliday swapped army experiences and talked poli-

[1] William N. Wishard, "The Eldership of the First Presbyterian Church, Indianapolis," in *Centennial Memorial (1823–1923): First Presbyterian Church Indianapolis, Ind.*, pp. 121–66. See also Louis Albert Banks, *Religious Life of Famous Americans*, pp. 237–48; Bliss Isely, *The Presidents: Men of Faith*, pp. 179–85. Harrison's eldership extended from his election in 1861 until his death in 1901.

[2] Jacob P. Dunn, *History of Greater Indianapolis*, II, 1221–23, hails Martindale as "one of the fathers of the Republican party." After buying the Indianapolis *Journal*, he still continued his rôle of confidential adviser to Oliver P. Morton. See *Sentinel*, October 15, 16, 1875.

[3] Dunn, *op. cit.*, p. 1082; Wishard, *loc. cit.*, p. 137.

[4] Dunn, *op. cit.*, pp. 1006–9, rated the *News* as "one of the great daily papers of the middle west."

tics with the General, while their wives planned church parties and evening socials.[5]

Though in demand as a hostess, Carrie also worked with the missionary society of the church and became quite a force among the younger women.[6] This, too, had its social compensation. For most of the young wives, already skilled with needle and paint brush, gathered at the Harrison home whenever their husbands joined the General in hunting and fishing—expeditions they made with religious regularity.

So, within a decade of his return to civilian ways, Harrison and his wife had built up a strong corps of friends who would stand by them a lifetime.[7]

While Harrison's victory in the Ida Fawkner case had been of great importance to him in furthering his career, it had also deprived him of a pleasant trip with Carrie to western Pennsylvania for the golden wedding anniversary of her parents, Dr. and Mrs. John W. Scott. During the trial, Mrs. Harrison and her daughter went alone to the family reunion, while young Russell, accompanied by two Indianapolis cronies, departed for old Lafayette "to dig for Greek roots and worry science." [8] Thus compelled to keep bachelor quarters for two weeks, the General anticipated a compensating peace and quiet. A sudden rush of church business and G.A.R. affairs intervened, however, starting Harrison on another round of activity.

First of all, there loomed for him and his fellow churchmen the distasteful prospect of losing the services of the Rev. Jeremiah P. E. Kumler,[9] their faithful pastor and Harrison's personal friend. Dr. Kumler had been graduated from Miami University the year after Harrison and came to Indianapolis from Evansville in 1871.[10]

[5] Evaline M. Holliday, "Some Women of the First Church in the Eighties," *Centennial Memorial, ut supra*, pp. 64–67.

[6] *Ibid.*, p. 66. Carrie Harrison "laughed readily and her gaiety and her intellectual gifts made her delightful. . . ."

[7] Wishard, *loc. cit.*, pp. 121–66; Herbert C. Tyson, "A History of the Columbia Club," in *The Columbian* (Historical-Roster Ed.), June, 1935, pp. 3–17.

[8] *Sentinel*, August 25, 1875. The Scotts celebrated their jubilee on August 18, 1875. Detailed accounts are preserved in the Benjamin Harrison Scrapbooks, (L.C.), Vol. 1.

[9] John H. Holliday, "Biographical Sketches of Ministers," in *Centennial Memorial, ut supra*, pp. 300–2.

[10] Kumler, after graduating from Lane Theological Seminary in Cincinnati, held pastorates in Greenville and Oxford, Ohio, before accepting the call to Evansville.

His fruitful four-year pastorate now prompted the elders to oppose his transfer to the Third Presbyterian Church of Cincinnati. The final decision hung fire while Elder Harrison addressed the presbytery "at some length and with considerable feeling, tears coming to his eyes during his most pathetic appeals." [11] He also extended his pleas to Kumler, but failed to dissuade him. The presbytery accepted Kumler's resignation in mid-September. General Harrison then headed an eight-man Committee of Supply to search out and recommend a new pastor.[12] He himself traveled to St. Louis to extend a personal call to Dr. James A. Brookes and, failing there, entered into correspondence with Dr. John A. Anderson, a minister and also president of the State Agricultural College in Manhattan, Kansas. Both men, graduates of Miami University in 1853 and close friends of the General, regretfully declined.[13] Not until the spring of 1877, and after a great deal of political maneuvering, did the Committee finally settle upon Dr. Myron W. Reed as their new pastor.[14]

During the fall of 1875, Benjamin Harrison also undertook another time-consuming, though interesting, task. After their September encampment in Parke County, he organized the 70th Indiana veterans into a committee which would greet other Indiana comrades at a general reunion in Indianapolis on October 14, 1875.[15] This date marked the birthday of the Seventieth Indiana Regiment Association, which chose Harrison as its first president. "Little Ben" was to be re-elected at each succeeding reunion, and in March, 1889, "the Boys," more than a hundred strong, would escort their General to the White House.[16]

[11] *Sentinel,* July 17, October 26, 1875.

[12] *The Centennial Memorial, ut supra,* pp. 282, 300, and the *Sentinel,* October 26, 1875, list General Harrison, Robert Browning, Thomas H. Sharpe, E. B. Martindale, Eb. Sharpe, Thomas McIntire, W. S. Armstrong, Chapin C. Foster, and Merrick E. Vinton as the committee.

[13] See *The Alumni and Former Student Catalogue of Miami University, 1809–1892,* pp. 57–59; and John A. Anderson to Benjamin Harrison, December 26, 1875, Harrison Home MSS. Anderson was pastor at Junction City, Kansas.

[14] Jacob P. Dunn, "The Last Fifty Years," *Centennial Memorial, ut supra,* pp. 167–82.

[15] *Sentinel,* August 18, September 8, 9, October 3, 1875.

[16] Minute Book of the Seventieth Indiana Regiment Association (from third annual meeting, October, 1877, to August 20, 1938). A copy of the Memorial, read at the 27th Annual Reunion, October 9, 1901, records that "there grew up between the colonel and the regiment a feeling of trust and confidence that can only be likened to that boundless faith of the superb Army of the Cumberland in their idol, the sturdy Thomas—the Rock of Chickamauga."

Busy with church, legal, and veterans' affairs, Harrison did not overlook emerging political patterns within his own state and across the nation. Bankruptcy threatened the Republican party and political morality sank to new depths. The appalling revelations of dishonesty and corruption in the national government had particularly damaged the Republican cause, prompting many to turn to the Democratic party for reform. Also, after the Panic of 1873 money scarcity, unemployment, and farmer and labor unrest due to low prices combined to lessen Republican prestige. With the rise of an inflationist movement, the G.O.P. faced a sectional split. Eastern financiers wanted hard money and legislation to restore greenbacks to the gold level by January 1, 1879.[17] In the West and Midwest, such political leaders as Indiana's Senator Morton and Illinois' Senator John A. Logan favored more greenbacks and moderate inflation.[18] Public faith in Republican policies grew weaker and weaker, and the party faced defeat in 1876 both on national and state levels.[19]

Despite this dismal picture, Senator Morton, a perennial Presidential aspirant, tossed his hat into the ring early in 1875. Favorable notices by the New York *Times* aroused the Democratic press in Indianapolis to a series of editorial attacks on Hoosier Republican rule in general and on Morton in particular. Between July and November, this political assault continued.[20] The *Daily Sentinel*, while acknowledging Morton's power in Indiana and "his great tact in political management," stated ruthlessly that to win the Republicans must produce a candidate with an unblemished reputation. This, it was argued, would rule out Oliver P. Morton.[21] The Hoosier Senator, however, seemed impervious to criticism, and remained determined that his state machine should back him and no other at the coming national convention in Cincinnati.

General Harrison kept his own counsel on the subject of politics during the early fall of 1875, making only a brief speech of

---

[17] Eugene H. Roseboom, *A History of Presidential Elections*, pp. 234–38.

[18] William Dudley Foulke, *Life of Oliver P. Morton*, II, 102, 389.

[19] Malcolm Moos, *The Republicans: A History of Their Party*, pp. 144–46. Changing currents, caused by the money question in Indiana, are detailed by William G. Carleton, "The Money Question in Indiana Politics, 1865–1890," *Indiana Magazine of History*, 42 (1946), 117–32.

[20] *Sentinel*, July 1, 15, "Morton and the Presidency", August 26, "The Results of Republican Rule"; September 2, 6, editorials; September 30, "The Republican Party"; October 14, 15, 16, and 18, "Morton vs. Grant"; October 18, "Morton as a Revolutionist"; October 21, "Morton on the Resumption Bill" (all in 1875).

[21] Roseboom, *op. cit.*, p. 236. Also *Sentinel*, August 26, September 6, 1875.

congratulations to the Ohio Republicans who had elected Rutherford B. Hayes governor for the third time. This indication of party
power in Ohio increased Republican speculation in Indiana as
to its own gubernatorial race in 1876. Benjamin Harrison certainly led the list of possible candidates; even the Democratic
Sentinel referred to him as "the coming man" and "the strongest
man in the party for that position if he could secure the support
of Mr. Morton." And this was believed possible, in view of Morton's own probable candidacy for the Presidency.[22] Still, Harrison
retained the memory of the Republican State Convention in 1872,
and there is no evidence that Morton himself had in any way mod-
erated the spirit of rivalry "always manifested toward Mr. Harrison." [23] Thus matters stood until the third week of November,
1875, when the Republican State Committee assembled at Indianapolis.

On Friday, November 25, L. M. Campbell, Harrison's trusted
friend from neighboring Danville, forced the issue. He advised
Harrison in a brief letter that "so frequently and favorably" had
he been mentioned as Republican candidate for governor, it was
now necessary for him to make a public statement. Asking for
authorization to propose Harrison's name at the February State
Convention, Campbell added: "I feel quite sure that the entire
Republican party in this county earnestly desire your nomination
and election, and such is undoubtedly the case in many other parts
of the state." [24] Campbell's request for a reply went unanswered
for a week, and a second week passed before Harrison's decision
was made public.

In declining to allow his name to go before the convention, Harrison wrote that he had but one regret: "the temporary disappointment of some very warm personal friends," among whom he
classed Campbell as the oldest and most partial. He admitted that
"to these, and to the somewhat wider circle of political friends,"
he felt "a very real obligation." Personal affairs, Harrison explained, made it unwise for him to abandon his legal practice.

22 *Ibid.*, October 14, November 25, December 7, 1875.
23 The *Journal* and the *News* had a controversy over Morton's opposition to the
nomination of Ben Harrison, and the *Sentinel*, on November 4, 1875, reminded the
Journal of Morton's feeling of rivalry in 1872.
24 L. M. Campbell to Benjamin Harrison, November 25, 1875, cited in the *Journal*,
December 6, 1875.

Pointing out that he had taken part in every political campaign since 1860, Harrison submitted that he had fulfilled his party obligations. He expressed the hope, however, that he would have some part "in the very important campaign which our State Convention will inaugurate," although, he added, "you must allow me to follow, and not to lead." [25]

The Democratic *Sentinel* seized upon Harrison's declination as an opportunity to editorialize on the undercurrent of rivalry within Republican ranks. Pointing out that General Harrison cherished political honors, the editor explored the possible reasons behind his peremptory refusal of such an obvious opportunity. He concluded that the delicate relationship between Morton and Harrison would necessarily forbid the General's acceptance of "any favors from such a source," adding:

There is a moral odor about Senator Morton's personal and political history that must be in an intense degree repulsive to Mr. Harrison. This has doubtless been the real source of estrangement between these two distinguished lights of the Republican party of Indiana.

The editorial went on to characterize the Morton-Harrison political relationship as a "sort of rivalry" that never came out into the open because "the party in the state has never arisen up to the plane or level of Mr. Harrison's delicate sensibility in matters of probity and general respectability." It attributed Morton's continued ascendancy to the fact that "Mr. Harrison, with more grace and a great deal of self-respect, has refrained from contesting the leadership." The account concluded by commending Harrison for "declining the honor of a nomination from a party that can do no more than nominate." [26]

Harrison's decision received an unqualified endorsement from his father. John Scott Harrison, writing from his Point Farm, expressed deep pleasure that his son had chosen "to avoid the cares and harassments of a political campaign and stick to the labors of your profession which are so much more profitable." While assuring Ben that he was "certainly the strongest candidate the Republicans could bring out," he rejoiced that Morton would not be the "task master." The old man concluded with a heart warm-

[25] Benjamin Harrison to L. M. Campbell, December 1, 1875, *ibid.*
[26] *Sentinel,* December 7, 1875.

ing prophecy: "Besides, you can afford to wait—that high political honors are in store for you in the future—no one doubts." [27]

In Indiana, however, Harrison's personal and political friends gave voice to their disappointment. William H. Calkins,[28] claiming spokesmanship for "the masses of the Republican party," wrote that although Harrison may have acted wisely from a financial point of view, he questioned whether the General fully understood the emergency confronting the party. "Just now," Calkins explained, "we want a *man* we can really rally around and a grand, central pivotal starting point, and if you could only appreciate how the Republicans of this vicinity were centering their thoughts and hopes upon you, I am sure you would have hesitated before blasting and dashing them to the ground." The letter from La Porte closed with the plea that Harrison reconsider.[29]

Meanwhile, a coterie of Harrison's friends in Indianapolis whispered that the General, in declining the gubernatorial nomination, had left himself "untrammeled and free to accept the nomination for the presidency." Almost at once the Cincinnati *Commercial* began to promote Harrison for the higher office. The *Journal*, Morton's mouthpiece, discreetly refrained from comment, but the *Sentinel* editorialized on the "New Presidential Aspirant," noting in the Cincinnati paper's move a serious effort "to supplant the war governor here in his own vineyard." The Democratic editor gleefully anticipated a fight between pro- and anti-Morton Republicans and announced that the *Sentinel* would not vigorously espouse either side, adding, however, that it would rather "give its leanings and occasional lifts to Gen. Harrison." [30]

Outside of Indianapolis, anti-Morton Republicans had not yet surrendered the hope that Harrison might be induced to run for governor. From Covington, county seat of Warren, came a strong letter begging the General to reconsider his refusal. "We have no doubt," it urged, "that you will receive the nomination with but

[27] John Scott Harrison to Benjamin Harrison, December 4, 1875, (L.C.), Vol. 7.
[28] Calkins, like Harrison, was Ohio-born and a lawyer who had served with distinction during the Civil War. He was active in state politics and served three terms (1877–1884) in the Congress of the United States. See *Biographical Directory of the American Congress, 1774–1949*, p. 937.
[29] W. H. Calkins to Benjamin Harrison, December 7, 1875, (L.C.), Vol. 7.
[30] *Sentinel*, December 10, 1875.

little opposition—the *Journal* to the contrary notwithstanding—
and without doubt be elected by a majority in October."[31] Harrison promptly sent another refusal, pointing out that "there are
others willing to make the race and under whom we can achieve
success" and insisting that "there is no public necessity for my
services." [32] By shutting the door on his own candidacy for governor, Harrison certainly did not aid Morton, whose chances for
the Republican Presidential nomination now appeared on the
wane.[33] Even President Grant favored Hayes of Ohio, a real soldier, over Morton, merely a soldier's friend.

Meanwhile, talk of "Harrison for President" spread from his
native Ohio to Indianapolis, his adopted town. On Christmas Day,
the General received an unexpected present from the *Sentinel,*
which reprinted from the Greenville (Ohio) *Courier* [34] a rabidly
partisan plea that the Republican National Convention name
Harrison as its Presidential nominee. If Democrats were amazed
to read so laudatory an account of a rising young Republican on
the editorial page of their party paper, it could only have been
because they missed the corollary exclusion of Morton as a fit candidate. The *Journal* ignored the proddings from Ohio until December 28, when it broke its dignified silence. It dismissed Harrison's qualifications "with a restless haste" that proved annoying
to the General's admirers. In an editorial on the following day,
the *Sentinel* chided the Republican organ for having declared
"for Senator Morton first, last, and always." [35]

When the *Journal* persisted in its editorial boycott, the *Sentinel*
and *News* retaliated by keeping the name and availability of Benjamin Harrison before the public.[36] The former printed an interesting report from Chicago that "another Indianian is looming
up and casts a shadow over Morton; between the two there is only

---

[31] George Nebeker, and others, to General Benjamin Harrison, December 21, 1875,
(L.C.), Vol. 7.

[32] Benjamin Harrison to George Nebeker, December 29, 1875, *ibid.*

[33] The *Sentinel,* December 22, 1875, indicates that Harrison belonged to the
"coterie of opponents" who refused to indorse Morton's ambitions.

[34] The *Sunday Courier,* established in Greenville, Ohio, about thirty-five miles
from Dayton, was less than a year old. It was a Republican weekly with a circulation exceeding eight hundred. *American Newspaper Directory, 1892,* p. 587. It was
quoted by the *Sentinel,* December 25, 1875, and the article reads as favorably as
the General's later campaign biographies.

[35] *Sentinel,* December 28, 29, 1875.

[36] *News,* January 1, 3, 4, 6, 7, 10, 11, 13, 15, 18, 19, 20, and 22; *Sentinel,* January
3, 8, 12, 14, and 20, 1876.

a show of cordiality and friendship, for secretly Morton fears Ben Harrison, the grandson of old Tippecanoe glory." [37]

The *Sentinel* agreed that "Morton will do his level best to beat down his rival," but added cryptically: "Ben is sly." In 1840, William Henry Harrison had captured the popular fancy with a log cabin and hard cider crusade. Now, in the centennial year 1876, some speculated that the grandson might easily stir up yesteryear's echoes. His supporters felt that Harrison needed only a local Samuel Bowles and a dynamic paper like the Springfield *Republican*,[38] to be known across the nation. The record shows that Harrison came within an ace of having just such a combination behind him.

John H. Holliday, in his seventh year as editor and founder of "the first two-cent newspaper . . . west . . . of Pittsburgh," had made a distinctive advance in the field of midwestern journalism with his *Evening News*.[39] Holliday had announced an editorial policy of "no political preferences, no affiliations which might prove restricting (or embarrassing), no friends to favor, no enemies to condone." By strong criticism of the foibles of the Grant era, he soon made the *News* popular, and its independence earned it a reputation as "the mouthpiece of the unrepresented rank and file of all parties." [40] Its growth was to be consecutive and substantial for nearly a quarter of a century. At the start of 1876, it was this newspaper that underwrote an effort to make Benjamin Harrison the Presidential candidate of the Republican party.

In opening his Harrison-for-President campaign, Holliday attacked the Grant administration for its greed, self-seeking, low

[37] The Evansville correspondent of the Chicago *Times*, who made this observation (reprinted by the *Sentinel*, January 3, 1876), also noted that "Ben is a kind of Charles Francis Adams of Indiana."

[38] For the role of the Springfield *Republican* as an independent force in political thought, see Frank Luther Mott, *American Journalism*, pp. 264-65, 346-47. The moral leadership of Bowles as an intelligent independent is ably set forth in George S. Merriam, *The Life and Times of Samuel Bowles*, II, 441-61, which contains a summary of his services. See also the *Journal*, January 3, 1876, for a correspondent's report on the "sturdy virtues of the celebrated Harrison ancestry" and the possibility of rekindling the "fires of 1840."

[39] Dunn, *History of Greater Indianapolis*, II, 1007.

[40] Hilton U. Brown, *A Book of Memories*, p. 121, styles Holliday as a conservative Democrat who was bent on conducting an independent newspaper. Brown knew Holliday intimately and testifies that the *News* "battled for what it believed in," and that Holliday distinguished between a "neutral" and an "independent" newspaper. "He [Holliday] designed to make the *News* independent and never neutral on public issues." See also Nolan, *op. cit.*, p. 195, and Dunn, *op. cit.*, p. 1007.

tone, unbridled power, loose morals, and cheap money. He stressed the need for change and reform under Harrison. At the same time, leaders in both parties were searching the political woods for acceptable timber. The Democrats dubbed Governor Thomas A. Hendricks a "favorite son" and saluted him as their likely nominee.[41] Republicans, however, still seemed hopelessly divided. Morton, Blaine, and Roscoe Conkling would need no coaxing.[42] But all three were opposed by independent and liberal Republicans in Indiana and elsewhere on the ground that the evils of Grantism would only be perpetuated under their leadership.[43] They preferred Harrison, if he was available.

The Democratic *Sentinel* soon editorialized that "the growing popularity and influence of Mr. Harrison threatens the bloody-shirt man with a scuffle for indorsement that bids fair to be lively." Harrison's friends were cautioned to use prudence in promoting the General's presidential chances at home, for, once the Morton machine is stopped, Harrison "will be accepted with enthusiasm East and West. Blaine, Hayes, Bristow, and even Grant himself, would . . . rather see Mr. Harrison nominated than Mr. Morton. The Republican party would come nearer to carrying Indiana, as the case now stands, with Mr. Harrison as the candidate than with Mr. Morton."

Harrison said nothing, but his supporters, and especially his good friend Holliday, were far from silent. The *News* editor agreed with the *Sentinel* that Harrison's strength was being recognized "at home as well as abroad," [44] and he predicted that the General could carry Indiana "by a large majority, even against so popular a candidate as Gov. Hendricks." [45] Holliday's editorial crusade for Harrison caused an uneasiness in the Morton camp and, of course, in the office of the *Journal,* which repeatedly claimed Morton's political supremacy in Indiana "by an over-

[41] *Sentinel,* January 12, 1876.

[42] *News,* January 1, 4, 1876, and Donald Barr Chidsey, *The Gentleman from New York: A Life of Roscoe Conkling,* pp. 200–4.

[43] *News,* January 6, 7; and *Sentinel,* January 3, 8, 12, 1876. For liberal opposition to Grant, Blaine, and Conkling, see E. McClung Fleming, *R. R. Bowker, Militant Liberal,* p. 68. On the exodus of Republicans in Indiana to form independent splinter parties, see John D. Barnhart and D. F. Carmony, *Indiana: From Frontier to Commonwealth,* II, 203 ff.

[44] *Sentinel,* January 12, 14, 20, 1876.

[45] *News,* January 6, 13, 15, 18, 19, 1876.

whelming majority." At the same time, it went out of its way to minimize the growing popularity of General Harrison.[46]

Both the independent *News* and the Democratic *Sentinel* refused to accept the *Journal's* sweeping statement that "ninety-nine per cent of all the Republicans of Indiana are for Morton against the field." [47] The *News* retorted that "Morton is not as strong in Indiana as Harrison by many thousands," adding that when this fact came to be better understood "the chances for Harrison's nomination will be greatly improved. Indeed this fact may force his nomination." [48] On the following morning, the *Sentinel* obligingly featured a "Harrison vs. Morton" editorial. Criticizing Morton as politically inconsistent and burdened with the threadbare issue of "the bloody shirt," the Democratic editor pointed out that Harrison, on the other hand, could go before the people as "an accomplished gentleman, lacking neither in moral character or ability." If the *Journal* continues to ignore the claims of General Harrison, continued the editor, "we can not do less than let them have a hearing." [49] Loathing for Morton rather than love for Harrison undoubtedly prompted this surprising Democratic propaganda for the latter. The *Journal* struck back obliquely by publishing the Richmond *Palladium's* observation that "the Indianapolis *Sentinel's* advocacy of Gen. Harrison for the presidency is rather thin and greatly overdone. If the General were a candidate, the *Sentinel* would be the first and the busiest to throw dirt at him." [50]

In the *News*, meanwhile, Holliday kept insisting that Harrison was the man of the hour. Morton, he maintained, "can't get as many votes as Gen. Harrison. He has hundreds of enemies, where the General has none. . . . The people of Indiana will support

[46] January 7, 10, 12, 14, 1876. "General Harrison's friends are worrying Morton's immensely by urging the former for the presidential nomination. It will only result in worrying them, however, as Benjamin will not find himself so popular as his friends seem to think." This was reprinted from the Indianapolis *Sun* on January 10, 1876.

[47] *Ibid.*, January 19, 1876.

[48] *News,* January 11, 1876.

[49] The *Sentinel,* January 12, 1876, likened Harrison in 1876 to Grant in 1868. Nothing on their records could prove in any way offensive to the Republican party. This was Harrison's opportunity to battle for Republican leadership in Indiana and in the nation. The Democrats, of course, preferred Hendricks but, "if in the mysterious way of providence this nation should have to endure the infliction of another Republican president, we would all the time prefer Harrison."

[50] Cited in the *Journal,* January 15, 1876.

him [Harrison] . . . as they would support no other man, and he would gain Democratic votes at the expense of even Gov. Hendricks." Holliday also announced that the Harrison movement had attained a "magnitude no one would have expected a month ago," and he interpreted this support as coming from men who "are Republicans from principle" and who "have no connection or hope with offices or officials." [51]

Throughout this period of shifting political patterns, Harrison held fast to his earlier decision that his legal and personal interests demanded a vacation from party affairs. Despite his continued refusal to be considered a candidate, even for the governorship, party pressure increased. This persistent effort to change the General's mind was interpreted by the watchful *News* as a command from the Morton forces. Holliday shrewdly warned that, should Harrison yield to this insistence, "Morton's point will have been made. Harrison will not only be put out of the way but will be made to add to his [Morton's] strength, and one more prominent man will be made to contribute to his election." [52]

Apparently oblivious of the heated cries of friend and foe alike, Benjamin Harrison continued with his profession. During mid-January, at the height of his presidential boomlet, he was busily preparing to defend one Hiram Brownlee in Federal Court. He made his opening argument before Judge Walter Q. Gresham and the jury on Tuesday, January 18, 1876. On the following day, while the trial was still in progress, he received a timely letter from his father, supporting his political decision. "My dear Benjamin," it began,

. . . I have noticed articles in the newspapers connecting your name with the Presidency. While complimentary notices—so honorable to you and so gratifying to your friends—do not mean much *now*—they are seeds that will bring future fruit.

I do not think [I'd] let my friends "force" me into a candidacy for the Governorship—a defeat would be fatal to your future aspirations—and the inducement for Morton's friends is too strong to trust them. Mor-

51 *News*, January 13, 1876.

52 On January 15, 1876, Holliday claimed that Morton and his friends were planning to draft Harrison as the party's candidate for governor. "This explains the language used in several county papers, that 'he must be made to take it, as Henry Lane was made to take it in 1860.' 'The Party demands the sacrifice.' " See also the *Journal*, January 4, 1876, which carried a notice from the Logansport *Journal*; also the *Journal*, January 15, 1876. Holliday argued that this was "the present program" and that time "would show how it fares." *News*, January 15, 1876.

ton fears you more as a quiet citizen than he does as an aspirant for state office. "Walk into my parlor, said the spider to the fly." In a *private* position he cannot injure your claims for higher honor. In an *candidacy* he has you in the *slaughter house* of his friends.[53]

If Morton's friends would play you fair, and your party could elect you governor, the distinction would aid you in your future political career, but defeat would destroy you. *Don't trust them!* . . .[54]

Father and son were apparently in agreement that, despite newspaper talk, 1876 was not a year of political opportunity for the General. Senator Morton's presidential ambitions, coupled with his undeniable control of party machinery, remained an obstacle. At any rate, Harrison, choosing to steer clear of political feuds, entered the Brownlee case with undivided attention.

As a federal case, Hiram Brownlee's alleged offense was not startlingly serious. He was an internal revenue officer, accused of having accepted a five-hundred-dollar bribe from a distiller in Evansville. On the surface it appeared to be a routine court action, but, since 1876 was an election year, Indianapolis was very much interested both in Harrison's course of action and in Brownlee's fate. On either count, the story merits repeating here.

Whiskey distillers in Evansville and elsewhere [55] had for several years been swindling the government out of considerable revenue by the systematic bribing of revenue officers. Many of these latter were in fact active partners in a conspiratorial group known as the "Whiskey Ring." [56] During the end of 1875, the ring was investigated by Secretary of the Treasury Benjamin H. Bristow, and several hundred people were soon indicted by the Government— including President Grant's private secretary, General O. E. Babcock. Indiana, too, felt the impact of the federal prosecution. In

[53] During the first three weeks of January, 1876, both the *Sentinel* and *News* featured editorials and stories that revealed the Morton strategy in operation: *Sentinel*, January 3, 8, 12, 14, 20; *News*, January 1, 4, 6, 7, 10, 1876. On January 11, 1876, the *News* printed a dispatch by the Washington correspondent of the New York *World*, alleging that "perhaps no politician in the country has wielded more absolute, personal power" than Morton. "In his own state he has been a despot whose word was law."

[54] John Scott Harrison to Benjamin Harrison, January 19, 1876, (L.C.), Vol. 7.

[55] Chicago, Cincinnati, Evansville, Milwaukee, and St. Louis were the major distilling centers where investigation and subsequent court action took place.

[56] See John McDonald, *Secrets of the Great Whiskey Ring*, for the account of Grant's appointee. Later and more reliable is L. E. Guese, "St. Louis and the Great Whiskey Ring," *Missouri Historical Review*, 36 (1942), 160–83.

Indianapolis alone, in December, thirty-one men were indicted by the Grand Jury. One was young Hiram Brownlee, revenue officer and son of a respected judge in Marion County.[57] He was charged with accepting a bribe. His trial, on the docket for the middle of January before Judge Walter Q. Gresham, evoked extraordinary interest in the Hoosier capital. An imposing array of legal talent was involved. The staff of prosecutors included Colonel Nelson Trussler, United States district attorney, and his two assistants, General Thomas M. Browne and Charles Holstein. To date they had a nearly perfect record—all convictions save one. Handling the defense were Harrison, Hines and Miller of Indianapolis, and George W. Steele of Marion, Brownlee's home town. Judge Brownlee, the defendant's venerable father, acted as honorary counsel. Behind the scenes, an altercation between Harrison and Judge Gresham over a point in constitutional law added to the interest in the case.[58]

When the General faced the twelve men in the box, including five farmers and four merchants, he addressed his appeal to "twelve unbiased minds, over none of which a shadow of a suspicion that my client is not innocent will come until the evidence in this case shall put it there." Harrison strove to remove from the jurors' minds any prejudice that may have been built up through the conviction of other officers indicted for the same crime as Brownlee. "My client stands before you clothed by the law itself in a robe of innocence." [59] He then launched a skillful attack on the Government's chief witness, John W. Bingham, a distiller who, after indictment, had turned state's evidence. He painted him as "a self-acknowledged perjurer on whose evidence the Government relied" for a conviction.[60] The following day the *Journal* reported that "General Harrison's statement was regarded as a masterly effort, and could not have failed to make a strong impression on the jury." [61]

When the Government presented its case against Brownlee, the

[57] *Sentinel*, January 19, 1876.
[58] Matilda Gresham, *Life of Walter Q. Gresham*, II, 443–53. Harrison had objected to Gresham's interpretation of the national Act known as *Section 860* of the *Revised Statutes of 1875*, which seemingly erased the distinction between public records and private papers. Harrison lost the legal battle, but not his feeling and conviction in the matter. The press is silent on the feud.
[59] *Sentinel*, January 15, 18, 19, 1876.
[60] Gresham, *op. cit.*, p. 449; *News*, January 25, 1876; also *Sentinel*, January 19, 1876.
[61] January 20, 1876.

morning papers in Indianapolis provided excellent coverage. Interest, already above average, grew. Visiting attorneys crowded the courtroom. It soon became apparent that the case for the prosecution rested mainly on Bingham's testimony. This gentleman told the jury that he personally had handed Brownlee a bribe of $500. The transaction, he said, took place in Brownlee's hotel room in Evansville, and he clearly recalled the fact that Brownlee was wearing white kid gloves, having just finished dressing for an evening wedding. As to the accuracy of these incriminating details, Bingham explained to the court that he had purposely refreshed his memory, having been warned that he was "going to be cross-examined by the best cross-examiner in the state." [62] In corroboration of Bingham's story, the court then admitted as evidence a telegram and a canceled check for $500.

Then came Harrison's cross-examination, which centered on Bingham's statement that Brownlee was wearing white kid gloves when he allegedly accepted the bribe. The witness re-affirmed his story, adding that he remembered this interesting detail explicitly because Brownlee, dressed as a groomsman, was on his way to the wedding of Harry Veatch, son of General James C. Veatch, Collector of Internal Revenue for the Evansville district.[63] At this point, Harrison peremptorily dismissed Bingham, and opened his defense of Brownlee. He first called General Veatch, who testified to Brownlee's good character and commendable record as a revenue agent. Then there paraded to the stand some of Marion's finest citizens: banker, judge, farmer, physician, and merchant. All bore witness that the "unimpeachable" Brownlee possessed a "moral character without a blemish," and that he had always been noted for his "honesty and integrity." [64] The key witness, however, was Henry Babcock, an Evansville merchant. It was his cousin who had been married to Harry Veatch, and both he and Brownlee had been members of the wedding party. Babcock swore that Brownlee had come to the wedding barehanded and that, just before the ceremony, he had had to be supplied with white kid gloves. In cross-examination, General Browne was unable to shake this critical testimony. Harry Veatch, the bridegroom, corroborated

[62] *Sentinel* and *Journal*, January 19, 20, 21, 1876. The press confirmed Bingham's praise of Harrison's skill in cross-examination, citing the court record.

[63] General James Veatch was the first in a long series of character witnesses; it was at his home that the son's wedding took place.

[64] *Journal* and *Sentinel*, January 21, 22, 1876.

Babcock's recital, and white kid gloves became the talk of Indianapolis. It was now Brownlee's word against Bingham's, and the jury, either at their lodging or during recess,[65] could have read the *Sentinel's* headline: "IS BROWNLEE GUILTY: OR DOES BINGHAM LIE?" [66]

In his closing address to the jury, Harrison pressed his advantage with "great force and ability." Court, jury, counsel, and spectators gave undivided attention [67] to the General's powerful summary of the contradictory evidence in the case. The *News* reported that "the earnestness and general manner of the speaker indicated that he was satisfied in his own mind of the innocence of his own client, and of his determination to impress the jury with the same belief." [68] General Browne closed for the Government with an able, dispassionate effort. He ridiculed the "white kid glove fraternity" [69] in an effort to bolster Bingham's original testimony. Finally, Judge Gresham began his instructions to the jury. The charge was fair to both sides, unless, as Mrs. Gresham intimates, her husband erred "in telling the jury that it was no contradiction of Bingham's testimony to show that Brownlee put on a pair of white gloves at General Veatch's residence" just before the wedding. "Where the white gloves were put on," instructed Gresham, "was not the controlling fact in the case." [70] The important question was: Did Bingham pay the defendant the money? Gresham's biographer is alone in stating that this section of the charge angered Harrison, but that he heard it out. In summary, the judge reminded the jury that "it was a rule of necessity that required the government to resort to an accomplice such as Bingham to get evidence, and that they might convict on such evidence properly corroborated." In his final two sentences Gresham stated the rule of law that "the

[65] Gresham, *op. cit.*, pp. 448–50; *Journal*, January 22, 1876. To allow a Captain W. W. Kellar, another groomsman at the Veatch-Babcock marriage, to leave his government post at Evansville and come to Indianapolis as a defense witness, Judge Gresham adjourned the case one afternoon. Meanwhile the jury was permitted to separate, "but with the admonition that they were not to talk about the case nor suffer any one to talk to them." (Gresham, *loc. cit.*)

[66] January 21, 1876.

[67] *News*, January 24, 1876. The *Journal* and *Sentinel* also commented favorably on Harrison's closing address to the jury.

[68] January 24, 1876.

[69] *Journal*, January 26, 1876. During the cross-examination of Babcock, Browne had been given a lesson in the etiquette of the era. "On wedding occasions it was not the custom of gallants to put on their white kid gloves at their hotels." Gloves, it was explained, were always put on at the residence of the ladies. See trial testimony in the *Journal*, January 22, 1876.

[70] Gresham, *op. cit.*, p. 450.

government is not bound to convince you of the defendant's guilt beyond all doubt. It is sufficient if you are convinced of his guilt beyond all reasonable doubt."

Even before the marshal took charge of the jury during its deliberation, press and public were speculating as to the verdict. The editor of the *Sentinel* felt that "Brownlee was still on the ragged edge" and that "the white kids" would hardly save him.[71] The *Journal's* court reporter observed that the "prevailing opinion in the court room was that the accused was 'in for it,' and that a verdict of 'guilty' would be returned," though the jury might deliberate a long time.[72]

Contrary to expectation, the jury was ready with their verdict within four hours.[73] At this word a considerable crowd collected in the courtroom. A hushed silence prevailed as the "clerk of the court stepped down from his place, took the verdict from the foreman, opened it tremblingly, and in a voice faltering with emotion read: 'We, the jury, find the defendant not guilty.'" A moment of surprised silence ensued and then the bystanders made a noisy demonstration of approval. Congratulations were tendered to Brownlee and his attorneys, and "General Harrison received many warm compliments on his great argument." [74] Nevertheless, the verdict served to deepen the Harrison-Gresham feud.

On the day following Brownlee's acquittal, the Indianapolis press moralized on the subject. The *Sentinel*, taking a dim view of "Brownlee's Escape," attributed the verdict to the "influence of eloquent pleading and the social position of the accused," pointing out that "the impression is current upon the streets that white kid gloves had very much to do with saving him." [75] The *Journal*, on the other hand, observed that the jury had rightfully rejected Bingham's testimony because he was a "villain of many colors." It praised "the twelve good and true men" who had declared "that previous good character is entitled to great weight, and that the honest work of a whole life cannot be destroyed by a breath of

[71] January 26, 1876. The jury retired on Tuesday afternoon, January 25, 1876.

[72] *Journal*, January 26, 1876.

[73] Gresham, *op. cit.*, p. 451. In the city, only the *News* forecast an acquittal, or a "hung jury" that would necessitate a retrial. *News*, January 24, 1876.

[74] *Sentinel, Journal*, and *News*, January 26, 1876.

[75] January 26, 1876. In the belief that justice had miscarried, the editorial concluded: "The moral is that if any one will connive at crooked whiskey, and visit the still house as an inspector, he should, to be safe, wear kid gloves."

poisoned air." [76] Finally, the *News,* the only local paper that had forecast an acquittal or at least a hung jury, considered the case a "great triumph for General Harrison, especially as General Browne had made such a gallant fight. It was a well-contested legal battle." [77]

Whatever the weight of public opinion, Harrison's warmest praise came from within the family circle in Ohio. His brother-in-law, who had judged that "the chances were decidedly against success," regarded the verdict as the most outstanding triumph of Harrison's "professional life." And John Scott Harrison wrote:

I can hardly express to you the pleasure that these triumphs of yours at the Bar afford me. I feel much prouder of them then I would of your success in politics. Any demagogue may obtain office, but it takes brains and learning to sway a judge and jury.

I congratulate you, my dear son, on your success in this case, and hope your client was in every way worthy of your powerful and effective "defense." . . .[78]

Had the elder Harrison lived through the next decade, young Brownlee would not have disappointed him. The trial over, he returned to Marion with his family, where he lived an exemplary life, ultimately commanding much respect as a judge in Grant County.[79] Meanwhile, the General's new courtroom victory served to underscore his present decision for law over politics. Not until some months later would the taunting phrase "kid gloves" be reassociated with his name.

---

[76] January 26, 1876. The paper also noted that Harrison had gained "the first acquittal in any of the whiskey cases, here or elsewhere."

[77] January 26, 1876.

[78] John Scott Harrison to Benjamin Harrison, January 27, 1876, (L.C.), Vol. 7. In an earlier letter the General had informed his father of the deep interest he felt in the outcome of the Brownlee case.

[79] Gresham, *op. cit.,* p. 451.

CHAPTER VII

The Office Seeks the Man*

ARRISON'S DECISION to remain aloof from politics in 1876 apparently pleased Morton's political chieftains, who still saw in the General a threat to the aging Senator's state leadership. Party managers at once began the search for another gubernatorial candidate, one who would satisfy Morton. This demanded close cooperation between Indianapolis and the national capital. Several days before Washington's Birthday, the date set for the opening of the Indiana Republican State Convention, party leaders in Washington finally settled upon former Congressman Godlove S. Orth as Republican standard-bearer in the gubernatorial race. At that time, Orth, "one of the best post-politicians and strongest electioneerers in the state," [1] was serving out his term as Minister to Austria.[2] Definitely a Morton man, his name and record stirred no enthusiasm among the reform element in the party. The report that his nomination would be practically unopposed irked many Hoosiers. On the eve of the Convention, therefore, a large delegation called upon General Harrison, but he met their urgent appeal for his candidacy by a firm, final refusal.[3]

The State Convention at Indianapolis proved a dull affair. Nominations, decided in advance, met one test only: would they advance Senator Morton's presidential plans? The Convention

* Former Vice-President Schuyler Colfax wrote Harrison on August 10, 1876, (L.C.), Vol. 8: "We ought to win in Indiana, for now . . . our Gubernatorial nomination has sought the man instead of the man seeking the office, exactly as in the case of President and Vice-President."

[1] *Journal,* February 24, 1876.

[2] *News,* February 15, 1876.

[3] In the hope that General Harrison would change his mind they promised him a unanimous nomination for governor on the convention floor. Their last-minute pleadings had little effect.

believed with Morton that "waving the bloody shirt" could win another Hoosier election. No one seemed to question the political potency of this much used device. When from his Washington stronghold Morton let it be known that he would wage his campaign on the old battleground, it was an invitation to the Indiana delegates. Unanimously they endorsed him for the Presidency and resolved to present his name to the National Convention in Cincinnati the following June.[4] Orth was then unanimously nominated for Governor, despite the fact that he was still at his post in Vienna.

General Harrison took no active part in the State Convention. The official proceedings mention his name but once, when, with Thomas H. Nelson, he was chosen presidential elector for the State-at-large.

Two weeks after Godlove Orth's nomination, the engine in his political machine began to sputter. An attack, spear-headed by the Democratic press, gained momentum. Though the rank and file of the Republican party stood by their absent candidate, independents openly expressed doubt as to Orth's integrity as a public servant. Through his *Evening News*, Editor John H. Holliday, always an ardent Harrison supporter, closely scrutinized Orth's political past. His paper posed the usual question: had the malodor of the Grant administration extended to Orth? Evidently some Hoosiers thought it had. Judge Walter Q. Gresham, for example, voicing the opinion of the independents, stated: "I even fear that our candidate for Governor will not escape; . . . I don't believe that Orth is an honest man. Don't [*sic*] it look like we are rapidly drifting into the condition that Louisiana and Arkansas have been in for several years? . . . Certainly we will be overwhelmed with corruption at no distant day, if the people continue to ignore the duties of citizenship in the blind adherence to party leaders." [5]

4 *Journal*, February 23, 1876.
5 Gresham had opposed Senator Morton's candidacy before the Cincinnati Republican National Convention by supporting the reform candidate, Benjamin Bristow of Kentucky. See William D. Foulke, *Life of Oliver P. Morton*, II, 396 ff. Gresham also seemed to reflect Harrison's viewpoint as well as that of the General's former law partner, Albert G. Porter, when he said: "The leaders of the Republican party are as corrupt as the leaders of the Democratic party, but there is still this important difference between the two parties . . . the masses of the Republican party are vastly better than the masses of the Democratic party. But the people in our party can only express themselves through the medium of party machinery, and that machinery is in the hands of leaders, who as a class, are cor-

Meanwhile, Harrison was in the East. Carrie's mother, Mary M. Scott, had died at Jefferson, Pennsylvania, on March 1, 1876.[6] No sooner had the Harrison family returned home from her funeral than a telegram arrived from the Point Farm in Ohio. John Scott Harrison was desperately ill. The General left immediately for his father's bedside, where he remained until the crisis had passed.[7] Consequently, during March and part of April Harrison remained out of touch with political crosscurrents in his home city.

By the time the General resumed his neglected law practice, the Democrats had gathered in Indianapolis for their turn at a state convention on April 19. Party leaders, hoping to take advantage of the scandals exposed in the Grant administration,[8] had concluded that a political unknown would be a sizeable asset as their own gubernatorial candidate, provided that he could combine a clean record with popular appeal. Democratic leaders in Washington now believed they had found such a phenomenon. He was the Honorable James D. Williams, "ugly, well-to-do, six-foot-four-inch" Wheatland farmer, a Democratic member of the House of Representatives. Loved for such homely quips as "I just grew up between two corn rows," [9]—his commentary on his height—he also sported overalls, which had earned him the immortal nickname "Blue Jeans." His humble attire had also caught the public fancy as an external sign of inward integrity, a relatively rare virtue in the scandalous seventies. Such a reputation was tempting to Democratic leaders, both national and local.[10] As for popular appeal, "Uncle Jimmie" Williams had that, too. Strikingly similar to Abraham Lincoln in looks and stature, he was often seen with mud on

rupt. Unless the present leaders are thrown overboard the Republican party in the future will be no improvement on what it has been for the several past years." Gresham to Slaughter, March 4, 1876, Gresham MSS, Vol. 3.

[6] *News*, March 2, 1876. The death was not unexpected. Mrs. Harrison and her daughter Mamie had attended Dr. and Mrs. Scott's golden wedding anniversary celebration on August 18, 1875. Benjamin Harrison Scrapbooks (1871–1875), (L.C.), an unidentified but dated newspaper clipping.

[7] *News*, March 30, 1876.

[8] For example, Columbus Delano's administration of the Interior Department was infamous. Two others in Grant's cabinet were also unmasked: William W. Belknap, Secretary of War, and George M. Robeson, Secretary of the Navy.

[9] J. B. Martin, *Indiana: An Interpretation*, p. 69.

[10] *News*, April 7, 1876, *passim*. The paper's Washington correspondent, "Regulus," kept its Hoosier readers informed of Williams' availability. He was described as knowing "nothing of diplomacy and the disreputable wild shifts of small politicians. . . . Uncle Jimmy is of the people and has always identified himself with them and with their most intimate interests."

his boots. Thus, on the eve of the Democratic State Convention, "Blue Jeans" Williams seemed made to order for the gubernatorial nomination.[11]

Meanwhile, state Republicans grew uneasy in the knowledge that reform filled the air. One disgruntled leader admitted that "Indiana needs elevation in moral tone more than any other Northern State." [12] Others agreed, but felt that the necessary reform should come from within the Republican party. Almost to a man, these "reform" Republicans agreed that Grant's administration had done more to demoralize the country than the Civil War itself.[13] Against this background of Republican fear and a moderate desire for reform, the Indiana Democracy unanimously nominated James D. Williams to make the race for governor. The *Evening News* at once predicted that this "horny-handed son of toil, rude of speech and uncouth of garb . . . would wear his blue jeans and raise his lank form in every Hoosier County so that a unified Democracy could rally round" [14] plain, honest, old Uncle Jimmie. There can be little doubt that the choice of Williams to oppose Orth—whose integrity was already under suspicion —reflected political wisdom. The one vulnerable spot in the Democratic armor was Williams' uncompromising opposition to the Civil War. A "bloody shirt" campaign, argued the Republicans, might be the very thing to defeat the Indiana Congressman.

Once the local slates in Indiana had been chosen, the coming national conventions drew the spotlight. Cincinnati was playing host to the Republicans, St. Louis to the Democrats. As to Benjamin Harrison, the party press speculated endlessly but failed to elicit either private or public comment from the General, who

11 Williams' strength rested on the fact that he would be a compromise candidate. A dog fight had ensued between the forces of Holman and Landers, who controlled approximately 900 votes each, with 950 necessary to a choice. Though Williams collected only 28 votes on the first ballot, he won going away on the second ballot. In the end, the chair decided that Williams' nomination was "unanimous," although there were not less than a dozen votes opposing. *News,* April 19, 20, 1876. Howard R. Burnett, "The Last Pioneer Governor of Indiana—'Blue Jeans' Williams," *Indiana Magazine of History,* 22 (1926), 118–19, describes the bitter fight that permitted compromise candidate Williams to win the nomination. This account relies upon the *Sentinel* and the *Journal,* April 20, 1876.

12 Walter Q. Gresham to Thomas E. Slaughter, March 12, 1876, Gresham MSS, Vol. 3.

13 They aimed at the "purification of the government" and at preventing the nomination of Blaine, Conkling, or Morton. See Foulke, *op. cit.,* II, 396, and Matilda Gresham, *The Life of Walter Q. Gresham,* II, 454 ff.

14 *News,* April 20, 1876.

spent most of April and May in court and took no part in local party councils. Personal feelings would scarcely allow him to pronounce publicly for Morton; between James G. Blaine, the "Plumed Knight" of Maine and Benjamin Bristow of Kentucky he did not choose.[15] It was reported privately, however, that Harrison favored Blaine. When the St. Louis *Globe-Democrat,* vigorously endorsing Blaine's candidacy, suggested that "General Ben Harrison, of Indianapolis, would make a first class candidate for vice-president on the ticket with Mr. Blaine," [16] it was not too surprising. For six weeks prior to the Cincinnati convention, the St. Louis paper urged the nomination of the Blaine-Harrison team. No one in Indianapolis, including Harrison, regarded the nomination as likely. The *Evening News* suggested that the *Globe-Democrat* combination be reversed to read "Harrison and Blaine," [17] boldly asserting that "there would be the greatest enthusiasm and heartiest support" should Harrison run as a "dark horse." [18]

The *News* was speaking wishfully. As events proved, Rutherford B. Hayes of Ohio, a quasi-reform candidate, was nominated on the seventh ballot. Blaine, Conkling, and Bristow—even Morton—fell by the wayside. When the latter released his Indiana delegation to Hayes, with Bristow of Kentucky and Conkling of New York following suit, the switch in votes counted Hayes in and Blaine out. The "unknown" selected for second place was not Harrison but William A. Wheeler, a New York lawyer.[19]

Two weeks later, at St. Louis, the Democrats countered by nominating Samuel Jones Tilden of New York on the second ballot. For a Vice-Presidential candidate, they turned to the doubtful state of Indiana and chose Governor Thomas A. Hendricks. The Democratic combination showed ingenuity. Reformers found

15 Foulke, *op. cit.,* II, 397, details the Indiana sentiments with care. Most of the "reform" Republicans leaned to the nomination of General Bristow. This was true of Gresham, Holliday, and Porter, Harrison's former law partner. In evaluating Bristow's strength in Indiana, Gresham was silent on Harrison. W. Q. Gresham to T. E. Slaughter, March 4, 12, 1876, Gresham MSS, Vol. 3.

16 As cited in the *News,* April 21, 1876.

17 April 21, 1876.

18 The *News,* June 1, 1876, favored Bristow and Hayes, in that order. For a good summary of the preconvention phases of the 1876 Republican Convention, see William Hesseltine, *U. S. Grant,* chap. 24. In May, the Chicago *Times* also carried an editorial advocating Harrison's claims for the nomination. See E. T. Guenwalt to Harrison, August 5, 1876, (L.C.), Vol. 7.

19 William S. Myers, *The Republican Party,* pp. 225 ff. Wheeler's nomination was calculated to appease the Conkling forces in New York.

a champion in Tilden, while Hendricks, the Hoosier lawyer, held a reputation for ability and integrity even among Republicans.[20]

Immediately after the national conventions, political interest centered upon Indiana. Leaders of both parties wanted the Hoosier State's electoral vote. Consequently the state campaign for governor aroused national interest. General Harrison, by his own choice, appeared destined to witness from the sidelines what was to develop into one of the hottest gubernatorial races in Indiana history. Early in August, however, an unexpected event occurred that was to lead directly to Harrison's rapid rise in Republican circles: Godlove Orth quit the ticket.

Having resigned his Austrian commission, Orth had arrived stateside shortly before the Cincinnati convention. The former Congressman, long recognized as a power in the "inner history" of the Grant administration,[21] had been trained in the O. P. Morton school, and at his first public appearance, his senatorial master praised him unstintingly. Reform Republicans, however, withheld approbation. With the Democrats they awaited Orth's answer to one specific question: could the Republican candidate for the governorship of Indiana explain his rumored congressional connection with a group of swindlers known as the "Venezuela Ring"?[22] From the beginning, Orth chose silence on the subject,

[20] Alexander C. Flick, Samuel J. Tilden, p. 290.

[21] Allan Nevins, Hamilton Fish: The Inner History of the Grant Administration, pp. 357–63, 724, and 812, n. 1.

[22] The question of Orth and Venezuela was aired at great length by the Washington correspondent of the Evening News on July 26, 1876. In summary the article said: In 1866 a treaty between Venezuela and the United States settled all claims against both governments. While the Venezuelans acted in good faith, it was alleged that the U. S. representatives, Commissioner David M. Talmadge, Counsel Juan N. Macahado, Minister Thomas Stillwell, and Attaché William P. Murray, had organized a ring to speculate in these claims. Unless a claimant's case was presented through this quartet, his chances for justice were small. Senator Sumner, chairman of the Senate Committee on Foreign Relations, denounced the ring and was removed from his position. The Venezuelan Government complained, but sought a revision of the commission's findings rather than abrogation of the treaty. It was in 1870–71, when the Venezuelan protest came before the House Committee on Foreign Affairs, that Congressman Orth claims he first had any knowledge of the matter. Afterwards he was employed by Stillwell and Talmadge to assist them in recovering their percentage paid by the Venezuelan Government under protest of these awards, and in persuading Congressmen to pass a law confirming them. As late as July, 1873, Orth corresponded with the State Department on behalf of Talmadge in regard to the affair.

discreetly avoiding the word "Venezuela" in every stump speech.[23]
Day after day the independent *Evening News* charged Orth with
being no better than Belknap, Babcock, and men of like stamp in
the Grant regime. Had Orth not heard of *Crédit Mobilier* and the
Whiskey Ring? Did he not know that fraud and corruption threatened the country with ruin? [24] There were no answers from Orth—
or from Morton.

"Blue Jeans" Williams naturally made political capital out of
the situation. As a result of a striking speech in the House of Representatives and innumerable appearances among Indiana farmers,
Uncle Jimmie grew in popular favor. In addition, the fierce editorial lashing administered to Orth by the *News* created a tonic
effect in the Williams camp. Even old-line Republicans, long under
Morton's spell, began to suspect that Orth was too heavy a load
for the party to carry in Indiana. Public pressure upon Orth to
withdraw for the good of the party soon caused Republican leaders more embarrassment. One editorial urged Orth to resign, observing that it was not too late to change leaders. Independents
suggested several alternate candidates who could make a real race
against Williams. Most prominently mentioned was Benjamin Harrison.

Meanwhile Harrison, seemingly unconcerned with the political
happenings, was no longer in the city. On July 6, accompanied
by his partner, Judge Hines, and several other friends, he had set
out for Sault Sainte Marie for a few weeks of good fishing in good
company. Mrs. Harrison and the children planned to join the
General in early August for a restful family vacation—the first
in a long time.

In the blue waters of Lake Michigan, Harrison and his party
found the bass running well. Home in Indiana, however, the political waters were muddied and troubled. When Godlove Orth

[23] Orth chose to speak on practically every subject except his part in the Venezuelan claims. As the press put it, Orth chose to "exhaust his energies in manifesting
a lime-kiln degree of wrath against the 'confederate democracy.'" The *News*, May
26, 1876, pointed out that Orth had not cleared himself as one of the "jobbers" or
thieves, against whom loyal Republicans were dead set. Also O. B. Carmichael, "The
Campaign of 1876 in Indiana," *Indiana Magazine of History*, 9 (1913), 292, stresses
Orth's arraignment of the Democrats and his defense of Republican policies.
[24] *News*, June 1, 1876.

steadfastly refused to clear the record before the House Committee on Foreign Affairs, he found himself in a particularly bad light. The *Evening News* headlined the fact that Orth was "dodging an investigation" into his connection with the Venezuelan swindlers' ring. Then, on July 26, "Regulus," Washington correspondent for the *News*, struck the critical blow. Four columns of concise, dispassionately written charges finally disposed of Orth's candidacy:

> . . . He has aided and abetted one of the most disgraceful swindles ever perpetrated in the name of the National Government, nay, he has become a *particeps criminis* by partaking of the ill-gotten plunder. He has prostituted his office to that of procurer for thieves and swindlers, and in the prosecution of his shameful work, he has not scorned to cover his real purpose by the use of a man of straw. Orth is no more to be blamed than any other members of the ring, but he desires to cut a larger figure before the public . . . [and] aspires to be governor of Indiana on a platform which promises a reform of all abuses. . . .[25]

The private embarrassment among Republican leaders in Indiana now changed to open confusion. Samuel Bowles, seasoned and respected editor of the Springfield (Mass.) *Republican*, declared that Hoosier political chieftains were anxious "to get Orth's name off their state ticket at the earliest possible day."[26] The only Indiana paper to deny this was the *Journal*, Morton's mouthpiece. On July 31, the *Evening News* expressed the opinion of local independents in an editorial attack captioned "Mr. Orth Must Retire." At this point Orth's guardian angel gave up. Senator Morton withdrew public support, feigning surprise at his candidate's implication in the Venezuelan scandal.[27] When asked what he thought Orth ought to do, Morton replied piously that that was a matter for Orth himself to decide; no one else could decide for him.[28]

On Wednesday, August 2, 1876, Godlove Orth, after hastily consulting with the Republican State Committee, announced his withdrawal. "Feeling satisfied," he wrote in an open letter, "that I

[25] *Ibid.*, July 26, 1876.

[26] This opinion of the *Republican* was cited in the *News*, July 27, 1876. Editor Bowles recommended cleaning up Indiana politics. See George S. Merriam, *The Life and Times of Samuel Bowles*, II, 281–82.

[27] Gresham claimed that Senator Morton not only knew of but was intimately connected with Orth's guilt.

[28] Foulke, *op. cit.*, II, 415. "When Morton was further pressed: 'What would you do if such charges were made against you?' he growled, 'What would *I* do?' and nobody asked anything more."

shall not receive the united support of the Republican party, so essential to success in the approaching election, I hereby tender . . . my declination as a candidate for Governor." [29] Beyond doubt, the Indianapolis *Evening News* had caused Orth's retreat under fire.

As to Orth's successor, Republican leaders agreed that they faced a difficult task, "except in the event that Gen. Ben Harrison could be induced to accept the honor." To this end, State Chairman George W. Friedley called a meeting of the entire Central Committee at Indianapolis for Friday, August 4, at seven in the evening.[30] However, the fact that General Harrison was found to be en route from Michigan complicated the planned action of the Committee; party prestige would be seriously damaged should Harrison on his return refuse a nomination made in his absence. It was important to reach him first. Early on August 4, therefore, several urgent telegrams were directed to General Harrison at various stopping points, in care of the conductor of his southbound train. At Sturgis, Michigan, and again at Fort Wayne, Indiana, the wires caught up with an astonished General. In each, the urgent message read: "The Central Committee and Republicans throughout the state demand your candidacy for governor. They feel that this is a time when you should sacrifice private interest for public good. Your friends who justified your declination before now think that you should accept. It weakens us to tender the nomination and have it declined. The committee meets at 7 P.M. Give us a favorable answer before that time." [31] In spite of all efforts, Harrison received the Committee's appeal too late for a reply to the scheduled meeting.

Although forced to act without benefit of Harrison's personal feelings in the matter, the Committee was not unsupported by the press. On the editorial page of Thursday's *Evening News* it had been stated that General Harrison was probably "the most popular

[29] *News*, August 3, 1876. As Burnett, *loc. cit.*, p. 120, n. 73, points out, "A Congressional investigation later declared that Orth had no criminal connections with the Venezuelan claims." Yet at the time of his resignation his guilt was still an open question. Many believed that he had accepted an attorney's fee of $70,000 for pressuring a bill through Congress.

[30] Action upon Orth's declination could take either of two forms: the Committee could appoint their own candidate, or issue a call for another state convention. Political prudence in the face of public opinion favored the former procedure. See *News*, August 3, 1876.

[31] The wire was signed by all the members of the Committee, (L.C.), Vol. 8. General Lew Wallace also tried to persuade the General by telegram.

man in Indiana." [32] Even more reassuring was the *Journal*, which now happily raised the Harrison flag and reminded its readers that the General "is not only one of the ablest, but also one of the purest and best men in the state . . . a man of splendid intellect." [33] All of this was lost on Harrison, still traveling calmly towards Indianapolis. But it reinforced the Committee members, who determined to nominate the General *in absentia*, despite the danger of a split with the Morton machine. The Democratic *Sentinel* cannily warned its Republican friends that Harrison's nomination "would bring confusion and disorganization into ranks at once. Mr. Morton's well known jealousy of Harrison would defeat him, if his over-zealous friends should attempt to urge him on the Central Committee . . . [as this] aims to place the party in the hands of Mr. Morton's enemies." [34]

At the appointed hour, the twelve men of the Central Committee met in the United States courtroom in Indianapolis. At eleven o'clock, Chairman Friedley emerged to announce the unanimous nomination of General Harrison. The news, "received with a hearty three times three," sped over the wires to every important newspaper in the state. In the early hours of Saturday, August 5, return messages of congratulation addressed to Harrison began to pour into the Western Union office in Indianapolis.[35]

At noon on Saturday in Fort Wayne, Harrison himself was finally informed of the Committee's decision. He immediately wired a personal friend in Indianapolis: "I heard nothing of it at all till my arrival here. I cannot answer without a fuller understanding of the circumstances. Will be home tonight at 10:30 by Bee Line." [36]

This first word from Harrison reminded the Committee that they had better organize their case well lest the party still be without a candidate. An advance group of prominent Republicans, headed by Colonel Friedley, journeyed north to Muncie, where they planned to meet the General and escort him home.

[32] August 3, 1876. The other candidates most prominently mentioned were Albert G. Porter, Jonathan W. Gordon, David C. Branhan, and Daniel W. Pratt.

[33] *Journal*, August 4, 1876. The editor was eating crow, and he knew it.

[34] August 4, 1876. This editorial sagely concluded that inasmuch as "Harrison had declined a race when he could have helped Morton's presidential aspirations, Morton's friends would not now consent to let him have the field."

[35] Many of these telegrams were subsequently reprinted in the press; others are to be found in (L.C.), Vols. 7 and 8.

[36] Benjamin Harrison to George Martindale, August 5, 1876, (L.C.), Vol. 7

When the train carrying the Harrison family rolled into the Muncie station, the engine's headlight shone upon a waiting crowd of more than a thousand. The local band blared strains of "We Are Coming, Father Abraham" as an eager welcoming committee entered Harrison's compartment. They found the "nominee" sitting quietly with his family, "perfectly unconscious of the furore caused by his arrival." [37] In less than two minutes forty men had grasped his hand, meanwhile hurrying him to the platform where the amazed vacationer found himself addressing a friendly, cheering crowd. Harrison thanked them warmly for their demonstration of generosity and loyalty, assured them that he was not insensible to the duty he owed his country as a citizen, and said that he would "seriously consider the matter" and make reply "at an early day." [38] Obviously the General was not to be stampeded.

The remainder of the short trip to Indianapolis was scarcely an express run. The train slowed down at the smaller stations while Harrison waved genially from the platform. But at Daleville and Pendleton huge bonfires and great crowds necessitated full stops and brief speeches from the General. The train was due in the Indianapolis Union Depot at 10:35 P.M. and here a real Hoosier welcome had been arranged. By 7:30, a marching band had been mustered for the rôle of musical escort. At 9:30, the cannon was hauled to the station and feverishly readied for a thirty-seven gun salute.[39] Carriages full of excited citizens lined the streets where volunteer bands played military airs. When the train pulled in at last and ground to a slow stop, nearly five thousand spectators jammed the small station. Their first glimpse of the new candidate set off a wild demonstration over the din of which roared the cannon. Harrison reacted warmly, one reporter fearing that his hat brim "would wear out in the duty of acknowledging the many manifestations of delight at his appearance."

Now a procession formed and paraded north to Delaware Street, where the General's neighbors had brilliantly illumined and decorated the Harrison home. After the cheering and demonstrations had somewhat subsided, Judge Porter, standing beneath the por-

---

37 *Journal*, August 7, 1876.
38 *Ibid.*
39 One salute for each state in the Union, and one more for Colorado, which had entered the Union on August 1, 1876.

tico, extolled Harrison's gifts of character and intellect. The eminent jurist drew loud applause when he characterized Harrison as possessing "sober judgment . . . a power to see the right and the will to do it; . . . [and] an ability to make clear to others what is right, and to inspire them with the will to do it." In conclusion, Porter appealed: "General, put yourself at the head of the column and let us move on!"

At this, hats were tossed in the air and cheers resounded. General Harrison was visibly moved. He labored to control his emotions as he described exactly how he felt at that moment. He had had no idea that he was needed at home, he said, save in professional pursuits. After alluding briefly to the vigorous efforts needed to preserve the fruits of peace, Harrison protested that his own abilities were being vastly overestimated. Nor had he yet decided to accept the nomination. "My fellow citizens," he concluded,

I am not ready to say to you tonight what my answer will be to your central committee. I may say to you confidentially, however—[*laughter and applause*] I don't at present see how I am to get out of it. [*Cries: "Let's have it now; spit it right out"—laughter*] I shall not require so much time as Hendricks and Tilden have required. [*Loud laughter and applause*] But I promise you that very early in the coming week I will state my decision, and I will endeavor to make it plain. [*Cries of: "Spit it out quick; let us hear it tonight"—great laughter*] I am sure you will not ask me to give it to you tonight for the reason that there are some matters in connection with this that will require time for thought and consultation with my friends. Let me thank you for this expression of your good will toward me; words are inadequate to express to you my feelings tonight.

It was well after midnight when Harrison's more intimate friends left the house. With each went the conviction that "the General could not withstand the unanimous call of the people." [40]

Harrison needed sleep and time for reflection. The previous day's demonstrations of affection and approval were one thing; the bitter memory of his humiliation at the 1872 convention was another. He had been treated then, as the Cincinnati *Commercial* reminded its readers, "to a liberal portion of gall and wormwood," and it was not easy to forget undeserved abuse and vilification. And now this sudden turn in public opinion—was the mill of the gods

40 Drawn from the *Journal,* August 7, 1876.

grinding with unusual speed? Were the protestations of 1876 amends for the rejection of 1872? Had he himself changed?

Most probably Harrison entertained these and kindred thoughts at morning prayer, as regular in the Harrison household as breakfast.[41] Then came the usual Sunday morning service in the First Presbyterian Church. There, his mind at peace, he may have weighed the pros and cons of a decision that could appreciably alter the course of his life. One thing was certain. He had already committed himself, as presidential elector, to canvass the state on behalf of both local and national tickets. Consequently, only a limited number of additional speeches would be necessary if he should accept the nomination. A point which gave Harrison pause, however, was nicely stated in the Democratic press: How far would he have to bend under Morton's leadership, and to what extent would he be compelled to adopt the Senator's political philosophy and strategy? [42] Finally—and on this score Harrison was a realist— his election as governor would practically end a pleasant and lucrative legal practice. Here again was the old familiar stumbling block.

A stack of letters and telegrams from a half-dozen states and the District of Columbia awaited the General's return from church. Each message urged his immediate acceptance of the nomination. From all the Republican Congressmen from Indiana: "We beg you to accept the nomination for Governor, the interest of the country demands it." From the great Senator Morton: "I congratulate you upon your nomination for Governor, and hope you will accept. I have no doubt of your election." [43] And from a sobered Godlove Orth: "Accept the nomination and they will elect you." [44]

Harrison later admitted that he was most persuaded by his own personal friends. Reassuring letters had come from many of these even before the nominating committee met. John Defrees wrote

[41] J. Robert McKee of Indianapolis, Harrison's son-in-law, knew the General's personal habits as well as anyone. Though he had little or no love for his father-in-law in later life, he had great respect for his deep religious convictions and practices. He once remarked that the head of the Harrison household crawled out of bed and was on his knees early every morning. (McKee was talking to the late Bernard R. Batty, executive trustee of the Arthur Jordan Foundation, which bought and restored the Harrison Home as an historic shrine.) Bernard R. Batty to the author, personal interview, May 21, 1951.

[42] *Sentinel*, August 7, 1876.

[43] Sent from Washington, D. C., August 5, 1876; reprinted in the *Journal*, August 8, 1876.

[44] *Ibid.*

that a majority of the leading Republican Senators and Congressmen, including General Garfield, were eager for him to enter the race.[45] Lawyer Charles C. Binkley sent a typical note from Richmond, Indiana: "I hope before I die to be permitted to vote for you for President of this Nation and have expected it for some time, but it is my conviction that you made a mistake and missed reaching one of the stepping stones when you declined the race for Governor during this campaign." [46] Nor were the General's Civil War comrades silent. Colonel Dan Ransdell, for one, laid all the cards neatly on the table. "You can save the state. Most likely the state will decide the National Contest in which event your future will be secured." [47] There were other letters that appealed to the General's stern sense of duty. An Indianapolis bank president wrote: "*Vox populi, vox Dei* is such in the case that I know you will not, nor can resist. It *means much more for the future* . . . you can trust *your friends* . . . I write this note in your absence and deposit it with your waiting mail as a humble reflection of the Republican heart of the State." [48] Also, more than one old-timer who had helped to elect William Henry Harrison now came forward to promise the grandson "a campaign just like 1840" and to beg him not "to go back on us in this our hour of peril." [49]

While General Harrison wrestled with his mail in Indianapolis, his father was penning him another letter from the Point Farm. The elderly gentleman began his lengthy epistle by expressing serious regret "that this responsibility has been thrown upon you . . . but as the negroes say—'they have been gone and done it' and you are compelled to decide between party obligations and your private and personal interests. I am curious to know which 'horn of the dilemma you will choose.' " On the whole, John Scott Harrison believed the race would be close. He did not, oddly enough, proffer his son any advice. "Your own judgment," he wrote, "after all is your best guide, and I confidently leave you to its dictates." [50]

[45] John D. Defrees to General Benjamin Harrison, August 3, 1876, (L.C.), Vol. 7.
[46] C. C. Binkley to General Benjamin Harrison, August 3, 1876, *ibid*. Other letters from Richmond also poured into Harrison's mail basket.
[47] Daniel M. Ransdell to Benjamin Harrison, August 3, 1876, *ibid*.
[48] J. M. Ridenour to General Ben Harrison, August 5, 1876, *ibid*.
[49] David W. LaFollette to Ben Harrison, August 6, 1876, *ibid*., Vol. 8.
[50] John Scott Harrison to Benjamin Harrison, August 7, 1876, *ibid*.

The letter, dated August 7, 1876, could not have reached Harrison in time to influence his final decision, every possible consequence of which he had weighed. By sundown on the Sabbath Day, August 6, he had already decided to make the race.

CHAPTER VIII

"Kid Gloves" Harrison vs. "Blue Jeans" Williams

O N THE DAY following Harrison's decision, the *Journal* featured his letter of acceptance and congratulated the party. For once the independent Republicans also rejoiced and joined ranks with the regulars. The *Daily Sentinel*, on the other hand, champion for "Blue Jeans" Williams, attacked Harrison editorially, deriding especially his aristocratic manner and his successful defense of well-to-do Hiram Brownlee in the recent whiskey fraud case. "Give Harrison a kid-glove client," sneered the Democratic daily, "and a two-thousand-dollar fee, and no matter how guilty the culprit may be, his intellectual grasp will really separate crime from such respectability." [1]

On the very morning of the *Sentinel's* blast, Harrison received a letter of congratulation from former Vice-President Colfax, containing a timely warning: "You will exchange congenial professional labors for public life which—in its best estate—is full of toil, exactions, misrepresentations. But I have always believed that, if you had been nominated in '72 you would have beaten Mr. Hendricks, and destroyed in advance the prestige that gave him this year the nomination of V.P. . . ." [2]

Harrison promised as vigorous a general canvass of the state "as the time and my strength will allow." His first address he

[1] The *Sentinel*, August 9, 1876, charged that the "poor feeble-minded subordinates of the same gang [as Brownlee] are now sweating behind bars . . . [because] they are not in the habit of wearing kid-gloves and could not raise the fee necessary to employ Harrison to defend them."

[2] Schuyler Colfax to Benjamin Harrison, August 7, 1876, (L.C.), Vol. 8. Willard H. Smith, *Schuyler Colfax*, p. vii, points out that "few men have risen to greater

scheduled for Friday, August 18, at Danville, Indiana, permitting himself ten days of grace in which to study the campaign issues and feel the pulse of public opinion. Political advice poured in from near and far, almost every informant suggesting a different "major issue."

Colfax urged Harrison to warn the voters that a Democratic victory would mean high taxes and misappropriation of funds. Throw the culprits out of Indiana, he counseled grimly, and keep them out of the nation's capital. From Washington, John D. Defrees advised the General to wave "the bloody shirt" in the Hoosier campaign. Stress must be placed, he insisted, on the "odiousness of the Rebel Democracy" as "the only thing that will save the Republican Party." [3] A former member of Harrison's brigade put it even more bluntly: "General, we today hear that same old yell that greeted us at Resaca, Kenesaw, and Peach Tree Creek and well do we know the meaning of 'tighten your belts, boys, and give them the cold steel.' " [4]

The astute John W. Foster, later Harrison's Secretary of State, cautioned him against the "greenback element, which is threatening to nominate an independent ticket. . . . The other danger to our success is the paralyzed condition of business and industry, the multitude of people out of employment, and the consequent dissatisfaction and desire for some change of policy, with the hope of revival of business. These people thoughtlessly say that any change of administration will be better than the present." [5] After seriously considering Foster's advice, Harrison decided to offset the "greenback" craze by offering a program to alleviate hard

---

heights of popularity and then fallen to greater depths of obscurity than Schuyler Colfax." Consequently, Harrison could well appreciate the meaning of the "toil, exactions, and misrepresentations" of which Colfax wrote.

[3] John D. Defrees to Benjamin Harrison, August 17, 1876, (L.C.), Vol. 8. Harrison's subsequent speeches reveal that he put particular stock in the political observations of Defrees, his wartime confidant and, from 1862 to 1882, Government Printer. Harrison came out boldly against fiat money, but Williams proclaimed that "the greenbacks are the best currency we can get." *Sentinel*, August 17, 1876. Also William G. Carleton, "The Money Question in Indiana Politics, 1865–1890," *Indiana Magazine of History*, 42 (1946), p. 133.

[4] G. H. Blakeslee to Benjamin Harrison, August 12, 1876, (L.C.), Vol. 8.

[5] John Watson Foster, grandfather of John Foster Dulles, President Eisenhower's Secretary of State, was closely associated with Harrison in both political and legal matters. See John W. Foster to Benjamin Harrison, August 15, 1876, (L.C.), Vol. 8. On the prevalence of economic discontent in 1876 and the farmers' small return on corn and wheat, see Carleton, *op. cit.*, pp. 133–34. The chief issues in the campaign were financial.

times. He had to admit, however, that the unpopularity of Grant's administration would lose thousands of votes for the Republican party.

While the General reconnoitered, storing up political ammunition for his opening foray at Danville, Republicans prepared to welcome none other than commander in chief Morton himself, who had decided to sound the keynote for Harrison's canvass. The Democrats interpreted his hasty return from Washington as a favorable omen. But Morton's actual efforts were lamentable. He delivered a disappointing two-hour arraignment of the Democracy with little or no reference to positive Republican views on the financial crisis or on the vital question of civil service reform. The Senator's weak address gave the independent *Evening News* grounds for the sarcastic comment that it "would have been a good speech, even as late as 1870 but has a moldy flavor now." [6]

Harrison, on the other hand, was in top speaking form. After the routine "three cheers" for the Senator by faithful party members, the General moved to the front. The *Sentinel* noted that he "was received with ten times the demonstration of applause that had greeted Mr. Morton at any time, and in the few moments that he spoke he showed at least that he stands higher with his neighbor than the distinguished gentleman who occupied the evening." [7] Actually, since the hour was late, Harrison refused to make a speech. Instead, he suggested that the doxology be read, after which the rather limp meeting was concluded.

Candidate Williams, blue jeans and all, got the jump on Harrison by a week. He opened his campaign at Salem with an exceptionally fine speech, leaving the impression of being shrewd, hardheaded, and experienced. If Harrison read the papers, he knew he was in for a rough fight.

An all-night downpour preceded Harrison's initial campaign speech on August 18, at Danville, the "little capital" of Hendricks County, directly west of Indianapolis. The weather in no wise dampened the spirits of Harrison's supporters: the Indianapolis and St. Louis Railroad provided five cars to carry the General's

---

[6] August 12, 1876. Editor Holliday further characterized the speech as "narrow, inadequate, and unadapted to the present exigency."

[7] August 12, 1876. On the same date, the *Journal* observed that Harrison's appearance "was the signal for prolonged cheering, so hearty and demonstrative that it must have assured the General . . . of the general satisfaction his nomination gives to the party whose leader he is. . . ."

personal cheering section. Escorted by more than seventy-five of the newly organized Hayes-Harrison Guards, the train pulled out of the Indianapolis Union Depot amid a rousing demonstration. Danville, overhung by a lingering mass of dull rain clouds, produced four thousand enthusiasts to greet the new Republican candidate. A guard of honor, composed of men who had voted for William Henry Harrison in 1840, conducted the grandson to an open-air platform which bore, outlined in evergreen, the motto "The Office Seeks the Man." No sooner had Harrison launched into his remarks than a torrential rain drove both speaker and crowd to shelter. A long delay convinced the Republicans that the rain was Democratic and could not be dissuaded. Some 1,500 persons then crowded into a spacious courtroom, where Harrison finished his address, volleying "solid shots of fact . . . [which] found lodgement in appreciative and confident hearts." [8]

Since this first speech of Harrison's covered much ground and typified his entire campaign, it might bear some analysis here. On the reform question, he took a higher ground than Morton, promising to punish every wrongdoer and "to hold all public officers to a rigid responsibility." High in his own ideals, the General realistically admitted: "We will always have some fraud in office until the good time comes of which the Bible tells us, when the evil doers shall go to their own place. As the Scriptures say, offenses come, but the motto of the Republican party is: 'Woe unto the man by whom the offense cometh'!" [9]

The "hard" versus "soft" money question agitated politicians and financiers alike in 1876, for in the previous year the Republican-controlled Congress had passed the Resumption Act, under which gold payments were to be resumed in 1879 and greenbacks redeemed. Until his nomination Harrison boasted no special wisdom in money matters since, as he confessed, "the record of my own financial operation would not support the claim." He was, however, a careful student, and during the week before his opening speech he engaged in diligent research that convinced him that the war had been the primary cause of Indiana's present cur-

[8] *Journal*, August 19, 1876.
[9] *News*, August 18, 19, 1876. Harrison said that if elected he would prosecute and punish all who betrayed official trusts.

rency problem.[10] While Colonel Harrison had been busy drilling troops and guarding railroad lines, gold had been gradually disappearing from circulation. Congress had then authorized the issuance of "greenbacks"—paper money—with national credit as the sole support. This war-financing measure soon resulted in a plentiful supply of cheap money, and by the time Lee surrendered to Grant almost $400,000,000 in greenback currency was outstanding.[11]

In the post-bellum years, the Treasury planned to retire these greenbacks and resume payment in specie, hoping thereby to exercise an effective control of currency, high prices, and inflation. This policy evoked a violent protest from debtor groups, especially in the Midwest where borrowing had been heavy. The crisis came when city creditors demanded payment in gold worth a hundred cents on the dollar, while debtor-farmers, who had borrowed in paper money worth seventy-five cents on the dollar, naturally wished to pay their debts in greenbacks. In order to forestall another panic like that of 1873, the Republicans, in 1874 and 1875, produced the Resumption Act as a protective measure. "Howls of disapproval came from the still debt-ridden Midwest, and Greenbackism momentarily merged with the railroads and the trusts as a political issue."[12] In Indiana, in 1874, a new party was launched, called the Independent party. A mixture of many elements, its "Greenback" adherents proved the most numerous and active. Agitating doggedly for paper money and lots of it, this party became well organized on both state and national levels, even to the extent of entering "Peter Cooper, the millionaire Eastern reformer, in the presidential campaign of 1876."[13] Consequently,

[10] Don C. Barrett, *The Greenbacks and the Resumption of Specie Payments* (No. 36 in the "Harvard Economic Studies"), p. 3. Chapter 1 gives a clear picture of the "Origins of the Greenbacks." See also *News*, August 21, 1876.

[11] Russell B. Nye, *Midwestern Progressive Politics*, p. 53. In reality, the Government bought property during the war without paying in full for it. For example, the Union Army secured shells, guns, soldiers, battleships, transports, clothing, etc., for nothing except strips of paper of small value. See Barrett, *op. cit.*, p. 79.

[12] Barrett, *op. cit.*, pp. 199–203; Nye, *op. cit.*, p. 54.

[13] The Independent party of Indiana sponsored a conference on November 26, 1874, at Indianapolis. Delegates from seven states attended. This conference recommended the formation of a national party and scheduled a convention at Cleveland, Ohio, on March 11, 1875. Here representatives from twelve states met and formed the National Greenback Party. E. A. Olleman, editor of the *Indiana Farmer*, and James Buchanan, editor of the Indianapolis *Sun*, were chosen to serve as the party's first chairman and secretary. Their first national convention met at Indianapolis on May 17, 1876, where 240 delegates, representing 18 states, nominated Peter Cooper

Greenbackism seriously threatened Republicanism; this was Harrison's chief worry as a candidate for the governorship of Indiana.[14]

A major portion of his Danville speech was therefore devoted to the greenback issue. His analysis of the situation was simple and effective. The greenback, he stated, is a promise on the part of the government to pay money; it says: "The United States will pay the bearer one dollar, or five dollars." "It is precisely the same thing," the General declared, pointing to one of his audience,

as if I had your note in which you promised to pay me so much money: "I promise to pay to Benjamin Harrison," so much money. . . . I understand there are some people now who would have what they promised to pay wiped out. Instead of "United States will pay one dollar," they would have the government print upon its notes, "This is a dollar." That proposition is well illustrated by the story of the milkman who changed the printing on his tickets, which had been "Good for one pint of milk," so as to read: "This is a pint of milk." The ticket would not do in the coffee. The pasteboard would not answer for the cream. Our greenback friends refuse to follow their logic to its conclusion.

Harrison then declared he was firmly convinced that the government would maintain its honor before the world by redeeming greenbacks whenever and wherever necessary. He argued, however, that the government's promise to pay as set forth on one greenback is not canceled by issuing another in its place. This, he pointed out, was the false assumption of the Greenback party. He asserted that the obligation of the government—as expressed on a greenback—could only be discharged in coin. The universal expectation that the government will sometime or other pay those notes, the General concluded, is precisely what gives them their purchasing value.

Harrison hammered away at the need for sound money, especially for "the poor man, the laboring man—the men who are most liable to be deceived by those who have better opportunities for information in regard to matters of finance." When a fluctuating currency goes up, he reminded his hearers, labor is the last party

---

of New York as presidential candidate. Earlier, on February 16, 1876, the Independent Greenback Party of Indiana, as the state organization came to be known, convened at Indianapolis and nominated a slate of candidates for the state offices. For a summary, see John D. Barnhart and Donald F. Carmony, *Indiana: From Frontier to Industrial Commonwealth*, II, 203–4.

[14] On Benjamin Harrison's chagrin that the Republican party had not come out definitely for sound money in their state platform of 1874, see Carleton, *loc. cit.*, p. 121.

to feel the rise; when it goes down, labor is the first to feel the depression. Under present conditions, he claimed, greenback currency is a stable currency and it "is a currency with which I believe the people will never consent to part." [15] On the practical question of legislation to stabilize the national currency and thus safeguard the poor, General Harrison admitted there was room for much difference of opinion, but he maintained that the country was on the right road, one paved with "national honor and personal interest."

At this point in his Danville speech, Harrison boldly shook out the "bloody shirt." "It is clear to my mind," he thundered, "that we ought not to entrust this practical work to the rebels who loaded us with the debt of the war, or to their northern allies who have always been the defamers of our national credit." [16] Warming to the subject of money and the Democratic party, the General charged that in his opinion "the Democratic platform, with its stony face looking towards hard money in the East and soft money in the West, was an attempt to reconcile irreconcilables. Democrats tell us they want a 'sound currency,' that implies the one we have is rotten. And what objection do they make to the one we have? They say they cannot get coin for it. Then they say next they want 'to restore the public credit and maintain the national honor.' Restore the public credit to what? To what it was when the Democrats had charge of the government." Harrison continued his attack with a snap of the political whip:

Gentlemen, when the feeble and palsied hand of Buchanan let go its struggling hold on our national finances, a government loan, made to pay the ordinary expenses of the government, was put on the market at 15% discount. Is that the condition of things which they wish to restore? . . . Is it not a shame that these fellows, coming right out of rebel congresses and blood-stained rebel armies, should go into a political convention and proclaim themselves the custodians of the nation's honor? They taunt us with our failure to make good our promise to pay the legal tender notes in 1865, right upon the close of the war, and yet they are honeying up to the greenback men at the same time they are denouncing the Republican party for not beginning resumption the very

[15] *News,* August 21, 1876.

[16] *Ibid.* By far the best account of the greenback issue as it affected Indiana politics in the campaign of 1876 has been written by O. B. Carmichael, "The Campaign of 1876 in Indiana," *Indiana Magazine of History,* 9 (1913), 276–97.

year the war closed. That was the first year ex-rebels had any interest in our currency, and it may be they felt the failure to resume all the more deeply on that account.[17]

Harrison then drove home his final point: while the Democratic Convention had repudiated the Resumption Act as injurious to the interest of the country, their own platform was capable of no other construction than that resumption ought to have taken place long ago. With this twist of the dagger he concluded, and the meeting ended after brief addresses from Senator Newton Booth of California and Will Cumback of Indianapolis.[18]

Harrison's speech, more than two hours in length, was something more than a success. Speaking without a manuscript as usual, the General achieved close contact with his audience. A political reporter observed that "it has rarely happened in the memory of the oldest campaigner to see an audience and speaker in more complete accord." [19] He predicted that the speech would go far. Particularly pleasing to old Republican hearts was their candidate's devastating arraignment of the Democracy and his bold attempt to show that Tilden was a rebel sympathizer at heart. To political independents, however, Harrison's diatribe against election-time frauds was of particular importance, with its emphasis on "the necessity of throwing some additional safeguards around the ballot box." [20] This remained a cardinal point in Harrison's political philosophy; some thirteen years later it came to haunt him in the White House.

The *Evening News* supported Harrison's stand against dishonesty at the polls by publishing a trenchant editorial, "Guard Your

[17] *News*, August 21, 1876. Actually, Harrison favored Senator John Sherman's position on resumption. See Barrett, *op. cit.*, p. 198. Basically, Sherman favored the plan of accomplishing resumption through the establishment of a gold reserve.

[18] *News*, August 19, 21, 1876. Newton Booth, a native Hoosier, studied and practiced law in Terre Haute. He first moved to California in 1850, where he was elected Governor in 1871 and Senator in 1874.

[19] *Journal*, August 19, 1876. As early as August 8, the editor of the *Journal* predicted Harrison's success as a campaigner from "the Lake to the Ohio, and from the Wabash to the eastern boundary." On August 21, his follow-up comment read: "In the light of the rallies at Danville and Anderson it was not too much to say that the fires of 1840 were being kindled from the Lakes to the Gulf."

[20] *News*, August 21, 1876. "It is impossible that our institutions should survive the general prostitution of the ballot box. To rob a legal voter of his fair measure of influence in directing public affairs is a crime of the very highest order. Democratic framers of our Constitution have, by loose and unguarded provisions, opened the wide and easy door for fraud."

Liberty." The *Daily Sentinel,* on the other hand, charged the Republican candidate and his party with bad faith. The Democrats, with some foundation, alleged that Republican National Chairman Zach Chandler was planning to employ a "corruption fund" to prop up the failing fortunes of the Hoosier Republicans. It was no secret that the National Committee was more concerned with carrying Indiana for Hayes and Wheeler than they were with winning New York's large electoral vote. National headquarters had been warned by Senator Morton that there would be a "close, ugly contest" [21] on Indiana soil.

During September, while rival papers waged a fierce war of political propaganda, Harrison and Williams covered every corner of the Hoosier State. Special trains, chartered river boats—occasionally the horse and buggy—carried the two candidates to population centers large and small. Each party looked upon Indiana as a national political barometer and no amount of personal effort was considered too great. At each campaign stop Harrison stressed the currency issue, adopting the position that the Republican party had always been the friend of the greenback, the Democratic party its enemy. The General was failing, however, to convince the independent Republicans and Democrats, now linked together in the Independent Greenback party. As their own candidate for governor, they had nominated a former Republican, Anson Wolcott.[22]

During the first two weeks of September, Harrison made major speeches at Fort Wayne, Terre Haute, Evansville, and Jeffersonville. The *Journal* termed his campaign a victory march, and noted that Republican enthusiasm had reached "the boiling point." [23] Special campaign speakers brought from out of state to stump

[21] R. C. McCormick to Wm. E. Chandler, August 21, 1876, Wm. E. Chandler Papers, Vol. 43. It was alleged that the corruption fund was created by political assessments on Washington department clerks. McCormick admitted that Zach Chandler was "much disgusted with the large demands from Ind. but will send Tyner out in a few days with $10,000 to begin on." McCormick to Chandler, August 27, 1876, *ibid.*

[22] The Greenback Convention actually nominated Franklin Landers for governor. Carmichael, *loc. cit.,* p. 288. When he failed to secure the Democratic nomination as well, he withdrew; Anson Wolcott then became the candidate. Long a citizen of Indiana, Wolcott was recognized as an early and able champion of the American monetary system. He accepted the nomination on the Independent Greenback ticket in the hope that he might hasten financial reform, first within the state, then throughout the nation. *Journal,* October 6, 7, 1876.

[23] September 12, 1876.

Indiana [24] confirmed the bright outlook for Harrison, who meanwhile continued to "wave the bloody shirt." When taunted for this by the Democrats, he never failed to reply with warmth. Particularly eloquent was his Morgan County rejoinder. Surrounded by fifty or more gray-haired veterans, and speaking with grave emphasis, he said: "For one, I accept the banner of the bloody shirt. I am willing to take as our ensign the tattered, worn-out, old gray shirt, worn by some gallant Union hero, stained with his blood as he gave up his life for his country. . . . When they purge their party of the leprosy of secession . . . we will bury the 'bloody shirt' in the grave with the honored corpse who wore it and not before." [25] These words received national as well as state recognition, and throughout the remainder of the campaign the Indianapolis *Journal* featured them proudly on its masthead. To his old friends, the battle-hardened veterans, the General appealed directly: ". . . I would rather march by your side on the dusty road under the dear flag of our Union, and wear the old army shirt stained with drops of blood, than to do service under the black banner of treason." [26]

As the campaign entered its last three weeks, Harrison's mail reflected the increasing support of his fellow veterans.[27] Meanwhile at Republican National Headquarters in New York, party leaders carefully weighed the importance of the G.A.R. vote. Full realization of its potential might well be the deciding factor in the doubtful states. In the Indiana and Ohio campaigns, the needle fluctuated between plus and minus. One day word would come that "things look better in Indiana"; the next day "a shade of doubt" would be reported.[28] This uneasy state of affairs convinced

---

[24] Some of these were: Eugene Hale of Maine, John Kasson of Iowa, Edward McPherson of Pennsylvania, J. C. Burrows of Michigan, C. H. Joyce of Vermont, William P. Frye of Maine, P. B. S. Pinchback of Louisiana, and William B. Allison of Iowa.

[25] *Journal*, August 24, 1876.

[26] *Ibid.*, August 25, 1876. Mary R. Dearing, *Veterans in Politics*, p. 228, observes that in the art "of stirring half-forgotten passions" Harrison "was not to be surpassed by his more experienced colleagues."

[27] H. A. Kenyon to Harrison, August 29, 1876, (L.C.), Vol. 8, represents the trend of the correspondence. Kenyon, who had served under the General, claimed that Harrison's success at the polls would "prove the chosen instrument of administering another rebuke to the duplicity and dishonesty of the same old enemy."

[28] Z. Chandler to Hon. R. B. Hayes, September 12, 1876, Z. Chandler Papers, Vol. 6. "Never has it been so difficult to raise money for a political campaign as now. It was far easier to raise $5,000.00 in 1872 than $1,000.00 now. . . . Maine has done

several leading Republicans that the party should concentrate at once on the various veterans organizations. If anyone could save Indiana for the party, they reasoned, it would be the "Boys in Blue." Hence, it was not without reason that Indianapolis was selected as the site for the annual G.A.R. encampment some two weeks before the state elections. The local press urged that soldier demonstrations be spectacular, for the "party must carry Indiana."

Harrison's own canvass was indeed stimulated by the national encampment. Top Republican campaigners assembled in the General's own back yard, where everything possible was done for the incoming conventioneers. "Local committees had canvassed the city for provisions and equipment. Indiana veterans had been instructed to bring 'a torch, 2 blankets and a tin cup, or canteen' apiece. Citizens contributed over 400,000 sandwiches and lent their saddle horses. Wholesale grocers donated 3,350 pounds of coffee, to be steamed in barrels at the Blind Asylum Wash House. When the warriors arrived, they found the city 'blossoming with bunting and ablaze with enthusiasm,' and three camps waiting to house them." [29]

On September 20, 1876, Indianapolis had a new look. Brass bands, drum corps, parading veterans, cheering civilians, and ornate orations substantiated General Garfield's feeling that "war issues were dwarfing all others." To the enthusiastic crowds of ex-soldiers Senator Morton made the speech of welcome [30] to which James A. Garfield replied.[31] All the speeches that day, and the next, had but one object: "the revival of war hatreds." [32] A seemingly endless procession of veterans, with General Garfield in command, brought the affair to a climax. The line of review extended

---

wonderfully well and Indiana will do better. . . ." See also R. C. McCormick to Wm. E. Chandler, September 17, 1876; Wm. E. Chandler Papers, Vol. 43; and W. S. Dodge to William E. Chandler, September 18, 1876, ibid.

[29] Dearing, op. cit., p. 226.

[30] The amount of work performed by Morton in the encampment and during the campaign was enormous. He generally spoke twice a day and each of his speeches was usually two hours in length. William D. Foulke, Life of Oliver P. Morton, II, 425.

[31] James A. Garfield recorded in his diary for Sunday, September 17, 1876, that he had dined in Columbus, Ohio, with Presidential-candidate Hayes and his family. Carl Schurz also sat in on their political discussions. Garfield and Hayes felt that "the prospect of the return of the rebels to power has absorbed all other issues in the public mind." Garfield MSS. Also the entry for Wednesday, September 20, 1876, ibid.

[32] Dearing, op. cit., p. 226. Morton's point was: "To forgive the South is one thing, to give them the control of the government is another thing."

nearly three miles. Towards evening, General Harrison joined Garfield in a nostalgic ride through all the "camps." Not only were wartime memories re-awakened on that occasion, but new political fires were set ablaze.[33]

After the veterans broke camp, Harrison directed his energies to the last two weeks of the campaign. Greenbackers and northern Democrats bore the brunt of the General's final, blistering attack. "We will all go down together," he shouted, "in one vast abysmal depth of bankruptcy, beggary and ruin" if Confederate representatives are aided by enough Democrats to obtain control of the administration and the treasury.[34] Just a week before the election, Republican feeling in Indiana ran high. On Wednesday, October 4, the *Journal* featured an editorial on "Why We Can Carry Indiana." As the editor saw it, the chief causes for optimism centered around the return to party ranks of the liberal Republican element that had supported Greeley in 1872. Moreover, the "Tippecanoe" movement had furnished a rallying point for the old men of the state—"those worthy patriots who voted for Harrison in 1836 and 1840." [35] Finally, declared the *Journal*, "the young men of the state are enthusiastic for Harrison. Himself a comparatively young man, he unites all the elements which a generous youth can respect, admire and love."

General Harrison's first major victory in the political arena was at last within reach.

Harrison's political sky, promisingly bright during eight weeks of active campaigning, suddenly grew overcast six days before the Indiana gubernatorial election. On Wednesday, October 4, 1876, Wolcott, the Greenback candidate, withdrew from the race. News of this surprise move reached the public through the columns of the *Journal* where, in an open letter to the chairman of the Independent Greenback Central Committee, Wolcott set forth the

[33] The Diary of James A. Garfield, entry for Thursday, September 21, 1876, Garfield MSS.

[34] *Journal*, October 3, 1876.

[35] Howard R. Burnett, "The Last Pioneer Governor of Indiana—'Blue Jeans' Williams," *Indiana Magazine of History*, 22 (1926), 122, describes the monster celebration at the Tippecanoe Battleground in Lafayette, September 26, 1876. "Log houses on wheels, large wagons filled with young ladies in uniform, canoes on wheels, and wagons carrying banners" attempted to revive the scenes of 1840. Carmichael, *loc. cit.*, p. 295, alleges that "the plan was practically a failure," and that in 1876 the Democrats were the log-cabin party.

reasons for his unexpected course of action. Having despaired of his own election, the respected Greenbacker had concluded that "the sacred cause of the people and the work of financial reform cannot at the coming state election be materially advanced." Wolcott was equally convinced that his candidacy, supported chiefly by independents and liberal Republicans, would serve only to insure a victory for the Democratic party. Of this Wolcott wanted no part. "Censurable as in some respects the Republican party is," wrote Wolcott, "it is the party which preserved the unity of the nation; and it . . . still has for a cardinal principle the enduring purpose of maintaining a perpetual union of the states." He firmly refused to aid in turning over the government to the Democratic party, "many of whose late leaders yet reek with the crimes of unrepented treason." In this frame of mind, Wolcott had weighed the merits of his two competitors, and now made public appeal to the voters of Indiana to vote as he himself would:

General Harrison . . . a Union soldier, is a man of tried patriotism, pure character, of a splendid intellect, and learned in all the lore of statesmanship; a man whom the office would not exalt, but who would dignify the office. Mr. Williams is a man who has always been a strictly partisan Democrat; a man who during the trying ordeal of the war evinced no special patriotism; who indeed, stood with his party in Indiana, and that party was on the verge of active treason. His qualifications for the high office of Governor of one of the principal states of the nation, are generally conceded to be greatly below the requirements of that exalted place. Politically and personally his qualifications compare most unfavorably with those of General Harrison for whom I shall cast my vote.[36]

Wolcott's last-minute withdrawal threw Hoosier political leaders into a frenzy of excitement. Earlier in the campaign, Senator Morton had gone on record to the effect that "the Greenback party . . . draws four-fifths of its voters from our side." [37] This

[36] Written on October 4, 1876, the letter appeared in the *Journal* on October 6, 1876. On the surface, this appeal could be counted as an important factor in Harrison's potential victory over Williams. Both Carmichael and Burnett, *loc. cit.*, ignore Wolcott's withdrawal. Carleton, *loc. cit.*, p. 134, styles Wolcott's conduct as mysterious and unexplained.

[37] The Diary of Rutherford B. Hayes, August 13, 1876, as cited in C. R. Williams, *The Life of Rutherford Birchard Hayes*, I, 478–79. It should be borne in mind that the Greenback meetings during the campaign had been well attended and marked by intense enthusiasm. Yet these gatherings do not seem to have voted as they cheered. As Carmichael, *loc. cit.*, p. 295, observes, "many that sympathized with them certainly voted with one or the other of the old parties through fear of losing their votes if they cast them with the Greenbacks."

became the basis for an immediate Democratic charge that Republicans and Greenbackers had entered into an infamous bargain—the sale of the gubernatorial office by collusion. Soon the battle-cry of "sold but not to be delivered" rang through independent ranks, inspiring Democrats to intense activity on behalf of " 'Blue Jeans' Williams, the honest farmer." Simultaneously, vehement denials came from Colonel Friedley, Republican State Chairman, and from E. A. Olleman, the Independent Greenback political coordinator. The Greenback party chairman assured Wolcott's irate followers and the suspicious half-Democrats that his own "deliberate judgment, observation, and information" fully confirmed the conclusions reached independently by candidate Wolcott. He disclaimed collusion, repudiated charges of a corrupt bargain, and endorsed everything Wolcott had stated in his open letter of October 4. In addition, he pronounced the opinion that Wolcott's position commended itself "to the approval of every patriotic, thoughtful Greenback voter in the state." [38] In this, however, a large faction of the Greenbackers failed to concur. By a last-hour nomination they substituted Henry W. Harrington for Wolcott and kept their ticket in the field.[39]

The last four days of the campaign were remarkable. The personalities of Williams and Harrison were overshadowed by the speculation, gossip, and newspaper comment following hard on Wolcott's withdrawal. Democrats cried fraud; Wolcott's friends found themselves both angry and confused. Even liberal Republican Judge Walter Q. Gresham believed that Wolcott had been purchased.[40] Benjamin Harrison, who had had no foreknowledge of Wolcott's action, ignored such imputations. Choosing to regard the Democratic charges as the usual assortment of political fireworks, he simply continued through his schedule of speeches.[41]

---

[38] The *Journal*, October 7, 1876, carried a letter from Col. G. W. Friedley to the editor, enclosing the following resolution (first published in the Indianapolis *Sun*): "Resolved: that upon full investigation, this committee is satisfied that no person or persons, except Anson Wolcott, E. A. Olleman and the Republican State Central Committee had any part in the attempt to betray the independent party." In justice to all parties concerned, Friedley issued a complete denial of the *Sun* resolution by asserting that there was no communication at any time among the several people mentioned. Independently, but in the same issue of the *Journal*, Olleman stated that he agreed with Wolcott and denied collusion.

[39] Barnhart and Carmony, *op. cit.*, p. 204, n. 34.

[40] W. Q. Gresham to T. E. Slaughter, October 19, 1876. Gresham MSS, Vol. 3.

[41] An unidentified newspaper clipping enclosed in a letter from A. Wolcott to General Harrison, October 19, 1876, (L.C.), Vol. 8.

At Crawfordsville on Friday, October 6, thousands, headed by General Lew Wallace, greeted Harrison and Congressman Eugene Hale of Maine. This meeting climaxed a glorious celebration at Peru only the day before. So impressed was the Congressman, Harrison's junior by three years, that he immediately wrote to General R. C. McCormick, secretary of the National Republican Committee: "Harrison with whom I have been all week is very strong with the people and will run ahead. If we don't carry, I am a dead guesser." [42] Hale echoed the sentiments of Indiana's war veterans, as expressed in a frequently heard political ditty:

> The Boys in Blue and soldiers true
> Are shouting loud for General Ben.
> While from the river to the lakes
> He draws a host of loyal men.
> But nowhere in the Hoosier State
> A single voice or vote he gains
> From Copperheads or ex-Confeds
> For they all march with Uncle James.[43]

On the final week end of the campaign, General Harrison made speeches at South Bend, Muncie, and Rockville, ending his tour at Lebanon on election eve. Here, at the conclusion of his ninety-minute address, a glee club led the crowd in singing the "Battle Hymn of the Republic," and the Indiana Republican campaign of the Centennial Year was over.

The state election took place quietly on Tuesday, October 10. Despite the fact that both parties scattered voting money liberally,[44] neither violence nor rowdyism characterized the contest. Actually, the close vote kept the contest in doubt for two days. Nevertheless, on the morning after the election the *Journal's* headline read: "Gallant Benjamin Harrison Runs Ahead of his Ticket in all Directions." "A fitting conclusion," the editor observed, "to

[42] Eugene Hale to R. C. McCormick, October 6, 1876, Z. Chandler Papers, Vol. 6.
[43] Benjamin Harrison Scrapbooks, (L.C.), Vol. 3, p. 2, col. 1.
[44] W. Q. Gresham to T. E. Slaughter, October 19, 1876, Gresham MSS, Vol. 3. ". . . a man told me last night, and he knew whereof he spoke, that the National Committee sent to Indiana $75,000. And I know that quite a large sum was raised here by private subscription. What became of all that money?" Editorials in the *Journal, Sentinel,* and *News* made frequent mention of "slush funds"—a fact confirmed by correspondence in both the Wm. E. Chandler and Z. Chandler Papers.

a campaign unequalled in the history of the state." [45] State Chairman Friedley claimed the election for Harrison by a four to six thousand majority. But enthusiasm soon gave way to reality; on Thursday morning, October 12, the *Journal* somberly admitted that the vote was close "and a victory is claimed by both sides." While this particular Republican daily was now willing to await the tabulation of votes before making any further guesses, another party paper, the Cincinnati *Commercial*, ventured a cautious headline: "Blue Jeans Probably Elected by a Small Majority." Democrats, on the other hand, were jubilantly confident that "Blue Jeans Williams had won a clean-cut victory." Party members soon were singing a triumphant tune celebrating "Williams' Walk Over the Political Grave of the Grandson." [46]

On Friday, October 13—a fitting date—the Republicans admitted defeat. The *Journal's* leading editorial consoled weary party workers by distinguishing between "such a thing as a successful defeat and a disastrous victory." [47] It rationalized Harrison's defeat by some 5,000 votes as a moral triumph. "Though not elected governor, the position occupied by General Harrison before the people of the country today is infinitely superior to that occupied by his successful competitor." It further observed "that the General has won the lasting gratitude of the party and a secure place in the affections of all its members." [48]

Victory-fed Democrats interpreted the results quite differently. The voters, they argued, had spoken out against corruption, extravagance, and the twin evils of slander and hatred. Followers of Tilden, Hendricks, and Williams also agreed that the people had reduced "the bloody shirt" to the value of a cipher in American politics. "It may still be red enough to infuriate a 'sitting bull,' but it has lost the power to goad the masses to suicidal madness."

[45] October 11, 1876.

[46] *Sentinel*, October 12, 1876.

[47] Even Gresham admitted that "the Republican party was not defeated last week; it was Morton's party that failed, for the campaign was Morton's program. . . ." W. Q. Gresham to T. E. Slaughter, October 19, 1876, Gresham MSS, Vol. 3.

[48] The heavy correspondence in Vol. 8 of the Harrison MSS substantiates the claims made by the *Journal* editorial. For example, Ben Butterworth to Benjamin Harrison, October 13, 1876; Lewis D. Stubbs to Harrison, October 13, 1876; *et passim*. Presidential-candidate Hayes instructed his private secretary to thank Harrison, "not for what he has done for individuals but what he has done for Republican principles." Edward Crassey to Harrison, October 14, 1876, *ibid*.

Perhaps Harrison himself winced at the *Daily Sentinel's* editorial, which placed the blame for his defeat at Morton's door:

General Harrison, the defeated candidate, is perhaps the strongest man in his party in this state. His commanding ability, his high character, have not been assailed in the canvass, and he owes his defeat, in great measure, to his blunder in adopting the brutal opinions and tactics of Morton.[49]

In a later press interview, however, he stated that he thought Wolcott's withdrawal had the most to do with his defeat. "The fact that he withdrew in my favor at the 11th hour," he said, "gave rise to suspicion in the minds of many that there was a monied inducement, and the time was too short to convince them to the contrary."

The *Sentinel* commented dryly that not even "the Angel Gabriel himself could have carried Morton, Logan, Holloway, Ingersoll, Kilpatrick, and Wolcott, together with fraud, bribery, iniquity, abuse, corruption, etc." [50] Rank and file Democrats were content to believe that Williams' victory was one of "blue jeans over blue blood."

[49] October 13, 1876.

[50] *Ibid.* Perhaps the best analysis of the Republican defeat has been furnished by Carleton, *loc. cit.*, p. 134: "For governor, Williams had a total vote of 213,219 of the aggregate vote. Harrison had 208,080, and Harrington polled 12,710." None can deny that the Greenbackers held the balance of power, and Carleton concludes that "the Greenbackers continued to draw more heavily from the Republicans."

CHAPTER IX

Political Debits
and Personal Credits

HARRISON REACTED with philosophic calm to his first major setback at the polls. "My own defeat," he wrote Anson Wolcott, "does not matter much if we shall elect Hays [*sic*] as I believe we will." [1] The General's personal prestige and popularity had not been diminished by his failure to beat Williams. Just four days after his defeat, Indianapolis Republicans, at a mass meeting for Hayes and Wheeler, gave Harrison a standing ovation that completely eclipsed previous demonstrations in his honor. Visibly moved, the General exclaimed to the crowd: "I am glad I am a Republican!" Cheers followed his characteristic statement that "though victory has not perched on our banners in this campaign, I had rather be beaten on the side of truth than win on the side of ignorance and error. I don't feel whipped at all." One fact alone grieved him: that "Indiana, our grand old state, should have seen fit to answer the Confederate Roll Call." [2]

At the announcement of the official state vote, it became clear that the General had run ahead of the state ticket by almost two thousand votes. [3] In addition to gratifying Harrison personally, this fact also bolstered hopes in the Hayes camp. Easterners reported that they "never saw a state election which produced such

[1] Benjamin Harrison to Anson Wolcott, October 20, 1876, (L.C.), Vol. 8.
[2] *Journal,* October 16, 1876.
[3] Lew Wallace, *Life of Gen. Ben Harrison,* pp. 265–66, notes that thirteen Congressmen were voted for on the same day, and the combined vote of those on the Republican side was 204,419. From this comparison it would seem clear that General Harrison was from three to four thousand votes stronger than the Republican organization in the state at that time.

general and national interest and excitement." [4] From Chicago, an historically minded lawyer observed of the Harrison-Williams duel that "no state contest has attracted so much attention since the debate between Lincoln and Douglas in 1858." He pointed out that "although Mr. Lincoln was defeated in the immediate results of that contest, yet in the greater result which followed he won the battle." [5] There was a growing feeling, based on Harrison's strong showing, that Indiana would go Republican in November. Even Presidential-candidate Hayes admitted that Indiana Republicans had done far better than he had expected. "I feel sure we shall carry the state in November," [6] he told Harrison, to which the latter replied quickly, "We will continue to fight and do our best." He meant this, and personally assured Hayes that he would regard his defeat as nothing short of a "crowning *calamity.*" [7]

During the third week of October, legal business took Harrison to Chicago, giving him an opportunity to fulfill his promise to Rutherford Hayes. On the night after his arrival, the General addressed a capacity crowd in famed Farwell Hall, where, according to the Chicago *Tribune,* round after round of applause greeted "the gallant Harrison." The General responded with one of his better oratorical efforts. When he spoke of Abraham Lincoln as "the grand old pilot who safely guided the ship of state through the stormy sea of rebellion," the assemblage rose as a man and "for several minutes the hall resounded with cheers." [8]

Even prior to Harrison's Chicago success, the National Committee had scheduled him for several speeches in New Jersey, another doubtful state. But as word of his triumph at Farwell Hall got around, strong pressure was put upon him to make a major address at Philadelphia, the Centennial host city. Harrison

[4] Elizabeth (Scott) Lord to "Dear Brother Ben" and "Sister Carrie" (Harrison), October 14, 1876, (L.C.), Vol. 8. Elizabeth, Carrie's sister, was then living in Princeton, New Jersey. She had to entertain visitors at the Centennial celebration in Philadelphia and mixed with a good number of the people and political leaders. The Lords frequently entertained the Harrisons in the East. In 1896, Mary "Mame" Lord, then the widow of Walter Erskine Dimmick, married General Harrison, a widower since 1892.

[5] James P. Root to General Harrison, October 14, 1876, *ibid.*

[6] Charles R. Williams, *The Life of Rutherford Birchard Hayes,* I, 480, n. 1.

[7] Benjamin Harrison to Hon. R. B. Hayes, October 16, 1876, (L.C.), Vol. 8.

[8] *Journal,* October 19, 1876, as taken from the report in the Chicago *Inter-Ocean.* The citations included in the text are taken from this source.

accepted and left for his eastern tour in particularly good spirits. When he appeared at Horticultural Hall, scene of his Philadelphia address, he was greeted with profound applause. This warm reception could only have been a tribute to Harrison's reputation for gallantry and eloquence because his physical appearance "disappointed general expectations." Most Philadelphians, the Philadelphia *Times* noted, "had pictured General Harrison as a man of commanding presence, large, well formed, and possessed of personal magnetism." The reverse was true, and thanks to the same meticulous reporter, we can judge for ourselves perhaps the best pen picture ever made of Harrison the political campaigner as he appeared in late October, 1876:

He is about 5' 6" in height and slenderly built. A well-formed head rests upon a square pair of shoulders. The face of the General is adorned by a full, light brown beard, cut close, and a heavy mustache appears under his shapely nose. The forehead is of medium height and retreats to a luxuriant mass of light hazel-colored hair, slightly tinged with gray. A pleasant pair of little blue eyes and a clear cut mouth complete the picture of the orator. He was dressed in a black broadcloth frockcoat, black vest and gray pantaloons. While speaking he is all energy, nervous and wiry, gesticulates rapidly, putting a full point to each sentence with a rapid motion of clenched fists. It cannot be said that he is an eloquent speaker; his forte seems to be clear enunciation, rapid delivery and emphasis. If Ingersoll is the Cicero of the campaign, Harrison is the Demosthenes.[9]

In the audience that night were the General's daughter Mamie and his niece, Lizzie Lord. The two girls cheered loudly each reference to Indiana, especially when Harrison assured his audience that Hoosier Republicans were determined to win the election for Hayes and Wheeler. "Why, we have got a little mad over this thing," he exclaimed. "Now, when men get mad, they are bent on winning the fight. We don't rest upon our oar; we don't go into camp to refit. We have ordered the column forward and the march onward to victory." [10] Before his speech was over, Harrison had won a host of new friends and admirers, many of whom became his ardent supporters in the Senate and later in the White House.

New Jersey was no less cordial. Speaking enthusiastically at Newark, Harrison told a large Republican turnout that victory

---

[9] Philadelphia *Times*, October 26, 1876, as cited in the *Journal*, October 30, 1876.
[10] *Ibid.*

was within their grasp if only they would work hard during the last week. And he reminded them triumphantly that neither he nor the Republican party was dead.[11]

General Harrison returned to the Midwest for the final week end of campaigning. At Bloomington, Illinois, he spoke for three hours "in an eloquent and impressive manner, holding the undivided attention of the crowd to the last." [12] Afterward, wearied by more than two weeks of extensive travel and long speeches, Harrison returned to Indianapolis, and on Tuesday morning, November 7, cast his vote for the electors of Hayes and Wheeler. This act terminated a campaign fraught with personal significance for Harrison. Though numerically defeated in his contest for the governorship, the forty-three-year-old "Hoosier Warrior" had successfully thrown off political anonymity and emerged a national figure in party circles. It is somewhat of an anomaly of history that Harrison's defeat was so successful that it inevitably made him a leader of his party, not only in fast-changing Indiana but also throughout the country. As he walked away from the Indianapolis polling booth in 1876, Harrison was less than five years away from the United States Senate and only two presidential elections away from the White House.

The first reports on the Presidential election of 1876 proved no more encouraging to General Harrison than had the final verdict of his own race in October. The tally showed that Samuel J. Tilden had carried Indiana as well as the doubtful states of Connecticut, New Jersey, and New York. Moreover, it appeared that the Democratic nominee had polled a popular majority of nearly a quarter of a million votes. Still, the electoral vote promised to be close, and there were other rays of hope for the disappointed and gloomy Republicans. Oregon and California, considered doubtful, were now reported in the G.O.P. column, along with the Republican-ribbed states of New England and the Middle West.[13] The final verdict rested with the South, still slow to tabulate and report an accurate vote. Also, the New York *Times* refused to concede a

[11] New York *Times*, October 27, 1876.

[12] *Journal*, November 4, 1876.

[13] H. J. Eckenrode, *Rutherford B. Hayes, Statesman of Reunion*, pp. 176 ff., gives a useful summary of the election in Chapter 8 of this biography. This life is more critical and scientific than the official life written by Charles R. Williams.

Tilden victory based on the presumption of a solid Democratic South, and this encouraged the Republican National Chairman and his staff. If the votes of Florida, Louisiana, and South Carolina did not belong to Tilden, then the New York reformer had only 184 electoral votes, with 185 necessary for election. In short order, in each of the three doubtful states, Republican leaders read practically identical telegrams: "Can you hold your state? Reply immediately." The result was that early on the morning of November 8, National Chairman Zachariah Chandler was able to assume the offensive and release his famous dispatch: "Hayes has 185 electoral votes and is elected." [14]

Louisiana particularly interested Republican leaders. They felt that a fair election and a fair count in the Bayou State would give Hayes a large majority, which had already been claimed by the Tilden forces. Hayes' supporters immediately decided to send their own representative to New Orleans to witness the recounting of the ballots. Consequently, on November 11, President Grant directed a telegram to Benjamin Harrison: "I would be gratified if you would visit New Orleans to witness the count of the vote." [15] On the same day, several other leading Republicans of national reputation received similar messages. Harrison declined, however, apparently satisfied that his close friends, Generals Lew Wallace and John Coburn, would represent Indiana in holding the fort for Hayes in Louisiana. Later that same week, he refused a second appeal from Zachariah Chandler to appear in South Carolina as one of the "visiting statesmen." [16] Adopting a hands-off policy, he calmly resumed his legal chores, leaving to his fellow-politicians in the South the task of legal and political compromise.[17]

On New Year's night, 1877, General Harrison became ill and for a week was confined to bed. By the time Russell departed for his last term at Lafayette College,[18] his father was on his feet again,

[14] Eckenrode, *op. cit.*, pp. 182–85. The two men most responsible for getting Zachariah Chandler to take any action at all were his brother William and John C. Reid, managing editor of the New York *Times*.

[15] W. G. Grant to Benjamin Harrison, November 11, 1876, (L.C.), Vol. 8.

[16] Zachariah Chandler to General Ben Harrison, November 25, 1876, (L.C.), Vol. 8.

[17] Malcolm Moos, *The Republicans: A History of Their Party*, pp. 149–54.

[18] Earlier plans calling for Russell's enrollment at Cornell had been dropped in favor of Lafayette. J. J. Perling, *Presidents' Sons*, pp. 238–39; also Indianapolis *Star*, February 4, 1936.

although still quite weak. For nearly a month he engaged in a minimum of activity, paying little or no public attention to the acrimonious dispute in Washington over the creation of an electoral commission to pass judgment on the still contested electoral votes in the South. This inactivity and lack of support displeased Senator Morton, who had counted on complete backing from Indiana Republicans of his own contention that the electoral commission had no power to go behind the returns made by the state canvassing boards. When Morton did not obtain Harrison's help, the gap between the two leaders widened.[19]

Recovering slowly from the fatigue of two arduous campaigns and his resultant illness, Harrison had by no means lost his quiet sense of humor. Margaret Peltz, an intimate family friend living in St. Louis—lovingly addressed as "Cousin Mag"—had made "Cousin Ben" some extremely fancy night-shirts as a Christmas gift. The convalescent Harrison, still mindful of his defeat by "Blue Jeans" Williams, sent her a playful letter of thanks:

The garments were, I believe, intended for the Governor of Indiana, but they were too short for him and much too dainty, so I have taken the liberty of keeping them. Mrs. Harrison thought I would not wear ruffled and pleated *"robes de nuit"* and was surprised to see how kindly I took to the finery. Strange as it may seem, I have never had more *unruffled* sleep.[20]

[19] Eckenrode, *op. cit.*, p. 208. If the Commission had gone behind the returns in Florida, Hayes' case would probably have been lost. While the Electoral Commission bill was pending in the Senate, a dispatch was sent to Senator Conkling, signed by Harrison, Gresham, and a half-dozen other prominent Republicans of Indiana, urging passage of the bill. This dispatch was read on the floor of the Senate by Conkling, "with a great flourish of trumpets," to show that Morton did not represent the Republicans of Indiana in opposing the bill. As an editorial in the Cincinnati *Commercial*, January 25, 1876, pointed out, in the "debate . . . between Senators Conkling and Morton . . . the latter was decidedly the loser in the contest. His [Morton's] own record was quoted against him, and the petition of some of the leading Republicans of his own state in favor of the bill was pressed home upon him so sharply that he was not able to efface the impression created by the counter-statements by the gentlemen whose names were not given in the Senate." See also Williams, *op. cit.*, p. 23.

[20] Benjamin Harrison to Margaret Peltz, January 13, 1877. The holograph copies of these letters are in the possession of Mrs. Clarence W. Messinger of Houghton, Michigan, granddaughter of Margaret Wilson Shelby who had married Samuel Peltz of Philadelphia. From this union came three daughters: Eugenia, called "Eugie"; Margaret, called "Maggie"; Mary, called "Daisy." The Harrison and Peltz families were on very intimate terms, and when Samuel Peltz died in 1875 in St. Louis, General Harrison took charge of Mrs. Peltz's legal and business affairs. The families visited and corresponded with one another until their deaths. The author is extremely grateful for copies of the handwritten letters Harrison sent to Mrs Peltz ("Cousin Mag") between 1877 and his death in 1901. Mrs. Messinger's interest

This light spirit indicated the return of normal health and a pleasant outlook on life, both of which Harrison needed. The first three months of 1877 had brought him heavy financial outlays— Mamie's school bill of $444.03, for example—and made substantial fees more imperative than ever.[21]

Even before the electoral commission assured Hayes of the Presidency, the Ohio Republican had considered Benjamin Harrison for a Cabinet post. On January 17, the President-elect confided to his diary: "I think well of General Harrison of Indiana." [22] Several close mutual associates in Ohio and Indiana believed that Hayes' first choice for a Secretary of the Navy was Harrison, "whose gallant though unsuccessful campaign to win Indiana to the Republican cause" must not go unrewarded.[23] A month later, some two weeks before the inauguration, Murat Halstead, owner-editor of the Cincinnati *Commercial* and on the best of terms with influential politicians, informed Harrison that Hayes "has an almost extravagant feeling of admiration and affection for you." However, he added, "one thing would prevent him from offering you a place in the Cabinet; he would not like to give an Indiana appointment in defiance of the opposition of Morton." Then, to make the situation even clearer to Harrison, he concluded: "If Gov. Morton would convey to Hayes the understanding that he would not be displeased if you were appointed to the Cabinet, it is my judgment that nothing more would be required to secure your appointment." [24]

Both Morton's continued opposition and Hayes' friendship puzzled and nettled Harrison. For a time he refrained from comment "lest," he wrote Halstead, "it be attributed to the interest of an office seeker." He assured his old college crony that the mere

---

and generosity made these copies possible. (Hereafter the papers will be cited as the Messinger MSS. Copies are now in the possession of the author.)

[21] In addition to school bills for Russell and Mamie, the General met the taxes on the North Bend (Ohio) property, his father's personal and financial needs, church obligations, and several contributions to charity. Each item is detailed in Harrison's "Perpetual Diary for 1877 and 1878," preserved in the Harrison Memorial Home at Indianapolis.

[22] As cited in Williams, *op. cit.*, II, 17.

[23] For example, see Edward Crassey to Benjamin Harrison, October 14, 1876, (L.C.), Vol. 8 *passim*. There is a great deal of confirmatory evidence on this point.

[24] M. Halstead to Gen. Benjamin Harrison, February 22, 1877, *ibid.*, wrote that he would undertake the task of reaching Morton, "but my relations with him are not such that I can get at him." Harrison received several letters which made the same point: have Morton on your side and you have a Cabinet office.

knowledge that he enjoyed the new President's confidences and affection deeply gratified him. "It is worth having without an office at the end of it. . . . Gov. Hayes may be absolutely certain that I will not allow any supposed claims of mine to embarrass him in the slightest degree. If the good will and cooperation of others depend on official favor, mine does not."

On the delicate question of Morton's opposition, Harrison was cautious. "You assume it exists and is strenuous," his letter continued. "Do you know this, or only infer it from what you have understood of our former relations?" Judging others by his own standard of conduct, Harrison could see no reason for Morton to obstruct his political advancement. "Our personal relations have always been pleasant," he reminded Halstead, "and I have never opposed him in any ambition he has entertained." He did concede that his feeling for Morton had not extended to any excessive admiration for the man. As he dispassionately put it: "Somewhat independent, I have been somewhat less of a personal follower than others."

Halstead, more astute and experienced in practical politics than his friend, could not fathom Harrison's noncommittal attitude. Did he want the Cabinet post or not? The Cincinnati editor could find no clue in the General's final careful comment: "His [Morton's] great public power and pre-eminent abilities I have always cheerfully conceded and have often publicly extolled. Some of us have thought that his rule was too absolute at times, and the disposition to proscribe for difference of opinion too strong. But of this Gov. Hayes must judge when he disposes of Indiana affairs." [25]

Senator Morton once again had his way. The aged but fiery Richard Wigginton Thompson [26] received the Navy portfolio in

[25] Benjamin Harrison to Murat Halstead, February 24, 1877, *ibid.* This letter contains the best reflection of Harrison's mind on bothersome questions of his relations with Senator Morton. The General explained his position with regard to the telegram on the electoral commission which had been read in the Senate by Conkling: "It was presented to me while engaged in a trial in court and was signed, with a limitation, because it expressed my views of the true policy of our party. No thought of such a use as was made of it ever entered my mind. All this and Gov. M's reported statements in the Senate have been explained between us." Harrison was equally certain that any appointment could be made by Hayes even over the "opposition as you apprehend. When the matter is pressed, and all that is personal to M. is out of the way, I shall have to go East to have a full talk with the President."

[26] Thompson was nearly twenty-five years Harrison's senior. He was Virginia-born but moved to Indiana, where he commenced the practice of law in 1834, the year after Harrison's birth. He served four years as a Whig Congressman and was

the Hayes cabinet. Harrison's backers thereupon saw signs of a new political war between the Morton faction and the General's younger friends. Halstead, in a *Commercial* editorial, argued that Thompson's appointment served only to throw "Harrison into the attitude of the leader of the anti-Morton Republicans in Indiana." [27] Harrison himself, in his letter of congratulation to the new Secretary of the Navy, successfully concealed whatever chagrin he may have felt. At any rate, he drew satisfaction from the fact that Evarts, Sherman, and Schurz had entered the Cabinet. These appointments marked a change for the better and gave hope to all civil service reform advocates.

He delayed writing to Hayes until a full Cabinet had been named, fearing that his letter might be interpreted as a plea for office. He then sent the President his solemn promise: "Whatever influence I have in Indiana is fully pledged to the support of your declared policy." At the same time, Harrison wrote to one of Hayes' closest Washington friends that the new man in the White House "has set for himself a task which will try his patience and his fortitude, but if he holds out, only two presidents will take rank before him." [28]

Morton's attitude towards Harrison—that of an undeclared but active enemy—served to teach the younger man, still a political neophyte, what he needed to know about practical political warfare. Still, it took Harrison almost a decade to learn that to appease or compromise with Morton meant nothing less than surrender on the installment plan. His position at the end of 1876, despite his party loyalty and great ability as a speaker and votegetter, confirmed this. Hence, when the czar of Indiana politicians

---

the noted orator of nine presidential campaigns. Despite the age gap, Thompson and Harrison were quite intimate. See Charles Roll, *Colonel Dick Thompson: The Persistent Whig*, pp. 286–91.

[27] Cincinnati *Commercial*, March 8, 1877.

[28] Benjamin Harrison to General John G. Mitchell, March 8, 1877, (L.C.), Vol. 8, put his cards on the table: "I have good reason to believe that Senator Morton, directly or indirectly took ground against my appointment to a Cabinet place, and I want to know the *facts*." One sentence in Harrison's letter was crossed out. He claimed he was asking for the facts "not because I feel the slightest disposition to object to Col. Thompson's appointment nor because I am foolish enough to think I had any claims upon a Cabinet place, but solely that I may not do Gov. Morton an injustice [the following scratched out: "but may know exactly his disposition to me"]. My friends believe he took this opposition to show that I am no sorehead and no political invalid."

marshaled his forces early in 1877 to capture another term as United States Senator, General Harrison led the opposition, as Halstead had predicted, heading a host of young Republicans who had determined to send Indiana's colorful chieftain to the rear.[29]

Harrison's break with Morton, although not aired in the press, became evident soon after Hayes' inaugural. He began to by-pass the Senator, especially in patronage matters, using Secretary of the Navy Thompson as his Washington contact. His letter of May 5 was typically frank: "You know, Colonel, as well as I that many of the Indiana appointments have heretofore been very bad. There is a very strong determination not to submit to it any longer. . . . I have heard it said President Hayes was not giving us much Civil Service Reform in Indiana. . . . We naturally look to you, so far as you properly can do so, to cast your influence for the betterment of Civil Service here." [30] This determination to strike out for himself and to lead the liberal Republican faction in Indiana marked Harrison's political coming-of-age.

June, 1877, was a pleasant month for Harrison. Mamie had just completed her sophomore year in college; Russell, now twenty-two, was about to be graduated from Lafayette. Mrs. Harrison and the General decided to mark this occasion with another vacation trip to the East. They would attend the commencement ceremonies at Easton, Pennsylvania, stop off at the home of Carrie's sister in Honesdale, pay President and Mrs. Hayes a visit at the White House, then return to Indianapolis with their daughter and son.

The Harrisons set off on their journey in mid-June. Unlike his quick campaign trip to the East, this leisurely excursion in early summer permitted the General to observe closely industrial and labor conditions in key cities along the coast. It was not a promising picture. Everywhere, laboring men were restless and dissatisfied. They felt that as a class they were not receiving a just share of the profits which abundant natural resources and the almost daily perfecting of machinery had made possible.

29 See A. Denny to Hon. John Sherman, March 25, 1877, John Sherman Papers, Vol. 139. Secretary of the Treasury John Sherman early learned that Harrison had intended to take the lead in Indiana politics.

30 Benjamin Harrison to Hon. Richard W. Thompson, May 5, 1877, (L.C.), Vol. 8. Harrison pointed out: "I have no personal ends in view and will only be too glad if Senator Morton will himself take the lead in this reform."

As Harrison toured the East, the basic causes of American industrial conflict were already apparent: long working hours, inadequate wages, perennial fear of foreign competition, and unsafe working conditions. Many laborers talked revolt. Finally, the match was lighted that fired the conflagration. In June, 1877, the owners of four eastern trunk lines jauntily announced a ten per cent cut in wages, the second since the panic of 1873. Although poorly organized, the railroad workers struck. Alone they could have accomplished little, but they had the support and sympathy of a huge army of hungry and desperate unemployed. With traffic suspended on the trunk lines and railroad employees becoming demoralized, the railroad strikes of 1877 spread rapidly, gripping practically every large industrial center from the Atlantic to the Pacific. Pitched battles between local militias and unruly mobs took place in Baltimore, Pittsburgh, Buffalo, Chicago, and San Francisco. When a reign of terror seized Pittsburgh, federal troops hastened to the scene. Scattered reports had the fatalities in the hundreds, and property damage at more than ten million dollars. The inevitable storm headed for Indianapolis.

On Friday, July 13, the Harrisons returned home from their trip to find the city still relatively calm.[31] Apprehension increased, however, as word spread that only thirteen soldiers were on guard at the United States Arsenal located within the city. Usually available federal forces were already engaged in other strike-ridden areas, leaving Indiana little hope for such aid. By Saturday evening, July 21, the state of public alarm in Indianapolis reached fever pitch. It was feared that when the strike came, hordes of railroad workers aided by sympathizers could easily arm themselves from military stores in the inadequately protected Arsenal, and re-enact the bloody scenes of Pittsburgh. Even the normal quiet of the next day's Sabbath failed to relax the mounting tension; Indianapolis churchgoers grew more apprehensive with the distribution of challenging handbills:

Attention, railroad men! Rise up and assert your manhood. There will be a meeting held in the State House Yard on Monday evening, July 23, 1877, at eight o'clock sharp, for the purpose of sympathizing and

31 Benjamin Harrison Diary, entry for July 13, 1877, Harrison Home MSS. The *Journal* of this date carried no reports on the impending railroad crisis. On the other hand, its editorial page carried a friendly notice of Harrison's return and the speculation that President Hayes had perhaps tendered him "an office commensurate with his talents and public services."

taking action with our starving brothers in the East who are now
being trampled under the feet of railroad bond holders. Everybody
invited that believes in equality and justice to all mankind. Let us all
have a hand in the breaking of the backbone of this railroad monopoly.[32]

The call to strike had reached Indianapolis. At two o'clock Monday afternoon, July 23, 1877, the employees of the Vandalia Line
walked off their jobs, soon inducing the firemen of the Indianapolis and St. Louis Line to join them. The strikers then marched
to the Union Depot where they tried unsuccessfully to stop a
passenger train, departing for St. Louis. Incensed by this failure,
strike leaders appealed to the excited mob that had assembled in
the State House Yard for the advertised meeting. Stirred to violence by inflammatory speeches, the crowd soon moved along in
a second march on the depot, which they seized as strike headquarters. Disconnecting all cars except those carrying mail, the
strikers forced both owners and federal receivers to abandon their
lines. With the Union Depot under mob rule and rail transportation crippled, the battleline between property owners and strikers
was clearly drawn.

At this point, politics complicated the crisis. Governor ("Blue
Jeans") Williams, while declaring that the state would protect
life and private property, refused to extend similar protection to
the mails and the federally operated railroad lines. Fearing to lose
the labor vote, he pursued instead a "hands-off" policy. In this
stand, he had the support of Mayor John Caven, the Sheriff of
Marion County, and the local chief of police. The latter official,
however, making a somewhat incredible gesture of compromise,
appointed several of the strike leaders as special policemen.[33]

With state and city officials standing aloof, and federal assistance
impossible, the situation demanded action. On Monday, July 23,
therefore, a group of leading citizens hurriedly met in private
conference. General Harrison took the lead in discussing with
Judge Walter Q. Gresham, Colonel A. W. Hendricks, and several
other lawyers how to handle the strike.[34] All agreed that a call
should be issued at once for a volunteer citizens' force, which could
maintain order if the Governor and Mayor should fail to act. To

[32] *Journal*, July 23, 1877.
[33] W. Q. Gresham to Judge Thomas Drummond, July 24, 1877, Gresham MSS,
Vol. 3. Also Indianapolis *Journal*, July 24, 1877.
[34] *Ibid.*

execute this plan, they constituted themselves a Committee of Public Safety. On the same day, General Harrison telegraphed Washington on his own initiative, offering federal authorities the aid of "two hundred men to protect government property" in Indianapolis.[35]

On Tuesday the 24th, Judge Gresham summoned all citizens interested in self-protection to a noon meeting at the Federal Court House. A heated discussion soon arose. Some insisted that public order could best be preserved by citizen volunteers; others contended that such action would only enrage the strikers and encourage them to violence. With lives and property at stake, a worried Gresham asked Harrison for his opinion. The General's answer was forthright. First, he stated, "order must be maintained" and "all attempts at interference with the operation of the railroads in violation of the law ought to be suppressed." He then pointed out that there were two sides to the strike question,[36] and moved that the strikers' grievances be heard by a mediation committee. Adopting Harrison's suggestion, the citizens also passed a resolution to recruit an emergency militia.

During the next seventy-two hours of crisis, Carrie and the family saw little of the General. Within a few hours of the Tuesday conference, volunteers filled two companies of one hundred men each. From hastily arranged headquarters in the Federal Building Harrison commanded one, General George H. Chapman the other.[37] The court house and other public buildings became sleeping quarters. At the rear of the Post Office Building stood tarpaulin-covered wagons loaded with muskets and ammunition. Beside them waited the volunteers, prepared for any emergency. Their ranks were soon strengthened by the arrival of General Lew Wallace and his Montgomery Guards. Later that evening (July 24), Harrison ordered his company to the Arsenal, not only to protect it but to secure a second base of operations if necessary.[38]

On the next morning, after a watchful night in uniform, General Harrison re-enacted for a time his earlier rôle of lawyer-medi-

[35] *Ibid.* A reply from Washington, "sent through Capt. Arnold, the commandant," thanked the General for his offer, and assured him that "if necessary, he would be called upon."
[36] Indianapolis attorney Charles W. Smith, an eyewitness, has preserved details of these and similar meetings, as well as Harrison's remarks, in an undated memorandum in the Gresham MSS, Vol. 3.
[37] *Ibid.*
[38] Matilda Gresham, *Life of Walter Q. Gresham,* I, 390.

ator. He and General Albert Porter, his former law partner, became spokesmen for the newly formed Committee of Mediation. The first meeting of the strikers with the Committee lasted all day Wednesday, July 25. The striking employees aired their grievances, and at the conclusion of the session Harrison put his powers of courtroom summation to good use. While counseling exact obedience to the law, he expressed his firm opinion "that the wages, as stated, were too low" and should be raised. He promised "to use his influence with those in authority in favor of this desired increase." [39] Thus the first day of discussion ended in a friendly spirit. The meeting adjourned until the following morning, at which time the strikers were asked to present a written and detailed statement of their wage demands, covering all classes of workmen.

The follow-up conference, however, did not run smoothly. Impatient citizens had urged the Committee of Safety to send the militia against the strikers and put an end to the business. This Harrison opposed vehemently. Believing a peaceable settlement possible, he declared: "I don't propose to go out and shoot down my neighbors when there is no necessity for it." [40] When belligerency marked one part of the session, Harrison arose and addressed the representatives of the strikers. He warned them of the serious evils arising from their present course of stopping transportation and thereby destroying property. "Businessmen," he said, "have been nearly bankrupted by the stoppage of their drafts." He then posed the question that incensed the strikers: "Have you a right, while you are breaking the law, to appear before a committee of law-abiding citizens with an appeal to redress the wrongs you claim to be suffering from?" At this point the strikers made for the door—whereupon Harrison sat down. Striker spokesman Warren Sayre immediately checked the walkout and possible violence by ordering the men to return to the conference table. After accepting an apology, Harrison continued.

Although the strikers were in no frame of mind to listen to arguments, Harrison continued to speak straight from the shoulder. He advised their immediate return to work at the current pay rate, and pledged the influence of the citizens' committee to secure pay increases and other benefits from the companies. He himself

39 Wallace, op. cit., p. 325; Journal, July 26, 1877.
40 Wallace, op. cit., p. 331.

promised to do his utmost in their behalf if they would obey the law. "Citizens will not long tolerate mob rule," he argued, "it has been tried again and again. The sooner you realize that you are breaking the laws of the land . . . the sooner you will regain the sympathy and confidence of the public and gain your ends." These recommendations were taken under advisement by Sayre and his committee, and a third day of meeting was scheduled for Thursday, July 26.

The Committee of Public Safety meant business. It requested the volunteer companies to present a dress parade near the Arsenal as an effective argument. Harrison marched at the head of his column, where, noted a *Journal* reporter, "under the transforming influence of a rubber overcoat, he developed a striking resemblance to Napoleon." That evening, wives, relatives, and lady friends visited the arsenal grounds with some of the comforts of life "thought necessary to existence." The whole affair was reminiscent of Civil War days—even to the quintet which serenaded the boys for over an hour. Good spirits prevailed, but the citizens' show of strength had its effect on the striking railroad workers.

At its final meeting, the Committee of Mediation issued a series of recommendations in line with Harrison's speech of the previous day. In presenting the resolutions, Attorney Albert Porter attempted to show that no labor reforms had ever been accomplished by violence. He voiced Harrison's own sentiments when he told the strikers: "You have called public attention to your grievances and this is the only good such a rebellion can accomplish." [41] Only a brief consideration preceded acceptance of the mediation committee's recommendations. This mutual agreement ended fear of violence and bloodshed. Hence, Governor Williams' official proclamation organizing the militia on July 26, 1877, came as an anticlimax. [42]

Certain legal aspects of the strike, however, still had to be settled. Sayre was put under technical arrest and several other strike

[41] *Journal*, July 27, 28, 1877.

[42] Newspaper accounts show that Governor Williams was slow to take positive action. On Monday, July 23, he said in private conference that the "railroads will be left to run themselves, but the lives and the property of the citizens will be protected." He added that "no trouble is anticipated from the strikers whom we propose to treat kindly." Within three days the *Journal* was running editorials to the effect that the city was under the control of a mob without "the first element of lawfulness about it." Then came the appeal for the "people to take the matter in hand" and restrain the law defiers and the lawbreakers. *Ibid.*, July 26, 1877.

leaders were held for contempt of court. General Harrison appeared for them voluntarily and begged that they not be punished. He argued that they were all good men; that their claims were founded in justice; that they erred simply in the course taken to safeguard their rights. Federal Judge Drummond viewed his plea favorably and discharged the men.[43]

All in all, Harrison emerged from the strike crisis a much respected public citizen.[44] If the strike served to strengthen the Republican party as the exponent of law and order, it had also enhanced Harrison's personal prestige.[45] The press had especially noted the delicacy of his dual rôle of soldier and mediator. The strike was no sooner settled than the General was hailed "as the most available candidate for the United States Senate." [46] To importuning friends Harrison conceded that "the average Republican in Indiana has had a good deal to bear. I am in hopes that there is a prospect of improvement." But on the question of his own candidacy for the Senate in opposition to Morton, Harrison said he wanted no part of it. "For myself official life is not attractive, and I am not willing to consider at present any plan which proposes to bring me forward as a candidate for any office." [47]

Three days later, while on a trip to the West Coast, Senator Morton suffered a stroke in San Francisco. It left him paralyzed and his family had him brought back to Indiana in a special train.[48]

Oliver P. Morton's illness and painful return trip to Indiana made news across the nation. The press spoke of him as aged and broken, but the controversial former war governor, barely turned fifty-four, was Harrison's senior by only ten years. In a greatly

[43] Wallace, *op. cit.*, pp. 330–31. On the other hand, in the cases of the Ohio and Mississippi strikers charged with violence at Vincennes, Harrison was retained by railroad counsel C. K. Beecher to assist the prosecution. Harrison lost the case. Gresham, *op. cit.*, I, 403.

[44] A facsimile of the emergency militia's muster roll (which General Harrison receipted for his pay as captain for a company) reads: Benjamin Harrison; rank: Captain; Period of Service: July 27–30; Number of days: 4; pay per month: $150; Amount received: $20.

[45] Cyrus T. Nixon to E. G. Hay, August 28, 1877, Eugene Gano Hay MSS, Vol. 1, gives a good cross section on political feeling in Indiana, where the Republican party gained strength by handling the strike without bloodshed. "The fact that the Republican Party, under all circumstances, sustains the law and order, is its great source of strength before the American people. It is truly the only hope the country has for permanent peace and prosperity." ·

[46] Thomas M. Browne to J. M. Clements, July 29, 1877, (L.C.), Vol. 8.

[47] Benjamin Harrison to James M. Clements, August 4, 1877, *ibid.*

[48] W. D. Foulke, *Life of Oliver P. Morton*, II, 493–96.

weakened condition, the Senator, in residence at his mother-in-law's in Richmond, Indiana, failed rapidly. Early in September, he rallied sufficiently to receive a visit from President Hayes, to whom he expressed his hope of resuming his seat in the Senate.[49] This seemed to be a distinct possibility, for on October 15 he went home to Indianapolis, where he gained strength daily and occupied himself in writing. A week of this activity took its toll, however. During the last week of October, his condition became critical, and in the early hours of November 1 hope was abandoned by his wife and family. Shortly after five in the afternoon, the once powerful frame of Oliver Perry Morton lay lifeless.

Indiana, particularly Indianapolis, paced the nation in paying tribute to Morton's memory. Harrison himself was asked to serve on four different committees to do honor to a Hoosier hero, and he joined with veterans and lawyers in an effort to memorialize Morton's contribution to national and local history. He helped to phrase the veterans' "In Memoriam," which read:

A great man has gone from amongst us. In a few days all that will be left us will be the memory of his life and his deeds.

Citizens have met and have done great honor to a great citizen; lawyers have assembled and testified to the pre-eminent powers of the great lawyer and advocate; we, as citizens who have been soldiers, instinctively think of him as the soldier and the soldier's friend. For he was a soldier not by virtue of any man's commission, but by the voice of the people, commander-in-chief of the forces of a great state, by the divine right of splendid mental and physical endowments, a ruler of rulers.[50]

Upon resolution, the veterans formed an organization to erect a suitable monument to Morton's memory. Every Indiana soldier was invited to contribute to the magnificent statue that now fronts the State House in Indianapolis. General Harrison headed the committee on permanent organization of the Morton Monumental Association, and on his motion General Lew Wallace was named president. Before Harrison turned over the Association to Wallace, he had received the first offering for the monument in a letter postmarked Petersburg, Kentucky. Its sender wanted it credited to "an Indiana soldier."

At the Senator's elaborate funeral, Harrison marched with Indiana's veteran soldiers. Accompanied by his friend and former partner, William P. Fishback, the General also represented the

49 *Ibid.*, p. 495.
50 *Journal*, November 1, 5, 1877.

Indianapolis Bar. Harrison had never known Morton as a practicing lawyer, so he attempted neither a speech nor a eulogy.[51] Instead, he recalled his long association with the Senator in public life. For particular praise he singled out Morton's ability and "remarkable power" as a speaker. "Although his utterances were the result of close thought, they . . . were so direct and logical that everyone was able to understand them." He pointed out that Morton had withdrawn from the field of law to follow other not "less honorable, and perhaps even more useful pursuits. We may be sure had he not done so, he would have honored our profession to the very close of his life."

There then fell from Harrison's lips a somewhat incredible statement, even for an earnest Republican surrounded by his lost leader's sorrowing friends: "No man either at the bar, in the Senate, or on the stump, could ever impeach the honesty of Gov. Morton's utterances; he spoke from conviction; no one could challenge that statement; even his bitterest enemy would concede such to be the case, while that characteristic was the admiration of his friends." If Harrison, heir-apparent to Morton's political mantle, had tongue in cheek here, he was seriously truthful as he concluded that

. . . in his life and methods of thought, as statesman, orator and lawyer, we may find food for reflection . . . thought and meditation, and his profession may take warning from the calamitous results which came to him from excessive work.[52]

Of personal differences and political enmities Harrison made no mention. At this solemn moment the General preferred to let the laurels fall without comment, as when the immortal Hoosier poet, James Whitcomb Riley, wrote in the opening verse of "Morton":

> The warm pulse of the nation has grown chill
> The muffled heart of freedom, like a knell
> Throbs silently for one whose earthly will
> Wro't every mission well.[53]

---

[51] Harrison remarked that "an appropriate eulogy of Gov. Morton could only be one that had been carefully prepared." He claimed he did not know the deceased in the capacity of a lawyer, for "I cannot recall a single occasion on which I saw him in a court of Justice taking a professional part." *Journal*, November 3, 1877.

[52] *Ibid.* It is interesting to note that this is the only section of Harrison's speech quoted by the "reformer" William Dudley Foulke. Foulke, *op. cit.*, II, 502, n. 1.

[53] The *Journal*, November 2, 1877, published Riley's poem in full on the day after the Senator died.

Before 1877 came to a close, twin shafts of personal sorrow struck deeply in the Harrison family circle. First, the General's niece, Mollie Eaton, passed away in the late fall. She was followed to the grave on December 1 by Major Henry Scott,[54] Carrie Harrison's devoted brother and the General's former law clerk and his captain in Company A of the 70th Indiana Volunteers. In both instances, Harrison willingly bore the funeral expenses.[55] The wheel of gratitude had turned full cycle, for Mollie Eaton's mother and father had made possible Harrison's first study of law in Cincinnati,[56] and Major Scott had always been his faithful friend. Shadows of sorrow lingered over the Harrison home through and beyond the Christmas season, and for the first time since moving to their house on North Delaware, the Harrisons did not hold open house on New Year's Day.

Prolonged periods of personal sorrow, and the renewed pressure of legal work once more began to undermine Harrison's health. At this juncture, he took his own remarks on Morton's overwork to heart. He purchased a $36 rowing machine, guaranteed to afford safe and pleasant exercise. What sold the serious-minded attorney on this device is uncertain. Still preserved among his papers, however, is the advertiser's blurb that "one of the first and marked results of rowing is the almost irresistible tendency upon rising from the machine to straighten up, throw back the shoulders, and step squarely to the front." [57] This strange investment was perhaps sounder than the General realized, for in 1878 he would indeed be challenged to "step squarely to the front."

[54] Major Henry Scott died in faraway Oregon on December 1, 1877. He was Harrison's junior by six years and had studied law with Harrison before and during the war. See Harry J. Sievers, *Benjamin Harrison: Hoosier Warrior*, pp. 168–71. A lengthy obituary appeared in the Indianapolis press on December 2, 1877, and a copy is preserved in the Benjamin Harrison Scrapbooks, (L.C.). See also *Journal*, December 3, 1877.

[55] Harrison's Expense Account, under "gifts to Relatives—1877," shows a marked generosity to the entire Eaton family. He supplied funds to Mollie before her death, supported her brother Archie, and made liberal allowances to his widowed half-sister, Bettie. Mollie's funeral expenses came to $154. On the other hand, the funeral of Major Scott was costly. The body had to be shipped from Oregon at a total expense of well over $500. Harrison MSS.

[56] See Sievers, *op. cit.*, p. 69.

[57] S. Baldwin to Benjamin Harrison, November 21, 1877, (L.C.), Vol. 8.

CHAPTER X

The Harrison Horror

IN THE EARLY SPRING of 1878, Benjamin Harrison visited the Point Farm in North Bend, Ohio, where his father, John Scott Harrison, now white-bearded and seventy-three, was spending many absorbing hours in literary pursuits. In demand as a local speaker, the former Congressman had delivered a number of lectures during 1877. Ironically enough, the most successful lecture of this almost bankrupt farmer was entitled "The World's Race for Wealth," in which he rode hard over skinflints and money-lovers. He himself had never refused to endorse a note for a needy friend.[1]

On this particular visit, the General found his father hard at work on his next subject, "The Lay Element in the Church." In good health and spirits, he seemed to enjoy his new occupation and told Ben that he anticipated another successful season on the lecture platform. After his son returned to Indianapolis, John Scott wrote to report that he had made good progress on his latest lecture and had been invited to deliver it at the local Town Hall. Another letter told of his continued outdoor exercise, including a twelve-mile trip on horseback to pay his last respects to Augustus Devin, his daughter's 23-year-old nephew who had died suddenly on May 18.[2]

Meanwhile at his own home, the General also had pen in hand as he prepared the text of his next important political address. After Senator Morton's death, Hoosier Republicans had chosen Harrison their leader. This meant that at the State Convention, scheduled for Indianapolis on June 5, he would deliver the keynote address.[3]

[1] *Journal*, May 27, 1878. Generosity rather than business acumen marked John Scott Harrison's later life. Only the solvency of Benjamin in Indianapolis prevented foreclosure of the Point Farm.
[2] Cincinnati *Commercial*, May 20, 1878.
[3] *Journal*, June 4, 1878.

On Sunday morning, May 26, 1878, the Harrisons returned from church to find awaiting them a short, shocking telegram from the Point. During the night, it read, death had claimed John Scott Harrison. There were no details and the grief-stricken son threw himself at once into the task of learning just what had happened. Slowly, reports from those at hand told the sad story.

On the day of his death, John Scott Harrison had been revising "The Lay Element in the Church" lecture; on his desk lay several paragraphs extolling the value of training given by a Christian mother. His last evening on earth had, like most of his life, been spent quietly. After dinner he had talked awhile with his son Carter and his family, then excused himself for a quick review of his lecture headings before retiring for the night. Early the next morning a grandson had discovered his partly dressed, lifeless body.[4]

General and Mrs. Harrison departed immediately for the old family homestead, where Ben's brothers and sisters soon joined them. Hundreds of friends and neighbors came from miles around to pay their final respects to the last son of President William Henry Harrison.[5] The funeral was set for Wednesday, May 29, at the Presbyterian Church in Cleves. It was "The Little Church on the Hill," erected with the help of William Henry Harrison and his wife. Political and social acquaintances crowded the small edifice, and by the time the funeral procession had arrived from the Point, it was difficult to find even standing room. Among the honorary pallbearers were William S. Groesbeck,[6] who had defeated John Scott Harrison for re-election to Congress in 1856, and the elderly attorney S. S. Smith who, forty-seven years earlier, had acted as pallbearer for Harrison the President.

Two eulogies were delivered. Blind and infirm Horace Bushnell, John Scott Harrison's most devoted ministerial friend, spoke first, praising the deceased as a "consistent Christian, a faithful husband and a kind and just father." [7] Dr. R. E. Hawley then spoke

---

[4] Cincinnati *Commercial*, May 27, 29, 1878. A paroxysm of angina pectoris was given as the cause of death.

[5] *Ibid.*, May 30, 1878.

[6] A native of Rensselaer County, New York, Groesbeck moved to Cincinnati with his parents in 1816. A graduate of Miami University (Ohio) in 1835, he served as a Democrat in the 35th Congress (1857–1859). He represented President Johnson in the impeachment trial of 1868, and died in Cincinnati in 1897.

[7] Cincinnati *Commercial*, May 30, 1878. Citing scripture copiously, Bushnell compared John Scott Harrison to the prophet Elijah, who, after many trials and vexations and much weariness of spirit, approached his end with calmness.

as acting pastor, sketching briefly the life of the former Congress-man, and commenting significantly on his baptismal name, John Scott.[8] When the minister finished, General and Mrs. Harrison led those who filed past the coffin. The funeral procession then formed and slowly wound its way to Congress Green Cemetery, where the Harrison family plot lay on a broad hill, commanding a beautiful view of the Ohio. There the earthly remains of Ben's father were placed next to those of his mother, near the vault of President Harrison.[9]

One thing marred the burial. As the mourners walked towards John Scott's grave, some noticed that the resting place of Augustus Devin, just recently interred, had been disturbed. The earth seemed to have been rooted, as by hogs, and some thought this was the cause. To the majority came the chilling thought—body-snatchers had been at work.

A cursory examination showed that young Devin's body was missing. Two precautions seemed necessary: first, to hide the dis-covery from the widowed mother until the body could be recov-ered; second, to safeguard the remains of John Scott Harrison. The General assumed this latter task; with his younger brother John he supervised the lowering of his father's body, encased within a metallic casket, into an eight-foot grave made secure by a number of cemented marble slabs. Two watchmen were hired.[10] If ghouls in human form had stolen and sold young Devin's body to a medical school for anatomical research, John Scott's sons would see that their father's remains were safe.

Since the General had only a few days in which to finish his keynote address, he and Carrie returned to Indianapolis by train

[8] He was named after Dr. John Scott of Lexington, Kentucky, who knew William Henry Harrison intimately and had frequently attended Mrs. Harrison at childbirth. Dr. Scott returned the compliment by calling one of his own sons, William Henry Harrison. See Freeman Cleaves, *Old Tippecanoe*, p. 43.

[9] This cemetery possessed a wealth of historic associations. On "the Mound" rested the old family vault that held the remains of the former President, his wife, Anna, and one of his daughters, a Mrs. Thornton. Near the center of the enclosure was the Harrison lot, containing a score or more of the graves of the descendants of the ninth President and those of John Cleves Symmes. For photographs of this entire area, the author is indebted to Dr. Francis Forster, dean of the Georgetown Univer-sity School of Medicine.

[10] Cincinnati *Commercial*, May 31, 1878. For the stern instructions given to the watchmen, as well as for a detailed description of the grave, see Harry J. Sievers, "The Harrison Horror," pp. 6, 37 (n. 18). This 52-page, illustrated pamphlet, published in 1956 by the Public Library of Fort Wayne, Indiana, is hereafter cited as the "Harrison Horror."

late on the day of the funeral. Other family members retired to the Point—all except young John Harrison who stayed in Cincinnati to make a thorough search for young Devin's body. In this he was to be aided by his nephew, George Eaton. Early the next morning, armed with a search warrant and assisted by Constable Lacey, Detective Snelbaker, and one other officer, the Harrison kin set forth on a determined quest.

Their only clue, a weak one, sent them first to the Ohio Medical College on the south side of Sixth between Vine and Race Streets. At three o'clock that same morning, they were told, a wagon had rattled into the alley beside the college building and stopped at the door of the chute where "resurrectionists" usually deposited their subjects. Before the wagon pulled away, they were informed, some thing or some body had been taken out. On the suspicion that Ohio Medical might be in collusion with body snatchers, the searchers thought the "thing" might well have been a corpse, although they believed that the body of their young kinsman had been stolen and sold much earlier in the week.

The officers suggested a thorough search of the building, and a recalcitrant janitor, A. Q. Marshall, showed them various rooms and closets, protesting that no bodies would be found. Still, the five-man team persevered, even peering into a deep shaft through a side door opening out of the dissecting room on the top floor, using a lantern to illuminate its blackness.

After unsuccessfully ransacking every nook and corner, young John Harrison and George Eaton were about to look elsewhere. Constable Lacey, however, noticed a rope attached to what proved to be a windlass installed in the shaft. It was pulled taut. He ordered Detective Snelbaker to haul up its load. This was no easy task, for as the windlass was turned the weight at the bottom seemed to grow heavier. Slowly, however, there emerged into the light something covered with cloth. As the thing rose higher, it appeared that the fabric concealed only the head and shoulders of a corpse—that of a very old man. John Harrison said: "That's an old man; we're after a young man." "Never mind," replied Constable Lacey, "we'll see what it is." He ordered the janitor to help them pull in the body and lay it on the floor. He then took a stick and lifted the cloth away from the dead face. As he did so, John Harrison started back with a cry of horror, exclaiming, "My God, that's my father!"

His eyes bulged from their sockets as he gazed at the awful

spectacle. He had come to this dreadful spot in Christian charity, seeking a widow's son. He had found instead the corpse of his own father, lovingly entombed less than twenty-four hours before. The sight before him was almost beyond belief—John Scott Harrison's body, caught by a rope around its neck, hidden in a black hole in the Ohio Medical College. In his daze the youngest of the Harrisons could think only of the grave at North Bend—a grave bricked in, "covered with nearly a ton of stone slabs, cemented, and then covered with earth." [11]

Deeply agitated, John Harrison engaged a local undertaker to care for his father's body until he could consult with his older brothers and other relatives. Above all, he determined to keep the matter secret. But rumor was already abroad. A reporter from the Cincinnati *Commercial* heard part of the startling story from the boys in the fire-house next to the college. He tracked down Harrison, Eaton, and the undertaker, and found that none of them would talk. The undertaker, sworn to silence, would not even admit that it was John Scott Harrison's corpse which had been discovered.

When the news finally broke, its dateline was not Cincinnati—but North Bend. Three relatives had visited the tomb early in the morning and saw for themselves what had happened. [12] Immediately young Archie Eaton was sent to Cincinnati to inform his brother George and Uncle John that they now faced a second, even holier task, the recovery of the stolen body of John Scott Harrison. At the last moment, Carter Harrison decided to join Archie in the short trip to the city.

The first words of the two brothers as they met in Cincinnati form one of the strangest greetings in history. Just as John Harrison cried out to Carter: "I've found . . . father's body," Carter Harrison exclaimed: "John, they've stolen . . . father's body." It was a moment of profound grief, mingled with a bitter satisfaction. [13]

Telegrams alerted Indianapolis to the tragedy; the first dispatch reached Benjamin Harrison less than twenty-four hours after his return home. This early report told only of the robbery, not of the

[11] Cincinnati *Commercial*, May 31, 1878.
[12] The "resurrectionist" showed great skill in stealing the body. See "Harrison Horror," pp. 36–39.
[13] Cincinnati *Commercial*, May 31, 1878.

recovery of John Scott Harrison's body. Aroused to a terrible anger, the General immediately requested the chiefs of police in the principal midwest cities to institute searches for his father's body. He also employed the Pinkerton Detective Agency to conduct a private investigation,[14] after which he boarded the 5:45 P.M. Cincinnati-bound train. Further details of the gruesome situation reached Indianapolis after his departure, and young Russell Harrison released them to the press. The graphic stories which ensued shocked the entire Hoosier community. Expressions of horror and indignation were outnumbered by offers of assistance "in detecting and bringing to punishment the perpetrators of the outrage." [15] Prominent members of both the Indiana and Ohio Bars volunteered their services to the Harrison family and public feeling ran high.

The Cincinnati *Commercial* retold the story in a dramatic editorial, whereupon it flared into national news. Baltimoreans, Philadelphians, New Yorkers—all soon know how General Ben Harrison's younger brother John,

seeking the body of the widow's son, and not knowing of the desecration of his father's grave, found the honored father at the Ohio Medical College, with a rope about his neck, by which he was suspended until wanted in the dissecting room.

They heard, too, that the citizens of Cincinnati and North Bend were

excited and distressed in an extraordinary degree, and anxious to take vengeance on the responsible parties. It is doubtful whether the law would be allowed to take its course in case the guilty was speedily discovered.[16]

Police efforts to find the guilty had so far been fruitless. The few suspects taken into custody soon had to be released for lack of sufficient evidence. Public indignation remained at fever pitch, however, and the search was intensified.

Before Benjamin Harrison arrived on the scene, his older brother, Carter, visited the Ohio Medical College to examine the spot where his father's body had been discovered. Here he encoun-

---

[14] Harrison's partial diary for 1878 and a receipted bill show a payment to Pinkerton in the amount of $101.35. Harrison Home MSS.
[15] *Journal*, June 1, 1878.
[16] Cincinnati *Commercial*, May 31, 1878.

tered Dr. William Wallace Seely, professor of clinical ophthalmology and otology and secretary of the College.[17] It was an unfortunate meeting. The eminent eye specialist, angered by newspaper criticism of the faculty, brutally remarked to the grief-filled son that the entire "affair matters little, since it would all be the same on the day of resurrection." Neither the public nor the Harrison family forgave or forgot that comment.[18]

At about the hour of Benjamin Harrison's arrival in Cincinnati, his brother Carter was swearing out a warrant before a justice of the peace for the arrest of A. Q. Marshall, the college janitor. Marshall was shortly booked on the charge of receiving, concealing, and secreting John Scott Harrison's body which had been "unlawfully and maliciously removed from its grave." [19] Marshall was no sooner committed to Cell 61 of the county jail than the entire College faculty rushed to his defense. Pooling their resources, the medical men posted a $5,000 bond for Marshall's release on bail. This show of sympathy for one whom the public had come to regard as the accomplice of grave robbers angered the citizens of Cincinnati. Several friends of the Harrison family called on the General and his brothers in their quarters at the Grand Hotel and suggested mob action, in defiance of the law. This was quickly vetoed by General Harrison, but at the same time he made it clear that he was determined to hunt down and punish those guilty of the outrages, and thus insure justice both to his family and that of Augustus Devin. It was at this time that he fired a verbal volley against the "know-nothing" attitude of those in charge of the Medical College.[20]

[17] Seely had graduated from Yale in 1862 and from the Ohio Medical College in 1864. He gave nearly thirty-five years of service, including twenty years as secretary and dean of the faculty. See Otto Juettner, *Daniel Drake and his Followers*, pp. 269–70.

[18] *Journal*, June 1, 20, 1878. On this latter date the *Journal*, reprinting from the Cincinnati *Gazette*, stated: "As there is a great demand . . . for bodies for anatomical purposes, physicians [should] donate their bodies after death. . . . Perhaps they could be induced to contribute the bodies of their families to the cause of science. It doesn't matter, you know, what becomes of the body after death."

[19] Cincinnati *Commercial*, May 31, 1878. The charge was worded according to an Ohio statute enacted on May 5, 1877. For careful research on the general statutes concerning the subject of body-snatching in Ohio between 1846 and 1881, the author is indebted to Professor Roscoe Barrow, dean at the University of Cincinnati College of Law. For a detailed description of such Ohio statutes prior to 1878, see Linden F. Edwards, "The Ohio Anatomy Law of 1881," *The Ohio State Medical Journal* (December, 1950, February, 1951), Vols. 46–47.

[20] Cincinnati *Commercial*, June 1, 1878.

With the rest of the Cincinnati community, the faculty of the Ohio Medical College expressed their deep regret over the repulsive circumstances connected with the crime. They evidenced particular chagrin that John Scott Harrison's body had been found in their college building, but they pleaded complete ignorance of the transaction. Their chief concern was for the odium now brought upon the dissection of human bodies. They complained that the attitude of the press had made future procurement of cadavers more difficult and the price of anatomical subjects prohibitive. On the whole, the medical profession felt that unjust legislation was mainly responsible for the outrage.[21]

The College finally decided to bring their case to the public. As their spokesman they selected Dean Roberts Bartholow, a strange child of genius, branded by his contemporaries as "the embodiment of cold cynicism."[22] In a statement handed to the press on the morning of June 1, 1878, the frigid dean stated flatly, with a show of sarcasm, that "under existing circumstances bodies necessary for the instruction of medical students must be stolen." He appealed to reason. If the three hundred students at Ohio Medical were to be adequately instructed, a large number of "resurrected subjects" must be provided. While he confessed that he could not condone unscrupulous means of procuring bodies, still it was his opinion that neither the faculty nor the janitor should be held responsible for "the resurrectionist, unknown to us, who . . . short of funds, took this means to replenish his exchequer."[23]

The position adopted by Dean Bartholow was frowned upon by the press. In New York, the influential *Tribune* administered an editorial scolding to both dean and faculty. If bodies must be stolen for anatomical research, the editor reasoned, "then medical instruction of that kind must cease."

Doctor Bartholow admits that the resurrection men with whom he deals are unscrupulous scoundrels only fit for the state prison, but he intimates that he shall keep on dealing with them all the same.[24]

[21] *Ibid.* Medical men gave a plausible argument· ". . . anatomical knowledge is required of all who practice medicine surgery. Suits for malpractice are constantly before the courts, and physicians and surgeons are cast into damages for a lack of that anatomical knowledge which the law denies them an opportunity to obtain." The Cincinnati *Gazette,* May 31, 1878, contended editorially that "the responsibility for this outrage rests ultimately upon the legislature."

[22] Juettner, *op. cit.,* p. 260.

[23] "Harrison Horror," p. 12.

[24] New York *Tribune,* June 6, 1878.

As to Bartholow's argument that the body snatchers were "unknown to the faculty": "This," observed the *Journal*, "is not precisely credible, but suppose it is true. Is the school any less a party to the felony because it does not know the name of the felon with whom it cooperates?" [25]

The general conclusion of the press was this:

If this is the best case the Ohio Medical College can make out for itself, it would have been better for it to have said nothing. As it is, it has said altogether too much. And heroic doses of the Ohio Penitentiary are the best medical treatment the people of Cincinnati can prescribe for it.[26]

Until the morning on which the medical faculty made its case public, General Harrison had talked with friends on the subject of the outrage "with the greatest freedom and with characteristic calmness and intensity." As far as he could ascertain, "resurrectionism" had fallen into the hands of a class of people who were rough, reckless, and brutal. "The system of grave robbing in the vicinity of Cincinnati," he said, "had recently been characterized by most hideous outrages." His own family's suffering was just another example of how other citizens had been and would be victimized. He advised one group of friends that

the people of Cincinnati should not allow this thing to go on, with nobody found out, no punishment inflicted, nobody responsible. If they did permit that to be the result . . . it would be an advertisement of immunity for all possible outrages of that character.[27]

When Harrison read Dean Bartholow's press interview of June 1, however, its heartless conclusions stung him to an indignant rage. He could admit the necessity and value of anatomical research, but as to the Medical Faculty's denial of complicity with the "resurrectionists," this, he thundered was "cant and hypocrisy." In an open letter "To the Citizens of Cincinnati," Harrison answered Bartholow. Gratefully he acknowledged the city's solicitude and sympathy, adding a strong plea that God would keep "their precious friends from the barbarous touch of the grave robber,"

25 June 30, 1878.

26 New York *Tribune*, June 6; *Journal*, June 11; Cincinnati *Gazette*, June 14, 1878.

27 Cincinnati *Commercial*, June 1, 1878. After a personal investigation, one reporter concluded that "if any good, healthy, reasonably discreet body-snatcher wanted to get a body out of any of the large cemeteries about the city, they would eight times out of ten, find little trouble in doing so."

and preserve themselves "from the taste of hell, which comes from the discovery of a father's grave robbed and the body hanging by the neck, like that of a dog, in a pit of a medical college." [28]

While the public argued both sides of the controversy, the body of John Scott Harrison was quietly re-interred in the vault of a family friend at Spring Grove Cemetery, near Cincinnati. Here the family was met by a citizens committee from Lawrenceburg, Indiana, who requested permission to remove the remains of William Henry Harrison from Congress Green, now touched with horror, to a new and stately cemetery in Lawrenceburg. When the Hoosiers then revealed to the grieving family their plans to erect a fitting monument over the former President's grave, the offer may have appeared to carry insulting overtones. At any rate, the family refused to consider it and the delegation returned to Indiana.[29]

Reports of John Scott Harrison's quiet reburial helped to keep public indignation at a peak in the Queen City. Excited citizens and morbid sightseers were observed "in the vicinity of the college building staring at its blank walls as if trying to discover in them the names of the perpetrators of Wednesday night's sacrilege." Crowds milled in and out of the alley, attempting to peer into the now celebrated "cadaver chute." Local reporters interviewed as many as possible and concluded that a fear-hysteria was growing. The question on the lips of thousands was: "What can we do with the bodies of our loved and lost ones to save them from the ignominy of the 'chute and windlass and dissecting knife of the Medical College?' " [30]

Tuesday, June 4, also provided moments of intense bitterness for Benjamin Harrison and his brothers, Carter and John. In a renewed effort to recover young Devin's body, the General, heading an eight-man party, searched the Ohio Medical College premises from cellar to attic. Failing in their quest, the Harrisons did discover the garments in which their father had been buried. This

---

[28] Cincinnati *Times,* June 1, 1878; *Journal,* June 3, 1878. This somewhat lengthy letter, closely reasoned but not without emotional overtones, ranks as one of the most potent documents ever written by Benjamin Harrison. See also "Harrison Horror," pp. 14–15. The Benjamin Harrison Scrapbooks, (L.C.), Vol. 52, p. 90, also contains a copy of the letter.

[29] The crumbling brick of the vault at North Bend had prompted the Hoosiers to begin negotiations for the transfer. A feud between Indiana and Ohio over the remains of William Henry Harrison was kept alive until 1924, the year in which the present monument was erected along the Ohio.

[30] *Journal* and Cincinnati *Commercial,* June 1, 1878.

unexpected evidence both angered and grieved the General, for it flatly contradicted the Medical Faculty's statement that no one in the college had been connected with the unlawful acceptance of John Scott Harrison's body. It also helped the Grand Jury, which continued to take testimony.

On the evening of that same hectic day of discovery, General Harrison had to return to Indianapolis in order to address the State Convention, which was to open at ten o'clock the next morning. While Harrison worked over his speech en route, the members of the Ohio Medical Faculty were comparing notes in Cincinnati. Each had received a summons to testify before the Grand Jury "as to their knowledge of the resurrecting of the body of the late John Scott Harrison, and its transfer to the dissecting rooms" of their college.

On Wednesday morning, in the Metropolitan Theater of Indianapolis, the Republican State Convention was called to order and Benjamin Harrison was introduced as president of the assembly. As he stepped forward into his new rôle of state leader, Harrison faced a friendly, enthusiastic crowd, "every one of whom probably knew him personally." Waiting for the cheers to die down, Harrison appeared to one reporter "greatly cast down by the dastardly outrage at North Bend." His self-command was complete, however, and his first keynote speech—brief and crisply delivered— was a creditable one. He had designed it as a commentary on the party's platform, pledged to the "maintenance of the great principles of the Republican party" as being essential "to the peace, permanency, and prosperity of the nation." [31] Skilled in rhetoric, he had the 1,500 delegates laughing and applauding before he had completed five sentences.

His speech reached its climax when he touched on the much discussed questions of capital, labor, and cheap money. "It is to delay our return to prosperity to keep laborers' wages down," he asserted, "for it is certain that prosperity can never return or continue in the midst of turmoil. Capital is a timid bird, and seeks close shelter in times when the elements are disturbed." It was only in his closing words that he at last confessed his personal feelings:

[31] New York *Tribune,* June 6, 1878.

I have spoken today under circumstances that have sadly tried me. I did not know whether I should have been able to serve you today. I thank you for the cordial manner in which you have received me and the patience you have shown me.[32]

After playing his part in the Convention, Harrison returned to Cincinnati at once, leaving Carrie and the children to pore over his press notices. Much unfinished business awaited him in the Queen City. Janitor Marshall was scheduled for a hearing before Squire Wright, and Devin's body was still missing.

During Ben's brief absence, Carter and John Harrison had remained on the job. They were busy evaluating new evidence uncovered by a *Commercial* reporter to the effect that their father's body had been stolen from its grave by a notorious resurrectionist from Toledo, Ohio—Charles O. Morton by name. It was charged that Morton, whose wife assisted him (disguised in men's clothing), had contracted with the Ohio Medical College to provide them with a specified number of cadavers yearly.[33] While local police investigated and drew up plans to apprehend Morton, Carter and John Harrison publicly exonerated the Miami Medical College, thereby directing a hard slap at the authorities of the Ohio Medical College.

On Thursday morning, June 6, Squire Wright arraigned Marshall; the hearing took place less than a square from the scene of the alleged crime. The Medical Faculty retained Attorney Thomas Logan to defend Marshall, while General Harrison himself, assisted by a local firm, Cooper and Morton, prepared to examine Marshall and establish to the satisfaction of the court that he had willfully and maliciously secreted a human body "snatched from a grave by a resurrectionist."

The tiny office of Squire Wright was "crowded to suffocation" by the time the court announced that the hearing was open. The onlookers registered disappointment when Attorney Logan rose to waive examination in behalf of his client. This settled the legal question, for now Marshall would be under the jurisdiction of the

[32] The *Journal*, June 6, 1878, described Harrison's effort as having "the ring of true metal in it . . . in harmony with the declarations of the [Republican] platform . . . a platform in itself, and one that will repay a careful perusal."

[33] The Cincinnati *Gazette*, June 14, 1878, revealed that "resurrectionist" Morton, operating under several aliases, had made similar contracts with many medical schools.

grand jury without benefit of a preliminary hearing. The Squire would have closed the proceedings at this point except for Logan's unexpected charge that both the warrant for Marshall's arrest and the search warrant permitting an investigation within the walls of the Ohio Medical College were clearly invalid. This touched off an animated exchange between General Harrison and Counsel Logan, which served to highlight several underlying issues.

Logan charged that Harrison had acted most unfairly in publicly accusing the Ohio Medical Faculty specifically in his open letter to the citizens of Cincinnati. He termed this an attempt at indictment by public rumor, nourished by insinuation and innuendo. In reply Harrison calmly stated that he recognized the defendant's right to waive examination and to let his case go to court without a preliminary investigation of the facts involved. He argued, however, that justice would prevail more readily in an open, public hearing. He further contended that public scandal and public infamy could best be established or corrected by a preliminary public hearing—the very course of action Logan had chosen to avoid.

After a heated exchange, Logan concluded with a statement that sounded curiously like a threat: "I understand that General Harrison invited the bringing of a civil suit, and expresses a wish to have the matter thoroughly tried. He may yet have an opportunity to defend his position in a civil suit." [34]

Harrison declined further argument, saying that there was no legal question at issue. Only the question of bail remained, and the proceedings ended with the court's decision that Janitor Marshall should continue in $5,000 bail.

Table talk, gossip, and the press combined to keep the "Harrison Horror" and the "art of resurrecting" main topics of conversation until the middle of June. Though the General had returned to his practice of law and politics in Indianapolis, the morning papers kept him abreast of developments in Cincinnati, where a corps of clever reporters had successfully pumped grand jury witnesses for news. Scraps of testimony, secretly given by professors of the Ohio Medical College, soon leaked out to a news-hungry public. The Faculty had admitted that their institution, like most

[34] The Cincinnati *Commercial*, June 7, 1878, carried a full account of the hearings held on June 6. For an account of the verbal clash between Harrison and Logan, see "Harrison Horror," pp. 23–24.

other American medical schools, was under annual contract with "certain persons" who guaranteed to furnish them with bodies for dissection and anatomical demonstration. The public was chilled to learn that these "cadaver-producing contracts obliged the resurrectionist to prepare the bodies for immediate use." Moreover, it became common knowledge that Cincinnati had become a shipping center of this "dead traffic," which then moved on to such smaller cities as Fort Wayne and Ann Arbor. This fact afforded the clue which led to the ultimate discovery of young Augustus Devin's body, stored in a charnel house near Ann Arbor. Fortunately the gruesome details connected with this and similar cases, brought grave robbing into such prominence that the Ohio Legislature quickly enacted more stringent and more constructive laws in an effort to curtail, if not eliminate the dreadful practice.[35]

Harrison, whose rôle in closing the Devin case had been chiefly financial, returned to Cincinnati with Carrie in order to pay final tribute to young Augustus' memory. When the funeral procession reached Congress Green, the small company of mourners had swelled to a large concourse. Just four weeks to the day had elapsed between the first and second interment.

Although the Hamilton County Grand Jury indicted both Charles O. Morton and A. Q. Marshall, and Harrison filed suits for $10,000 in exemplary damages on behalf of the widow and his father's estate, time has obscured the results; perhaps the case was finally settled out of court. The General himself last referred to the matter after a torrid summer of work and campaigning. On October 11, 1878, he wrote:

I expect I will have to go to Cin. sometime this month to try that case for the stealing of my father's body. You know how I dread to go over the details of that horror again—but I don't see how it can be avoided.[36]

The General had been deeply wounded. The affection and respect between father and son had been strongly rooted, and twenty-five

[35] *Journal,* June 14; Cincinnati *Gazette,* June 14, 1878. The story surrounding the discovery and identification of young Devin's body in the Ann Arbor charnel house chills the blood. A detailed account may be found in "Harrison Horror," pp. 48–50, which is based on an eyewitness account published in the Cincinnati *Commercial,* June 15, 1878.

[36] Benjamin Harrison to Margaret Peltz, October 11, 1878, Messinger MSS.

years of political differences had not weakened the bond of their mutual love. Indeed, lest a flood of bitter memories engulf him, the word "father" rarely crossed Harrison's lips throughout the final two decades of his own life.

Compared with the lasting social benefit gained by the American people as a result of the "Harrison Horror," the outcome of both the criminal and civil suits is relatively unimportant. Within two years Ohio had set an important landmark in medical history and the slow task of public education was under way. An 1880 law increased the maximum penalty for "body-snatching," and soon legitimate sources were found. This gradually lessened the odium associated with anatomical research.[37] Young surgeons became more adept, people began to live longer, and the horror of "resurrectionism" was at last relegated to a dark, almost forgotten page of history.

[37] According to the Cincinnati *Commercial*, June 18, 1878, Harrison's prime motive in prosecuting the case was to "protect society at large." New state legislation accomplished this purpose. As Dean Barrow states: "In my opinion, a fair appraisal of the effect of the John Scott Harrison incident is that it resulted in a more effective statute against the removal of corpses from a place of sepulture for medical and anatomical study than had previously existed in Ohio." Roscoe L. Barrow to the author, August 2, 1951.

CHAPTER XI

The Road to Washington

BETWEEN 1878 and 1880 Indiana proved itself an excellent political workshop, where Benjamin Harrison could complete his apprenticeship for the high offices which lay ahead. A contemporary historian writes: "In regard to population, wealth, progress, enterprise, commerce, manufactures, agriculture, intelligence, the State of Indiana is in all senses a First Rate State." [1] The capital city furnished much of the driving force behind Hoosier progress. It supported a National League baseball team which drew large crowds. Road shows stopped regularly and, in addition, local drama enthusiasts formed a talented Thespian group of their own. The city invited activity. One could cycle or stroll along the canal, every park boasted a bandstand, and the capacious German gardens featured beer and music. Rowboats on the White River produced a mobile lovers' lane. Parades, almost an everyday occurrence, enlivened Washington Street, a roomy one hundred and twenty feet from curb to curb. For General Harrison in these hopeful, progressive years, the Hoosier State and its capital provided every opportunity.

Now leader of the Republicans in his state, and spokesman for the party's young bloods, Harrison was accepting full responsibility for uniting a party badly divided on the financial question.[2] During his gubernatorial campaign of 1876, he had noted

---

[1] J. B. Martin, *Indiana: An Interpretation*, pp. 89–90.

[2] *Journal*, March 9, 1880. In a lengthy address to the Young Republicans' Club, Harrison expounded in detail the divided condition of the party along the lines of a money philosophy. In 1878, the two inflation parties (Democratic and Greenbacker) polled 56.50 per cent of the popular vote. This was radicalism's greatest victory. Returning prosperity in 1879 and 1880 swung the political pendulum to a conservative Republicanism. See William G. Carleton, "The Money Question in Indiana Politics," *Indiana Magazine of History*, 42 (1946), 138–43.

the exodus of dissenting Republicans into the Greenback party. It seemed to Harrison, in 1878, high time to consider a reformation of Republican principles.

He was at last in a position to devote more time to politics. The firm of Harrison, Hines and Miller held one of the highest ranks in legal circles so that a steady and considerable income would permit sufficient time for campaigning in the fall. At home, Carrie, busy with her strawberry beds and grapevines,[3] was healthy and happy. One of her chief joys was Mamie, now twenty and charming. The skating parties, buggy rides, and strolls along shaded lanes which her vivacious daughter described reminded Mrs. Harrison pleasantly of her own girlhood in Ohio.[4] Russell, his Lafayette College days over, was beginning his own career. His father's influence with John Sherman, Secretary of the Treasury, had won him an assayer's position at the Philadelphia Mint.[5]

With both children grown, Carrie, too, found more time at her disposal and she and Mamie were frequently away on trips. This left the home on North Delaware a bachelor's sanctuary, an ideal place in which to plot new strategies for the coming state campaign. Old-line Republicans, confident of recapturing the State Legislature, early planned to send Judge Gresham to the United States Senate.[6] Harrison, however, harbored some misgivings. Currency problems, continuing labor unrest, and a mounting dissatisfaction, first with Grant's, then Hayes' reconstruction policies, had seriously reduced Republican majorities in Congress at the mid-term elections.[7] But, as the summer of 1878 wore on, political conferences and organizational meetings exhausted the General less than the torrid temperatures. During July he wrote, with humorous exasperation: "We are having a higher degree of heat than I supposed was possible outside of St. Louis and one other place that we read of in the Good

[3] General and Mrs. Harrison cultivated strawberries and grapes each season. Benjamin Harrison to Margaret Peltz, July 16, 1879, Messinger MSS.

[4] *Ibid.*, January 15, 1879.

[5] H. R. Linderman to Benjamin Harrison, July 11, 1878, (L.C.), Vol. 8. Philadelphia was to be a temporary assignment, for Russell was seeking the position of assayer of the New Orleans Mint, then in construction, and Senator Conkling had assured his confirmation. Eventually, however, Russell received an appointment to the Helena, Montana, office. New York *Tribune*, March 24, 1880. Also Roscoe Conkling to Benjamin Harrison, December 14, 1878, (L.C.), Vol. 8.

[6] Thomas Slaughter to Walter Q. Gresham, July 10, 1878, Gresham MSS.

[7] H. J. Eckenrode, *Rutherford B. Hayes: Statesman of Reunion*, pp. 300–1; William S. Myers, *The Republican Party*, p. 248.

Book." [8] He added that he was preparing notes for a vigorous speaking tour in August, including a campaign opening address at Richmond, Indiana.

The heat wave broke early in August, just before Harrison set out for the hustings. At Richmond he sounded the keynote of the state campaign. History would prove, he said, that "the Democratic party had a stronger instinct for the wrong side of every question than any other political organization the world ever saw." In his opinion the rival party could show no record of constructive legislation. Challenge them to produce evidence of even one great public measure, said Harrison, and the Democrats would chorus, "We have appointed investigating committees." Yes, quipped the General, but "the spade of the investigator" too often "turned up a Democrat!" [9] Turning from humor, Harrison lashed out at the Potter Investigating Committee, which he termed "tragedy turned farce," since its rules excluded the presentation of evidence of any Democratic frauds.[10]

Harrison's campaign oratory struck at personalities as well as issues. He singled out Daniel W. Voorhees, Indiana's eloquent and popular United States Senator, charging that the "Tall Sycamore of the Wabash" had declared war on the Federal Army in the South and attempted to invalidate President Hayes' power to use the troops to enforce the decisions of federal courts. Harrison warned Hoosier voters that a victorious Democracy would quickly liquidate Southern war claims. He proposed a hypothetical case:

If a Democratic Congress should pass an act to indemnify Jeff Davis for the loss of his wardrobe, including his hoop skirt and bonnet, . . . or to pay General Beauregard for his personal effects destroyed by our bombardment of Charleston, would Mr. Voorhees attempt to maintain that these laws were unconstitutional? [11]

[8] Harrison could not recall nights "so absolutely intolerable," with "sleep out of the question." Harrison to Margaret Peltz, July 13, 1878, Messinger MSS.

[9] *Journal*, August 10, 1878.

[10] The Potter Committee originated in a resolution passed by the General Assembly of Maryland, which attacked directly the title of President Hayes. For the most recent readable summary concerning the investigation, see Harry Barnard, *Rutherford B. Hayes and His America*, pp. 467–79. Barnard concludes: "Whether or not there was serious intent behind this investigation to pave the way for ousting Hayes by court proceedings or impeachment will never be known." Barnard exonerates responsible Democratic leadership of such an attempt.

[11] *Journal*, August 10, 1878. Voorhees, in a speech at South Bend, had cited Section 4 of the 14th Amendment, which provides that neither the United States nor any State should be responsible for debts incurred in aid of insurrection or rebellion against the United States. C. B. Swisher, *American Constitutional Development*, p. 330.

Throughout his two-month canvass, Harrison defended President Hayes' Southern policy as the only instrument gauged for the "even administration of the law to all classes and the untrammelled exercise of political rights." No plant can grow, he declared, in a soil salted with injustice and discrimination. He asked the voters to remember that Lincoln's party

has given to the laboring man a free homestead on public lands . . . has emancipated four million laborers from slavery, and brought by the same charter free labor itself to an honor it could not attain while companioned with slavery.[12]

Three key ideas characterized the new party chief's political philosophy. First, he called for the repression of "lawlessness, Communism and class hatred." Second, he specified the need of "currency on an honest basis" so that "those who buy and sell and those who work know when they contract what the dollar of payment is to be." Finally, the General appealed for a spirit of national confidence based on faith in God and in the brotherhood of man.[13]

The General's initial efforts as state leader evoked high praise. His printed speeches gave evidence that Harrison had become one of the foremost political orators of his day.[14] Nevertheless, Election Day, 1878, once more put Indiana in the Democratic column. Even so, the General was not disheartened. A few days after the election he wrote lightly to "Cousin Mag" in St. Louis:

Well, the campaign is over and the Dems have beaten us again—more badly than before. But you know I am not enough of a politician to be very unhappy about such results. If our people prefer "Blue Jeans" and Dan V [Voorhees]—let it be so. My law practice is a more attractive field for me . . .[15]

Enthusiasm for church and community affairs soon matched Harrison's interest in law and politics. Also, the Indianapolis

[12] *Journal*, August 10, 1878. In this speech and elsewhere, Senator Voorhees bore the brunt of Harrison's attack. Governor Williams had appointed Voorhees to fill the Senate vacancy caused by Morton's death. As an inflationist, Voorhees championed the West. See Leonard S. Kenworthy, *The Tall Sycamore of the Wabash*, pp. 97–124. Also Carleton, *op. cit.*, pp. 141 ff.

[13] *Journal*, August 10, 1878. Harrison appealed for industrial peace and maintained that "only security and confidence can call it [money] back to its natural partnership with labor."

[14] *Ibid.* Also G. F. Hoar, *Autobiography of Seventy Years*, I, 413, writes that Harrison was "an eloquent orator, capable of uttering great truths in a great way."

[15] Benjamin Harrison to Margaret Peltz, October 11, 1878, Messinger MSS.

Literary Club [16] was an interesting source of mental stimulation. Its members included notables in practically every profession: such famed scholars as Demarchus C. Brown and Byron K. Elliott; eloquent ministers such as Bishop William A. Quayle and Harrison's own Presbyterian divine, Myron W. Reed; such distinguished novelists and journalists as Booth Tarkington and Meredith Nicholson, Louis Howland and John H. Holliday; also the Hoosier poet, James Whitcomb Riley. Gradually, prominent lawyers were added to the roster, but Harrison's three close associates, Fishback, Gordon. and Gresham were charter members.[17] The General took an active part in the club's programs; on the evening of January 11, 1879, he addressed his fellow members on "The Chinese Question," [18] a problem currently perplexing not only to Congress and President Hayes but especially to the people of the Pacific Coast.

When the Harrisons were in town, evening prayer meetings summoned them to the new $100,000 Presbyterian Church on the southwest corner of New York and Pennsylvania Streets.[19] While religion had always played a significant rôle in the General's life, it took on a new depth under the influence of Myron W. Reed, one of the most popular preachers Indianapolis ever had. "If he did not call sinners to repentance," remarked one of his contemporaries, "he at least called them to church." [20] His war record, a nonclerical appearance, and a cordial manner attracted many, while his keen mind, blessed with courage and a pungent wit, "reconciled all to his lack of conventionality." Reed exerted a strong influence on Harrison. The General soon went beyond the exercise of his office as elder and headed a missionary effort that led to the establishment of the city's Ninth Presbyterian Church.[21]

[16] J. P. Dunn, *History of Greater Indianapolis*, I, 520. This club, formed in the early 1870's, was originally called the Gentleman's Literary Club.

[17] C. G. Bowers, *Beveridge and the Progressive Era*, pp. 51–52. The club later boasted one President (Harrison) and three Vice-Presidents (Hendricks, Marshall, and Fairbanks).

[18] Harrison's views on this subject will be considered in the chapter on his career as United States Senator. Benjamin Harrison to Margaret Peltz, January 10, 1879, Messinger MSS.

[19] Dunn, *op. cit.*, p. 581.

[20] *Ibid.* Also Dunn's chapter, "The Last Fifty Years," in *Centennial Memorial of the First Presbyterian Church*, pp. 167–82, details Reed's unusual background and character.

[21] Dunn, *History of Greater Indianapolis*, p. 587.

Religion to the General was not just a matter for Sunday contemplation. It lay beneath his daily life and imbued him with the strong sense of responsibility towards his fellowmen that formed an integral part of his character and played an important part in preparing him for his political destiny.[22]

During the spring of 1879, Harrison tried the now celebrated "Election Fraud" cases. Assisted by William Henry Harrison Miller, the General represented the Government. Keen competition was furnished by a tough and competent defense team, headed by former Governor Thomas A. Hendricks, his brother A. W. Hendricks, and future United States Senator David Turpie. The accused was James Wilkinson, Democratic candidate for treasurer of Jennings County; the charge, illegal conspiring to transport 125 voters from one Congressional District to another in order to give a clear majority to a Democratic candidate for Congress. In the twenty-two-day trial, more than 130 witnesses were called. Political feeling ran high and Harrison in closing his case gravely warned the jury that it would be a sad day for our country "when so much as a spray from the waves of politics . . . can be felt in the face of a jury or judge." Harrison won a jury verdict. Sitting as judge in the case was Walter Q. Gresham, a man who would continue to figure largely in Harrison's career.

On June 21, 1879, the 46th Congress, in answer to the South's annual plea for constructive help, passed a bill creating the Mississippi River Commission, a seven-man board to be appointed by the President. Each year millions of acres of the richest lands in four states were "subject to floods for the lack of an adequate system of levees and flood control along the Mississippi." [23] At the same time, the river was "a grand highway of commerce, furnishing the cheapest outlet to the sea for the immense products of the Northwest." [24] The task of the Commission was to devise methods of improving navigation on the river and protecting its banks. Of the seven appointees, three were to be Army engineers, three civilians, and one a Coast and Geodetic Survey employee. Their job was a difficult one. Countless commercial interests demanded

[22] Bliss Isely, *The Presidents: Men of Faith*, pp. 180–81. See also Louis A. Banks, *The Religious Life of Famous Americans*, pp. 238–39.

[23] C. Vann Woodward, *Origins of the New South, 1877-1913*, p. 30.

[24] *Journal*, June 30, 1879.

protection, as did thousands of farmers, boatmen, and other citizens.

On June 28, President Hayes, in a surprise move, appointed Harrison one of the civilian Commissioners.[25] Engaged at the time as defense lawyer in a first-degree murder trial, Harrison had no foreknowledge of it. On hearing the news, he quickly telegraphed Hayes, declining the appointment; but when the President's personal letter and official commission arrived soon afterwards, he sent a second telegram: "If it will relieve you of any embarrassment I have no objection let it [the appointment] stand." [26]

Harrison decided to confer with the President in Washington later in the summer. Meanwhile he spent the greater part of July on various legal errands. Of late his firm had worked on railroad settlement cases in Chicago and New York, and these took him out of Indianapolis from time to time. He returned home on July 22 to help adopt a constitution for the State Bar Association,[27] thus becoming one of fifty-three charter members, and was appointed its delegate to the National Bar Association meeting in August at Saratoga, New York.[28] This honor inspired plans for an East Coast vacation with the family, now visiting in Yonkers, New York. The General would join them there after his interview with the President, then head for the seashore, where he could "dip his weary form in the briny deep, and take an undisturbed rest, with no bands, balls, or bores, to molest him." [29]

Harrison left Indianapolis on August 1 and on the 4th met with the President at the White House. Hayes assured the General that as a civilian member of the Commission his duties would not prove too time-consuming. His friendly persuasion won Harrison's assent; on the following day he wrote Hayes a letter of formal acceptance from his New York hotel room. In it he explained that his "hesitation grew out of the fear" that he could not "discharge the duties

25 *Ibid.*, editorial page. The appointment came as a complete surprise to Hoosiers. Also, Hayes' action may be interpreted as a palliative to Harrison, who in his bid for the United States Senate had suffered defeat at the hands of the Indiana legislature early in 1879. Radical Voorhees received 83 votes to 60 for conservative Harrison. See Carleton, *op. cit.*, p. 141.

26 Benjamin Harrison to Hon. R. B. Hayes, Winchester, Indiana, June 30, 1879, (L.C.), Vol. 8 (photostat). There is no record of the first wire in either the Harrison or Hayes MSS.

27 *Journal*, July 23, 1879. According to city historian Dunn, *op. cit.*, p. 565, the preliminary meeting was held on November 30, 1878.

28 *Ibid.* The National Bar Association had been organized at Saratoga in 1878.

29 *Journal*, July 24, 1879.

of the place without sacrificing my law practice to an extent that would result in a considerable loss. Our conversation yesterday satisfied me that this will not be the case." Nevertheless he added a cautious proviso: "Should I find that I cannot give the necessary time to this important trust, I will promptly ask you to relieve me." [30]

Harrison served on the River Commission for twenty months, during which time he worked closely with Captain James B. Eads, another Hoosier. Hailed by one historian as "the greatest civil engineer of the nineteenth century, American or foreign," Eads was famed as the designer of the great St. Louis Bridge and for his system of jetties which opened to commerce the mouth of the Mississippi River. [31] Rumor had it that the Commission was committed in advance to this type of jetty-and-levee plan," [32] and Harrison was warned by an Indiana Congressman that the whole Commission "business was set on foot . . . as the entering wedge to a grand scheme for depleting the Treasury in the interests of the Southern politicians." [33]

Harrison strove to keep an open mind until he had studied the reports submitted by the engineer members. It thus developed that when the Commission itself made its report to the Secretary of War in March, 1880, Harrison and C. B. Comstock, Major of Engineers, both dissented from an unqualified recommendation of the levee system. [34] This apparently prompted Randall L. Gibson, a Louisiana Democrat, to introduce a bill to "remodel" the Commission by reducing its membership to six, with only two civilian appointees, both of whom must be civil engineers. Harrison, suspecting this as a method of dropping him from the Commission because of his minority report, wrote to Garfield, [35] who replied that there was no chance of such a scheme passing the House. Tom Browne, an Indiana Congressman, agreed in this opinion, but admitted that the general impression in Washington was that the

[30] Benjamin Harrison to Hon. R. B. Hayes, August 5, 1879, (L.C.), Vol. 8. A photostat from the Hayes Memorial Library, Fremont, Ohio.

[31] Dunn, op. cit., p. 384; Hoar, op. cit., pp. 271–74.

[32] Journal, July 16, 1879. It was proposed to lower the level of the stream by decreasing the volume of water. This would mean constructing side cuts in favorable places, by which excess water might be drawn off and danger of overflow averted.

[33] Thomas M. Browne to General Harrison, May 16, 1880, (L.C.), Vol. 8.

[34] Minority Report of the Mississippi River Commission (46th Cong., 2nd Sess., Ex. Doc. 58), pp. 21–23.

[35] April 19, 1880, Garfield MSS, Vol. 70.

"levee system is intended more for the improvement of land than for water navigation." [36] Harrison's advance report had been based on this very point. In his opinion such an intention raised a serious constitutional question concerning the use of public funds for the benefit of private individuals. Further discussion was postponed, however, until 1882 when, as Senator from Indiana, Harrison himself raised the question. The second, and last, report of the Commission, signed by Harrison, was submitted to the Secretary of War on January 8, 1881, in good time to furnish material for a sharp debate in the 47th Congress. On March 3, 1881, Harrison tendered his resignation to Hayes, effective immediately.[37]

In August, 1879, Harrison had done Hayes a personal favor in accepting a post on the River Commission. In October of the same year, the President returned the compliment in some measure by spending an evening with the Harrisons at their home on North Delaware. The Presidential party had come to Indianapolis in order to head one of the city's most talked-about industrial parades. Carrie watched proudly as her husband marched by with General Sherman and other dignitaries. But for her, the event of the day was the lawn party that she arranged for President and Mrs. Hayes. It was a triumph, duly noted as such in the *Journal's* society column.[38]

Political campaigns were routine in the fall of 1879, and Harrison did not confine his speaking engagements to Indiana. Crossing into Ohio, he made several eloquent speeches for Charles Foster, banker and Republican candidate for governor. After Foster won the election, Harrison continued the friendship, which became a lasting one, and in 1891 appointed him his Secretary of the Treasury.[39]

In October of 1879, however, Harrison missed an exceptionally

[36] J. A. Garfield to General Benjamin Harrison, April 22, 1880, (L.C.), Vol. 8. Garfield wrote: "Should there be any such measure you may rest assured your friends in Congress will keep watch of it." Also Thomas M. Browne to General Harrison, May 16, 1880, *ibid.*

[37] Benjamin Harrison to the President (R. B. Hayes), March 3, 1881, (L.C.), Vol. 8. A photostat from the Hayes Memorial Library, Fremont, Ohio.

[38] G. L. Harney, *The Lives of Benjamin Harrison and Levi P. Morton*, pp. 150 ff.; *Journal*, October 3, 1879.

[39] Four times elected from Ohio to the House of Representatives (1871–1878), Charles Foster served four years as governor, and, except for his service in Harrison's cabinet, pursued banking as his career.

fine chance to make political capital. The Society of the Army of the Cumberland had scheduled its annual meeting for November 19 in Washington. Illness and death canceled the appearance of the announced orators and the Executive Committee appealed to Harrison to give the principal address.[40] James A. Garfield had already agreed to speak at one of the events, the unveiling of General Thomas' statue. Since Indiana soldiers had fought largely with the "Rock of Chickamauga," who better than "Little Ben" could speak for them? This was put strongly to Harrison by his outspoken friend, John D. Defrees,[41] yet the General turned down flatly an opportunity which such an alert politician as the late Senator Morton would have seized gleefully.[42]

Harrison kept his reasons to himself. It is probable that he was again simply overloaded with legal, literary, and Commission duties, none of which he would neglect. There is evidence that one absence, occasioned by a trip down the Mississippi, cost him the opportunity of presenting James G. Blaine's name to the National Convention at Chicago in 1880. An unanswered wire compelled the Blaine forces to look elsewhere for a speaker.[43]

The year 1880 marked the turning point in Benjamin Harrison's political career. From now on, he would go forward, never back. His expanding and lucrative legal practice had made him known in several Eastern seaboard cities, and his duties as Mississippi River Commissioner had carried him into many Midwest and Southern States.[44] The Indianapolis *Journal* had already heralded him as a "dark horse" Presidential candidate, though other papers throughout the state preferred him as Blaine's running mate.[45]

[40] Gen. McCook to Harrison, telegram, October 12, 1879, (L.C.), Vol. 8.

[41] John D. Defrees to General Harrison, October 13, 1879, *ibid.* Defrees wrote: "You are a comparatively young man, and have a laudable ambition to serve your country in a position of great trust. . . . You have never had an opportunity for making yourself a national reputation such as is now presented you. *It is greater than years in Congress.* . . . You should avail yourself of the present opportunity . . . [for] prominence and publicity."

[42] Mary R. Dearing, *Veterans in Politics*, pp. 110, 247.

[43] Eugene Hale to Harrison, telegram, May 20, 1880, (L.C.), Vol. 8. "It is the earnest desire of Mr. Blaine's friends that you will present his name to the convention, please answer." On the back, W. H. H. Miller, Harrison's partner, wrote: "Harrison absent—not known where to address him, nor when he will return."

[44] John G. Williams to General Harrison, February 21, 1880, *ibid.* Williams was General Counsel for the Vandalia Railroad and Harrison was associate counsel. Thousand-dollar fees were not unusual. Also Harrison to Margaret Peltz, February 7, 1880, Messinger MSS; and Carrie Harrison to Mamie Harrison, April 30, 1880, (L.C.), Vol. 8.

[45] *Journal*, January 8, 15, 31, February 24, 1880.

Outside Indiana his stock had also risen. The Des Moines *Register* argued that Harrison "as a lawyer . . . has already proved himself the peer of the ablest; . . . he traces doctrines to their sources and proves them to their foundations. . . . He is not a smiling politician of the school of Colfax . . . [yet] those who consider him first cold and distant soon change their impressions." [46]

The Hoosier State, always doubtful and sometimes pivotal in national elections, controlled thirty nominating votes. More frequently than not, the head of either ticket would choose a Hoosier running mate. Though the state favored Blaine, the Grant forces were ready to bargain at almost any price. As delegate-at-large and chairman of the Indiana delegation to the national convention, the General was at last in a strategic position.

Harrison's only preconvention address was an impromptu speech to the Young Men's Republican Club of Indianapolis. He chose for his setting the Bates Block, a spot charged with political and historical significance. Here Lincoln, the first President-elect to visit Indianapolis, had spoken en route to his first inauguration.[47] The General took advantage of such memories to review his own twenty-five years as a Republican campaigner. "While the Republican party may not always have been right," he observed, "it has always been nearer right than any political party that has existed contemporaneously. . . ." Even so, integrity bade the Indiana leader confess that "the party has not always been successful in selecting the best men for offices and public trusts. . . . The party has been dishonored by unfaithful public servants." But, he went on, a Republican characteristic has always been both to know the truth and, with a ready mind, to receive it. He assured the younger party members that, despite the serious failings of certain Republicans and the undeniable scandals connected with the Grant administrations, he himself was convinced that Republicanism "represented the moral conscience of the people of America." A warm tribute to the workingman concluded a speech that earned Harrison prolonged cheers and won the allegiance of young Republican hearts.[48]

[46] Des Moines *Register,* as quoted in the *Journal,* January 31, 1880.
[47] Dunn, *op. cit.,* p. 213.
[48] *Journal,* March 9, 1880.

At noon, June 2, 1880, the great amphitheater of the Chicago Interstate Exposition Building threw open its doors to a crowd of more than 18,000, including 756 delegates. So began the longest Republican National Convention on record. Representatives from the 38 states and 9 territories settled down for more than a week of deliberations.[49]

The rôles which Harrison and Indiana would choose to play remained nebulous. But there were clues. The General's Indianapolis speech had showed him unsympathetic to Grant's cause. Indiana's polite but studied indifference to pressure from the Blaine forces indicated that her delegation was independent, but strongly anti-Grant. Finally, on the eve of his departure for Chicago, Harrison confided his intentions to President Hayes: "We are very apprehensive that the interests of persons rather than those of the party" may rule the convention. "Our state has preferences but *no pets*. I will be ready to support any good man who can unite the party." [50] This appeared to be the view shared by a majority of the uninstructed and unattached delegations.[51]

At the outset, Harrison instructed his delegation not to place his name before the Convention in any capacity. He hoped by this to offset the persistent rumor that "Gen. Ben Harrison was in good form for second place." Talk persisted, nevertheless, that in the event of an eastern Presidential candidate, Harrison would receive the "vote of Virginia, the Tennessee Valley, . . . part of Iowa, Colorado, and also a few of the Michigan delegation." [52] If Blaine, the "Plumed Knight," won, "Wisconsin was also solid for Harrison for vice-president." [53] Also, the delegation had received a constituents' wire reading: "Nominate Ben Harrison for President and Indiana will go 20,000 Republican." [54]

The entire story of the torrid eight-day convention cannot be

49 H. L. Stoddard, *Presidential Sweepstakes*, p. 71.

50 Benjamin Harrison to Hon. R. B. Hayes, May 30, 1880, (L.C.), Vol. 8. A photostat from the Hayes Memorial Library, Fremont, Ohio.

51 Senator James F. Wilson of Iowa also expressed the same common concern. Be "for the reliable Republican who can most certainly lead us to victory. . . . To this end I would sink personal preferences." Wilson to J. S. Clarkson, January 9, 1880, J. S. Clarkson MSS, (Des Moines, Iowa). Uninstructed delegates were, however, a minority. See Eugene H. Roseboom, *A History of Presidential Elections*, pp. 253–56.

52 *Journal*, June 2, 1880.

53 J. B. Cassoday to Harrison, June 11, 1880, (L.C.), Vol. 8.

54 A telegram from "Many Republicans" to the Indiana delegation (c/o E. G. Hay) sent from Madison, Indiana, at 8:55 P.M., June 1, 1880, E. G. Hay MSS, Vol. 2.

told here.[55] Active from the beginning, Harrison brushed shoulders with the best. His humor set off several of the few laughs to ease the tense atmosphere. His early plea for a fair time limit on debate was much appreciated: "I sympathize with every delegate here in the inconvenience of this protracted stay in Chicago. I have found my former visits here pleasant, but from the bottom of my heart to my much trodden toes I have been anxious to get away this time." After a short but friendly dispute with Roscoe Conkling over time for the Alabama delegation,[56] Harrison pushed through a resolution limiting debate to twenty minutes on each side.

The wrangling between the Grant and anti-Grant forces lasted four full days. Blaine of Maine loomed large, especially when the convention defeated the unit rule of voting.[57] At last, on the evening of the fourth day, the nominating speeches began. "The most telling" were "those of Conkling when he proposed the name of Grant, and of Garfield in proposing Sherman." Actually Blaine, placed in nomination first, had his thunder stolen by Conkling and Garfield. At midnight on Saturday, the Convention adjourned over Sunday.[58]

Balloting began with the Monday session. The first count gave Grant 304, Blaine 284, Sherman 93, with 75 votes divided among four other candidates. Harrison and the Indiana delegation now tipped their hand by throwing 26 votes to Blaine, 2 to Sherman, and 1 each to Grant and Washburne. Twenty-seven ballots followed without material change, except that on the third ballot Harrison himself was presented with 1 vote—the gift of an unidentified Pennsylvania friend. At about 10:00 P.M. further balloting was postponed to Tuesday morning. The first half-dozen ballots of the new day recorded no appreciable change. Grant kept his strength at 306 or better, and Blaine had not been able to close

[55] The definitive research on the 1880 Republican Convention has been done by the Rev. Herbert J. Clancy, S.J., and is incorporated in his volume, *The Presidential Election of 1880.*

[56] *Proceedings,* p. 27.

[57] The Grant men were conspiring to force their candidate upon the convention. Their scheme was to impose the unit rule upon the state delegations, which would mean that the votes of all the delegates from the large states of Illinois, Pennsylvania, and New York would go to Grant despite the opposition of many of those delegates. See R. N. Current, *Pine Logs and Politics, A Life of Philetus Sawyer,* pp. 151–52.

[58] Myers, *op. cit.,* p. 257; *Proceedings,* pp. 175–79.

the gap. Neither of the leading candidates had come within striking distance of the necessary 378 votes.

Finally, at the end of the roll call on the thirty-fourth ballot, Wisconsin cast 16 of her 20 votes for a dark horse—James A. Garfield. Blaine later wrote that "the great body of the delegates saw at once that the result was foreshadowed." The next time around, Harrison cast 27 of Indiana's 30 votes for Garfield, swelling his total to 50. According to Blaine, "the culmination was now reached" [59] and the swing to General Garfield had started. As the thirty-sixth ballot opened, other states, beginning with Connecticut and Illinois, followed the lead of Indiana and Wisconsin. The Ohioan now polled 399, a sufficiency. On a motion of Conkling, the Grant lieutenant, Garfield's nomination was made unanimous.[60] The Vice-Presidential nomination fell to New York's Chester A. Arthur on the first ballot—a sop to the disappointed Grant supporters.

Harrison returned to Indiana a stronger man, politically speaking, than before the Convention. The Wisconsin delegation rightfully claimed credit for the initial break to Garfield,[61] but even the chairman of that delegation felt constrained to throw a bouquet to Harrison. On June 11, J. B. Cassoday wrote from Janesville, Wisconsin:

Allow me to congratulate you upon the part which you and your delegation formed at Chicago. I was glad for the assurance that your vote gave that no vice-presidency would be allowed to stand between you and duty. Had the nomination . . . gone East, our delegation had substantially agreed to support you for Vice-President. But country—party—duty are higher than office, and I was pleased to notice that spirit in you.[62]

The General had, of course, simply been true to his political philosophy. He had supported the "good man" who could "unite the party."

[59] James G. Blaine, *Twenty Years of Congress: From Lincoln to Garfield*, II, 666.
[60] Before the nominations and balloting for a Vice-Presidential candidate got under way Harrison had received telegrams of congratulation and advice. M. Halstead to Harrison, George H. Chapman to Harrison, W. Q. Gresham to Harrison, June 8, 1880, (L.C.), Vol. 8. Two days later, Halstead wrote that his idea of the probable ticket had been Harrison and Hawley: "It would have been better than the one nominated. However, I do not feel unhappy and the next Ohio man who is President will know more about you than the present one has revealed." Halstead to Harrison, June 10, 1880, *ibid.* This prediction was fully realized.
[61] Current, *op. cit.*, p. 154.
[62] (L.C.), Vol. 8.

In Chicago, Indiana Chairman Harrison made the final speech seconding Conkling's motion for Garfield's unanimous nomination. Half seriously, half in fun, Harrison announced himself as "the only defeated candidate for the Presidency on the floor of this Convention [*laughter*]—having received one vote from some misguided friend from Pennsylvania, who, however, unfortunately for me, did not have 'staying qualities,' and dropped out on the next ballot." He assured the Ohio delegation that he bore Garfield "no malice," which brought renewed laughter from the weary delegates.

Harrison's speech concluded with the serious promise: "Mr. President, I will defer my speech until the campaign is hot, and then, on every stump in Indiana, and *wherever else* my voice can help this great Republican cause on to victory, I hope to be found." [63] On that same evening, he was appointed one of an official committee charged with the pleasant duty of notifying Garfield and Arthur of their respective nominations. Out of this was born the invincible Garfield-Harrison entente. From that moment and until Garfield's assassination sixteen months later, Harrison remained steadfast in the rôle of intimate friend and adviser to the man from Mentor.

Now the real struggle was at hand. Hoosier Republicans faced two critical campaigns, state and national. On October 12, the nation would know whether Judge Albert Gallatin Porter, Harrison's lifelong friend, had recovered the governorship for the Republicans. And in November, the party would depend heavily on Indiana to give victory to Garfield and Arthur over General Winfield Scott Hancock and William H. English. In June and early July, state leaders were confident. "The political pot boils beautifully," wrote United States Marshal Dudley from Indianapolis. Porter, he felt, was a "tower of strength" locally and he termed "the nomination of Hancock . . . a confession of weakness on the part of the Democracy [which] insures us Indiana." [64] Creed Haymond, leading California Republican, visited Indianapolis in July and sent a wire to William E. Chandler at the Fifth Avenue

[63] *Proceedings*, pp. 279–80, 296.
[64] W. W. Dudley to E. G. Hay, June 24, 1880, Eugene Gano Hay MSS, Vol. 2; W. W. Dudley to J. A. Garfield, July 13, August 10, 1880, Garfield MSS.

Hotel headquarters: "Indiana is sure for Garfield." [65] Such Republican boasts spurred Hoosier Democrats to greater efforts. English, their Vice-Presidential candidate, was a native son who had been an Indiana Congressman from 1853 to 1861. Garfield's adviser and friend, Whitelaw Reid, owner-editor of the powerful New York *Tribune*, pictured him as "mediocrity, pure and simple," but warned against his vote-getting power "in his own very important state." [66] Harrison attributed English's influence to his unlimited capacity for cheating, and there is little doubt that the General feared this "banker with a 'barrel.'" [67]

In late July, the battle was joined. In a rush for position, the Democrats unleashed what has been called "one of the most disgraceful and contemptible campaigns against the private character of General Garfield." [68] Confronted simultaneously with the task of harmonizing a discordant party, the Ohio candidate turned to Indiana for help. The Hoosiers at once issued a circular effectively denouncing "the whole pack of infamous campaign slanders." On the other score, General Harrison offered to accompany Garfield to New York City in order to reconcile party factions by means of personal conferences.[69] He joined the worried candidate at his home in Mentor, Ohio, where, awaiting his arrival, were John A.

[65] Creed Haymond to W. E. Chandler, July 3, 1880, William E. Chandler MSS, Vol. 49. Chandler was a member of the Executive Committee of the Republican National Committee.

[66] Royal Cortissoz, *The Life of Whitelaw Reid*, II, 30–32. Cortissoz notes the "almost fraternally intimate terms" of the relationship between Garfield and Reid.

[67] B. Harrison to J. A. Garfield, September 13, 1880, Garfield MSS, Vol. 92. The usually conservative Harrison wrote: "The State is ours unless we are cheated out of it. The capacity of English and Barnum for that sort of work is unlimited and the money will be abundant." An examination into the William H. English MSS, (housed in the Delvan Smith Division of the Indiana State Library), yielded evidence that on August 9, 1880, English contributed $1,250 to the Democratic State Central Committee. During the course of the campaign, an Indianapolis newspaper published a list of mortgages held by banker English; this filled two newspaper pages. See Carleton, *loc. cit.*, p. 143. Although English had many warm admirers, Republicans regarded him with deep suspicion. See Manton Marble to W. H. English, May 8, 1871; George F. B. Carr to W. H. English, November 7, 1879; Thomas F. Bayard to W. H. English, November 3, 1879; D. W. Voorhees to W. H. English, January 12, 1880, (English MSS). Roseboom, *op. cit.*, p. 257, refers to him in the rôle of Vice-Presidential candidate as "a banker with a 'barrel.'"

[68] Myers, *op. cit.*, p. 264. See also T. C. Smith, *Life of James Abram Garfield*, II, 863 ff.

[69] W. W. Dudley handled the preparation of the circular and branded the charges "senseless and vapid and trumped up," yet he confessed that one of the anomalies of our national politics is that such charges can be made public, and although groundless, have to be met. Dudley to Garfield, July 13, 1880, Garfield MSS.

Logan of Illinois and Omar D. Conger of Michigan.[70] Their subsequent New York meeting served to solidify the party. Closing ranks, Blaine, Grant, Hayes men, independents, and reformers, all agreed to fight for the same cause. Even the sullen Conkling, though refusing to appear at the "harmony meeting" itself,[71] promised to stump for Garfield in Indiana and Ohio.

On returning to Indianapolis, Harrison described his mission as "interesting . . . but very tiresome." He confessed he was "about played out. I had to be speaking almost all the time and my voice was badly used up." [72] A side trip to Cleveland and a sudden call to meet with the Mississippi River Commission in Detroit had allowed him little chance for recuperation. Nor was there any rest in Indiana, where Republicans were now fighting an uphill battle.

In mid-August, John Hay, the Hoosier literary giant and future diplomat, wrote from Washington in praise of "the importance of the work . . . and the magnificent fight which the Republicans of Indiana are making." Carry the state in October, he urged, and "it is to you that the honor of Garfield's election belongs." [73] The Hoosiers were in battle trim. A report to Garfield from every county in Indiana revealed "an efficiency of work never before attained in the history of our state Republican organization." [74] Harrison was in the thick of it. From Auburn, Indiana, he wrote Cousin Mag:

I am here on a political tour. . . . It's dreadful weather for speaking. I am as wet as if I had been dipped—after every speech I have to change all my clothes. My meetings have been very fine and everybody very kind and complimentary.[75]

Meanwhile, in Ohio, General Garfield was conducting a fruitful front-porch campaign at his Mentor farm. His correspondence reveals a keen interest in Indiana's state campaign. Indeed, one

[70] Whitclaw Reid to J. A. Garfield, July 29, 1880, Garfield MSS.

[71] Cortissoz, op. cit., pp. 37–38.

[72] Harrison to Margaret Peltz, August 10, 1880, Messinger MSS. In most instances, Carrie Harrison accompanied the General on his shorter trips of a nonpolitical nature. In a letter postmarked September 1, 1880, Harrison admitted that his wife was lonely at home during his political tour of Indiana. Ibid.

[73] John Hay to E. G. Hay, August 18, 1880, E. G. Hay MSS, Vol. 2. John Hay was born in Salem, Washington County, Indiana, but could trace no kinship with Eugene Gano Hay, also a friend of Harrison.

[74] W. W. Dudley to J. A. Garfield, August 10, 1880, Garfield MSS.

[75] Harrison to Margaret Peltz, September 1, 1880, Messinger MSS.

letter served to turn the tide for the Hoosiers. "We are gaining every day . . . prospects are good," he wrote Stephen B. Elkins in New York, but "we ought to throw all our available resources into the October states, especially into Indiana. Nothing is wanting except an immediate and a liberal supply of money for campaign expenses to make Indiana certain. With a victory there, the rest is easy." [76]

Garfield's plea for funds for Indiana was in answer to calls for help from the Hoosier battleground. The Democrats were plotting election-day bribery and worse, in an all-out attempt to win Indiana. An urgent report from W. W. Dudley at Indianapolis had warned Garfield that William Henry Barnum, money baron and chairman of the Democratic National Committee, had brought $20,000 to Indiana for "preliminary expenses" and assured party leaders of an "abundant supply on election day."

Also, according to Dudley's report, Vice-Presidential candidate English had proposed a sordid program to be followed on Indiana's voting day. Its five points were: 1) "Buy voters . . . on election day"; 2) "import professional repeaters and bulldozers from large cities"; 3) "use money on Republican inspectors—not to stuff boxes or commit any affirmative act of fraud—but to go out for a drink, or turn the head at a critical juncture of the count"; 4) "have every Negro challenged and prevented from voting by acts of violence or intimidation"; 5) "cast upon the results, if unfavorable, suspicion . . . of Republican frauds." [77]

[76] J. A. Garfield to S. B. Elkins, September 3, 1880, S. B. Elkins MSS, (West Virginia University Archives). Elkins became a strong Blaine supporter in 1884 and an untiring supporter of Harrison in 1888. A survey of the W. H. English MSS for 1880 reveals the operation of a Democratic counterplan of liberal spending "that Indiana may safely be taken from the list of doubtful states." See Sen. J. E. McDonald to Hon. William H. English, June 13, 1880. Also W. H. Barnum to W. H. English, June 27, August 9, 10, 17, 19, and 21, 1880, for convincing evidence that the Democrats were ready to match Republicans dollar for dollar in order to win Indiana. These letters support the claim of E. Joy, Jr., of Chicago that "we can displace as many Republican votes as you want to carry Indiana." Joy to English, July 9, 1880, (English MSS).

[77] W. W. Dudley to J. A. Garfield, September 9, 1880, Garfield MSS. This was in reply to Garfield's letter of September 6. "What we need is money now—for our close counties. We feel the influence against us, and are powerless to counteract them. Our enemy has caught 'his second wind' and is pressing us hard." Dudley was a match for Barnum and there seems little doubt that both parties planned to use "soap" in an effort to gain Indiana's electoral vote. While Dudley complained about Barnum's slush fund, Barnum himself confided to English that Harrison and New had a plan to carry Indiana for Garfield. See W. H. Barnum to W. H. English, August 9 and 10, 1880, (English MSS).

Wrote Dudley: "If we succeed in the prevention of one half of these facetious schemes, we shall carry the state handsomely." "Counter-money" was desperately needed, he said, for "those legitimate uses by which enthusiasm is wrought up and votes gotten into organization, etc." Every word of this shocking report was soon confirmed by Harrison, who added facts of his own from personal correspondence. He predicted, however, that "we have 'boom' enough to outvote them—allowing pretty liberally for fraud." [78]

Garfield quickly referred these reports to Republican National Headquarters in New York. Within a week, the National Chairman wrote Harrison that $21,000 had been sent to Indiana, which state, he said, "is going to be backed at this end of the line in all proper ways, and to an extent commensurate with her wants. Our affairs look very well generally. Of course we all know that Indiana is the battleground, and we all here expect it to be carried by the Republicans." [79]

Early in September the opportunity arose for Harrison to seal his personal friendship for Garfield. Tom Hendricks, the General's old political antagonist, had attacked Garfield in a vicious and vitriolic speech. He charged that in 1876 the Ohioan had criminally helped to steal the Presidency from Tilden. When the Hendricks speech appeared in the press, Harrison's friends in Indianapolis wired Garfield to send material for an answering speech from the General. That same evening Garfield wrote Harrison, and also shipped to his home two volumes of testimony taken by the Potter Committee, with slips of paper marking those pages bearing his own testimony. He later sent Harrison another letter containing facts powerful enough to silence Hendricks, whom he described as "exceedingly short of material . . . and excessively sore over his loss of the Vice-Presidency." [80]

[78] Harrison to Garfield, September 13, 1880, Garfield MSS, Vol. 92 (see *supra*, n. 67). In this letter Harrison also observed that "in Kentucky, Missouri and even as far south as New Orleans appeals are being made for money for Indiana. I have no doubt that ten thousand rebels could be found who would pay their own expenses for the privilege of putting in a Dem. vote in Indiana. You know that our election laws favor frauds at the ballot box. Our Committee is taking every precaution to expose and prevent fraud and our people will fight if there is any attempt at bulldosing [*sic*] by imported roughs."

[79] Marshall Jewell to Hon. Ben Harrison, September 23, 1880, (L.C.), Vol. 8. Jewell admitted that the letter was written at the suggestion of Mr. Forbes of Boston, "who is my principal financial backer."

[80] J. A. Garfield to Ben Harrison, September 7, 1880, *ibid*. Garfield had no qualms about Republican action in Louisiana and had convinced Hayes of the honesty of his election there. See Barnard, *op. cit.*, pp. 333–35.

Although Harrison considered Hendricks' attack "so intemperate and . . . so weak that it was scarcely worthy of any notice" he agreed with other friends of Garfield that "it offered a good opportunity to give Mr. H. a drubbing . . . I consented to speak Saturday night and did so." [81] Mrs. Harrison sent a newspaper copy of the speech to Garfield, who wrote Harrison at once, expressing relief and gratitude. He told Harrison that his rebuttal had put Hendricks "in a very unlovely position before the country. I have rarely seen a more miserable piece of pettifogging in a man of his standing." This, he noted, will not take a "single vote from us; and I do not think he needs any further notice, unless he attempts some additional assault. Accept my cordial thanks for your masterly reply." [82]

Anxious Republicans kept a close watch on the Maine elections, the initial skirmish in the Presidential contest. On September 13, Maine voted, and the next day Blaine wired a report to Garfield. The outcome was scarcely encouraging. Although three of the five Congressional districts went to the Republicans, they lost the governorship by two hundred votes. Garfield notified Harrison of this result, commenting gravely: "This should arouse our people to still greater effort and thus assure the victory by greater diligence." On September 22, Harrison showed Garfield that he for one was overlooking no opportunity to further the cause. Seizing a good chance he had rejected a year earlier, he delivered the annual address to the Society of the Army of the Cumberland at their Toledo, Ohio, reunion. Garfield himself followed Harrison with a brief fifteen-minute speech, noted in his diary as "just a fair one." [83]

As the hectic fall days raced by, political fever mounted in Indiana. Everywhere citizens reveled in the excitement of marching bands, torchlight parades, and almost nightly meetings with big-

---

[81] Harrison to Garfield, September 13, 1880, Garfield MSS, Vol. 92. Harrison excused himself for failing to answer Garfield's two previous letters—"too much on the go to answer them sooner." Even this letter was handwritten from Connersville— a trip Harrison had begun at 4:00 A.M. from Indianapolis. A contemporary press report claimed that Harrison showed Hendricks up "as a garbler of testimony, a misrepresenter of the truth of history, and a public calumniator of private character." Benjamin Harrison Scrapbooks, (L.C.), Vol. 1 (unidentified clipping).

[82] J. A. Garfield to Harrison, September 14, 1880, (L.C.), Vol. 8.

[83] Garfield Diary, September 22, 1880, Garfield MSS. For text of the address, see Benjamin Harrison Scrapbooks, (L.C.), Vol. 1, No. 42.

name, out-of-state speakers to help attract crowds. These visitors were impressed with the colorfulness of Hoosier political rallies. They reported that the Republicans had a "drill club wearing white breeches, very baggy, white coats with red trimming and blue caps." Then there were "pole raisings," which were the climax of exuberancy. The "Democrats used a hickory tree and the Republicans a poplar." [84]

Out in the field, with one speaking engagement following another, Harrison impressed his associates with "a sense of fairness." John L. Griffiths, who campaigned with him for ten days, characterized his speeches as "very different from the ordinary campaign addresses. They were thoughtful and logical, and frequently eloquent." As to his effectiveness as a speaker, Griffiths wrote:

He dominated his audiences through the nobility of his character and the strength and integrity of his intellect. He used the anecdote sparingly—in fact seldom resorted to it but had the keenest wit, which is so much finer than story-telling.[85]

As state leader, Harrison welcomed to the Hoosier battleground many Republican dignitaries, among them S. W. Dorsey, Secretary of the Executive Committee of the Republican National Committee, Senator Roscoe Conkling of New York, and Senator William B. Allison of Iowa. They reported to New York headquarters that Indiana "looks quite hopeful." [86] At Mentor, Garfield received an election-eve report from his close friend Burke A. Hinsdale. After spending "fifteen working days" and making "sixteen speeches" in Indiana, Hinsdale summed up the situation:

All the data . . . point to a Republican victory Tuesday. But there are said to be 30,000 merchantable votes in the state, and which side will manage to buy most of them is the question. This is not the universal understanding of Republicans, but it is the common understanding. . . . I have an idea that the Republicans of Indiana expect to carry the State, and Harrison told me Thursday that he was confident of success. Gains are being made this week, and every day.

Hinsdale concluded with the ambivalent statement: "I am going home now, but think I will come to Mentor Tuesday evening to be at the *wedding* or the *funeral*." [87]

[84] "Reminiscences of Charlie Wesler" in *Indiana History Bulletin*, 31 (1954), 111–12.
[85] Chicago *Inter-Ocean*, March 14, 1901.
[86] W. B. Allison to Whitelaw Reid, October 4, 1880, Whitelaw Reid MSS.
[87] B. S. Hinsdale to J. A. Garfield, October 9, 1880, printed in Mary L. Hinsdale (ed.), *Garfield-Hinsdale Letters*, pp. 460–61.

On the eve of the election in Indiana, Harrison, in a final speech, strongly endorsed his former law partner, Albert G. Porter, for governor. The next morning he voted earlier than usual so as to be "at my desk, ready once more to attend to my own business and to that of my friends which I have been neglecting." Writing Cousin Mag, he confessed: "I am just dead tired out by so much speaking, but a few days of rest will make me all right again. I have invitations to go east to speak, as well as to several western states but I don't think I will do much of it." [88] This was Harrison's mood on October 12.

When the smoke of battle cleared, the two parties had spent "something over half a million dollars" [89] and the people of Indiana had chosen the Republican ticket. Porter, swept into office as governor, had a working majority in both houses of the state legislature. This also guaranteed that a Republican would replace Democratic Joseph E. McDonald in the United States Senate. Buoyed by this new party spirit and quickly forgetting his weariness, Harrison joyfully reported to Cousin Mag:

The success of the Republicans in this state has elated everybody— so much so that the city is in an uproar. Crowds in front of my office are picking up every leading Republican and making them speak. They picked me up this morning and carried me about a square. . . . You'll be glad on my account, won't you? [90]

Ohio joined Indiana in a Republican victory, but the party's national leaders had no intention of surrendering to complacency. There were other states still to be won. Chester A. Arthur telegraphed Indiana headquarters, stressing the importance of carrying New York State. In particular he called for Harrison: "The withdrawal of General Harrison at this time would result in great detriment. . . . Our own speakers left us for the Indiana campaign at a time greatly needed here. They have returned disabled and unfit to help us for the time being. The Democrats are desperate and will throw their whole strength upon us. We need Gen-

[88] Harrison to Margaret Peltz, October 12, 1880, Messinger MSS.

[89] Dunn, *op. cit.*, p. 292. Dunn presents an interesting picture of Barnum, chairman of the Democratic National Committee, and Dorsey of the Republican National Committee, coming to Indiana in person to supervise "the organization of the state," and spending "something over half a million dollars in the effort." Strangely enough, these men were business partners: Barnum president and Dorsey secretary of the Bull-Domingo Company.

[90] Harrison to Margaret Peltz, October 13, 1880, Messinger MSS.

eral Harrison." [91] The word was passed on to General Harrison who, back at his law desk, had believed that his arduous work for the state victory had. earned him a respite. He soon found that what he had thought were invitations to speak in the East and Midwest were in reality "command performances," already advertised in the New York press. A personal wire from Arthur advised him: "Your appointments are all made and cannot be cancelled without giving the greatest trouble and disappointment. We helped Indiana all we could and I appeal to you to stand by us now." [92] In response, Harrison consented to return to the stump on behalf of the party.

There were a number of reasons, in addition to Arthur's wire, for Harrison's consent: pressure from National Committee headquarters; his Convention pledge to go "wherever else my voice can help"; his genuine party loyalty; and another, quite personal reason. On October 16, he had confided to his closest friend, Robert S. Taylor of Fort Wayne: "I have made up my mind to be a candidate for the Senate and will be obliged to you for everything you may feel disposed to do for me." [93] This decision had not been easy or made without some misgivings. Friends close to both Harrison and Garfield had intimated that should the Republicans win in November, President-elect Garfield would most certainly wish Harrison to enter his Cabinet. This was a disturbing thought to the General. Close friends agreed with him that a seat in the United States Senate would "be more congenial to your tastes and profession." [94] As he himself expressed it to Cousin Mag: "I prefer the Senatorship to a place in the Cabinet because I can keep up my law practice and be at home a considerable part of each year." [95]

Although his decision to stand for the Senate was independent of friends' opinions, he must have been pleased and reassured by a frank note received in November from John D. Defrees, his Washington adviser. In Defrees' judgment, the "Senate is your

[91] Chester A. Arthur to C. C. Riley, telegram, October 16, 1880, (L.C.), Vol. 8.

[92] C. A. Arthur to General Ben Harrison, telegram, October 18, 1880, *ibid.* John C. New, Indiana representative to the National Committee, was in New York at the time and he concurred in the contents of the Arthur telegram.

[93] Harrison to R. S. Taylor, October 16, 1880, *ibid.* Taylor was an unsuccessful candidate for Congress in the 1880 election. Harrison wrote that his defeat had caused "the only real taint of bitterness . . . you will not be forgotten."

[94] John W. Foster to General Harrison, October 23, 1880, (L.C.), Vol. 8.

[95] Harrison to Margaret Peltz, October 18, 1880, Messinger MSS.

proper place. A great mistake exists in the public mind as to the desirableness of a Cabinet appointment." He went on to discuss other possible Government posts, then reverted, in colorful language, to a diatribe against the current senatorial types. The Senate, he wrote,

should be composed of men of brains, culture, intelligence, good morals, and gentlemanly deportment. I have seen it when it *was* such. But, alas! of recent years, very few such men have been members of that body. The result of the election in Indiana has given it a position in National politics never before reached, and it should not be *fooled* away by sending blattering *nincompoops* to Congress. Of late years *money*, not brains and merit have secured seats in each House, but more notably in the Senate. It is time this thing should end.[96]

Harrison made his first return to the hustings in Illinois, where he spent a week and delivered three rousing speeches. In Bloomington, he came within an ace of martyrdom for Garfield and Republicanism. He had just given the Democrats a verbal bombardment of "shot balls, bombs, canister and shell" when an old Confederate rebel from Kentucky, sitting near the platform, called him a liar. Harrison faced him calmly and sent off a few more well-placed "shots" for his benefit. The man suddenly pulled out a gun, pointed it—but his nerve failed. He was immediately seized and dragged from the hall but Harrison's cool attitude won many admirers, who often afterwards spoke of his nerve, if not his judgment.[97]

After a week-end rest at home, he spent the final days of the national campaign in New York. He returned in time to register his vote for Garfield, who carried Indiana by a plurality of 6,642 votes. Approximately the same number of votes marked Garfield's national plurality over General Hancock, although the Republican won 214 electoral votes—59 more than the Democratic nominee.

Harrison preferred "to wait until the rush was a little over" before expressing his congratulations to the President-elect. Instead of "using the wires," the General sat in his law office and wrote a brief, sincere letter to Garfield:

You must know how sincerely I rejoice over your success. Outside your own family I am sure no man in the country can be happier than I

[96] John D. Defrees to General Benjamin Harrison, November 22, 1880, (L.C.), Vol. 8. Defrees' illness prevented an earlier letter.

[97] Recalled by T. N. Pusey in a letter to Benjamin Harrison, July 7, 1888, (L.C.), Vol. 32.

am over your elevation to the presidency. Whoever else *might* have been elected, you have been—and this justifies those who were not of the "mystic 306." Indiana has splendidly vindicated the action of her delegation at Chicago. . . .

After reciting several personal details, Harrison boldly laid his cards on the table: "I have made up my mind to be a candidate for the Senate. There are four or five others in the field who are very busy—still, I think I shall succeed. When I see you I want to have a full talk over Indiana affairs." [98]

Garfield acknowledged the letter by return mail and expressed his own congratulations to Harrison on the great victory won in Indiana "and the conspicuous part you have taken in achieving it." [99] He added the hope that both the General and Mrs. Harrison would visit him at Mentor before too long.

Harrison had begun the final mile of the road leading to Washington. One question remained: would he be in the capital as the junior Senator from Indiana, or would Garfield persuade him to accept a Cabinet position?

[98] Harrison to Garfield, November 4, 1880, Garfield MSS, Vol. 104.
[99] Garfield to Harrison, November 6, 1880, (L.C.), Vol. 8.

CHAPTER XII

United States Senator:
Freshman Year

AFTER Harrison's private announcement of his candidacy for the Senate, many Republicans spoke out in his favor. As two county leaders put it: "If General Harrison wants the position, he will get it without effort." [1] From politically influential Richmond came the report: "The feeling here is that Harrison should be the Senator." [2] In and out of the state, the belief grew that the new Republican majority in the Indiana Legislature would endorse Benjamin Harrison with "a spontaneous and unanimous vote" [3] as successor to Senator Joseph E. McDonald, the incumbent Democrat. Soon two former "Morton machine" men fell into line. Former Vice-President Schuyler Colfax, disavowing his own candidacy, declared that Indiana had scores worthy of the Senate but Harrison had "especially . . . earned it." [4] From Washington came the endorsement of Secretary of the Navy Richard W. Thompson. The Secretary's "uniform kindness," as Harrison expressed it, gave "a presumptive case to start on." [5] This kind of political support meant prestige, but it needed the local support of organized workers. The plain hard work essential to any canvass would depend on Harrison's lieutenants in every corner of the state.

[1] F. Macartney to R. S. Taylor, October 20, 1880, R. S. Taylor MSS, (Indiana State Library); also M. M. Browne to Harrison, November 17, 1880, (L.C.), Vol. 8.

[2] I. Jenkinson to R. S. Taylor, October 18, 1880, R. S. Taylor MSS.

[3] J. W. Foster to Harrison, October 23, 1880, (L.C.), Vol. 8.

[4] Schuyler Colfax to Harrison, November 5, 1880, ibid. See also Willard H. Smith, Schuyler Colfax: The Changing Fortunes of a Political Idol, p. 421

[5] Harrison to R. W. Thompson, December 4, 1880, (L.C.), Vol. 8. This brought a reply from Thompson on December 6, in which the Secretary pledged his full support until the end.

The Harrison camp boasted unheralded but thoroughly trusted party men like his old friends Robert S. Taylor of Fort Wayne, M. M. Browne of Winchester, W. R. ("Riley") McKeen of Terre Haute, W. H. Trammel of Huntington, D. S. Alexander of Indianapolis, and some twenty others. Each prepared to strike a blow for Harrison in his respective community. For example, Taylor made frequent trips through each Congressional district just to make sure that the Republican state representatives "felt right" about General Harrison.[6] In Indianapolis, the General received a stream of confidential reports from practically every county, each correspondent listing the "certain and solid votes."[7] Nevertheless, there were other strong contenders for the coveted office.

Energetic Will Cumback, whose fortunes at the polls never quite equaled his ambitions for office,[8] was tramping the entire state alone, "making a personal appeal to each member" of the legislature. This information disturbed Harrison less than the report that "some men are working for Gresham." When the judge's friends pronounced Harrison "the only man in the state that could worthily represent it in the *Cabinet*," the General viewed this flattery as a disguised effort to sidetrack him in the Senate race. "How much better to be frank," he commented, "than to dissimulate in this way." Still, prudence dictated that he "keep peace in the family" and he tried to "restrain any over-zealous friends"[9] from personal animosity.

In the middle of November, Harrison and his lieutenants devised a political plan calculated to weaken Gresham's position for the Senate seat. The strategy called for the concentration of speakers and practical politicians on New Albany, the Gresham stronghold. Here Harrison supporters extolled their candidate's legal ability, his record for sound finance, and his growing national reputation. Without mentioning Gresham's name, they claimed that in Washington only Harrison would serve the best interests

[6] In (L.C.), Vol. 8 *passim*, more than fifty letters reveal the hard work done for Harrison by his friends throughout November, December, and the first two weeks of January, 1881.

[7] Harrison to Taylor, November 13, 1880, *ibid*.

[8] Cumback, at the age of twenty-five, had represented the new party in the 34th Congress (1855–1857), but was defeated for re-election in 1856. He served as State Senator in 1866, as Lieutenant Governor in 1868, and campaigned unsuccessfully for the United States Senate in 1869. The governorship also escaped him in 1896.

[9] Harrison to R. S. Taylor, November 13, 1880, (L.C.), Vol. 8. Harrison admitted that Walter Q. Gresham "may have more strength than I know—but I hear nothing that alarms me. . . ."

"of the Republican Party and the country. . . . Indiana would honor herself by honoring him." [10] Harrison now formally announced his candidacy, a move which evoked a flood of favorable comments.

In December, Harrison returned from St. Louis, where he had been visiting relatives, still wearing the smile of confidence.[11] But the opposition forces had not yet surrendered. Murat Halstead, editor of the Cincinnati *Gazette* and former classmate of Harrison's, warned that a "combination" had been formed against him in Indianapolis. On December 14, General A. D. Streight, hostile to Harrison, called a secret Republican caucus in an attempt to divide the party. He urged Greenbackers to bolt Harrison on the score that he did not favor cheap currency.[12] Thanks to the presence of many of the General's friends the attempted coalition failed. In fact, reported John Wildman, it boomeranged into a Harrison rally. One participant, initially antagonistic to the General, concluded that "Harrison should be senator . . . the people want him, and [state] representatives will not reflect the sentiments of their constituents if they do not vote for him." [13] This outcome pleased Harrison, who noted that none of his real friends had joined the "Indianapolis Ring." [14]

Even Christmas preparations failed to interrupt the regular flow of political correspondence from every corner of the state. By this time Harrison's only rivals for the senatorship were two former Republican congressmen, Will Cumback and Godlove Orth. All other candidates had quit the race and thrown their strength to Harrison, who was particularly happy that "Judge Gresham's friends . . . are warmly and sincerely for me." He also noted that "Cumback is not gaining any . . . rather the re-

[10] W. Q. Gresham to G. F. Chittenden, November 16, 1880, George F. Chittenden MSS, (Indiana State Library); also J. A. Wildman to O. A. Sommers, November 14, 1880, O. A. Sommers MSS, (Indiana State Library).

[11] Harrison to R. W. Thompson, December 4; R. W. Thompson to Harrison, December 6; Harrison to M. Halstead, November 27, 1880, (L.C.), Vol. 8.

[12] A. T. Wright to Harrison, December 25, 1880, and Harrison to R. S. Taylor, December 14, 1880, *ibid.* Aware of the coalition strategy that "I must be beaten for the Senate," Harrison blamed State Senator Moses Poindexter, a Greenback leader whom he characterized as "decidedly frisky" and as nurturing a desire "to be the Atlas of the Legislature." Harrison, however, remained confident that his friends would not desert him under fire. The *Sentinel*, December 15, 1880, gave good coverage to the caucus, held in Room 39 of the Grand Hotel.

[13] J. A. Wildman to E. G. Hay, December 17, 1880, Eugene Gano Hay MSS, Vol. 2.

[14] Harrison to the Rev. C. B. Bartholomew, December 20, 1880, a Tibbott transcript, (L.C.), Vol. 8.

verse." [15] Concerning Orth, whose reputation still suffered from the Venezuelan scandal of 1876, Harrison made no comment.

With the help of Frank Tibbott, a skilled stenographer, Harrison appealed to all parts of the state, and especially to doubtful counties. Each message emphasized the fact that he was a party man who favored sound money and the protective tariff. He promised that "the new and younger element of the party and the soldier may expect an appreciative recognition from me." [16]

With the Indiana Legislature convening on January 6, 1881, and senatorial nominations scheduled for the 17th, Harrison, now carefully schooled in practical politics, intended to use all the tricks of the trade. He arranged headquarters near the State House well beforehand; then invited trusted friends to come as his guests to Indianapolis for the opening session of the Legislature. Taylor of Fort Wayne, upon whom Harrison relied most heavily, received a special invitation: "Make your arrangements to stay with me. I shall have a room at the Grand and between that and my house we can find a place to sleep and eat that will suit our engagements . . . I see nothing to create any alarm . . . but I would like to make a good show of outward force." [17]

Nor did the senatorial aspirant overlook the opportunity provided on January 10 by the inauguration of his friend Albert G. Porter as chief executive. The press duly commented on Harrison's prominence during the colorful ceremonies.

On the eve of the legislative decision, both Cumback and Orth withdrew from the Senate race, leaving Harrison a clear field. [18]

[15] Harrison to J. Gardner, December 27, 1880. *Ibid*. See Martha Alice Tyner, "Walter Q. Gresham," *Indiana Magazine of History*, 29 (1933), 297–338. Writing of Gresham's senatorial aspirations in 1880, Tyner observes that "the strength of Harrison finally caused him [Gresham] to withdraw from the fight." *Loc. cit.*, p. 309.

[16] Harrison to C. B. Bartholomew, December 20; Harrison to W. H. Trammel, December 23; Harrison to N. Cadwallader, December 27; Harrison to J. B. Lewis, December 27; and Harrison to B. Wilson Smith, December 27, 1880, Tibbott transcripts, (L.C.), Vol. 8. To Trammel, one of his most trusted lieutenants, Harrison emphasized the fact that "my views on financial questions are those of my party . . . I do not differ from . . . Porter . . . Orth . . . Cumback."

[17] Harrison to Taylor, December 29, 1880, *ibid*. Harrison extended similar invitations to Congressman Tom Browne, W. H. Calkins, and business-bankers Joseph I. Irwin of Columbus and W. R. McKeen of Terre Haute.

[18] *Journal*, January 11, 1881, carried Cumback's letter to Harrison and the General's gracious reply. Orth announced his withdrawal in a public letter published in the same edition. County papers copied immediately, and the state soon knew that the election would go to Harrison. See Petersburg *Press*, January 14, 1881. Also Benjamin Harrison Scrapbooks, (L.C.), Vol. 3 *passim*.

On Tuesday, January 11, 1881, Senator Jesse J. Spann of Rush County presented Benjamin Harrison's name to the Republican Senatorial caucus, held at the Grand Hotel. The speech was described as untheatrical, "yet beautifully and delicately expressed," and the sustained applause which followed indicated Harrison's popularity. Representative Vinson Carter of Harrison's home county, Marion, seconded the nomination. Then came the motion that the nomination be made by acclamation, seconded by Orth's chief supporter, Senator Robert Graham. A rising vote carried the motion, with "every Senator and Representative springing to his feet and capping the nomination by three rousing cheers and general handshaking." Graham and Representative J. B. Kenner of Huntington were appointed a committee of two to notify General Harrison. After many disappointments, his hour of political triumph had come.

Within a few minutes the committee reappeared, the General arm-in-arm between them. Reporters described the resultant ovation as "an old-fashioned soldiers' yell." Overcome with embarrassment "mingled with intense emotion," Harrison's "face turned ashen." First with uplifted hand, then with bowed head, he tried to stop the demonstration in order to express his gratitude. When quiet was restored, however, his first words caught in his throat and he could not be heard beyond the front rows. The nomination, he repeated again and again, was "an honor greatly beyond his deserts." Then, warming to his speech, he said he rejoiced that mud-slinging and personal disparagement had had no part in his campaign or in that of his Republican rivals. His platform called for legislative efforts to solve the currency problem and to regulate interstate commerce. It underscored the need for a long-range study of other national problems. He also promised to maintain "very pleasant relations with the incoming administration of General Garfield . . . because I feel it will be liberal in its statesmanship and stalwart in its Republicanism." He concluded with the characteristic statement: "Don't let us be afraid of the people," after which the caucus members surged forward to congratulate him.[19] For half an hour after his speech, Harrison shook hands

---

[19] Among other Indiana papers that printed the speech in its entirety, the Frankfort *Banner* led in editorial praise for Harrison. Stressing his ability, reliability, and worthiness, it said that the General "has, by nature and education, one of the

with the friends whose unwavering support was to win him a seat in the United States Senate.

On Tuesday, January 18, the Indiana legislature cast a majority of votes for Harrison, and the new Senator accepted the tally-sheet as a memorial.[20] Congratulations from congressmen, judges, fellow lawyers, and personal friends across the country soon deluged his home and office.[21] Harrison complained laughingly that his "desk . . . had the appearance of a brush heap." [22] In reading his correspondence, however, he was able to relive in memory some thirty-five years. Letters came from classmates of College Hill and Miami University days, and from comrades of his old command, the 70th Indiana Volunteer Regiment. In particular, a letter from Lieut. J. S. Parker, Co. F, touched his heart:

I write to congratulate you on your election as U. S. Senator. As one of your own boys, being with you throughout the war, it pleases me to hear of your success. . . . I will never forget . . . going into battle . . . at Resaca . . . tears was [sic] in your eyes; you said, some of my poor boys will not come out and that was true, for many of our men fell there . . . I have always been proud of my leader, Harrison, have watched your career, have spoken of you to my friends always in honor . . . I shall still watch your future career, Colonel. You will excuse this letter but it is from the heart.[23]

All his correspondents did not agree that Harrison could best serve his country in the Senate. One of these was Federal Judge Thomas Drummond, before whom Harrison had argued many cases, who wrote: "I don't like to see a lawyer like you leave his profession and go into politics." [24]

---

first minds in the country . . . greatest lawyer in the state . . . an able debater . . . soldier of distinction. His Republicanism has never been questioned; at all times, whether victorious or beaten at the polls, Gen. H. has stood at the front and demanded equal rights and exact justice for all men." The phrase "Don't let us be afraid of the people" was characterized as "Harrisonian."

[20] The clerk, Cyrus T. Nixon, Harrison's friend and admirer, sent him the unofficial tally (now in [L.C.], Vol. 1, Second Series). The Republicans controlled the joint session of the general assembly by 81 to 62. See Barnhart and Carmony, *Indiana: From Frontier to Industrial Commonwealth*, II, 313.

[21] (L.C.), Vol. 8. There are several letters from Indiana, Ohio, Kentucky, Illinois, California, New York, Maryland, Wisconsin, Iowa, and the Territories of Montana and Wyoming.

[22] Harrison to A. Moore, January 12, 1881, *ibid*.

[23] J. S. Parker to Harrison, January 21, 1881, (L.C.), Vol. 1, Second Series.

[24] Thomas Drummond to Harrison, February 9, 1881, (L.C.), Vol. 8.

Harrison answered each morning's mountain of mail with the help of a clerk. One letter, however—from President Hayes—he answered in longhand:

Your letter of congratulations was very unexpected and very gratifying. That you should think with so much interest of my election to the U. S. Senate, and should express yourself with so much personal kindness is very pleasant. I can scarcely hope to realize the position and influence in the Senate which you kindly anticipate, at once, for I am relatively unfamiliar with public life. I feel, however, I am put under bonds by the kindness of my friends both at home and abroad to make the fullest return possible to their great expectations.

It must be exceedingly gratifying to you to know that both the country and the Republican Party have come out of weakness to great strength under your administration.[25]

With Harrison's election to the Senate, a difficulty emerged that he and other state leaders would have to solve. Indiana deserved a place in Garfield's cabinet, but, if Harrison refused, would the President-elect be satisfied with anyone else? The General himself had prepared a list of available Hoosiers; however, since expressing his own preference for the Senate he avoided the subject in letters to Garfield, who had already invited Harrison to Mentor for a "quiet little talk." The General accepted for the week end of January 22–23, thus deferring his conference and visit until the Indiana Legislature had balloted for the new Senator on January 18. On Saturday night, January 15, Carrie Harrison met with an accident which frightened her husband and made it impossible for her to go with him to Mentor. He wrote Cousin Mag a detailed description:

She started across the Street [N. Delaware] to Mr. Miller's and entering their gate fell on the ice striking her head and face on the pavement. She was so stunned that she could not get up till help came. Someone passing called Mr. Miller and they helped her into the house and sent for me.

Harrison forgot Garfield, Cabinet, and Senate. When he arrived Carrie still "bled from the nose but her face was not cut at all." Two days later, her eyes turned black and she was purple with bruises. "She will hardly be presentable for some time," wrote Harrison, somewhat needlessly. When it was determined that there

[25] January 18, 1881, *ibid.*

was no permanent injury, Harrison's sense of humor returned: "I have arranged to take the deposition of the Miller family," he wrote his cousin, "to prove that it happened away from home." [26]

Harrison wired Garfield that he would come to Mentor alone, arriving on the noon train, Saturday, January 22. Against his better judgment, he brought Garfield a letter signed by a committee of Hoosier congressmen, requesting an interview with the President-elect. They wished to persuade him to name an Indiana man to his Cabinet. Harrison had pointed out that this request went beyond good taste, adding that he doubted Garfield's willingness "to have a formal call from a large Com'tee." [27] The congressmen insisted, and the letter went into Harrison's pocket. His trip to Mentor, Ohio, was made through a typical midwestern snowstorm, which made the train an hour late in arriving. Harrison recalled later that the cold outside contrasted sharply with the warmth of Garfield's welcome. On the farm, alone and uninterrupted, the two talked all afternoon and well into the night. They discussed national and local politics and the coming administration. Finally, Harrison reluctantly gave Garfield the letter he had brought. Before reading it, the President-elect predicted dryly: "They wish me to choose a Cabinet officer . . . but I understand they are not agreed upon anyone." At this point, Harrison gave his personal estimate of such men as Gresham, Taylor, Tyner, Dudley, and several other leading candidates for a Cabinet post. Garfield listened patiently, then told his friend that if he chose anyone from Indiana it would be Harrison himself. For, on the previous Sunday, the President-elect had confided to his diary a list of possible Cabinet officers. In this entry he mused, "If I were compelled to make a Cabinet today . . . Harrison of Indiana. . . ." [28]

When Harrison retired for the night, Garfield again took out his diary. Harrison "is in doubt whether he ought to leave the

[26] Harrison to Margaret Peltz, January 17, 1881, Messinger MSS.

[27] Harrison to Hon. Calvin Cowgill, January 17, 1881, a Tibbott transcript, (L.C.), Vol. 8. This mass pressure annoyed Harrison, though he readily admitted that General Garfield "will be glad to talk individually with all the leading Republicans."

[28] Garfield Diary, January 16, 1881, Garfield MSS. Others included in this list were: Blaine for the State Department; James or Morton of New York for the Postmaster Generalship; MacVeigh of Pennsylvania for Attorney General; Lincoln of Illinois for Secretary of War; Knox or Allison of Iowa for the Treasury. One appointment was to go to the South, either Phillips or Morgan, and another to Harrison of Indiana. Garfield had not determined whether he would ask Harrison to be Secretary of either the Navy or the Interior; a blank space followed his name.

Senate," he wrote. "I like him." The snow continued on the next day, and so did the two-way discussion. Only the arrival of Burke Hinsdale, Hiram College president and intimate friend of Garfield, turned the conversation along broader lines. At 2:45 P.M. Harrison departed. Sometime later that day, Garfield told his diary that Harrison "thinks he ought to stay in the Senate, but a place in the Cabinet was neither refused nor tendered." [29]

The General arrived in Indianapolis with the feeling of one who has accomplished a mission. Although he had promised Garfield to think over their conversation before writing him a final decision, he felt he had made it clear he preferred to be Senator. He was also sure he had convinced Garfield that Indiana should be represented in the Cabinet. The next day he wrote to Washington to assure leading Republicans that the President-elect "feels very kindly toward our state. I argued with him so far as I could the propriety of giving us a place in the Cabinet. I did not get and did not expect an answer as to what he would do." He then added shortly what he knew they wanted to hear: "Gen'l G. consented to see a Com'tee." [30]

Harrison found his desk "looking like a Post Office" and he therefore put aside all legal affairs in favor of more letter-writing. There was also more fence mending to do. He paid visits to all Republican leaders of national influence and assured each one that he would cooperate fully with the Indiana delegation in Congress. He went out of his way to promote party harmony. To Godlove Orth, still disappointed by his failure to gain the senatorship, he wrote a "peace" letter in which he branded "jealousy and suspicion" as "unmanly and uncomfortable." [31]

When it was known that Garfield had consented to receive the Hoosier committee at Mentor, all Indiana buzzed with proposals. Meanwhile, Harrison had decided not to accompany the delegation. The committee members objected vigorously, insisting that

[29] January 22, 23, 1881, *ibid.*

[30] Harrison to Hon. R. B. F. Pierce, January 24, 1881, a Tibbott transcript, (L.C.), Vol. 8.

[31] Harrison to Orth, January 25, 1881, *ibid.* Harrison tried to smooth Orth's hurt feelings by calling on him at his Lafayette home, but he was out of town. Somewhat later, Orth sent a letter of congratulations, which Harrison in reply claimed was not "at all spoiled by your frank statement that you would rather have succeeded yourself."

the absence of the Senator-elect would imply dissension within the ranks. This persuaded the General to change his mind and he sent a wire to Garfield informing him that the committee would call on him on Monday, January 31. He added somberly: "I shall be with the Committee, though I would have preferred it otherwise." Under the same cover, Harrison enclosed a confidential communication designed to avoid embarrassments after the group reached Mentor. Explaining that he would "not have an opportunity for any private conversation," he told Garfield that he had made up his mind:

I avail myself today of your suggestion that . . . I should write to you. I am most decidedly of the opinion that I could not, without a breach of faith towards some of those who supported me for the Senate, vacate that place for any other. And if I were personally free to do so, I am very sure that it would not tend to the harmony of the party in Indiana. I hope you will believe me when I say there is no personal sacrifice that you could expect, that I would not make to promote the success of your administration. But I have said repeatedly to my own friends and the friends of other gentlemen who have been named among us for Cabinet positions, that if elected to the Senate, I should expect to remain there.

I hope therefore that you will not think it necessary to do anything that would subject me to the most painful embarrassment and criticism. I yet hope that you may be able to find someone in Indiana who will answer the high demands of the position in your Cabinet. But if you should think not—you will still not be without the means of showing a generous appreciation of the support which this state has given you.[32]

So matters stood between Garfield and Harrison when the latter led a 28-man delegation [33] from Indiana to Ohio. The President-elect received them cordially and listened attentively to their pleas for Hoosier recognition in his Cabinet. Harrison noted, however, that Garfield lacked his usual urbanity, and this disturbed him. Immediately upon his return to Indianapolis, he wrote to Mentor: "You looked troubled yesterday, and I was sorry to see it. It is hard for a real friend to know how to help you . . . do the best you can and then stand by it—the country will sustain you." [34]

Nothing came of the committee's pilgrimage to Mentor. Garfield made it clear that a Cabinet member must possess a "national

[32] Harrison to Garfield, January 28, 1881, Garfield MSS, Vol. 126.

[33] In the delegation were four members of Congress and at least one representative from each of the thirteen election districts. In addition to Harrison there were four delegates from his home county (Marion).

[34] Harrison to Garfield, February 1, 1881, Garfield MSS, Vol. 127.

reputation, abilities of a high order, an unsullied name, and . . .
the entire confidence of the commercial interests." He felt that
in Indiana only Harrison met these requirements. The General
himself attempted to end this impasse by a letter suggesting to
Garfield that he appoint General Lew Wallace, Harrison's intimate
friend for over thirty years. In addition, Wallace had fought with
Garfield at Shiloh. "If you think well of the suggestion," Harrison
added, "I think I can pave the way for its acceptance by our delegation." [35] This enthusiastic endorsement was, of course, a definite
departure from Harrison's own announced policy, but he justified
the action to his friends by saying: "If we are to succeed, our
urgency must be in the *line* of Garfield's preferences and not
against them." [36] Garfield did not choose Wallace and Indiana's
prospects for a place in the Cabinet dwindled.

With Garfield's inauguration fast approaching, Harrison planned
to leave for Washington on Friday, February 18, via Cincinnati.
He sent his itinerary to the President-elect and confessed, "I do not
desire to say anything further on the Cabinet . . . except that
before you commit yourself to any selection from our state, I
would be glad to know of it." In reply there came from Mentor
a final invitation to enter the official family:

After the best reflection I have been able to give to the case, I do not
see that I can make a selection from Indiana, for the Cabinet, unless it
will be agreeable to you, and consistent with your views of duty to
take a place.

I have long hoped we could be thus associated; but I will not press you
beyond your wishes or views of duty.

Please write me your latest thoughts on the subject before you leave
for Washington.[37]

No written reply to Garfield's request has been preserved. Carrie had been ill and Harrison was unable to leave for Washington
until February 21. It may be that he presented in person a reluctant
"no" to Garfield's last appeal. It was a difficult decision to make,

[35] *Ibid.*

[36] Harrison to Stratton, February 2; and to H. L. DeMotte, February 9, 1881, Tibbott transcripts, (L.C.), Vol. 8.

[37] Harrison to Garfield, February 14, 1881, Garfield MSS, Vol. 130; also Garfield
to Harrison, February 15, 1881, *ibid.* (a letterbook for 1881, p. 110), added that "in
case Indiana does not go into the cabinet, I shall cheerfully do what I can to give
her fitting recognition. . . ."

but it is to Harrison's credit that he did not break faith with the friends who had elected him United States Senator.

The Harrisons decided to make March 4, 1881, a day of family reunion at the nation's capital. Russell came on from Montana to join his father, mother, and sister at the Riggs House. A number of the newly elected Senators and Representatives had also taken temporary quarters there, and the Harrisons soon found themselves happily surrounded with old Indiana and Ohio friends.

Before the inaugural ceremonies commenced, Harrison walked to the Capitol for the special session of the Senate. Here, with his wife and two children watching from the visitors' gallery, Harrison took the oath prescribed by law. He then joined his proud family for Garfield's inauguration. The civic, military, and social display, more elaborate than in 1877, impressed the Harrisons, who shared the general "feeling of hopefulness and confidence in the new administration." [38] "Hayes looked . . . sweet and lamblike," but "Garfield's face looked worn" as he shouldered the burdens of office. This might be partly explained by the fact that his inaugural address had not been completed until 2:30 that morning.[39]

On the next day, Vice-President Chester Arthur called the Senate to order, and Harrison found himself assigned to Seat 20, close to that of Arthur. Directly in front of Harrison were Orville Platt and General Joseph Hawley of Connecticut and William Windom of Minnesota.[40] On his right sat William Sewell of New Jersey, also a former Union general, and on his left, Eugene Hale of Maine, an understudy for James G. Blaine, now Secretary of State. These completed the immediate semicircle of friendly colleagues. Such legislative luminaries as George Hoar, William Allison, and George Edmunds ranked as veteran policy-makers. Roscoe Conkling and newcomer Tom Platt, faces familiar from the Chicago Convention, would represent the Empire State until their resignations in May.[41] In the opposition party, besides his fellow

[38] *Appleton's Annual Cyclopedia, 1881,* p. 317.

[39] Harry Barnard, *Rutherford B. Hayes and His America,* p. 500.

[40] Harrison knew Hawley as a soldier and was well acquainted with Windom, who took charge of the Treasury Department during Garfield's brief term in office. Windom returned to the Senate when Arthur became President.

[41] Both resigned their seats on May 16, 1881. Platt, who soon earned the title "Boss" in New York politics, wore a Prince Albert coat and fine side whiskers. Some

Hoosier, Daniel W. Voorhees, Harrison was soon to respect the abilities of Thomas Bayard, James Cameron, and George Vest. One of Harrison's oldest and closest friends was John Sherman of Ohio, a shrewd though somewhat colorless individual, who had just quit the Treasury Department for a seat in the Senate. He had served with John Scott Harrison in the troubled days of the 34th Congress [42] and it was natural that he should now counsel and help the son of his fellow Buckeye.

The Senate counted 37 Republicans, 37 Democrats, and 2 Independents, Judge David Davis of Illinois and General William Mahone of Virginia.[43] Its only true unanimity came on the second day, when Garfield's Cabinet was to be confirmed.[44] Then followed a two-week delay while both parties fought for control of the important committees. Neither had a clear majority vote and Davis leaned to the Democrats while Mahone favored the Republicans. A fierce dog fight deadlocked the formation of committees until Vice-President Arthur cast his vote for the Republican list. Freshman Senator Harrison found himself appointed to four Committees: Indian Affairs, the Military, Territories, and Rules. He then became chairman of the Committee on Transportation Routes to the Seaboard.[45]

The work of the Committees, however, would not get under way until the Senate could agree on its own organization. This battle for control continued through March and all of April, while Harrison observed the maneuvers silently. Three weeks of political bickering in the Senate and a month of interviewing office seekers from Indiana disappointed the new senator. He wrote to Taylor, his successor on the Mississippi River Commission: "I am not sure

---

claimed that daylight politics blinded him for he could only work under cover. See W. A. White, *Masks In A Pageant*, pp. 35–40; also Thomas C. Platt, *The Autobiography of Thomas Collier Platt*, p. 139, for his version of the resignations.

[42] John Sherman, *Recollections of Forty Years in the House, Senate and Cabinet*, pp. 80–105. For the rôle played by John Scott Harrison in the 33rd and 34th Congresses, especially during the "bloody Kansas" days, see Harry J. Sievers, *Benjamin Harrison: Hoosier Warrior*, pp. 116 ff.

[43] Mahone had been elected by the readjuster wing of the Democratic party in Virginia. Nelson Blake, *William Mahone of Virginia*, chap. 7, draws heavily on the standard monograph by Charles C. Pearson, *The Readjuster Movement in Virginia*, in depicting Mahone's rôle as a political insurgent.

[44] Three Senators went into the cabinet: Blaine, Windom, and Kirkwood; their places were filled by Frye, Edgewater, and McDill.

[45] *Congressional Directory* (47th Cong., 1st Sess.), pp. 86–91. Harrison's personal copy is now in the library of the Harrison Memorial Home in Indianapolis.

but I am ready to *swap* with you." [46] To another friend he confessed: "It is very distressing business to me—this attempt to furnish places for those who deserve them, when the places won't go around." [47] He did succeed in having Colonel W. W. Dudley named Commissioner of Pensions and John C. New appointed Assistant Secretary of the Treasury.[48] Other local appointments in Indiana stirred up petty jealousies and allowed the junior senator little rest. At the same time, working conditions in the Senate Chamber taxed Harrison's patience:

The weather has been *very* hot here and the sessions of the Senate held in a chamber that has no window opening out doors, makes a stay of 6 hours in it very oppressive. I have to wipe my face every few minutes while I write. There's no telling when we will get away from here. . . .[49]

Just before this perspiring session ended, Senators Tom Platt and Roscoe Conkling resigned. Harrison must have been pleased to see the New Yorkers stalk out of the Senate Chamber. Already he had come to regard Conkling, whom he had battled in Chicago, as a public nuisance, endorsing the opinion of his law partner, Miller, that the gentleman from New York "always seems to be looking around to see where he can find a man in his own ranks to throw his javelin at. . . ." [50] With the hostile New Yorkers out of the picture, Garfield's appointments in that state were confirmed almost without opposition.[51]

On May 20, the Senate adjourned. Without having uttered a word on the floor, Harrison had thrown in his lot with Garfield.

[46] Harrison to R. S. Taylor, March 19, April 7, 1881, (L.C.), Vol. 9.

[47] Benjamin Harrison to Dr. George F. Chittenden, March 30, 1881, George F. Chittenden MSS, (Indiana State Library).

[48] In (L.C.), Vol. 9, there is a list of twelve persons recommended by Harrison and agreed upon by the entire Indiana delegation. Only Dudley and New received appointments. For the significant part Dudley played as Commissioner in the development of the pension system in response to G.A.R. pressure and political interest, see John William Oliver, *History of the Civil War Military Pensions*, chap. 4, "Pensions and Politics," pp. 90–108. Also Leonard D. White, *The Republican Era: 1869–1901*, pp. 218–21.

[49] Harrison to Margaret Peltz, May 12, 1881, Messinger MSS.

[50] W. H. H. Miller to Rev. Samuel Miller, April 19, 1881, W. H. H. Miller Letterbooks, in possession of the author. The drama behind the double resignation has been ably recounted by Donald Barr Chidsey, *The Gentleman from New York, A Life of Roscoe Conkling*, chap. 30, "As of Thunder," pp. 329–41. Garfield's courage earned him the bullets of an assassin.

[51] William H. Robertson was appointed Collector of Customs in the Port of New York, and Edward A. Merritt, incumbent Collector, was appointed Consul General at London.

Soon an assassin's bullet and a new President from New York would cause him endless political embarrassment and a severe loss of patronage. Ten weeks had opened few avenues of advancement to the freshman senator.

Harrison returned to Indianapolis at the end of May with a guilty conscience. "I have been kept away from my law office all Spring . . . and my partners have had to do all the work," he wrote Cousin Mag. Moreover, Miller had been quite ill and needed a long vacation. Harrison therefore decided to postpone his plan to visit the western territories, where he had hoped to gain first-hand knowledge for future committee work.[52] This decision was fortuitous. In June, political hell broke loose over federal appointments in Indiana. Harrison took up the cudgels for his political friends, especially Charles Kahlo, a popular manufacturer from Logansport, recently appointed Consul-General at Berlin. Charges of "incompetency and incapacity" had been preferred against him and word now reached Indianapolis that these charges chagrined President Garfield. Vexed by this news, Senator Harrison vigorously defended Kahlo. He asked Colonel Dudley to confer with the President and Secretary of State Blaine, and followed this action with a series of long, sharp letters to Garfield.[53] The Senator won his point and Kahlo was vindicated.[54]

Political headaches and 101-degree weather greatly discouraged Harrison in early July.[55] "Can't sleep," he complained, "wander about the house from one room to another and from chair to bed all night." [56] This mood of self-pity ended abruptly on July 2.

[52] Harrison planned to go first to Montana. Harrison to Margaret Peltz, May 12, 1881, Messinger MSS.

[53] Harrison to Garfield, June 7, 1881, (L.C.), Vol. 1, Second Series; Harrison to Garfield, telegram, June 13, 1881, Garfield MSS, Vol. 143; also a letter, Harrison to Garfield, June 15, 1881, *ibid*. It is interesting to note that Harrison knew Kahlo from the campaign of 1876 and had entertained him at his home. As state senator from Cass County, Kahlo helped Harrison obtain his Senate seat. His appointment had been endorsed by leading Indiana Republicans.

[54] *Ibid*. Kahlo did not serve under President Arthur. Harrison admitted that "I may have oversized the man or undersized the place," but in view of his almost universal endorsement he felt that the President and Secretary of State should allow the man a fair chance "and save his family from needless hurt."

[55] *Journal*, July 1–31, 1881. Sunday, July 10, was the hottest day on record in the city, but the thermometer in Cincinnati read 103.5 degrees and in Pittsburgh a cool 103.

[56] Harrison to Margaret Peltz, July 14, 1881, Messinger MSS.

Washington dispatches carried the news that Garfield lay critically wounded, victim of an assassin's bullet. A *Journal* reporter rushed to the Senator's law office with the shocking story of how Guiteau felled Garfield. Harrison's instant anxiety for his chief made a public statement of his feelings "almost impossible." He said that he knew Guiteau, who had fired the shot, but he did not consider him insane. "I met him frequently about the Riggs House. . . . He used to accost me every day about his prospects, and was really a nuisance." Harrison added that he thought Guiteau had been in line for a consulship. As the Senator hurriedly prepared for a quick trip to the President's bedside, he told reporters that "it would be cruel and unjustifiable to attribute . . . such fiendishness" to any of Garfield's political opponents within or without the party. He especially condemned the idea of any conspiracy led by Vice-President Arthur. "There can be no cause assigned for committing the deed other than the pure meanness of the scoundrel." [57] That same afternoon, he boarded a Washington-bound train.

Harrison had difficulty making his way to the Executive Mansion; the gateways were "thronged with people awaiting the issuing of bulletins on the President's condition." Newspapermen jammed the steps and vestibule. The fear had spread that "the President would not survive the night." Harrison remained at the White House about half an hour, speaking with Mrs. Garfield, "the most heroic woman I ever knew." He deemed it prudent, however, not to enter the President's bedroom. "I could have seen him had I so desired, but I knew it would only add to the danger he was in, were he allowed to converse, which, in all probability he would have done, had I or hundreds of others who were there been admitted to his room. We could render him no more service than he was receiving." [58]

On Monday, July 4, Harrison returned to the White House to consult with Dr. Bliss and the other physicians attending the stricken Chief Executive. Afterwards, he wired Indianapolis that Garfield was "better than anticipated. . . . Nature is making a

[57] *Journal*, July 4, 11, 1881. Of the thirty or forty public figures interviewed in the city, no one attributed the shooting to the President's political opponents.

[58] *Ibid.*, July 4, 5, 11, 1881. Fond of Mrs. Garfield, Harrison commented publicly on the "presence of mind she exhibited . . . I do not believe there is another woman in the country who could have acquitted herself so magnificently. . . ." If Garfield recovered, he said, "it will be greatly due to the heroism and courage displayed by his wife and family." Colonel Dudley stayed at Garfield's bedside that night, giving the President all the ice he wanted.

splendid fight, and may yet win, though the odds against her are great. Garfield's great courage has not failed him for a moment. God help him and the country." [59] He stayed three more days to assure himself that Garfield was actually on the mend. On Thursday night, he left Washington, stopping on the way home at Deer Park, Maryland, where his daughter Mamie was vacationing.

Back in Indianapolis, Harrison spent the week end answering hundreds of anxious questions and awaiting each new bulletin from the White House. He told friends that he had seen Arthur "as he returned from his interview with Mrs. Garfield," and that the Vice-President was "all anxiety." Again Harrison scolded those who suspected Arthur of conspiring with Guiteau, labeling such gossip silly and groundless. He warned that "there are hundreds of people who will cling for a lifetime to a first impression . . . that . . . will . . . never be eradicated." His own family history provided him with a striking parallel:

Some people who were Whigs in the day of that party, still believe that my grandfather was poisoned while he was President. . . . There was nothing more absurd than to believe that he was poisoned. The same may be said of the talk about the alleged conspiracy on the part of the Vice-President or any of the stalwarts so-called.[60]

The nation continued its long vigil as Garfield bravely fought his seesaw battle with death. Between July 4 and September 19 the *Journal* rarely failed to carry front-page medical bulletins. During these uncertain days, numerous constitutional and political questions were raised and a general controversy raged over the question of "Presidential incapacity." Several politicians rushed into print, but Harrison made only one public statement, then pursued a course of determined silence. It was his opinion that "as long as the President retains his mental faculties, he . . . is not incapacitated from acting as President. . . . The clause of the Constitution which speaks about incapacity does not apply to

[59] *Ibid.,* July 5, 1881, contains Harrison's wire sent to Congressman Peelle.
[60] *Ibid.,* July 11, October 1, 1881. Harrison met Arthur during the 1880 campaign, when he visited New York with General Garfield. Attracted by Arthur, Harrison invited him to speak in Indiana. Yet Harrison was quite convinced that Arthur made "a great mistake by going to Albany and taking the part he did in the Conkling fight." This, Harrison believed, gave the public grounds to regard Arthur as a conspirator.

the present case. . . . He is now competent to attend to business and doubtless would, were his physicians to allow him." [61]

Harrison caught up with his legal work by mid-July and decided to carry out his wish to see the far West. Miller agreed to accompany him on a six weeks' vacation. On July 22 they left for Chicago, where they met Senator John Sherman and a party of dignitaries which included the senator's brother, General William Sherman, Justice William Strong, late of the Supreme Court, and Governor Frederick A. Potts of New Jersey. The group traveled together along the Union Pacific route as far as Salt Lake City. Here the travelers separated, Harrison and Miller branching off on their own, and the Sherman party continuing to Yellowstone Park. [62]

Harrison spent most of his western vacation in the Territory of Montana, where Russell was working both in the U. S. Assay Office and as a private rancher. The Senator was pleased that his son, now a dues-paying member of the Helena Presbyterian Church, had apparently succeeded in his cattle business. [63] Mr. Miller was sufficiently impressed to lend Russell $1,000 for expansion. [64] Throughout their Montana stay, Harrison and Miller received frequent bulletins on Garfield's condition, but the reports promised little. The two partners returned home during the first week of September and Harrison again cleared his desk of unanswered mail. On September 8, he left for Chicago where work on the firm's railway cases kept him for several days. It was here that the news of Garfield's death reached him on September 20.

Harrison returned immediately to Indianapolis, where he attended a citizens' meeting at the Grand Opera House to honor the martyred President. Under the stress of marked emotion, the Senator rose to address the huge gathering of saddened people from every walk of life. "As I look over this great assembly," Harrison slowly began, "I see sorrow in every face. It is not often that a calamity is so widely felt as this. . . . It has cast darkness, not only on the porticos of the rich, but it has come into the

[61] *Ibid.* The *Journal* and *Sentinel* carried numerous articles from July to September on the topic of "incapacity."

[62] Sherman, *op. cit.,* pp. 651–53; and *Journal,* July 22, 1881.

[63] Items in the Russell B. Harrison MSS, (Terre Haute, Indiana), June 1, August 2, 1881. On July 21, 1881, just before his father and Miller arrived, Russell bought two horses for $250.

[64] W. H. H. Miller to Mrs. C. M. Bunce, October 4, 1881, W. H. H. Miller Letterbooks.

humblest home with its shadow." Echoing Garfield's own sentiments expressed on the occasion of Lincoln's death, Harrison reminded his listeners that "God reigns and the government at
Washington still lives." Then, continuing extemporaneously, he
recalled his intimacy with the President. Their friendship, he
said, had begun at the Grand Pacific Hotel in Chicago before the
1880 convention, where "I had once taken pleasure . . . in his
nomination. Yesterday," he went on, in the same hotel, "all
seemed to come back to me as a cause of grief, and I seemed to
stand, with all others, responsible for the shadow that has fallen
upon those hearts that were so near to him." Harrison praised
what he believed were Garfield's two finest characteristics: the
gift of speaking with "the utmost delicacy and appropriateness"
and "a family life that was deep with devotion and inspiration."
He concluded with an appeal to all citizens to support President
Arthur: "Let no friend of Garfield dishonor his generous friend
by meeting his successor with suspicion." [65] Harrison attended
the funeral in Washington; then accompanied the President's
body to Cleveland for burial. Perhaps as he rode in that sorrow-
ful journey he regretted not having entered Garfield's cabinet,
where for six months he might have served the President more
closely.

On October 10, President Arthur convened the Senate in the
expected extra session, and the contest to elect a temporary president of the upper House got under way. At the end of the day,
Senator Bayard [66] of Delaware was elected, but on the following
day, with the swearing-in of three new Republican senators, the
permanent office went to one of the Independents, Judge David
Davis of Illinois. Davis, a man of enormous bulk, had difficulty
squeezing into the largest armchair in the chamber,[67] and the fact
that the new presiding officer "had to be surveyed for a new pair
of trousers" helped turn party bitterness into good-natured laughter.

The death of Rhode Island Senator Ambrose E. Burnside, a
Hoosier-born Union general, brought Harrison an invitation to

[65] *Journal*, September 21, 1881.
[66] See Charles C. Tansill, *The Congressional Career of Thomas F. Bayard*, for
a definitive and scholarly study based on the voluminous Bayard Manuscript Collection.
[67] G. F. Hoar, *Autobiography of Seventy Years*, II, 65–69.

Above, in order: Harrison's wife, Carrie; his son, Russell; daughter, Mamie; father, John Scott Harrison: and his constant correspondent, "Cousin Mag" Peltz. *Below:* Harrison after his election to the U.S. Senate.

The Harrison home at 674 (now 1230) North Delaware Street, Indianapolis. The picket fence shown was later torn down by visiting throngs after Harrison's Presidential nomination.

General Harrison's desk in his law office, with an early set of the *Indiana Reports* edited by him shown above. *Right:* The Wright Block on East Market Street, Indianapolis. Campaign bunting decorates Harrison's law firm windows. Also in this block was *Evening News* Editor John H. Holliday's office and the literary retreat of James Whitcomb Riley, famed Hoosier poet.

Destruction of the Pittsburgh Union Depot and Hotel during the Great Railroad Strike of 1877, soon afterwards to terrify Indianapolis. *Above, left and right:* "Blue Jeans" Williams and Benjamin Harrison, while contending for the Indiana governorship, 1876. As governor in 1877, Williams' failure to act in protecting Indianapolis from strikers was offset by Harrison's prompt action.

Veterans of the 70th Indiana Regiment hear Harrison speak at their 1888 reunion at Clayton, Indiana.

Harrison with friends and guide proudly poses with trophies after one of his frequent duckhunting trips.

The 1888 Republican National Convention in the Auditorium Building, Chicago.
Inset: Indiana Attorney General Louis T. Michener, master mind behind Harrison's campaign.

The July 7, 1888, issue of *Judge* carried this tribute to Harrison on its front cover, following his nomination at Chicago. The caption read: "The Hour Has Come, The Man Is Here."

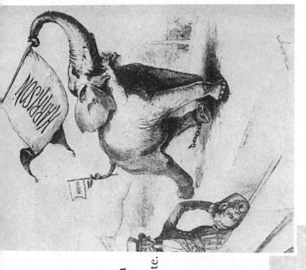

Left: Harrison greets the Danville delegation a few hours after his Presidential nomination. *Right:* "Harrison Broken Loose," a *Harper's Weekly* post-convention tribute. Cartoon by W. H. Rogers.

Left: The famous Cumberland campaign ball arrives at Harrison's Delaware Street home after some 5,000 miles of travel from the east.

Election night in 1888 at Madison Square, New York, as Benjamin Harrison carried the Empire State. Drawn by Charles Graham for Harper's Weekly.

deliver the eulogy. Experienced orator though he was, the junior senator felt exceptionally nervous as he slaved over the rough draft of what was to be his initial oratorical effort in the Senate. As he read over the results with much dissatisfaction, a friend from Indiana walked into the office. Seating his visitor, Harrison said: "I wish you would read this over," and handed him several manuscript sheets bearing evidence of many changes. "I want you to scratch out anything in it that you don't like," he said. "Scratch it all out, if you think best," he added in a discouraged tone, "and write in whatever you wish." [68] The visitor carefully perused the manuscript, then handed it back, advising the overwrought Senator to deliver it just as it stood.

Harrison spoke the next day and the speech was a triumph. The veteran Republican Senator George F. Hoar walked to his side and "congratulated him very warmly in the presence of the entire Senate upon the manner in which he acquitted himself." He was followed by the eloquent Democratic senator from Mississippi, Georgia-born Lucius Q. C. Lamar. Later, Wade Hampton of South Carolina, who had also eulogized Burnside, "accorded to Senator Harrison the honor of having made one of the most efficient addresses . . . he had ever listened to." The freshman Senator had passed his formal test.

Harrison spoke for the second time two days before adjournment. The General's soldier friend from Indiana, one-legged Colonel W. W. Dudley, himself an astute politician, had come before the Senate for confirmation as Commissioner of Pensions. His appointment was savagely attacked by Senator Bayard, and Harrison took the floor to defend his old comrade. His speech was later reported as "strong and aggressive," but so "politic and conciliatory that . . . the Senators crowded around him and congratulated him." One prominent Democrat rose to announce that "after such a conciliatory effort . . . he could not do otherwise than vote for Mr. Dudley's confirmation." Another Democrat, Voorhees himself, followed Harrison and spoke "perfectly in accord" with his fellow Hoosier, after which Dudley was confirmed by an overwhelming majority.[69]

[68] A clipping in an unidentified Milwaukee, Wisconsin, newspaper under date of March 17, 1901, Russell B. Harrison Scrapbooks, Vol. 1, (Indiana State Library).

[69] *Journal,* October 24, 1881. Eight votes were cast against Colonel Dudley, the man destined to play a leading rôle in Harrison's Presidential campaign in 1888.

After a brief detour to Virginia for the centennial celebration of the Battle of Yorktown, Harrison again returned home. His political leadership had not yet been tried under fire, but both parties were already speculating on Tom Hendricks' remark that Indiana's new senator "came as near as anybody" to filling Morton's shoes, yet "I doubt if Harrison proves any such leader as Morton was." [70] The answer to this still lay in the future, through and beyond the General's remaining five-and-a-half years in the Senate.

[70] *Ibid.,* August 30, 1881. In an interview by "Gath," former Governor Hendricks described Morton as a "man of undoubted ability and force" who belonged to what he called "the group [of] . . . great senators and party leaders."

CHAPTER XIII

Tariff Tempest and Protection

ONE OF THE bright spots for Harrison in that first Washington fall had been the arrival in mid-October of Mamie Harrison, now 24, attractive, and accomplished. She and her mother planned to move to the Capital before the opening of the regular session in December and try their hands at senatorial housekeeping. Father and daughter went house hunting and finally rented a "floor of four rooms and bathroom" from a boarding house at 825 Vermont Avenue, where "the table is very good." [1] Even the prospect of excellent meals may have seemed small recompense to Mamie, whose cousins were already whispering, "She does not think Washington a very pleasant place for young ladies as there are so few young gentlemen." Her father was pleased, however, since he had found his repeated separations from Carrie and home life a trial.

Before leaving for Indianapolis, Harrison had accomplished one other important piece of business. On October 31, he had conferred with President Arthur, who received him with much cordiality. After a general discussion of state and national politics, Arthur concurred in Harrison's belief that in Indiana many political fences would have to be rebuilt in order to sustain a Republican majority in so doubtful an area. Back in his Senate office that same day, Harrison drew up a detailed memorandum of the meeting, with a view "to the best interest of the Administration and for Indiana Republicanism." [2] He entrusted the President's copy to Colonel Dudley for personal delivery and further clarification. This done, he felt that his first months in the Senate had not ended in too great a state of futility.

[1] Harrison to Margaret Peltz, October 28, 1881, Messinger MSS.
[2] Benjamin Harrison to President Arthur, October 31, 1881, (L.C.), Vol. 10.

Harrison's letters during the latter part of his first senatorial year indicate that he had undergone a period of self-examination in the light of the criticism and advice with which friends and constituents alike had inundated his desk. The General admitted privately that he was "not cut out for a 'Boss'" and possessed "few of the elements of a 'leader,'"[3] but added in his own favor that he "was prepared, like Burnside at Fredericksburgh to take the responsibility."[4] He was proud of the fact that he had won his seat without having committed his honor to any man's keeping:

I tried to conduct my canvass for the Senate upon a high plane . . . no living man can say that I promised anything for his support, or suggested any motive to influence him that was not consistent with his honor and mine. Since I came to the Senate I have tried with unobtrusive industry to win the respect of my fellow senators, and I may say to an old friend, with fair success, I think.[5]

As a Republican state leader and the people's representative in the Senate, Harrison knew that he faced the difficult task of party reform in Indiana; he did face it, though not as squarely as other, more ardent statesmen. Even personal friends who shared Harrison's political views found fault with the Senator's indirect methods of opposing political rascality. "Too quiet . . . you get no credit for it . . . you are unjustly suspected of having fellowship with the workers of iniquity, because they claim you as their friend."[6] Some branded as "corrupt and extravagant" the Marion County and the Indianapolis city governments, but this indictment Harrison refused to consider until he had been provided with a "bill of particulars."

As to the complaints that national politics had sunk to a disgraceful level, he replied realistically:

I am, as you know, ready to cooperate in the most effective way for the improvement of political methods and morals. But I do not hope to rid our party of all but the Saints while we are in control of the office.

---

[3] Harrison to Fishback, April 29, 1882, (L.C.), Vol. 11.
[4] Harrison to Robert S. Taylor, January 5, 1882, ibid.
[5] Harrison to Fishback, April 29, 1882, ibid. This letter affords a rare insight into the Senator's views on practical politics.
[6] William P. Fishback to General Harrison, April 26, 1882, ibid.

When it came to practical politics, he confesssed a preference for expediency in some matters, and a taste for compromise. "I haven't a good stomach for a 'row.' . . . There are many things in political life exceedingly distasteful to me . . . I find it only possible many times to do second or third best . . . instead of the first as I would like." [7]

Harrison returned to Washington with optimism. Conscious that he had mended some political fences back home, he was also aware that Carrie's charm would make the expected "afternoon receptions" more a pleasure than a duty. As for Mamie, she had congratulated herself that their position only required them to make "the *first calls* on the old Senators, & the Judges & the President."

When Harrison answered the Senate roll call on December 6, 1881, he began twenty years of national service, ten in Washington and ten as a private citizen. As Lord Bryce observed, the Senate contained many men of great wealth.[8] An increasing number were senators because they were rich; a few were rich because they were senators; in the remaining cases, the same talents that had won success in law or commerce had also brought their possessor to the top in politics. Benjamin Harrison fitted into this third category, for until 1882 he had been considered merely a "capable Hoosier rather than a national figure." [9] Now, with his foot on the first rung to national fame, he had the great advantage of a large, friendly acquaintance in both parties. After a few months Harrison, with service on some five committees, found the Senate a congenial arena in which to exercise his already sharpened legal talents. He learned early that Republican leaders ran most sessions without serious recourse to floor debates. The real business of the nation was conducted in the less formal atmosphere of the committee room. Here Harrison formed close relations with a small but powerful group with all of whom he became fast friends.

[7] Harrison to Fishback, April 29, 1882, *ibid.*

[8] Richard N. Current, *Pine Logs and Politics: A Life of Philetus Sawyer*, p. 195, points out: "From Nevada hailed James G. Fair, 'Bonanza Fair,' the wealthiest of them all; he had extracted a fortune of thirty millions from the silver mines." Others included Leland Stanford, builder of the Central Pacific; Senator Joseph E. Brown, large stockholder in southern railroads; Don Cameron and Matt Quay, who stood for the Pennsylvania Railroad and Standard Oil; and Aldrich of Rhode Island, champion of corporate interests.

[9] New York *Mail and Express*, March 14, 1901.

This coterie, known in political circles as the "School of Philosophy Club," conspired to control the mechanism of government. Perhaps the most constructive of the "Philosophers" was Senator Orville Platt of Connecticut, noted as a "creator and a builder." [10] Another important member was William Boyd Allison, the Hawkeye, whose diplomacy enabled him to soothe ruffled feelings and to reconcile party differences.[11] Eugene Hale, the freshman senator from Maine, represented an aggressive element in the group. Likewise included was Major General William Joyce Sewell, a novice senator from New Jersey and a respected railroader. His friendship for Harrison extended beyond Washington to the marshes of lower New Jersey where they both enjoyed duckshooting.[12] Still another first-term senator, Nelson W. Aldrich of Rhode Island, successor to the late Senator Burnside, was destined within a few years to become leader of this select company of legislators. He and Harrison formed an immediate and lasting friendship based on mutual admiration. Aldrich's biographer states that the man from Rhode Island had much in common with his Hoosier comrade:

Both were natural aristocrats, both were instinctively in opposition to the crowd, both were firm, quiet, unexcitable, without the qualities that captivate men in the mass. Both lacked and both despised all the arts of the rhetorician, the mere orator, and the demagogue. Each was predestined to unpopularity and each was indifferent to the fact.[13]

Perhaps their mutual respect and admiration can also be explained as an attraction of opposites. On the one hand, the six-foot Aldrich's steel eyes, powerful jaw, projecting chin, and firm mouth proclaimed a dominant personality.[14] Harrison, on the other hand, short and with a pronounced tendency to rotundity, remained the painstaking, detail-minded lawyer who could electrify a crowd but otherwise, strangely enough, lacked personal magnetism. Rather it was his "poise, characterized by rugged honesty and political conservatism" that made Senator Harrison

---

[10] Claude G. Bowers, *Beveridge and the Progressive Era,* p. 313.

[11] Professor Leland Sage has authored the definitive biography of *William Boyd Allison: A Study in Practical Politics,* and has generously shared many important items with the author.

[12] Norwich (Conn.) *Record,* March 21, 1901.

[13] A memorandum by Nicholas Murray Butler in the Aldrich MSS; also Nathaniel Wright Stephenson, *Nelson W. Aldrich: A Leader in American Politics,* pp. 68–69.

[14] O. O. Stealey, *130 Pen Pictures of Live Men,* pp. 26 ff. See also Bowers, *op. cit.,* p. 313.

"loved by his party and personal friends and hated by his political opponents." [15] His contemporaries apparently held no middle ground in his regard. They either liked and admired Harrison, or they ignored him.

In the early 1880's, one of the major national problems facing political leaders was an unprecedented surplus in the Treasury. As Harrison observed, "the debt, under which the nation groaned, has become a plaything." [16] He was definitely aware that the accumulations of enormous revenues in the Treasury invited "all sorts of jobbery and official rascality." Even with the question of "grab" set aside, the country's sound financial situation prompted many constituents to ask, "how shall the pudding be divided?" [17] Potential log-rolling schemes, including tariff legislation, railroad and other grants were geared, as the public suspected, to take the money out of the pockets of one man and put it into the pockets of another.

Several major national policies hinged on the surplus, but the one which most interested Harrison as an old soldier was a more liberal pension policy for Civil War veterans. In his eyes "the fellowship of war" extended beyond state lines. This was no time, he declared, "to use an apothecary's scale to weigh the rewards of men who saved the country." [18] Such practical interest in veterans' welfare endeared Harrison to many Grand Army organizations.[19] Advised by "Pink" Fishback, his former law partner, that the "abuses of the Pension Law as administered by Dudley are simply scandalous," [20] Senator Harrison demanded evidence, writing tersely: "I do not know of any facts impeaching Dudley's management of the Pension Office or his integrity. If you do, you ought not to withhold them.", [21] The requested evidence was not

[15] Kansas City (Mo.) *Times* and the Atlanta *Journal*, March 14, 1901.
[16] *Journal*, August 30, 1882.
[17] W. P. Fishback to General Harrison, May 4, 1882, (L.C.), Vol. 11.
[18] *Report of the Benjamin Harrison Memorial Commission* (77th Cong., 1st Sess., House Doc. No. 154), p. 145.
[19] Mary Dearing, *Veterans in Politics*, pp. 268-307.
[20] Fishback to Harrison, April 26, 1882, (L.C.), Vol. 11.
[21] Harrison to Fishback, April 29, 1882, *ibid*. Charles Latham, Jr., "Benjamin Harrison in the Senate, 1881-1887," p. 47, suggests that Harrison's espousal of "Dudley is less easy to understand. Perhaps Dudley's political usefulness outweighed his lack of scruples."

given, and Harrison continued to trust his Indiana lieutenant and fellow veteran with a simplicity almost childlike.

The biggest boon to the pension-hungry soldiers had been the Pension Arrears Act of 1878–1879, which by 1885 had cost the government close to two hundred million dollars.[22] In his first regular session as senator, Harrison spoke heatedly against the repeal of this act, urging the Republican party to honor its "profuse and liberal promises" made to Union volunteers. He even stretched his Presbyterian conscience by supporting a private bill to relieve a veteran discharged for drunkenness in 1878. His alcoholism, the Senator argued, had been caused by the stress and strain of military service.[23]

This was just the beginning. As a member of the Military Committee during the next six years, Harrison introduced 101 special pension and relief bills. The record shows no important instance where he ever blocked a pension grant. On the contrary, Harrison's devotion to his fellow veterans led him to father legislation during the 49th Congress that resulted in the more than liberal Service Pension Act, which was later to become law over his own Presidential signature. In the course of his blind determination to aid any and all ex-Union soldiers, Harrison did make some blunders. As the Democratic press was to point out in 1888, some of the bills he sponsored were "so very bad" that President Cleveland was forced to veto them, one of the proposed beneficiaries having been a man who had deserted.[24]

In 1882, Secretary of the Treasury Folger counseled Congress to reduce the surplus by a tariff revision. To this, Senator Harrison gave only halfhearted support. He believed that the Secretary, along with such Democrats as Bayard of Delaware, had become unreasonably excited over the surplus. He agreed in principle with the Democratic contention that "a nation may be crippled in its resources and disabled from performing its just obli-

---

[22] Dearing, *op. cit.*, p. 250. By 1885, the Treasury had paid $179,400,000 under this Act. This sum does not include the numerous claims inspired and paid by the liberal legislation. Dearing's study is solidly based on William H. Glasson, *History of Military Pension Legislation in the United States,* chap. 5, "Civil War Pension Legislation, Arrears Act to 1890," pp. 88–107.

[23] *Congressional Record,* 47.1; p. 1013.

[24] *Nation,* 47:45, July 19, 1888. Latham, *op. cit.*, p. 42, assigns the motive that Harrison "underneath [was] a generous, warm-hearted man."

gations by bad management" [25] of the bloated Treasury, but as late as 1884 he saw no "imminent danger." Of the 413 million dollars in the Treasury, some 242 millions were held for the support of gold and silver certificates, while the remaining 141 millions were needed to bolster the 346 million greenbacks then in circulation.[26] A close survey of the *Congressional Record,* 1881–1887, reveals that Senator Harrison supported, as a general rule, measures that either tended to drain off the surplus, or presupposed its bountiful and continued existence. Though he might have had to plead guilty to a charge of overindulgence of veterans, no one ever accused the Indiana senator of any spending sprees.

In the 47th Congress, tariff talk filled the Senate Chamber. Harrison was among those who voted for the establishment of a nine-man Tariff Commission, for, like many other legislators, he "did not have time to give to intricate tariff problems." [27] This is not to say that he had joined the ranks of those unenlightened politicians who had asked during the 1880 campaign, "Who is Tariff and why is he for revenue only?" [28] Quite the contrary. "Tariff and encouragement to American industry" was in his blood. In 1840, it had been one of the campaign slogans of "Old Tippecanoe," his grandfather, and Harrison followed the question closely from the passage of the revised Morrill Tariff in 1864 until the Dawes Act of 1872. He approved only that type tariff that protected home industry. From the time of the Garfield campaign until his death, Harrison stood on protection ground. When free traders claimed that protection failed to help appreciably the wool, iron, and shipbuilding industries, their arguments left Harrison unconvinced. He likewise refused to believe that the stiff tariff on raw materials had proved hurtful to home industry. To the charge that the protective tariff forced up domestic prices, Harrison replied that he could never be in "sympathy with this demand for cheaper coats, which seems . . . necessarily to involve a cheaper man and woman under the coat." [29]

25 *Journal,* September 26, 1884.
26 Latham, *op. cit.,* pp. 25–28.
27 C. C. Tansill, *Congressional Career of Thomas F. Bayard,* p. 289.
28 Albert B. Paine, *Thomas Nast: His Period and His Pictures,* p. 438.
29 *Report of the Benjamin Harrison Memorial Commission,* p. 141. In 1887, during an Indianapolis speech given on December 20, Harrison said: "I think I saw the other day, in one of our Indianapolis papers, a good overcoat advertised for $1.87,

Free trade advocates further confronted Harrison with the argument that protection to industry in his native Indiana had served not only to mulct the consumer but to make manufacturing a parasite on agriculture. State statistics, Harrison could retort, told an entirely different story. When he assumed his Senate seat in 1882, Indiana's agricultural produce totaled more than $153,847,961, with six million acres of wheat and corn accounting for two-thirds of the total value.[30] The total product continued to rise under the protective tariff. In the same year, Indiana ranked fourth in national coal production, and manufacturing had advanced along parallel lines. More than 12,000 establishments produced $167,067,443 worth of manufactured articles. It seemed strange to Harrison that Indiana Democrats would declare, in their 1882 convention, that they stood for "a revision of the present unjust tariff," especially when Senator Voorhees, Harrison's Democratic colleague, had publicly stated: "I stand here declaring that I am a protectionist for every interest which I am sent here by my constituents to protect."[31]

Throughout his senatorial career, Harrison was firmly convinced that the protective tariff had accomplished three things: the stimulation of an already growing industrialism, the amelioration of American working conditions, and an impetus to the immigration of workers from abroad. In 1883, he told a cheering audience of Iowa farmers that "every honest and intelligent advocate of free trade must admit that if we abandon our system of protective duties, the wages of labor must be reduced."[32] Political overtones can be detected in Senator Harrison's defense of the protective tariff. He often highlighted the fact that industries build up our cities "and the cities cannot wall in the influences

---

and it must be a pretty mean man that wants to get one for a dollar . . . whenever the market price is so low that the man or woman who makes the article cannot get a fair living out of making it, it is too low." Lew Wallace, *Life of Gen. Ben Harrison*, p. 295.

[30] *Appleton's Annual Cyclopedia, 1882*, pp. 420 ff. After wheat and corn the Hoosier farmer produced oats, rye, and barley in great quantity. Statistics showed hay, tobacco, peaches, and potatoes on the increase between 1881 and 1887.

[31] Wallace, *op. cit.*, p. 291. Voorhees made this remark on February 27, 1883, in debate with Senator Zebulon Vance.

[32] *Iowa State Register*, October 22, 1883. Although 1879–1881 were boom years, Harrison's argument ignores the depressions of 1882 and 1884, when the farmers and laborers of his own state sustained heavy losses. See William G. Carleton, "The Money Question in Indiana Politics, 1865–1890," *Indiana Magazine of History*, 42 (1946), 145–46.

which enhance the value of property. They are not free cities, but must pay tribute to the outlying fields and to the farmer who tills them." Then, eyeing the manufacturer, he would say: "If the tariff were lowered, our mills would close and English goods would come in, but there would be less goods all around; there would be more demand for the goods; the price would go up; and we would be just as badly off as we were before, except that the Englishman would have all the business, and our workers would be unemployed." [33]

Despite these fixed ideas on the necessity of a protective tariff, Harrison particularly welcomed the establishment of a nine-man Tariff Commission. His work day, which frequently extended into the night, scarcely permitted a close study of rates and the constantly changing conditions of industry and trade. He complained to "Cousin Mag" that life in Washington

is slavish to those who feel like conscientiously trying to do their duty. You know I used to be a hard worker at home but I usually had my evenings for rest. Here I have no time out of bed that is my own, and bed time is very late, which you know must be a grief to me.[34]

The Tariff Commission reported to the 47th Congress during its short session. President Arthur, having studied its recommendations, asked for new legislation to effect substantial reductions in duties on cotton, iron, steel, sugar, molasses, silk, wool, and woolen goods. Harrison, with a majority of his Republican colleagues, agreed to a 25 per cent reduction on the items suggested by the President and the Commission. On other items, Senator Harrison was not so amenable. Pressure from home made him cautious and he voted to safeguard the interests of the Hoosier glassworks in New Albany and objected to reducing the duty on jute bags by 10 per cent, maintaining that any rate lower than the current 20 per cent "would put the Indiana baggers out of business." [35] Harrison defended his vote by pointing out other senators who had pursued a similar course when it came to protecting "home" constituents. Was not Sherman successful in raising the schedules on pig iron, wool, and lumber so as to help Buckeye industrialists? [36] Did not

33 Latham, *op. cit.*, p. 30.

34 Harrison to Margaret Peltz, March 29, 1882, Messinger MSS. Harrison voted affirmatively when, by a vote of 39 to 15, the Senate passed the House bill to create the Tariff Commission. See Appleton, *op. cit.*, p. 139.

35 *Congressional Record*, 47.2, p. 2562.

36 Latham, *op. cit.*, p. 33.

Democratic leader Thomas F. Bayard refuse to reduce the tax on matches for those who "were not a light unto themselves?" [37] Yet the bill as it left the Senate was a big step down the free traders' road. In the lower House, however, the parliamentary juggler "Czar Reed" contrived to put the proposed bill into joint conference. The net result satisfied the New England protectionists because it made only slight concessions to the public demand for a more moderate tariff system.[38] Harrison voted for this revised bill, which became law by a strictly party vote of 32 to 31.

In theory, Harrison appeared willing to solve the problem of surplus by reducing tariff schedules; yet in practice he supported his party's demand for almost universal protection. There still remained another way: stop the inflow of taxes into an over-full treasury. Consequently he supported the Kelley Bill, which aimed at the reduction of internal revenue by $23,000,000. It proposed stripping taxes down to the barest essentials in order to reduce the surplus. "In my opinion," Harrison told his constituents, "whiskey and tobacco should be the last on the list from which the hand of the tax-gatherer is lifted . . . these articles are luxuries." [39] The Senator would not say whether by "luxuries" he meant these items were either good or bad. "I dodge that question." Harrison himself was known as a "regular smoker" to the Indianapolis dealer who supplied him with mild, small cigars by the hundreds.[40] His favorite brand was the Daniel Webster, although he would smoke any clear Havana after dinner, "imported or domestic."

In the Senate debate which followed introduction of the bill, Harrison exercised his talent for debate by challenging his Democratic fellow Hoosier, Voorhees. Speaking more than an hour, he achieved what has been enthusiastically termed "one of the most brilliant and masterly efforts ever made on the floor of the Sen-

[37] *Journal,* August 30, 1882.

[38] F. W. Taussig, *Tariff History of the U.S.,* pp. 249 ff., observes that the actual reductions were 1) where the duty was still high enough to keep out foreign goods, or 2) where without duty domestic manufacturers could control the domestic market.

[39] *Journal,* August 30, 1882. Harrison argued that unless the internal revenue taxes were reduced, the evil of an overfull treasury would be perpetuated.

[40] St. Louis *Post-Dispatch,* July 1, 1888, a clipping in Benjamin Harrison Scrapbooks, (L.C.), Vol. 6, p. 57. Charles F. Meyer (15–17 N. Pennsylvania) testified that the Senator was a moderate smoker but paid $8 to $11 for Havanas, which he bought by the hundreds.

ate." [41] During his remarks, he coined a phrase to describe "the perverse disposition to oppose everything proposed by" Republicans as the "strawberry mark" by which one can always identify a Democrat. After one full session in Washington, the Indiana senator was ready to make political capital by dismissing the opposition as "public scolds" who

since 1860 have sat in the cage to which public opinion consigned them, chattering like enraged parrots, while the work of saving and regenerating a constitution and a country which they had torn, was going on outside; or, to change the figure they are discredited witnesses who for twenty years have been annually approaching the great inquest of the country with their accusations, and instead of being accepted in the witness box have been put in the dock.[42]

Periodic scolding of the opposition may have pleased a great majority of the Republicans in Indiana but some thinkers back home took Harrison to task for failure to lead a reform movement within the party. The Senator had sponsored John C. New for the post of Assistant Secretary of the Treasury. Unfortunately one of the Senator's closest friends regarded New as "a damned fraud." [43] Fishback, too, warned that the men who composed the Republican ranks would not stay with a party "which shows its unwillingness or confesses its inability to denounce and punish or at least discountenance its rascals and disreputable men." The Senator's former law partner made it painfully clear that, while "I do not hold you responsible for these things," still "if you serve out your term without making it distinctly apparent that you hate thievery . . . and prefer the 'flavor of honesty' and purity of private life to men of bad morals and sullied integrity, I have made a great mistake in my estimate of your character." The epistle ended on a conciliatory note: "I am persuaded of better things of you . . . you are a greater man than you think. You are in the Senate because of your character and ability." [44]

Harrison gave evidence of this ability midway through the session when a bill for the improvement of the Mississippi River

[41] James P. Boyd, *Life and Public Services of Benjamin Harrison*, p. 75. See also *Congressional Record*, 47.1, pp. 6247–49.

[42] *Journal*, August 30, 1882.

[43] Murat Halstead to Benjamin Harrison, February 11, 1882, (L.C.), Vol. 11.

[44] Fishback to Harrison, May 4, 1882, (L.C.), Vol. 11. In his previous letter of April 26, 1882, Fishback had cautioned Harrison that he was not fully employing his opportunity for influence.

came before the Senate. Here, his experience as a River Commissioner put him on familiar ground. He lost no time in drawing a sharp line between appropriations for land reclamation and appropriations for river improvement. The former, he argued, were outside the scope of Congressional power. In two exhaustive speeches on "The Levee Question," one on April 18 and the second on April 21, 1882, Harrison outlined precisely his unpopular position:

The improvement of the navigation of the Mississippi River is clearly a national matter, both as to jurisdiction over the subject and as to the benefits to be obtained. The admiralty control of the United States unquestionably extends over the entire navigable length of the river and over the vessels that sail upon it. This jurisdiction has been repeatedly asserted by the Supreme Court and still more frequently exercised by Congress. It is impregnably entrenched not only in judicial and legislative precedent, but in good reason.[45]

He willingly voted for an appropriation of $15,000,000 to improve navigation on the Mississippi, but with this strict proviso: ". . . no part of the said sum . . . shall be used in the construction or repair of levees for the purpose of preventing injury to lands by overflow, or for any other purpose whatever except as a means of deepening the channels or improving the navigation. . . ." This limitation was aimed at preventing the government from entering into the land reclamation business. Why? Under the Constitution, Harrison argued, Congress had no power to appropriate money for the reclamation of land. On the other hand, the Constitution did grant to the government admiralty control over the river. The Indiana Senator made it clear that he in no way objected to the erection of levees which might *incidentally* serve to reclaim land. He felt, however, that it was an unconstitutional use of public money, when and if levees were erected under the Admiralty clause for the *express purpose* of reclaiming land. Here was the nub of the question. Did Congress enjoy the wide power to appropriate funds to reclaim lands held by individual owners? In Harrison's view, the answer was a clear no.

The proposed appropriation to improve the Mississippi "in an unrestricted fashion" amounted, he told the Senate,

[45] Edward McPherson, *Handbook for Politics, 1882*, pp. 129–130. It should be noted that Harrison's two speeches were based on his own minority report as a member of the River Commission.

to saying that we have here as Congressmen the right to donate money to fence men's farms, to build their houses, to enrich them in any way we please, and so an act to appropriate $10,000 to fence John Smith's farm would be a constitutional and valid law.

Harrison maintained that "we could not float out of the Treasury on the tide of our sympathies, probably fifty million dollars" for a levee system nonessential to channel improvements.[46] The political tinge to the question was immediately evident. The Constitution, Harrison warned, would not permit the South, impoverished though it was, to foist upon the nation the state duty of protecting alluvial lands.

Immediately, Senator George Vest of Missouri and Senator Augustus Garland of Arkansas attacked Harrison. They accused him of "waving the bloody shirt" and asked him how he justified his previous vote to give $150,000 to flood sufferers in the light of his refusal to grant $15,000,000 for levees.

In reply, Harrison stated that he did not attack the levee construction in a spirit of bitterness against the South. The controlling question concerned river improvement. To the charge of inconsistency in voting flood relief Harrison pleaded guilty. "Justification flowed from the emotional well of his sympathetic heart." The question was how big was the N in Nation and how large the S in State. At this point the constitutional doctrine of John C. Calhoun was debated. Harrison cited the apostle of the states rights doctrine to prove that the South Carolinian himself believed that the federal government possessed no legal power to grant money for the reclamation of alluvial land held by individual owners.

On one plan only would Harrison yield his constitutional position: let there be joint participation by nation, state, and private individuals, each holding an interest in the land to be reclaimed. To this Senator Vest would not agree. "In less than fifty years," he prophesied, "the wonder will be that any senator from a sovereign state ever stood on this floor and questioned the right and duty of the National Government . . . to reclaim that magnificent alluvial territory from the ravages and desolations created by the property of the Government itself." History has underwritten Vest's position. Even in 1882 many people failed to see how Harrison could vote to protect industries and at the same time

46 Harrison's Senate speech, April 21, 1882. *Congressional Record*, 47.1, pp. 2983–88

scruple in appropriating public funds to protect land. At the time, Harrison made his own defense:

. . . I believe it is entirely possible and altogether fair that these Southern states should by some method levy a tax for this purpose, and that there are methods by which we may co-operate with them and aid them in connection with the improvement of the river that will greatly lessen the cost of this work to them. . . . It is possible for those states to inaugurate a system of legislation by which the help of the General Government may in some proper way be given to them, and at the same time not to put upon the Public Treasury and the tax-payers of the whole country the entire burden of building a system of works that is intended to reclaim their own lands.[47]

Harrison's minority position received newspaper support in Indiana and brought congratulations from his friend Fishback: "What is needed now in public life is men who say the right thing because it is the right thing . . . and who are known as the inveterate foes of scoundrelism in or out of the party."[48] A week later "Pink" added a further accolade: "The Levee scheme has, I think,. been beaten in argument. You absolutely left . . . Garland nothing to say. You have made a line of demarcation for land reclamation and protection outside the scope of congressional power for river improvement. Bye and bye, the thing will appear in some log-rolling scheme for dividing the surplus revenue."[49]

[47] Latham, op. cit., p. 74, and the Congressional Record, 47.1, pp. 3134–38.
[48] Fishback to Harrison, April 26, 1882, (L.C.), Vol. 11.
[49] Ibid., May 4, 1882.

CHAPTER XIV

Problems of a Senator

A T THE END of the first session of the 47th Congress, patronage problems still plagued Harrison. Yet he had no one but himself to blame. Having announced a policy of favoritism for veterans, their pleas quickly clogged his file on appointments. Known as "a prince in Indiana," Harrison strove desperately to avoid becoming "a scrub in Washington." [1] Also, as he soon discovered, his Indiana appointments were raising a storm of criticism back home. Particularly trying was the selection of Hoosier postmasters, where the skirmishing for office sent nine out of ten applicants away disgruntled. Acrimonious Republicans in Fort Wayne spoke out against their senator, charging that his appointments were a series of "egregious blunders." [2] His friends denied this, but Harrison continued to feel the pressure in Washington. [3]

Old friends of President William Henry Harrison and cronies of John Scott Harrison descended upon the junior Senator in droves. For the most part penniless, they sought any kind of employment. Typical was elderly Sam Morrison who had been a drillmaster under "Old Tippecanoe." Orphaned at seven and crippled at twelve, Morrison was a self-educated civil engineer and surveyor, who had helped Grant plan the capture of Vicksburg. [4] Now unemployed, he begged Harrison to help him obtain work as a printer. In this case, the Senator was successful. Almost at once, scores of disappointed office-seekers cried out their resentment. [5]

---

[1] W. H. H. Miller to D. S. Alexander, April 27, 1882, W. H. H. Miller Letterbooks.
[2] Harry Sempler to R. S. Taylor, January 8, 1882, R. S. Taylor MSS, (Indiana State Library). "So far as Senator Harrison committing such egregious blunders, as some Ft. Wayne papers would like to have us believe, I fail to see wherein they lie; that he errs is but to say that he is human."
[3] *Ibid.,* and Harrison to Taylor, January 14, 1882, (L.C.), Vol. 11. This volume and Volume 12 contain countless letters on Post Office matters.
[4] Morrison to Harrison, March 15, 1882; December 1, 1882, *ibid.,* Vols. 11 and 12.
[5] *Ibid.*

Such reactions fired Harrison's interest in the growing problem of civil service reform. Ever since Garfield's death, Harrison had realized the evils inherent in the spoils system, characterized by Fishback as "a veritable devil in the Republican party." [6] Still, he attempted to steer a safe course between the Sunday School and the penitentiary in the matter of appointments.

Fitness for office and integrity, coupled with loyal party service, were the standards against which he tried to measure his army of applicants.

Halfway through the session, Harrison returned to Indianapolis for a brief speech in which he told his audience: "I want to assure you tonight that I am an advocate of Civil Service Reform." [7] Reformers found the mild word "advocate" hard to swallow. Harrison, they felt, was a follower of the movement rather than a pioneer in it. After all, he had been raised in the atmosphere of practical Hoosier politics, where the spoils system reigned. When he entered the Senate, he had insisted that in the matter of Indiana appointments the President honor the celebrated rule of senatorial courtesy. To insure the worthiest men of offices, Harrison had relied upon the discretion and good judgment of a close circle of friends in the four corners of the state. He therefore used, but sincerely believed that he did not abuse, the spoils system. To him it was a distasteful necessity and he voiced his real feelings on the subject in August, 1882:

My brief experience at Washington has led me often to utter the wish with an emphasis that I do not often use that I might be forever relieved of any connection with the distribution of public patronage. I covet for myself the free and unpurchased support of my fellow-citizens, and long to be able to give my time and energy solely to . . . public affairs. [8]

Before debate began on the Pendleton Bill—now a landmark in the crusade for an airtight civil service—Harrison played a singularly unimpressive rôle in the reform movement. One of the national reform agitators, E. P. Wheeler, regarded Harrison's course

6 Fishback to Harrison, May 4, 1882, *ibid.*, Vol. 11.

7 *Journal*, August 30, 1882. See also William D. Foulke, *Fighting the Spoilsmen*, p. 287.

8 *Journal*, August 30, 1882.

in the Senate as that of an "inveterate spoilsman." [9] Carl Schurz confirmed this, maintaining that neither Harrison's "profession nor his antecedents stamp him as a man who would resist the demands of the influential politicians of his party." [10] Yet after President Arthur, in his second annual Message in December, 1882, insisted that legislation for civil service reform "should no longer be postponed," Senator Harrison voted for the Bill, which passed the Senate and became law in January, 1883. Though he took only a minor part in the debate, he spoke out strongly against a proposed amendment forbidding federal employees to contribute to party campaign funds.[11] Harrison contended that once a man had earned his pay from the government, he had a natural right to use it for any legitimate purpose whatsoever. The fact that an individual worked for the government, argued Harrison, should not deprive him of the liberty to use his own property.[12] This argument, which he was to use again in defending a case before the Supreme Court, helped defeat the amendment.

There were times when Harrison saw fit to depart from the party line and cast his vote with the minority. The Chinese Exclusion Bill of 1882 was such a case. It was a statesman's answer to the "hoodlums' cry that 'the Chink' must go." [13] Controversy had centered about the increasing influx of Chinese laborers into California. After the gold rush of 1849, that state's demand for cheap labor had been largely satisfied by an influx of Chinese immigrants. Later, the construction of transcontinental railroads made this coolie labor even more welcome. During this "era of good feeling" Anson Burlingame, somewhat of a visionary "whose enthusiasm

---

[9] E. P. Wheeler, *Sixty Years of American Life*, p. 138.

[10] Carl Schurz, *Speeches, Correspondence, Political Papers, IV*, 513.

[11] Ellis P. Oberholtzer, *The United States Since the Civil War*, I, 152. The Act, in its final form, forbade the levying of political campaign assessments on federal officeholders and protected the latter against ouster for failure to make such contributions.

[12] *Congressional Record*, 47.2, p. 639. See Carl Russell Fish, *The Civil Service and the Patronage*, pp. 223–37. Chapter 10, "Period of Civil Service Reform, 1865–1901," pp. 209–28, is particularly valuable.

[13] E. G. Hay to Thomas M. Browne, March [?], 1882, Eugene Gano Hay MSS, Vol. 3, No. 534. Hay compared it to the slavery issue and warned the Indiana Congressman against taking the same stand as the proslavery men of the ante-bellum days. He said it was ridiculous to say that a protectionist in order to be consistent must be an opponent of Chinese immigration. A man's liberty and right to immigration should not be equated with the rights of trade and manufacture.

for Chinese culture ran away with his political judgment," [14] concluded a treaty with China. Approved by the Senate in 1868, this
guaranteed the rights of Americans in China while providing that
Chinese subjects visiting or residing in the United States should
enjoy the same privileges, immunities, and exemptions in respect
to travel and residence as may be enjoyed by the citizens or subjects
of the most-favored nation. One authority estimates that by 1876
approximately one quarter of a million Chinese had come to the
States. Of these, nearly 100,000 resided and worked in California,
accounting for almost ten per cent of the state's population.[15]

As armies of white labor came from the East, the welcome for
Chinese labor ceased. The coolie, however, proved too strong a
competitor, and this added fuel to the fire of anti-Chinese sentiment on the Pacific Coast. Soon states passed discriminatory laws,
but these were nullified by the federal courts. The issue quickly
became a political football to be bounced around the halls of
Congress. In 1879, Congress tried to abrogate the Burlingame
Treaty by making mandatory the registration of Chinese immigrants and by restricting the number who could come to the States
in one ship. President Hayes vetoed this action on the ground
that Congress had exceeded its constitutional powers by repudi-
ating the "honorable contracts of the nation." [16] This merely delayed matters until a new pact could be concluded with China.
On November 17, 1880, the new treaty went into effect, pleasing
the Pacific Coast. The American Government now claimed the
right to "regulate, limit or suspend" the entry of Chinese laborers
into the United States, although it could not "absolutely prohibit"
such entry. The treaty further specified that the "limitation or
suspension" must be reasonable.[17]

A hassle over interpretation of the treaty terms soon sparked

[14] Charles C. Tansill, *The Congressional Career of Thomas F. Bayard*, p. 302.
[15] Oberholtzer, *op. cit.*, IV, 215. For a satisfactory monographic account of the
bases for anti-Chinese sentiment in California and that state's agitation for restriction and exclusion, see Elmer C. Sandmeyer, *The Anti-Chinese Movement in
California*, pp. 9–111.
[16] Oberholtzer, *op. cit.*, IV, 215.
[17] As Tansill, *op. cit.*, p. 301, points out, "it was apparent that the Chinese Government thought that it had made an important concession in granting to the United
States the right to regulate but not to prohibit the entry of Chinese laborers, a
term which included both artisans and unskilled laborers." For a detailed statement
of the diplomatic and public documents surrounding this treaty, Paul Hibbert
Clyde, *United States Policy Toward China*, chap. 22, "Controlling Chinese Immigration, 1880–1894," pp. 140–58, has arranged and selected the material.

a debate in both Houses of Congress. Compromise resulted and a bill was passed restricting Chinese immigration for a period of twenty years. Harrison, engaged in a Congressional investigation at the time, took no part in the debate and did not vote.[18] President Arthur vetoed the bill on four counts,[19] forcing the Senate to reconsider its terms. Harrison made an unsuccessful attempt to refer the bill, the Presidential veto, and all other papers to the Committee on Foreign Relations. He then voted against the repassage of the bill, which fell short of the necessary two-thirds majority. He had parted company with a majority of his Republican colleagues, and he made his views clear in the subsequent debates on a new anti-Chinese bill which had passed the House by the overwhelming vote of 203 to 37.

Harrison, it appears, had no objection to the legislation in principle. But he entertained constitutional scruples on one section which overruled the 1880 Treaty. Section 15, Harrison argued, used the word "laborers." He insisted that this term must be understood in precisely the same way as it had been when incorporated into the treaty:

I take it that it is not in the power of Congress to enlarge the meaning of that word. Whatever it meant in the treaty it would mean the same thing as used in the law; we cannot make it mean more than that. Therefore, why not let it stand in the law as in the treaty, and let the use of that word include what it will?

LaFayette Grover, a Democrat from Oregon, and John Franklin Miller, a Republican from California, disputed Harrison's contention by declaring that the Commissioners who had drawn the bill had already agreed that the word "laborers" as used in the treaty meant the same thing in their bill. Harrison, singularly unconvinced by this, proceeded to tell the Senate a personal experience which explained his opposition:

It reminds me of a will case that I was once trying when the lawyer who drew the will was on the other side. There was a great deal of controversy about its meaning, and he undertook to settle it by saying that he wrote the will and knew what it meant. It seems to me that is a parallel case with our Commissioners undertaking to say what the word means.[20]

18 *Congressional Record*, 47.1, March 9, 1882. Harrison was engaged, with Sewell of New Jersey and Hampton of South Carolina, in an investigation of the Soldiers' Home.

19 Veto message of April 4, 1882, J. D. Richardson, *A Compilation of the Messages and Papers of the Presidents*, VIII, 112–18. See also *Sentinel*, April 6, 1882.

20 *Congressional Record*, 47.1, p. 3359.

Harrison was adamant. He held that the bill abrogated the treaty, and he voted against it. When the bill passed by a party vote of 32 to 15, Harrison's stand was severely criticized in the far-Western states, and its ghost was to haunt him in 1888 during his Presidential campaign. Yet he never retracted his position. On the contrary, he let his desire to restrict Chinese laborers from the Pacific Coast be known far and wide. He held an unalterable belief in John Marshall's decision that a treaty is, in its nature, a contract between two nations, not a legislative act.[21] As such, he contended, it could not be distorted by act of Congress. His vote against the Exclusion Bill did not mean, however, that he was indifferent to the interests of his fellow-citizens on the Pacific Coast. Before he left the Senate in 1887, Harrison helped to steer through the Committee on Foreign Affairs an Exclusion Bill that he believed to be both constitutional and beneficial to American interests.[22]

The Washington winter of 1882 had not been kind to Carrie Harrison, who was frequently reported ill. Only when the traditionally pleasant spring weather reached the capital and the "Parks and Public grounds" became "bright and beautiful" [23] again did she begin to regain her health and spirits. Mamie had cheerfully assumed the task of companion and nurse to her mother, but the young daughter's interests were divided. She spent much time writing to Bob McKee, her Indianapolis beau. Russell, too, was involved in romance and was a frequent visitor at his parents' Vermont Avenue boarding home, which was but a short distance from the residence of Nebraska's Senator Alvin P. Saunders on 14th and G Streets. Here lived Mary ("May") Saunders, "a charming blonde," whose popularity as the current "Belle of Washington" made Russell understandably jealous.[24] Montana was a long

[21] A more detailed account of Harrison's part in voting against the Exclusion Bill of 1882 is given by his campaign biographer, Lew Wallace, *Life of Gen. Ben Harrison*, pp. 336–48.

[22] In House Doc. No. 154 (77th Cong., 1st Sess.), p. 134, it is observed that Harrison had taken this unpopular stand on Chinese immigration because he refused to let the United States lightly repudiate a treaty obligation before the constitutional machinery was put in motion. For a fuller discussion of his restriction and effort at exclusion, see Roy L. Garis, *Immigration Restriction*, pp. 292–96.

[23] Harrison to Margaret Peltz, March 29, 1882, Messinger MSS.

[24] *Journal*, January 11, 1884.

distance from Washington, even for a man not in love—and Russell was.

In spite of the pleasant distraction caused by the sight of his children in love, Harrison was not happy. Carrie's illness and his own hard work in the Committee rooms were wearing him down. "I am worked to death here and am getting right tired of the long session," [25] he wrote his brother Carter. It was the end of May and the legislative mill was due to run until mid-August. The Senator's work was important, but routine. On only one occasion before adjournment did he make the Washington and Indianapolis headlines. His Indiana colleague in the Senate, Daniel W. Voorhees, in an attempt to win some soldier support, had posed as a friend of the veterans. This aroused Harrison to an angry speech, and veterans and friends applauded his efforts. From Charlestown, Indiana, came congratulations "upon your successful *felling* of the 'Tall Sycamore' last week in the Senate . . . you did not hit him a lick amiss." [26] Harrison had pointed out that while the Senate was under Democratic control, Confederate soldiers had been preferred in an 8 to 1 ratio over Union veterans. When Harrison finished his address, which ultimately became a report of the Military Committee, one admirer rejoiced to see Dan Voorhees, the "policy politician," successfully "punctured." He added the hope that Harrison might "have still other opportunities to tear off his borrowed lion's skin." [27]

On August 8, 1882, Congress finally went home for the summer. So did the Harrisons, although Carrie, who had been convalescing at Deer Park, Maryland, arrived at their Delaware Street home before her husband [28] Harrison was in time to preside over the Marion County Republican Convention, held in the Indianapolis Park Theatre. After being elected permanent president, the Senator delivered a brief, partisan speech. He ridiculed the Democrats for not being able to "tell a trade wind from a squall." Indeed, he alleged, "the old Democratic ship had her sails set for opposite winds, . . . and was whirling around on her keel." In a lively fashion, he discussed the usual issues: tariff, woman's suf-

[25] Benjamin Harrison to Carter Harrison, May 21, 1882, (L.C.), Vol. 11.

[26] M. C. Hester to Harrison, July 24, 1882, *ibid.*, Vol. 12. This letter is a bitter indictment against Voorhees as a political turncoat.

[27] *Ibid.*

[28] W. H. H. Miller to Mrs. M. W. Peltz, August 10, 1882, W. H. H. Miller Letterbooks.

frage, and prohibition. Then, quite unexpectedly, a gentleman in
the gallery arose. He identified himself as an Illinois Republican
who believed that "as Indiana goes, so goes the Union." The un-
invited speaker declared that the "Republicans of Illinois wanted
no less a presidential standard-bearer in 1884 than the present
chairman of the convention, Benjamin Harrison." The *Evening
News* reported that "the cheers that followed . . . were terrific"
and the audience saved three of them "for the fellow in the gallery." Stunned but not speechless, Senator Harrison denied that
any "presidential bee was buzzing in his bonnet." History, he
said, had taught him how "fatal the presidential disease was" and
he hoped it "would never catch himself." Despite this protest,
the *News* editorial goodnaturedly warned the Senator to fumigate
himself, since "a touch of the presidential fever . . . is contagious." [29]

Harrison now began a two-and-a-half month political tour
through Indiana, Ohio, and Maine, including a side trip to Boston. During this period the Senator renewed his personal friendship with James G. Blaine, who entertained him lavishly at his
Augusta mansion. Here Harrison arranged for the controversial
Maine Republican to make a few speeches in Indiana,[30] thus
strengthening a bond that was to yield political dividends during
the next ten years.

On the whole, the state elections of 1882 went against the
Republicans. When Harrison returned to Washington for the
new session of Congress, he told the press that "we were all
beaten together," and all should take the blame "until our forces
get into line for the next battle." [31] Questioned as to the possibility of his nomination for President at the next Republican
National Convention, Harrison replied:

I have not at all entertained the idea that such a thing was contemplated, or that it could be desirable in a party point of view. My public
career has been too brief and inconspicuous to make the thought more
than a passing reference of a *friend* (?). The Presidential fever has
blighted the lives of so many of our public men that I have determined
not to expose myself to that contagion.

29 August 12, 1882. The Illinois Republican was identified as H. W. Magee of
Chicago.

30 Harrison to Blaine, September 9, 1882, (L.C.), Vol. 12.

31 G. J. Langsdale to Harrison, November 21, 1882, *ibid.* Harrison had said that
"it is nonsense to try to win a fight with our ranks divided into hostile factions."

The present work is, I think, to heal division, pull the party together, and make some issues about which the intelligence and conscience of the people can rally. When this is done—we will send out for a man who will at least be as strong as the party.[32]

Carrie Harrison's health sank to a new low in January, 1883, and she stayed under doctor's care in New York until the middle of March. Surgery kept her hospitalized and Russell came on from Montana, staying three months at the Metropolitan Club so as to be near his mother during her slow convalescence. Meanwhile Mamie kept house for her father on Vermont Avenue, and commuted to New York on week ends to visit her mother. As often as possible, her father went with her. By Lincoln's Birthday the Senator felt thoroughly depressed. To Cousin Mag he wrote: "Never have I been so busy and so much harassed as during this session. We have been holding sessions 10 or 12 hours a day, and have never had a single Sat. even for rest. I have had to run back and forth to New York several times, and above all, in the way of worry, I have had several desperate Post Office fights raging around me. It has been altogether the most trying and disagreeable winter I have ever spent since the war." [33]

While Harrison yearned for the 4th of March and the end of Congress, he kept a close check on legislative trends. In his December, 1882, Message to Congress President Arthur had criticized the existing tariff structure and advocated what Harrison had promised on the stump: a substantial reduction in duties on cotton, iron, steel, sugar, molasses, silk, and wool. When the Tariff Commission reported, it advocated similar reductions.[34] With these recommendations from both the President and the Commission to back him, Harrison set to work to fulfill tariff promises he had made as a freshman senator. This took courage, for he encountered strong opposition from Wharton Barker, Philadelphia industrialist, rich Republican, and self-appointed spokesman for the steel industry. Barker, who had evidenced a keen interest in Harrison's political future, begged the Senator to abandon the tariff bill. In a pointed reply Harrison refused

[32] Harrison to A. V. Dockery, December 7, 1882, ibid. Dockery sent the Senator the following notation: "We now need worse than ever 'to send out for a man' at least as strong as his party."

[33] Harrison to Margaret Peltz, February 12, 1883, Messinger MSS.

[34] Ida Tarbell, The Tariff and Our Times, pp. 102–10.

to do this, although he added a word of comfort: "I think it is still possible to get the bill into such a shape as to save our industrial interests from serious misfortune." He also included some explanation of his support:

I can readily see that if after having done our utmost to revise the tariff, we should fail, without our fault, the situation would be one of political advantage to us. I have felt, however, that we must make it very clear, that we had honestly intended to do the work.[35]

Harrison's observation at this time that "the situation of [the] parties in the Senate is quite unfavorable to the best work" on the subject of tariff [36] was decidedly an understatement. During the last hours of the legislative session, the "mongrel bill of 1883" was finally passed by Congress and received President Arthur's signature.[37] Styled by tariff historian Ida Tarbell "a tariff of abominations," this act, according to Senator John Sherman, "laid the foundation of all the Tariff complications since that time." [38] James G. Blaine, however, spoke in its favor, saying that he felt "very strongly that even an imperfect bill was better than no bill at all." [39]

Harrison left Washington without delay, staying with Carrie in New York until she was strong enough to return with him to Indianapolis. Back in their North Delaware Street home by the end of March, Harrison busied himself with law and some very important political maneuvering. The Senator had had a bad jolt in April. When President Arthur decided to choose his new Postmaster General from Indiana, he had selected Judge Walter Q. Gresham for the post. Since the growing enmity between Harrison

[35] Harrison to Wharton Barker, February 16, 1883, Wharton Barker MSS. Harrison wrote: "I fully realize the gravity of the situation in Congress at this time, but am not able at present to agree with you. . . . We are pledged to tariff revision; the law creating the Tariff Commission implied that, and almost every Senator has personally committed himself to it on the stump. All of our party newspapers have promised it . . . I do not see how we can abandon the Tariff Bill."

[36] *Ibid.*

[37] Tansill, *op. cit.,* p. 308.

[38] Tarbell, *op. cit.,* p. 131; and John Sherman, *An Autobiography: Forty Years in House, Senate and Cabinet,* p. 671.

[39] Royal Cortissoz, *Life of Whitelaw Reid,* II, 82–83. As owner-editor of the powerful New York *Tribune,* Reid, at Blaine's importuning, had sounded several "old fashioned bugle blasts" for protection interests. Reid thought Blaine could go before the country in 1884 with the benefit of having the tariff as an issue. This cemented an already strong friendship.

and Gresham was by now common knowledge, many interpreted this as a direct slap at Indiana's Republican leader. In addition, Arthur had wired Harrison appointing him bearer of the good news to Gresham.[40] This rubbed considerable salt into the Senator's wound. The President was quite aware of the political implications involved and his action served to erect a wall of quiet hostility between the Chief Executive and the Hoosier senator.[41] Harrison complained to his friends that control of state patronage had passed out of his hands. He felt that Postmaster General Gresham would now dictate Indiana appointments. In this the Senator was entirely correct.[42]

As an added bitterness, Harrison soon found himself overruled by another member of Arthur's cabinet. This time it was Secretary of the Treasury Charles W. Folger who struck a blow against the Senator. Over Harrison's protests that it was contrary to the best interests of both state and nation, Folger consolidated the four revenue districts of Indiana into three. In this affair, as well as in the matter of federal appointments, Harrison suffered a serious loss of prestige. Accordingly, when July and torrid temperatures reached Indianapolis, the General willingly talked of taking his family "down to West Baden Springs, a resort, among the hills in the southern part of the state." [43] It was an ideal spot. Carrie could avail herself of the celebrated mineral baths, and Ben himself could find leisure in which to take inventory of his political

40 Arthur to Harrison, April 3, 1883, (L.C.), Vol. 1, Second Series. The *Sentinel,* April 5, 1883, confirms the procedure used by the President, and indicates that Harrison had neither blocked nor supported Gresham. Harrison had told Arthur that Indiana should get the appointment, adding that any good Republican would be satisfactory. An editorial concludes that both Harrison and Gresham were surprised.

41 J. W. Foster to Harrison, April 8, 1883, *ibid.* In this detailed, handwritten letter, marked "confidential," Foster denied that he suggested the Gresham appointment. He said that when President Arthur asked his opinion, "I told him I regarded Gresham well fitted for the position, that I knew him well, we had been schoolmates and comrades in the war and in politics . . . but that I feared there were serious objections to his selection . . . his appointment would not be agreeable to you and possibly impolitic." For a discussion of the reasons behind Gresham's appointment and press reaction to the announcement, see Martha Alice Tyner, "Walter Q. Gresham," *Indiana Magazine of History,* 39 (1943), 297–338. This article is an abridgement of a master's thesis (Indiana University). The postmastership is treated on pp. 309–11.

42 Gresham to Harrison, July 2, 1883, (L.C.), Vol. 1, Second Series; Harrison to Embree, May 5, 1883, Lucius C. Embree MSS, (Indiana State Library).

43 W. H. H. Miller to Rev. Samuel Miller, June 23, 1883, W. H. H. Miller Letterbooks; Harrison to Margaret Peltz, July 21, 1883, Messinger MSS.

stock.[44] For it began to appear to him that he was on the brink of a major setback within his own party.[45]

As the summer of 1883 wore on, Harrison's political rating began to climb once more. Invited to stump Iowa and Ohio in September on behalf of the off-year elections, he canceled all plans for a family vacation in order to prepare his speeches and also to ready himself for an appearance before the United States Supreme Court in October.[46]

Iowa awaited Harrison's coming with interest. The Des Moines *Register* spared few laudatory adjectives in its enthusiasm. It described Harrison as "at once the scholar and the statesman" and "calm, cool, deliberate, polished, candid, dignified and strong." [47]

Encouraged by such a glowing press, Harrison set out for Waterloo, Cedar Rapids, Marshalltown, Charlton, and Des Moines, where he was to deliver five speeches in five days. In the Hawkeye capital, three days before Harrison arrived, the leading news article prophesied: "General Harrison will deliver one of the greatest speeches of the campaign at Moore's Opera House on Friday evening, September 21st." [48]

That Friday night in Des Moines, General Harrison lived up to his advance notice. The "quiet great man of Indiana" delivered a speech "dealing with the tariff nearly in full." "His candor and fair-dealing," wrote a reporter in the next day's Republican press,

carried with it those whom invective can never win—and his ready conversance with public affairs, and with the details of government, and his remarkable use of such knowledge, prove his mastery both in statement and argument. Strong and commanding men alone can pitch discussion on the high plane that he did last night and make political discussion noble in itself.[49]

Democrats in the audience disagreed rather violently with Harrison. At one point, when he was speaking of the war and its issues,

[44] Jesse L. Spann to Harrison, June 28, 1883, (L.C.), Vol. 1, Second Series, indicates careful planning by Harrison for the next state campaign. Harrison's watchwords were: "the law favors the diligent" and "victory is for those who deserve victory."

[45] Thomas M. Browne to Harrison, July 13, 1883, *ibid*.

[46] D. S. Alexander to R. B. Harrison, October 15, 1883, R. B. Harrison MSS, (Terre Haute Collection, Indiana University, Bloomington, Indiana).

[47] As cited in the *Journal*, September 28, 1883.

[48] *Iowa State Register*, September 18, 1883. Ladies were extended a special invitation to attend the address.

[49] *Ibid.*, September 22, 1883.

a hostile voice rang out: "The bloody shirt again!" The General's "eyes flashed fire at the words and springing forward to the footlights, and holding his right hand towards the person interrupting," he thundered out a response "with electrifying power, which swept the audience like a storm":

Yes, the bloody shirt again! I have seen thousands of them on the field of battle wet with the blood of loyal men—and I would a thousand times rather march under the bloody shirt, stained with the life-blood of a Union soldier, than to march under the black flag of treason or the white flag of cowardly compromise.[50]

From Iowa, Harrison went to Ohio for five more speeches, three of them major efforts at Youngstown, Cleveland, and Toledo. Here, as in his other addresses, the Senator emphasized the tariff but also gave much time to the hotly contested question of a civil rights act.[51]

Harrison had been focusing his attention on this latter problem. He had made it his business to be in the Supreme Court when a decision respecting the rights of Negroes was handed down. He afterwards reassured colored citizens that it had not been a question of their losing their legal status or rights as electors, or their privileges in connection with the public schools. The case before the Supreme Court had rather concerned the emotion-packed problems of whether the Negro "shall have the right to sit in the front seat in the theatre," and of how he shall "be treated by the railroads, and of what rights" he shall enjoy "in hotels." On these still burning social questions, Benjamin Harrison took an enlightened position some seventy-five years in advance of his time, saying how he rejoiced to see on his way downtown "numbers of colored boys and girls going to High School along with the white boys and girls." [52]

[50] *Journal*, September 26, 1883, as copied from the Des Moines *Register*. Leland L. Sage, *William Boyd Allison, A Study in Practical Politics*, p. 193, testifies to the help given by General Harrison in the re-election of Senator Allison.

[51] *Journal*, September 17, 1883. Harrison spoke at Youngstown and at Cleveland on successive nights, September 28 and 29; at Toledo on October 1, 1883.

[52] *Ibid.*, October 23, 1883. The Civil Rights Cases (109 U. S. 3) were five cases where Negroes had been refused equal accommodations or privileges allegedly in defiance of the 1875 Civil Rights Act. That act was declared invalid for protecting social rather than political rights. The Court held that the 14th Amendment prohibited invasion by the states of civil rights, but did not protect the invasion of civil rights by individuals unaided by state authorty. Also see *Sentinel*, October 23, 1883, for full text of Harrison's speech on the decision. Made in the spacious audience-room of the Second Baptist Church before a mixed audience, his address counseled obedience to the court and amelioration by future state legislation.

The off-year elections gave the Republicans a majority of four in the United States Senate, and as Harrison prepared to return to Washington, he did so with the knowledge of having won fresh laurels and new friends. No one was more grateful than Iowa's celebrated senator, William Boyd Allison, who thanked Harrison for his "very great service" in his state, and promised "service in return." [53]

In addition to the major problems confronting him as senator, Harrison also faced two personal matters which demanded immediate and serious consideration. Russell had announced himself victorious in love, and his prospective bride, May Saunders, had set the wedding date for January 9, 1884, in Omaha, her home town. The Harrisons now spent much time over the dinner table, happily discussing plans for the journey to Nebraska by Carrie and the General.

The other problem, even more personal to the Senator, and over which he could exercise some control, concerned his own political future. During the Christmas holidays in Indianapolis, Harrison had received a three-page, personal letter from Wharton Barker, the Philadelphia steel magnate. Barker had his eye on the 1884 Presidential election. "It will not be possible to postpone much longer the serious consideration of candidates for the Presidency," he wrote Harrison. It was plain, he went on, "that the selection of Mr. Arthur, like that of Mr. Blaine, would be altogether injudicious. . . . The candidate must be strong in his hold on public questions and he must be unobjectionable in his private character . . . he must command respect alike of the Regulars and the Independents. There are only a few such men in public life at this time. Mr. Edmunds and Mr. Evarts in the East and you in the West." In Barker's view, the nomination

must fall either to you or to Mr. Evarts. In the East Mr. Evarts would command the Independent vote perhaps in some measure better than you would, but in the West he would not nearly be so strong. You have the advantage of position because from your seat in the Senate you can lead the Republican party in the financial struggle now upon us.

After a full discussion of the issues and personalities involved, Barker concluded his letter with the invitation which was causing

[53] W. B. Allison to Harrison, October 16, 1883, (L.C.), Vol. 1, Second Series. "I want to thank you cordially and heartily for what you did for our party and for me especially in the late campaign. . . ."

Harrison serious reflection: "I wish you would come here [Phila-delphia] on your way to Washington to discuss all the questions, political and economic, which are at hand." [54]

The provocative letter stayed on Harrison's desk until New Year's Eve. Finally, on New Year's Day, 1884, he began to draft a reply to his powerful friend. He regretted that a visit to Philadel-phia was presently out of the question. Russell's marriage in Omaha on the 9th and the unveiling of Oliver P. Morton's statue in Indianapolis on the 15th would keep Harrison away from the Senate long beyond the end of the holiday recess. He was there-fore undertaking a written reply. Two rough drafts done in pen-cil, and a final copy give ample evidence of studied phrases and tortured thought.[55] The letter speaks for itself:

Indianapolis,
January 1, 1884

My dear Sir:

Your kind favor of the 27th ult. has been upon my desk for a day or two—but until now I have not found time to answer it. I regard the indisposition to discuss Presidential candidates . . . as favorable to a wise choice and so to party success.

My hope for the party is in a free, unpledged, representative conven-tion. Every friend of mine knows—and the more intimate the better he knows—that I have not allowed a Presidential ambition to get a lodg-ing in my mind. I can understand why Edmunds or Evarts should be thought of, and would give either the heartiest support. My own public life has been brief and inconspicuous. I have never sought occasions for display—or attempted to do anything brilliantly or for applause. A somewhat prosy—perhaps stupid—habit of trying to discharge quietly but to my best, such few public duties as have been cast upon me, is hardly likely to make of me "Presidential timber." But I am sure that you will allow that I may be innocent of this ambition and yet very gıatıfied to you for your too partial judgment of my "chances."

Two things I have settled for myself—first that we must not abandon the protection idea in our tariff duties, and second, that we ought not to set whiskey free. Perhaps the surplus may not be so formidable when we have attended to the obvious building of the navy, and aiding public education etc.[56] I will be frank and say that I have not been able

---

[54] Wharton Barker to Harrison, December 27, 1883, a copy in the Barker MSS. The original is in (L.C.), Vol. 1, Second Series.

[55] Harrison's original drafts are in (L.C.), Vol. 15. The copy received by Barker is in the Wharton Barker MSS, 1882–1892, Harrison Box.

[56] Harrison's original draft included the phrases "liberal appropriations for education" and "putting our great ports in a condition of defense."

to accept the idea of a national tax collected *for the purpose of* distribution to the states. I agree that there is something very attractive in the proposition to lighten the direct local tax burdens by the proceeds of indirect general taxes—in the shape of excise duties.[57]

I am not willing, however, that this second attempt at an interview should fail, and will see that it does not. If you are not in Washington soon, I will run over to Phila. some Friday evening and spend a few hours with you.

Very truly yours,

BENJ. HARRISON

So Harrison entered the New Year of 1884—with caution.

[57] In the rough draft, Harrison had inserted a clause: "Why not have the government use the money, if it is to be collected, for education and instruction and internal improvements—instead of turning it over to the states for those uses?" This section he deleted in the final copy, but it throws a light on his legislative thinking in 1884.

CHAPTER XV

Love and Legislation

OMAHA BUZZED with excitement on the eve of May Saunders' marriage to Russell Harrison. Trinity Cathedral was chosen for what promised to be a brilliant event in Nebraska social circles. Society reporters from the Omaha *Daily Republican*[1] and the Indianapolis *Journal* remarked upon the bride's wedding gown of white satin, lace, plush flowers, and diamonds, artfully designed to complement the charms of a young lady already blessed by nature.[2] Her wedding ring was fashioned of gold taken from Russell's own Montana mine. There were also interesting political overtones in this union of "Nebraska's fair daughter" with the son of a senator whom many thought would be the next President of the United States. The bride's family, too, had a proud political history. Her father, Senator Alvin Saunders, had been territorial governor for Nebraska from 1861 to 1868; friends recalled that a renewal of his commission had been signed by President Lincoln only two or three hours before the grievous episode at Ford's Theatre on the night of April 14, 1865.[3]

[1] On December 23, 1883, the Omaha *Daily Republican* announced the proposed marriage: "a valuable secret, for some days back . . . is now divulged as a delightful little morsel for friendly gossip."

[2] The *Journal*, January 11, 1884, described the wedding gown, "mostly imported from Paris," as a "white satin dress en train [sic], trimmed with point lace, the front embroidered with opal beads and appliquéd with plush flowers, and . . . adorned with diamonds." On December 30, 1883, the Omaha *Daily Republican* had reported that the trousseau "is said to do credit to a cultivated taste and the New York modistes."

[3] In an interview with Marthena Harrison Williams, a daughter of Russell Harrison, and now a resident of the Georgetown section of Washington, D. C., the author was informed that Alvin Saunders' commission was believed to have been the last signed by President Lincoln before he left for the Ford Theatre and his death. The signed paper was discovered on Lincoln's desk the following morning, with several other routine documents left unsigned due to the lateness of the hour.

On January 8, 1884, Russell was given a bachelor's farewell party, which his father was unable to attend. Carrie Harrison was confined to bed in Indianapolis,[4] and the Senator had stayed at her side, both hoping until the last minute that she might recover in time to be at the wedding. Finally, Harrison was forced to leave without her. He and his party boarded a special car on the Vandalia Line, arriving in Omaha in time for the ceremony on the evening of the 9th. With him came Mamie Harrison and Robert McKee, her intended husband, who on this occasion were content to play the respective rôles of bridesmaid and usher. A large crowd assembled in the Cathedral, its nave a sea of white flowers. At the exchange of vows, Russell was "audible and firm," and his bride answered "in a low yet earnest tone." [5] Afterwards, a reception was held at the Hotel Paxton, where guests toasted the bride and groom as they stood under an umbrella of flowers. At the banquet which followed, "salads, oysters, ices, wine jellies, claret punch, and all imaginable dainties and temptations to the hungry or thirsty were plentifully provided."

On the next afternoon, the wedding party, still "in the highest spirits," left for Indianapolis where, in spite of her illness, Carrie Harrison was preparing a second reception. Russell and May enjoyed this first lap of their six weeks' honeymoon in the privacy of the palatial car of the director of the Union Pacific. At the Harrison home, where over five hundred guests had gathered, Carrie welcomed her new daughter-in-law and presented the newlyweds with a set of silver.[6] After the reception, the joyful couple resumed their wedding journey with no specific plans other than to start housekeeping in Helena, Montana, on or about March 1.

The day after the Indianapolis wedding reception was one of lasting importance in Harrison's life. He had delayed his return to the Senate in order to attend the elaborate ceremonies that

[4] Harrison to Howard Cale, January 8, 1884, Howard Cale MSS, (Library of Congress).

[5] Omaha *Daily Republican*, January 10, 11, 1884.

[6] *Ibid.* Carrie Harrison had selected this gift personally while engaged in a New York shopping spree. Carrie Harrison to Russell, December 9, 1883, R. B. Harrison MSS, (Terre Haute Collection). ". . . silver teaspoons, table spoons, forks, and gravy spoon of the handsomest and heaviest pattern. Mamie [Harrison] also got a very heavy soup ladle to match."

would mark the unveiling of Oliver P. Morton's statue, now a landmark in Indiana's capital. A capacity crowd filled the Opera House to hear the eulogy delivered by Colonel R. W. Thompson, "the silver-tongued orator of Indiana." The program did not call for Senator Harrison to make a speech, but the audience did. "Reluctantly" he came forward.

There were two reasons, he began, "why I should not speak to you today. One belongs to you, the other to me." He was unwilling, he said, to detain them "until the shades of evening shall obscure the outline of the loved Governor's face." Also, he felt it was unfitting to match his own unprepared remarks with Thompson's "finished eulogy." Still, there was something in his heart that he would like to express:

It cannot be inappropriate . . . that I should suggest to you this thought . . . that we should build in Indianapolis another monument . . . a stone which will keep fit company with that bronze statue which we are soon to unveil. An impersonal statue, one upon whose base no name shall be written; upon whose summit shall stand the typical soldier of the Union.

Here Harrison recalled that

in one of the Southern states they have built, in a beautiful cemetery, a monument to commemorate the Confederate dead. A soldier stands upon a shaft with his gun reversed and his head bowed over his musket. Not thus shall we typify the soldier of Indiana [cries of No, no]. He shall stand with head erect, with arms at the shoulder, fitly typifying the victory he won . . . we will write no name upon the stone, but the sons and daughters of every soldier who went to battle for the country, as they stand at the base of that monument, may speak of their own dead and be able to say, "That is his monument." [7]

After Harrison's moving remarks, the audience filed out and reassembled in Circle Park. Here Governor Albert Porter and former Governor Conrad Baker mounted a temporary stand erected beside the veiled statue. All eyes, however, were focused on the bright-looking nine-year-old grandson of the celebrated war governor. The youngster, also named Oliver Perry Morton, cut the thread which held together two large American flags. As they fell apart, the bronze effigy of Morton was at last revealed.[8] The band

[7] *Journal,* January 16, 1884, clipping in the Benjamin Harrison Scrapbooks, (L.C.), Vol. 2.
[8] *Journal,* January 16, 1884.

struck up "Hail, Columbia," and another chapter in Indiana history came to a close.[9]

When Harrison boarded the Baltimore and Ohio train for Washington and the resumption of his senatorial duties, he merely expected to represent Indiana in the rôle of delegate-at-large at the Republican National Convention in June.[10] He had expressed no other political aspirations for 1884. In fact, he frequently told his friends that he was not going to Chicago as a Presidential candidate. What he was working for was harmony within the state party and he repeatedly urged close and influential friends to make sure that "the delegation to Chicago will be made up of good men and left entirely free to do the best at the time." It was his plan to draft "uninstructed and unpledged delegates" who would consider party first and candidate second.[11]

Harrison's feelings, however, were not shared by most of his friends, who were convinced as early as February that the nomination would probably go to Indiana.[12] In which case, as an enthusiastic newspaper editor expressed it to Harrison: "You are the only man whom Indiana can think of placing at the head of the National ticket." [13] Similar frank letters had already reached Harrison's desk. One from old Vincennes, ever a Harrison stronghold, assured the senator that "while you might not be willing to declare yourself a candidate," still "unrestrained friends might do much cheerful work for you." [14] This unsolicited support was not confined to Hoosiers. A tour of eleven states prompted a former

[9] Harrison's moving suggestion for a victory monument in Indianapolis soon prompted the erection of a splendid 285-foot shaft surmounted by a 38-foot statue of Victory, adorned with the bronze figures of George Rogers Clark and Governors William Henry Harrison, James Whitcomb, and Oliver Perry Morton. Henry G. Alsberg (ed.), *The American Guide*, pp. 446–47.

[10] The convention to select the four delegates-at-large was scheduled for April 17 at Indianapolis. Senatorial duties precluded Harrison's presence, but he was assured of the honor. J. A. Wildman to Harrison, February 24, and Cumback to Harrison, February 26, 1884, (L.C.), Vols. 15 and 16.

[11] More than a hundred letters, (L.C.), Vols. 15–17, reveal Harrison's political thinking. Particularly pertinent are Michener to Harrison, February 28, and H. C. Hartman to D. S. Alexander, April 7, 1884.

[12] Wildman to Hay, February 13, 1884, Eugene Gano Hay MSS, Vol. 4; also Cumback to Harrison, February 14; Harrison to Michener, February 16, 18; McLain to Harrison, February 23; and Ransdell to Harrison, February 28, 1884, (L.C.), Vol. 16.

[13] Dick Morgan to Harrison, April 1, 1884, (L.C.), Vol. 16. Morgan was editor of the Terre Haute *Daily and Weekly Courier*.

[14] S. N. Chambers to Harrison, February 16, 1884, (L.C.), Vols. 15 and 16 *passim*.

member of Congress to write: "I find everywhere you are considered a possible, if not probable, presidential nominee." [15]

Under such constant pressure from well-meaning friends, the most impatient and influential of whom was Wharton Barker, Harrison wavered. He at last consented to meet the Philadelphia financier in March at the Riggs House in Washington, "for," as Barker wrote him, "the time has come for us to have a frank talk and clear understanding as to the course of action required." [16] This meeting resulted in plans on a national scale: to enlist support for Harrison from within the camps of both Arthur and Blaine. Barker himself promised to secure the backing of New York and Pennsylvania independents and reformers.

The Harrison wing now went into action. Barker got in touch with George William Curtis, an East Coast reform leader, while Louis Michener, Harrison's closest political friend, entered into correspondence with Theodore Roosevelt, now inching towards the threshold of party prominence. Michener knew that the New York reformer considered Blaine "our greatest danger" because "of his decidedly mottled record" and Arthur "the very weakest candidate we could nominate." [17] Young Roosevelt actually favored Senator George F. Edmunds of Vermont. Hence, Michener had to convince him that Benjamin Harrison possessed all of Edmunds' qualities and, in addition, could control a large block of Western votes. Michener accordingly arranged a pre-Convention meeting at Chicago so as to "agree on some definite plan of action." [18]

This undercover work by friends failed to change Harrison's public policy. Deeply conscious of the kindness of those who regarded him as a Presidential prospect, he determined not to let "ambition possess or disturb me." In mid-April, he accepted the

[15] Cumback to Harrison, February 14, 26, 1884, *ibid.*, Vol. 16.

[16] See Barker to Harrison, February 29, and Harrison to Barker, March 3, 1884, Barker MSS. Even after Harrison's letter of disavowal (January 1, 1884), Barker continued to sound out politicians in almost every state. He had concluded that the Harrison-for-President boom should originate in New York or Pennsylvania, not in Indiana. To this end, he corresponded with such reform Republicans as R. R. Bowker and George William Curtis.

[17] Theodore Roosevelt to Henry Cabot Lodge, May 5 and May 26, 1884, in Elting Morison (ed.), *The Letters of Theodore Roosevelt*, I, 68–70. Roosevelt was serving his second term in the New York State Assembly, having been re-elected in 1883 from New York City's 21st District.

[18] T. Roosevelt to L. T. Michener, May 5, 23, 1884, Michener MSS. Carleton Putnam, *Theodore Roosevelt, The Formative Years, 1858–1886*, I, 425–50, has detailed Roosevelt's rôle prior to the Chicago Convention of 1884. This account fails to credit Michener with the attempt to win Roosevelt's support for Harrison.

office of delegate-at-large, and thereafter steadfastly maintained that he was not going to Chicago "with the expectation that my name will be presented." Nevertheless, his supporters were encouraged by his quiet assurance that should the country want an Indiana Republican, and should the finger point to him, "I would of course retire from the Convention." [19]

The question in the minds of Wharton Barker and Harrison's other friends in the East centered on the inclinations of the Indiana delegation. Accordingly, their primary aim was to create a "healthy feeling for General Harrison." Then, "if the time should come when it was thought proper to present his name," the General could count on "the united vote of this state." The Harrison camp knew, however, that "a man cannot be boomed into a nomination for President." [20] And there was always the Senator's unpredictable new rival, Judge Walter Q. Gresham. On the very eve of the Convention, Barker predicted success for Harrison, "if only your Indiana delegation will abandon Mr. Gresham and without any reservation declare at once for you." [21]

It was known by this time that Gresham and his friends held the balance of power; indeed, their hatred of Harrison was undisguised. Heading the anti-Harrison forces in Indiana was James H. McNeely, outspoken editor of the Evansville *Journal*. In a confidential letter dated March 2, 1884, McNeely displayed considerable bile:

Senator H. will never be President, nor do I believe he will ever get the support of Indiana in convention. He is too cold-blooded and cold-hearted to secure the support of a warm-hearted party. He has done very little since his election for his friends who placed him in his present position, except to place a lot of his relatives and Indianapolitans in office, consisting of his personal friends and cronies. If you could hear him cursed and denounced, as I have, by prominent and active Republicans, it would open your eyes. . . . Your advocacy of his cause is "love's labor lost." . . . General Harrison has the last office that he will ever get at the hands of the Republicans of Indiana. I have heard dozens of them say that they would "knife" him, politically, if the opportunity were ever offered.[22]

[19] Harrison to A. V. Dockery, May 24, 1884, (L.C.), Vol. 17.
[20] J. A. Wildman to E. G. Hay, February 13, 1884, Eugene Gano Hay MSS, Vol. 4. The *Sentinel*, March 7, 1884, admitted, however, that the Harrison boom enjoyed great strength during January and February.
[21] Barker to Harrison, May 25, 1884, (L.C.), Vol. 17. Original in Barker MSS.
[22] J. H. McNeely to F. S. Howall, March 2, 1884, (L.C.), Vol. 16. On the back of this letter Harrison simply noted: "Jas. McNeely's letter to Howall abusing me."

McNeely was inclined to favor General John Logan of Illinois. "He is a brave, fearless man and a legislator. He is warm-hearted, and in comparison with Harrison, is like a volcano to an iceberg." [23]

While Harrison's friends were busy meeting the challenge of the Greshamites, the Senator himself was giving almost undivided attention to the many legislative tasks confronting the 48th Congress. In early February, his pledge to push pension legislation was partially redeemed by his introduction of "a very humane and just bill for the relief of disabled soldiers and their widows." [24]

This bill, which pleased G.A.R. organizations, embodied Harrison's pension philosophy, namely, that the "Government should accept the muster of the soldier as a *prima facie* fact that he was sound at the time, and should undertake to pension those who are disabled without reference to the fact whether they were in prison or serving with their commands." [25] When the Committee on Pensions was slow to act, Senator Shelby M. Cullom of Illinois reintroduced Harrison's bill, "almost exactly as I had introduced it," [26] in an effort to get prompt action. Harrison meanwhile was overwhelmed with touching appeals that tugged constantly at his heart.[27] Help for the disabled soldier and his family became a passion with Harrison and he was willing, if necessary, to endorse an expenditure of 246 million dollars for that purpose.[28]

Harrison's work with the Committee on the Territories was more fruitful. His bill providing civil government for Alaska passed the House of Representatives on May 13, 1884, and its pro-

---

[23] *Ibid.* As Martha Alice Tyner, "Walter Q. Gresham," *Indiana Magazine of History,* 39 (1943), 313, observes: "Gresham's friends supported President Arthur. An Arthur-Gresham ticket would satisfy them."

[24] O. Aborn to Harrison, February 26, 1884, (L.C.), Vol. 16. Appreciative letters from various societies of disabled soldiers came to Harrison during March.

[25] Harrison to R. A. Connor, May 26, 1884, a Tibbott transcript, (L.C.), Vol. 17.

[26] Harrison to Collins, June 11, 1884, *ibid.*

[27] Soldiers' widows and maimed veterans detailed their sufferings in most vivid language. The effect of the sentimental side of the pension question has been competently discussed by Donald L. McMurry, "The Political Significance of the Pension Question, 1885–1897," *Mississippi Valley Historical Review,* 9 (1922), 19–25.

[28] Harrison to Small, June 18, 1884, (L.C.), Vol. 17. Harrison expressed his belief that the sum required would not be as large as Commissioner of Pensions Dudley estimated. The record shows that on June 30, 1885, there were 324,968 Civil War pensioners borne on the rolls. This cost the government over $62,000,000. See John W. Oliver, *History of the Civil War Military Pensions, 1861–1885,* p. 118.

visions brought praise from the press.[29] This encouraged him to increase his efforts to win statehood for South Dakota. As chairman of the committee, Harrison was able to force action here, where intolerable delay had been the rule. In one of his most forceful speeches on the floor of the Senate, he urged the passage of the bill. He pointed out that this southern portion of the Dakota Territory had a population of approximately 300,000 and offered proof that its total produce far exceeded that of Nevada and Colorado together. Since the territory was predominantly Republican in sentiment, the largely Democratic Senate delayed its vote[30] until just before Christmas, 1884, when Harrison's bill (S. 1682) was passed by a margin of six votes. It was not considered in the House.[31] At each succeeding session of the Senate, Harrison sponsored similar legislation, and each time the House failed to take action. To Harrison this was partisanship at its worst. His similar efforts for the admission of Washington, Montana, Wyoming, and Idaho were also unsuccessful. Not until his Presidency, when the Republicans dominated both Houses of Congress, were these territories granted statehood.[32]

Harrison had come to the Senate in 1881 determined to protect his country's natural resources. These had been treated as political gifts which senators could vote into their own possession or that of influential lumber and railroad magnates. Harrison's position was this: he insisted that in granting land to construction companies, "The grant should be only for the railroad right of way and not for speculative land with which to finance the railroad building." During his work on the Committee on the Territories, Harrison became increasingly aware of the need to preserve the natural beauties of the country. In each of the three

[29] Harrison to Captain H. D. Rogers, June 25, 1884, a Tibbott transcript, (L.C.), Vol. 17.

[30] *Congressional Record*, 48.2, pp. 107–111. Also Harrison to Hon. N. C. McFarland, Commissioner General, Land Office, December 3, 1884, (L.C.), Vol. 17. On the same day, Harrison wrote for the latest facts and figures that could be supplied from the Comptroller of Currency and the Postmaster General.

[31] Charles Latham, Jr., "Benjamin Harrison in the Senate, 1881–1887," p. 105. Also, Howard R. Lamar, *Dakota Territory, 1861–1869: A Study of Frontier Politics*, p. 247, links Harrison's interest in Dakota statehood to his friendship with Arthur C. Mellette, whose appointment as U. S. Land Commissioner he had secured. Mellette was a Hoosier and the representative of several Indiana investors interested in Dakota speculation. Lamar seems to conclude (p. 272) that sectionalism rather than financial gain motivated Senator Harrison. This squares with the Harrison MSS.

[32] *Report of the Benjamin Harrison Memorial Commission*, pp. 134–36.

Congresses in which he served, Harrison introduced a bill to set apart a certain tract of land lying on the Colorado River, specifying that it was to be in the Territory of Arizona and used as a public park. His foresight in wishing to set aside what is today Grand Canyon National Park was not appreciated in his day. Positive action on his proposal was not taken until 1919.[33]

In the matter of appropriating federal funds for improving the Mississippi River, Harrison followed Calhoun in advocating states rights. But in the area of public education, he found himself endorsing the use of broader powers by the federal government. His part in the enactment of the Blair Common School Bill as amended is distinguished by an oddly modern point of view, based on strict justice, but still new to the times. Energetic but irascible Henry W. Blair of New Hampshire had introduced an education bill designed primarily to improve school conditions in the financially exhausted South. It provided for the expenditure of some $120,000,000 by the federal government, to be disbursed in proportion to the illiteracy in any given state.

Harrison favored federal aid to education in principle, but objected strenuously to Blair's norm of distribution. Convinced that the federal government should match state appropriations regardless of the illiteracy involved, Harrison refused to vote for the Blair Bill. Such a giveaway program, he argued, would relieve backward states of responsibility and encourage them to remain backward. Harrison caught the attention of his colleagues with a plea from the floor "to give wisely" to the cause of education in the South. He warned, however, against indiscriminate federal spending and spelled out his own position that

. . . there is a giving that pauperizes; there is a giving that enfeebles. It is against that sort of giving that I protest. . . . giving should always be so regulated as to save self-respect and awaken in the mind of the recipient a lost faith in his ability to take care of himself. We should carefully avoid that giving which creates a disposition to lean and to

[33] Latham, *op. cit.*, pp. 88–110. Harrison was willing to revoke the lavish grants of previous Congresses to transcontinental railroads, especially where the conditions of the grant remained unfilled. He consistently refused to vote for charters which provided for extra franchises for any company. By advocating the conservation of natural resources and the parceling out of small pieces of land at a time, he showed concern for the rights of both the Indians and the homesteaders.

expect; which takes the stamina and strength and self-dependence and industry out of men.[34]

At this point Harrison proposed an amendment to the Blair Bill: [35] that no state should receive more in federal grants for the common schools than it spent out of its own funds. This, he declared, would stimulate "a generous rivalry . . . as to which state will show the smallest percentage of illiteracy. . . ." After a brief discussion of Harrison's amendment and a previous one by Kansas Senator Preston Plumb, both amendments were withdrawn in favor of a new one offered by Harrison. This touched off a spirited debate.

The Indiana senator argued for three things: 1) the federal government should match state money in support of the common school system; 2) these federal grants were to be made available only on condition that state governors file an annual report of their school systems with the proper Washington agency; and 3) Negroes and whites should be given equal opportunities, though a segregated school system might be adopted. This last provision, Harrison informed the Senate, "was intended to prevent discrimination against the colored people." Democratic Senators James Groome of Maryland and John Morgan of Alabama raised strenuous objections to Harrison's proposals, Groome accusing Harrison of raising a new issue for the purpose of furthering his candidacy for the White House. The amendment was approved, however, by a vote of 28 to 15 and the bill itself passed the Senate, 33 to 11.[36]

In many ways the debate on the Blair Bill and its amendments showed Harrison at his best as a legislator.

[34] *Congressional Record,* 48.1, pp. 2242–44. Blair objected to Harrison's interpretation of "wise giving." By way of rebuttal, Harrison argued that "it is an open question whether we shall do an injury to this scheme of education by curtailing its propositions. In my judgment we shall be doing a real benefit." As Professor C. Vann Woodward, *Origins of the New South, 1877–1913,* pp. 63–64, points out, "the South would receive the lion's share of the appropriations—$11,000,000 out of the first $15,000,000. . . ." This was reported as more than the entire sum spent on the public schools of the South in 1880.

[35] *Congressional Record,* 48.1, p. 2244. The Blair Bill was S. No. 398 ("to aid in the establishment and temporary support of common schools"). Harrison's proposed new amendment actually amended that of Senator Plumb. Blair objected that the Harrison proposal would rob the South of $3,654,848 in some fifteen states.

[36] *Ibid.,* pp. 2693–2707. The House of Representatives gave no consideration to the bill. Senator Bayard of Delaware regarded it as an invasion of the federal government into the field of public education. See C. C. Tansill, *The Congressional Career of Thomas F. Bayard,* p. 309.

Coupled with Harrison's concern for education for both white and colored was his deep-seated anxiety that Southern freedmen were being deprived of their civil rights. He deplored the lack of general interest "in the Southern question" and apologized to one Negro leader because he had failed "to make a bolder reference" to the problem in his Senate speeches. He was convinced that "massacre and outrage have become so old a story that they ceased to move the popular mind." He believed, nevertheless, that "there are many people still who are interested in honest elections, and in the decent and human treatment of the colored people." He was candid in his admission that he did not know "what the solution is to be," but he was confident that repeated outrages would "stir symptoms of interest and indignation in the North" which could prove "healthful." In the newly healed union of the states, he believed that the North would not allow the South to legalize injustice. "The men who put down the rebellion," he said, "will insist upon having an equal voice with the Confederates in the administration of the Government." [37]

Some Republicans were ready to use the Treasury surplus as a wedge with which to split the "solid South." [38] Harrison's legislative philosophy would not permit him to join in this. Rather, he hoped to capture the South for the party through the sounder medium of education. This accounts, in part, for his partisan pleading in the Blair Bill debates.

As a member of the Committee on Indian Affairs, Harrison also developed a keen interest in the problems of the red man. He visited reservations and made on-the-spot investigations as to the Indians' living conditions. On the Senate floor, he frequently spoke against granting railroad rights of way which served to carve territory allocated to the Indians. He also urged that the Indians be provided with the same schooling facilities as the white settlers. Although the *Congressional Record* reveals but three bills sponsored by Harrison in behalf of the Indians,[39] there is more than ample testimony that he worked hard in the committee room to protect their interests. His faithful and "unobtrusive industry"

[37] Harrison to M. C. Garber, December 6, 1884, a Tibbott transcript, (L.C.), Vol. 18; also Harrison to D. W. Eidier, September 8, 1884, *ibid.*

[38] Wharton Barker to John A. Logan, November 17, 1884, Barker MSS.

[39] Latham, *op. cit.*, p. 11; *Congressional Record*, 47.2, p. 1612; also Harrison to Fletcher, December 3, 1884, and Harrison to Wiley, January 27, 1887, (L.C.), Vols. 17 and 18.

in the Senate had not led to his becoming a colorful public figure, but those who knew his character felt that he was indeed Presidential timber. Thus, while Harrison toiled in committee his political friends busied themselves in consolidating the Harrison-for-President movement.

CHAPTER XVI

The Chicago Story:
Law, Libel, and Losses

THE SPRING MONTHS of 1884 saw the emergence of many Presidential hopefuls, but until the actual opening of the Republican National Convention in Chicago on June 3, no one candidate had captured political sentiment. President Arthur had his friends, but they were few. Abraham Lincoln's son, Robert, was an active candidate but lacked the popular appeal of veteran politician James G. Blaine, the "Plumed Knight" of Maine, and Senator George F. Edmunds of Vermont was relatively unknown outside of the East. The Massachusetts delegation, headed by Senator George F. Hoar, favored General William T. Sherman, but his backers were soon informed that "our people do not want a Father Confessor in the White House." [1]

The Indiana and Pennsylvania friends of Benjamin Harrison, led by Barker and Michener, continued to groom him as the "dark horse," although they knew the odds were long. For example, George William Curtis, president of the newly organized National Civil Service Reform League, when approached by Barker on behalf of Harrison, coldly informed him that the Indiana senator was unknown in New York and that "his attitude upon the question of Civil Service Reform . . . is not satisfactory to the Independent voters." [2] In vain Harrison pointed to his practical amend-

[1] George F. Hoar, *Autobiography of Seventy Years*, I, 407–8. General Sherman was a Protestant, but it was generally known that his wife was a Catholic and his son a Jesuit. According to George W. Curtis, head of the New York delegation, this knowledge caused an "insurrection" and the idea was dropped.

[2] George William Curtis to Wharton Barker, March ·6, 1884, Barker MSS. Although the nineteenth-century biography of George William Curtis by Edward Cary is adequate, the best portrayal of the Curtis rôle is in E. McClung Fleming, *R. R. Bowker: The Militant Liberal*, chap. 13, "The Mugwump Crusade, 1880–1891," pp. 196–224.

ments to the Pendleton Civil Service Act.[3] Barker was satisfied but Curtis was still not impressed.

With the arrival of April, public interest in the various candidates mounted. From the editorial rooms of the Cleveland *Leader*, Edwin Cowles wrote that Harrison's nomination "will be the best and safest under all the circumstances surrounding the case." He warned the General, however, that straw votes cast in April had indicated Blaine and Lincoln as the strongest team.[4] Despite this popular trend, many believed that the New York delegation, convinced of Blaine's weakness in the Empire State, would name another candidate who could swing the big electoral vote. With this in mind, Michener was in constant touch with the New York delegates. Michener and Barker had two vital things to accomplish: one, to make the Indiana delegation solid for Harrison; the other, to convince New York that Harrison could carry the doubtful states.[5]

Harrison's fate rested mainly with the independent delegates at Chicago, who were awaiting a candidate who could win for them and who would effectively develop and execute reform measures already begun.[6] Harrison's lieutenants now held a conclave in Washington and decided to wage a promotional campaign for him in the national press.[7] Soon thereafter a score of telegrams flooded into New York, Philadelphia, Cincinnati, and Chicago newspaper offices, proclaiming Benjamin Harrison as

[3] Harrison to Barker, March 20, 1884, Barker MSS. In reply to Barker's request for a clarification of Curtis' opinion, Harrison sent two extracts from speeches delivered in Indianapolis and Des Moines in 1883: "I think some Eastern people at the time took exception to my remarks . . . on the ground that they contained a 'slighting allusion' to the *theorists*. I was responsible for the provision in the civil service law, requiring the examinations to be practical. I believed that catch questions and too high a standard of scholarship would break the laws down."

[4] Edwin Cowles to Harrison, April 5, 1884, (L.C.), Vol. 16.

[5] D. S. Alexander to E. G. Hay, May 1, 1884, Eugene Gano Hay MSS, Vol. 4. "In my opinion the outlook for the Senator is flattering . . . he has made many warm friends in the Senate and his name is in the minds of the best men who will go to Chicago. . . . Allison of Iowa, Cullom of Illinois and Ingalls of Kansas are very friendly and would encourage any movement in his favor."

[6] Andrew D. White, president of Cornell University, had written to Barker: "These, with me, are . . . the only questions. Compared with them, men are nothing. I feel deeply that now is the turning point with the Republican Party." A. D. White to Barker, May 12, 1884, Barker MSS.

[7] D. S. Alexander to R. S. Taylor, May 14, 1884, R. S. Taylor MSS, (Indiana State Library); also D. S. Alexander to E. G. Hay, May 14, 1884, Eugene Gano Hay MSS, Vol. 4.

"the one and only person in Indiana whose name will be presented by the Indianians to the Chicago Convention." [8] This gambit aroused public interest in the Senator, and by May 14, Michener felt that Harrison "has reason to be hopeful." [9]

The Senator himself was far from helpful. He still refused to announce his candidacy. Nor did he attempt to cultivate the favor of the eastern independents, though he was urged to do so. In mid-May, he went to New York for a week-end visit with Mamie. "I shall not seek to see any of the Independent delegates," he wrote an anxious Michener, "but if any of them shall call, will see what their temper is." [10] While in New York, the Senator, surprisingly enough, posed for a news picture,[11] but he "saw no one to talk politics with." Quite by accident, however, he did encounter Theodore Roosevelt and Henry Cabot Lodge on the street. Still in search of a suitable candidate, these two proposed a more formal meeting in Washington the following week. At that time, Harrison's friends held a full discussion of his merits and reported, rather ambiguously, that both Roosevelt and Lodge "spoke of the Senator very kindly, mentioning also Senators Sherman and Hawley." [12] Apparently Roosevelt's chief goal was "to avoid the Blaine devil." He and the reform faction of the party were convinced that in the event of either Blaine's or Arthur's nomination "we are lost." [13]

In good time, Harrison reserved rooms at Chicago's Grand Pacific Hotel, and on May 31 arrived to assume personal leadership of the Indiana delegation. En route to Chicago he held a last-minute conference with Wharton Barker, who was now confident

[8] *Ibid.* Harrison to Michener, May 15, 1884, a Tibbott transcript, (L.C.), Vol. 17.

[9] Michener to R. S. Taylor, May 14, 1884, R. S. Taylor MSS, (Indiana State Library). Michener added: "I think he will be the nominee."

[10] Harrison to Michener, May 16, 1884, Michener MSS, Box 1.

[11] Harrison was sensitive about his appearance in news photographs. "I have been so fearfully caricatured in woodcuts that I am a little reluctant to put myself even in the power of a friend." During his New York visit, he asked Mamie to send a Chicago paper a favorite picture taken in New York in 1883 by Bogardus. Harrison to William Penn Nixon, May 19, 1884, a Tibbott transcript, (L.C.), Vol. 17.

[12] A false report appeared in the New York papers that Harrison met in conference with independent and Republican leaders. D. S. Alexander to Barker, May 21, 1884, Barker MSS. Carleton Putnam, *Theodore Roosevelt, The Formative Years,* I, 429, does not list Harrison as a subject of Roosevelt's preconvention thinking.

[13] T. Roosevelt to Lodge, May 26, 1884, in Elting Morison (ed.), *The Letters of Theodore Roosevelt,* I, 70.

of Harrison's nomination. At the hotel, a cheerful telegram awaited the Senator. Signed by Colonel G. W. Friedley, chairman of the Indiana State Republican Committee, it read: "Indiana delegation ought to nominate you at the outset and stand by you." [14]

In the strategy of Harrison's friends, bold and decisive support for him on the first ballot was imperative. It would convince the New York independents and eastern reformers that only Harrison could stop Blaine's nomination.

Officially, the Indiana delegation would come to Chicago uninstructed; unofficially, it had very nearly agreed to unite on Harrison.[15] If Indiana placed Harrison's name before the Convention on the day set for nominations, nobody knew better than his political advisers that the nomination would have to be made with unanimous enthusiasm or not be made at all. For two days and two nights, therefore, the Hoosier delegates discussed the Senator's candidacy, he himself being the only one absent. Finally on Convention eve and by a vote of 28 to 1, the delegation resolved to present Benjamin Harrison as Indiana's candidate,[16] slating former Secretary of the Navy Thompson to make the nominating speech. Informed of this, the General relinquished his position as delegate-at-large to his alternate and returned to Indianapolis to await the results. No sooner had he left Chicago than Hoosier committees began visiting other state delegations to solicit votes for their "favorite son." Harrison's most vigorous spokesman was Stanton J. Peelle, through contacts arranged by the indefatigable Michener and Barker. The greatest pressure was brought to bear on the Edmunds delegates in general and on New York's young Theodore Roosevelt and Massachusetts' Henry Cabot Lodge and Governor John Davis Long in particular. Among them, this coterie of reformers and anti-protectionists represented 100 votes.

Peelle's untiring efforts met with success. Senators Preston B. Plumb of Kansas and Hoar of Massachusetts joined with Roosevelt

[14] G. W. Friedley to Harrison, May 31, 1884, a Tibbott transcript, (L.C.), Vol. 17.
[15] The friends of Senator Harrison believed they controlled sufficient strength to compel the Gresham supporters to abandon hope. Barker to Harrison, May 25, 1884, *ibid.*
[16] *Journal*, June 4, 1880. "The unanimity with which the delegation adopted the resolution was a surprise, in view of the previous wrangle." At least four delegates were suspect. Some of Harrison's friends felt that this was a trap to kill the General's candidacy by a unanimous vote on the first ballot and a withdrawal of votes on the second.

of New York, Barker of Pennsylvania, and others outside of Indiana in agreeing that Harrison should enter the race at the outset.[17] Here the Senator's bubble burst and the friends of Walter Q. Gresham entered the picture. They objected strenuously to Harrison's nomination on the first roll call.

Though Postmaster General Gresham was not a candidate as long as President Arthur was still in the running, his friends felt that he might very well be the "dark horse" of the Convention if Arthur chose to withdraw his name. Yet if Harrison were endorsed as Indiana's "favorite son," how could Gresham enter the race at all? This impasse brought deep-seated hostilities to the surface and threatened to destroy both the Harrison and Gresham camps. At the last minute, the Indiana delegation caucused and determined that it would be unwise to present the Senator's name in the face of such strong opposition. The first news Harrison received was in a wire from W. H. H. Miller, who had stayed at Chicago: "Your name not presented. We were all agreed about it. Circumstances greatly changed. Stay in Indianapolis." [18]

Harrison did stay at home, and on the fourth ballot Blaine received the nomination. General Logan of Illinois was chosen as his running mate, a position the Senator would not accept.[19] According to Barker's detailed report to Harrison, the discord in the Indiana delegation had made Curtis, Lodge, Roosevelt, and other Edmunds men hesitate. This delay played directly into the hands of the Blaineites, who showed "their great joy when Indiana made no nomination and gave Mr. Blaine 18 votes. The trouble in Indiana was due, of course, to Mr. Arthur, Mr. Gresham and Mr. Foster and upon them must rest the responsibility of the nomination of Mr. Blaine. They did their work with vigor, with great directness and with telling effect. Too much honor cannot be done the gentlemen from Indiana who were your support. I want to say further that Mr. Blaine and his friends understand your position and appreciate your course." [20]

If Harrison felt chagrin at this outcome, he concealed it com-

17 *Ibid.*, June 3, 1884.

18 W. H. H. Miller to Harrison, June 5, 1884, (L.C.), Vol. 17.

19 C. W. Fairbanks to Harrison, telegram, June 6, 1884, *ibid.* "Several Blaine friends and supporters asked me to a conference to know if you or Judge Gresham will take second place. I submitted this to Judge Taylor and Mr. Alexander. They think it best that you should at once be advised. Will be necessary act at once if you consent." Harrison did not act.

20 Barker to Harrison, June 9, 1884, *ibid.*

pletely. Many of his letters written after the convention indicate that he never felt there existed sufficient reason for his nomination [21] and that he believed the contest lay between Arthur and Blaine. "In that contingency," he wrote, "I was for Blaine, believing him to be the much stronger man in our part of the country." [22]

The Convention had barely adjourned before Harrison left Indianapolis for Washington, where several hundred letters greeted his return. To his many friends he wrote that he had no regrets, personal or political, over the Chicago ticket. This attitude must have puzzled many of his supporters. Theodore Roosevelt, for example, considered Blaine "as most objectionable, because his personal honesty, as well as his faithfulness as a public servant, are both open to question." [23] Yet, publicly at least, Harrison voiced complete satisfaction, noting that Blaine's selection "is very well received in Indiana." [24] To his chief lieutenant, Louis T. Michener, Harrison expressed personal gratitude, which was spontaneous and complete:

I did not get to see you after the Chicago Convention, and so had no opportunity to express verbally my gratitude for the very earnest and unselfish efforts you made in my behalf. It was a rare evidence of friendship which you and others gave me at Chicago—standing by me who was not likely to have any power to give you more than gratitude in return—I did not hope for success—but as I had often said to you, there was an Indiana aspect of the question in which I felt a very deep interest. I felt that had been taken care of—and was glad to have you give our state an advanced standing in securing the nomination of Mr. Blaine.[25]

The "Indiana aspect" was a phrase for Gresham, who now seemed to occupy Morton's old place in Harrison's life; as to the rest, the General was still for party first, candidate second.

[21] Harrison to Mrs. W. W. Denny, June 10; to George W. Gordon, June 10; to S. F. Horral, June 10; and to John Lenhart, June 10, 1884, *ibid.*

[22] Harrison to George W. Gordon, June 10, 1884, *ibid.*

[23] Theodore Roosevelt to Anna Roosevelt, June 8, 1884, in Morison, *op. cit.*, pp. 70–72. For a clear insight into the ambivalency of Roosevelt's reaction to Blaine's nomination, see Putnam, *op. cit.*, pp. 445–50. The treatment is comprehensive and sympathetic.

[24] Harrison to H. H. Harding, June 10, 1884, a Tibbott transcript, (L.C.), Vol. 17. Both privately and publicly, Harrison chose to ignore Blaine's blameworthy record. Perhaps like young Roosevelt, Harrison deemed the collapse of the party a greater evil than Blaine's record.

[25] Harrison to Michener, June 11, 1884, *ibid.*

There can be little doubt that Blaine's candidacy pleased the rank and file of the Republican party, but it is interesting to speculate as to how far respectable party leaders had to stretch their consciences in order to support him. Characteristically, Theodore Roosevelt was the most outspoken. He pointed out, ironically, that the Blaine camp did not include "men of the broadest culture and the highest character," nor those prominent "in the professions or eminent as private citizens . . . who were possessed of a keen sense of personal and official honesty, and who were accustomed to think for themselves." Even those who were most critical of Blaine were soon "captivated," he pointed out, "by the man's force, originality, and brilliant demagoguery." [26]

June 19 was the date set for Washington Republicans to ratify the work of the Chicago convention. On that day, at dusk, a brilliant display of fireworks, countless marching bands, and a surging mass of enthusiastic Republicans turned the capital's Judiciary Square into a beehive of activity lasting until midnight. Platforms surrounded three sides of City Hall and speechmaking continued for three straight hours. A Washington reporter noted that "among the most forceful remarks were those of Senator Harrison," who did not speak until nearly eleven. Cheers frequently interrupted his brief, extemporaneous address, which amounted to a plea to canonize the man from Maine:

Bring forward the best and ablest men of the nations; assemble the greatest men, not only in our land, but in others; let the summons go out to the nations of Europe; let Bismarck and Gladstone be in the company, and we will not fear to have their measure applied to our candidate. [*Good! good!*] Blaine will stand among them all a representative of whom the American people need not be ashamed.[27]

Blaine's campaign managers were more than pleased by the key Harrison struck, and they made immediate plans for the Senator to speak in the pivotal states as the race for the Presidency progressed.

The Democrats moved into Chicago for their national convention a month after the Republicans departed. On the second bal-

[26] Theodore Roosevelt to Anna Roosevelt, June 8, 1884, in Morison, *op. cit.*, I, 71–72. This opinion reflected the reform viewpoint of the original Mugwumps. See Fleming, *op. cit.*, pp. 196–224.

[27] The *Journal*, June 20, 1884, reported that Harrison's speech was dotted with applause "and approving interpolation from the thousands who heard him."

lot, Grover Cleveland, dedicated to reform and the doctrine of free trade, was declared the party's candidate. Thomas A. Hendricks, Harrison's political antagonist for more than a quarter of a century, received second place on the ticket. This was a shrewd move, for as a one-time governor of Indiana, Hendricks' popularity with Hoosiers could well prove to be the decisive factor in carrying that state for Cleveland.[28] And if Indiana were counted in the Democratic column, the chances were that the White House would be occupied by the first Democratic President since before the war.

Bank failures in Indianapolis in July, and twin bombshells dropped on the campaigns of both Blaine and Cleveland, kept Harrison more than busy in his own back yard. He had been preparing his campaign notes so as to discuss the tariff, civil service reform, and other national issues, but circumstances would soon force him to fight on the plane of moral issues rather than political principles.

Republicans exploded the first bomb on July 21, when they published far and wide the fact that Cleveland while a young man had fathered an illegitimate child.[29] The effect this would have on the minds of Victorian-bred voters galvanized worried Democrats into a determined search for a like skeleton in the Blaine closet. Acting on the theory "that all is fair in politics and war, and that the best defense is a spirited offense," [30] they soon unearthed a bomb of their own: that Blaine had been married in Pennsylvania on March 29, 1851, and that a son had been born on June 18, 1851. This bold but simple arithmetic shocked an already shocked public when, on August 8, it read the ugly tale in the Democratic *Sentinel*. The slashing, vituperative account made no mention, however, of the fact that the Blaines had gone through an earlier ceremony (although one open to legal attack) on June 3, 1850. The partisan *Sentinel's* version of the facts withheld no venom:

[28] Allan Nevins, *Grover Cleveland: A Study In Courage*, p. 154.

[29] The Buffalo *Evening Telegraph*, on July 21, 1884, first carried the story of Cleveland's affair with Maria Halpin. The story was garnished with unctuous details and telegraphed all over the United States. See Nevins, *op. cit.*, pp. 162–69.

[30] A. T. Volwiler (ed.), *The Correspondence Between Benjamin Harrison and James G. Blaine, 1882–1893*, p. 6.

There is hardly an intelligent man in the country who has not heard that James G. Blaine betrayed the girl whom he married, and then only married her at the muzzle of a shot-gun. . . . If Mr. Blaine was the scoundrel to betray an innocent girl; if, after despoiling her, he was the craven to refuse her legal redress, giving legitimacy to her child, until a loaded shot-gun stimulated his conscience—then there is blot on his character more foul, if possible, than any of the countless stains on his political record.[31]

Stunned, and bitterly indignant at this cruel attack on his family and morals, Blaine hotly wired Harrison on August 21 to institute criminal proceedings for libel against the *Sentinel.* He demanded $50,000 damages, and directed that the suit be filed "without an hour's delay" in the Indianapolis courts.

This peremptory request placed Harrison in a difficult position. He advised the Republican Presidential candidate, still in Maine, that criminal prosecution in Indianapolis would involve an exceptional risk. "The judge is a Democrat," wrote Harrison, "and has been a somewhat active local politician. His bailiff, who would ordinarily select the jury, is also a Democrat and is very smart in his line. We would be in great danger of having a jury so made up as to prevent a verdict." In Harrison's opinion a civil case in the federal courts would afford "a better chance of having a jury of high-minded and unprejudiced men—not of one party, of course, but of men who could rise above party in trying such an issue." Harrison warned Blaine that "it is at the best, and in any Court, a very difficult matter in such a case, and at such a time to get a fair and impartial jury." He pointed out that suit might be brought in any county of the state where the *Sentinel* was circulated. This, Harrison felt, was equally unfair and impolitic. "If we were to go out to some Republican county and drag the accused there for trial, it would be said that we were seeking a partizan advantage."

The General expressed a decided preference to try a civil case before a federal jury in September, the defendant to be John C. Shoemaker, editor-publisher of the *Sentinel,* and a Democratic state official. He gave Blaine the opportunity, however, to reassert his determination to press a criminal prosecution against Shoemaker. In the event of a criminal trial, Harrison advised Blaine, his presence in Indiana would be "indispensable; . . . come here

---

[31] "Can Blaine Afford It?" was the title of the *Sentinel's* attack.

and make the affidavit yourself, confront the accused, and demand an immediate trial." He added, in closing his letter, that he "felt the embarrassment of consulting at long-range." [32]

While awaiting a further directive from Blaine, Harrison opened both state and national campaigns with a keynote speech at Indianapolis on Saturday night, August 23, 1884. He confined his remarks to national issues as seen from the Senate floor, making no reference to Blaine's impending libel suit or to the *Sentinel's* story. Harrison himself felt that he had not struck nearly so popular a note as in his ratification speech in Washington. He laid the blame on the fact that his notes had been "prepared in the midst of a medley of distractions." [33] But the chief reasons for his failure to capture his audience probably lay in the fact that they had come to the meeting fresh from discussions of the Blaine scandal and had expected more in the same vein. This morbid curiosity of the public was being pandered to by the rival political organs, the *Sentinel* and *Journal,* which daily treated their readers to new lurid details, denials, and charges.[34] The truth could be supplied by Blaine alone, and more than ever Harrison watched anxiously for a return communication from Maine.

Meanwhile, national leaders were urging him to "push things in the Blaine suit for an early trial." Indiana Republicans regretted "that such an outrage should have been committed" in their state; it "is enough to make us all blush, and calls for quick expiation." [35] Blaine himself acted as quickly as possible. On Tuesday, August 25, probably the day on which Harrison's letter reached him, the "Plumed Knight" got word to the Senator to come at once to Maine. Harrison, regarding it as important to see Blaine personally, canceled his Indiana speaking appointments at once, and advised both the press and friends that he was going to Maine to make three or four speeches before the state election, slated for the first week in September.

Harrison received a warm welcome from Maine Republicans despite the fact that his brief visit would permit only five speeches.

[32] Harrison to Blaine, August 21, 1884, copy in Volwiler, *op. cit.,* p. 22.

[33] Harrison to C. W. Ernst, Esq., September 8, 1884, a Tibbott transcript, (L.C.), Vol. 1, Second Series.

[34] Between August and December, these two papers printed many articles and editorials dealing with the suit. The author has based his account on these two files. Also, there exists a volume of newspaper clippings labeled "Blaine's Libel Suit" in the Toner Collection, (Library of Congress).

[35] W. W. Dudley to Harrison, August 24, 1884, (L.C.), Vol. 17.

After an address at Waterville on August 30, an effort made with Blaine looking on, the Presidential candidate and his counsel boarded a Pullman for Blaine's home in Augusta where they spent the week end.[36] No record of their conversation has been preserved. Subsequent correspondence, however, reveals Blaine's explanation of the equivocal dates, which exonerated him from the *Sentinel's* sensational but false charges.

Blaine began his story by recounting his employment from 1848 to 1851 as an assistant professor in the Western Military Institute in Kentucky. Here he met Harriet Stanwood, an instructor in a nearby girls' school. They fell in love, and after a two-year courtship, were married on June 30, 1850, at Millersburg, Kentucky. Wishing to continue teaching, and since Kentucky school regulations forbade the employment of married teachers, the Blaines and their two witnesses kept the simple ceremony a secret. They later found that their failure to procure a license from the clerk of the county court in accordance with Kentucky statutes had made their marriage legally invalid. Consequently, on March 29, 1851, the Blaines had their marriage solemnized in Pittsburgh, again before two witnesses.[37] A son, Stanwood, was born to them on June 18, 1851, and died three years later. Only political mudslingers would have attempted to sully the Blaines' marriage by emphasizing the 1851 ceremony and ignoring as non-existent the witnessed, but technically invalid contract of 1850. Blaine's explanation satisfied Harrison as a lawyer and relieved his mind, both as a Republican and as a church member. He continued on to New York where he brought the gratifying facts to the National Committee and incidentally impressed them with Indiana's need for name orators and additional campaign funds.

Harrison had been home only a week when tidings of a state victory in Maine reached him. Some two thousand rejoicing Hoosier Republicans joined in a spontaneous "monster jollification meeting" on Market Street on the evening of September 11. Maine's action, they believed, foreshadowed the inevitable result in Indiana. Typical of the spirit of the times was the "unorganized

[36] Kenebec (Maine) *Journal*, August 30, September 1, 1884.
[37] *Journal*, September 22, 1884. S. L. Blaine and Sarah C. Stanwood were the Millersburg witnesses; John V. LeMoyne and David Bell were witnesses at Pittsburgh.

joy" of that September demonstration in nineteenth-century Indianapolis. As soon as a sizeable crowd had gathered at one of the
gaslit street corners, speakers by the dozen were immediately available for their entertainment. At length Harrison was recognized
in the crowd and called to the "temporary stand . . . erected on
the Market Street sidewalk" for a brief speech. The gaiety of Harrison's ensuing talk perfectly reflected the spirits of his listeners.
"I feel tonight," he said, "as if song, and shout, and trumpet blast,
rather than speech, are best expressive of our feelings over the
news from Maine! . . . Did any state ever before give a man such
an endorsement as Maine has given Blaine? Did you ever hear
before of a state election where every county went Republican?" [38]
The Senator went on to hail the re-election of Thomas B. Reed, a
"gallant and noble fellow," who had cross-examined Samuel J.
Tilden about the cipher dispatches calculated to buy Florida's
returning board and electoral vote in the celebrated Presidential
conflict of 1876.[39]

Harrison, ever sensitive to audience reaction, found that September 11 an occasion not to be neglected. The Senator reminded
the crowd before him of the Democrats' boast that they had compelled the Republicans to fight a defensive campaign for Blaine.
As his audience roared, he saw he had hit the mark. And now Harrison the attorney for Blaine joined cause with Harrison the political leader, who had promised the Hoosier vote for the Republican
candidate. In a ringing voice, he proclaimed:

The Plumed Knight of Maine never fought a defensive battle and never
will. What does it mean that among the people who knew him when,
in obscurity and poverty, he began that brilliant career that will cul-
minate in the White House, his party should receive such a large majority, if it is not indicative of their confidence and affection in him?
It matters little what men say who do not know him, when his own
neighbors have said that they believe in him as a man and as a statesman, that they indorse his public career.

At this the crowd cheered wildly and Harrison raised his voice
in a challenge: "Comrades of the Republican Party! . . . Can we
need a stronger stimulation and inspiration than what Maine Re-

[38] *Ibid.*, September 12, 1884.
[39] For Tilden's part in the cipher dispatches, see Harry Barnard, *Rutherford B.
Hayes and His America,* pp. 474–78.

publicans have done? We have met the vanguard of the enemy and have conquered. When the main action comes on, shall we be less true and courageous?" Then, sure of his audience, he closed with the never-failing appeal of the "bloody shirt," as he pleaded

. . . for the sake of the old Flag, for the sake of those brave boys that we put to everlasting sleep in their narrow beds in the South, I beg of you to give the vote of Indiana to the men who stood by the country.[40]

Harrison's rôle in the still pending Blaine libel suit made his presence in Indianapolis imperative. He had therefore canceled all plans to campaign for the national ticket in states other than Indiana and Ohio. Then, in mid-September, Blaine decided against bringing his suit to judgment before election, perhaps fearful of the resultant publicity. His unexpected directive to Harrison read: "*Now*—confidentially & earnestly—I want the case to stand just as it is until after election. You must not appear to waste time—*but you must let it drift.*" [41] Blaine's decision embarrassed Harrison at the time, and even more so four years later when, during his own Presidential canvass, enemies within the party alleged that he had purposely mismanaged the case so as to eliminate Blaine as a future political rival. In 1884, little was gained in Indianapolis by delaying the suit. The facts pertinent to Blaine's double ceremony were again fully aired in both the *Sentinel* and *Journal*, the former newssheet declaring with some insolence that Blaine would never consent to a court trial any place in Indiana.

Throughout the campaign, Blaine was particularly anxious to win the doubtful Hoosier State. He mistrusted John C. New, Indiana's representative on the National Committee, and arranged for him to ". . . be gently put aside, by detailing a sub-committee of the National Committee for headquarters at Indianapolis." He also warned his astute political manager, Stephen B. Elkins,[42]

---

[40] *Journal*, September 12, 1884.
[41] Blaine to Harrison, September [17?], 1884, cited in Volwiler, *op. cit.*, pp. 24–25.
[42] Elkins (1841–1911) practiced law and held various offices in New Mexico before moving to West Virginia. Here his investments in railroads, oil, and coal increased his wealth. During the last sixteen years of his life he served as United States Senator. Even in 1884, Elkins was a leader in the councils of the Republican party. He was on intimate terms with Blaine, and was one of his staunchest and most trusted supporters. In 1888, he transferred his allegiance to Harrison and in 1891 entered his Cabinet as Secretary of War.

that "Indiana must have your careful overlook." [43] Blaine was finally persuaded to stump Indiana in person during October.

The logical place for the Presidential candidate to stay while in Indianapolis was with the Harrisons. Consequently, the household prepared early to provide the traditional Hoosier hospitality. [44] Carrie Harrison did her charming best to soothe Blaine's naturally wounded sensibilities, but as the campaign progressed, it was soon evident that Blaine's feelings would continue to be ruffled if something were not done to increase his popularity with Indiana Republicans. On October 20, the "Plumed Knight" had encountered a chilly reception at Fort Wayne. [45] When he attempted a speech at that city's Aveline House, he was angered to have "his voice drowned by large cheers for Cleveland and Hendricks." Although Blaine was later more successful with a twelve-minute address at Liberty Hall, Harrison was disappointed and chagrined. He determined that Indianapolis, Terre Haute, Evansville, and Lafayette must make reparation to Blaine. To make sure of this, he penned personal notes to his friends in those cities and helped arrange a rather effective plan "for giving the people a chance to see him in most places." [46]

In the meantime, Harrison rolled up his sleeves and worked hard to dissipate a certain apathy which had pervaded Republican ranks in Indiana. Michener and other state leaders rejoiced that "Harrison is making able speeches, and the people are not afraid to shake his hand." Still, cautioned Harrison's friend, "Hard work, very hard work, is now needed." [47] No one knew this better than the Senator. Yet as the campaign grew in excitement, he remained relatively calm. In Indiana, as in the rest of the nation, great torchlight parades and blaring brass bands obscured the political issues, but not the personal scandals. The Democratic hosts clamored in unison:

[43] James G. Blaine to S. B. Elkins, August 5, 1884, Elkins MSS, (West Virginia University Archives).

[44] Harrison to Dr. George F. Chittenden, October 4, 1884, Chittenden MSS, (Indiana State Library).

[45] Benjamin Harrison Scrapbooks, (L.C.), Vol. 4, October 21, 1884.

[46] Harrison to Hon. R. W. Thompson, October 13, 1884, (L.C.), Vol. 17 (a photostatic copy from the R. W. Thompson MSS). The plan was to have "uniformed companies form in open order so as to make an open way for his [Blaine's] carriage to drive between and give everyone a chance to get a glimpse as he goes by."

[47] L. T. Michener to E. G. Hay, October 16, 1884, Eugene Gano Hay MSS, Vol. 5.

Blaine, Blaine, James G. Blaine,
The Continental liar from the State of Maine,
Burn this letter! [48]

and the Republican cohorts chorused back:

Ma! Ma! Where's my pa?
Gone to the White House,
Ha! Ha! Ha! [49]

During the last two weeks of the 1884 campaign Harrison put up a brave front, but he was gravely concerned over the complexion of the next Indiana Legislature, which in 1886 would decide his future as a senator. On October 25, despite a lacerated hand and a lame finger, he scribbled a plea for funds to Wharton Barker. He complained that the National Committee "has done almost nothing for us. Up to this time only $5,000 has been furnished by them to our campaign. The outlook is very favorable and I have great confidence in carrying the state, but we are without friends and in debt." He added dolefully: "Our adversaries seem to have a good deal of money." [50]

Barker responded with his customary generosity, sending to Indianapolis a check for $2,250, of which $1,500 represented his personal contribution. He apologized to Harrison for the small amount, but explained: "I have called upon all those who are in the habit of giving money for campaign work and find all have given more than they think their share." [51] Harrison, quick to acknowledge Barker's "generous interest" predicted in a surge of optimism that the Republicans "will, I believe, carry the state by a handsome majority—and gain at least three Congressmen." [52]

[48] The letter referred to was, of course, one of the "Mulligan letters." This was a series published in the Boston *Journal* in mid-September, clearly indicating unorthodox financial transactions and subsequent perversions of the truth on Blaine's part. One letter in particular had a damaging effect. Blaine had sent it to an old business associate and warned "Regard this letter as strictly confidential. Do not show it to anyone." He also wrote on the back of it: "Burn this letter."

[49] Nevins, *op. cit.,* p. 177.

[50] Harrison to Barker, October 25, 1884, Barker MSS. E. H. Roseboom, *The History of Presidential Elections,* pp. 268–69, notes that Daniel Manning, William Whitney, and Arthur Gorman "collected a larger campaign fund than usual from a segment of business and from Democratic state and municipal office-holders." Republicans used the same methods, but not as early or effectively.

[51] Barker to Harrison, October 30, 1884, Barker MSS.

[52] Harrison to Barker, November 1, 1884, *ibid.*

In 1884, Election Day fell on November 4. The five days which preceded it were nothing short of a nightmare for Blaine's Indiana supporters. On the evening before the polls opened, the state looked safe for Blaine. Harrison was outwardly cheerful: "Everywhere I have been in the state we have been making decided gains, and I have great confidence in our gaining a very decided victory tomorrow." [53] The Indiana senator also pinned Republican hopes on the large Irish vote in the East which Wharton Barker had promised to deliver to Blaine.[54] In Harrison's mind, however, there remained one serious reservation. In Indiana, he wrote a friend that same night, "we have a large floating vote that is not much influenced by argument or conviction." [55] In a closely contested election these "floaters" could turn the Hoosier tide. Although later Cleveland's biographer seemed to feel that "the Democrats were unfortunately hampered by a lack of funds," [56] Harrison learned too late that in several Hoosier counties the Cleveland forces "had $4,000 to $6,000" [57] for efficient Election Day use.

Oddly enough, disaster did not strike Blaine from the Midwest. There, Ohio's victory balanced Indiana's defeat. New York City, originally unscheduled for a speech by Blaine, was to be the scene of a fateful error. A group of obscure clergymen had been invited to meet Blaine on October 20 at the Fifth Avenue Hotel. A local Presbyterian minister, the Rev. S. D. Burchard, acted as spokesman. In the course of his remarks, he glibly referred to the Democrats as the party of "Rum, Romanism, and Rebellion." [58] Irish Catholics, scores of whom had pledged their allegiance to Blaine, were more than affronted. Thus, a religious issue, weighted with prejudice and angry passion, cost Blaine many votes in a state that

[53] Harrison to H. C. Lockhart, Esq., November 3, 1884, a Tibbott transcript, (L.C.), Vol. 17.

[54] Barker to Blaine, November 17, and Barker to Dr. William Carroll, November 18, 1884, Barker MSS. On November 21, 1884, Barker reported to Harrison that "the Irish vote which I assured you would be cast . . . we were able to carry . . . without this vote Mr. Blaine would have been defeated by such a vote that the people would have been convinced that the Republican party had met final defeat. My friends Prof. Thompson, Dr. Carroll, Mr. Powderly and Mr. Ford are the men who lead and direct the Irish vote. When you are here I want you to meet these gentlemen." (L.C.), Vol. 17.

[55] Harrison to Waters, November 3, 1884, a Tibbott transcript, ibid.

[56] Nevins, op. cit., pp. 180–1, feels that the contributions by chief donors in the amount of $460,000 comprised "a meagre sum."

[57] Harrison to Barker, November 25, 1884, Barker MSS.

[58] Nevins, op. cit., pp. 181–5, judged that, in a truer sense, the affair fitted "logically into the pattern of the unprincipled campaign which the party was conducting, and their penalty was deserved."

was maddeningly close.[59] Whitelaw Reid was convinced that "tactless alliteration had lost the day." [60] More than one Republican leader wished that Dr. Burchard had suffered a hopelessly sore throat that evening. His incredible folly was to be long remembered.

Harrison was slow to admit defeat. Preoccupied with the lavish wedding of his daughter Mamie to Robert McKee on November 5, the day after election, the Senator did not get down to letter-writing again until November 8. The loss of the state to Cleveland amazed him. One of his first comments reflected his confusion: "We gained largely where we had no reason to expect it, and lost where we ought to have gained." In regard to New York State he died hard. On November 8, he was still unwilling to concede defeat here. "The official count of New York may yet give the electoral vote to Blaine, but perhaps it is too much to expect as the Democrats have the machine and New York has been notorious for election frauds." [61] Later the same day he was still uncertain: "It is a great misfortune that New York should be so close; and it is exceedingly disgusting too, I think, that Republican mugwumps have beaten us—if we are beaten." [62]

With the official count, gloom settled in earnest. It was all over for the "Plumed Knight." Benjamin Franklin Tracy (a Brooklyn attorney who later served as Harrison's Secretary of the Navy), wrote Elkins on November 9 that the cause was lost. "There appear to be clerical errors in our favor which, when corrected, will increase Cleveland's majority." [63]

For Harrison, a few days of duckhunting along the Kankakee River and in its mysterious marshes were sufficient to recoup his usual composure. By Thanksgiving Day, he was himself again, adamant in his opinion that "Blaine made a magnificent fight. . . . He was beaten by several little things, some of which were made apparent only at the very close of the campaign." [64] Moreover, he

[59] For three days the election remained in doubt and the vote was dangerously close. Cries of fraud came from both parties and an official recount was demanded. It should be noted that a change of 575 votes in New York would have given the Presidency to Blaine. See Putnam, op. cit., p. 504, and Roseboom, op. cit., p. 273.

[60] Royal Cortissoz, The Life of Whitelaw Reid, II, 97.

[61] Harrison to Lockhart, November 8, 1884, a Tibbott transcript, (L.C.), Vol. 17.

[62] Harrison to C. B. Walker, ibid.

[63] Benjamin F. Tracy to S. B. Elkins, November 9, 1884, Elkins MSS.

[64] Harrison to Dr. W. H. Melrath, November 22, 1884, a Tibbott transcript, (L.C.), Vol. 17. Three days later Harrison sent his personal analysis to Wharton Barker: "The victory seems to be what the candidate is, an accident. The events of great

agreed with Wharton Barker's gallant statement that "the Republican Party has been beaten but in no way broken." [65] In a longhand letter of reply, the Senator assured his Philadelphia friend that "as to the future, I can see nothing to discourage us. Discipline and tribulations will disrupt them [the Democrats]—even if serious divisions on questions of policy are avoided—which I do not think possible." [66]

Harrison's renewed faith and optimism were in large part due to the same qualities in his followers. For example, the Young Republicans of Patriot, Indiana, resolved soon after their party's defeat to convert their temporary organization into a permanent one, "with a view to prevent a recurrence of defeat in the future." They voted to call themselves the "Harrison Guards" and advised the Senator that their new name was a unanimous choice "in respect for you, whom we esteem and honor for your party and public service, and as a representative of a name endeared to us by tradition." [67] Harrison's warm reply reflected his approval of a group "stimulated rather than discouraged" by disaster.[68]

As he boarded the train for Washington, Harrison carried with him Wharton Barker's letter of November 21, containing this statement: "Great power rests in your hands and of course great responsibility also. You can take the lead in the Senate and in Congress. The Republican Party will follow you. . . ." [69]

---

portent turned on small hinges. I cannot but think Mr. Blaine was, taking everything into account, as strong, possibly stronger than any other candidate would have been. He lost some votes that another would have held, but I do not know another candidate who could have been certainly successful in the Pacific States, or who could have secured so many Catholic votes. In our state, the temperance vote, nearly 4,000, and a liberal use of money by the Democrats, accounts [sic] for the result." November 25, 1884, Barker MSS. In addition to the unforgettable occurrence of Blaine's last fatal week, Nevins, op. cit., p. 169, lists five principal factors, three of which militated against Republican success. These were: the distrust of Republicans caused by Pension Bureau officials; the Prohibitionist vote, cutting into Blaine's strength; and a lingering distrust of the South coupled with the business depression of 1884.

65 Barker to Harrison, November 21, 1884, (L.C.), Vol. 17.

66 Harrison to Barker, November 25, 1884, Barker MSS. Harrison also noted the principal reason for the Democratic victory in his own city of Indianapolis: "We had here (in this city) a very weak local ticket—and one that was attributed to the 'Court House Ring.'"

67 G. W. Olcott to Harrison, November 17, 1884, (L.C.), Vol. 17. Olcott was the group's corresponding secretary.

68 Harrison to Olcott, November 22, 1884, a Tibbott transcript, ibid.

69 Wharton Barker to Harrison, November 21, 1884, ibid.

CHAPTER XVII

Storms on the Senatorial Sea

THE WASHINGTON to which Senator Harrison returned at the end of November, 1884, was in a changed mood. Republicans, deprived of the power they had held for nearly a quarter of a century, were gloomy with foreboding. Victorious Democrats, on the other hand, turned to the task of leadership with enthusiasm. They interpreted the election of Grover Cleveland as a popular mandate for general reform, especially in the civil service. Independents were even more optimistic in their plans for political reformation.[1] Cleveland was expected to be a blunt, hard-hitting President, though perhaps somewhat cautious at the outset. The country was not facing any definite crisis, but the farmer, laborer, and the trust-minded business world were nursing problems which the new government would do well not to ignore.

As Harrison resumed his seat in the Senate, he was well aware of these disturbing undercurrents, and he determined to pay closer attention to national needs. He now felt himself a free agent. As he put it, "I am practically shorn of all power"[2] over federal appointments. Relieved from his previous burden of appeasing Hoosier office seekers, the Indiana senator determined to make the most of the four-month "lame-duck" session which would precede Cleveland's inauguration, although he admitted that "the Democrats are on horse-back and . . . the Republicans will be expected to journey on foot."[3]

But in response to Wharton Barker's suggestion that Harrison

[1] E. McClung Fleming, *R. R. Bowker: Militant Liberal*, p. 210, cites the advent of the new Administration as "a splendid proof of the important fact that, in the darkest days of political corruption, party tyranny, and moral depression, there exists in the American people a reserve power" to affect a political reformation.
[2] Harrison to Capt. A. B. Patterson, November 22, 1884, (L.C.), Vol. 17.
[3] Harrison to R. Bell, March 5, 1885, a Tibbott transcript, *ibid.*, Vol. 19.

assume the Senate leadership of the party, the Senator hedged: "I can say while I hope to 'lend a hand' . . . I would not like my performance given so pretentious a name." [4] Nevertheless, with the second session of the 48th Congress only a week old, he was on the Senate floor leading the old fight for South Dakota's statehood. Armed with fresh facts and figures, Harrison introduced his bill, and on December 8, 1884, opened the debate which followed. [5] Although Bill S. 1682 passed by the narrow margin of six votes and was never considered in the House, it represented an important landmark for the junior senator. He would keep trying.

Christmas of 1884 was a strange one for Ben and Carrie. For the first time in years, they were alone at that happy season, unable to return to Indianapolis and old friends, since committee work was keeping Harrison close to his desk. After the holiday recess, important differences between the two Houses on various bills would have to be ironed out in joint committee. Harrison was therefore content to spend his free time in the office and the library where he prepared for discussion of the Naval Bill in particular by studying the Monroe Doctrine and background material on the Isthmian Canals. [6] He had become painfully conscious that the American Navy had sunk to its lowest level of efficiency. [7] To remedy this, he had decided to recommend that Congress ". . . should at once expend a large sum of money for coast defense and guns; . . . [make] large appropriations for the Navy and . . . aid by suitable appropriations our Merchant Marine." [8] This opportunity for uninterrupted study of foreign and domestic policy enlarged Harrison's perspective on his senatorial responsibilities and made his enforced Washington holiday worth while.

While in the Senate Harrison earned and enjoyed a reputation as "the soldier's legislator," but the farmers of the Midwest and

[4] Harrison to Barker, November 25, 1884, Barker MSS.

[5] Harrison to W. W. Slaughter, March 6, 1885, a Tibbott transcript, (L.C.), Vol. 17, shows the extensive research made by the Senator in support of his Dakota statehood bill (S. No. 1682). Much data was supplied by the Commissioner General of the Land Office and by the Comptroller of the Currency.

[6] Harrison to R. W. Thompson, January 7, 1885, ibid., Vol. 18.

[7] C. C. Tansill, The Congressional Career of Thomas F. Bayard, p. 304. With the launching in 1884 of the Dolphin, first of a group of steel cruisers, twenty years of steady naval decline ended. Captain George Dewey commanded this newest Navy ship. See Richard S. West, Jr., Admirals of the American Empire, Part Two, "Naval Decline and Resurgence, 1865–1890," pp. 65–133.

[8] Harrison to E. W. Fox, December 14, 1886, a Tibbott transcript, (L.C.), Vol. 27.

South were also seeking a friend in court. The problem was railroad rates. Farming interests felt these were unfair and that interstate commerce should be placed under federal control. Their angry protests were first heard in the House, where gaunt John H. Reagan of Texas, former Postmaster General of the Confederacy, declared that the government should deal gingerly with the abuses engineered by the nation's common carriers. He then offered a bill for debate. This encouraged the Granges to hope for Senate support of House action, and several Hoosier counties petitioned their junior senator to this effect.[9] In Harrison they found a friend who was willing to help, although he had ideas of his own on the subject because of his long experience as a railroad counsel.

While the House deliberated on the Reagan Bill through January and early February, the Senate, after a special committee had conducted nationwide hearings, drafted the Cullom Bill to establish a commission for the regulation of interstate commerce. Harrison, though he "had one cold chasing on the heels of another all winter," [10] gave long hours of study to both bills. He concluded that Reagan's bill was weak and "would utterly disappoint those who urge its passage." He advised his rural petitioners that the "two great faults in railroad transportation" were the "inequitable rates as to local traffic, and discrimination between shippers." Both the Senate and House bills made these practices misdemeanors, punishable by heavy fine. Harrison favored the commission plan of the Senate which would protect and aid people "who suffered unjustly at the hands of the Railroad Company." In explaining his stand to the farmers of Indiana, he wrote, on January 31:

I believe the special strength of the Railroad Companies is the fact that the private litigant cannot contest with them. Therefore I think that the Senate bill, which provides a commission whose duty it is, at the expense of the Government, to look into complaints that are lodged, and which can have access directly to the books and papers of the Railroad Company, is better than the Reagan bill, which contains no such provision, but leaves the shipper to find out for himself that he has been discriminated against, and to pursue his suit at a disadvantage.

The Senate bill requires the District Attorneys of the United States to bring suits for citizens upon request.[11]

[9] Harrison to J. M. Case, January 31, 1885, *ibid.*, Vol. 18.

[10] Harrison blamed his colds on near-zero weather, long sessions, and a closed hall. Harrison to John B. Elam, January 30, 1885, *ibid.*

[11] In a letter to the Secretary of the Grange of Franklin County, Indiana, Harrison replied that he had given careful consideration to the plea that the Reagan Bill

Four days later, Harrison argued convincingly before a full Senate in favor of the commission plan to stop railroad abuses. A reputable commission, he argued, could "open the secrets of the railroad companies" whose clandestine schedule of rates made trusts more monopolistic and squeezed out small business. As a precedent, he cited "the power of the State of New York wielded through a legislative commission," which put an end to discriminatory rebates in favor of the Standard Oil Company. Such a plan, the Senator explained, "has the power to concentrate public sentiment upon any practice of the railroad company that is thought to be unjust. . . . Take the humblest man in any of our towns; he cannot make himself heard beyond the village he lives in. He has no influence; the railroad managers would laugh at him; he is but a pigmy in this contest and he is contending with giants."

The Indiana senator's lengthy but powerful speech showed him far from the camp of vested interests. Hoosier farmers joined other abused shippers throughout the nation in applauding the relief such legislation would afford. Once an individual or a company filed a complaint, he would no longer be obliged to pursue the case at his own expense. At long last, Harrison declared, "the United States Government has thrown itself into the scale in behalf of the citizen in this contest." [12]

The Indiana senator continued to use the passes customarily furnished him by leading railroads, but this in no way weakened his determination to vote for a permanent administrative commission "to hear complaints, bring witnesses before its bar, and enforce the law." [13] Finally, after a long deadlock between Reagan's supporters and friends of Senator Shelby M. Cullom of Illinois, sponsor of the bill that incorporated Harrison's legislative thought, the Interstate Commerce Act became law early in 1887 over Cleveland's signature.

The most troublesome question before the Senate in February was the silver bill. East and West were already divided on the expediency of continuing the silver coinage, but politicians pre-

---

receive his support, but he begged to show its inadequacy. Harrison to J. M. Case, January 31, 1885, *ibid.*

[12] *Congressional Record,* 48.2 (February 3, 1885), p. 1154.

[13] Allan Nevins, *Grover Cleveland: A Study In Courage,* p. 355.

ferred to avoid the issue. Harrison advised his constituents that he thought "the politics of the situation was to let Cleveland, or his Secretary of the Treasury, make some recommendation on that subject." [14] The situation grew more serious, as the government was compelled to accept silver from its debtors while it paid out gold to its creditors.[15] In this crisis, the President-elect, as yet without official power, defied the silver enthusiasts by recommending an immediate suspension of the purchase and coinage of silver. Two days later, the House rebuffed Cleveland, as Harrison had predicted,[16] by decisively defeating the movement to suspend silver.

Although Harrison shared Cleveland's concern over the worsening currency situation, he could not help noting jubilantly that the first Democratic President in a quarter-of-a-century had been slapped in the face by his own party before he took his seat. To Louis T. Michener he confided: "Cleveland's silver letter has produced a wide and a bitter break in his party in Congress. . . . If we are left half a chance, we can beat them in 1886." He also criticized the new Cabinet. Cleveland had selected two New Yorkers, Daniel Manning and William C. Whitney, as Secretaries respectively of the Treasury and Navy. Harrison termed these men "monopolists" whose appointments had "produced outspoken disgust" in the West and Midwest.[17] In addition, his friend, W. W. Dudley, was to be replaced as Commissioner of Pensions by John C. Black.

As to the Senator's opinion of Cleveland, some hint is contained in the story he told a Hoosier friend on Valentine's Day, 1885:

The Democrats who have been over to see Cleveland are not very talkative when they return. They evidently feel like the man who had carried a bucket of water and emptied it into a cistern! They have brought back only empty buckets, and they seem to be somewhat in doubt

[14] Harrison to Michener, February 7, 1885, a Tibbott transcript, (L.C.), Vol. 18, admitted that no Senate bill on silver "would have the smallest chance of passing the House. See also Harrison to M. L. Essick, January 13, 1885, *ibid.,* Tibbot transcripts, Box 2.

[15] If the United States refused to pay creditors in gold, there was a well-grounded fear that the government's credit would be ruined. Yet this very practice threatened the $100,000,000 in gold held as a reserve to protect the redemption of greenbacks.

[16] Nevins, *op. cit.,* pp. 202–5. On Cleveland and silver, as well as a discussion of the split within the Democratic party on the question, A. Barton Hepburn, *A History of Currency in the United States,* pp. 292 ff. affords a clear summary and interpretation.

[17] Harrison to Michener, March 1, 1885, a Tibbott transcript, (L.C.), Vol. 19.

whether the cistern will hold water. They have made a "catch," but whether it is a salmon or a dog-fish they do not yet know.[18]

What promised to be an easy week of final Senate sessions for Harrison soon developed into an enduring agony. In addition to the chairmanship of his own Committee on Territories, he was compelled to assume the same position on the Military Committee. Then, in an effort to avoid an extra session, the Senate held two all-night deliberations just before Cleveland's inauguration and Harrison yearned for adjournment and the peace of his Indiana home. Unfortunately for him, the new Chief Executive called a special session at the time excited letters from Hoosier friends spoke of political pandemonium in Indiana as the result of a Democratic *coup d'état*.

Early in 1884, Harrison had recognized the weakness of his state party. To his political confidant, Michener, he wrote: "I have very little hope of making Indiana a Republican state with 4,000 Republican Prohibitionists and 8,000 Republican Green-backers voting separate tickets." [19] As state leader, his continuous problem had been how to keep "our temperance friends in line" [20] and how to allay the fears of the silver-loving Greenbackers.[21] Then a more serious threat to Republican fortunes in Indiana presented itself. Political friends in the state capital warned Harrison that the newly elected Democratic majority was preparing to gerrymander the state so as to "disfranchise our people." These initial reports reached Harrison on February 19, and whatever ice he had in his veins melted as his blood came to a slow boil. He immediately took the helm and barraged his Indiana followers with warnings and advice. He cautioned them against haste, but counseled vigilance and, if necessary, desperate remedies. He urged John C. New,

---

[18] Harrison to Hon. Stanton J. Peelle, February 14, 1885, *ibid.*, Vol. 19. Peelle was a former Indiana Congressman, a great supporter of Harrison, and one of the delegates to the 1884 Republican National Convention.

[19] Harrison to Michener, January 13, 1885, *ibid.*

[20] Harrison to Col. James H. Jordan, February 12, 1885, *ibid.* William G. Carleton, "Why Was the Democratic Party in Indiana a Radical Party, 1865–1900?" *Indiana Magazine of History*, 42 (1946), 226–28, explains how the liquor issue weakened the Republican party.

[21] Harrison to Michener, February 7, 1885, (L.C.), Vol. 19. William G. Carleton, "The Money Question in Indiana Politics, 1865–1890," *Indiana Magazine of History*, 42 (1946), 147, notes that the Greenback vote had fallen off considerably in 1884 and concludes that by the winter of 1885 "the financial issue was no longer paramount."

owner of the Republican *Journal* to expose the scheme at once and to stir up "some hot talk." [22] His own title for the Democratic bill to reapportion the Hoosier State was: "A Bill to Prohibit the Election of A Republican to the United States Senate From Indiana." [23]

The outraged senator was too far away to exercise any oratorical influence; for the moment he had to depend on the effectiveness of State Senators James Huston and William Foulke and State Assemblymen George Adams and Warren Sayre in fighting the bill. These Republicans were ordered "to engage in all methods of delay" and "make combinations with dissatisfied Democrats," even to "secure resignations *if imperatively necessary and advisable.*" These were only slender weapons, and with each day's mail Harrison took a dimmer view of the affair. Republican leaders on the State Central Committee were equally disheartened. One of the letters which arrived just before the Inauguration was from Michener, who wrote despondently:

If this bill passes, I very much fear that none of us will ever live to see a Republican in the United States Senate, unless there should be a disintegration of the D— party. It appears that no landslide, or earthquake, of a political kind can ever, under this bill, put a R— majority in the General Assembly. It is an open secret that it was drafted so as to make sure the calling of Isaac P. Gray to your seat in 1887.[24]

If the Democrats succeeded in slicing Indiana's election districts to their own advantage, no one doubted that they could and would rub Republican "noses to the grindstone for four years" and oust Harrison from the Senate in 1887. This latter prospect might be a personal blessing for the Senator and his family, but a deadly blow to the party. Benjamin Harrison was "Mr. Republican" in Indiana. However, the General was still in the field. Writing to State Senator Nicholas Ensley, he said, "I could leave the Senate and return to my home and to business without any personal regrets, for I find it a place of hard work and many annoyances. But I feel I owe it to the Republican party to make the best fight possible, and shall do so." [25]

---

[22] Harrison to Hon. John C. New and to Hon. J. N. Huston, February 18, 1885, (L.C.), Vol. 19, declared that the "unjust bill ought to be resisted until the last; almost any methods are justifiable in resisting it."

[23] Harrison to T. P. Keator, February 19, 1885, (L.C.), Tibbott transcripts, Box 2.

[24] Michener to Harrison, February 26, 1885, (L.C.), Vol. 19.

[25] Harrison to Nicholas Ensley, February 18, 1885, *ibid.,* Vol. 18.

In Harrison's opinion the Democratic gerrymander was "the most infamous piece of legislation ever attempted outside of a Rebel State." Only "the closing hours of the session" kept him on the Hill, frustrated by his inability to give on-the-spot advice to his dismayed Republican forces. To direct any real defensive action from far across the Alleghenies was, he reasoned, "a good deal like General Grant undertaking to fight the battle of Nashville instead of leaving it to General Thomas." [26] Two days later, on March 1, Harrison learned that the hopeless contest was lost. The reapportionment bill became Indiana law on Cleveland's inaugural morning. The next day Harrison prophesied bitterly, his mind on local affairs, "Only a popular revolution will be able to give us the legislature, or more than two Congressmen." He knew now that his stay in the Senate would terminate early in 1887. But meanwhile, the lines were already re-forming for the next battle and the General himself coined the Republicans' rallying cry: "Brave men have won more desperate fights than this . . . we will not give them a walk-over." [27]

At the close of the special session of Congress on April 2, 1885, Harrison hurried home to take inventory of smashed fences, design a vigorous political policy for 1886, and, by far a more pleasant duty, map out for Carrie and himself an itinerary that would take them as far west as Portland and perhaps as far south as lower California. It would be a two months' business-pleasure jaunt, occasioned by Harrison's chairmanship of the Sub-Committee on Indian Affairs which had been directed to take testimony relating to the leasing of Indian lands by the cattlemen.[28] Part of this journey would therefore be devoted to work by the Senator, who would be accompanied by the two other committeemen and a clerk.

In the immediate present, however, Harrison had before him a mountain of work at his Indianapolis law office. Between court

[26] Harrison to Gen. Fred Knefler and to J. A. Wildman, February 28, 1885, *ibid.*, Vol. 19.

[27] Harrison to Hon. Benjamin S. Parker and to L. T. Michener, March 5, 1885, *ibid.* Political corruption characterized both parties in Indiana between 1865 and 1888. See J. P. Dunn, *History of Greater Indianapolis*, I, 292–93. Other historians have chosen to ignore the 1885 gerrymander by the Democrats.

[28] Harrison to Perry S. Heath, May 4; and to L. D. M. Sweat, May 16, 1885, (L.C.), Vol. 19.

trials in Indiana during his law partner's illness, and brief trips to Washington for political reasons, the spring of 1885 seemed short to the Senator. To his close political friends, however, this same period called for long, hard work at rebuilding the state party. Heading this grim task force was Louis T. Michener, whose devotion to Harrison was unwavering. "I regard him as being one of our best and greatest men," Michener wrote a friend at this time, "and, if kept in public life, his chances are bright for the future." [29]

Such stalwarts as Michener, Miller, Hay, Peelle, and Taylor formed the core of Harrison's strength in Indiana. They urged their chief to take a vacation from politics for the month of April and leave reorganization plans to them. This the Senator found easy to do. With pleasure he joined Carrie in gardening and planting on the north side of their home on Delaware Street.[30]

As he and Carrie contentedly gardened, or basked in the April sun, Harrison's mind was at work on the problem of "redeeming our state from Democratic control." [31] On May 5, he was ready to go into action to secure his own re-election as Senator. In a carefully thought-out letter to Eugene Hay, now at his Madison, Indiana, home, Harrison outlined his plans for a frontal attack:

I want to open the campaign of 1886 now. It will be a desperate fight but there is a chance to win and we must take it. If we can get to work at once and I can find a few friends in each county who will organize early with a special reference to the Legislative ticket I shall have great hopes of success.

Here indeed was a new Harrison, well in control of his forces. The Republican defeat, he wrote, was due primarily to "unfortunate or weak" nominations. He warned that "there must be no more such mistakes, and the only way to avoid them is to canvass the matter in advance." Voters should be reminded, he told Hay, that he had secured federal aid and patronage for them; he had also

[29] L. T. Michener to E. G. Hay, April 4, 1885, Eugene Gano Hay MSS, Vol. 5. Michener felt that the Republican defeat would be a blessing in the end, as "the perspiring statesmen in our party will now have a chance to rend the enemy instead of one another. Our party will once more be on the offensive—and it excels in attack. . . ." Hay, an Indiana attorney, was at this time beginning a new and successful practice in Minnesota, but still retained his Madison, Indiana, home.

[30] Harrison to R. S. Taylor, April 25, 1885, (L.C.), Vol. 19 (copy by courtesy of the Hayes Memorial Library, Fremont, Ohio).

[31] Harrison to W. W. Slaughter, April 14, 1885, ibid.

procured a levee for Jeffersonville, across the Ohio from Louisville, Kentucky. Nor was he silent as to the "very many soldier friends who will help me." But, most important, he warned that each county must put up its best candidate:

Who is the man—that is the first question and ought not to be settled hastily. He must also be a man who can get Dem. votes. Get out a search warrant for him. The further plans of work I will submit to you after awhile.[32]

For the next month and a half, Harrison wrote letters furiously, overpowering his secretary with work. Into each of the state's ninety-two counties poured his appeals, calling on Republican leaders and personal friends to join in the task of "overcoming . . . the gerrymander." Keep a fast hold on all certain counties; use vigilance and prudence in debatable districts—this was Harrison's theme. In particular, he advised them to look to the ranks of doctors and lawyers for help; to approach G.A.R. members whom he knew would offer unlimited service; and to choose candidates known as churchgoers in their communities. He was personally convinced, he concluded, that "we have the material to achieve victory." [33]

Before the Harrisons and his senatorial colleagues left for the West, a flood of spirited political reports reached the Senator from various parts of the state. They indicated, Harrison triumphantly wrote his supporters, that Hoosier Republicans "are very much aroused . . . they will, for a time at least, forget their quarrels in the larger quarrel with Cleveland and his confederate supporters." [34]

It was clear now that Harrison planned to lay stress on national issues in the next state campaign, and in particular on that legacy of the Civil War known as the "suppressed Republican vote of the South." As early as March, 1885, in fact, he had composed a letter that revealed his determination to take action to remedy the situation:

If any prophet had arisen during the war and had predicted such a condition of things as we now see, he would have been stoned to death

[32] Harrison to E. G. Hay, May 5, 1885, Eugene Gano Hay MSS, Vol. 5.
[33] W. H. H. Hart to Harrison, May 11, 1885, (L.C.), Vol. 1, Second Series. This volume, as well as Vol. 19, contains copies of Harrison's epistolary efforts to secure his re-election in 1886.
[34] Harrison to Hon. W. D. Owen, May 16, 1885, ibid., Vol. 19.

without the camp. No soldier would have credited a prophecy which involved the placing of the Rebel who was confronting him in battle over the Pension Office.

The disfranchisement of Republicans in the South is a question, the gravity of which cannot be exaggerated; but what can we do? We may place the U. S. Marshals at the polls, if we ever recover the Presidency again; but it has been demonstrated that local sentiment is such that conviction for any violations of election laws is impossible.

Possibly, if we could unite the North and get control of both Houses of Congress and the Presidency, we might take some steps to deprive the South of representation in Congress and the Electoral College, based upon this suppressed vote.

Harrison was realistic enough, however, to predict that the South's representation in Congress would never be curtailed. In the same letter, he had maintained that "a division of the White vote in the South furnishes the only possible solution," that "the tariff or some other financial question" could divide the voting power of whites in the South.[35] As he packed for the West, however, he filed this thorny problem under "unfinished business," promising himself not to forget it.

The Harrisons started their western vacation with a parting, the Senator heading for Washington to join his fellow committee-men, and Carrie and Mamie leaving for St. Paul, where they would await his arrival. On reaching the capital during the first week in July, Harrison approved a six-weeks itinerary for his Sub-Committee on Indian Affairs, which included himself, Senator James K. Jones of Arkansas, who had served in the Confederate Army, and Senator John J. Ingalls of Kansas, a former newspaper editor who had been a lieutenant colonel in the Union Army. For the office of clerk to the sub-committee, Harrison had selected Colonel Elijah W. Halford, editor of the influential Republican *Journal*. This was a shrewd political choice, but it also resulted in a warm friendship which would bring Halford to Washington in 1889 as President Harrison's private secretary.[36]

[35] Harrison to W. W. Slaughter, March 14, 1885, *ibid.* For a fair discussion of Harrison's attitude toward the South between 1889 and 1893, see Vincent P. DeSantis, "Benjamin Harrison and the Republican Party in the South," *Indiana Magazine of History,* 51 (1955), 279–302.

[36] Harrison to Perry S. Heath, May 4, 1885, (L.C.), Vol. 19. Harrison felt that the *Journal* should be recognized and Halford was his choice. Perry Heath, the paper's Washington correspondent, had also desired the position.

None of the foursome was happier to start for the West than Senator Harrison, who could now forget how industrious Vice-President Hendricks was "in picking up the crumbs" [37] of patronage for job-seeking Democrats. He could also laugh at Senator Dan Voorhees, mobbed by spoilsmen hungry for office. Half way through the investigations held at various Indian reservations, Harrison was joined by his law partner, William H. H. Miller, who accompanied the group as far as Helena, Montana. Law, politics, and old soldiers' yarns filled the travelers' leisure hours and lightened their official duties.[38]

At St. Paul, Harrison met his wife and daughter for a brief reunion, after which the ladies journeyed ahead to Helena, where Russell and his wife awaited them. The Senator joined the family circle in mid-August when his committee had finished its work.[39] It was a happy time for Carrie and Ben. Both their children were happily married, and their son seemed to be on the road to success. In addition to working in the United States Assay Office in Helena, Russell was skillfully managing the Montana Cattle Company.[40] When their pleasant visit was over, Carrie and Ben set off alone on what might be termed a second honeymoon. They made "a flying trip to the Pacific Coast" heading from Washington to Oregon and on down through California.[41] Turning eastward, they stopped at Yellowstone Park before continuing home. They reached Indianapolis on September 7, just three weeks after leaving the Montana Territory. The next morning Harrison was back at his law office, briskly dictating more letters.[42]

His legal work had so accumulated during his seven weeks' absence that Harrison was forced to decline many speaking invi-

[37] Harrison to Capt. J. H. Bush, May 4, 1885, *ibid.* This remark was occasioned by the dismissal of one of Harrison's friends from the Capitol police force.

[38] Charles Latham, Jr., "Benjamin Harrison in the Senate, 1881–1887," p. 111. The usual routine at each reservation was to spend two days in examining the records and in holding council with the Indians. Also Harrison to Herbert Welsh, January 8, 1886, (L.C.), Vol. 22.

[39] Harrison to Margaret W. Peltz, July 10, 1885, *ibid.*, Vol 19.

[40] W. H. H. Miller to A. A. Wheeler, October 8, 1885, W. H. H. Miller Letterbooks. Miller and his son, Sam, had joined the Harrisons at Helena. This letter was to the president of the Montana National Bank. "You can congratulate Russell for me . . . on the sale and on the fact that he has come out on top in all matters pertaining to the Assay office. . . . am quite willing to agree to a larger salary. . . ."

[41] Harrison to Howard Cale, August 15, 1885, Howard Cale MSS, (Library of Congress). Passes for Senator and Mrs. Harrison were issued by the Northern Pacific.

[42] Harrison to Capt. J. M. Sligh, and to Charles Beardslay, September 8, 1885, (L.C.), Tibbott transcripts, Box 2.

tations during the fall of 1885.[43] He made one exception. His father's old friend, John Sherman, was seeking re-election as Ohio senator and had asked for help. Although it meant Harrison's missing the eleventh annual reunion of the old 70th Regiment,[44] his tour of the Buckeye State just before its October 13 election was widely acclaimed and Senator Sherman was profoundly grateful. Citizens of his birth state assured Harrison that he would have their "earnest and early support in any council of national character." The General was as pleased as Senator Sherman himself when the 13th brought to Ohio a decisive Republican victory, including an individual triumph for Sherman. Indiana was enjoying an off-year, but Ohio's success raised Harrison's hopes for 1886.[45]

The date set for the opening of the first regular session of the 49th Congress was December 7, but Harrison planned to go to Washington several days in advance for a meeting of party leaders. His return was delayed, however, by the unexpected death of Vice-President Thomas A. Hendricks in Indianapolis on November 25, 1885. Like Harrison, the late leader of the Indiana Democracy was Ohio-born but Hoosier-bred. Implacable foes in politics, they had been friendly competitors in law. Harrison served on the funeral committee in Indianapolis, but confined his eulogistic remarks to praise of Hendricks' private character and personal traits.

The 49th Congress had no sooner met than an underground war broke out between Cleveland and the Republican side of the Senate on the vital matter of federal appointments.[46] Still stunned by their 1884 defeat, the Republicans were in a hostile mood towards the Chief Executive. Since his inauguration, Cleveland had removed more than five hundred Republicans from office. Ohio's John Sherman, who nursed a perpetual hope of reaching the White House,[47] led the Republicans in protest. Ready to join

---

[43] *Ibid.* From a political viewpoint the most important refusals concerned the Iowa state campaign and an address to the Society of the Army of the Cumberland, which had scheduled its 1885 reunion at Grand Rapids, Michigan.

[44] Harrison to J. F. Snow, October 12, 1885, *ibid.*

[45] Isaac W. Monfort to Harrison, October 8, 1885, and John Sherman to Harrison, October 13, 1885, (L.C.), Vol. 1, Second Series. See also John Sherman, *An Autobiography: Forty Years in House, Senate and Cabinet,* pp. 717, 726 ff.

[46] Nevins, *op. cit.,* pp. 253 ff. The historical details of the "Tenure of Office Battle" are fully developed here.

[47] John A. Logan to S. B. Elkins, December 11, 1885, Elkins MSS. Logan claimed he bowed out of the convention race in favor of Sherman, who was "so anxious on

forces against the President were Senator Harrison and a host of others who felt they should openly challenge the issue. Others, more timid, thought they should wait for elections. Frequent caucusing found Harrison eloquent in helping to outline strategy for a political assault on Cleveland. It was felt that a challenge to the President's popular leadership might serve to restore their party's prestige.

On December 10, 1885, however, just four days after the session got under way, Harrison came out in the open. He wrote several friends, stating that he did not "intend to offer a factious opposition to Cleveland." He felt that the President might have been led by bad advice in making certain appointments, but pointed out that "self-respect, as well as my public duty, requires a vigorous opposition to the confirmation of unworthy persons." [48] He was also determined, he wrote in another letter the same day, to see to it that in all cases of removals upon charges, where there is afforded no opportunity to see the charges and meet them, such persons "shall have the opportunity before the Senate Committee." [49] This shaft was aimed at Postmaster General William F. Vilas in particular, whose callous treatment of Republican office-holders Harrison branded an "outrage." "Whatever may be done by other Senators," he wrote on the 11th, "a good while ago I made a program for myself as to removals from office in Indiana." He assured his constituency and persuaded his colleagues to follow his lead in pledging that no Republican "shall be made a victim of Civil Service false pretensions of the Administration." [50]

By his open, positive efforts to bring civil service regulations into proper perspective, Harrison gradually won the support of many, including reform leader William Dudley Foulke, with whom he corresponded frequently. By the week before Christmas, the Indiana senator felt able to predict that "the hypocrisy of the Administration in its professions of Civil Service Reform and its practice probably will be exposed before this Congress is

---

the subject much as he felt that this would be a stepping stone for him to the Presidency, and feeling assured that the whole people were hankering for him, I thought it was right for a little fellow like myself to give way."

[48] Harrison to Benz, and to Calkins, December 10, 1885, (L.C.), Vol. 20, wrote that "the President himself will be glad to have a chance to correct such mistakes."

[49] Harrison to Johnson, December 10, 1885, ibid., reaffirmed that "it is not my purpose . . . to make opposition to the confirmation of reputable men appointed by Cleveland to vacancies."

[50] Harrison to Coulson, December 11, 1885, ibid.

over." [51] To hasten this end, he invited any and all evidence that might serve to illustrate such simulations on the part of the President or members of his Cabinet. Harrison assured Foulke that "during the holiday recess I shall classify them [the papers] and study them sufficiently to have some judgment of my own as to what I ought to do in each particular case." [52] Particularly annoying to Harrison was the peremptory removal or dismissal of ex-soldiers. By Christmas, such instances were as "thick as black-berries in August." He was especially angered at the ". . . un-American course of Vilas in removing officials upon charges without advising them of their character or giving them any opportunity to defend against it."

Disappointed office seekers from among the Indiana Democrats also furnished Harrison with illustrations of what they termed unfair removals from office. This was what Harrison wanted—names, dates, and places. He promised to use such information "judiciously." [53] The uncompromising struggle between the Republican senators and the Chief Executive was nearing a crisis. Only the Christmas recess postponed open battle, as Cleveland went his own unbending way. He knew he had captured the popular fancy. As John B. Elam, Harrison's junior law partner, observed, "outside of politicians the people are well satisfied with the administration of Cleveland." [54] Much as the thought irked him, the Senator knew Elam was right. Nevertheless, if the President, dependent on public approval, could be weakened, even humiliated, in the course of his distribution of spoils, Harrison was willing to carry the fight to the White House.

Senator Harrison worked doggedly through most of Christmas Day, 1885, sending out several letters without a mention of the

[51] Harrison to Williams, December 18, 1885, ibid.

[52] Harrison to Foulke, December 18, 1885, ibid., Vol. 21. For a fuller discussion of apportionment methods and limitations, even after the passage of the Pendleton Law of 1883, consult the U. S. Civil Service Commission, Annual Report, 1886–1887, pp. 56–64. An excellent summary is contained in Leonard D. White, The Republican Era, 1869–1901, pp. 360–61.

[53] Harrison to Sexton; to Robbins; and to Anderson, December 23, 1885, (L.C.), Vol. 21.

[54] John B. Elam to Harrison, December 24, 1885, (L.C.), Vol. 1, Second Series. Elam, like Harrison, was a graduate of Miami University and a Phi Delta Thetan. He had joined Harrison and Miller shortly after completing his term as prosecuting attorney in 1882. See Harvey W. Elam, The Elam Family (privately published, Xenia, Ohio, 1933), p. 126.

fact that it was Christmas. He and Carrie had rented a new and more spacious apartment in the Woodmont on Iowa Avenue, but it was a barren substitute for a real holiday back home. The General regretted what could not be helped. He was finally on the verge of playing the rôle that Wharton Barker had seriously urged upon him, that of leader of his party in the Senate. But before he could lead, he must have ammunition. There was still much work to be done, much evidence to be gathered. Most of all, he needed something to make Cleveland and the Democrats squirm.

CHAPTER XVIII

The Assault
on Grover Cleveland

ARRISON REJOINED his Senate colleagues in January, 1886, satisfied that his intensive work through the holiday recess had prepared him for some of the legislative battles ahead. Though he might be starting his last year in the Senate, he had made up his mind to make every day count. While continuing to sponsor bills for the aid of needy and disabled veterans, he would remain on the alert for the strategic moment of attack on Cleveland and his federal appointment policies. Meanwhile, his perennial battle with southern and western Democrats was waiting to be refought. Once more he had prepared a carefully drafted Dakota statehood bill, first on his agenda. To introduce it, he was armed with a "full and formal speech," hoping that this year his favorite measure would finally pass both Houses.

As chairman of the Committee on the Territories, Harrison commanded sufficient prestige to induce the Senate's consideration of his new Dakota statehood bill on Wednesday, January 27. It would bring on a partisan fight, he knew, and again he had reminded hopeful Republicans in the Territory that there was only "one reason that can be given for keeping her [South Dakota] out, and *only* one, and that is that there are not enough Democrats in the Territory." [1]

The Indiana Senator opened debate with great moderation, but political feelings soon got the better of him as Senator Matthew C. Butler of South Carolina opened the Democratic attack by saying that the Harrison bill had been instigated by the executive

[1] Harrison to Hipple, January 23, 1886, a Tibbott transcript, (L.C.), Vol. 22.

committee of a political party.[2] This Harrison denied in strong terms, and the battle was on. The ensuing wrangle continued day after day until February 4, with Harrison challenging all objections with a sheaf of unbeatable facts. The tone of the debate was set on the third afternoon by Senator George G. Vest, Missouri Democrat, who claimed that the Dakotans were lawless and therefore not worthy of statehood. Harrison bristled back with an indignant reply and the debate went into a fourth day.

Mail now began to pour into Harrison's office, and continued throughout the strenuous debate. Dakotans vied with Hoosiers in praise of his staunch defense of the Territory. His answers all carried the same comment: "The opposition to . . . Dakota is absolutely partisan—it is the solid south." But he would make no compromise:

I will not consent to the admission of the territory as one state. It contains nearly a hundred and fifty thousand square miles. Divided as I propose, on the 46th parallel, South Dakota would be eighth state in size in the Union. And, taking its productive capacity in connection with its area, I think it would take a still higher place.[3]

In the Senate chamber on Wednesday, February 3, 1886, the political storm over Dakota had reached blizzard proportions. Outside, nature kept pace. Within three days Washington was blanketed "with a deeper snow than the oldest inhabitant recalls," [4] On the floor of the Senate, John Logan of Illinois was speaking: ". . . there never were so many merely technical and flimsy objections by men called statesmen . . . against the rights of any people." Senator Butler rose, reasserting that Dakota's admission appeared "to be controlled and influenced by a political clique." Before Harrison could get the floor, Logan lashed back with the pointed observation:

[2] *Congressional Record*, 49.1, pp. 952–75. Howard R. Lamar, *Dakota Territory, 1861–1889: A Study of Frontier Politics*, pp. 248–56, details the background of the statehood movement and shows that Butler raised a plausible and constitutional objection.

[3] *Ibid.*, Harrison to Williams, and to Andrews, February 2, 1886, Tibbott transcripts, (L.C.), Vol. 22, reiterated his conviction that "there is abundant precedent for Dakota, and no just ground of opposition to her admission. It is purely and solely a partisan question." Harrison over-simplified Vest's position. The Missourian argued that the Dakotans themselves were engaged in a task of "dubious and obviously partisan nature." He chided the Dakota state legislature for electing senators "without congressional permission as an ex-sovereignty." See Lamar, *op. cit.*, p. 257.

[4] Harrison to Alexander, February 6, 1886, (L.C.), Vol. 22.

I believe when a people having sufficient population and all the necessary requisites, believing in this Government, want to be admitted as a state, statesmanship should rise to that height that it would not inquire as to cliques or politics, Democratic or Republican. . . .[5]

Butler, eager to let pass so embarrassing an issue, turned his fire on Harrison, and the debate and the bickering dragged on until the storm outside prompted a motion to adjourn while there was still some daylight.

On the following day, February 4, Harrison spoke for two-and-a-half hours in an effort to bring his bill to a vote. Annoyed by the constant interruptions of John T. Morgan of Alabama, James Z. George of Mississippi, and, of course, Butler of South Carolina— a formidable trio of Democratic orators—Harrison ironically congratulated the Senate. "It is no longer necessary," he observed, "to shell the woods to locate the enemy." Their delaying tactics he called "the Atlanta campaign over again." After a few other cogent remarks, he went on to review the history of Democratic opposition to Dakota's admission since 1881. The Presidential election of 1884, he said, had postponed Dakota's statehood lest its votes add "an uncertain element to the electoral college on the very eve of a great national contest." And now, Harrison exclaimed angrily,

We hear the suggestion from the distinguished Senator from Alabama that Dakota shall wait until 1889. . . . Another Presidential election must be passed before Dakota can receive the hand of fellowship from the Senator from Alabama. I ask him, I ask the country, how long shall three hundred thousand American citizens, as justly entitled as he or the people of his state to participate in the great decision of a Presidential election, be kept out in order that the chances of a Democratic succession may be increased or the power and influence of other states magnified?[6]

Following a bitter retort from the Alabama senator, Harrison spoke for two hours and twenty minutes, while tempers flared intermittently. The Senate adjourned without a vote, but on the next day, Friday, February 5, just before adjournment for the week end, Benjamin Harrison's Dakota bill passed the Senate by a strictly party vote of 32 to 22 (with 22 senators absent). Oddly enough, the only convert to the Dakota cause was Harrison's Dem-

[5] Congressional Record, 49.1, p. 1090.
[6] Ibid.

ocratic colleague, Dan Voorhees.[7] Although the bill had only dim prospects in the House, its passage by the Senate and his remarkable handling of the debate had marked Harrison as a party leader of national stature.

After a week in Indianapolis to try a case and to advise with state party leaders, Harrison returned to Washington on February 18, where he was immediately engulfed in a nightmare of activity: committee work, preparation of notes for Senate debate, the study of national problems, special meetings, the daily mountain of mail—and always his letter writing, often as many as fifty a day. One, written on the day of his return, reveals his viewpoint on the growing problems of labor. Harrison offered a simple statement of his position: "I am sympathetic with the laboring man and I shall always be found supporting such measures as are for his interests. No country can be prosperous that does not have a well-paid and contented laboring population." [8] He cooperated cordially with various assemblies of the Knights of Labor, but in no instance would he support a program of violent action. He believed that "well-digested reforms" in "orderly procession" were the best means of improving labor-capital relations and of keeping labor from adopting "the fierce and destructive doctrines of the Anarchist and his bloody work." [9] To this end, he had pledged himself to help correct the "overcrowding, ill-ventilation and unhealthful surroundings" [10] which too often were the laborer's lot in the world of the 1880's.

Pension bills always claimed much of Harrison's attention, but in the spring of 1886 he was especially interested in the welfare of those disabled veterans whom Congress had apparently neglected. He therefore sponsored a bill of his own, while confiding to ex-soldier friends that "he was laughed at by many . . . who

[7] Harrison to Alexander, February 6, 1886, a Tibbott transcript, (L.C.), Vol. 22. Harrison claimed he could not say Voorhees was a convert. "He was compelled in his son's interest to support the bill for the Washington Territory, and could not of course do that and go back on Dakota."

[8] Harrison to Kentwell, February 18; and to Harris, February 24, 1886, *ibid.*, Vol. 23.

[9] Fort Wayne boasted 2,000 and Indianapolis some 7,000 Knights of Labor who endorsed Harrison's course of action. See T. P. Keator to Harrison, March 11, 1886, (L.C.), Vol. 1, Second Series. Also Harrison to Hopper, March 15; to Hess, March 20; to Wilson, March 20; and to Hopper, March 29, 1886, (L.C.), Vols. 23 and 24.

[10] *Journal,* September 16, 1886.

said I was playing the demagogue."[11] Nevertheless, Harrison continued his work on behalf of the "Boys in Blue" and succeeded in winning a few Senatorial converts.[12]

Meanwhile, as spring wore on, relations between the Republican Senators and President Cleveland grew more strained. For months, Harrison had been studying the evidence that Republican civil officers were being thrown out of their positions for no stated reason, and then were not granted hearings. One strong letter of protest had come to his desk while he was involved in the Dakota debate. It was from General John Coburn, territorial judge in Montana. He had been summarily dismissed from office by Cleveland, and he was appealing to Senator Harrison, his friend, to challenge the President's action:

What can I do, to protest against these despotic acts of the President, to assert my innocence of any blame, to insist that I have done my whole duty fairly as a judge, and to appeal to my friends in the Senate to see that my reputation, which is my only earthly possession that I prize, may not be tarnished for all time to come by the joint action of the President and the Senate, while I am as powerless as an infant to do or say anything.[13]

With such letters as this in his collection of scores, Harrison felt that the case against Cleveland was very nearly complete and that his weeks of tedious research would soon end in definite action. Verbose testimony to unjust removal or suspension from office of Indiana Republicans crowded his files. Additional letters containing proofs of dismissal on secret charges came in daily in reply to his own letters, seeking additional evidence.[14]

During the last week in February, Harrison and his friends decided they were ready to bring the fight to the floor of the Senate. As attorneys, John Sherman of Ohio and George Edmunds of Vermont, chairman of the Judiciary Committee, agreed with Harrison that the attack should be based on the Tenure of Office Act, authored by Edmunds in 1867. This had provided that no

---

[11] Harrison to Power, March 8, 1886, a Tibbott transcript, (L.C.), Vol. 23.

[12] Harrison to T. S. Brooks, March 18, 1886, *ibid.* Senator Sherman was listed as the chief convert to the cause of more liberal pension legislation.

[13] Coburn to Harrison, January 31, 1886, (L.C.), Vol. 1, Second Series. This ten-page letter, one of several from Coburn, confirmed the Republican belief that such Presidential action was an arbitrary exercise of power. The Coburn Papers (Indiana State Library) throw no additional light on this problem.

[14] Harrison to Sayre, Peelle, Dudley, March 11; Harrison to Fisk, March 26, 1886, (L.C.), Vol. 23.

civil officer appointed with the consent of the Senate could be removed without the Senate's approval.[15] A modification in 1869 weakened the act in three respects: 1) the President might now suspend an officer "at discretion" instead of only in cases of misconduct or crime; 2) the President was no longer required to submit to the Senate evidence and reasons for dismissal; and 3) if the Senate refused to concur in a removal, the President was free to make nominations until one was accepted by the Senate.

Edmunds, Sherman, and Harrison now agreed that Edmunds should bring out a resolution on the floor, carrying a statement of the Republicans' policy of approving Presidential nominations in all cases where dismissal of the previous officeholder seemed justified. It would also state the Republicans' demand that the President henceforth send to the Senate full information as to his suspensions and new appointments. Harrison felt that this would straighten out the federal appointment "muddle" by calling it to public attention. Thus began a celebrated battle between Grover Cleveland and the Senate. Though he could scarcely foresee it, the "Hoosier Warrior" was on the eve of his most widely heralded speech as a member of the United States Senate.

Grover Cleveland was correct in stating that "the Spoils System is involved in my controversy with the Senate." [16] He was even heroic when, unsupported by a majority of his party, he pledged that all conscientious public servants "might hold their offices until the end of their terms." [17] This policy endeared him to the Senate's civil service reform bloc, who continued to support the President until it became known that officeholders were being dismissed on secret charges and without subsequent hearing. The reformers broke openly with the Administration in March, 1886, while the Edmunds resolution was in debate in the Senate. This produced the effect Harrison and his friends had hoped for, giving everyone a chance to come out in the open. Cleveland was dismayed by the sudden, savage barrage of criticism from both Demo-

15 Allan Nevins, *Grover Cleveland: A Study in Courage*, pp. 255 ff. Also Harrison to Edmunds, January 13, 1886, a Tibbott transcript, (L.C.), Vol. 22.

16 Cleveland to Silas W. Burt, March 2, 1886, Burt MSS, (New York Historical Society).

17 *Congressional Record*, 49.1, p. 2790. Harrison stated: "The President of the United States repeatedly put himself under pledge, not simply in his public utterances but in private letters, voluntarily written, in favor of such a policy."

crats and Republicans. Especially acceptable to friend and foe alike was the stipulation in the resolution that secret charges must be made public before any officeholder could be suspended or removed. The President was in trouble. He pleaded with his erstwhile reform friends not to choose such an hour for an attack of their own. He said he felt he had the "right to ask, as the man did of God when he was fighting the bear: 'If you can't help me, don't help the bear.' " [18]

The real "bear" in this case was Harrison, who had not yet been heard from. It was now March 26 and so far, as an experienced courtroom attorney, he had been dissatisfied with the tone of the speeches. Except for a sharp one by Senator John Ingalls of Kansas, the senatorial debate that droned on seemed to lack drama. Harrison, listening, felt strongly that there was a human side to the situation "that was much more attractive in the popular sense." [19] Then his Democratic colleague, Dan Voorhees, rose for one of his celebrated bursts of oratory, and Harrison was stirred to emulation. He had planned to save his own speech until the next day, Saturday, March 27, but his orator's instinct told him to follow in Voorhees' wake. His audience was aroused; now was the time to speak. With only a handful of scribbled notes and an assortment of Indiana newspaper clippings to guide him, Harrison asked for the floor. Leaving aside the constitutional question involved, he put tears and indignation into an address that drew applause from senators and gallery alike. But he had still to dramatize the human effects of the "patronage" evil.

He therefore told the story of Isabelle De la Hunt, widow of a Democratic veteran and mother of an orphaned son.[20] She lived at Cannelton, a small Indiana town on the Ohio River, where for years her father had been postmaster. Isabelle had served as his deputy until old age compelled his retirement. At Harrison's re-

[18] Cleveland to Burt, March 2, 1886, Burt MSS.

[19] Harrison to Michener, and to Wildman, March 27, 1886, (L.C.), Vol. 24, noted that some of the passages of Ingall's speech were "simply inimitable" and that "Democratic Senators, including our distinguished Voorhees, nodded approval in the most emphatic way of what he said."

[20] Harrison stated that Major De la Hunt, who had served with the 26th Indiana Volunteers, was a Democrat before, during, and after the war. He had been shot down twice and compelled to return home, where the Democracy of Perry County elected him to several offices. A sorrowing wife and an only son watched him walk slowly to the grave. No details that could draw a tear were overlooked by Harrison, who was later distressed to learn that the Washington correspondent for the Indianapolis *Journal* was absent from the gallery at the time of this speech.

quest, Frank Hatton, Postmaster General under President Arthur, had appointed the widowed mother to the position. Reciting his story with the skill of an actor, Harrison brought each detail into bold relief: Major De la Hunt's service in the Union Army; his early death as the result of war wounds; his widow's mounting financial needs; the plight of her young son and aging father. He emphasized the fact that the major had been a loyal Democrat. Finally, he said, this widow, mother, and loyal daughter, struggling to make ends meet, had—without a chance to defend herself—been dismissed from her small federal post.

Mrs. De la Hunt had appealed her removal, said Harrison, demanding to know the charges against her. Democratic Congressman John Jay Kleiner, Union veteran and former mayor of Evansville, had investigated her case in the late summer of 1885. Within two days she had received his curt reply: "Evidence deemed sufficient to cause your removal has been filed, and your removal was ordered on account of offensive partisanship shown in the conduct of the office during the campaign just closed."

Now, with a warmth that captured the Senate, Harrison read aloud the correspondence between Congressman Kleiner and Mrs. De la Hunt, after which he offered the widow's gallant defense of herself. Solemnly he held up the letter she had written to the press, and said, "Now hear . . . the woman." He began to read:

. . . Had the Government seen fit to remove me without alleged cause, as it had an undoubted right to do, I should remain silent; but when I am sacrificed by falsehood I may be excused if I protest against it.

I have this to say, that whoever has sworn to any act of partisanship on my part in the conduct of the post-office here has committed willful perjury, and I dare him to appear before any open tribunal and make good his accusation. I call upon him to stand forth in the glare of honest sunlight and exhibit himself to this community as the author of this calumny. Let him do this and bring from the files of the star-chamber court at Washington the specifications to which he has affixed his infamous name and I pledge myself to prove their utter falsity. So conscious am I of the rectitude and the impartiality of my conduct in the discharge of my official duties that I do not hesitate to appeal to you, one and all, irrespective of your political preferences, for the truth of this assertion.

Somebody in this community has sworn to a lie to accomplish that which could not be done through the instrumentality of truth. For this I now brand him publicly as a perjurer. I do not propose to lie under the false accusations of any untruthful coward who thus resorts to secret assassination of character to accomplish an unjust object. Hence I appeal in this public manner to the honor and conscience of all honest men and women to condemn, as I know they must, this infamous attempt to do me an injury.

Republican senators realized what was happening, as Harrison read on and the silent public in the galleries strained to catch every word. The Hoosier was not only dramatizing their complaint against Cleveland. He was getting the point through to the people.

I say to the Government—take your post-office, but not under false pretenses. Do this, and I will utter no word of complaint, however unjust it may appear.

Excuse me, my friends, you who have known me from my childhood and are witnesses of my daily and official life—excuse me if I manifest some feeling over this wrong; I cannot help it. War, with its natural and inevitable results, struck down my husband, my protector and support. It was the act of an open foe on the field of battle; whom I try to forgive; but that the Government, to preserve which he sacrificed his life, should connive with secret enemies and false witnesses to strike down his family without an opportunity of vindication is a national disgrace, and an act too cowardly and base for absolution.[21]

The Senator had finished, and the applause from the galleries was spontaneous. Democrats urged Voorhees to reply; the Administration and the party could ill-afford silence. But Edmunds and Logan spoke for the Republicans while Harrison waited for the dynamic voice of the "Tall Sycamore of the Wabash." Voorhees, however, remained in his seat. No other Democrat uttered a word.[22]

The constant stream of visitors, hundreds of letters, and the number of requests to the Government Printing Office for copies of Harrison's now celebrated patronage speech failed to turn his head. At first he ordered only 5,000 copies printed for personal distribution in Indiana, but within three days, congressmen subscribed for 20,000 more. Several Indiana papers and the St. Louis

[21] The John J. Kleiner and Isabelle De la Hunt correspondence, as cited by Harrison in the *Congressional Record*, 49.1, p. 2794. All details are from the *Record*.

[22] Harrison advised constituents that he had it by the "grapevine" that Voorhees said he could not reply because "it was too damned true." Harrison to Holstein, April 1; and to Cole, April 2, 1886, (L.C.), Vol. 24.

Globe-Democrat reproduced the Senator's speech in full. The spirited and touching De la Hunt letter came in for special commendation, so much so that Harrison and the State Committee ordered it reprinted in each county organ in Indiana.

On April 5, the Senator sent a modest reply to a grateful letter from Isabelle De la Hunt:

You are largely entitled to whatever credit I am getting for my speech. Everyone here agrees that your letter was admirable and very touching. I read it to Senator Frye in my Committee Room a day or two before the speech, and with moist eyes he said it was worth all that had been said on the subject by the Republican Senators.[23]

On the same day, Harrison wrote in longhand to his favorite confidante, Cousin Mag, whose limited finances were his concern. After mentioning various family plans, he commented glumly:

I am born to be a drudge, I think, and don't look for any rest until the Democrats beat me for the Senate next fall—if they do I shall shed no tears, for life here is not to me enjoyable.[24]

Perhaps popular acclaim, like family responsibility, rested heavily on Benjamin Harrison. His own diagnosis was simpler. In chiding a friend, John Morris of Fort Wayne, for refusing to run for office, he had written: ". . . the great weakness in your character, as in mine, is modesty!" He was quick to add, however, that "there is no better school for the cure of modesty than Washington." [25] Indeed, many contemporaries felt that Harrison's career in the Senate had left him with quite another malady—ambition. According to one newspaperman, "ambition never left him, and sometimes was unpleasantly conspicuous." [26]

Whatever his inner conflicts at the time, Harrison had little time for reverie. On the night he posted his "born to be a drudge" letter, the telegraph wires burned with the news that the Republicans had recaptured the city government at Indianapolis and made solid gains at Fort Wayne. Similar dispatches from his home county of Marion made Harrison hopeful of victory in the fall

23 Harrison to Mrs. De la Hunt, April 5, 1886, *ibid.*
24 Harrison to Margaret Peltz, April 5, 1886, Messinger MSS.
25 Harrison to Morris, March 29, 1886, (L.C.), Vol. 24.
26 William Allen White, *Masks In A Pageant*, p. 72. White interprets Harrison's ambition as "the glory-dream of a stunted boy coming true. Nothing succeeds like a well-ordered inferiority complex, pushing a good brain and a kindly heart to a high goal." In what respect Harrison had an inferiority complex escapes him who reads the Harrison MSS.

state elections. Still, his re-election by the state legislature called for an uphill campaign. Only four months remained to perfect the local organizations founded early in 1885. Harrison busied himself in seeing that every Republican worker, from state chairman to district leaders, was alerted, briefed, encouraged, and amply armed for the campaign wars.[27] He spent several stolen week ends in Indianapolis on this urgent work. Carrie Harrison was there, too, indulging in a long visit with her daughter and son-in-law in the North Delaware Street homestead.

At the end of April, Harrison helped to dedicate the new City Hall and remained long enough to enjoy the annual music festival. Tibbott, his secretary, held the fort meanwhile in Harrison's Woodmont apartment. Mountains of free garden seeds and new government publications had to be mailed to the Senator's home state constituents to remind them to vote the right ticket in November.[28]

As the spring of 1886 merged into summer, Harrison found more reasons for return trips to Indiana. Once it was to argue a case before the Indiana Supreme Court; again it was to address the Grand Army Campfire.[29] Each time there were talks with farmers, laboring men, and other citizens. There were also political parleys with State Chairman James Huston and State Secretary Louis Michener who, with Harrison's blessing, was to run for the attorney-generalship. In all these conferences, whether in Indiana or Washington, the Senator made it clear that he would not enter into any schemes to buy a Republican majority in the state legislature, even though national leaders hinted that they might tap the coffers of wealthy eastern industrialists and corporation heads.[30]

The remainder of the first session of the 49th Congress was to keep Harrison busy in Washington until August 5, 1886. As

27 Harrison directed personally the distribution of his speeches as campaign leaflets and cooperated with every G.A.R. post and Knights of Labor assembly in the state.

28 The volume on "Aquatic Animals" was popular in Indiana, as was the report from the Committee on Education and Labor. Harrison to Maxwell, April 15; and to Power, April 20, 1886; et alii, (L.C.), Vols. 24 and 25. To labor leaders he sent copies of Robert P. Porter's book entitled Bread Winners Abroad—an eyewitness account of the conditions of workmen in Europe.

29 Harrison to Huston, May 25, 1886, a Tibbott transcript, (L.C.), Vol. 25.

30 Harrison to Huston, June 30, 1886, ibid., Vol. 26. Also James G. Blaine to Charles Emory Smith, October 20; and R. W. Thompson to Michener, October 20, 1886, Michener MSS, Box 1.

much as a candidate for re-election can, he took part in Senate debates and carried on the tedious work of drafting bills in the summer heat of the committee room.[31] Spring and early summer in Washington taxed Harrison's patience and physical endurance. Temperatures and humidity soared, and Mrs. Harrison suffered a violent illness which the Senator feared had been caused by her "constantly working on . . . tapestry painting." Despite a new cook, who "can't make soup, or much of anything else," Ben nursed his wife back to health and they were soon able to enjoy their regular evening drives to the Soldiers' Home.

On May 7, 1886, the Ohio Society of New York invited the General to speak at its first annual banquet at Delmonico's. Among the notables present were Senators John Sherman and Henry Payne, former Governor R. M. Bishop, and the power of the *Tribune*, Whitelaw Reid, all of whom Harrison regarded as close friends. Presiding was Thomas Ewing, attorney and son of the late Ohio senator. The meeting of these "men from Ohio," at which Carrie was present, was covered by colorful George Alfred Townsend of the Cincinnati *Enquirer*, who captured the Hoosier's strong personality in the following words:

Ben Harrison, senator from Indiana, who is a native of Ohio, showed his metal in a considerable speech, delivered with a vigor and style that carried to my mind the idea that he was an abler man than his distinguished ancestor, the President of the United States. In appearance he does not generally impress people as he goes about the streets, with his head somewhat down and no particular "get-up" about him. But when he rises to speak you see that he is broad-shouldered, full-chested, healthy and strong, square-headed, firmly planted on his feet, aggressive, loud and incisive—very much of a leader of men. In all he made the strongest impression of any speaker of the night.[32]

After the New York address, the Harrisons made an excursion to the ancestral homestead along the James River before returning to Washington. Back at his senatorial labors, Harrison again became depressed at the routine overwork, of which he complained in a letter to his junior partner, Elam. "I am worn out and disgusted with the Senate. We were in continuous session the other day and night for 13 hours and a half; and all of our

[31] *Congressional Record*, 49.1, pp. 5018–19, 5717, 6050, 6431.
[32] James H. Kennedy, *History of the Ohio Society of New York, 1885–1905*, pp. 20–21.

sessions run from 11:00 A.M. till nearly 7 P.M. This breaks up all regular living and I am suffering from it. . . ." Two weeks later, his elder partner, Miller, heard much the same lament:

It is terrifcly [sic] hot here. Exposure to the sun is dangerous and the Senate Chamber is a heated furnace. I do not feel as if I could stand it many days longer. I am worn out; and when I contemplate what is before me this summer and fall I am fairly sick of the whole business.

I do not dare say this to the public but I will greatly enjoy the opportunity to attend to my business and let politics alone.[33]

No one, outside the immediate family circle, knew Harrison the man as well as did the members of his law firm. Judge C. C. Hines, former partner of Harrison and Miller,[34] now living on his farm in Proctorsville, Vermont, also received one of Harrison's "mood" letters. In his almost unintelligible scrawl, Harrison wrote:

After my campaign is over, and I am beaten (with honor) my purpose will be to make as much money as you have and then go into philosophical retirement like you. If by any chance I am re-elected and have to spend six more years here, I may have to spend my time passing a bankruptcy law and pay your debt that way. I will not for another term impose upon my law partners or share their profits when I can't share their work. I don't like the life I have had here. No man can be a statesman comfortably on $5,000 a year. When you hear of my romping and roaming this summer in the campaign you will conclude that what I have said is insincere—but it is not.[35]

Two days after Congress adjourned on August 5, 1886, the Senator hurried home for active participation in the state campaign. During the next three months, Harrison and his party workers would have to face the giant problem of persuading Hoosier Republicans that they could win despite the effects of the 1885 reapportionment law. Harrison knew that he had fighters under his command, but he also knew they had been demoralized by the 1884 rout. It was his task to furnish the leadership, the hope, and the inspiration.

[33] Harrison to Elam, July 16; and to Miller, July 30, 1886, Tibbott transcripts, (L.C.), Vol. 27.

[34] Hines, one of Harrison's most trusted friends, had served as one of his financial advisers in the area of first mortgage railroad bonds, and had also given much business advice to Russell Harrison.

[35] Harrison to Hines, June 28, 1886, (L.C.), Vol. 26.

Before Harrison could win a victory over the Democrats, he had to win a victory over himself. Two problems, one physical and the other spiritual, pressed on him heavily at the end of August. He had returned from Washington completely "used up," and was obliged to spend two weeks under the doctor's care. However, a "diet of iron with strychnine and quinine" soon helped to restore him to physical health.[36] His spiritual problem was not so easily solved. For almost five months he had been tortured by a deep-seated anxiety over his son Russell. The younger Harrison was in a financial tangle because of some ill-conceived ventures in cattle and mining enterprises at Helena. This had resulted in catastrophe; only the consideration of one of the Senator's newspaper friends had kept a disgraceful story out of the press.[37] Russell, now nearing thirty-two but still immature in business matters, shared neither his father's dread of indebtedness nor his prudence in the management of his affairs. On May 28, 1886, the Senator wrote his only son the first of a series of letters which reflect a father's kindness as well as his anguish. Written in longhand from his Senate office, this "My dear Son" letter throws a strong light on Harrison's inner self. It begins:

I am greatly troubled that you should be so much troubled. If you could get your matters into a shape that would enable you to sit down at home to some regular business that would give you a comfortable support I should be more pleased than you can know, as much excitement and care is not good for you—wealth cannot compensate either you or me for such a strain & so much risk. You have shown an amount of industry and enterprise that has won the admiration of your friends and your Ma and I have felt great pride in you. I was always fearful that you had not enough of your father's dread of debt & have often given you a father's most affectionate counsel upon this subject. But it is not profitable to talk of the past, I want to help you now and would make any money sacrifice that was not unjust to your Mother and Sister to do so, and they no doubt would be as glad as I to make any sacrifice in your interest.[38]

36 Harrison to Margaret Peltz, August 22, 1886, Messinger MSS.

37 Harrison to Russell Harrison, April 21, 1886, (L.C.), Vol. 25. Harrison informed his son that the proprietor of the Helena *Independent,* who had charge of press dispatches coming through St. Paul, had taken the responsibility of smothering the story.

38 Benjamin Harrison to Russell B. Harrison, May 28, 1886, R. B. Harrison MSS, (holograph). This large manuscript collection was salvaged by the Vigo County (Indiana) Historical Society of Terre Haute. The papers had probably been stored in the basement of the Terre Haute Savings Bank when Russell went to the Spanish-American War.

At the time of this first worried letter from his father, Russell was not yet in desperate straits. Harrison therefore advised him to seek the counsel and help of Judge Hines, confessing that he himself was not conversant with Wall Street tactics. He closed his four-page letter with advice badly needed by his son: "Do not be obstinate—no one plan is essential—a wise man adapts himself & does not always go over obstacles. Be patient with those who differ with you." [39]

For a short while after this Russell seemed to have revised his get-rich-quick ideas. Unfortunately his craving for speculation soon revived, and he opened an office at the Hoffman House in New York City, where he renewed his dreams of a financial empire. Again, by letter and in a personal visit, the Senator offered his son a guiding, and restraining, hand.[40] When he found Russell unwilling to accept any supervision, Harrison forbade future speculations without paternal approval. Outwardly obedient to his father's wishes, Russell was unable to resist his urge to financial scheming. Determined to try his hand once more he turned for advice not to his father but to Stephen B. Elkins, mine owner, railroad operator, lawyer, and James G. Blaine's chief political lieutenant.

There were aspects of this new friendship which could cause complications if things went wrong. Elkins, who might be classified as "Robber Baron, junior grade," held considerable power as one of the leaders of the Republican party. He knew Harrison's friend Michener well, and was consequently well disposed toward the Senator himself. This was important, should Blaine choose not to be a Presidential candidate in 1888. In addition, the Harrisons had been invited to attend the marriage of Elkins to Hallie Davis, eldest daughter of West Virginia Senator Henry G. Davis.[41] Harrison was therefore not too pleased to learn that Russell was planning, with Elkins' blessing, to turn "a substantial Montana enterprise . . . into a New York City speculation." William H. H. Miller, whose own money was involved, distrusted both Russell's plan and Elkins' judgment. In his letter on the subject to

[39] *Ibid.* Both Judge Hines and W. H. H. Miller advised Harrison that his son was headed in the wrong direction.

[40] Harrison to Russell Harrison, June 6, 7, 1886, *ibid.*

[41] Harrison to Miller, January 7, 1886, a Tibbott transcript, (L.C.), Vol. 22. The Elkins-Davis wedding took place in Baltimore on April 14, 1875. See Oscar D. Lambert, *Stephen B. Elkins; American Foursquare,* pp. 49–50.

young Harrison there was more than just a suspicion of hostility: "I gather from the letter what I knew before that your trust is in Elkins in whom I have no confidence at all. I further gather that you are very sanguine of results, but when were you ever otherwise?" [42] Ten days later, at a stockholders' meeting, both Miller and Judge Hines voted against Russell's reorganization proposals.[43] Indeed, Miller made it clear that he would be very happy to dispose of his stock in the Montana Cattle Company—$15,000 worth.

This ominous drift in his son's affairs and the increased distrust of him shown by Hines and Miller were observed by Harrison with great foreboding. The state campaign was about to be officially inaugurated, but Senator Harrison's mind and heart were in New York, not Indiana. Between August 9 and 25, 1886, he sent off a half-dozen handwritten letters to Russell. State committeemen and local workers alike were forced to stand by while their state leader finished one of these carefully phrased, fatherly documents. He was determined, in spite of the grief and regret it caused him, to force the stubborn youth to yield to his father's experience and maturity.

Meanwhile, in New York, Russell was continuing to push "his scheme" for a financial killing, in spite of the fact that his stockholders disapproved. Miller, in particular, dressed him down with unmerciful severity. He told Russell bluntly that he was at "the point where you see failure staring you in the face, [and] are looking for someone upon whom to cast the blame." [44] Russell, it seems, was obsessed with the idea that no one had the right to differ with him. He had been warned by his father repeatedly against obstinacy, but the warning had been gentle. Now the older Harrison was forced to be less kind. Although he had written his son a long letter on August 8, he wrote again on the 9th, this time with a note of parental authority:

I have thought of nothing else except your affairs since and will give you my conclusion. And first I want you to understand that to the

42 W. H. H. Miller to R. B. Harrison, July 16, 1886, W. H. H. Miller Letterbooks.

43 Ibid., July 26, August 10, 1886. The scheme was evidently designed to enable stockholders in Russell's Montana Cattle Company to get their capital out of the concern, and at the same time, retain control and management. Miller and other stockholders failed to approve such a scheme and this made Russell quite angry.

44 Ibid. Miller, somewhat incensed by Russell's charge of interference, showed that the accusations were false and stated: "You will have to take the responsibility yourself."

extent of my ability I am willing to help you—but on your part you must not insist that you will only be helped in your own way.[45]

The General forbade his son to incur any new obligations and advised him to leave New York as soon as possible.

Harrison had decided that Stephen Elkins was the man who could best extricate Russell, and to this end he had been in communication with him. Fortunately Elkins appreciated Harrison's position and had promised his full co-operation.[46] Before he could confer with Russell in New York, however, that young man had already aroused his father to further concern by another wild proposition. He now pictured himself as the editor of a flourishing Montana daily. Harrison wrote posthaste from Indianapolis: "Adopt a conservative and economical element into your affairs . . . it would relieve me of great anxiety and give us a better hope of your ultimate success. You ought to give your Ma and me, as well as May [Russell's wife] relief from anxiety by making a resolution not to go into debt another dollar." [47]

The final two weeks of August found Senator Harrison in southern Indiana where, "beset with the demands of my campaign," he realized that his real concern was for his son's welfare. If necessary, he was ready to give up politics and property in order to rescue Russell from the brink of failure. On August 20, 1886, he again wrote his son, giving him a complete statement of his own financial standing. He reminded him that

. . . all my investments for six years have been in Montana and all of them now stand in your name—the Townsend Ranch—the Gulch property and the cattle stock. I do not know whether any of them could be sold or used in any way to help you. Here I have only our home, the Wash. St. property and the Penn. St. property. I have given the little 1st St. property to Robert and Mamie & they are going to put up a little house on it. Indianapolis real estate is low and hard to sell. But I can help you and will to the extent of my ability, if I can only see you and you will go over all your affairs with me fully and frankly.

45 Harrison to Russell Harrison, August 9, 1886, R. B. Harrison MSS, (holograph).
46 Elkins had been at Deer Park, Maryland, for the burial of a relative. Senator Harrison was willing to come to Deer Park himself if Elkins and Russell could not conveniently meet in New York. S. B. Elkins to Harrison, August 11, 1886, (L.C.), Vol. 27.
47 Harrison to Russell Harrison, August 11, 1886, R. B. Harrison MSS. Harrison expressed faith in his son's ability to work on a weekly; a daily, however, he felt would sink him financially.

You have been much too sanguine and have taken risks you ought not. I would like to bring my calmer judgment to a review of all your affairs —you can trust my affection and I hope my judgment to some extent.[48]

He offered to meet his son in either Chicago or New York and, if necessary, to accompany him to Montana. He felt that Russell should return to the West.

It does seem to me that with your property in Montana and some of mine your affairs can be brought out—if you will stop creating new obligations and can once get home & settle down to work & to the practice of economy. But the first requisite is that I should know all about your affairs—and this can only come by a meeting.[49]

The end of this serious domestic crisis, which had very nearly wrecked Harrison's re-election campaign, came with Russell's return to Montana, sobered by his father's words and his own experience. In his last letter on the distasteful subject, Harrison wrote:

If your hard experience this summer has taught you how oppressive debts may become—it will be a valuable lesson. I learned it very young —in small things. Let me *again* & *again* urge you to incur no new risks or debts, in connection with the *Journal* or in any other way—learn economy in small things—& you will yet succeed.[50]

Filled with relief over Russell's decision, the Senator turned with new zest to the task of winning the state in November. The September—October campaign of 1886 was now an old story to Harrison. He made speeches in almost every county and helped write the Republican platform at the State Convention. Mondays he saved for letter writing and "for work in connection with the Committee." [51] He felt optimistic and this feeling was heightened by the encouragement of national leaders. Blaine, Sherman, Allison, McKinley, and Dudley wrote reassuring letters and offered their personal help, either in raising campaign funds or on the stump.[52]

48 *Ibid.*
49 *Ibid.*
50 *Ibid.*, August 25, 1886.
51 Harrison to Alexander, September 20, and to Dorman B. Eaton, October 4, 1886, Tibbott transcripts, (L.C.), Vol. 27.
52 William McKinley to James N. Huston, September 15; R. W. Thompson to Michener, September 12; and John Sherman to Michener, September 25, 1886, Michener MSS. Senator Allison of Iowa was the only one to disappoint Harrison by a failure to speak in Indiana. Harrison to Allison, September 28, and Allison to Harrison, September 30, 1886, (L.C.), Vol. 27.

But the real work burden as usual fell to Harrison, as one of the party's most eloquent speakers. If anyone could speak against Cleveland's party, the Senator could.

He planned his speeches so as to enjoy the advantage peculiar to a sniper, whose fire need not be heavy if his single shots are well-directed. Where the soldier vote counted, Harrison reminded his audience that his veterans' pension bill had twice passed the Senate through Republican efforts, only to be buried by the Democrats in the House. He also accused Secretary William C. Whitney of neglect of duty in leaving the Navy with "old wooden vessels . . . to keep afloat or have no ships at all." Likewise, he deplored the country's lack of merchant ships, which the Democrats refused to build.[53]

These direct hits aroused security-conscious Hoosiers, as well as the rest of the nation, for they could believe what Senator Harrison told them. In the words of William Allen White:

The people trusted Harrison. They had never been told things by Harrison which they discovered after the campaign was over to be vote-catching tomfoolery. He never deceived them with promises he did not expect to keep. He did not try to flatter them by pretending to believe their judgment infallible.[54]

As the 1886 Indiana campaign drew to its close, Harrison realized the physical impossibility of visiting every part of the state and of meeting all the local leaders. On October 20, therefore, he composed a warm letter of encouragement to his men in the field, mailing nearly three hundred copies. In it, he begged them to put "heart and soul into the fight . . . look around you and see if you cannot win at least one vote for our whole ticket and especially for our Legislative ticket." He advised each one to spend the entire day at the polls, explaining that their presence would "tend to prevent any fraud that may be attempted by our adversaries and will greatly encourage our friends in their effort to secure a full and fair vote." [55]

[53] Harrison to Sanders, *ibid.*

[54] White, *op. cit.*, pp. 72–73. White, scarcely considered an artist in whitewashing, claimed that "Harrison worked effectively, and in six years came out of the Senate stronger than he went in, with clean hands and a good name. During these six years, before the chatter about high ideals became politically popular, Harrison exemplified quietly and without advertising it . . . a principle of civic righteousness."

[55] A copy of this circular letter is in the Michener MSS, Box 1. Michener wrote on the back that "some 300 were sent over the State by Harrison."

In the last few days before the election, Harrison rose to greater heights of eloquence, attacking the state's Democratic regime with fury. Michener, who as candidate for Attorney General, was often on the same platform, noted that the Senator lashed out against the Democratic apportionment law "with tremendous power, not only arousing the wrath of the disfranchised Republican voters but also receiving the votes of many thousands of disgusted Democrats." Harrison also demanded a thorough investigation of the state's penal, benevolent, and reform institutions, and called for new legislation to put them under nonpartisan control. His appeal on this score stirred the public deeply. Michener recalled later that Harrison's "audiences would weep openly, shout 'Amen' and 'Glory to God,' and cheer to the echo his eloquent denunciations of the wrongs perpetrated on helpless men and women confined in those institutions." [56]

This whirlwind finish resulted in a Republican victory. "We are elected by 4,000 and upward. We will return Harrison to the Senate." [57] So read the jubilant wire sent to Eugene Hay in Minneapolis by Attorney General-elect Louis T. Michener.

The Republicans' margin of victory was small; they had won just 7 of 13 Congressional seats.[58] Michener had been somewhat optimistic, therefore, in calculating the relative strength in the State Legislature which was to elect a United States senator in January. On November 6, 1886, Harrison himself was dubious. He confessed to a close friend: "It looks as if the Democrats had a 2 majority on joint ballot. We have the House, 55 to 45. A change of 15 votes would have given us two more members—close scratch, wasn't it!" [59] To Perry Heath, the *Journal's* Washington correspondent, he wrote: "I think I may have made some reputation

[56] A typed memorandum entitled "State Campaign of 1886," Michener MSS, discloses Michener's personal recollections.

[57] Michener to Hay, November 5, 1886, Eugene Gano Hay MSS, Vol. 5. Later the same day, Michener wrote in a letter to Hay: "We are claiming and expect to sustain the majority in the Legislature on the joint ballot and send General Harrison to the Senate." William G. Carleton, "The Money Question in Indiana Politics, 1865–1890," *Indiana Magazine of History*, 42 (1946), 148, indicates that the Greenback vote had dwindled to less than one per cent of the total vote.

[58] J. D. Barnhart and D. F. Carmony, *Indiana: From Frontier to Industrial Commonwealth*, II, 316.

[59] Harrison to Harley, November 6, 1886, a Tibbott transcript, (L.C.), Vol. 27. It is strange that the Harrison MSS make no comment on the election frauds in Indianapolis. Democrat Sim Coy, "undisputed boss" of Marion County, was indicted, convicted, fined, and jailed. See J. P. Dunn, *History of Greater Indianapolis*, I, 293–98.

in this campaign; but is it not likely to be in the line of the reputation in '76—the reputation of almost getting there!" [60] National party leaders sent congratulations from the East, but worded them cautiously. As an example, Stephen B. Elkins' letter, which also reflected Blaine's sentiments, was sanguine:

I congratulate you on your splendid fight, and I hope yet to congratulate you on getting a majority in the Legislature. Nothing in politics has attracted so much attention as the Indiana fight. Mr. Blaine, while here, often referred to it, and what you had done and were doing. . . . I hope yet you may pull through.[61]

On December 6, 1886, Harrison was due in Washington for the opening of the second session of the 49th Congress. Whether this trip to the nation's capital would be his last as senator, he could not guess. He did know that he had "come out of it with more friends and reputation than ever before." As to the senatorship, he had written Cousin Mag, "I have carried no anxiety about it— nor shall I." [62] Perhaps his hopes—and his ambition—were already turning towards another star. If so, his heart must have beat faster as he read the last lines of a letter from Preston B. Plumb, the influential Senator from Kansas:

Dear Harrison:

The news from Indiana about the Legislature is delightfully uncertain—though I begin to fear that you have lost. After so magnificent a fight it is a great pity to lose—and by so small a majority. You carried the state handsomely—and I believe it now possible to again put Indiana in the list of Republican states. Seriously the victory won in electing a State Ticket puts you in the line of Presidential promotion. It seems to me that you and a good New Yorker would make an invincible team.

Very truly yours,

P. B. PLUMB [63]

[60] Harrison to Heath, November 6, 1886, (L.C.), Vol. 27.
[61] S. B. Elkins to Harrison, November 13, 1886, *ibid.*
[62] Harrison to Margaret Peltz, November 12, 1886, Messinger MSS.
[63] Plumb to Harrison, November 10, 1886, (L.C.), Vol. 27, (holograph).

CHAPTER XIX

The Rejuvenated Republican

WHEN HARRISON returned to the Senate in December, 1886, he found Washington dull and lonesome. "I . . . have been doing the work that came to hand but not hunting anything up," he wrote Carrie. Since she was to stay in Indianapolis, they had given up the Woodmont apartment. In bachelor quarters at the Riggs House, the senator's evenings hung "very heavily." This was actually Harrison's own fault; he admitted that he "could find company no doubt but I am not a good hand at doing it." [1] Undoubtedly this inactivity coupled with the uncertainty of his own future contributed heavily to his moodiness. Nevertheless, when the press carried a false rumor that he had withdrawn from the race, he told reporters and friends that he "was bound to do all that can be honorably done to secure a re-election." [2]

Meanwhile political interest in Indiana deepened. There, ardent Harrison supporters vowed that nothing should block the Senator's re-election. First secretly, then publicly, the word spread through the Indiana General Assembly that Harrison's friends were preparing for battle and professing the political philosophy that "the end justified the means." [3] Republican papers warned that the Democrats would try to steal the legislature; and Democratic organs countered with similar charges against the Republicans. Hence, upon returning to Indianapolis for the Christmas recess, Senator Harrison found the Democratic press proclaiming that "the notorious Col. Dudley" was, according to the *Sentinel*,

[1] Harrison to Margaret Peltz, December 15, 1886, Messinger MSS.
[2] Harrison to Michener, December 12, 1886, a Tibbott transcript, (L.C.), Vol. 27; and Harrison to E. G. Hay, November 26, 1886, Eugene Gano Hay MSS, Vol. 5.
[3] W. W. Thornton, "Benjamin Harrison's Candidacy for a Second Term in the Senate," a typewritten manuscript (Indiana State Library).

in the East, raising a large sum of money from the beneficiaries of the high tariff and other monopoly legislation to secure the re-election of Ben Harrison by bribery, if all other means fail. There is no doubt that the loot-hunting monopolies will make a desperate effort to keep Harrison in the Senate and retain a Republican majority in that body. Dudley seems to be the man relied on to carry out the scheme and no better selection could be made. . . .[4]

The story was only half true. The General's friend, William W. Dudley, was merely on a trip in the East. The unfavorable publicity annoyed Harrison, however. He summoned his close friends and advisers to his home for a meeting and proclaimed his willingness to contest legal and constitutional issues in court; but of bribery he would have none. When friends in Philadelphia offered to help defray court costs in connection with the celebrated case of Lieutenant-Governor Robert S. Robertson, in which Harrison was to appear as chief counsel,[5] he refused, saying, "I will not . . . avail myself of your kind offer of assistance until the contest is over." [6]

A vacancy in the office of lieutenant-governor had already complicated the state campaign of 1886. Both parties had run candidates, but the Republican nominee, Robert S. Robertson, had won a surprise victory and anticipated a routine installation by the Joint Assembly scheduled to convene in January, 1887. The president *pro tem* of the Senate, Alonzo G. Smith, was the Democrat's candidate for the office, and he had other ideas. He contested the validity of Robertson's claim to the office by insisting that the Indiana constitution allowed the election of a lieutenant-governor only once every four years. With the new legislature evenly divided between Democrats and Republicans, the vote of the lieutenant-governor loomed large in determining Benjamin Harrison's quest for re-election to the United States Senate.[7]

Party leaders on both sides rallied their forces. But whether the contest would be waged in the local senate chamber or in the

---

[4] LaPorte *Argus,* December 31, 1886, which carried the *Sentinel* story. Harrison received these and several other clippings from George L. Andrews in a letter dated December 31, 1886, (L.C.), Vol. 28.

[5] Lew Wallace, *Life of Ben Harrison,* pp. 129–73.

[6] Harrison to Joseph Wharton, January 19, 1887, a Tibbott transcript, (L.C.), Vol. 28.

[7] Wallace, *op. cit.,* p. 130.

state courts, or in both at the same time, had yet to be decided. If it took the shape of a legal controversy, the Smith-led Democrats felt safe insofar as they controlled the Supreme Court. If the battle were confined to the senate chamber, Smith as presiding officer could be relied upon to take care of himself. Should there be a resort to force, Governor Isaac Gray, also a Democrat, would exercise his prerogatives as commander in chief of the militia. By the time Harrison reached Indianapolis for the holidays, tension had already gripped the city. Public opinion refused, however, to tolerate physical violence which could undermine the very stability of the government. Feeling the lack of public support, Smith appealed to the courts to enjoin the secretary of state from delivering the election returns for lieutenant-governor to the speaker of the house. If this injunction stratagem worked, then the General Assembly's joint convention would have no votes to count, as required by the state constitution. In the Marion Circuit Court, Judge Alexander Ayres refused Smith's plea for an injunction. On appeal to the Supreme Court, Ayres' decision, to the utter amazement of the Democratic petitioners, was sustained. The Democratic judges of the Supreme Court, by holding that they had no authority in the case, refused to prostitute themselves.[8]

The Democrats refused to submit to this decision. Claiming that the Court had evaded the issue, they launched a vigorous attack on the supreme judiciary. Despite the fact that Democrats constituted a majority of the court, the *Daily Sentinel,* party mouthpiece in Indianapolis, carried a scathing editorial which exploded with the introductory sentence, "Damn their cowardly souls." [9] For some days this assault on the state's highest court eclipsed the legal issue itself. But more excitement was ahead. In the middle of January, the legislature met, calmly counted the votes, and proclaimed Robertson Lieutenant-Governor. In this crisis, Smith again appealed to law. He instituted a *quo-warranto* proceeding

---

[8] J. P. Dunn, *History of Greater Indianapolis,* I, 413. On January 4, 1887, the Supreme Court (with two judges dissenting) decided the question on the ground that it had no jurisdiction of the case since the Constitution made each House the judge of the election of its members and officers, and that it was not proper for the Court to decide what was the law unless it had jurisdiction in the case at bar. Harrison read the abstract of Michener's argument, and wrote him that "it seemed to my mind very comprehensive and conclusive. I congratulate you on your first appearance as Attorney General." Harrison to Michener, December 12, 1886, (L.C.), Vol. 27.

[9] Dunn, *op. cit.,* pp. 413–14.

in the Marion Circuit Court to settle title to the lieutenant-governorship. This time Judge Ayres, ruling that the suit was properly brought and the question determinable by the courts, issued an injunction forbidding Robertson to preside over the Senate or in any manner to exercise the functions of Lieutenant-Governor. Immediately, the State appealed to the Supreme Court. Senator Harrison, aided by W. H. H. Miller and Attorney General Michener, presented the oral argument in behalf of Robertson. Smith retained attorneys Jason Brown and David Turpie, the latter ranking as top Democratic choice for Senator.[10] This time the court sustained Smith's position,[11] thus striking a serious and unexpected blow at Harrison's chances for re-election.

During this legal conflict, the General Assembly began a battle of the ballots for a United States senator. The first count revealed that neither major party enjoyed the majority necessary for a choice. The balance of power rested with "a trio of independent voters" who, "day after day, by voting for a third candidate" prevented the election of either Harrison the Republican, or of Turpie, the federal district attorney favored by the Democrats. This stalemate prevailed through fifteen ballots.[12]

In February, 1887, on the sixteenth ballot, and by virtue of what Republicans called "a fraudulent and illegal majority," [13] David

10 Wallace, *op. cit.*, p. 136.

11 Dunn, *op. cit.*, p. 413, cites *Robertson vs. The State ex rel. 109 Ind.*, p. 79, as authority for his opinion that the court had reversed itself. Lew Wallace, on the other hand, with the inaccuracy of a campaign biographer, claimed that Harrison's argument before the Supreme Court had convinced that body that they had no jurisdiction of the person of Mr. Robertson and that the suit had been improperly brought to that court. A majority of the judges held further that the judiciary had no power to determine the question. Wallace, *op. cit.*, p. 137, concludes that "nevertheless Smith maintained his usurpation to the last, and as a result David Turpie was ultimately elected to succeed General Harrison as United States Senator from Indiana."

12 Thornton, *op. cit.*, p. 2. From an economic point of view, William G. Carleton, "The Money Question in Indiana Politics, 1865–1880," *Indiana Magazine of History*, 42 (1946), 107–150, explains the close vote in the General Assembly. Relying on the *Indiana Senate Journal, 1887*, pp. 420–22, Carleton, *op. cit.*, p. 148, details the struggle in the General Assembly without mentioning the hassle over the office of lieutenant-governor. "The Democrats had seventy-six on joint ballot and the Republicans seventy-four. . . . There was one Greenbacker elected as a Democrat, and three Greenbackers had been elected on the Republican ticket. . . . For many ballots the four Greenbackers voted for Jason H. Allen, and an embarrassing stalemate was created. It was not until the sixteenth ballot that the Greenbacker elected on the Democratic ticket voted for Turpie. His vote was absolutely necessary to give Turpie the necessary majority of one."

13 *Journal*, February 4, 1887.

Turpie [14] was elected to succeed Harrison. The Republicans began investigations but accomplished little. Leaving the task of fact-finding to subordinates, Harrison himself returned to Washington half hoping that a special session of Congress, beginning on March 4, might review the legality of his defeat. After two weeks, when no news had come from Indianapolis, Harrison appealed to John C. New, owner of the Indianapolis *Journal,* and to Attorney General Michener. He advised his newspaper friend that the vote of the Indiana General Assembly might well be impeached on the grounds of bribery.[15] And he urged Michener to seek redress from the Indiana Supreme Court.[16] Still nothing happened, and as the March 3 deadline neared, Harrison grew resigned to the reality of his defeat.

During his final three weeks as the senator from Indiana, however, he scarcely had time or reason to bewail his imminent retirement. Rousing receptions for him in Providence and New York not only eased the sting of departure but also promoted his national prestige. In Providence, the Young Men's Republican Club gave him a testimonial dinner in recognition of "brilliant service in the War of Rebellion and eminent statesmanship in the Congress of the United States." Governor George P. Wetmore's presence, the excellent food, and spirited band music provided an enthusiastic background for Harrison's address. The Senator rose to the occasion. Putting aside his personal defeat, he emphasized the fact of a newly found Republican majority in the Hoosier State. He promised that Indiana would join Rhode Island in sending a Republican to the White House in 1888. He also reminded his audience of the vital part politics should play in the average American community. "There are some people," he said, "who affect to despise politics, and speak sneeringly and slightingly of

[14] Turpie had been appointed United States District Attorney for Indiana in August, 1886. Five years Harrison's senior, Turpie had served in the United States Senate for less than two months in 1863, filling the vacancy caused by the expulsion of Jesse D. Bright. He left a profitable law practice in Indianapolis for the State Assembly where he was the Speaker in 1874 and 1875. Returning to the U. S. Senate in 1887, he stayed until 1899, at which time he was defeated for re-election. Carleton, *op. cit.,* p. 148, observes: "As a member of the Senate, Turpie became one of the leading inflationists in national politics."

[15] Harrison to New, February 17, 1887, Harry S. New MSS, (Library of Congress). Harrison had a report of a bargain that would impeach some votes and thus keep Turpie out of office.

[16] Harrison to Michener, February 22, 1887, (L.C.), Vol. 28. He feared that the court would give "a most marked illustration of judicial politics in the history of our state."

what they are pleased to call the machine." His next statement was memorable: "Unless free government is discreditable, or to be made discreditable, it is the duty of every American citizen to support that party to which he gives the allegiance of his heart and mind." [17]

Harrison devoted more than half of his address to national questions. In a crescendo of partisan oratory, he blasted the Cleveland Administration for trying to destroy the protective system, which guaranteed "an American market for the American people." [18] He styled the President's civil service reform a partisan blessing for Andrew Jackson's spoils system. Finally, as a solution to the nation's problems, he appealed to the Rhode Island Republicans to "make the nominee of the next Republican National Convention the President of these United States." [19]

In New York the following day, at the National Republican Club's annual Lincoln Day dinner at Delmonico's, Harrison responded to the toast, "Reform of the Party within the Party." This time he aimed his fire at the "Mugwumps." "If there are any barnacles on the old ship," he said, "it is a poor policy to scuttle her. Let us put her in dry dock and scrape her hull. Or, better still, take her into fresh water and these impediments will drop off of themselves." On the delicate question of reform within the party, he gave positive answers which drew rounds of applause and cries of "Good!" His concluding remarks contained one final dig at the Mugwumps:

I think . . . reforms must begin, and progress, and end within the party, because I do not know of any political organization outside of it that has any reformative power to spare. [*Laughter and applause.*] Certainly not the Democratic party. I know that our Mugwump friends think that they have a great deal of surplus reformative energy, but

[17] Providence *Journal*, February 11, 1887. Harrison reflected his own political philosophy when he observed that "it is in the primary that action is taken that will lead to results great and creditable or shameful and injurious. . . . I utterly despise that maudlin sentimentality that rejects participation in politics as not an indication of the highest manhood. . . . If the machine is out of order; if it does not run without jolt or jar, let us mend it, not smash it."

[18] *Ibid.* Harrison charged that the Carlisle wing of the Democratic party was unwilling to reduce the surplus in any other way than by breaking down the protective system embodied in the revenue laws. See also Allan Nevins, *Grover Cleveland: A Study in Courage*, pp. 374–75.

[19] Providence *Journal*, February 11, 1887.

the trouble with those people is that they have put themselves up on the shelf like dried cakes of Fleischmann's compressed yeast, and they can have no power upon the mass that they should leaven because they have ceased to have contact with it.[20]

The next day found Harrison back in Washington again, where he proceeded to finish his term "as quietly as possible." [21] On March 3, 1887, he finally yielded his seat to David Turpie, left the Senate Chamber, and turned his thoughts homeward.

Leaving Washington also meant leaving relatives and close friends. As the Harrisons made their rounds of farewells during the second week of March, the usual feelings of regret prevailed. For a short while after his return to a more permanent stay in their Indianapolis home, both Carrie and Ben felt lost. This feeling was very short-lived. Excitement, joy, and thanksgiving moved in at an early hour on March 15, 1887, as Mamie Harrison McKee gave birth to a son. General Harrison "was up all night," but the proud grandfather felt doubly rewarded when Mamie named the boy after him. Telegrams and letters of felicitation flooded the Harrison home. The General, probably from lack of sleep, refused "to make any comments on the event—the boy did enough of that last night," and he added that "if he don't [sic] do better tonight he is unworthy of his name." [22] Nevertheless, Benjamin Harrison McKee at the age of one week took all hearts. Despite repeated warnings from older relatives of "don't spoil the baby," [23] the new grandparents refused to check their natural inclination. Three times during his first week as grandfather, Harrison wrote enthusiastic longhand letters to Cousin Mag, all full of "Baby McKee":

Mame continues to get along nicely—no trouble of any sort. As to the baby, I told his mother to say to him that if he would be patient until the snow is gone, we would all move out on the roof and give him the house.[24]

[20] Unidentified clipping dated February 12, 1887, in the Benjamin Harrison Scrapbooks, (L.C.). The press described the Republican dinner at Delmonico's as the most notable of Lincoln Day celebrations.

[21] Harrison to Michener, February 22, 1887, (L.C.), Vol. 28.

[22] Harrison to Margaret Peltz, March 16, 1887, Messinger MSS.

[23] Elizabeth Scott Lord to Mrs. J. Robert McKee, March 17, 1887, Harrison Home MSS, wrote, "Don't spoil the baby. I expect your father and mother will be inclined to." Also J. S. Scott to Harrison, March 18, 1887, ibid.

[24] Harrison to Margaret W. Peltz, March 21, 1887, Messinger MSS.

Harrison's pressing need for more money from his law practice was quickly gratified. He spent June and part of July in court at Sullivan, Indiana, where in the Wise will case, involving about $300,000, he won a verdict and a substantial fee. The seven-week trial found him "somewhat used up," but ready to accept a sizeable retainer for another important case, on the docket for August 1. The reason for his willingness to overwork during that sizzling summer of 1887 [25] was no secret in the family circle: "I am not greedy," the General had commented, "but I owe some money and I want to pay it." [26] In his mind was a plan to bundle Baby McKee, the young parents, and Carrie off to Deer Park, Maryland, where he had arranged for a special vacation. He also planned to re-survey the shaky financial ground under his son Russell, who, amazingly enough, was "still wedded to his speculative schemes." [27]

Harrison's first impulse had been to go to Helena himself and help his son personally. Reflection, however, had counseled a review of Russell's financial status by mail—a task he had performed many times before. He sat alone in his study on August 8, and began the first of another series of letters. This one, however, was different. At fifty-four, the General was still striving to harmonize his own life with spiritual help, and he now recommended this path to Russell. "My dear son," the laboriously written epistle began,

There is nothing for you except to meet your difficulties bravely and squarely. You had too much courage in going into debt—and must not lose your pluck when it is needed. As a lawyer I have so often seen men under pressure do things that affected their standing and character that I am anxious for you. You may lose everything you have in the way of property but if no man can say that you have done a tricky or dishonorable thing, you have still a chance to recover. Do not let any pressure of seeming necessity draw you one inch away from the line of honor and duty. You will then retain the confidence of everyone— even if they have lost money by you.

I hope you will renew your Christian faith and duties. It is a great comfort to trust God—even if His providence is unfavorable. Prayer

25 The hot spell was disastrous as well as enervating. Harrison wrote his son Russell that "we have had a summer worse than that of 1881." August 8, 1887, (L.C.), Vol. 28.

26 Harrison to Margaret Peltz, July 18, 1887, Messinger MSS.

27 W. H. H. Miller to a Mr. McKammon, April 18, 1887, W. H. H. Miller MSS. Miller mentions a letter from Russell to General Harrison which put the losses in Montana at a minimum of 15 per cent.

steadies one when he is walking in slippery places—even if things asked for are not given.[28]

Where Harrison himself was concerned, this exhortation to confidence bolstered by a prayerful faith, told only half the story. He himself worked on the manly principle that God helps those who help themselves. Thus, he now wrote another letter on his own behalf to James J. Hill, the St. Paul financier. Known as the "Empire Builder," Hill at that moment was stringing railroad tracks across Montana.[29] Trusting this tycoon's knowledge of promising railroad stocks, the General hoped to invest wisely and so add to his shrunken income. Hill replied with an attractive offer that would enable Harrison to bid on bonds guaranteed to yield 12 per cent interest at the end of a year.[30] After some reflection, Harrison decided to accept the offer. More than one Republican leader owned stock in Hill's railroad, which enjoyed monopolistic prestige as "the only available route between Helena and the navigable waters of the Missouri River." [31]

When Harrison and his family finally arrived at Deer Park for the vacation he had planned, they found everything in readiness. The General's friend, ex-Senator Henry Davis of West Virginia, Stephen Elkins' father-in-law, had placed at their disposal a beautiful but unpretentious two-and-a-half-story frame cottage, painted sage green and sporting a red-shingled roof. In an adjoining cottage the Elkins family was already settled.[32] The weather was delightful, the company congenial, and the General's financial troubles well under control. While the ladies sewed and gossiped, the gentlemen talked politics, speculating on the Presidential prospects for 1888. Elkins had been Blaine's Warwick in 1884,

---

[28] Harrison to Russell Harrison, August 8, 1887, (L.C.), Vol. 28. This letter was catalogued and filed separately by the authorities of the Division of Manuscripts, Library of Congress. On April 11, 1946, the Library procured the document from the Carnegie Book Shop, 105 East 59th Street, New York. We may surmise that it had been long held as a family treasure but was eventually sold to a national dealer.

[29] Stewart H. Holbrook, James J. Hill: A Great Life in Brief, pp. 102–7.

[30] James J. Hill to Harrison, September 7, 1887, (L.C.), Vol. 28. Hill mentioned a Col. Broadwater whom Harrison knew well as a close associate with Russell in the Montana Cattle Company. Harrison himself was very familiar with the Territory from his committee work in the Senate. Free from the ties of official life, Harrison was ready to plunge.

[31] Holbrook, op. cit., p. 104. Harrison to Hill, February 20, 1888, (L.C.), Vol. 28.

[32] Although some of the homes at Deer Park were three stories high with as many as twenty rooms, they were known, in the fashion of the times, as "cottages," a word harmonizing with the privacy in the mountains. See Oscar Doane Lambert, Stephen Benton Elkins, American Foursquare, p. 103.

while Davis had supported Grover Cleveland. Half jokingly, half seriously, Davis and Elkins told Harrison that he himself was Presidential timber. Republicans, they argued, needed a citizen-soldier to oppose Cleveland in 1888. Senator Davis even promised to cross party lines to support his friend, and Elkins, as Blaine's trusted lieutenant, assured the General that only the "Plumed Knight's" renomination stood between Harrison and the White House. The General manifested little enthusiasm. He realized that Blaine could command the nomination if he wished to run a second time. So, although he showed himself a good listener, Harrison returned to Indianapolis convinced by Elkins' remarks that Blaine wanted to be President.

Since leaving the Senate, Harrison had played a relatively inactive rôle in national politics. As early as February, 1887, he had announced that he was in no sense a Presidential candidate. Ohio Senator John Sherman, still longing for the White House, had taken him at his word and asked him to pledge Indiana's vote for his own candidacy at the coming national convention.[33] In the middle of August, Harrison's adviser, Attorney General Michener, wrote a mutual friend that Harrison "is not a candidate for the nomination in 1888," adding, however, a meaningful line: "I have good reason to believe he will listen to the advice of his friends." [34] But all summer long, despite immense pressure from friendly leaders in over half the states,[35] Harrison himself neither wrote nor said anything privately or publicly that could be construed as a willingness to run.

During these same summer months, James G. Blaine, Republican nominee in 1884, had also refused to make any definite commitment. The acknowledged leader of the national Republican forces, he had, by silence or by ambiguous statements, both puzzled his friends and confused the political forecasters. He had hibernated through a Maine winter "as fierce" as Greenland's, deeply immersed in the preparation of his book, to be entitled *Political Dis-*

[33] Harrison to Michener, February 22, 1887, Michener MSS.
[34] Michener to Hay, August 11, 1887, Eugene Gano Hay MSS, Vol. 6. Michener felt that Indiana would send a delegation solid for Harrison, "if it is desired."
[35] Not only the Harrison MSS, Vol. 28 *passim,* but also the Elkins, Hay, and Michener Papers reveal the pressure exerted on Harrison to declare himself. Barker to Harrison, August 27, 1887, (L.C.), Vol. 28; also Barker's public letter to the citizens of Montgomery Co., Penn., December 21, 1887, *ibid.*

cussions. The magnetic leader frankly admitted that he had "been shut off and shut out from the world for more than two months." To Elkins, he had even confided, "I have been giving no heed to political currents—think nothing of them, know nothing, and, am almost ready to say, care nothing." [36] In June, the "man from Maine" decided to take a long European holiday, but not before a feminine member of his family had let it drop that Harrison was now Blaine's first choice for the next Republican standard-bearer.[37] If true, this news remained a secret not only to the General but to most Americans, despite the fact that after Blaine arrived in London, Sir Cecil Spring Rice,[38] British Secretary at the Washington Legation, reported that Blaine "intends to be Secretary of State and to run Harrison for President." [39]

In any event, while Blaine toured Scotland and Ireland, and half-a-dozen countries on the mainland, his enthusiastic followers in the States refused to abandon hope that he would return home in time to fight a second round with Grover Cleveland for the prize of the Presidency.[40] August 15, 1887, however, brought a letter from Mr. Blaine himself who, with the abandon of a vacationer, chanced to remark, "I have lost sight of politics." [41] Two months later from Paris he wrote Whitelaw Reid another letter that came as a sword to pierce the heart of the Blaine movement:

. . . personally I feel very strongly disinclined to run. In the first place and radically, I do not feel that I want the office—conceding the election. In the next place I do not want the turmoil and burdensome exactions of a canvass. . . .

[36] Blaine to Elkins, March 14, 1887, Elkins MSS. Blaine did say: "I shall revive my intelligence and awaken my interests by some good long talks with you . . . soon."

[37] Gail Hamilton, *James G. Blaine,* p. 651. Lambert, *op. cit.,* p. 155, confirms this report, stating that "Blaine was unselfish and looked only to the good of the party." The Elkins biographer in stating that Blaine and Harrison were not "closely associated in any other interests" overlooks the fact that Blaine had retained Harrison as counsel during the campaign of 1884. See A. T. Volwiler (ed.), *The Correspondence Between Benjamin Harrison and James G. Blaine, 1882–1893,* pp. 5–7.

[38] This British diplomat, noted for his charming wit, served as secretary of the Washington Legation in 1887–1888, 1889–1892, and 1894–1895. From 1913 to 1918 he was Britain's Ambassador to Washington.

[39] Stephen Gwynn (ed.), *The Letters and Friendships of Sir Cecil Spring Rice: A Record,* I, 68.

[40] C. J. Bernardo, "The Presidential Election of 1888" (unpublished doctoral dissertation, 1949, Georgetown University), pp. 132–42. Comprehensive and firmly based on much hitherto unused manuscript material, this thesis can well serve as a model of exhaustive research, though in 1948–49 neither the Elkins nor Reid MSS were available to its author.

[41] Hamilton, *op. cit.,* p. 644.

Although I think it probable I could be nominated there will be a contest, serious with Sherman and incidental and irritating with Allison, Lincoln, possibly Harrison and some other favorite sons. Above all I abhor the idea of becoming a chronic candidate. . . . At the proper time if the friends entitled to be consulted—of whom you are chief—shall agree upon with me, I will pull out, and do it in a direct, open, above-board way.[42]

Taken at face value, this letter should have solved the political puzzle, but more than one Republican leader kept tongue in cheek when apprised of Blaine's disinclination for a second candidacy.[43] Preston B. Plumb, Harrison's senatorial crony from Kansas, told the General that Blaine's absence in Europe was cleverly planned. Blaine "is lying in wait," he wrote Harrison cynically. "Of course he *can* be nominated—because he has the fellows to do it. He may come back from Europe next June, have a great throng to meet him and make a speech that will fire the heart etc." [44]

Meanwhile, Harrison himself continued a discreet silence as incoming mail told him that Blaine was far from dead as a candidate. As late as December, 1887, a New Jersey friend assured the General that "it is all bosh about Mr. B. not wanting a re-nomination. Our people must not be carried away by one speech or letter. All the brains of the country are not in one man's head." [45] Everywhere, Republican politicians remained puzzled by the course Blaine pursued. Even after Blaine's October pronouncement from Paris, many regarded it as merely a private letter to Whitelaw Reid and those who shared Reid's confidence. As long as no formal and public withdrawal was made, numerous wealthy backers felt justified in keeping the political home fires aglow for their hero.

Paradoxically, it was a Democrat, President Cleveland himself, who struck the blow that was to shatter Blaine's silence, at the same moment marking the ground on which the Presidential battle of 1888 would be fought. As Chief Executive and leader of his party, Cleveland had begged two Congresses to revise the tariff,

[42] Blaine to Reid, October 11, 1887, as cited in Royal Cortissoz, *The Life of Whitelaw Reid*, II, 113.
[43] Edward Stanwood, *History of the Presidency*, I, 459, proves this point. "It is doubtless safe to say that had the delegates to the convention been elected in December, 1887, there would not have been chosen a dozen in all the country who would have preferred any candidate to Mr. Blaine."
[44] P. B. Plumb to Harrison, October 1, 4, 1887, (L.C.), Vol. 28.
[45] Charles Scranton to Harrison, December 15, 1887, *ibid.*

"which was steadily rolling up a surplus in the Treasury, imposing an unjustified burden of taxation upon the people and taking tens of millions of dollars from their legitimate employment in the channels of trade." The tariff required close study, and Cleveland had proved himself tenacious in this respect. The more he studied the protective tariff system, the more he became convinced that "it was a ruthless extortion of the people's money and a violation of the fundamental principles of free government." [46] But convincing himself and convincing Congress were two different matters. In two annual messages, Cleveland had strongly urged Congress to reduce the tariff and twice his plea had been rejected.

Now the President decided to take his case to the people in as conspicuous and as striking a way as possible. Already feared and disliked by some leaders of his own party because he was "unmanageable, stubborn and plainspoken," Cleveland decided to leave his party behind [47] by assuming an advanced position on tariff revision. On December 6, 1887, he presented to Congress his famous message on the tariff, denouncing the whole protective system for establishing too close a relationship between the operations of the federal government and the business interests of the country. "The next day every important newspaper in the country published it in full, and it was read as no Presidential messages since Lincoln's had been." [48]

Both Harrison in Indianapolis and Blaine in Paris read Cleveland's message, though Blaine had only a condensed version to scan. Inside the Democratic lines it was like the explosion of a bomb; to the Republican party, however, it came as a twofold blessing. Bound to be an overshadowing issue in the coming 1888 Presidential contest, it would smoke out all aspirants for the office; but more especially it would compel Blaine, as head of the party, to answer the President's challenge. A vigorous rejoinder, they believed, would win a unanimous nomination for the "Plumed Knight" at the Chicago convention in June.

For a few weeks, the Blaineites saw their wishes gratified. On December 7, 1887, a reporter for the New York *Tribune* inter-

---

[46] David S. Muzzey, *James G. Blaine, A Political Idol of Other Days*, pp. 361–64.

[47] Nevins, *op. cit.*, p. 367. Also Muzzey, *op. cit.*, p. 361, who points out that a minority of the President's Democratic advisers were in sympathy, "but most of the party politicians regarded it with dismay."

[48] Nevins, *op. cit.*, p. 379. Also F. W. Taussig, *The Tariff History of the United States*, pp. 252–55.

viewed Blaine at his Paris hotel, and within two days the "Plumed Knight's" answer to Cleveland was printed by every important Republican paper in the United States. Expert politicians read it eagerly and immediately proclaimed that Blaine, and Blaine alone, must carry the party banner in 1888. Was he not already the celebrated champion of protection? Read the "Paris letter," Republicans chanted. Rejoicing party leaders already considered this reply a scathing indictment of Cleveland as well as a campaign masterpiece. To quote one of Cleveland's sympathetic biographers, the Maine Republican had "in twenty lines . . . managed to appeal to high protectionists, lovers of cheap tobacco, haters of England, temperance advocates, coast-defense enthusiasts, and those who thought that Cleveland was a poor Democrat compared with Tilden." [49] Republicans had delivered similarly good arguments many times in the past, but the real significance of the "Paris letter" lay in the prompt and willing way Blaine himself had accepted and returned the Democratic challenge. Intentionally or unintentionally, the Blaine rejoinder "created the impression among his followers at home that he was announcing his candidacy for the approaching presidential nomination." [50]

Messages of anticipatory congratulations followed Blaine from France into Italy. Even Theodore Roosevelt and Henry Cabot Lodge, hostile to Blaine's candidacy in 1884, now climbed onto the bandwagon.[51] From Washington, John Hay triumphantly declared that "you have given us our platform for next year." [52]

Increased public and private pressure soon conspired to make Blaine define his position once and for all. From Venice, in a private letter, he restated his previous determination that under no circumstances would he seek the Presidency. When close friends refused to take him at his word, Blaine drafted and issued a formal

[49] In giving the interview, Blaine chose to dictate answers to a series of questions. The interview was cabled to the *Tribune* and published in full on December 8, 1887. It was copied widely next day by the nation's Republican press. See Nevins, *op. cit.*, pp. 383–84.

[50] Muzzey, *op. cit.*, p. 367. Abundant manuscript evidence in (L.C.), Vol. 28. Also Lambert, *op. cit.*, pp. 116 ff.

[51] Cortissoz, *op. cit.*, II, 155. Whitelaw Reid reported that both men felt that nothing could prevent Blaine's nomination, and that they preferred it as "the strongest nomination possible and because they are particularly eager to beat the Mugwumps with you." Reid's optimism about Roosevelt and Lodge was premature. See Theodore Roosevelt to Henry Cabot Lodge, January 15, 17, 1888, in Elting E. Morison (ed.), *The Letters of Theodore Roosevelt*, I, 136–37.

[52] John Hay to Blaine, December 8, 1887, as cited in Muzzey, *op. cit.*, p. 367.

letter of withdrawal, which he released at Florence on January
25, 1888. In the plainest terms possible, he addressed B. F. Jones,
chairman of the Republican National Committee, and practically
swore an oath that "my name will not be presented to the national
convention." Faced with this "formal and final withdrawal from
the presidency," [53] close associates like Elkins and Reid were
confused but forced to believe. The *Tribune's* owner admitted
that Blaine "is perfectly sincere, red-hot, in fact, in insisting that
his name shall not be used." By the end of February, 1888, less
than two months after President Cleveland's tariff message, the
Republicans found themselves with a tremendously popular campaign issue, but without a popular candidate for the White House.

Even before Blaine had formally bowed out of the Presidential
picture, the supporters of Benjamin Harrison had spearheaded
an effort to make him the Republican choice in 1888. By early
January, Hoosier politicians were claiming that the General already enjoyed the prestige of a solid delegation from his native
state. Indiana State Chairman James Huston traveled East to feel
the political pulse of New York Republicanism. His diagnosis
was encouraging: ". . . enthusiasm for Blaine is becoming less
and . . . General Harrison is growing much stronger." [54] From
the nation's capital came reports that Harrison was favored as "a
straight Republican . . . involved in no factional animosities."
Wisconsin's Senator Spooner declared that "everybody who has
ever belonged to the Republican party can support" him.[55] Notwithstanding these friendly assurances from influential quarters,
Harrison continued to hold himself aloof. Also, he expressed a
strong desire that even the district conventions in his own state
refrain from endorsing him as a candidate. "I will not in any way

---

[53] Hamilton, *op. cit.*, pp. 604–5. In the spring of 1888, en route from southern Italy
to Paris, Blaine wrote to correct overzealous friends who had tried to interpret his
Florence letter as no withdrawal at all. "My Florence letter was, in my own mind, a
formal and final withdrawal from the presidency. It has been accepted as such by
thousands of my best friends. Candidates have come before the people who would
not have been there but for my action."

[54] Huston to Hay, January 2, 20; and Graham to Hay, January 12, 1888, Eugene
Gano Hay MSS, Vol. 6.

[55] Spooner to Harrison, January 27, 1888, John G. Spooner MSS, (Library of Congress). This item is in the Letterbooks, Vol. 4. Spooner commented on the favorable
way in which both senators and representatives viewed Harrison's candidacy.

promote any movement to make me a Presidential candidate." [56]

Dazed by Blaine's withdrawal, Republican national leaders treated with studied indifference those candidacies which had flowered before the Florence letter. Harrison's friends, however, had been discreetly cautious in their public statements, though they had privately assured the General that the previous solidarity for Blaine was slowly transforming itself into Harrisonian support. At Deer Park in September, 1887, Stephen B. Elkins had informed Harrison in "several conversations" [57] that the Blaine mantle might be his own, when and if the Maine man was scratched in the 1888 sweepstakes. Now, the day after the Florence letter, Elkins made it publicly known that Harrison, not Sherman, was the heir to Blaine's position as party leader. And on St. Valentine's Day, Elkins wrote a letter to Harrison that breathed devotion:

Sherman wants and expects the Blaine strength largely, but Blaine's friends have in mind that Sherman could have nominated him in 1876 and 1880 but would not do it. He has no real claim on Blaine's friends. This word has been passed around. You have more strength here in influential quarters than you think. You know I have thought for two years you were the strongest leader we had next to Blaine, and that your chances for nomination were the best next to Blaine's. I think so now. [58]

Elkins' support was essential to any aspirant to the White House. Indeed, candidates more sanguine than Harrison would have leaped at the chance to secure a promise that was almost equal to a nomination for the Presidency. Harrison, however, remained unmoved. He admitted the many kindnesses which Blaine supporters had shown him, but on February 18, 1888, on his return from a brief business trip, he replied to Elkins in a letter intended for him alone. "You know," he began,

I have not fired up much over your suggestion that Mr. Blaine might not be a candidate and that . . . I could be nominated. Neither event

---

[56] J. W. Study to Harrison, February 1, 1888, (L.C.), Vol. 28. Harrison kept a penciled draft of his answer, in which he expressed gratitude for the good will but repeated the answer he had sent to all his friends, that "no action" be taken.

[57] Elkins to Harrison, February 11, 1888, *ibid.*

[58] February 14, 1888, *ibid.* Harrison began a long correspondence with Elkins. An article in the Chicago *Tribune* prompted Harrison's letter to Elkins on January 30. The article charged Harrison with making public and offering to file in court Blaine's letter (giving his reasons for dismissing his libel suit against the *Sentinel*) when that letter was not intended for publication. The *Tribune* charged that Harrison's action was taken to prejudice Blaine politically in Indiana. The General's emphatic denial, bolstered by evidence, was accepted by Elkins.

seemed to me at all probable—and besides my ambition is not very inflammable. My friends have regarded me an obstructionist rather than a promoter. Even my good Democratic friend Senator Davis when I was at Deer Park last summer took me one side to say that I ought not to say or do anything to discourage my friends. I have always believed and said that Mr. Blaine would be nominated easily. He may yet be, as you say, but in that event his letter will prove to have been a great mistake, for it will be hard to prove to Sherman's friends that they have not been injuriously dealt with. . . . Disappointment don't [sic] reason, and is full of suspicion.[59]

Silence and apparent indifference made Harrison his own worst enemy. Blaine's withdrawal had increased the crop of Republican aspirants for the presidency, and each potential candidate, from Allison of Iowa to Sherman of Ohio, was far better known across the nation than was Indiana's favorite son.[60] When Elkins complained that these more prominent candidates were enjoying a favorable press day after day, Harrison gave the matter scant attention. To a query from Elkins as to how he stood in states other than Indiana, the General replied that "as to other states I can say very little. Of course I have had many letters but they have in the main been from persons not conspicuous in their state politics. I have had no bureau and no manager—and have not even looked over the states to see what friends I had in any of them." [61]

Harrison's personal inactivity puzzled many of his intimate supporters, not only in Indiana and the Northwest, but also in New York and Washington. Unavailing pleas reached him, saying that he "had better direct the flag," even if he did not come "out from behind the curtains." Some advisers, however, like former Postmaster General James N. Tyner, considered Harrison's strange silence golden. "Indifference and 'mostly inactivity' may now be the best policy," he wrote, since "an active personal struggle for nomination (such as Sherman is making) would undoubtedly leave you behind." Tyner added shrewdly that "mighty few ever get to the White House who enter the race as avowed competitors." He warned Harrison, however, to refrain from telling

[59] Harrison to Elkins, February 18, 1888, Elkins MSS.

[60] In addition to Allison and Sherman, there were other prominent candidates in the Republican ranks: Chauncey M. Depew of New York, Judge Walter Q. Gresham of Indiana and Illinois, General Russell A. Alger of Michigan, Senator Joseph R. Hawley of Connecticut, and William Walter Phelps of New Jersey. Depew's and Gresham's chances are evaluated by Bernardo, *op. cit.*, pp. 142–72. Also Leland L. Sage, *William Boyd Allison*, pp. 214 ff.

[61] Harrison to Elkins, February 18, 1888, Elkins MSS.

"others (your sincere friends) that you prefer the law to politics, and don't want position—as you wrote to me—for such people are too apt to conclude that they won't disturb a man's settled conclusion as to himself." [62]

As matters stood at the end of February, Harrison was heir-apparent to Blaine's strength, with Senator Allison his nearest competitor. Yet, in the estimation of a successful Washington attorney, Harrison's chances were better: "Your public record is not so long as his [Allison's], nor are there any chapters in it that might be revived (such as supposed warm friendship for the Pacific Railroad capitalists, etc.), and you were a soldier. Other things being equal the soldier record is an important element. You have never antagonized Blaine, but on the contrary have been very kind to him from the beginning. Proper management ought to give you a strong position with his supporters." [63]

Political management of Harrison was at best a difficult task. Since the General distrusted the professionals, he put himself at a decided disadvantage in both press and party circles. Accordingly, two friends, amateurs on the political stage of the nation, volunteered their organizing efforts. Indiana Attorney General Michener and Hoosier lawyer Hay, then practicing in Minnesota, joined hands to direct Harrison along the path to the Chicago nomination. Their success, they agreed, would be proportioned to their intimate knowledge of the General's virtues as well as his foibles. At the outset, Michener stated the prime problem to Hay: "We cannot organize a regular bureau for General Harrison, and get him puffed in the Chicago and New York papers. . . . He would never consent to it, and such fulsome flattery is so foreign to his character that I believe it would hurt him." [64]

Michener believed correctly that the Harrison boom had to be handled secretly, and in some instances without the General's approbation or supervision. The Attorney General therefore took on the duties of a manager without assuming the title. His first important move was to make sure of the Blaineites. To this end, and without Harrison's knowledge, Michener sounded out Elkins in New York. Relying on a friendship cemented at the 1884 national convention, Michener asked frankly for support in Har-

---

[62] Tyner to Harrison, February 20, 1888, (L.C.), Vol. 28.
[63] *Ibid.*
[64] Michener to Hay, February 24, 1888, Eugene Gano Hay MSS, Vol. 6.

rison's interest. First assuring Elkins that Indiana would vote solidly for the General at the convention and that "we shall do everything in our power to secure his nomination," he confessed that Harrison's nomination was impossible "without receiving the support and assistance from Mr. Blaine." He then laid his cards on the table:

We think we have the right to make some modest claims upon the friends of Mr. Blaine, such as yourself, for instance, because of the high character of our candidate, and the very material support given to Mr. Blaine at a critical juncture in the last convention, and which support was given with the cordial approval of General Harrison, and of every intimate friend of his. I presume the incidents are still reasonably fresh in your mind.[65]

Michener pursued this same frank approach with other influential party leaders, stating that he chiefly desired to get "them thinking" about Harrison. As it chanced, Elkins had already written confidentially to Harrison before receiving Michener's appeal. He told the General that "next to Blaine you are the strongest candidate; . . . you have more elements of strength than any other. In a quiet way, word is being passed around to the Blaine men that you are the choice of a great many of them." [66]

For Michener and Hay as amateur publicists, the problem of a favorable press for Harrison reached the crisis stage in late February, 1888. Despite Elkins' assurance that many papers, including the New York *Tribune* and the Minneapolis *Tribune,* were well disposed towards him,[67] Harrison soon realized that the real burden of popularizing himself rested squarely on his own shoulders. Publicity follows as well as precedes the spotlight of activity. In confining his efforts to the Indiana and Illinois courts, Harrison now realized that he had forfeited many an hour under the warm rays of a political sun. On Washington's Birthday, therefore, he changed his tactics. He went to Detroit where he broke almost a year's political silence in a speech at the annual Michigan Club banquet.[68] The Detroit Rink, crowded with Congressional and

[65] Michener to Elkins, February 27, 1888, Elkins MSS. As early as January 9, 1888, Elkins had declared for Harrison as "the only one we can elect." Lambert, *op. cit.,* p. 118.

[66] Elkins to Harrison, February 27, 1888, (L.C.), Vol. 28.

[67] Hay to Michener, March 3, 1888, Michener MSS; and Elkins to Harrison, February 14, 1888, (L.C.), Vol. 28.

[68] Charles Hedges (compiler), *Speeches of Benjamin Harrison,* pp. 9–10. The Michigan Club, largest and most influential organization in the state, had invited Har-

other Republican leaders,[69] provided an excellent arena for Harrison in tossing his own hat into the presidential ring. He was well aware of his position and in responding to the toast, "Washington, the Republican," his opening sentence hit hard on the nail of political expediency. "Mr. President and Gentlemen of the Michigan Club," he began,

I feel that I am at some disadvantage here tonight by reason of the fact that I did not approach Detroit from the direction of Washington City. I am a dead statesman [*No! No!!*]; but I am a living and a rejuvenated Republican. . . .[70]

That last expression caught the popular fancy and "rejuvenated Republicanism" became the keynote of the Harrison campaign. Throughout his speech, the Hoosier kept his eye on local interests. Spontaneous applause greeted his talismanic reference to Zachariah Chandler, whose memory in Michigan was warm and deep. "I am here," Harrison modestly stated, "to be helped myself, . . . by spending a little season in the presence of those who loved and honored and followed the Cromwell of the Republican party, Zachariah Chandler." The General soon won his audience, and amid cheers and laughter, filled his listeners with food for future thought. He also seized the opportunity to express his own views on each important question that would face the voters in November.

Harrison's Detroit address attracted national attention. Reporters called his oratorical performance "one of his greatest," [71] and Hoosier party workers and friends were stirred by his "magnificent reception" on Michigan soil. Republican State Chairman Huston, who regarded Harrison "as the hardest man the Democrats could have to beat," was elated because the General had finally manifested a "disposition . . . to go out and allow the people to see and hear him." Louis Michener quickly reported to Hay that the veterans were on the march after reading the General's address.

---

rison to address its third annual banquet. Directors of club to Harrison, January 30, 1888, (L.C.), Vol. 28.

[69] Senator Thomas W. Palmer presided at the banquet, whose distinguished guests and speakers also included General Joseph R. Hawley, Connecticut; Hon. William McKinley, Jr., Ohio; Hon. L. E. McComas, Maryland; Hon. James P. Foster, New York; and the three party leaders from Illinois: Joseph G. Cannon, John F. Finerty and Green B. Raum.

[70] Hedges, *op. cit.*, pp. 10–15.

[71] *Ibid.*

"The Grand Army Boys are going from the city tonight to all parts of the state thoroughly filled with the belief that Harrison is the coming man." [72]

At the end of February, Harrison resolved to take a brief vacation from both law and politics. This unusual decision had been prompted by the arrival of another grandchild. It was a girl this time, born to Russell and May Harrison on January 18, 1888, at the home of May's parents in Omaha. Great joy attended the family reunion in Nebraska. Russell was on hand, having accompanied his wife from Montana, where the high altitude had played havoc with her health.[73] The new baby, little Marthena Harrison, was already a healthy month-and-a-half old when Grandpa Ben and Grandma Carrie arrived. In short time, Baby McKee of Indianapolis had a worthy rival for his grandparents' affection. They stayed with Marthena, her parents, and the Saunders family until the middle of March. It was the beginning of the contest for affection that placed Benjamin Harrison McKee and Marthena Harrison among the most photographed and talked-about grandchildren ever to grace the White House.

An accumulation of mail greeted the General upon his return from Omaha. Many letters endorsed him as the party's best bet for a winner in the coming presidential race because he combined "fitness with availability." [74] Republicans agreed that a candidate was "fit" if he was an ex-soldier with a clean record and if he was a statesman who had an American rather than a foreign policy. "Availability" meant the ability to carry doubtful states at the polls in November, with special emphasis on Connecticut, New York, and Indiana.[75] Close friends, however, were seriously doubtful as to Harrison's availability on the West Coast, where the "Chinese

[72] Huston to Hay, February 23; and Michener to Hay, February 24, 1888, Eugene Gano Hay MSS, Vol. 6.

[73] Marthena Harrison Williams to the author (telephone conversation in Washington, D. C.), February 22, 1956. Mrs. Williams related that her mother had suffered nasal hemorrhages due to Helena's altitude. Under doctor's orders the expectant mother sought a more favorable location, finding it with her parents at the family home in Omaha. For similar details, see W. H. H. Miller to Sam Miller, February 1, 1888, W. H. H. Miller Letterbooks; and Harrison to Elkins, March 1, 1888, Elkins MSS.

[74] Harrison to Hawkins, March 1, 1888, (L.C.), Vol. 28.

[75] These three states meant 57 electoral votes to the candidate who carried them. On the importance of the soldier record, see Sage, op. cit., p. 215.

question" still sorely agitated the voters. On this score, Elkins asked Harrison for his voting record, explaining that rival candidates had publicly stated that "Harrison would be weak in California," and that anxiety on the Pacific Coast would block his nomination at Chicago.[76] The powerful Chicago *Tribune*, an organ devoted to the nomination of Harrison's long-time rival, Judge Gresham, led the attack on Harrison's Chinese record.

Even before the General's return from Omaha, Michener in Indiana and Perry Heath in Washington feverishly attempted to overcome an undercurrent of false impressions.[77] In a confidential letter dated March 9, 1888, Michener convinced Elkins that "Harrison's record is as good as that of any other Senator and is better than some of them on the subject. Our friends on the West Coast have nothing to fear so far as he is concerned. He voted with Sherman, Allison, Ingalls, Hawley, and others."[78] If Elkins and his Blaine men had any final doubts, Harrison himself put them to flight by detailing his own record on each vote and by pointing out that "the Fair Bill which was the last acted upon in the Senate while I was there was unanimously reported from the Committee of which I was a member and passed the Senate without a decision."[79] Blaine's friends felt reassured when both the Oregon and California senators expressed complete satisfaction with Harrison's attitude and vote on Chinese immigration.[80]

If General Harrison's Detroit speech had succeeded in "rejuvenating" him on a national scale, his next effort in Chicago four weeks later (March 20, 1888) marked him as a candidate of prestige and stature. Before the Marquette Club, a social and political organization for young Republicans, Harrison restated his belief in the party which "by faith saw Appomattox through the smoke of Bull Run, and Raleigh through the mists of Chickamauga." He took the popular position that the call for the "highest statesman-

---

[76] Elkins to Harrison, March 3, 1888, (L.C.), Vol. 28.

[77] Heath to Michener, March 3, 1888, *ibid.;* and Michener to Elkins, March 9, 1888, Elkins MSS.

[78] Michener to Elkins, *ibid.*

[79] Harrison to Elkins, March 12, 1888, *ibid.* The bill to which Harrison referred was not considered in the House. See Elmer Clarence Sandmeyer, *The Anti-Chinese Movement in California,* pp. 96–99.

[80] Opposition from Oregon had been expected. Senator Mitchell's letter, however, dissipated these fears. Harrison to Elkins, March 12, 1888, Elkins MSS.

ship" during the war had been answered by the Republican leaders, not only on the battlefield but also in the "matchless management of our diplomatic relations." Harrison also twisted the Lion's tail vigorously and frequently, referring with disdain to England's diplomacy as a "grasping avarice" that "has attempted to coin commercial advantages out of the distress of other nations." [81]

In his Chicago address, more than in any previous public speech, Harrison explained what the Republican party meant to him in terms of progress and prosperity:

We took the ship of state when there was treachery at the helm, when there was mutiny on the deck, when the ship was among the rocks, and we put loyalty at the helm; we brought the deck into order and subjection. We have brought the ship into the wide and open sea of prosperity, and is it to be suggested that the party that has accomplished these magnificent achievements cannot sail and manage the good ship in the frequented roadways of ordinary commerce?

The General begged eloquently that a Republican be put back on the ship's bridge. He charged that Cleveland, the Democratic captain, had radically changed the sailing course of the ship of state because "he has made the mistake of mistaking the flashlight of some British lighthouse for the light of day." This was an unmistakable repudiation of President Cleveland's free trade philosophy. The General appealed to his listeners to keep the tariff high. But party leaders and friends particularly noted his concluding remarks:

Defeated once, we are ready for this campaign . . . and I believe that the great party of 1860 is gathering together for the coming election with a force and a zeal and a resolution that will inevitably carry it, under the standard-bearer who may be chosen here in June, to victory in November.[82]

Before Harrison made his Chicago speech, his friends had been worried over the fact that there had been no crystallization of party sentiment.[83] Now Theodore Roosevelt, with Henry Cabot Lodge and other independent Republicans, nodded favorably in Harrison's direction as one of the party's most likely nominees.[84] "Harrison is a clean, able man, with a good record as a soldier and a

---

[81] Hedges, *op. cit.*, pp. 16–20.
[82] All citations are from Harrison's Chicago speech. See Hedges, *op. cit.*, pp. 20–24.
[83] Michener to Hay, March 30, 1888, Eugene Gano Hay MSS, Vol. 7.
[84] Roosevelt to Michener, March 12, 1888, Michener MSS.

Senator" was the verdict within the Roosevelt family circle.[85] On the very day of his address in the Windy City, the General received outspoken support in a letter from his friend Henry G. Davis, who, in addition to having served two terms in the Senate, was an influential West Virginia banker and railroad president. Himself a Democrat, Davis was already extolling Harrison to associates in both political parties. He now assured the General: "I tell Republicans you are the best man for '88 and tell Democrats, if you are nominated, they have *no* walk over and that I *cannot* help defeat you." [86]

After the press publicized Harrison's Chicago speech, as well as a similar effort at Fort Wayne, he was lauded as the party's hope "against the Democracy, the flesh, and the devil." That Harrison "has a head full of brains and is a born fighter" [87] became Hay's watchword on the Minnesota front. Stephen B. Elkins in New York kept a close eye on each new phase of the Harrison boom. He had counseled the General to utter kind words for Blaine at all times, and, in Chicago particularly, Harrison played the game as Elkins wished, referring to Blaine as the "matchless statesman" of 1884.[88] By the end of March, Elkins was satisfied that Harrison had the advantage. Only Blaine's nomination by acclamation could deprive the Hoosier of the highest gift within the party's competence.[89]

During April and May, sentiment for Harrison crystallized on a national scale.[90] New York reported that "Harrison is growing daily in the East," [91] and when the New York *Times* admitted that a "clean candidate . . . would be very strong" against Cleveland,

[85] Roosevelt to Anna Roosevelt, July 6, 1888, in Morison, *op. cit.*, I, 141–42.

[86] Davis to Harrison, March 20, 1888, (L.C.), Vol. 28.

[87] J. W. Macy to E. G. Hay, March 30, 1888, Eugene Gano Hay MSS, Vol. 7. J. W. Scott to Harrison, March 18, 1887, Harrison Home MSS. The phrase "Brainy Ben Harrison" was picked up by a Mrs. Lockwood, a Washington landlady, and had become a household word at 814 Twelfth Street, N.W., home of Carrie Harrison's relatives.

[88] Hedges, *op. cit.*, p. 17.

[89] Elkins to Michener, March 26, 1888, (L.C.), Vol. 28. Harrison had advised Elkins that Halford and Michener were very reliable friends and could be trusted with all information at any time. See Harrison to Elkins, March 21, 1888, Elkins MSS.

[90] Huston to Hay, April 11, 1888, Eugene Gano Hay MSS, Vol. 7. Theodore Roosevelt to Henry Cabot Lodge, April 7, 1888, in Henry Cabot Lodge, *Selections from the Correspondence of Theodore Roosevelt and Henry Cabot Lodge, 1884–1918*, I, 66–67.

[91] Michener to Elkins, April 10, 1888, Elkins MSS.

the General's stock rose above par.[92] Hoosier politicians came home from visits to Washington, Baltimore, and Philadelphia convinced that "the Harrison boom is growing . . . and looking up." [93] Even from the South, where funds for John Sherman had been lavishly spent, came the cheering news that Harrison had "votes in nearly every Southern State." [94]

On April 19, 1888, Indiana Republicans elected their national delegates and the contingent was solidly for Harrison.[95] This vote of confidence from friends and neighbors sparked more enthusiasm from the General than any previous expression of support by national leaders. Perhaps this accounts for the fact that a week later, at a Pittsburgh banquet honoring General Grant's birthday, Harrison at last appeared in the true light of a presidential aspirant. B. F. Jones, Republican national chairman, listened carefully to the General's "excellent and appropriate" speech and later wrote Elkins that Harrison had "the presidential fever in the severest form." [96] The tide was running so strongly to the Hoosier candidate, in fact, that the powerful Elkins finally "came to the mountain." He tried vainly, however, on three occasions to meet Harrison for a conference, suggesting for privacy a small, out-of-the-way town near the West Virginia-Maryland boundary line. A succession of court appearances prevented Harrison's compliance.[97]

During the first week of May, while Harrison was still detained in court, the Hoosier Republicans concluded the work at their

[92] An April 10, 1888, newspaper clipping cited by George William Curtis in his letter to Silas W. Burt, April 10, 1888, Burt MSS, (New York Historical Society).

[93] Huston to Hay, April 11, 1888; and S. J. Peelle to Hay, April 12, 1888, E. G. Hay MSS, Vol. 7.

[94] Michener to Hay, April 12, 1888, ibid.

[95] Michener sent the important news to Elkins at his New York address: "You have doubtless read in this morning's papers that Indiana yesterday chose a solid delegation of my loyal, faithful and sincere Harrison men. We will follow it up on the 3rd of May by choosing four delegates-at-large at the same time." Michener to Elkins, April 20, 1888, Elkins MSS. This, as well as confirmatory evidence in the E. G. Hay, Barker, Michener, and Harrison Papers, seems to possess greater validity than earlier judgments, based solely on newspaper research, that "Harrison did not carry a solid delegation to Chicago." See R. C. Buley, "The Campaign of 1888 in Indiana," Indiana Magazine of History, 10 (1914), 162–85, and Sage, op. cit., p. 366, n. 17. (Writing in 1914, Professor Buley did not have access to the above-mentioned manuscript collections.)

[96] B. F. Jones to Elkins, April 30, 1888, Elkins MSS. Jones was also president of the American Iron and Steel Works.

[97] Harrison to Elkins, April 4; Elkins to Harrison, April 6; Harrison to Elkins, April 12; Elkins to Harrison, April 16; Elkins to Harrison, May 2; Harrison to Elkins, May 6, 1888, Elkins and Harrison MSS. Elkins had suggested Deer Park as the rendezvous.

state convention with a unanimous resolution declaring "General Harrison to be the choice of the Indiana Republicans for the Presidency" and instructing "the delegates to work, vote, and exhaust every honorable means to accomplish his nomination." [98] Michener, "laughing all over," brought the news personally to the Harrison household on North Delaware. The four delegates-at-large and their alternates are "solid for your father" was Mrs. Harrison's pleased boast in a letter to Russell. She now threw political caution to the winds and began to count the days until the Chicago national convention would get under way.[99]

Five weeks of feverish activity preceded the meeting of the national delegates at Chicago on June 19, 1888. Committed to a jury trial in Sullivan County until June 10, General Harrison entrusted his political interests to Michener, whom he sent to New York for a strategic meeting with Elkins, influential Blaine backers, and other party leaders. Subsequent events proved that the General could not have chosen a more loyal and devoted manager than Louis T. Michener. The Hoosier attorney general knew from the start that he was dealing with a crafty politician in Elkins; at the same time he realized that without his support Harrison could not be nominated. Michener arrived in New York at a time of crisis. Elkins and other Blaine supporters were weakening in their belief that the "Plumed Knight" was sincere in his refusal to stand for the Presidency. On the surface, Elkins had spoken first and last for Harrison, with only an occasional warning that the Blaine craze was not yet spent.[100] But on May 8, 1888, the West Virginia Warwick had dashed cold water on Michener by writing that "everything now points to Blaine's nomination." [101] With other correspondents, Elkins was even more candid. He told J. S. Clarkson, Senator Allison's chief lieutenant, that "New York will demand" Blaine's nomination "with at least 630 delegates and I am certain that if nominated Blaine will not decline." Forty-eight hours later,

[98] Michener to Elkins, May 5, 1888, Elkins MSS.

[99] Carrie Harrison to Russell Harrison, May 7, 1888, (L.C.), Vol. 29. Mrs. Harrison rarely expressed a political opinion, but she knew that Russell was eagerly awaiting news as to his father's prospects. Also, she had caught some of Michener's enthusiasm.

[100] Elkins to Michener and Harrison, February–May, 1888, *ibid.*, Vols. 28–29. Also Lambert, *op. cit.*, p. 118.

[101] Elkins to Michener, May 8, 1888, Michener MSS. Elkins added a note in longhand: "This, however, may well be changed."

Elkins predicted a minimum of 349 votes for Blaine on the first ballot, and asked Whitelaw Reid to confirm his guess.[102]

Blaine's Florence letter of January had been conveniently forgotten by his friends in their "mad career" [103] of king-making. Michener, however, remained calm, even to the point of predicting on May 10, 1888, that Blaine himself would soon check the movement once and for all. On May 17, 1888, this prophecy came true. Blaine wrote a strong letter to Whitelaw Reid containing an explicit refusal to run. Published in the New York *Tribune* on May 30, just a week before Cleveland was renominated by the Democratic convention in St. Louis, Blaine's latest letter convinced everyone. Delayed in publication, its contents were already known to Elkins as he sat in conference with Michener.[104] It is obvious now that Elkins was still playing for time and on the alert for any and every advantage. But Michener was no longer worried.

"Harrison is going to be the nominee," he had told Hay before leaving for New York. "We are making no blow, doing no bragging, telling no lies, and are working quietly and diligently." During the next several days of "horse-trading" talk with Elkins at One Broadway, New York City, he pursued his quiet but unswerving course until, after five days, Blaine's letter was published. This cleared the path for Harrison. Fortunately Michener was on the scene and acted at once to steer the disappointed Blaineites into the camp of the General. He wired Eugene Hay in Minneapolis: "Work on Blaine delegates quick." [105] The race for the Republican nomination had begun in earnest. Only the Chicago convention could declare the official winner, but "the living and rejuvenated Republican" from Indiana had taken an early lead.

---

[102] Elkins to Clarkson, May 6, 1888, J. S. Clarkson MSS, Box 2, No. H. Also, Sage, *op. cit.*, pp. 215–16, and Elkins to Reid, May 8, 1888, Reid MSS.

[103] Michener to Barker, May 10, 1888, Barker MSS, Box 4.

[104] Michener remarked that many had written asking if Harrison would take second place to Blaine. Michener resolutely stated that Harrison would accept second place to no one.

[105] Michener to Hay, May 21, 30, 1888, Eugene Gano Hay MSS, Vol. 7.

CHAPTER XX

"You Are Put in Command"

TUESDAY, June 19, 1888, officially opened the Republican National Convention in Chicago. "Sobered a good deal by four years of adversity," [1] many delegates, and an increasing number of national and state chieftains, seemed willing to forget personal antagonisms in an effort to unite on a winning candidate. The goal was clear; the chief issue, protection versus free trade,[2] was set squarely. Only the selection of a standard-bearer remained in doubt. With Blaine presumably scratched from the race, political handicappers made John Sherman of Ohio the favorite by estimating his first ballot strength at over 300 of the 416 votes necessary to a choice. This early book-making pleased all the Presidential hopefuls, who readily agreed that Sherman would be a good pace-setter. Many felt that the Ohio senator would falter badly in the stretch, at which point the whip of the former Blaine support would be applied elsewhere.[3] General Harrison and his supporters believed they controlled most of the Blaine strength and that this would enable the General to win going away. In the preconvention trial runs Harrison had worked well, but few outside of the political leaders of Indiana, New York, and Pennsylvania realized how well organized the Hoosiers were in their determination to make Benjamin Harrison the next President.[4]

[1] William Starr Myers, *The Republican Party: A History*, p. 293.

[2] H. W. Furber (ed.), *Which? Protection or Free Trade*. This book, containing articles by eminent political economists and statesmen, was published and widely circulated in 1888.

[3] Sherman himself had been warned that ". . . if the Blaine men carry their enthusiasm to General Harrison he will be nominated and I have assurances that such a course has been adopted by them." Wharton Barker to John Sherman, June 14, 1888, John Sherman MSS, Vol. 448.

[4] "The National Convention of 1888," a typed memorandum in the Michener MSS.

The story behind the Indiana Republicans' effort to put their favorite son in the White House was a tale ghostwritten for Harrison by the state's attorney general, Louis T. Michener. He drafted the preface in Indianapolis early in 1888. At that time, Harrison himself felt that his "nomination could not be secured against such statesmen as Senators Allison and Sherman." [5] Michener, however, thought otherwise. Determined to make the attempt, he formed and headed his three-man "Committee for Harrison," including former congressman Stanton J. Peelle and party leader John A. Wildman.[6] This self-constituted triumvirate did not rest until they had persuaded the General to allow his name to go before the convention.

Having gained Harrison's passive cooperation, Michener increased his committee to six by securing the services of *Journal* publisher John C. New, former soldier Dan Ransdell, and Harrison's law partner, attorney John Elam. This sextet, each personally devoted to Harrison, contributed both money and brains. But it was Michener who spearheaded the movement and organized the work on a national scale. He also assumed the task of collecting and distributing all funds. The committee strove to produce, by "unseen management," a "spontaneous movement" for Harrison. Between February and May, 1888, this valiant nonprofessional organization secured favorable editorials in leading newspapers, obtained testimonials from business and labor, mailed thousands of Indiana papers into pivotal states, and persuaded the nucleus of the future Columbia Club of Indianapolis to take an active part in creating a local "Harrison-for-President" boom.

When Federal Judge Walter Q. Gresham was unexpectedly entered in the race, the committee for Harrison went into high gear. Secret efforts by Gresham's followers to secure Indiana delegates already pledged to the General "steamed the Harrison men to a high pitch and . . . much bitterness." [7] The final result, of course,

[5] Michener has left his recollections of the organization in a memorandum entitled: "The Harrison Campaign for Nomination in 1888." Michener MSS, Box 1.

[6] *Ibid.* Michener observed that this group called on Harrison to assure him that they did not share his views on unavailability. They kept on visiting the General until he authorized his candidacy. The active impetus came from Michener, not Harrison.

[7] George W. Curtis to Silas W. Burt, June 8, 1888, Burt MSS, (New York Historical Society). When B. F. Jones, chairman of the National Committee, settled on Chicago as the convention site, the State of Illinois promised not to enter a candidate. Since Gresham was sitting on the bench in Chicago, his candidacy was regarded as a violation of this pledge.

had been Indiana's unanimous endorsement of the General at the party's state convention in April.[8]

For weeks thereafter correspondence from all classes, but especially from bankers and businessmen, had revealed a substantial Harrison tide. Other state delegations had been individually polled by Michener, who used the mails vigorously and effectively. In Washington and in Indianapolis, party leaders had been interviewed, while Stephen B. Elkins in New York and Wharton Barker in Pennsylvania did their part in adding to Harrison's growing strength. Michener had consolidated these gains by a personal visit to the East, stronghold of business and vested interests. On his return to Indiana with the best of news, the General finally agreed to work actively with his committee.

Thereafter, Michener's burden was lightened. Week-end conferences at Harrison's home resulted in the pooling of information and sharing of suggestions; and his friends at last succeeded in arousing Harrison's latent ambitions. At this point, the committee decided to open headquarters in Chicago. With their leader now at the helm it was time to sail on the enemy. The committee of six valued their reluctant candidate in more ways than one. Michener later wrote that Harrison was "the ablest political strategist I have ever known; . . . strong . . . in the details of organization and the selection of methods; . . . a superb strategist and tactician in political warfare." As the committeemen set out for Chicago, therefore, they must have given much thought to the General's final warning: "Make no promises for me." [9] Harrison himself would stay in Indianapolis, working as usual at his law desk.

The Harrison Committee established headquarters in the Grand Pacific Hotel, where John C. New had engaged three rooms on June 12, a full week before the convention. Close by was housed the "disciplined" and "earnest" [10] Indiana delegation. Unusual harmony prevailed among these men, and total agreement characterized the daily briefing sessions conducted by the committee. Michener had achieved another prize here: the delegation had

[8] George W. Steele to Harrison, June 5, 1888, (L.C.), Vol. 29; S. B. Elkins to Whitelaw Reid, June 8, 1888, Whitelaw Reid MSS, (New York).

[9] Michener, "The Harrison Campaign for Nomination in 1888," Michener MSS, recalls that "he charged us to make no promises for him."

[10] Journal, June 15, 1888.

agreed to follow the policy of the committee and to remain subordinate to its decisions. Michener had chosen William W. Dudley [11] as his "constant associate" in this work. The Harrison Committee, now a strong seven with Dudley, was early enough on the scene to see to it that the Hoosier delegation received adequate representation on convention committees as well as its share of convention officers. One of its best strokes was the placing of *Journal* editor E. W. Halford [12] on the Committee on Platform and Resolutions. Halford, destined to become Harrison's personal secretary in the White House, was assigned one major objective: to design the planks in the party platform to harmonize with the political philosophy of the man from Indiana.

With the arrival in Chicago of some 10,000 Harrison supporters, cooperation between the committee and the Indiana delegation reached its peak. Recruited from every corner of Indiana, this volunteer but well trained army thronged the hotels and lodging houses of the Windy City; their voices could be heard everywhere, "earnestly, intelligently and persistently" [13] reiterating that only Benjamin Harrison could carry their doubtful state. Without Indiana, they argued, pointing to the Cleveland majority there in 1884, there would be no Republican in the White House as Centennial President. When questioned as to just how sure they were that Harrison could command victory in a state so closely contested, they replied that Harrison's

abilities as a vote getter had been proven in previous campaigns, such as 1860, 1864, 1884, and notably in 1886. His stainless record, oratorical powers, sound judgment, and excellent record in the Senate gave assurance that he would be particularly strong in other doubtful states and would be elected.[14]

The Hoosiers had a fight on their hands, however, and they knew it. As the sons and grandsons of men who had supported William Henry Harrison in 1840 began to arrive, rival camps caricatured

[11] Dudley, then a resident of Washington, became a vital cog in the organization formed to nominate and elect Harrison. Michener was ready to give Dudley the chairmanship, but the Committee voted otherwise. Michener, "The Harrison Campaign for Nomination in 1888," p. 3, Michener MSS.

[12] A close friend of Harrison's, Halford's favorable editorials in the *Journal* had been of conspicuous value in the promotion of Harrison's preconvention candidacy.

[13] C. J. Bernardo, "The Presidential Election of 1888," pp. 198 ff.

[14] Michener, "The Harrison Campaign for Nomination in 1888," p. 2, Michener MSS.

Harrison as a little fellow wearing his "Grandfather's Hat." [15] But the General's backers had facts to prove their candidate's personal abilities. As James G. Blaine's son Walker later noted, "General Harrison's reputation at the bar, his meritorious service in the field, [and] his admirable record in the Senate, served as an answer of triple strength." [16]

The underlying strategy of the Harrison forces had been carefully charted weeks before. The General had warned his committee, and Michener had agreed, that Harrison supporters must "give no offense to the friends of any other candidate" while attempting to secure first-choice votes. Far more important were the acquisition and hoarding of second-choice votes in increasing numbers until the final ballot. [17] This policy called for the repeated study and polling of every state delegation not irrevocably pledged to a major contender. By diligent, organized work, reasoned Michener, it could be calculated each midnight how the following day's ballot would read and how much leg work would be required of each willing supporter. Meanwhile, the tensions and excitement of the last preconvention hours mounted as each camp skirmished for support of its candidate. [18]

"Unless we blunder, you will be President next March." [19] This was Wharton Barker's bold prophecy to Harrison before the balloting began. Many of the General's congressional friends concurred in this judgment, and they urged him to have a "captain on the ground," for it is "desirable to have some one to whom we can go." [20] Louis Michener was, of course, that someone. In a sense, he knew Harrison's strength better than did Harrison himself. Influential leaders from the doubtful, and essential, state of

15 Following his selection by the convention in Chicago, the Democratic press pursued a campaign of cartoons entitled "Grandfather's Hat." See Michener, "Grandfather's Hat," a three-page memorandum, Michener MSS, Box 2.

16 Walker Blaine, "Why Harrison Was Elected!" *The North American Review* (December, 1888), p. 693.

17 Michener, "The National Convention of 1888," pp. 2–3, Michener MSS. Also see W. H. H. Miller to L. T. Michener, June 15, 1888, (L.C.), Vol. 29.

18 J. R. McKee to Mary Harrison McKee, June 18, 1888, Harrison Home MSS. ". . . the situation here. Chaos is a weak word for it, and yet it is about the only one that will cover it."

19 Barker to Harrison, June 4, 1888, (L.C.), Vol. 29.

20 George W. Steele to Harrison, June 5, 1888, *ibid.*, assured Harrison that at Chicago "we will doubtless be called upon for trades. . . . I am going to work in the ranks but want a captain on the ground and we will I really think win."

New York had already encouraged him by many promises of support. Equally strong pledges had come from the South and the West, where "the very friendly humor for Harrison" on the part of former Blaine men was undeniable.

Even before he left for Chicago, Michener confided to Eugene Hay that his mail was "full of letters of the most encouraging character." [21] In addition, the arrival of Indiana's enthusiastic volunteer army guaranteed vocal acclaim for Harrison in the great Exposition Hall, where Michener had instructed these workers to crusade against a possible "boodle ticket," to be headed by Governor Russell A. Alger of Michigan. It would be more in accord with the psychology of the American people, Michener told them, "to head our ticket with a poor man" rather than "with a man whose . . . qualification is that he has made a great deal of money." Even the capitalistic Elkins had to agree with Harrison's firm stand that "purchasing capacity" must not be allowed to supersede moral competency in the candidate to be chosen at Chicago. [22]

Among the thousands of Hoosiers who swarmed into Chicago to do battle for Harrison was the General's son-in-law, Bob McKee. Unschooled in politics, he lodged with two of its masters, Dudley and Michener, at the Grand Pacific. There he complained bitterly about Chicago's enervating humidity, adding grudgingly that his accommodations were as "comfortable as can be for the next Pres's son-in-law." This last may have been intended as irony, for his subsequent daily letters to the Harrison household, though full of convention chatter, were not oversanguine. Judge Gresham's supporters were still "talking big," he wrote Mamie. If Gresham "gets command," he continued, "rather than go down he will promise everything from Secretary of State down to coachman and may secure support not looked for." [23] This alarming

[21] L. T. Michener to E. G. Hay, June 7, 1888, Eugene Gano Hay MSS, Vol. 7.

[22] L. T. Michener to S. B. Elkins, June 9, 1888, Elkins MSS. Elkins and Michener carried on an almost daily correspondence. Law work kept Harrison from conferring with Elkins in the East; hence, the latter had visited Indianapolis on his way to the convention.

[23] J. R. McKee to Mary Harrison McKee, June 13, 16, 1888, Harrison Home MSS. The feeling between Gresham and Harrison supporters grew more tense and Bob McKee soon discovered this. He had been looking for the room of J. N. Huston, a party leader from Indiana, which he had been mistakenly informed was Room 210. "I knocked at 210," he wrote Mamie, "and imagine the surprise of two people when Mrs. Gresham opened the door. Katie [her daughter] stood behind her. Of course I excused myself and the door banged."

prediction of Bob's failed to worry the General's lieutenants. Professional politicians calmly reported: "Gresham is considered killed." [24]

Other flashes from McKee's pen, however, exposed the lighter side of the convention picture. The rooms hired by Governor Alger's wealthy supporters were located just across the hall from the Harrison headquarters. McKee observed cannily:

Alger seems to have a host of mysterious workers flying around; . . . a number of negroes . . . fly . . . very energetically. Evidently there is money and lots of it in the air.

Here there was danger, of course—money and promise of office. The entire New York delegation might be wooed into Alger's camp with a fat enough reward. Tom Platt, political boss of the Empire State, remained a question mark to most managers at Chicago, but it was suspected that his price was a Cabinet post.

Another off-the-cuff conclusion in Bob's letter home was that Blaine "is still the favorite of just lots and lots of people." [25] The arrival of the California delegation on June 15 had given some undaunted Blaineites among them a chance to demonstrate their strength. Large banners, shouting, and general noise-making highlighted a parade for the "Plumed Knight." Their enthusiasm was not contagious, however, and the last-stand movement for Blaine ended as "a significant failure." [26]

On the week end before the convention, confusion reigned wherever delegates gathered. "If any fellow can make heads or tails out of the grand hub-bub of claims, counter-claims, lies and a few truths that slap him on every side," commented the equally confused McKee, "he is more level headed than I am." The arrival of young Russell Harrison to join his father's staff of workers at the Grand Pacific did nothing to enlighten the son-in-law. At times, even Michener, usually cool and affable, lost patience with Russell's indiscretions and McKee's inexperience.[27] However, a steadying influence was soon added to the Harrison headquarters

24 W. W. Phelps to W. Reid, June 13, 1888, Whitelaw Reid MSS.

25 J. R. McKee to Mary H. McKee, June 13, 1888, Harrison Home MSS.

26 Bernardo, op. cit., p. 202. The dwindling Blaine enthusiasm was favorably noted in a telegram by Congressman Charles N. Grosvenor (R., Ohio) to Senator John Sherman, June 16, 1888, John Sherman MSS, Vol. 449.

27 J. R. McKee to Mary H. McKee, June 16, 19, 1888, Harrison Home MSS. McKee wrote that "Mr. Michener in a burst of disgust the other day exclaimed I wish both you and Russell had staid [sic] away. . . ."

when Russell's father-in-law, Alvin Saunders, former senator from Nebraska, rolled up his sleeves and began to work for the General.

Reports now began to reach Indianapolis that prospects are "very bright at this time." [28] Elkins, fresh from his conference with Harrison in Indianapolis, shared this optimism. By Sunday evening, June 17, even the cautious Michener conceded that much of the chaos had been dissipated. Everything was satisfactory, he reported; that is, almost everything, except how to handle Colonel Matthew Quay, the powerful Pennsylvania boss. A quick conference with the rest of the Harrison Committee convinced Michener that he ought to refer this delicate problem directly to Harrison. For the General's order, "make no promises," was still in effect.

Pennsylvania, where Matt Quay had long been the political overlord, had enjoyed but few favors during the long reign of the Republicans from 1860 to 1884. Little patronage and few offices had come that way. In 1888, therefore, Quay, to whom "politics was the breath of life, to win his only purpose," [29] had decided to step into the rôle of President-maker. He had already committed a majority of his delegation to John Sherman, whose stock was now beginning to decline. Better than a third of his delegates were already for Harrison.[30] Willing, therefore, to bargain with another candidate, Quay sent Thomas Bayne as emissary to Elam and Michener to advise that the Colonel was "ready to leave" John Sherman "at any moment, if Penn. can make a nomination by doing it." [31] Bayne assured the Indiana committee that Quay had Harrison in mind, but that as a practical politician he wanted "something in writing," either from Harrison's managers or from Harrison himself. The Pennsylvania boss suggested a blanket promise, couched in moderate and general language, that his state would receive a Cabinet post; with such a paper in hand, he would promise a solid vote for Harrison from the Key-

28 Michener to Charles P. Lane, June 14, 1888, (L.C.), Vol. 29.
29 See Henry L. Stoddard, As I Knew Them, p. 169, for Quay's Machiavellianism.
30 Bernardo, op. cit., pp. 204 ff. Wharton Barker's effective work, especially with the Irish vote, gave Harrison high hope. Barker to Michener, June 11, 1888, Barker Letterbook; and Barker to R. S. Taylor, June 11, 1888, R. S. Taylor MSS, (Indiana State Library). See also Sister Mary Lucille O'Marra, G.N.S.H., "Quay and Harrison from 1888 to 1892" (a master's thesis), p. 18.
31 John B. Elam and Louis T. Michener to General Harrison, June 17, 1888, (L.C.), Vol. 29.

stone State. Elam and Michener both appreciated the advantages and disadvantages of such a promise. They were not unmindful of Harrison's stern injunction, but they also remembered that Pennsylvania boasted 30 electoral votes in the Presidential contest and 60 votes in the nominating convention. So, by special courier, they dispatched to Harrison in Indianapolis the following letter, ready for his signature, together with the hopeful request to "let us know your views":

To: Hon. Thomas Bayne

Dear Sir:

I appreciate the kindly feeling of Senator Quay and his colleagues of the Pennsylvania delegation and I fully realize the claims of the great state of Pennsylvania. I write this to assure you and through you Senator Quay that in the event of my nomination and election to the Presidency, I shall regard the State of Pennsylvania as entitled to representation in my Cabinet and shall freely confer with Senator Quay and his confrères in making such selection.

Very truly yours,

What Harrison's thoughts were on receiving this no one knows. But he had already expressed his views very clearly. He scrawled a blunt "I said 'No' " on the letter, slipped it still unsigned into an envelope marked "Grand Pacific Hotel, Chicago," and returned the communication to his convention headquarters.[32]

By Monday, June 18, 1888, Chicago was in a turmoil. On convention eve, nearly 100,000 people were clamoring for the 7,273 seats available in Exposition Hall for the opening session. The outside view of the vast building, as yet uncompleted, was a disappointment. One correspondent described it as "an irregular heap of massive granite blocks averaging three stories in height, derrick-poles here and there like the dismantled masts of ships, piles of stone and mortar lying around in all sorts of places, and out of the center of all this four walls of rough brick towering far above everything around it." Yet these granite blocks formed little more than the foundation for the $2,000,000 combination

---

[32] The original documents are in (L.C.), Vol. 29. Stoddard, *op. cit.*, p. 171, recalls Harrison's instructions to his managers as: "Remember, no bargains, no alliances, no trades. I may like to be President, but if I am to go to the White House, I don't propose to go shackled."

hotel, theater, and office building that by the end of the following
year had risen ten stories high, with a tower soaring six stories
higher.[33] Within a few hours, the immense structure would become a human beehive whose swarming activity would continue
for nearly a week.

Good humor and enthusiasm radiated from delegates and visitors alike. Hundreds of local political clubs marched untiringly
in bright-colored uniforms and bands played unceasingly; tickets
for one day's session were peddled at ten dollars apiece. Tense
delegates and nervous friends of the various candidates skirmished
"in a most aggravating way for position . . . waiting to see where
the cat jumps." [34] A general feeling prevailed that the first ballot
would be of little consequence. Meanwhile, high spirits marked
the Harrison followers, who continued to stream into Chicago.
Many slept in Pullmans by night and visited various hotel headquarters by day. One Harrison delegate from Evansville, Jacob
Covert, an avowed representative of labor, actually found time to
describe the scene to his wife:

. . . The Palmer House and the Grand Pacific Hotels, each of which
look more like large public buildings, are the headquarters of all the
delegates, and halls, corridors and rooms are a seething mass of red-
hot perspiring Republicans. . . . am so glad I came up. In addition
to the little good I might accomplish for Harrison, it is a sight we
can never forget, and it is perhaps the most important convention
ever held on account of its peculiar complications.[35]

In the midst of the apparent pandemonium, the Harrison party
workers swarmed to their task. Literally thousands of Hoosiers

[33] Henry D. Northrop, *The Life and Public Service of Gen. Benj. Harrison*, p. 308.
This otherwise unsatisfactory campaign biography contains several graphic accounts
by correspondents who covered the National Convention. The Auditorium was located on Congress Street between Michigan and Wabash Avenues. Louis Sullivan
was the architect (1887–1889) of the building, which once housed the most famous
theater and hotel in America. See Henry G. Alsberg (ed.), *The American Guide*,
p. 519.

[34] J. R. McKee to Mary H. McKee, June 18, 1888, Harrison Home MSS.

[35] Covert to his wife, Ria Covert, June 19, 1888. A photostat of this letter was
made available to the author by Covert's great-grandson, Alan T. Nolan, Indianapolis
attorney. Covert was introduced to Lieutenant-Governor Charles W. Stone of Pennsylvania as "a Republican representative of the labor people," although today he
might be classified as a capitalist. A printer by trade, in 1888 he owned and operated his own newspaper. On June 17, Bob McKee reported that eight labor delegates from Indianapolis had arrived and were trying to hurt Harrison. Nothing
came of this movement.

like Covert scurried about, winning friends for General Harrison. Michener beamed with satisfaction and Bob McKee, vastly impressed, solemnly wrote his wife that "the Harrison men are working awful hard and show a devotion to your father's interest that ought to make him feel very grateful."

Comparable activity marked the organized efforts for rival candidates also. Russell Alger's headquarters showed the most evidence of the dollar sign until "the Allison crowd bloomed out in quarters . . . magnificently decorated with colors, smilax, hundreds of roses . . . the name 'Allison' over the door [in] Edison electric lights." McKee noted each detail with wide eyes; then reported knowingly to Mamie that "verily shekels play a big part in these things." He hastened to assure the home folks that his father-in-law's headquarters at the Grand Pacific "showed no signs of poverty," either. The decorations, he told them, were "fine and tasty" and everything was in "creditable style." As to his own opinion of where all this ostentation was leading, Harrison's son-in-law reasoned in sensible fashion that "where there is so much for so many candidates, it will neutralize itself." [36]

Until the convention reached its ultimate decision, the race for the nomination was always open. On June 18, however, few suspected that there would be a total of nineteen entries. Yet before the opening gavel fell even McKee knew there would be more than a few starters. To the family waiting on North Delaware Street he reported his impression that

the whole race seems to be like a lot of horses on a track. One runs to the front awhile, then another lays on the whip and forges ahead, but the horses cannot hold the gait clear around the track—so another lays on the whip in turn and comes to the front for a moment and so it goes. [37]

As far as General Harrison was concerned, his stable at Chicago was in good condition. Hitherto he had harbored a secret fear that Blaine might stampede the convention. But even this worry disappeared as he learned that in the poolrooms of Chicago the odds on Blaine were rising sharply: on June 11, it stood 1 to 5 that the man from Maine would be nominated; on June 18, the odds rose to 2 to 1.

[36] J. R. McKee to Mary H. McKee, June 17, 18, 1888, Harrison Home MSS.
[37] Ibid.

The convention was scheduled to open at noon on June 19. The crowd, however, started to assemble shortly after the breakfast hour. By ten o'clock, "panting pedestrians," with hoisted umbrellas, dotted the boulevard to the Auditorium. An army of lads sold fans, at triple their value, as a slight protection against the sweltering sun. By high noon every seat was filled, the galleries packed, and the aisles around and behind the desk of the presiding officer jammed. The new stage, second largest in the world, provided ample room for convention officials, party dignitaries, and prominent guests of the National Committee. Encircling the podium was a battery of newspaper correspondents. Directly in front of the reporters and their telegraphic wires sat the 832 official delegates and a like number of alternates.[38]

Called to order by Chairman B. F. Jones, at 12:30 P.M., the convention was at last under way. After the opening prayer, Chairman Jones delivered his welcoming address, a routine effort, and the convention hall grew noticeably quiet for the first and last time. It took just a bit of flamboyant oratory by Temporary Chairman John M. Thurston of Nebraska to bring the delegates to their feet. The magical name Blaine revived spirits wilted by the Chicago humidity.

When Thurston referred to the party's 1884 standard-bearer as "our uncrowned king, wielding the baton of acknowledged leadership," a round of cheers stopped the Nebraskan. Blaine, he finally continued, was not only the "nightmare of the Democracy" but was also "the greatest living American" and "the object of our undying love." Here the Blaine delegates rose in their seats, waving hats, handkerchiefs, and banners while the galleries yelled themselves hoarse. Although a thousand throats cried "No" when the speaker stated that Blaine "has denied us the privilege to support him in this Convention," the men of Harrison's committee knew that the Blaine threat had spent itself. Content in the conviction that this enthusiastic support for the Maine man would be General Harrison's at the opportune moment, they led the wild cheers of their own delegation when the chairman referred to the "gallant soldier" from Indiana.[39]

[38] Northrop, op. cit., pp. 309–12. In 1888, Milan's La Scala boasted the largest stage in the world. The delegates were arranged in a veritable pit, 120 by 246 feet, but the furthest distance from the speaker's stand for any delegate was 175 feet.

[39] Proceedings of the Ninth Republican National Convention, pp. 7–12. (Hereafter cited as Proceedings.) Thurston maintained that "though James G. Blaine may not be our president, yet he remains . . . supreme in the allegiance of his devoted fol-

The dull business of effecting a permanent organization for the convention took two days. Only the introduction of the party's first Presidential candidate, John C. Frémont, and a rousing speech by Negro leader Fred Douglass, who pleaded "in behalf of the millions who are disfranchised today," sparked life in a crowd impatient to get on with the nomination of candidates. Even Michigan's gift of a gavel "made from the wood of the oak under which the Republican Party was organized on the 6th day of July 1854 in Jackson . . ." failed to fire the delegates. The entire crowd laughed, however, at the chairman's promise to use the gavel "to pound the life out of the Democratic Party." [40]

Despite both afternoon and evening sessions on the second day, Wednesday, June 20, the convention made no progress other than accepting the report of the Committee on Credentials, once it had resolved a bitter conflict over the seating of delegates from Virginia.[41] The only diversion from routine proceedings was an offering of stirring band music, to which the audience sang lustily—and more than once—"Marching Through Georgia." Before the second session adjourned, however, Governor Joseph B. Foraker of Ohio delivered a partisan plea based on the theme that "he serves his country best who best serves the Republican party." Sustained applause greeted his hope that the convention would nominate a man who "will knock Grover Cleveland and the old bandana into 'innocuous desuetude.' " [42]

Between midnight and ten o'clock Thursday morning, June 21, the Committee on Platform and Resolutions, in closed session at

lowers, honored and respected by all honest and loyal men." General Hawley of Connecticut and General Gresham of Illinois were also mentioned as "gallant sol diers"—not by name but by state.

[40] Ibid., pp. 21–22. Significant to the Committee for Harrison was the observation that the gavel "has upon it copper, wool, iron, salt and wood—the five industries that the party now in power would ruin and abolish from the face of this country."

[41] Ibid., pp. 66–87. When the Wise faction was seated in preference to the Mahone-led delegates, the solution was regarded as another setback for John Sherman. See Bernardo, op. cit., pp. 210–11. William Mahone favored Sherman, while John S. Wise leaned to Gresham. See the unreliable Matilda Gresham, Life of Walter Q. Gresham, p. 585, and Nelson M. Blake, William Mahone of Virginia, pp. 241–42.

[42] J. B. Foraker, Notes of a Busy Life, I, 349, and Proceedings, p. 63. The "red bandana" referred to Democratic Vice-Presidential candidate Allen G. Thurman, the seventy-five-year-old "noble Roman" who was known and loved more for his appearance than for his principles. His red bandana, which he meticulously used after indulging in a pinch of snuff, became a political symbol. Stefan Lorant, The Presidency, p. 396, observes that when Thurman received his nomination "hundreds of red bandanas were waved enthusiastically in the convention hall."

the Union League Club, finished their report. It was read to a hushed convention by William McKinley, the avowed protectionist from Ohio. The platform, "a complete handbook of Republicanism," [43] satisfied delegates, managers, and all the candidates except Gresham, whose free trade views failed to harmonize with the party's plea for a protective tariff.[44] For Harrison, however, each plank in the document was in effect an endorsement of the voting record he had compiled in the Senate. Indeed, the resourceful Halford had executed his commission well, even to the extent of censuring Cleveland "for his numerous vetoes of pension measures." [45] Although there was some truth in the Democratic charge that the platform was "a general drag net, very skillfully contrived to catch any and all sorts of fish," [46] there was nothing in it that would embarrass Harrison in the event of his nomination.

Shortly before noon, the roll of states was called for Presidential nominees. California passed and Connecticut named Senator Joseph R. Hawley as her favorite son. Illinois then presented Judge Walter Q. Gresham in a flood of political oratory which lasted two hours. Delegates from Minnesota, Mississippi, Massachusetts, and Texas seconded the nomination. All five speakers took pains to emphasize such facts as that "Gresham . . . was a sound Republican—sound on the tariff and sound as to all other Republican principles and that it should not injure his cause that he was a favorite with the Mugwumps, who had defeated Blaine in 1884." [47]

After this "voluminous" presentation,[48] Indiana's name was called and Richard W. Thompson rose to announce that the Republican party of Indiana had selected Governor Albert G.

43 *Journal,* June 22, 1888.
44 Gresham, *op. cit.,* pp. 586–87.
45 *Proceedings,* p. 110.
46 Raleigh *News and Observer,* June 27, 1888, as cited in Bernardo, *op. cit.,* p. 221. Both the Richmond *Dispatch* and the Memphis *Daily Avalanche,* Democratic organs, claimed that so puerile a platform would invite the destruction of the party which had begun to disintegrate in 1884. The Indianapolis and Boston press warned that the "free whiskey" plank would certainly embarrass the Republican party.
47 J. B. Foraker, *Notes of A Busy Life,* I, 352; *Proceedings,* p. 19. Lynch admitted that Gresham was not Indiana's choice. This he attributed to the fact that the "friends and supporters of Walter Q. Gresham were more concerned, more anxious to maintain the unity, the harmony of the Republican Party in Indiana, than they were to secure the election of Gresham delegates." Michener flatly contradicted this statement by leaving a memorandum of how the Gresham men conducted a wide but ineffective "whispering" campaign against General Harrison. Michener MSS.
48 Foraker, *op. cit.,* p. 352.

Porter to present their candidate for the Presidency. It was a felicitous choice. Few men knew General Harrison more intimately than his former law partner, and few Hoosiers had commanded greater respect, whether in the courtroom, on the stump, or in the governor's chair. Porter ably stressed the political wisdom of choosing an Indiana nominee.[49] Briefly reviewing Harrison's career, he emphasized his stainless reputation, his shining military record, and the magical associations awakened in Virginia and the Old Northwest by the name Harrison. Grandfather and grandson, as well as great-grandfather, he reminded the Convention, "were woven into the very fabric of American history." Concluding, he said:

And now today in Indiana, among a people estimating highly the character and services of Gen. Benjamin Harrison, and holding in affection the memory of "Old Tippecanoe," the latch strings of the people are hospitably out to you, and their doors are waiting to fly open at your touch to let in the joyful air that shall bear upon its wing the message that Benjamin Harrison, their soldier-statesman, has been nominated for President of the United States.[50]

Harrison enthusiasts rocked the hall with a wild and prolonged demonstration that lasted beyond the luncheon recess. When the delegates reassembled, Congressman Jacob Gallinger of New Hampshire and E. H. Terrell of Texas seconded the General's nomination, the eloquent Texan contending, in a maze of adjectives, that General Harrison "stands the peer of any man mentioned for the high office of President." [51] Gallinger, no less forceful, won the applause of the galleries by observing the time-honored five-minute rule of the national House of Representatives.

---

[49] Most observers agreed that in 1884 Thomas Hendricks, as Vice-Presidential candidate, was responsible for 15 electoral votes in the Cleveland column. The fact that the Democrats did not choose a Hoosier in 1888 was regarded as making Harrison even more "available."

[50] *Proceedings*, pp. 122–25. Porter had in mind the promise that General William Henry Harrison made to his soldiers after the Battle of Tippecanoe: "If you ever come to Vincennes you will find a plate, and a knife, and a fork at my table, and I assure you that you will never find my door shut and the string of the latch pulled in." Porter was at pains to point out that Benjamin Harrison, whom he knew personally after his arrival in Indianapolis in 1854, never made "a first reference to his ancestors." Indeed, "he came poor in purse, but rich in resolution. . . . Self-reliant, he mounted the back of prosperity without the aid of a stirrup."

[51] *Ibid.*, pp. 126–27. A random excerpt reads: "In the prime and vigor of his manhood, free from the entanglements of faction, devoted to the interests and principles of his party; of unquestioned ability, untiring industry, and inflexible moral courage. . . ."

Referring to Harrison as "that grand man from Indiana," [52] he promised him the votes of the doubtful states of New England, which, added to the vote of doubtful Indiana, would, he declared, make him President.

During the remainder of the afternoon, Allison, Alger, Chauncey M. Depew, John Sherman, and two favorite sons, Edwin Fitler of Pennsylvania and Jeremiah Rusk of Wisconsin, were placed in nomination with the laurels well distributed to the speakers on each occasion. The greatest ovation was inspired by Ohio Senator John Sherman. The applause lasted for nearly half an hour, after which everyone again sang "Marching Through Georgia." Only Depew, earnestly presented by New York Senator Frank Hiscock, failed to arouse much enthusiasm. [53]

The first heat in the race to determine the party's standard-bearer got under way at 11:05 A.M. Friday, June 22, the fourth day of the proceedings. The opening prayer petitioned that "there be no doing of evil that good may come," [54] but the Sherman managers were soon convinced that either the Almighty or the Blaine supporters had not heard the parson's plea. In the roll call of the states, California amazed everyone by giving 16 unanimous votes to Blaine, who, of course, had not been placed in nomination. Pandemonium broke loose; friends of Sherman feared that "the Blaine lunatics" might stampede the convention. [55] As the roll call continued, however, the fear of a Blaine runaway proved groundless.

The anticipated indecisiveness of this first ballot became convention history. A total of 831 votes were cast, but Sherman, the preconvention favorite, captured only 229, [56] almost 200 short of

52 *Ibid.* Also Foraker, *op. cit.*, p. 352, notes that Gallinger's "modest manner but strong and effective speech made him a favorite with all who heard him, whether in strict accord with him or not."

53 *Ibid.*, p. 353. Robert G. Fraser of Detroit was perhaps the "readiest, most eloquent and most forcible of all the men who addressed the Convention" when he spoke for Alger.

54 *Proceedings*, p. 156. Senator Frank Hiscock was in the chair; the opening prayer was offered by the Rev. J. H. Worcester of Chicago.

55 Hanna to John Sherman (telegram), June 21, 1888, Sherman MSS, Vol. 450.

56 Bernardo, *op. cit.*, pp. 204-5, 215-16 shows conclusively that the vote received by Sherman reflected only negligible strength among the eastern and western states. The purchasable vote of the South was Sherman's mainstay.

the 416 necessary to elect. Harrison's total of 85 [57] clocked him as fourth, just a nose ahead of Allison and trailing both Gresham and Depew. Two more roll calls showed slight gains for all entries except Depew.[58] At 2:00 P.M. the convention recessed.

When the delegates re-assembled at seven for the evening session, they half-expected to ballot through the night. Depew, however, announced his withdrawal and intimated privately that although he had no candidate he had "been very much impressed by General Harrison" who was "a poor man with no corporate associations," and who could stimulate support by a battle cry like "Tippecanoe and Tyler too." [59] This freed New York's 72 votes and created tremendous confusion in the camps of rival candidates who called loudly for adjournment. Time was now of the essence for the supporters of such men as Sherman, Allison, Alger, and Gresham. Uniting in mutual concern, they carried the motion to adjourn until Saturday morning by a vote of 535 to 282.

The story behind Depew's withdrawal from the race goes a long way now in explaining Harrison's sudden surge to popularity. An almost solid opposition by western leaders to an eastern railroad president had gradually made Depew's candidacy too great a political risk. After the first three ballots, Depew recognized this fact and summoned former Senator Thomas ("Boss") Platt, New York gubernatorial candidate Miller, and United States Senator Frank Hiscock (the other three delegates-at-large from New York) to a private conference.[60] Then he announced his determination to retire, and in the ensuing discussion threw the weight of his influence behind General Harrison, a man whom he had never met.[61] Hiscock, Miller, and Platt hesitated, but Depew finally con-

[57] Vermont was solid for Harrison, and Indiana gave him 29 out of 30 votes on the first ballot. The one Hoosier vote for Gresham was anticipated and explained by Michener, and by the fourth ballot the Indiana delegation gave to Harrison its solid vote of 30. See Michener, "The Convention of 1888," Michener MSS. A scattered vote from 23 other states raised the total to 85.

[58] Depew dropped to 91 on the third ballot.

[59] Chauncey M. Depew to Cyrenus Cole, September 22, 1922, Depew MSS, (Yale University), as cited in Bernardo, *op. cit.*, p. 217.

[60] This conference preceded what Platt recollected as a "harmony dinner." See Louis J. Lang (ed.), *The Autobiography of Thomas Collier Platt*, p. 205.

[61] Depew said, in part: "There is one candidate here who at present apparently has no chance, but who, nevertheless, seems to me to possess more popular qualifications than any other, and that is Gen. Benjamin Harrison of Indiana. I do not

vinced them that the man from Indiana deserved the New York vote.

As its chairman, Depew then called a caucus of the entire Empire State delegation. His own account reads:

All were present. I told them of the action of the delegates at large and asked their opinions. Fifty-eight agreed with us, and 24 differed. No amount of persuasion could convince them that Harrison was the man to win.

Well, I thought the matter over for an hour and then invited the delegation to dinner. I did not try to convince the recalcitrants, I simply gave them good things to eat and good drink to enlighten their understanding. . . .[62]

There had been speeches after the black coffee, whereupon Senator Hiscock and State Senator Jacob Fassett joined Warner Miller and "Boss" Platt in an unqualified endorsement of Harrison. At the close of Depew's "harmony dinner," word soon reached the other delegations that New York was now in camp with the Hoosiers.

Meanwhile, at home in Indianapolis, Benjamin Harrison had continued his silent vigil. Telegrams from Chicago headquarters had brought conflicting stories. Now, however, one raised high his hopes: "I congratulate you in advance. Depew will withdraw in your favor. New York indorses you." [63]

On Saturday morning, June 23, the convention came to order for its fifth consecutive day. At first, the noise and disorder among the delegates almost drowned out the calling of the roll. Partial quiet was restored when William McKinley withdrew his name

---

know him, never met him, but he rose from the humblest beginnings until he became the leader of the bar of his state. He enlisted in the Civil War as a second lieutenant, and by conspicuous bravery and skill upon the battlefield, came out as a brigadier general. As United States Senator he became informed about Federal Affairs. His grandfather, President William Henry Harrison, had one of the most picturesque campaigns in our history. There are enough survivors of that "hard cider and log cabin" canvass to make an attractive contribution on the platform at every meeting, and thus add a certain historic flavor to General Harrison's candidacy." See *Report of the Benjamin Harrison Memorial Commission* (77th Cong., 1st Sess., House Doc. No. 154), p. 137.

[62] Rochester *Morning Herald*, November 9, 1888. This interview contained Depew's personal narrative of the inside workings of the New York delegation at Chicago. The figure "24" is evidently a typographical error, for it should read "14" to reach the proper total of a 72-man delegation.

[63] James W. Husted to Harrison, June 22, 1888, (L.C.), Vol. 29. This telegram was dispatched from Chicago at 7:08 P.M., some ten minutes before Depew made his speech of withdrawal.

from the ballot, for many had hoped that the Ohio major would sweep the convention as a surprise dark horse.[64] Then New York was called and Depew announced: "Harrison 59, Blaine 8, Alger 4, Sherman 1." Wisconsin followed suit by transferring her vote from Rusk to Harrison. The final tabulation showed Harrison a strong second, trailing Sherman by only 19 votes. On the fifth ballot Harrison gained more ground. Jubilant Harrison forces now flooded the convention hall with handbills headed: "STUDY THESE FIGURES." The illustration shown on page 349 approximates the original throwaway, which charted the strength of the remaining candidates and proved the "Hoosier Warrior" strongest in the doubtful states.[65] These states, every delegate was advised, must elect the next President.

With the fifth ballot, the convention got out of hand. The presiding officer blamed the noise and confusion on the delegates themselves rather than on the galleries. Only when the sergeants at arms cleared the aisles could the assembly agree to a four-hour recess.

At 4:10 P.M., the delegates filed back into the auditorium for the sixth ballot. Even before they were seated, however, Maryland moved that the convention adjourn without further balloting until 11 o'clock Monday morning. Disorderly cries of "No, no" and "Yes, yes" revealed a sharp division of sentiment. Michener led his followers in a struggle to keep the convention in session, but he could muster only 320 of the required 417 votes. With the week-end adjournment carried and the balloting delayed, Harrison's lieutenants knew they had suffered a temporary defeat.

On Saturday night and through Sunday, campaign headquarters for Harrison, Sherman, and Allison kept their lights burning, and the ghost of Blaine still haunted the convention.[66] Each manager worked cautiously and indefatigably. D. B. Henderson sent fre-

[64] Gresham, *op. cit.*, p. 596. Quay was rumored to have favored McKinley's nomination.

[65] One of these "throwaways" is in the J. R. McKee File, Harrison Home MSS. A handwritten note at the bottom reads: "Issued at time of Nat. Republican Convention at Chicago June 1888." Though Harrison received only 213 votes on the fifth ballot, 4 less than on the fourth roll call, he still came within 11 of front-running Sherman.

[66] William Henry Smith to Whitelaw Reid, June 24, 1888, Whitelaw Reid MSS.

quent telegrams to Iowa's Senator Allison at his Washington office, insisting that he could be nominated if he himself would only take "hold of it in earnest." [67] Senator Sherman, backed by Mark Hanna, had already done this; from Washington he predicted that he would most certainly be nominated on Monday.[68] But the time for bargains was at hand. In order to insure the choice of either Sherman or Allison, an alliance between those two camps was strongly urged.[69] Michener in the meantime concentrated his attention on the all-important New York delegation, for it was widely rumored that Boss Platt distrusted Sherman and that Depew would never consent to support Allison.[70]

On Sunday, Andrew Carnegie dissipated the Blaine fear once and for all. From Scotland, where the "Plumed Knight" was the house guest of the steel king, word came to Elkins that Blaine, steadfast in his refusal to run, wanted "Harrison and Phelps." [71] Elkins immediately pocketed the message, searched out Tom Platt, and joined him in a carriage ride. When Elkins returned to his hotel room, he had Platt's pledge of 72 New York votes for Harrison on the next ballot.[72] This Sunday excursion later led to the leveling of a "corrupt bargain" charge—denied and re-leveled many times since.[73] Only one thing is certain: the alliance between Indiana, New York, and all the former Blaine supporters was made strong and fast.

[67] Henderson to Allison, June 23, 24, 1888, (L.C.), Vol. 29. There were at least four telegrams from Henderson and one from Hines. Leland Sage, *William Boyd Allison, A Study in Practical Politics*, pp. 223–24, inclines to the judgment that "Black Friday" ended Allison's cause.

[68] John Sherman, *Recollections of Forty Years In House, Cabinet and Senate*, pp. 792–93.

[69] Hines to Allison, June 23, 1888, (L.C.), Vol. 29. Also, Wharton Barker, rushing to Washington from the convention, sent several wires to the leading candidates and their managers, urging them to hold their positions until he could arrive. See Wharton Barker to Swank, Sherman, Hoar, Miller, *et alii*, Wharton Barker MSS. All are dated June 23, 1888, initialed "W. B.," and filed in the "Harrison Box, 1882–1892."

[70] Bernardo, *op. cit.*, p. 216, n. 2. The opinion is strongly documented. Also Sage, *op. cit.*, p. 222.

[71] Burton J. Hendrick, *Life of Andrew Carnegie*, II, 327–28.

[72] Stoddard, *op. cit.*, p. 160.

[73] Sherman, *op. cit.*, p. 793, says: "I believed then, as I believe now, . . . that a corrupt bargain was made on Sunday which transferred the great body of the vote of New York to General Harrison and thus led to his nomination. It is to the credit of General Harrison to say that if the reputed bargain was made it was without his consent at the time nor did he carry it into execution." Reference here is that Platt was promised the Treasury post if Harrison were elected. Harrison, Michener, and Elkins all denied the allegations.

STUDY THESE FIGURES

HARRISON'S STRENGTH

ON

LAST BALLOT

	SHERMAN	HARRISON	ALGER	ALLISON	GRESHAM	BLAINE	McKINLEY
Democratic States	111	42	82	23	21	14	5
Republican States	108	74	47	57	55	26	2
New Jersey, New York, Connecticut, Indiana	1	91	7	12	6	6	7
Territories	4	6	6	7	5	2	
Totals, 5th Ballot	224	213	142	99	87	48	14

IT WILL BE SEEN BY THE ABOVE TABLE THAT GENERAL HARRISON'S STRENGTH COMES MORE LARGELY FROM DOUBTFUL STATES THAN THAT OF ANY OTHER CANDIDATE. THESE DOUBTFUL STATES MUST ELECT THE NEXT PRESIDENT.

By Sunday night, Hoosier headquarters in the Grand Pacific "showed that the current was running toward Harrison with a strength . . . believed to be irresistible." As the spirit of optimism increased, so did the unflagging efforts of the Harrison workers, who refused to be lulled into a sense of false security. Despite a telegram to Harrison, telling him that he would be nominated on Monday, Michener's Committee for Harrison refused to quit until all the votes were tallied. It would be too easy for Platt, for example, to change his mind and switch 14 of New York's 72 votes to another candidate.

At two o'clock Monday morning, Harrison's managers conferred with the section of New York's delegation that had already proved its dependability by giving Harrison 58 votes on Saturday. They learned that the full delegation would caucus at nine o'clock that same morning, just two hours before the sixth ballot. Michener and his co-workers asked New York's 58 Harrison supporters to move that the entire delegation "cast its vote for Harrison, and to continue to vote for him so long as Harrison's friends in the Indiana delegation should stand by him." The New Yorkers agreed to this; they also agreed that "when this motion was made it was to be seconded by an uprising of all who were willing to thus pledge themselves as Harrison men."

At nine o'clock Monday, as the New Yorkers went into caucus at their headquarters, Dudley and Michener stationed themselves in the hall near the door in order to follow the proceedings personally. Michener later recalled the scene:

We heard a little speaking followed by a round of applause, the big doors of the parlor were thrown open hurriedly, and Senator Platt rushed out into the hall, came to us, exclaiming excitedly that the New York delegation had just decided by a unanimous vote to stand by Harrison so long as his friends in the Indiana delegation stood by him, and asking that we furnish the delegation with Harrison badges.[74]

This news soon infected the other delegations. Runners informed them that New York was now solid for Harrison, thus increasing his anticipated vote by 14. Simultaneously, the rumor spread that General James S. Clarkson, coleader of the Allison forces with

[74] "No Promises Made," a typed memorandum in the Michener MSS. This memo was copied from a story by William E. Curtis, written for the Washington *Evening Star* and the Chicago *Record-Herald*. It appeared in the *Evening Star*, March 10, 1910.

Henderson, was preparing to withdraw the Iowan's name in favor of Benjamin Harrison.[75] The band wagon was ready to move.

The convention came to order at 11:07 A.M. on Monday, June 25, for its sixth day of work. A spirit of antagonism marred the first minutes following the opening prayer. Charles A. Boutelle, representative of the Maine delegation, was recognized by the chair as wishing to rise to a question of privilege. It was no secret that he was under orders to read two cablegrams from Blaine. Creed Haymond, delegate-at-large from California, took exception to the recognition of the Maine delegate. He blurted out that "nothing is in order now except a call of the roll, and if that is not in order I want to make a speech for Mr. Blaine when he is being betrayed in the camp of his friends." The chair chided Haymond and permitted Blaine's two dispatches of final withdrawal to be read to the disorderly crowd,[76] after which more pandemonium ensued.

Before he could establish order, the chairman threatened three times "to clear the galleries." Then the solemn roll call began. As the states announced their votes, both Dudley and Michener patrolled the aisles, working feverishly to persuade hesitating delegates to swing to Harrison. The sixth ballot showed the Hoosier's net gain at 18 votes, including the 14 additional votes delivered by New York. Still he had not caught Sherman. The seventh ballot, however, told a different story. California, third on the roll, left Blaine at last and gave 15 of its 16 votes to Harrison. Other delegations began to split their vote, with Wisconsin and Dakota Territories solid for the General. At the end of the ballot, Harrison had passed Sherman by 47 votes; this indicated that he would go further on the next roll call. Even as the eighth ballot got under

---

[75] *Ibid.* Michener wrote: "But other things had been occurring during that eventful night (Sunday). James S. Clarkson of Iowa, the leader of the Allison forces, had told us to be prepared for Allison's withdrawal Monday, and said that he expected that it would be made in such a way as to ask the Allison supporters to go to Sherman, but Clarkson said that he and those of the Allison men who would follow him would give their support to Harrison." Sage, *op. cit.*, p. 226, explains how Clarkson engineered the shift to Harrison.

[76] *Proceedings*, pp. 191–92. Blaine directed his cablegrams to Boutelle and Manley, Maine Delegation, Chicago. The first one, from Edinburgh, June 24: "Earnestly request all friends to respect my Paris letter (signed) Blaine." The second one, June 25: "I think I have the right to ask my friends to respect my wishes and refrain from voting for me. Please make this and former despatch public, promptly. (signed) James G. Blaine."

way, however, it became apparent that he would win. Not only Iowa, but a majority of Allison's total of 76 votes were coming to him. When Connecticut, Colorado, Delaware, and New Jersey also gave Harrison their votes and Wyoming Territory, last to be called, contributed her widow's mite, "two for Harrison," the race was officially over. The final totals read: Harrison 544, Sherman 118, Alger 100. He had beat Sherman by 426 votes, 128 more than necessary for the nomination.

In a matter of seconds, Foraker of Ohio sprang to his feet and moved that the nomination be unanimous. "Ohio came here all Sherman men. They are now all Harrison men," he cried. Michigan seconded, rejoicing that a soldier, even though not General Alger had been placed at the head of the ticket. Amid a flurry of speeches, every major group in the convention jumped on the Harrison band wagon: New York made him her adopted son; Iowa pointed to his "incorruptible life and gigantic intellect"; [77] Maine and California agreed that the convention had solved the problem of whether to choose a soldier or a statesman by endorsing Harrison—"a man who combines the wisdom of a statesman with the courage and the gallantry of a soldier." Judge John M. Thurston of Nebraska declared that the American people, "tired of avoirdupois and cussedness," are "ready for loyalty and statesmanship." The Southern states, too, promised to march in a November victory parade. William O. Bradley, Kentucky delegate, spoke for them all in his seconding speech:

We go into this canvass with Harrison and with the broad word of protection upon our banner—protection to American industries, protection to the persecuted people of the South, protection to the poor children who today in the South are laboring in ignorance, and protection to the grand soldiers who shed their blood upon the fields of battle that this Nation might live. In the name of Abraham Lincoln, in the name of Henry Clay whom Kentucky and this Nation are proud to honor, I second the motion to make this nomination unanimous. [78]

In a rising vote, the convention now gave Benjamin Harrison its unanimous nomination. With magnificent effect, the band burst forth with "Hail to the Chief" and a tumult of cheers rocked the convention. "Delegates stood on chairs, and waved flags, hats and

77 *Ibid.*, pp. 192–207.
78 *Ibid.*, pp. 208–13.

umbrellas. Ladies flung summer wraps in the air, waved small flags and . . . parasols, men hugged each other, and shouted until they were exhausted." [79] And at some time during the excitement, Louis T. Michener sent a wire to his chief in Indianapolis: "You are put in command." [80]

Shortly after 9:00 A.M., some two hours before the final balloting in Chicago, and as New York met in its fateful caucus, Harrison drove his own horse and carriage to his law office [81] on Market between Pennsylvania and Delaware Streets. Already at vigil in the inner office were William H. H. Miller, Howard Cale, Addison C. Harris, and a half-dozen others. Close at hand was the telegraphic instrument especially installed for the occasion. After the General arrived, a promising young reporter, Hilton U. Brown of the friendly *Evening News*, also joined the tense circle of friends. As the sixth and seventh ballots reflected the pro-Harrison trend, excited townsmen jammed the streets outside. The moment the victory flash came from Chicago, a triumphant shout from Harrison's office told its own tale to the eager crowd on the sidewalk below. Inside, according to reporter Brown, there was uncontrolled joy:

One of the ladies present in her exuberance and enthusiasm threw her arms around the General and gave him a hearty smack. Harrison himself was restrained in his comment but cordial to those about him.

When the General appeared for a moment on a little balcony to acknowledge the cheers and personal greeting, he could scarcely master his emotions. [82] Back in his office, the sense of the news overcame him and "he nearly fainted and had to lie down." Charles Hedges, Associated Press reporter, observed how Harrison's reaction differed from that of "phlegmatic Cleveland who never ceased

[79] *Journal*, June 26, 1888.

[80] Michener to Harrison, June 25, 1888, telegram, (L.C), Vol. 29.

[81] *Journal*, July 1, 1888. Every detail of what was an unpretentious law office became known across the nation. Harrison's private office, with its three windows opening on Market Street, a room about fifteen by twenty feet in size, was photographed time and again. His walnut desk, dingy red carpet, and brown spittoons became items of national interest.

[82] Hilton U. Brown, *A Book of Memories*, p. 173. This account is corroborated by Frank Tibbott who served so many years as Harrison's personal secretary. A 1938 letter, Tibbott to Hitch, filed in (L.C.).

eating his dinner when the bulletin came that he was nominated." [83]

News of Harrison's nomination spread rapidly over Indianapolis, particularly in the General's own neighborhood.[84] Before he could reach home, neighbors had congregated on his front lawn. The General's secretary, Frank Tibbott, "hot-footed it ten blocks to the Harrison home . . . and entertained the callers till the General . . . arrived." [85] Milling crowds of men, women, and children cheered the Republican candidate, and Harrison returned their tribute with a wave. "The children all seemed to know him and he seemed to know them, calling them by their first names." Catching sight of Frank Tibbott the General came to him and shook hands. The secretary later recalled: "There were tears in his eyes and he said, 'When a man receives the approbation of his neighbors, he is indeed blessed.' "

Meanwhile, souvenir hunters began busily to dismantle the white picket fence that surrounded the Harrison premises. Nothing could be done to stop them. But nobody cared, least of all Benjamin Harrison. He was ready to start his official campaign that same afternoon. With a glance at the crowd, he said to his secretary: "I suppose these folks will want me to say something, so you had better come in." [86]

Standing on the little "stoop" of his home, he gave the first of several "neighborly chats." Hundreds came and left before supper. By evening, the number of callers had swelled into the thousands. Delegations from Marion, Hendricks, Hamilton, and Howard Counties soon arrived, and Harrison extended to them a comrade's hand. Three times within an hour the new candidate spoke briefly. When "Harrison Clubs" from Danville, Plainfield, Kokomo, and Noblesville also arrived, they could not be denied personal greetings. Harrison's "front porch" campaign had begun. At a late hour, after the delegations from outlying towns had retired, nearly 5,000 Indianapolis residents assembled before the "picket-less" house

---

[83] Charles Hedges to William Henry Smith, July 21, 1888, William Henry Smith MSS, (Ohio State Archaeological and Historical Society Archives, Columbus, Ohio). See also *Report of the Benjamin Harrison Memorial Commission*, p. 138.

[84] In the Harrison home that day, as the first crowds began to swarm into her front yard, Carrie Harrison dropped her household duties and said to her daughter, "Well, Mamie, your father's got it." (Indianapolis *Sunday Star*, August 20, 1933, in a feature article commemorating Harrison's birthday centennial. Mrs. Harrison's comment was recalled by Sam Miller, W. H. H. Miller's son)

[85] Brown, *op. cit.*, p. 174.

[86] Tibbott to Hitch, *loc. cit.*, see n. 82.

on North Delaware Street, demanding another speech. Visibly moved, Harrison complied willingly:

Neighbors and friends, I am profoundly sensible of the kindness which you evidence tonight in gathering in such large numbers to extend to me your congratulations over the result at Chicago. It would be altogether inappropriate that I should say anything of a partisan character. Many of my neighbors who differ with me politically have kindly extended to me, as citizens of Indianapolis, their congratulations over this event. [*Cries of "Good!" "Good!"*] Such congratulations, as well as those of my neighbors who sympathize with me in my political beliefs, are exceedingly grateful.

The General rehearsed his thirty years as a resident of the Hoosier capital and predicted a future development for the town that would far outstrip its past. He concluded with the thought nearest his heart:

Kings sometimes bestow decorations upon those whom they desire to honor, but the man is most highly decorated who has the affectionate regard of his neighbors and friends. [*Great applause and cries of "Hurrah for Harrison!"*] I will only again thank you most cordially for this demonstration of your regard. I shall be glad from time to time, as opportunity offers, to meet you all personally, and regret tonight that this crowd is so great that it will be impossible for me to take each one of you by the hand [*cries of "We'll forgive you!"*] but we will be here together and my house will always open its doors gladly to any of you when you may desire to see me [*great cheering*].[87]

Meanwhile, back in Chicago, the convention had turned to the task of choosing Harrison's running mate. A spirited evening session concentrated on two nominees from the East, William Walter Phelps of New Jersey and Levi Parsons Morton of New York. Both candidates, strongly endorsed by party leaders, represented doubtful states. Blaine had already urged the selection of Phelps,[88] a Yale man who had turned from a good law practice to attend to his own banking and railroad interests. But New York's candidate, Levi P. Morton, won an overwhelming victory on the first ballot. While Morton's public life had been compressed into six years, two in Congress and four as Minister to France, the New York banker enjoyed great popularity. Californian Henry L. Gage, in seconding the nomination, declared him "a man who is better loved, and can poll more votes on the far-off Pacific shores, than

[87] *Reception Speeches by General Benjamin Harrison*, p. 4.
[88] *Biographical Directory of the American Congress, 1774–1949*, p. 1677.

any other man living upon this earth, save and except the great American Commoner, James G. Blaine." [89] As soon as word reached Indianapolis, Harrison wired Morton in New York: "Let me assure you that the association of your name with mine upon the ticket gives me great satisfaction."

Before the avalanche of congratulatory telegrams and letters at the Harrison home could be read or even sorted, the Republican delegates made a mass exodus from Chicago. Several delegations, including California, joined the home-coming Indiana contingent in a pilgrimage to Indianapolis to pay tribute to Harrison. This new crowd, reinforced by the candidate's friends and neighbors and a host of party workers, would not disperse from their stand in the General's front yard until he had addressed them. After complimenting the Hoosier delegation on its deportment at the convention, their candidate stressed the point that his nomination was a party, not a personal victory:

I do not feel at all that in selecting the candidate who was chosen, regard was had simply to the individual equipment and qualifications for the duties of this high office. I feel sure that if the Convention had felt free to regard these things only, some other of those distinguished men, old time leaders of the Republican party—Blaine, or Sherman, or Allison, or some of the others named—would have been chosen in preference to me.

I feel that it was the situation in Indiana, and its relation to the campaign that was impending, rather than the personal equipment or qualifications of the candidate that was chosen, that turned the choice of the convention in our direction. . . . And I feel sure, too, my fellow citizens, that we have joined now a contest of great principles, and that the armies which are to fight out this great contest before the American people will encamp upon the high plains of principle, and not in the low swamps of personal defamation or detraction.[90]

Self-satisfaction and complacency were not among the weapons in Harrison's arsenal as he armed for the Presidential battle of 1888.

[89] Robert McElroy, *Levi Parsons Morton: Banker, Diplomat and Statesman*, pp. 173–74. The first ballot results read 592 for Morton, 119 for Phelps, and 103 for Bradley. Actually Blaine himself, though he supported Phelps, had predicted Morton's Vice-Presidential candidacy as early as April, 1888. From Florence, Blaine had written Morton that "the tendency I think is towards a Western candidate for President. If this be so, you will have a splendid opening for V.P. if you desire it and set your New York friends to work. . . ." (*Ibid.*, p. 171.)

[90] *Reception Speeches by General Benjamin Harrison*, pp. 4–5.

CHAPTER XXI

The Making of a President

IN JULY, 1888, Indianapolis began to enjoy national prestige as far as the press was concerned. It became, in a political sense, a second capital for the nation's newspapermen. Scores of by-line articles were put on the wires from the Hoosier capital, and Benjamin Harrison soon found himself described, speculated about, and quoted in the papers of every state of the Union. Joining the army of reporters were numerous business and political leaders. Almost immediately, the city's already inadequate hotel facilities were overtaxed, and the newly constructed Union Depot seemed to have shrunk as Republican delegations and political clubs arrived in increasing numbers. Party enthusiasts, old soldiers, and boyhood acquaintances comprised the ranks of those who marched, accompanied usually by a band, from the railroad cars to General Harrison's front yard. Thousands more, unable to negotiate the trip, wrote or wired congratulations and predictions of success for the candidate who had promised protection at home and abroad.

In the thousands of hamlets that dotted the country from California to New York, Benjamin Harrison, his home, his law office, his family, and his personal habits dominated the news. Neither the secrets of his early life nor his private notes of contemporary activity were considered sacred to reporters clamoring for fresh copy. The country was assured that even though Harrison had not actually been born in a log cabin, he had at least begun his studies in a little log school house.

Next to the General's frontier and aristocratic ancestry, his rôle as a stout Presbyterian was widely heralded. This was traced in detail from a college campus revival, where a long-forgotten min-

ister had attempted "to convert the sinners of Oxford," [1] down to
Harrison's Bible classes and his eldership in the First Presbyterian
Church of Indianapolis. On the score of material possessions, the
Republican candidate was portrayed as a man of modest means
who, twelve years previously, had refused to run for governor
because he was too poor.[2] Rounding out the picture with a sketch
of the General's Hoosier connections, emphasis was placed on his
membership and active participation in the Indianapolis Literary
Club where he consorted with James Whitcomb Riley, Meredith
Nicholson, and "nearly every man of any real prominence in the
city."[3] Upon discovering that Harrison at the time of his nomination had been preparing for his club an essay on American foreign relations during the Civil War, reporters told their readers
that the new candidate had put aside this work in order to contribute a personal chapter to the nation's history during 1889–1893.

Full-blown accounts of him as "essentially . . . a family man"
also studded the daily press. These were often "planted" by Harrison's managers, and for good reason. Many citizens of Indianapolis who did not know him intimately had typed the General as
cold and aloof. They had mistaken his dignity and austerity for
pride. American newspaper readers now saw him as a man whose
"heart is wide open to view" [4] whether at the fireside, in his law
office, or during his leisure hours, when he could be seen taking
long carriage rides or equally long strolls about the city. Prospective voters were warned that Harrison was a man about whom
little by way of anecdote could be gleaned because "he does not
mingle with the good fellows of the town and slap people on the
back, as Garfield had the habit of doing and as Blaine does." His
good neighbors and close friends explained that he was not really
"stuck-up." It was just that he walked "with erect military attitude which so many mistake for aristocratic bearing." They
claimed that Harrison's critics "do not know the man." His mind

[1] St. Louis *Post-Dispatch*, July 1, 1888, a clipping in the Benjamin Harrison
Scrapbooks, (L.C.), Vol. 6. For details of this revival and conversion, see Harry J.
Sievers, *Benjamin Harrison: Hoosier Warrior*, pp. 58–59.

[2] R. T. St. John to Harrison, July 4, 1888, (L.C.), Vol. 32, wrote: "I recall a con-
versation we had in the U. S. Courtroom prior to the convention which nominated
G. S. Orth and that I there urged you to permit the convention to nominate you.
And your reply was 'St. John, I am too poor to make the race.' "

[3] J. B. Martin, *Indiana: An Interpretation*, p. 103.

[4] Smiley N. Chambers, in a speech to a joint session of the State and City Bar
Associations, March 16, 1901. See *Journal*, March 17, 1901.

preoccupied with business or affairs of state, he often passed acquaintances on the street without noticing them, but this was not
"from any sense or feeling of superiority." [5] As proof that he was
in reality a man endowed with warm, human qualities, there soon
appeared countless stories describing the General at home: his
cigar smoking, his periods of play with grandson Baby McKee,
an occasional light novel, chats over the back fence, his interest
in his grapevines, and his admiration for his wife's ability with
water colors. These and other domestic details filled in the public
portrait of Benjamin Harrison, the man and the candidate.

In 1888 scarcely a Republican had forgotten blundering Burchard's "Rum, Romanism and Rebellion" remark, with its three
little words that allegedly had felled Blaine in 1884's Presidential
battle. Consequently, before his nomination was even a few weeks
old, Harrison was deluged with letters cautioning the utmost cir-
cumspection in his speech at all times. Leading the host of friendly
advisers was a Roman Catholic priest, the Rev. P. A. Tracy, pastor
of St. Paul's Church in Burlington, New Jersey. Father Tracy
identified himself as "the acting leader of the Catholics" in the
Garden State, and professed his belief that "Rev. Mr. Burchard,
by his unfortunate alliteration killed Mr. Blaine's chances." With
this now in mind, he warned Harrison to be on guard against the
oratorical services of Robert G. Ingersoll, one of the party's most
famed speakers, but also notorious as "the great agnostic." Fearing
that Ingersoll's "offensive obtrusiveness" [6] would victimize Harrison as Burchard's intolerance had Blaine, the pastor reasoned
that a new alliteration, "Ingersoll, Independence, and Infidelity,"
might prove fatal to Harrison's chances.[7] The General quickly
acknowledged this and similar warnings: for example, that the
Democrats would claim he was for "free whiskey" when and if he

[5] St. Louis *Post-Dispatch*, July 1, 1888, Benjamin Harrison Scrapbooks, (L.C.), Vol.
6. After the 1880 campaign, the *Sentinel*, December 9, 1880, published a similar
explanation.

[6] In 1876, Robert G. Ingersoll, then the Republican party's most famous orator,
placed Blaine in nomination for the Presidency. By 1888 he was equally famous, or
infamous, as "the leading enemy of God in the United States."

[7] The Rev. P. A. Tracy to Harrison, July 9, 1888, (L.C.), Vol. 33, stated that "four
years ago I was the first priest and most influential Catholic in New Jersey to declare
in favor of Mr. Blaine. My letter on that occasion was utilized by the Republicans
as a valuable campaign document."

gave unqualified endorsement to the platform adopted at Chicago.[8]

There was also much professional advice. For example, New York's elderly Senator, William Evarts, saw victory as certain so long as Republicans kept uppermost in their minds the fact that an election campaign "is a fight, and not a feast." [9] With equal sagacity, Congressman D. B. Henderson, who had been Senator Allison's chief spokesman at the Convention, wrote Harrison: "I have faith in you . . . my heart is with you. Your great work will be in seeing to it that every Greek Warrior is in the field and fighting to reduce the modern Troy: *Get every chief at your side.*" [10]

Harrison took both advice and warnings in good part. He resolved not only to have "every chief" at his side but every fighting man as well. This, of course, included his beloved and powerful veterans. When it came to meeting and speaking with former comrades at arms, the old commander of the 70th Indiana Regiment proved matchless. On the evening of June 30, 1888, several thousand citizens—this time a nonpolitical group—paid their respects to General Harrison at his home. At the head of the Hoosier column marched four hundred Union veterans, commanded by Moses G. McLain. Their spokesman was a prominent Democrat, Major James L. Mitchell. To his congratulatory address Harrison responded briefly with some gracious, nonpartisan remarks. Then, especially moved by the presence of the veterans, he directed the remainder of his speech to them, vowing that "the comradeship of the war will never end until our lives end," for "the fires in which our friendship was riveted and welded were too hot for the bond ever to be broken." In conclusion, the General requested "the privilege now, without detaining you longer, of taking by the hand every soldier here." [11] Thus, as a citizen-soldier, Harrison gracefully returned Indianapolis' tribute to her adopted son.

Three days later, Senator Allison in Washington congratulated the General, characterizing the speech as "a gem" which "ought to have been sent everywhere." [12] As a matter of fact, it already had been; Michener had seen to that. He knew good copy when he saw it, and Harrison's words had a ring that his Democratic

[8] Senator Preston B. Plumb to Harrison, July 3; Senator Frank Hiscock to Harrison, July 7; and Senator Eugene Hale to Harrison, July 7, 1888, *ibid.*

[9] William M. Evarts to Harrison, July 1, 1888, *ibid.*

[10] D. B. Henderson to Harrison, July 2, 1888, *ibid.*

[11] Charles Hedges (compiler), *Speeches of Benjamin Harrison*, pp. 32–33.

[12] W. B. Allison to Harrison, July 3, 1888, (L.C.), Vol. 32.

opponent, Cleveland, unversed in war, could never surpass. The speech had also dignified both the Southern states and their former slaves.

Later on that same evening of June 30, the Harrison League of Indianapolis, numbering three hundred colored men, assembled on what had once been the lawn of the Harrison home to congratulate the Republican nominee through its spokesman, Ben D. Bagby. Despite the late hour and his weariness from a day and evening of speechmaking, Harrison made an address which reflected his sincere respect for and interest in the American Negro. Drawing on boyhood memories, he recalled how he once wandered through his grandfather's orchard at North Bend, then the natural boundary line between the free state of Ohio and the slave state of Kentucky.

. . . in pressing through an alder thicket . . . I saw sitting in its midst a colored man with the frightened look of a fugitive in his eye . . . attempting to satisfy his hunger with some walnuts he had gathered. He noticed my approach with a fierce, startled look, to see whether I was likely to betray him; I was frightened myself and left him in some trepidation, but I kept his secret.

This anecdote brought shouts of "good!" from his listeners, and Harrison went on to review the progress made by the Negro race, both before and after his own arrival in Indiana. As a lawyer, his memory went back to the "Black Code" that had prevented Negro witnesses from testifying in Indiana courts when a white man was party to a suit. To cries of "Amen to that" and to rounds of applause, Harrison expressed his pleasure that he "had lived to see this unfriendly legislation removed from the statute-books and the unfriendly section of our State Constitution repealed. I have lived not only to see that but to see the race emancipated and slavery extinct." He closed by painting a vivid picture of "the kneeling black man at the feet of the martyred President, with the shackles falling from his limbs," [13] and promised his audience a free and honest vote, as well as a just participation in the national government, if he were elected President. Then, with a handshake for each man, he bade the three hundred League members goodnight.

[13] Hedges, *op. cit.*, pp. 33–35. Aware of the political importance of the delegation, Harrison stressed the faithfulness of the Negro throughout the war, especially during the Union march through North Carolina, between Raleigh and Richmond.

On July 2, 1888, two days before the official Notification Committee arrived in Indianapolis, General Harrison received an
unannounced, neighborly visit from Francis Silas Chatard, the
distinguished Catholic Bishop of Indianapolis, who lived but a
stone's throw away. The Bishop's fragmentary diary reveals a picture of Harrison at home:

I found him walking on the lawn (674 N. Delaware St.) with his little
grandson in his arms. He received me very cordially and made the
servant conduct me into the house, while he said a few words to some
ladies and relatives who were at the gate. Almost immediately he came
in and expressed in a cordial manner his appreciation of my visit, and
repeated it.

The prelate had called to offer his congratulations on the honor
shown Harrison by the entire country. He commented on the fact
that "this was the first time a nomination for the Presidency had
fallen to the state," and from discussing the whys and wherefores
of that fact, they went on for a chat that lasted more than an hour.
In reviewing the General's campaign, then already under way,
Chatard later recalled that Harrison spoke bitterly of "trials" and
referred to campaign lies "that come up out of the ground." One
accusation in particular, it seemed, had bothered the General. It
was the Democrats' charge that he, Harrison, was unsympathetic
to labor, and that during the violent railroad strikes of 1877 he had
maintained that a dollar a day was sufficient wage for any workman. Chatard's diary records the vehemence of Harrison's statement

. . . that he had never advocated "90 cts a day as enough for a workingman"; that in 1877 he had stood for law against resistance to law.
He spoke of his appreciation of the Church's stand with regard to
social order, and obedience to authority, and temperance without
fanaticism. He also said in reply to a remark I made regarding the influence of the church in keeping her people out of secret organizations, that he had always been opposed to such societies, had never
been a member of one, except at College (in the Greek Society); though
he had voted the Know-Nothing ticket, he never belonged to them and
had refused to join them.[14]

14 "Diary of Francis Silas Chatard," in Chatard MSS, (Cathedral Archives, Indianapolis). For the effort on the part of the Democrats to show that Harrison was
unfriendly to organized labor, see R. C. Buley, "The Campaign of 1888 in Indiana,"
Indiana Magazine of History, 10 (1914), 35–36.

Two days afterwards—fittingly enough on July 4—the gentlemen of the Notification Committee, headed by Judge Morris M. Estee of California, were escorted through the rain to Harrison's house. The chairman's speech was not remarkable except for its brevity, and the General's reply was equally brief. He accepted the nomination, he assured them, "with so deep a sense of the dignity of the office and of the gravities of its duties and responsibilities as altogether to exclude any feeling of exultation or pride," and predicted that the Republican campaign would stimulate an unusual popular interest.

Commenting on the fact that it was the Fourth of July, Harrison then offered a few patriotic remarks that nicely entwined the ideals of the party with those of the Revolutionary and Civil wars. Returning to more current matters, he observed that he had examined the statements of the Republican platform with some care and that, for the most part, they were in harmony with his personal views. He reserved the right, however, to discuss these points in detail when he had completed his "formal letter of acceptance." The informal occasion closed with the Committee's presentation to him of an engrossed copy of the declarations comprising the party's 1888 platform.

July 4, 1888, was also memorable to General Harrison and his wife for a visit less historic, but closer to their hearts. From the Tippecanoe Club of Marion County, a political association composed exclusively of veterans who had voted for General William Henry Harrison in 1836 and 1840, came a unique tribute. The average age of this group was seventy-five years, with one member, James Hubbard of Mapleton, over one hundred years old. Nearly all who were still able-bodied had labored tirelessly at the Chicago convention for the nomination of "Old Tippecanoe's" grandson.

Now, on the afternoon of the Fourth, ninety-one of these veterans, commanded by their marshal, Isaac Taylor, marched to Harrison's home through a continuous downpour of rain. Their speech of congratulation stirred the General, for he had known many of them for more than thirty years as political, business, or family friends. The affection they had borne his grandfather had become the grandson's heritage, and upon this foundation he had built his own modest structure of personal respect. Such moving support added spiritual strength to his own campaign. Still, Harrison, struggling to rid himself of the mocking "Grandfather's Hat" refrain, insisted that the American rule of judging each man by his character alone be applied to himself. "He will not build high," he told the old veterans, "who does not build for himself. I believe also in the American opportunity which puts the starry sky above every boy's head, and sets his foot upon a ladder which he may climb until his strength gives out." Harrison also wove into his speech a tribute to the old Whig principles of his visitors. Chief among these, he reminded them, were a "reverent devotion to the Constitution and the flag, and a firm faith in the benefits of a protective tariff." The veterans responded with cheers, after which they crowded into the Harrisons' dining room, where Carrie served "some simple refreshments." [15]

Prior to the formation of the Republican National Committee in New York in early July, 1888, men, money, and methods had loomed large as a political necessity. Harrison himself had long been aware that his party possessed an undeniable advantage in the shrewd and wealthy high-tariff associations that had favored his candidacy. At least a half-dozen such groups, the foremost of which was James M. Swank's American Iron and Steel Association, wielded an immense political influence in the North, particularly in the Eastern states. Industrial power, coupled with an almost bottomless purse and civic prestige, made them and the great industries their members controlled a leading political factor in the seventies and eighties. They "warwicked" congressmen, exercised a determining control over Republican state committees, and lobbied effectively at both national and local levels. Alarmed by Cleveland's espousal of free trade, these groups now lent their strength to Harrison's support.

Meanwhile, practical advice came to Harrison by the carload. Typical was the view expressed by John L. Stevens, one-time chairman of Maine's Republican state committee, and at that time editor of the Kennebec *Journal*. In a confidential note, Stevens wrote Harrison that he attached the highest importance to "minute and careful organization," as well as to "the honest and prudent expenditure of campaign funds by tried and specially gifted men."

[15] Hedges, *op. cit.*, pp. 36–37, and *Reception Speeches by Gen. Benj. Harrison*, p. 10, a pamphlet published by the Indiana Republican State Central Committee in 1888.

He pictured the election as a contest "between the American manufacturers and workmen on the one side and Cleveland's officeholders and the English importing interests on the other." Though Stevens assured Harrison that "circumstances and the drift of events are in our favor," he set as a minimum campaign fund the sum of one million dollars.[16] The chief source of so large an amount would come, Stevens predicted, from liberal contributions by manufacturers, if properly solicited by responsible and trusted persons. Fortunately, to fill this rôle, there already existed one such man: the able Philadelphia financier, Wharton Barker, one of Harrison's earliest and firmest supporters. Barker, as financial guardian of the protectionist weekly, the *American*, used the magazine as a channel for propaganda among the farmers of the Midwest, who required special attention where tariff matters were concerned.[17] Barker had already informed Harrison that he was organizing the Irish labor vote and that he had committed himself to spend some $30,000 to cover the campaign costs of the Irish leaders.[18]

Particularly encouraging to Harrison's managers was the substantial support received from the Protective Tariff League. Organized several years earlier by such men as Cornelius N. Bliss and Vice-Presidential candidate Levi P. Morton, this group was supported by the "One Thousand Defenders of American Industries," each of whom "pledged a hundred dollars yearly." [19] In addition, Harrison's chances for victory were enhanced by a great number of already existing political clubs recently federated under the title National Republican League, with national headquarters in New York City. By August, 1888, 6,500 member clubs were reported, with an estimated total membership of one million voters. The central organization scattered "protectionist documents like pollen on the wind and sent its agents" [20] into doubtful states to enroll Republican voters. In many instances, the work of these clubs superseded the regular party machinery; it even reached down into the colleges by sponsoring senior essay contests on the topic of protection. While these vote- and money-garnering efforts were

---

16 John L. Stevens to Harrison, July 10, 1888, (L.C.), Vol. 33, predicted that the Democratic National Committee would be supplied with more than a million dollars by officeholders and English importing interests.

17 Allan Nevins, *Grover Cleveland: A Study in Courage*, p. 419.

18 Barker to Harrison, July 14, 1888, (L.C.), Vol. 34.

19 Nevins, *op. cit.*, pp. 418–20; New York *Herald*, June 17, 1888. The League's membership embraced manufacturers from all over the North.

20 *Appleton's Annual Cyclopedia, 1888*, p. 780; and Nevins, *op. cit.*, p. 419.

being made from the East, Harrison directed his own special attention to the organization of the National Committee. To that end, he sent the omnipresent Louis T. Michener to New York with full power to represent him.

Before naming a national chairman and forming an executive committee, Republican leaders held several confidential meetings in Indianapolis, New York, Washington, and elsewhere. Most prominently mentioned for the chairman's post was General James S. Clarkson, the Iowan whose prowess as an editor, coupled with his impressive record in the 1884 campaign, made him greatly respected within party circles. He had helped in a major way to nominate Harrison at Chicago and enjoyed the complete confidence of Michener and Dudley.[21] While Clarkson himself did not desire so conspicuous a position as chairman, he assured Harrison that he "was willing to take a working place," and readied himself "to report for duty in any field to which you might assign me." [22] This left the choice up to Harrison and Morton, and opened the door to the selection of a chairman from the industrial and tariff-conscious East. When Stephen B. Elkins also expressed a preference to work on the sidelines, or behind the scenes, a majority of the National Committee leaned in the direction of Pennsylvania Senator Matthew Stanley ("Boss") Quay.[23] When this Quay-for-Chairman sentiment began to crystallize, serious doubts crossed the minds of Hoosiers and other western members of the National Committee. From Levi P. Morton's study at Rhinebeck, New York, just four days before the choice of a chairman, Indiana committeeman J. N. Huston sent a pessimistic message to Harrison:

[21] Clarkson, in the documented opinion of Allison's biographer, shifted "Iowa's vote from Allison to Harrison and started the Harrison bandwagon on the road to victory." Clarkson attributed his action to "his love for old Hoosier friends, Louis T. Michener and William W. Dudley (Harrison's managers) and to "his desire to fulfill his father's pledge of devotion to the Harrison family." Clarkson's father had helped to nominate William Henry Harrison in 1839, "so now his son could carry out his father's wish and help nominate old Tippecanoe's grandson." See Leland L. Sage, "The Clarksons of Indiana and Iowa," *Indiana Magazine of History*, 50 (1954), 429-46. Confirmation of Clarkson as the leading contender for the chairmanship is found in Michener's typed memorandum, "The Organization of the National Committee in 1888," Michener MSS.

[22] J. S. Clarkson to Harrison, July 3, 1888, (L.C.), Vol. 32. Clarkson spent Saturday, July 7, with General Harrison in Indianapolis.

[23] Harry H. Smith to Harrison, July 9, 1888, *ibid.*, Vol. 33. Elkins and T. B. Reed favored Quay.

I am quite apprehensive that serious mistakes will be made. . . . I think it will be attempted to place the national committee in control of the East, and this means, in my judgment, an awful hard fight, with a good chance of our being beaten in Indiana. . . . With the Executive Com. that controls speakers, printed matter, and money in the hands of Eastern men and under the control of New York politicians, it would stand little chance. The feeling is strong that we can carry New York, but I do not think so, still if the opinion is true, we can do without Indiana, but I don't care to win under such circumstances.[24]

Harrison received similar warnings against excessive Eastern influence on the National Committee. Particularly chary, therefore, of the power of Boss Platt and his New York machine, he adopted the position that Indiana must be carried. Even if he were swept into the White House by a substantial majority of electoral votes, Harrison knew that the loss of Indiana would greatly weaken his administration. This, and kindred questions, Harrison discussed with Michener before the latter left for New York and the organization of the committee. To Michener he confided that Quay would be acceptable as chairman, provided the direction of the Executive Committee remained in the hands of a competent and discreet Hoosier already proved in his loyalty to the General's personal interests. But carrying New York must not be subordinated to winning Indiana.

With these instructions in mind, Michener arrived in New York. He spent only forty-eight hours with the party leaders; yet he accomplished a result most pleasing to his chief in Indianapolis.[25] Quay was unanimously [26] elected National Chairman and a Hoosier acceptable in all respects was named head of the Executive Committee. This was Harrison's friend, John C. New, publisher of the Indianapolis *Journal*. General Clarkson accepted the post of vice-chairman; Colonel Dudley, another Hoosier, became

24 *Ibid.*, July 8, 1888.

25 "The Organization of the National Committee in 1888," Michener MSS. See also Moses McLain, July 8, Harry H. Smith, July 9, and Edwin H. Terrell, July 9, 1888, to Harrison, (L.C.), Vol. 33.

26 Frank William Leach to A. T. Volwiler, July 20, 1938. In 1938, the 83-year-old Leach, in reply to the late Professor Volwiler's request, detailed his rôle as Quay's secretary, and added: "I was largely responsible for his election to the chairmanship of the Republican National Committee." While Quay was vacationing near Atlantic City, Leach, after conferences with Tom Platt and James M. Swank, telegraphed Michener in Indianapolis, urging Quay's selection. When the National Committee unanimously elected Quay, Leach wired his vacationing boss and won his acceptance. The personal secretary likewise recalled that Cabinet positions were not discussed, and that "Quay did not try to get promises from Harrison until after the election."

treasurer, and J. Sloat Fassett of New York consented to serve as secretary. According to Michener's report, "the officers were all skilled and industrious party managers and organizers and they led a most efficient and successful campaign." [27]

Even the Democrats recognized the Republican organization as "a model of energy and shrewdness." [28] Matthew S. Quay, who had learned his politics in the unscrupulous Cameron school of Pennsylvania, was not only a United States Senator but perhaps the most prominent representative of the alliance between big business and politics. Veterans, of course, applauded the choice of W. W. Dudley, who had lost a leg at Gettysburg, and who had been a generous Commissioner of Pensions. [29] So far as organization went, the two pivotal states of Indiana and New York were in the experienced hands of James N. Huston and Thomas C. Platt. Party leaders also reacted favorably to the new National Committee, and Senator John Sherman assured Harrison that Quay's appointment was a good selection: "He is shrewd, able and a skillful political manager—and has a wonderful facility in gaining the good will of those with whom he comes into contact. Better than this he is an honorable man. He will be true to his promise without evasion or reserve." [30]

Almost every American is familiar with *Ben-Hur,* one of the most popular historical novels of all times. Few, however, know anything of *Ben-Hur's* Hoosier author, General Lew Wallace. [31] In July, 1888, however, fate so acted as to link the fortunes of "Ben-Hur" Wallace with those of Ben Harrison, Presidential candidate. The result was a 65,000-word campaign biography, written by Wal-

[27] "The Organization of the National Committee in 1888," Michener MSS, Also Sister Mary Lucille O'Marra, G.N.S.H., in her excellent master's thesis, "Quay and Harrison from 1888 to 1892," p. 11, observes, "Quay was an extremely able machine politician. His talents lay in organization. . . . The outstanding traits he usually displayed were 'secretiveness and indefatigability in the pursuit of an object.' He had 'will power, infinite patience and a genius for details, a great power to compromise differences in his party, the firm strength to keep his word.' "

[28] Nevins, *op. cit.,* p. 417. Also, an appraisal of Quay's record has appeared in *Harper's Weekly,* January 22, 1887.

[29] *Nation,* November 8, 1888. See also the highly partisan account by Matilda Gresham, *Life of Walter Q. Gresham,* II, 478; also Nevins, *op. cit.,* p. 418.

[30] July 13, 1888, (L.C.), Vol. 33. This was also Michener's considered judgment. See L. T. Michener to S. B. Elkins, July 30, 1888, Elkins MSS.

[31] Irving McKee, *"Ben-Hur" Wallace,* pp. 170–88.

lace, authorized by Harrison, and bearing on its cover the somewhat cumbrous title: *Life of Ben Harrison by the Author of Ben Hur.*[32] At first, General Wallace had declined the literary task "but upon the urgent solicitation of many eminent men of the party, and General Harrison's assurance that everything needful should be placed at his disposal, so as to make it the strictly authentic and only authorized biography, he yielded to the call and . . . agreed to complete the work for publication by Hubbard Brothers of Philadelphia early in August."[33]

For a year prior to the Chicago convention, Lew Wallace had played the rôle of gentleman of leisure and letters. He enjoyed the nickname "Ben-Hur," a well-earned tribute conferred by appreciative neighbors in Crawfordsville, "the Athens of Indiana."[34] As the day of the Republican National Convention approached, Wallace had forsaken his happy hunting grounds amid the marshes of northern Indiana for "a place of honor on the platform of Chicago's auditorium." Here he had made herculean efforts for Harrison, and when the actual nomination was secured, lady reporter Mary Hannah Krout of the Chicago *Inter-Ocean*, herself a literary figure from Crawfordsville, pointed out that the choice was due in no small degree to Lew Wallace.[35] Others also told Harrison that Wallace had been a powerful friend at Chicago. This was not too surprising, for through the years he had come to expect nothing but the best from the entire Wallace family.[36] "Old Tippecanoe" had given "Ben-Hur's" father his start in life, and early in 1850, while still a student at Miami, Benjamin Harrison himself had become acquainted with young Lew, five years his senior. The author later recalled that initial meeting with vividness:

I see him distinctly, small, delicate, not yet a man; his hair thin and white; his brows white; his complexion pallid even to bloodlessness. His eyes were steel-blue, and he had a pleasant voice.

[32] Dorothy Ritter Russo and Thelma Lois Sullivan, *Seven Authors of Crawfordsville, Indiana,* pp. 335–40. The title page of Wallace's book reads: *Life of Gen. Ben Harrison.*

[33] An unidentified newspaper clipping enclosed in a letter of O. H. Hibben to Harrison, July 13, 1888, (L.C.), Vol. 33.

[34] The term "Hoosier Athens" was also applied to Indianapolis in the 70's, but as early as 1836 a toast was offered at a local Fourth of July celebration to "Crawfordsville—the Athens of Indiana." For details see Russo and Sullivan, *op. cit.,* p. vii.

[35] McKee, *op. cit.,* p. 230. Mary H. Krout covered the entire convention for the Chicago *Inter-Ocean*.

[36] Sievers, *op. cit.,* pp. 17, 96, 97, 104–5 ff.

Through the years, their friendship had deepened. They had both gone to war, and on their return had reminisced and marched together at soldiers' reunions. As attorneys they had worked together in courtrooms, and on the battlefield of politics they had been staunch allies. When the Democratic gerrymander ousted Harrison from the Senate in 1887, outspoken Lew Wallace had denounced the coup as "disgraceful, a bloody revolution . . ." and smacking of "usurpation and nullification." [37] With "Little Ben" now the man of the hour and "Ben-Hur" the author of the day, mutual friends and advisers saw great possibilities in a Harrison campaign biography from the pen of so renowned a comrade. Harrison's friend Robert S. Taylor, writing from a vacation spot in Colorado, expressed the general feeling in a haunting pun: "I see by the papers that Genl. Wallace is to biograph you. That is excellent. He did so well on *Ben-Hur* that we can trust him with *Ben Him*." [38]

Given only a month to write the biography, Wallace accomplished the task at the Indianapolis home of his sister-in-law, Mrs. A. H. Blair, a Harrison neighbor. This facilitated the author's work, for he frequently required detailed information from the General himself. With this, Harrison's cooperation ended, for Wallace has noted that the General "neither read nor heard read one line of the text; neither was he consulted as to the topics treated nor the arrangement adopted." Having decided on his friend as his official biographer, the busy Harrison put the rest in his hands.

Wallace dictated rapidly. He covered Harrison's ancestry, boyhood and college days, military, legal, and political pursuits in some 65,000 words, 15,000 of which were his own, 50,000 quoted from Harrison's speeches and notes, and other materials "from the record." [39] "Ben-Hur" met Ben Harrison's deadline, but he regretted that because of the "whip and spur" of rapid dictation, the biography was marred "by many crudities in the way of unstudied sentences and inapposite paragraphing, not to speak of words badly chosen." [40] This lack of literary polish, however, went unnoticed by scores of stump speakers, greedy for the facts of Harrison's

[37] From Wallace's uncompleted "Autobiography" (1901), cited by McKee, *op. cit.*, p. 230.
[38] R. S. Taylor to Harrison, August 5, 1888, (L.C.), Vol. 37.
[39] McKee, *op. cit.*, p. 231.
[40] Wallace, *op. cit.*, author's preface, p. v.

career and his statements on national issues. Advance copies were available in late August, 1888, but it was the first week of September before the public could buy them. Murat Halstead, the Cincinnati newspaper editor who had been Harrison's schoolmate, obliged Wallace by reading the biography in page proof. His word for the finished product was "bright." [41] Other reviews reflected political rather than literary judgment. Democratic papers considered it less than a "pot boiling" effort, while Republican reviewers greeted it with high praise. Be that as it may, the literary effort of "Ben-Hur" on behalf of his friend survived not only two Presidential campaigns but also some seventy years as the best biography of the only Hoosier to become President of the United States.[42]

Benjamin Harrison, meanwhile, was unwittingly writing his autobiography during the weeks before and after the publication of Wallace's book. His voice took the place of his pen, however, in revealing to crowds in Indianapolis and, through newspaper reports, to thousands of other men and women across the nation, the inner man and his political beliefs. The record of Harrison's unique and unexpected front-porch campaign speaks for itself. Between July 7 and October 25, he delivered over eighty extemporaneous speeches to nearly 300,000 people who visited him at Indianapolis. Friends feared for his health as day after day, frequently several times in one day, he spoke without preparation to visiting throngs numbering anywhere from 50 to 50,000. At the outset, some of the more experienced political leaders frowned upon these numerous impromptu talks. General Dan Butterfield warned him: "If you were under my command as of old, I should say steady—no speeches—no letters—we will carry you through." [43] From Washington came the nervous advice to "be careful—the enemy are watching and will misconstrue most anything you can say, and we are afraid, too, that your health may suffer." [44]

Such considerations as these carried weight with Harrison's managers in Indianapolis. As the towns neighboring on the Hoosier

[41] Murat Halstead to Harrison, August 4, 1888, (L.C.), Vol. 37.
[42] Lew Wallace to Harrison, August 13, 1888, *ibid.*, Vol. 38. At least six other campaign biographies were published. Harrison, however, refused to authorize any but that by Lew Wallace.
[43] Dan Butterfield to Harrison, July 15, 1888, *ibid.*, Vol. 34.
[44] H. B. Stanley to Harrison, August 2, 1888, *ibid.*, Vol. 35.

capital began to send large delegations, it soon became apparent that even the spacious lawn fronting the Harrison home could accommodate neither the local crowds nor the greater multitudes expected from other states. A discreet committee on arrangements (nucleus of today's distinguished Columbia Club) was hastily formed to handle all correspondence and to schedule all proposed visits. It also inspected in advance the addresses that political pilgrims had prepared for delivery. Its marching band and entertainment sub-committee met each delegation at the Union Station.[45] Before the parade to the speaker's stand in University Park, the visiting chairman's speech was re-examined to make, as Michener put it, "assurance doubly sure." Harrison invariably walked the mile from his home to the park, frequently accompanied by Attorney General Michener. There he listened attentively, often drawing from the speech a topic for his own extemporaneous reply. Delegations came into town at the rate of two or three a day; on one occasion, however, Harrison was obliged to speak seven times.

Even before the "Columbia Club" committee took over and transferred Harrison's speaking campaign from his front porch to University Park, the General had reached a national audience. His secretary, Frank Tibbott, took down his speeches in shorthand, supplying the General with transcripts for correction. Each evening, they were on the Associated Press wires, assuring publication in full on the following morning. Local reporters, like Hilton U. Brown of the *News*, took down the substance of Harrison's speeches in longhand and Indianapolis citizens were able to read them that same night.[46]

For this excellent publicity, however, Harrison paid the price of a near nervous collapse. Secretly, the General's intimate friends grew uneasy, despite the fact that the Republican *Journal* persisted "in declaring him in 'robust health.'" On the other hand, the Democratic *Sentinel* reported Harrison as "physically and

[45] Organization of the Harrison Marching Club, formed to promote Benjamin Harrison for the Presidency, was formally announced on August 17, 1888. Articles of association for the Columbia Club itself were filed by members of the same political group on February 13, 1889. See "History of the Columbia Club," *The Columbian*, 28 (February, 1957), 3, 45.

[46] Hilton U. Brown, *A Book of Memories*, p. 174. An Associated Press reporter claimed that Harrison reviewed carefully each stenographic report of his speeches before they were put on the wires. Both Tibbott and J. W. Fesler, a student in Harrison's law office, recalled that Harrison made no changes of consequence in the copy.

politically played out" at the beginning of the third week in July. Although the actual truth rested somewhere between these two accounts, the *Sentinel* came closer to the facts. Charles Hedges, the Associated Press representative assigned to cover Harrison's campaign, soon confirmed grave fears that the General would "utterly collapse before the campaign is half over." His report to Associated Press general manager William Henry Smith ran as follows:

. . . the General himself is exceedingly sensitive regarding the subject of his health and his staying powers, and at times persistently resists his physician, his family, and the Central Committee in their efforts to hold him in check and save his strength. Chairman Huston privately thinks the Genl. has not more than one half the vital energy he had the day he was nominated; this loss of strength is largely due to the earnestness with which he does everything, thus employing his nervous as well as his muscular system.

The first danger signal was a noticeable change in Harrison's even temper. "He has grown cross and ill-tempered even to those of his family," noted Hedges. Rest was the obvious remedy. The General agreed to a four-day respite, during which time the Associated Press dispatches generously intimated to a wondering public that "the Genl. may have better staying powers than his alarmist friends credit him." Reporter Hedges added privately: "If he can control his nervous exhaustion, he may get through the campaign all right." [47]

[47] Charles Hedges to William Henry Smith, July 21, 1888, William Henry Smith Papers (Ohio Historical Society Archives, Columbus, Ohio). Hedges gave considerable space in his dispatches to Harrison's health, always giving the candidate the benefit of the doubt.

CHAPTER XXII

A Lap in the Presidential Race

THE FIRST PHASE of Harrison's personal campaign for the Presidency lasted six weeks, stretching from July 7 until August 21. During this period of feverish activity, the General spoke to and shook hands with people from every walk of life. Among the first to visit him were five hundred commercial travelers from Philadelphia, Cincinnati, St. Louis, and Louisville. To them, as to all groups of mixed political beliefs, he gave a humorous reception. He refused to open before them "any store of flattery" or to indulge in "any stale compliments." When he expressed his regret that his own home was not large enough to receive them all, a voice called from the crowd jocularly: "There will be more room in the White House. . . . We will take your order now and deliver the goods in November." [1]

In his public speeches Harrison early prepared the ground for his later stand on the protective tariff. For an example:

We have men who boast that they are cosmopolitans, citizens of the world. I prefer to say that I am an American citizen, and I freely confess that American interests have first place in my regard.

Frequent applause greeted his argument that real Americanism could be harmonized with international comity or with "that philanthropy which sympathizes with human distress and oppression the world around."

We have been especially favored as an apart nation, separated from the conflicts, jealousies and intrigues of European courts, with a territory embracing every feature of climate and soil, and resources capable of supplying the wants of our people, of developing a wholesome

[1] Businessmen, army comrades, workingmen, and farmers came in droves, frequently accompanied by their wives. Harrison's speech of July 7, 1888, to the "Gentlemen of the Commercial Travellers' Association and Visiting Friends," Charles Hedges (compiler), *Speeches of Benjamin Harrison*, pp. 40–41.

and gigantic national growth, and of spreading abroad, by their full establishment here, the principles of human liberty and free government. I do not think it inconsistent with the philanthropy of the broadest teacher of human love that we should first have regard for that family of which we are a part.[2]

This philosophy fixed the foundations of Harrison's contention that fuller development of domestic manufacturing interests would lead to the upbuilding of a better home market for the products of American farms and thus afford the best opportunity for a rapid growth in national prosperity. To this end he insisted that "we should be slow to abandon that system of protective duties which looks to the promotion of the highest scale of wages for the American workingmen." In countless other speeches, Harrison steadfastly maintained that national development "must be on those lines that benefit all our people. Any development that does not reach and beneficially affect all . . . is not to be desired, and cannot be progressive or permanent."

Harrison opened his campaign by discussing the principles of government and proposing "a plan altogether above personal consideration." He referred frequently to a just "social order" pledged to the promotion of education, which in turn would influence the enactment of "just, equal and beneficent laws." As he proclaimed these convictions, his legal training and love for the law was apparent:

. . . the law throws the aegis of its protection over us all. It stands sentinel about your country homes to protect you from violence; it comes into our more thickly populated community and speaks its mandate for individual security and public order. There is an open avenue through the ballot box for the modification or repeal of laws which are unjust or oppressive. To the law we bow with reverence. It is the one king that commands our allegiance. We will change our king, when his rule is oppressive, by those methods appointed, and crown his more liberal successor.[3]

On the labor question, Harrison's views paralleled the thinking of the Knights of Labor in that both called for "protection to

2 Harrison's third speech, July 12, 1888, to the "Citizens and Comrades of Benton County, Indiana," *ibid.,* p. 44. The General repeated these sentiments on July 18, while addressing the Lincoln Club of Kokomo, Indiana.

3 *Ibid.,* pp. 45–53. On July 19, 1888, Harrison expressed the conviction that the streams of prosperity "shall flow bank full." He encouraged labor by referring to their individual rights, and "a manly concession of equal right to every other man." This, in the General's book, was the "boast and the law of good citizenship."

American labor against the pauper labor of Europe," by boycotting, or levying duties on articles from abroad that might take the place of domestic goods in the American market. But Terence V. Powderly, 39-year-old General Master Workman for the Knights of Labor, went further than the Republican candidate. He complained that he "did not like to see all of the profits of what is charged at the port of entry find their way into the pocket of the man who owns the glass factory instead of the men who operate it at the expense of sweat, strength and health."

Actually, Harrison offered no solution to this basic difficulty beyond endorsing organized labor in general terms.[4] When upwards of 3,000 Clay County coal miners visited him on July 26, 1888, he delivered what became known as "The Gates of Castle Garden" speech. In it he said it was not necessary to resort to statistics to prove that the American workingman's condition is better than his European counterpart. One fact was sufficient:

The tide of emigration from all European countries has been and is towards our shores. The gates of Castle Garden swing inward. They do not swing outward to any American laborer seeking a better country than this.

It was Harrison's repeated contention that America already threw about the workingman social and political safeguards that guaranteed social justice. Nevertheless, an intelligent, thrifty, and contented working class was vital to any nation's peace and prosperity.

Can we look for contentment if the workingman is only able to supply his daily necessities by his daily toil, but is not able in the vigor of youth to lay up a store against old age? A condition of things that compels the laborer to contemplate want, as an incident of sickness or disability, is one that tends to social disorder.

Time and again the Republican Presidential candidate hammered home the question to the representatives of labor: "What policy as to our tariff legislation will best subserve your interests, the interests of your families, and the greatness and glory of the

---

[4] T. V. Powderly to Louis Arrington, July 7, 1888, Letterbooks in the Powderly MSS (The Catholic University of America Archives). Powderly refused to ally himself or his group with either political party. On July 13, 1888, in talking to the railroad workers of Indianapolis, Harrison said that "any policy that transfers production from the American to the English or German shop works an injury to all American workmen." Hedges, *op. cit.*, p. 48.

nation of which you are citizens?" A high tariff under a Republican President, he asserted, signified the "highest possible prosperity" with "wages that not only supply the necessities of life, but leave also a substantial margin for comfort and for the savings bank." [5]

In the East, some complained that the Presidential campaign was dull and uninteresting.[6] Indianapolis, on the other hand, was gay with evening parades, whose brightly burning torches lighted up dozens of log cabins, cider barrels, coons, eagles, and other Harrison campaign emblems. The noisiest demonstrations were those sponsored by the veterans' Harrison and Morton clubs, and by the octogenarians who had supported William Henry Harrison for President in 1840.[7] "Marching Through Georgia" became the top political tune wherever ex-soldiers gathered. In an emotional appeal to veterans, new words were put to the old melody:

> Grover Cleveland sent a substitute where
>   he did not dare to go,
> Into the Union Army to face a rebel foe;
> There he left this poor old German to die
>   a death of woe
> While he was boasting of our Union victory.[8]

In theory, the Grand Army was nonpolitical, but in practice the uniformed veterans spearheaded countless Republican rallies in every section of the country. There the "Boys in Blue" cheered Harrison's high-tariff speeches and indulged in wild ovations at the mere mention of a more liberal pension policy. Nor did Harrison disappoint them. On August 1, speaking to 2,000 visitors from Morgan and Brown Counties, a delegation which included thirty survivors of the General's former command, Harrison vividly detailed his old comrades' wartime toil, suffering, and sickness. He reminded them of how "anxiety dwelt perpetually with those you left behind." At the close he said:

---

[5] *Ibid.*, pp. 51–60. On July 18, 1888, Harrison had formulated this question: "What legislation will most promote the development of the manufacturing interests of your country and enlarge the home market for the products of your farm?" (p. 51)

[6] Allan Nevins, *Grover Cleveland: A Study in Courage,* pp. 414–19.

[7] Even with the mercury registering 99 degrees on August 3, 1888, fifty voters of 1840 headed a column led by Major D. K. Pierce, aged 92.

[8] See Mary L. Dearing, *Veterans in Politics,* pp. 383–84. Copies of this and similar campaign songs are in (L.C.), Vols. 33–48. G.A.R. officers repeatedly assured the public that the organization was nonpolitical and instructed posts to refrain from partisan activities.

We remember gratefully the sacrifices and sufferings of the fathers and mothers who sent you to the field, and, much more of the wives who bravely gave up to the country the most cherished objects of their love. And now peace has come; no hand is lifted against the flag; the Constitution is again supreme and the Nation one. My countrymen, it is no time now to use an apothecary's scale to weigh the rewards of the men who saved the country.[9]

As a general pledge of pension liberality, this speech, which went further than the Democrats dared, definitely helped to herd the soldier vote into the Republican column.

In New York, the National Committee soon regarded Harrison himself as the whole show. Chairman Quay, who earlier in the campaign had opened his morning paper fearful that something unwise had been said to or by Harrison, completely changed his feelings in August. At that time, when Michener visited headquarters, Quay's first question concerned Harrison's health. Then he asked if the General "would continue making those wonderful speeches to the end of the campaign." When Michener replied affirmatively, the converted chairman humorously remarked that "if Harrison has the strength to do that we could safely close these headquarters and he would elect himself." [10] The records reveal, however, that Quay not only did not close national headquarters, but actually augmented his staff by acquiring the cash and services of Philadelphia's department store magnate, John Wanamaker. The merchant immediately took charge of an advisory board "made up of business men, with its own treasurer, and given unrestricted power in raising and deciding upon the expenditure of funds." [11]

Once Wanamaker was in the financial saddle, Republican fervor in the East matched the enthusiasm for Harrison in the Midwest. Wanamaker's plan was simple. He enlisted the help of Thomas Dolan, chief of a Philadelphia political syndicate, and ten other

[9] Harrison to the Morgan and Brown County delegations. See Hedges, *op. cit.,* p. 71. This allusion to the "apothecary's scale" was spread broadcast during the campaign and was included eventually by Charles M. Walker in "Gems from General Harrison's Speeches," *Hovey and Chase,* p. 96.

[10] "Harrison's Speeches in 1888," memorandum in the Michener MSS.

[11] Herbert Adams Gibbons, *John Wanamaker,* I, 257. According to Quay's personal secretary, F. W. Leach, Wanamaker was approached by Quay and offered outright the chairmanship of the Finance Committee. See F. W. Leach to A. T. Volwiler, July 20, 1938, a copy in (L.C.).

businessmen in the area. Each subscribed $10,000 for a "campaign of education." With this sum as a nucleus, and the tariff issue as the argument, manufacturers were approached, and additional contributions were collected. Philadelphians, boasting of Wanamaker as a peerless fund collector, predicted that he would raise more money than any other man east of the Allegheny Mountains. Democrats, quick to castigate the unholy alliance between the vested interests of the nation and the Republican party, charged that Wanamaker had collected and distributed some $400,000. This the chairman of the finance committee denied. "We did not need $400,000, and we did not raise it. But we raised more than $200,000 . . . so quickly that the Democrats never knew anything about it."

Wanamaker justified his actions by expressing the belief that it "was right to ask business men in various parts of the country to provide the sinews of war," on the principle that it is better "to insure good times than to have to start to build them up again." [12] The huge Republican campaign fund, Wanamaker insisted, was expended legitimately in an educational campaign calculated to convince voters of the soundness and advantage of the protective tariff over free trade. To this end, he employed stump speakers on salary, and had tons of "protection" literature printed for distribution in all sections of the country. This stimulated the charge that the Republican party had bargained away its right to represent the average man by its unconditional surrender to the money power,[13] an allegation that Harrison denied during the campaign and throughout his public life. The Hoosier candidate never deviated from his own beliefs, as expressed below:

Wealth should neither be the object of our enmity nor the basis of our consideration. The indiscriminate denunciation of the rich is mischievous. It perverts the mind, poisons the heart and furnishes an excuse to crime. No poor man was ever made rich or happier by it. It is quite as illogical to despise a man because he is rich as because he

[12] Gibbons, *op. cit.,* pp. 258–59; 380–82. See also John Wanamaker, *Quayism in Pennsylvania Politics,* p. 160. Wanamaker's biographer stated that "defense of the large campaign fund was hard to answer." Wanamaker himself pointed to the unblemished reputation of the men who were not politicians that he had gathered around him. He denied any misuse of funds.

[13] Amasa Thornton to Harrison, July 13, 1888, (L.C.), Vol. 33. Democrats "are making capital against us by saying that we are the party of trusts, and a good deal of capital, too." He pleaded with Harrison to spike this gun in his Letter of Acceptance.

is poor. Not what a man has, but what he is, settles his class. We cannot right matters by taking from one what he has honestly acquired, to bestow upon another what he has not earned.[14]

In the heat of the campaign of 1888, Harrison also endorsed his party's platform plank "against all combinations of capital, organized in trusts or otherwise, to control arbitrarily the condition of trade among our citizens." [15] He took the position that "ordinarily, capital shares the losses of idleness with labor; but under the operation of a trust, in some of its forms, the wageworker alone suffers loss, while idle capital receives its dividends from a trust fund." Harrison also pointed out what most monopolists preferred to overlook: that the "producers who refuse to join the combination are destroyed, and competition as an element of prices is eliminated." [16] Campaigning on a specific promise to correct these abuses by an effective antitrust law, Harrison's unequivocal declaration scarcely sat well with some men high in party circles. But he had enunciated his principle and did not waver. This may well have been the factor that determined Republican success in the state of New York.[17]

Until the middle of August the spotlight of political interest had shone almost exclusively upon Hoosierdom and Harrison's front-porch campaign. Occasionally the press directed attention to New York and Philadelphia where Quay and Wanamaker were effectively invigorating the Republican workers. But Harrison, informed by code of every move, sought to retain executive control by directives from Indianapolis.[18] No political blunders had been committed; surface indications promised success in November. Congressman John A. Anderson, Harrison's old college chum, sent words of encouragement from the nation's capital on August

[14] From Harrison's celebrated address on "The Obligations of Wealth," delivered before the Union League Club, Chicago, February 22, 1898. It is reproduced in Mary Lord Harrison (compiler), *Views of An Ex-President*, pp. 331–57.

[15] *Appleton's Annual Cyclopedia, 1888*, p. 776; also C. J. Bernardo, "The Presidential Election of 1888," p. 383.

[16] General Harrison's Letter of Acceptance, September 11, 1888, in Hedges, *op. cit.*, p. 113.

[17] Amasa Thornton to Harrison, July 13, 1888, (L.C.), Vol. 33, urged Harrison to speak out clearly on the subject. He wrote that "the statesman says and does things not like the politician and from different motives; one loves his country, the other himself. We believe you are a Statesman. . . . That kind of service will tell at the polls this year. This is to be a campaign of principle."

[18] Charles E. Smith to Michener, August 2, 1888, Michener MSS.

5, 1888: "I want to tell you how much you have gained by your meaty speeches—without making a mistake. Both sides here recognize the severity of the task and the very great ability you have displayed. . . . You don't know how rapidly you are growing in public esteem for common sense and great intellectual ability." [19] This encomium, with several others,[20] reached the General on the eve of the Republican State Convention, scheduled for Indianapolis on August 8. On that day a tumultuous demonstration, lasting nearly ten minutes, greeted "the next President," [21] who in turn congratulated the convention on its choice for governor: General Alvin P. Hovey, veteran of two wars, and his own personal friend.[22] In the course of his remarks, Harrison referred to another event which was capturing national attention: the return from Europe of James G. Blaine.[23]

Enthusiasm ran high as the new liner, *City of New York*, steamed through the Narrows on August 10, 1888, and was edged into her Hudson River pier. "Excursion boats thrashed down the harbor, with bands and hurrahing crowds," [24] to extend a dynamic greeting to Blaine. A committee of welcome aboard private yachts formed an escort for the new leviathan, but most of the dignitaries were either unaware or unconcerned that the ship herself had made a record maiden voyage. Harrison, still in Indianapolis,[25] had asked Murat Halstead, Whitelaw Reid, and William Walter Phelps to represent him. The trio rushed to the bridge in order to wring Blaine's hand before he hurried ashore. That evening the

---

[19] John A. Anderson to Harrison, August 5, 1888, (L.C.), Vol. 37.

[20] See Levi P. Morton to Harrison, August 14; and John Sherman to Harrison, August 4, 1888, *ibid.*, Vols. 37 and 38.

[21] Hedges, *op. cit.*, p. 81.

[22] A. P. Hovey to Harrison, August 15, 1888, (L.C.), Vol. 38. "Your advice shall be my law, for I regard your success as paramount to all other considerations." R. C. Buley, "The Campaign of 1888 in Indiana," *Indiana Magazine of History*, 10 (1914), 162–85, concludes that "the machine didn't particularly want Hovey but was determined to defeat Robertson." At the time of his nomination Hovey was representing Indiana in Congress.

[23] Hedges, *op. cit.*, p. 82. In referring to Blaine, as "that great Republican and that great American," Harrison said he hoped he would soon hear his powerful voice in Indiana.

[24] Nevins, *op. cit.*, p. 431, and the New York *Herald*, August 9, 10, 11, 1888.

[25] Harrison to Blaine, August 5, 1888, cited in A. T. Volwiler, *The Correspondence Between Benjamin Harrison and James G. Blaine, 1882–1893*, p. 32, conveys cordial greetings: "We would have sent a delegation from Indiana, but our State convention assembled . . . and those who would otherwise have gone were needed here." David G. Muzzey, *James G. Blaine, A Political Idol of Other Days*, p. 382, claims that an Indiana delegation did join the crowd at the harbor.

man from Maine, who shared with Harrison the love of the Republican party, addressed a huge crowd from a grandstand in Madison Square. Climaxing as it did two days of political parades for Harrison in New York and Brooklyn, his speech filled the leaders of the Democratic forces with foreboding. One of Cleveland's chieftains gloomily remarked: "As it stands today, the Republicans have got us on the run on the free trade issue. Their whole procession last night was an organized cry of 'No, no, no free trade!' " [26]

Blaine left immediately for Maine where he promised to produce an overwhelming majority in the September state election, so that Harrison had time to check the battle lines of the national campaign. Pleased by uniform assurances of party harmony, the General took particular delight in reports from the pivotal state of New York. There the old-time Conkling and Blaine controversies had evaporated, and the so-called "Stalwarts" and "Halfbreeds" were making common cause. Due directly to Harrison's refusal to make promises or play favorites, this end to party dissensions deeply impressed William H. H. Miller, who confided to his brother in upstate New York:

I confess that it has been a great gratification to me to know, as I do know, that not only have no promises been made to anyone, but none have been sought by those from whom such seeking might possibly have been expected.

If Gen'l Harrison becomes President, he will enter upon the discharge of his duties untrammeled and free to serve the country and deal fairly by all members of the Republican Party.[27]

Harrison's purpose in settling upon Middle Bass Island in Lake Erie for a fortnight vacation between August 21 and September 4 was twofold. His body needed rest, and his mind needed leisure for the painstaking composition of his formal Letter of Acceptance. Before he could leave home for Toledo, where former Gov-

[26] Nevins, op. cit., p. 422.

[27] W. H. H. Miller to Curtis Miller, August 14, 1888, W. H. H. Miller Letterbooks, tried to impress upon his brother that all Republicans in New York would have fair treatment at Harrison's hands. ". . . I can say to you with absolute truth, that there has not been either before the nomination or since, any arrangement made with any person or party in reference to what course would be pursued in the event of success, except simply that all affairs will be administered with a single view to the good of the country and according to the principles of the Republican party."

ernor Charles Foster of Ohio had his yacht, *Ligona,* in readiness
for the Harrison family, the General twice delayed his departure.
On August 17 and 18, some 11,000 commercial travelers from
Illinois, Indiana, and Ohio called for a speech in reply to their
greetings. Harrison seized the opportunity to repeat his belief that
the "provincialism that once existed in this country has largely
disappeared." The credit for this, he asserted, belonged to the
commercial travelers, whose business pursuits afforded them "a
fuller comprehension, not only of the extent of this country, but
of the greatness and unity of its people." Laughter and applause
greeted his remark that the "prophet Daniel must have had a vision
of the commercial travellers when he said that in the last days
many should run to and fro and knowledge should be increased."
But the General turned serious in his final suggestion:

Let me suggest but this one thought. Do not allow anyone to persuade you that this great contest as to our tariff policy is one between
schedules. It is not a question of a seven per cent reduction. [*Applause*]
It is a question between wide-apart principles. [*Cries of "That's right."*]

The principle of protection, the intelligent recognition in the framing
of our tariff laws of the duty to protect our American industries and
maintain the American scale of wages by adequate discriminating
duties [*cries of "That's right!" "That's it!"*] on the one hand, and on
the other a denial of the constitutional right to make our customs
duties protective, or the assertion of the doctrine that free competition
with foreign products is the ideal condition to which all our legislation
should tend. [*Applause*].[28]

That was Harrison's final public speech before his vacation.
There remained, however, one important private conference.
Shortly after Harrison's nomination, the officers of the National
Civil Service Reform League had begun to pressure the General
for a statement "as to how he should, if elected, manage the civil
service." Now Lucius B. Swift, Indiana leader in the civil service
reform movement,[29] sought and secured an interview with Harrison at his home. Swift's diary records that Harrison told him

---

[28] Hedges, *op. cit.,* pp. 93-94. Just the day previous to this address Senator John
Sherman had written from Washington that "as a rule both letters and speeches from
any candidate for the Presidency are dangerous but so far you have wisely steered
between Scylla and Charybdas [*sic*], and you have gained so much credit as a 'skillful
pilot,' that we do not fear your discretion will fail you." Sherman to Harrison, August
17, 1888, (L.C.), Vol. 38.

[29] Lucius B. Swift crusaded for the overthrow of the spoils system from the time
he made a speech in the Garfield campaign until his death on July 3, 1929. He was

. . . that the Pendleton Act should be enforced in spirit and letter, without evasion or violation; that within this law there should be no removal without cause. In the unclassified service he was more vague. He said "You know I do not consider offices as a source of strength but of weakness to a party." [30]

In effect, Harrison promised only to follow the Chicago platform.[31] But the Reform League wanted a more definite pledge concerning the unclassified service. Urged to confer with Harrison again, preferably before he had completed his Letter of Acceptance, Swift sought a second meeting, to which Harrison agreed. On August 20, Swift pleaded with the General to become a crusader. "I asked him why he did not set out to do something very great for the country and added that the greatest thing now was to transfer the civil service to a business basis." This point the General conceded, but added that "he did not see how it could be done." With regard to the unclassified service, which was wholly outside the Pendleton Act, he admitted that he had no "fixed principle except that to remove the Democrats and put in Republicans, with rare exceptions, must improve the service." The conference ended with Harrison's suggestion that Swift return in September and examine the civil service section of his Letter of Acceptance before it was released. This was a reassuring gesture but that was all. At the door, the General merely took his neighbor's hand and said that there would be "a strict enforcement of the law and that outside of that he would do his best so that at the end of his term some progress should have been made in civil service reform." [32]

---

celebrated for several speeches as well as for his important book, *How We Got Our Liberties*. He conferred frequently with Cleveland, Harrison, and Theodore Roosevelt in the interests of civil service reform. Harrison liked him as a fearless foe of every form of political corruption, while Roosevelt admired the fact that he kept a sane and well-balanced judgment as a rein on his crusading zeal. See William Dudley Foulke, *Lucius B. Swift: American Citizen*.

[30] Swift Diary, entry for August 21, 1888, in the Lucius Swift Collection (Indiana State Library). Also Foulke, *op. cit.*, pp. 36-37.

[31] This portion of the platform read: "The reform of the civil service, auspiciously begun under the Republican administration [of 1880-84], should be completed by the further extension of the reform system already established by law to all grades of the service to which it is applicable. The spirit and purpose of reform should be observed in all Executive appointments, and all laws at variance with the object of existing reform legislation should be repealed, to the end that the dangers to free institutions which lurk in the power of official patronage may be wisely and effectively avoided." *Appleton's Annual Cyclopedia, 1888*, p. 777.

[32] All quotations are from the August 21, 1888, entry in the Swift Diary, Lucius Swift Collection. Throughout the talk Harrison declared that "he did not want to promise more than he could do—but rather less." This position Swift commended. He also praised General Harrison for saying that "not for the Presidency would he be in the position regarding his promises that Cleveland is in."

The next day, August 21, accompanied by Mrs. Harrison, four family friends, and a corps of press representatives, the General boarded the 7:00 A.M. Wabash, heading for Toledo.[33] The departure was secret, and only at Defiance, Ohio, did a large demonstration stop the train and extract a few words from Harrison. The arrival in Toledo, however, had been well advertised in advance. A detachment of the Ohio militia and several thousand citizens formed a reception committee to escort the party to the residence of William Cummings, whose guests the Harrisons were to be.

That evening at Toledo's Memorial Hall Square 10,000 people gathered in an open-air mass meeting. Former Governor Foster spoke first. Harrison was then introduced as the man who came for "rest and quiet" and had only consented to a reception "upon one condition—that he was not to make a speech." In a particularly good humor, Harrison won the crowd's close attention by his opening sentence. He complimented his audience on being both "magnificent and instructive," adding: "I say instructive, for that public man is dull indeed who does not gather both instruction and inspiration from meetings such as this." Inasmuch as a large segment of the audience represented the laboring class, the General's address traversed the familiar ground of protection, as opposed to free trade. But they gave the approbation of silence to his challenge: "If there is anyone here present tonight that knows of any land that spreads a more promising sky of hope above the heads of the poor and the laboring man than this, I would be glad if he would name it." The Republican candidate closed the evening with an appeal "to settle it [the tariff question]; settle it in November, so that we shall be free for years to come from this agitation in behalf of free trade." [34]

Early the next morning his party, augmented by Ohio Governor J. B. Foraker and his wife, boarded the Foster yacht, which sailed a leisurely course for Middle Bass Island, where the Lake Erie fishing was reported as good.[35] Just before his departure, the Gen-

33 Charles Foster to Harrison, August 17, 1888, (L.C.), Vol. 38. W. H. H. Miller's son Sam, as well as Judge William A. Woods, his wife, and daughter, completed the party that left Indianapolis.

34 Hedges, op. cit., pp. 94–96.

35 Charles Foster to Harrison, August 17, 1888, (L.C.), Vol. 38. After a week's fishing, the General reported to his wife's niece: "It is too early for good fishing—though some are being caught. Your Aunt Carrie fished faithfully yesterday but did not get a bite." He admitted, however, that they were enjoying fine boat rides "and

eral was admonished in a letter from a resident of the National Military Home, Leavenworth, Kansas: "For God's sake, Benjamin, do not get a fishing reputation at the start; . . . take a fool's advice, and watch Public Opinion, and let Grover Cleveland go fishing." [36] But for once Harrison was deaf to the plea of a veteran.

In every respect, his two weeks' retreat to Lake Erie proved highly beneficial to Harrison. What rod and reel can do for frayed nerves and a tired throat many men understand. With his Letter of Acceptance to write, he was grateful for this period of thought and reflection. So, before settling down to the final draft, he leisurely perused one of Count Tolstoy's books. [37] The task still awaiting him he viewed realistically.

He did not entertain the hope that his remarks would create "any sensation" or give "any special impetus" to the campaign. His chief concern was to avoid mistakes which his political enemies could seize upon. [38] He had brought to the island a folder of suggestions that had accumulated since the convention, and these he carefully weighed, along with the warnings of trained politicians and the special pleas of reformers. In the final writing of his letter, however, he took counsel with his own principles. By the end of August, he had completed the document and was ready to attend a reception in his honor on neighboring Put-in-Bay Island.

To Harrison, this particular meeting was more than just another political rally. When the Foster yacht brought him to the appointed rendezvous, excursion boats from Cleveland, Detroit, Sandusky, and Toledo had already landed several thousand enthusiasts. Every visitor knew the spot. Here, within earshot of Put-in-Bay, Perry's guns had signaled his triumph over the British fleet after the celebrated Battle of Lake Erie. The General knew by heart, as did his political admirers, the laconic message his Presidential grandfather had received from Captain Oliver H. Perry: "We have met the

a good airing." Harrison to Mary Lord Dimmick, August 30, 1888, James Blaine Walker MSS.

[36] Leroy Walker to Harrison, August 17, 1888, (L.C.), Vol. 38. It was then common knowledge that many G.A.R. members had been incensed when they learned that President Cleveland had spent one Decoration Day with rod and reel.

[37] Harrison did not reveal which of Tolstoy's works he had been reading on this occasion. He did intimate, however, that he was disappointed and would "very willingly have substituted" Tourgee's Letters to a King, had he remembered to pack it in his bag. Harrison to Hon. Alvin W. Tourgee, September 5, 1888, (L.C.), Vol. 39.

[38] Harrison to William Boyd Allison, September 14, 1888, Allison MSS, Box 262, and Harrison to E. G. Hay, September 26, 1888, Eugene Gano Hay MSS, Vol. 7.

enemy, and they are ours." [39] Under such circumstances, Harrison was at his best. "If we had stood," he began, "where we stand today we could have heard the guns of Perry's fleet. If we had stood where we stand today we could have welcomed him as he came a victor into Put-in-Bay." Sustained applause followed his observation that they were paying tribute to an event and a story closely allied with "the formation and defence and perpetuation of our magnificent institutions." [40] In his closing remarks, he pledged himself to continue the "American Way of Life" if he were elected.

Harrison's vacation ended on Labor Day. [41] After a night's rest at Toledo, he and his party boarded an early train for the short run to Indianapolis. The General hoped to be back in his own home by early afternoon. Such a schedule proved impossible. Five times the engineer was compelled to stop the train to allow the candidate to address crowds ranging from two to seven thousand in number. Industrially prosperous Fort Wayne gave Harrison the warmest reception, but Huntington, Peru, and Kokomo were not far behind. In the latter city the darkness was dispelled with a brilliant illumination by natural gas. At Noblesville, the last stop before Indianapolis, a special train, carrying the now uniformed Columbian band and marchers, met Harrison and escorted him to the Union Station where some 15,000 people had waited several hours for the arrival of his train. Accompanied by the blaring band, veterans from his old regiment, and the Railroad Men's Club, the General reached the door of his home just before midnight. There, despite the hour and his fatigue, Harrison launched—almost without thinking—into his sixth speech of the day. [42]

His two weeks' absence had only added to Republican enthusiasm, and visiting delegations again began to pour into Indianapolis. The General had grown accustomed to merchants, politicians, and old soldiers, but September 8, 1888, provided something for his memory to hold. A group of young girls between the ages of seven and fifteen had organized a junior Harrison Club. Dressed

[39] Perry's naval victory over the British on September 10, 1813, the occasion of the famous dispatch, was a prelude to General William Henry Harrison's military success at the Battle of the Thames where Tecumseh was killed and the American frontier re-established.

[40] Hedges, *op. cit.*, pp. 97–98.

[41] This was only the sixth celebration of the day, instituted in 1882 by the Knights of Labor. The holiday was first nationalized by an Act of Congress in 1894.

[42] Hedges, *op. cit.*, pp. 99–105. All of Harrison's speeches on this day manifested a deep concern for the workingman.

in red, white, and blue uniforms, carrying Japanese lanterns, and led by a six-year-old lad mounted on a pony, the children marched four abreast to the General's home. A drum corps of eight young lads kept the young ladies in perfect parade step. After a few stanzas of the inevitable "Marching Through Georgia," the six-year-old boy dismounted, presented Harrison with a bouquet, and made an address on behalf of the small delegation. The General, visibly moved, complimented them not only on their charming appearance, but also on the excellence of their chorus and the proficiency of their drill. "Children have always been attractive to me," he told them gently. "I have found not only entertainment but instruction in their companionship. . . . Some of the best friends I have are under ten years of age, and after tonight I am sure that I will have many more, for all your names will be added." [43]

On September 10, 1888, after submitting the document to a special meeting of the Cabinet for criticism, President Cleveland made public his own Letter of Acceptance. Laborious in style, it came close to being an echo of his December Message to Congress, in which he had dealt with the tariff alone. Now the President wrote: "Unnecessary taxation is unjust taxation. . . . our people ask relief from the undue and unnecessary burden of taxation now resting upon them. They are offered instead—free tobacco and free whiskey." [44] To most Democrats, Cleveland's letter was an unflinching and courageous restatement of his free trade principles, but to industry-minded Republicans it appeared replete with "dull, phlegmatic egoism" sprinkled with "unbridled audacity." [45] Ponderous and lengthy, the Letter possessed little popular appeal.

Two days later Harrison's Letter of Acceptance was published. Eminently clear, it seemed superior to Cleveland's effort and at once evoked public interest and praise. Blaine wired his congratulations from Maine: "Your letter . . . covers every point most admirably, not a word too many, not a word too few, not a word

43 *Ibid.*, p. 107.
44 Nevins, *op. cit.*, pp. 433 ff. The President revealed his purpose to Pennsylvania attorney Chauncey F. Black, September 14, 1888, Cleveland MSS, by writing that ". . . this campaign is one of information. . . . Every citizen should be regarded as a thoughtful, responsible voter, and he should be furnished the means of examining the issues involved in the pending canvass for himself."
45 James Scovel to Harrison, September 12, 1888, (L.C.), Vol. 40.

amiss." [46] Senators Allison of Iowa and Hoar of Massachusetts also telegraphed their deep satisfaction, Allison saying "in all its details very good" and Hoar "your letter seems perfect." [47] More important perhaps, from the popular point of view, was future Speaker Joe Cannon's observation from Washington: "Our people here are delighted with your letter of acceptance. It satisfied the trained politician, while millions will read, understand and approve." [48] This prophecy was quickly verified. Scores of approving letters and telegrams poured into Indianapolis for Harrison, although press reaction followed strictly partisan lines.[49] From a representative of labor came the pious message: "I wish I was as sure of going to heaven—as I am that you will be elected." [50]

As for the document itself, Harrison surprised no one by emphasizing his views on the protective tariff. For him, as for his backers, it was the paramount issue of the campaign. From the outset, he had agreed with Senator John Sherman's judgment that it was far better for the Republicans that "the contest take place on the principles of the Mills Bill" with its undisguised and "manifest tendency towards free trade." [51] Congressmen, still deep in legislative work, read both letters carefully. Harrison kept in close touch with party leaders on the Hill, and he concurred with their judgment that it was politically more expedient that no specific Republican substitute for the Mills Bill be sponsored before the election. To offer one would, he felt, only serve to give an election eve advantage to the Democrats. As it was, he knew that many Democrats rested uneasily, fearing that they had been saddled with the obnoxious features of both Mills' plea and Cleveland's crusade for free trade. Consequently, Harrison preferred to keep the President and his supporters on the defensive to the end of the campaign,

[46] James G. Blaine to Harrison, *ibid.*

[47] *Ibid.* On September 12, Senators Sherman, Allison, and Hoar joined a chorus of representatives who congratulated Harrison on an important task well executed.

[48] Joseph G. Cannon to Harrison, *ibid.* North Carolina-born, Cannon had lived in Indiana and Illinois from the time he was four. He was in nine successive Congresses (1873–1891) before his defeat in 1890. Re-elected in 1892, he served in ten successive Congresses and was Speaker of the House from 1903 to 1911.

[49] *Public Opinion*, September 15, 1888, offers the most handy summary of press reaction. C. J. Bernardo, "The Presidential Election of 1888," p. 286, following the view of the Boston *Post*, September 12, 1888, concludes that Harrison's pronouncement compared unfavorably "with the clear and direct utterances of Cleveland's letter."

[50] James Scovel to Harrison, September 12, 1888, (L.C.), Vol. 40.

[51] John Sherman to Harrison, *ibid.*

even if this meant keeping Congress in session until late October, thus robbing both parties of their most celebrated stump speakers.[52]

On September 1, 1888, General Lew Wallace's campaign biography appeared and quickly enjoyed a wide distribution. Its pages brought Harrison closer to the people, who could now read for themselves his "terse and pointed speeches on tariff, trusts, labor, civil service, currency and surplus." [53] The man in the street now had a chance to know for whom and for what he would be voting. Resounding Republican victories in Maine and Vermont in early September pointed to national triumph in November. Congressman John R. Thomas of Illinois sent word from Washington that "the star in the East illumines the pathway for loyal Republican feet, and at the same time proclaims the downfall of the present Anglo-American viceroy." [54] And Blaine had already estimated the General's chances at "90 . . . in the 100." [55]

Two days after the publication of his Letter, Harrison wrote to Senator Allison: "I suppose I am now fairly embarked again on a sea of delegations and speechmaking." [56] Even he did not realize, however, that in the final six weeks he would be compelled to make nearly forty more speeches to some 20,000 visitors who crowded Indianapolis day after day. At the same time, reports came into his Indianapolis headquarters from vantage points in every part of the country. Quay and New in New York, Wanamaker in Philadelphia, Blaine in Augusta, Halstead in Cincinnati, Elkins in West Virginia, Medill in Chicago—all joined with West Coast correspondents in briefing the commander in chief of the Republican forces. All urged him to stay in Indianapolis and speak only to visiting delegations, lest stumping the doubtful states in the East endanger his health or permit him to be trapped as was Blaine in 1884.

On only one occasion did Harrison fail to follow this advice. On

---

[52] Harrison to Allison, September 14, 1888, Allison MSS, Box 262, shows the General was aware that "in some respects" it is "rather a misfortune to have Congress in session so late. . . . It keeps out of the campaign many of you whose services we need" and there "is the temptation towards the use of legislation for extreme party ends."

[53] John I. Mitchell to Harrison, September 19, 1888, (L.C.), Vol. 41.

[54] Thomas to Harrison, September 11, 1888, ibid., Vol. 40.

[55] Blaine to Harrison, September 15, 1888, ibid.

[56] Ibid., September 14, 1888.

September 13, 1888, the survivors of his old command, the 70th Indiana Volunteers, held their fourteenth annual reunion at Clayton, in neighboring Hendricks County. As the group's perennial president, the General was there to call the "old boys" to order.[57]

As the campaign moved into its final stages, there was outwardly a calm serenity that seemed to promise an election governed more by genuine issues and principles than by vilification, personalities, and attempts at fraud. Beneath the surface, however, tension was building up that could not long be denied. Indeed, a political storm was about to break that would cause near shipwreck to both Harrison and Cleveland.

[57] Minutes Book of the Seventieth Indiana Regiment Association, entry at Clayton, Indiana, September 13, 1888. The group's secretary noted that "we have all heard the Gen'l many times before, but never have we heard him excel this effort. . . . the words of eloquence which flowed from the speaker touched the hearts of all the veterans." This volume is preserved at the Benjamin Harrison Memorial Home in Indianapolis. It covers 64 meetings from 1877 until 1938.

CHAPTER XXIII

In the Low Swamps of Slander

A T THE OUTSET of his Presidential campaign, Benjamin Harrison
had hopefully prophesied: "We have joined now a contest
of great principles, and . . . the armies which are to fight
out this great contest before the American people will encamp
upon the high plains of principle, and not in the low swamps of
personal defamation or detraction." [1] Despite some doubts gen-
erated by memories of the 1884 canvass, "probably the dirtiest on
record," [2] the first three months of the 1888 contest had borne out
the General's prediction. In all the political demagoguery displayed, the major campaigners had failed to charge corruption,
venality, religious bigotry, or general immorality to either Cleveland or Harrison. New revelations about illegitimate children had
been conspicuously absent, and by the end of September, 1888,
"free whiskey" [3] and "Rum, Romanism, and Rebellion" [4] were
memories, not issues. The nation at large appeared to have forgotten "the marathon of filth, lies and slander" [5] which had re-
volted so many in 1884.

[1] Charles Hedges (compiler), *Speeches of Benjamin Harrison*, p. 31.

[2] W. Dean Burnham, *Presidential Ballots, 1836–1892*, p. 136. Running a close
second in bad taste was the 1828 contest between John Quincy Adams and Andrew
Jackson. See also Eugene H. Roseboom, *A History of Presidential Elections*, pp. 90–91.

[3] The Republican platform called for a repeal of the tax on spirits "used in the
arts." In some sections this was interpreted as an attempt to foist "free whiskey"
upon the country. Chicago *Tribune*, June 23, *Sentinel*, June 27, and Boston *Post*,
July 26, 1888. Since 1880, Temperance and Prohibition had been the watchwords of
the third party movement. See Mary Earhart, *Frances Willard: From Prayers to
Politics*, pp. 212–27.

[4] The fear of undue Catholic influence had not died with the 1884 election.
Blaine's backing of Harrison in 1888 made news of the fact that Blaine's mother
was a Roman Catholic and a cousin of his mother superior of a convent. Roseboom, *op. cit.*, p. 271.

[5] Burnham, *op. cit.*, p. 140. Allan Nevins, *Grover Cleveland: A Study in Courage*,
pp. 417, 422; and A. T. Volwiler, "Tariff Strategy and Propaganda, 1887–1888,"
American Historical Review, 36 (1930), 76 ff.

Meanwhile, political forecasters had begun to believe that the national voting patterns of 1880 and 1884 would be repeated in 1888. This meant an extremely close popular vote,[6] a situation in which a stroke of luck or an unexpected last-minute move by an enterprising politician could easily swing some doubtful state whose electoral vote might spell the difference between victory and defeat. Important, therefore, was the question as to where "luck" might strike or "enterprise" appear to add the critical weight to the scale. Eyes were focused principally on four states, Connecticut, Indiana, New Jersey, and New York. By the beginning of October experienced politicians agreed that the electoral votes of these four states would decide the Presidency.[7] Cleveland knew this only too well. Narrow pluralities in those states in 1884 had put him in the White House, but not without some anxious moments. Even in his home state of New York, the President's margin of victory had been only 1,143 votes. Now, in 1888, these same four doubtful areas, totaling 66 electoral votes, represented the balance of power. Indiana and New York in particular merited the closest scrutiny.

It had become apparent early in August that Republican prospects for carrying the Empire State ranged from good to excellent. The Harrison supporters, led by Dudley, Quay, and Platt, had gotten the propaganda jump on the Democrats. They had gained this initial advantage by bombing business-conscious Manhattan with an abundance of high-tariff literature, and by preaching protection to industry and labor incessantly and persuasively.[8] Their success worried Cleveland, who felt that in this vital respect his own managers were failing him.[9] Buffalo, for example, reported that high-tariff Republicans were "working very hard" while Democrats

[6] Hamilton Wilcox to Daniel Lamont, June 26, 1888, Cleveland MSS. A representative letter, indicating that both political organizations were evenly matched and that "no walk over" was in sight. Also Burnham, *op. cit.*, pp. 129–56, classifies 1880–1892 as "The Period of No Decision."

[7] Nevins, *op. cit.*, p. 148, styles Indiana and New York as critical. In the Harrison camp a similar feeling prevailed. See O. W. Nixon to Harrison, September 17, 1888, (L.C.), Vol. 41.

[8] Roseboom, *op. cit.*, p. 281. The strategy was clear: convince businessmen that the security of their investments depended on Republican control, and they would be willing to support the campaign with money as well as votes.

[9] Nevins, *op. cit.*, pp. 415–16. It seems evident that Cleveland's two managers, Calvin S. Brice and William H. Barnum, both typical products of big business, would have been more at home in the Harrison protectionist camp.

stood by and watched their rivals use "the old tactics of inducing manufacturers and large employers of labor" to cajole, entice, or bully their employees into the Harrison camp. Some Buffalo factory owners, Democrats complained, had taken "their men out on picnics and . . . labelled [them] with Harrison badges." [10] In Troy, other enterprising Republicans were threatening unemployment for the city's collar workers should Harrison be defeated.

Equally propitious to the Republican cause in New York State was the newborn party unity already described. While the G.O.P. at last worked in peace and harmony, the Democratic party in New York found itself badly disorganized by the renomination of David B. Hill, the incumbent governor. Cleveland and his supporters, who had never borne Hill any love, had been outnumbered at the state convention. The President had steadfastly refused to interfere, but several of his principal backers castigated Hill as "an unprincipled and slippery politician, unfit to rule over a great state." [11] Even after Hill had won his renomination, Cleveland stubbornly continued to refuse his endorsement. This provoked Democratic Chairman Calvin Brice into reminding the President that he had freely endorsed other candidates. Nevertheless, and although New York's 36 electoral votes hung in the balance, Cleveland persisted in his refusal. Finally Brice felt compelled to point out to his chief that "Governor Hill is as much a Democratic nominee as yourself." The President replied: "I don't care a damn if he is—each tub must stand on its own bottom." [12]

As the Cleveland-Hill feud continued through October, Democratic hopes of carrying New York began to fade. Soon a report became widespread that many Democrats who had supported Cleveland in 1884 would now shift to Harrison in the national election, but continue to support Hill on the state ballot. This defection from the Democratic national ticket soon caused a "Harrison and Hill" movement which began to spread rapidly throughout the state. In some old Democratic strongholds "Harri-

10 S. S. Cary to Cleveland, August 3, 1888, Cleveland MSS. Cleveland had been warned well in advance that his famous tariff message would produce such results. See DeAlva Stanwood Alexander, *Four Famous New Yorkers*, p. 105.

11 Nevins, *op. cit.*, p. 424. Alexander, *op. cit.*, pp. 112 ff., explains the opposition to Hill by resolute Democrats and Independents. Uncritical is the unpublished biography of David Bennett Hill (New York State Library at Albany, N. Y.). George Bixby, Hill's secretary, is the author.

12 Louisville *Courier-Journal*, April 11, 1904, as cited by Nevins, *op. cit.*, p. 427.

son and Hill" banners were openly displayed. Cleveland supporters raised the cry of "corrupt bargain" and began to scan the writing on the wall for signs of the fine Italian hand of New York's Republican boss, Thomas C. Platt.[13]

During the final month of the campaign, two powerful dailies in the metropolitan area, the *Times* and the *Evening Post,* upheld Cleveland by attacking Hill. This action, however, only widened the breach between the New York Governor and the President. Mutual recriminations built a barrier of hurt feelings that blocked all hope of a reconciliation. There is also little doubt that many Harrison leaders in the state worked feverishly to keep alive a squabble that could only redound to Harrison's advantage at the polls. Consequently Platt and Whitelaw Reid conspired to fan the factional fires flickering within the Democratic party.[14]

Despite the beneficent effects of this cold war between Cleveland and Hill, General Harrison soon had troubles of his own. His mood of growing optimism had been quickly shattered by a report that some upstate New York Knights of Labor were spreading a campaign canard that denounced Harrison as the enemy of the workingman. Along the Erie tracks in Steuben County,[15] circulars calculated to drive every laboring man from the Harrison camp appeared. These tracts pictured the General as breaking the Indianapolis railroad strike of 1877 at the point of a bayonet and as saying that "a dollar a day is enough for any workingman." [16] He was also supposed to have faced the strikers and barked: "I would force you to work by the bayonet, or I would shoot you down like dogs." [17] This particular attack, conceived by Edwin F. Gould, a half-crazed labor agitator, was not

[13] David S. Muzzey, *James G. Blaine, A Political Idol of Other Days,* p. 387. Sixteen years later, Cleveland exonerated Hill of any treachery to the Democratic national ticket. Alexander, *op. cit.,* pp. 129–31, and Roseboom, *op. cit.,* p. 282, offer no new evidence.

[14] T. C. Platt to Whitelaw Reid, September 21, 1888, Whitelaw Reid MSS. Platt's idea was to weaken both Hill and Cleveland by encouraging independents to bolt the entire Democratic ticket.

[15] The circular was published by Local Assembly 263, Knights of Labor, at Canisteo, New York, during the last week of September.

[16] The "dollar a day" story originated shortly after Harrison's nomination at Chicago. It was picked up by the *Sentinel* and copied by other Democratic papers throughout the country.

[17] The *Sentinel, Journal,* and *News* all covered the local phase of the 1877 strike, but none attributed anti-labor sentiments to Harrison.

new to Harrison. The same canard had died a natural death in Indiana where Harrison had refused to dignify such malicious and unfounded statements with public denial. But in the East it was novel to the laboring man and hence, at such a late hour in the campaign, real political dynamite.

Although New York City's *Sun* and *World* both denounced these anti-Harrison rumors as silly and untrue, the "dollar a day" tale continued its rounds, becoming more vicious with each re-telling. Small-town papers and local political chieftains, "as well as the speakers of the Democratic party generally," worked industriously to spread the canard further and faster in a last-ditch effort to win the workingman's vote. Anti-Harrison sentiment began to mount wherever he was personally unknown and especially where townspeople had only one partisan newspaper to guide them. As the slanders continued to mushroom, Harrison himself grew anxious and irritable. Repeated daily in the clippings and letters brought to his desk, this one story took on dozens of forms—all caricaturing Harrison as the outspoken foe of labor. Some accounts had it that the Republican candidate had once advocated only two meals a day for the laborer, including a cold lunch at noon. One report claimed that Harrison had recommended cheap and coarse meat for a cheap and coarse class of people.[18] Another story pictured the General in the 1877 strike as thundering to the pickets, "Were I Governor of Indiana or Sheriff of Marion County, I would force you back to work . . . if I had to wade in blood up to the tips of my fingers." [19] But the lie that most incensed Harrison originated with agitator Gould who had characterized him as a "gun-happy" despot in 1877. It described how Harrison had organized a private militia company, armed them with the latest Springfield rifles, drilled them, and finally, without authority, led them to the Indianapolis railroad depot in an effort to break the strike by force. Gould claimed that Governor Williams tried to check Harrison's troops, whereupon the General allegedly shouted: "We'll shoot the dogs, anyway; hanging is too good for them." [20]

[18] This was an embellishment of Gould's original charges.

[19] These, and other versions, were collected by the Republican State Committee at Indianapolis. Their recital appeared as part of a broadside that quickly achieved popularity as a campaign document.

[20] Since Governor Williams had asked Harrison to take command of all militia forces during the emergency, the allegation is even more ironical.

These vilifications were not confined to New York and the great labor centers east of the Alleghenies. California, Colorado, and Missouri soon reported that the Gould lies had wings and had now flown in to prejudice laboring men in those states.[21] A correspondent from Kansas wrote the General that Edwin Gould himself had come to the state and was engaged in a series of stump speeches bolstering his earlier printed attacks.[22] News of this scurrilous onslaught, which Harrison attributed to the Democratic party itself, ended the General's patience and his silence. Summoning State Chairman James N. Huston to his home, Harrison reviewed for him his actual rôle during the 1877 Indianapolis strike. He wanted the truth to be told. In short time, Huston and his staff issued a circular entitled "Origin, History and Refutation of the Dollar a Day Lie," which exposed the trickery behind the political blackmail.

Huston backed this document by re-offering a $2,000 reward to anyone who would swear to an affidavit in support of Gould's allegations.[23] This proved Gould's undoing. No one claimed the reward, but more than thirty citizens came forward, including members of Harrison's Citizens' Committee of 1877, members of the Mediation Committee that had acted at the time, and even some of the strikers themselves. All denied under oath the Gould story. Huston incorporated these testimonials into another circular which became a most effective campaign weapon. Shortly afterward, an Indiana assembly of the Knights of Labor repudiated Gould, and endorsed Benjamin Harrison as labor's friend. This favorable turn of events was mirrored in newspaper retractions of the old stories maligning the General. In addition, the Gould fantasies were categorically denied by Calvin Brice, Democratic national chairman, and by six influential Democratic journals in Chicago and New York.[24]

[21] W. H. H. Miller to Samuel D. Miller, October 3, 1888, W. H. H. Miller Letterbooks; also W. H. H. Miller to J. S. Clarkson, October 5, 1888, ibid.; and L. T. Michener to M. H. DeYoung, October 12, 1888, (L.C.), Vol. 43. Here Michener admits "these lies have done and are doing us . . . injury."

[22] J. S. Judson to Harrison, October 2, 1888, (L.C.), Vol. 42.

[23] Senator Joseph E. McDonald, who served on Harrison's 1877 Citizens' Committee, spoke out against the lie. See Harrison MSS, (Indiana Division, State Library, Indianapolis), entry under "Personal," June 4, 1937.

[24] The Chicago Times and Chicago News, joined by the New York World, Sun, and Brooklyn Eagle, repudiated the personal attacks on Harrison. See campaign document: "Origin, History and Refutation of the Dollar A Day Lie," p. 16, (L.C.).

The slow Harrison anger was soon roused again, this time from another quarter. He learned that Democrats were now attacking him as a bigot and as a "slanderer of the Irish." This charge was based on an alleged incident at Bloomington, Illinois, during the 1876 Presidential campaign. Here, a local grocer now recalled, Harrison had once made a speech in which he specifically praised all nationalities *except* the Irish. When Harrison had finished, an elderly gentleman possessing a distinct brogue called out from the rear of the hall: "How about the Irish, and where were Meagher, Sheridan, Shields, Mulligan, and the others?" The Bloomington audience, hissing the questioner, shouted for his ejection. It was during this gentleman's eviction that Harrison had allegedly slandered the sons of Erin. The grocer reported Harrison as saying: "It is easy to know that man's race; you all know what they are; if it were not for them we would not need half of our penitentiaries, which are almost full of them; they have no intelligence; they are only good to shovel dirt and grade railroads, for which they receive more than they are worth, as they are no acquisition to the American people." [25] This was the version of the grocer, by name William Condon, Sr. Now, at the very peak of the 1888 campaign, he gave his story to the Bloomington *Bulletin,* a Democratic daily. The paper in turn warned all Irishmen against elevating Harrison, "the cold-blooded, bigoted aristocrat," to the high office of President.

Like the "dollar a day" tag, this new "anti-Hibernian bigotry" label also made good copy for the Democratic press. Journal after journal excoriated Harrison for his "coarse, brutal and indefensible arraignment of the Irish-Americans as a class." Other eager Democrats, in an attempt to gain votes for Cleveland, approached Roman Catholic clergymen, many of whom already sported sprigs of green on their black suits. Late in September, Harrison learned that "every priest in the country" had received a copy of grocer Condon's condemnation. Although the Republican daily in Bloomington, the *Pantagraph,* had loyally defended Harrison and had charged Condon with spreading unmitigated falsehoods, the Republican cause had suffered. Denials by Harrison's friends only served to stimulate countercharges by enraged Irishmen. A Ro-

[25] The clipping, in (L.C.), is from the Rock Island *Argus,* September 5, 1888. The story was first published in the Bloomington *Bulletin,* a Democratic daily, and rapidly copied by the party press.

man Catholic cleric in Iowa, although he himself knew the bigotry charges were false, reported that the anti-Harrison feeling was solid [26] among his Irish parishioners. Meanwhile, Harrison chafed under this new scurrilous attack and, when the national press failed to vindicate him completely, determined to bring his own case before the voters. It was now mid-October, a mere three weeks before the election.

General Harrison chose October 25 as the day for attack, for this date marked the climax of labor's efforts on behalf of the Republican ticket in Indiana. Several prominent labor representatives from the East who had just completed a tour of the state for the party were scheduled to meet that day at a labor rally in Indianapolis. Among these, the most distinguished was Charles H. Litchman, recent secretary-general of the Knights of Labor, who had resigned his post in order to take the stump for Harrison.[27] A day of welcome and special events had been planned and the General himself was to be the principal speaker. By noon, more than ten thousand visiting Republicans had swarmed into the capital from every corner of the state. The colorful parade of political clubs and a stirring demonstration by contingents of workingmen thrilled the afternoon crowd of spectators. Harrison, with Carrie and Secretary Litchman at his side, reviewed the passing columns. On the same platform sat future President McKinley, accompanied by Senator Henry Blair of New Hampshire and Senator John Spooner of Wisconsin. When Harrison and Litchman stepped to the front, they were accorded an ovation of fully five minutes.

The presiding officer of the day was L. W. McDaniels, an Irishman who ranked high in the strong and well-organized Typo-

[26] John Fletcher Lacey to Harrison, September 20, 1888, (L.C.), Vol. 41. In 1888, Lacey was the successful Republican candidate for Congress, defeating James B. Weaver of Iowa. The Catholic priest at Brooklyn, Iowa, handed Lacey the clipping from the Rock Island *Argus*, and explained how it was harming Harrison. Harrison had been shouldering the weight of these attacks since early July; on July 4, 1888, in a conversation with the Catholic Bishop (Chatard) of Indianapolis, the General had expressed his deep annoyance and concern. See *supra*, p. 362.

[27] Powderly, Grand Master of the Knights of Labor, censured this move by Litchman. See T. V. Powderly to J. A. McCurdy, September 7, 1888, Powderly MSS, (The Catholic University of America Archives). Powderly himself was a neutral in the campaign but personally favored the protective tariff. He was unwilling, however, to involve the Knights of Labor in politics. See T. V. Powderly to James Campbell, October 16, 1888, *ibid.*

graphical Union.[28] Before introducing Harrison to the crowd, McDaniels apologized for the lies which, he said, a few credulous workingmen had spread and believed about the Republican candidate. The union spokesman pointed to Harrison's senatorial record as proof of his being the sincere friend of labor. It was Harrison, McDaniels reminded his listeners, who had insisted on arbitration as the fairest means of settling labor-capital disputes. It was Harrison who as Indiana's senator had voted to exclude "contract labor from our shores." [29] The prolonged cheers which frequently interrupted McDaniels' remarks, stirred the General and filled him with a sense of kinship with this vast assembly of workingmen.[30] As he rose to speak, therefore, the psychological setting for what he wished to say to them was little short of ideal.

Harrison launched at once into his memorable apologia. He spoke of the "number of false and scandalous stories relating to my attitude towards organized labor." He censured the press and the speakers who had circulated these tales of alleged treachery. He charged that Democratic campaign managers had secretly endorsed such trickery; the lies had been paid for "by their funds and circulated under their auspices." He branded the stories once and for all as "malicious, scandalous, and utterly false," whose only "purpose . . . was to poison the minds of the workingmen." After a noisy pause for flag-waving and tumultuous cheering, the General continued: "The story that I ever said one dollar a day was enough for a workingman, with all its accompaniments and appendages, is not a perversion of anything I ever said—*it is a false creation.*" [31]

Passing over other campaign slanders, Harrison took up the new charge, that he was a bigot. "I will only add that it is equally false that anywhere at any time I ever spoke disparagingly of my fellow-citizens of Irish nativity or descent." The General's sin-

[28] Diplomacy and strategy demanded that the party honor McDaniels. It would offset the labor difficulties encountered by Whitelaw Reid's New York *Tribune* and John C. New's Indianapolis *Journal*. At Harrison's suggestion, both editors had already modified their non-union policies, one cause of labor unrest.

[29] Hedges, *op. cit.*, p. 182. This measure had protected the West Coast Irish laborers who were seriously threatened by Chinese immigration. McDaniels also stressed Harrison's senatorial vote for a bill to outlaw convict labor on federal projects and forbid government purchase of articles produced by convict labor.

[30] Important Indiana labor leaders, as well as many from out of the state, were on hand. Not a few, like Jeremiah Murphy of New York, represented active blocks of Irish-Americans.

[31] Hedges, *op. cit.*, pp. 182–83 (the italics have been added).

cerity was heartfelt. "Many of them are now enrolling themselves on the side of protection for American labor—this created the necessity for the story." By way of conclusion he repeated his own code for political campaigning: "I want to say again that those who pitch a campaign upon so low a level, greatly underestimate the intelligence, the sense of decency, and the love of fair play of the American people." [32]

October 25, 1888, lived long in the memory of Republicans within and without the Hoosier State. Harrison, by his eloquent sincerity, had at last won his way to the hearts of the American people. His blazing words of self-defense had impressed even hardened political leaders. Stephen B. Elkins wrote immediately from New York: "Your speech made last night in some respects is the best of your many good speeches." [33] A flood of other congratulatory messages poured into Indianapolis. Editor John Sleicher of the Albany *Evening Journal,* after praising the General's effort, added that "the politics of New York City, as a rule, are the politics of Albany 24 hours later. Here in the capital, the political center, the indication that reaches me from every section of the state warrants the prediction that we will win and by a very decisive majority." [34] This statement was underscored by the General's own son, Russell, who wired from New York that the trend in the Empire State was definitely Republican.[35]

The honeymoon glow of near victory shone from the West Coast as well. From San Francisco, Thomas B. Reed, veteran congressman from Maine, who had just finished stumping California for Harrison, assured the General that victory would perch on his banner in November. So confident was the next Speaker of the House of Representatives that he added: "I shall not go home to vote, for we carry Maine with such a majority that my vote would not be needed. . . . While I deeply regret being deprived of the personal satisfaction of voting for a candidate who has always fully met my idea of what a man in public life should be, I promise myself the greater satisfaction of having aided his election by every means in

[32] *Ibid.*
[33] Elkins to Harrison, October 26, 1888, (L.C.), Vol. 44. Elkins himself had been speaking most effectively in West Virginia during October. See Oscar Doane Lambert, *Stephen Benton Elkins: American Foursquare,* pp. 122–25.
[34] John Sleicher to Benjamin Harrison, October 26, 1888, (L.C.), Vol. 44. "Pat, laconic and forcible" was Sleicher's judgment on Harrison's effort.
[35] Russell Harrison to Benjamin Harrison, October 26, 1888, *ibid.*

my power." [36] With both coasts thus apparently assured in the last week of October, Harrison and his political advisers turned their full attention to Indiana.

From the beginning, the strategists of both parties had agreed that the decisive battle of the campaign might well be fought on Indiana soil. The Democrats drew some consolation from the fact that Cleveland had been victorious in Indiana in 1884, besting Blaine by more than 6,500 votes.[37] Now the incumbent Democratic governor, Isaac P. Gray, grew confident that his party would maintain, perhaps even increase, its margin of victory in 1888. Grover Cleveland, however, remained uneasy in the knowledge that he was fighting in Harrison's back yard. He complained to Governor Gray that Hoosier Democrats "were relying too much on surface indications" and had neglected to make their party organization "as close and complete as it ought to be." [38] Meanwhile, Indiana Republicans optimistically claimed their state's 15 electoral votes for their favorite son by "several thousands." [39] While Harrison himself expressed an outward confidence that his own state would support him, he complained privately to the National Committee in New York that few good stump speakers were being assigned to Indiana. Already upset by the ordeal of campaign lies, he wrote a particularly strong letter to J. S. Clarkson, the hard-working vice-chairman of the National Committee, and persuaded his partner, Miller, to do the same.[40]

Actually, the outcome in Indiana was very much in doubt.[41] This fact, perhaps more than anything else, prompted Harrison to assume personal direction of the campaign in his home state. Pro-

[36] Reed to Harrison, October 26, 1888, ibid.

[37] Burnham, op. cit., p. 391.

[38] Allan Nevins (ed.), Letters of Grover Cleveland, p. 190. This differed from the report sent East by Republican Chairman Huston that the Democrats were importing hundreds of illegal voters. See Huston to Elkins, October 15, 1888, S. B. Elkins MSS, (University of West Virginia Archives).

[39] James N. Tyner to Louis T. Michener, September 21, 1888, (L.C.), Vol. 41, a copy from the Michener MSS.

[40] Benjamin Harrison to James S. Clarkson, October 5, 1888, Harrison MSS (Indiana Division, State Library, Indianapolis). Also W. H. H. Miller to J. S. Clarkson, October 5, 1888, W. H. H. Miller Letterbooks.

[41] Countless letters in both the Cleveland MSS and the Harrison MSS forecast a close vote despite the fact that the Republican nominee was a Hoosier. See R. C. Buley, "The Campaign of 1888 in Indiana," Indiana Magazine of History, 10 (1914), 162–85.

testing that he did not want to appear "hoggish at all," he still demanded a free hand in directing home-front strategy. Familiar with the reactions of his fellow Hoosiers, he sensed that Cleveland's 1884 popularity in Indiana might well be on the wane. The veterans in particular, Harrison argued, had been deeply disaffected by the President's veto of pensions and equally outraged by the Executive Order that had restored to the Confederate rebels their captured battle flags.[42] From the General's viewpoint, President Cleveland had also shown a poor sense of public relations. Had he not refused to visit Lincoln's tomb? Had he not maintained a studied silence at the Gettysburg ceremonies? And had he not peremptorily canceled his visit to the St. Louis encampment of the G.A.R. in 1887? With the veterans' vote so important, these actions, he felt, should be stressed by every Republican speaker.

Harrison, who knew the country of the Wabash, undoubtedly wanted to bank a surplus of political capital in Indiana. He therefore demanded the party's most sought after orators for the closing weeks of the Hoosier campaign. He knew from experience what Cleveland and his advisers knew only in theory, that "Indianians dearly love a speech, but it must be bright and sparkling, not too deep, or abstract, or technical." [43] Harrison cherished a well-founded belief that James G. Blaine, above all others, could put sparkle into Indiana's final rallies. In 1888, just as in previous Presidential campaigns, the magical name Blaine was a drawing-card. In the full floodlight of hero worship, many could not see the stains of former unethical associations that marred the reputation of the man from Maine.

Harrison's desire to have Blaine tour Indiana was not an unpremeditated campaign necessity. The idea had been hatched shortly after the Chicago convention and had grown to maturity before Blaine's return from abroad.[44] The General envisioned a monster rally at Indianapolis sometime in October, with Blaine featured as guest orator. For additional prestige, Harrison had urged Senators Allison and Sherman to attend, but with the Senate

---

[42] Roseboom, *op. cit.*, p. 276.

[43] Nevins, *op. cit.*, p. 422.

[44] Harrison to Blaine, August 5, 1888, in A. T. Volwiler (ed.), *Correspondence Between Benjamin Harrison and James G. Blaine*, p. 32. General Harrison had entrusted a personal message for James Blaine to his son, Emmons Blaine.

still in session, both men begged off.[45] Nevertheless, Harrison did manage to commandeer several other prominent politicians from the East and Midwest and scheduled his "Blaine rally" for Thursday, October 11.[46]

At this point, the National Committee crossed swords with their independent candidate. In an effort to use Blaine more widely in doubtful New Jersey, New York, and Connecticut, eastern headquarters proposed to cancel the "Plumed Knight's" appointments in equally doubtful Indiana. Harrison rebelled but Blaine became incensed. The 1884 standard-bearer misconstrued the National Committee's attempt to keep him in the East as a sign that neither Harrison nor the Hoosier State leaders cared to have him speak in Indiana. News of the suggested change in schedule had reached the sensitive man from Maine through the columns of a Democratic newspaper while he himself was in Detroit. Immediately he requested Harrison to cancel the Indianapolis rally, claiming a desire "to turn my face Eastward . . . where I shall be sure of a warm welcome." [47] Only quick action by the General smoothed Blaine's ruffled plumes. By promptly rebuking the National Committee for undue interference, Harrison won back his speaker; a reassuring wire to Blaine completely disarmed him.[48] The General's ability to lead was never more important to his political success than at this critical juncture. Had Blaine and his host of friends been alienated, the Republican ranks in Indiana and elsewhere might well have broken.

Thursday, October 11, 1888, became in point of numbers the greatest demonstration of the Indiana campaign. More than 75,000 Hoosiers dropped their ordinary business and surrendered to "the sweet intoxication of politics." [49] Flanked by Blaine and several

[45] Allison to Harrison, October 7, 1888, (L.C.), Vol. 43. Allison, the party wheelhorse in tariff matters, had to stay on the Hill. See the excellent biography by Leland L. Sage, *William Boyd Allison*, pp. 230–34. Sherman, on the other hand, excused himself on the score that it would be "too embarrassing" for him to appear on the same platform with Blaine. Sherman to Harrison, October 1, 1888, (L.C.), Vol. 42.

[46] Massachusetts, New York, and Pennsylvania sent representatives, while Illinois, Michigan, and Ohio spoke for the Midwest.

[47] Blaine to Harrison, October 7, 1888, in Volwiler, *op. cit.*, pp. 34–35. Evidently Blaine first got wind of the proposed cancellation from a hostile newspaper.

[48] Harrison to J. S. Clarkson, October 9, 1888, Harrison MSS, (Indiana Division, State Library, Indianapolis).

[49] Hedges, *op. cit.*, p. 170, estimates a more conservative figure of 50,000, although newspaper accounts claimed a crowd of 75,000.

other celebrities, General and Mrs. Harrison viewed the exciting scene from the balcony of the New Denison Hotel, noting with pleasure that "dusky faces as well as fair" lined the streets already gay "with the dazzling uniforms of young girls" marching in parade.[50] The Harrisons added their own voices to the lusty cheers that greeted a nine-divisioned, solid phalanx of 25,000 marchers in what the Associated Press described as "probably the greatest political parade ever witnessed in this country outside the City of New York." [51] Even so, the festivities were just beginning.

After the grand review, 30,000 gathered at the Exposition Grounds to hear Blaine excoriate the Democrats as unfit to be trusted with the government of the country. The main address, however, came that evening when more than 6,000 packed Tomlinson Hall. There, the famous "Plumed Knight" disappointed no one. He charged the Cleveland administration with ineptitude and vacillation abroad and at home, censured the country's weakness in dealing with England, and deplored the continued suppression of a free ballot in the South.[52] Harrison listened approvingly to his future Secretary of State. Blaine had helped to nominate him—most people knew this to be true.[53] Yet even more dynamic was this personal effort of his to help elect for the first time a Hoosier to the Presidency.[54]

Blaine left Indiana well galvanized with political rhetoric. Superficially, at least, the Republicans held the advantage. Yet Blaine had not finished. He continued to cover the Midwest with his oratory, climaxing his efforts in Chicago on October 20 with a thundering endorsement of Harrison and the party.[55]

As for the Presidential candidate himself, he still refused to travel. Mindful of Burchard's folly in 1884, he stood by his own philosophy. "I have a great risk of meeting a fool at home," he confided to Whitelaw Reid, "but the candidate who travels cannot escape him." [56] Hence, during the final days of the 1888 campaign, Harrison remained at Indianapolis, now a veritable Re-

[50] St. Paul *Pioneer Press*, October 16, 1888.

[51] Hedges, *op. cit.*, p. 170.

[52] Muzzey, *op. cit.*, pp. 383–84; 386–87.

[53] Lambert, *op. cit.*, pp. 115–20; also Sage, *op. cit.*, pp. 225 ff.

[54] Nevins, *op. cit.*, p. 433, admits that "Cleveland was unfortunate in having no speakers who attracted nationwide attention in the way that Blaine and Harrison did."

[55] Murat Halstead to Benjamin Harrison, October 16, 21, 1888, (L.C.), Vol. 44.

[56] Benjamin Harrison to Whitelaw Reid, October 9, 1888, Whitelaw Reid MSS.

publican Mecca for political pilgrims. On "German Day" in mid-
October, large delegations from Chicago and Milwaukee traveled
to the Hoosier capital, where they united with local Republicans
of German extraction to give Harrison a full vote of confidence.
To this, the General responded by delivering a eulogy on German
virtues.[57]

One of the most significant receptions of the entire campaign
took place in front of the Harrison home on Saturday, October
20. A parade of commercial travelers, estimated at upwards of
40,000 and led by drummers from eleven states, marched north
on Delaware Street. As was by now customary,[58] Carrie Harrison
and her husband appeared at the front door to watch the parade and welcome the oncoming crowds. One particular feature
brought an earlier phase of the campaign back to the General's
mind. In the parade, the center of attraction was a huge bull
covered with a white cloth banner bearing the slogan "JOHN BULL
RIDES THE DEMOCRATIC PARTY AND WE RIDE JOHN BULL." Leading
the bovine was a marcher dressed as Uncle Sam, and astride the
beast itself rode a drummer bedecked undeniably in an emerald-
colored suit. This unusual twist of the British Lion's tail, a tech-
nique common to most Presidential campaigns of the era, seemed
to please Harrison immensely.

That same evening, full of the spirit of the parade, which he
had interpreted as a plea for protection, the General walked to
Tomlinson Hall to address still another throng of commercial
travelers, some of whom were in Indianapolis for the fifth time
since the convention. Again Harrison pitched his speech on the
key of commerce. "You," he observed, "whose hand is every day
upon the business pulse of the people . . . have concluded that
the policy for America is the policy of a protective tariff." The hall

[57] Hedges, op. cit., pp. 172–74.

[58] Mrs. Harrison's niece, Mary Lord Dimmick, has left eyewitness accounts of
what usually transpired in the Harrison home as the multitude crowded at the
front gate. ". . . Little Benjamin [Baby McKee, Harrison's grandson] looked all
eyes and ears, and someone took him where he could see and hear them. Uncle
Ben and Aunt Carrie stood by the front door. . . . after a little while . . . little
boys passed through the house shaking hands, and Benjamin held out his hand also,
and so many shook hands with him. . . ." As for the commercial travelers, "they
wore linen dusters, high hats and carried parasols made of red, white and blue
handkerchiefs. . . . Cheers upon cheers went up continually until Uncle Ben spoke,
and then, as always, you could have heard a pin drop." Mary Lord Dimmick to her
mother (Elizabeth Scott Lord), undated (July–October, 1888). James Blaine Walker
MSS, (privately held).

housed many workingmen also, and for them Harrison had a message that summarized the chief issue of the campaign:

Two propositions . . . now stare our working people—and the whole country—in the face . . .: competition with foreign countries, without adequate discriminating and favoring duties, means lower wages to our working people; a revenue-only tariff, or progressive free trade, means larger importations of foreign goods, and that means less work in America.[59]

Sustained applause greeted the General's terse statement. No one could doubt now the ground of protection on which the party stood and on which Harrison himself was building his hopes of election.

As to "John Bull" in the October 20th parade, the story goes back to 1886, when Democrats and Republicans alike were fishing for political advantage in the troubled waters of Anglo-American diplomacy. Cleveland's administration had long been plagued by a series of vexatious clashes in Canadian waters, the direct outgrowth of a Canadian-American feud over respective rights "to inshore fishing, bait-purchasing, and the transshipment of cargoes within Canadian waters." [60] When, in 1886, Canadian cruisers and schooners began arresting American vessels for alleged violations,[61] protests in the United States against both Ottawa and London had launched a wave of ill-feeling that swept New England and lashed at the shores of Great Britain. In fish-catching-and-packing Maine and Massachusetts, the fires of Anglophobia burned brightly, and the blame was placed on Cleveland and the new Democratic administration. Even when Washington brought pressure on Canada to stop the boarding and seizure of Yankee ships, New Englanders had not been satisfied. Led by Massachusetts Congressman Henry Cabot Lodge, a Republican freshman in the House,[62] the Yankees talked retaliation. Lodge declared that "whenever the American

[59] Hedges, op. cit., pp. 177–79.

[60] Nevins, op. cit., p. 405. Also see John Bassett Moore, International Arbitrations, I, 725 ff., for a discussion of the abrogation of American rights in 1885.

[61] Particularly enlightening are chapters 6 and 7 in Charles Callan Tansill, The Foreign Policy of Thomas F. Bayard, a monograph based on the Bayard MSS and other collections.

[62] Lodge entered Congress on March 3, 1887, two months short of his thirty-seventh birthday. He served in the House of Representatives for three terms before taking a Senate seat, which he held until his death in 1924. See James L. Harrison (compiler), Biographical Directory of the American Congress, 1774–1949, pp. 1470–71.

flag on an American fishing smack is touched by a foreigner, the great American heart is touched." [63] Spurred on by such sentiments as these, the House passed a bill authorizing President Cleveland to close American ports to Dominion ships and trade. In Gloucester, Portland, and Boston, talk of an armed clash filled the air. Cleveland, however, chose diplomatic channels rather than force, though he signed the retaliatory legislation.[64]

Nevertheless, agitation over the fisheries had continued until February, 1888, when the draft of an Anglo-American treaty was completed. But this, unfortunately, was a presidential year; consequently, with eyes on the ballot box in November, a Republican dominated Senate killed the treaty.[65] It was a purely political effort, aimed at robbing Cleveland and the Democrats of any credit for settling the bitter dispute. Republicans lost no time in seizing the opportunity. George Frisbee Hoar of Massachusetts, Harrison's old senatorial friend, declared that while Grant was in the White House no petty British officer had ever hauled "Old Glory" down from an American masthead. Other Republicans, not unmindful of the Irish vote, warned all Americans that Cleveland stood on the brink of yielding substantial American interests [66] to the British. Finally a Democratic senator, Harrison Holt Riddleberger of Virginia, ventured the canard that the Cleveland administration was "pro-English from the President down to the last Cabinet officer" [67]—and this delighted the Republican strategists.

Coupled with the unsettled fisheries dispute remained the undeniable fact that Great Britain, in 1888, was the world's outstanding "free-trade" nation. This now inspired Republican posters, picturing Cleveland under the British flag and Harrison under the American. By August, 1888, slogans to Harrison's advantage had become legion: "PROTECTION TO AMERICAN LABOR, NO FREE TRADE FOR US"—"AMERICA FOR AMERICANS—NO FREE TRADE"—"AMERICAN WAGES FOR AMERICAN WORKINGMEN"—"CLEVELAND RUNS WELL IN ENGLAND." Republican propagandists even cited the London Times, erroneously, to the effect that "the only time England has

[63] New York Nation, May 19, 1887.

[64] Though he had no intention of immediately enforcing it, Cleveland signed the Bill into law in March, 1887. See Thomas A. Bailey, A Diplomatic History of the American People (3d ed., 1946), p. 438.

[65] The aspects of the Republican strategy are fully treated by C. J. Bernardo, "The Presidential Election of 1888," pp. 270–82.

[66] Nevins, op. cit., p. 412.

[67] Public Opinion, August 25, 1888, p. 428.

any use for an Irishman is when he emigrates to America and votes for free trade." [68] It now became Cleveland's turn to bog down in the low swamps of slander.

On August 23, 1888, therefore, with both Houses still in session, Cleveland sent a stinging message to Congress, demanding a new retaliatory law against Great Britain (nominally aimed at Canada). He thus tossed the pro-British issue back into the laps of the Republicans. If they supported his recommendation, Cleveland would be absolved of all pro-British leanings. Failure to act might easily mean the loss of Anglophobe support for Harrison. Nevertheless the Republican Senate refused the President's request,[69] although the House had acceded. Instead, while scores of Irish-Americans blessed the President for his "devotion to old Erin," [70] the Republicans turned to a shabby but effective electioneering trick to regain the Irish vote.

In Pomona, California, lived George Osgoodby, prominent attorney and active Republican, who had had at least some correspondence with General Harrison. In June and July, they had an exchange of letters concerning Harrison's stand on the question of excluding pauper immigration and cheap contract labor from China. Harrison had thanked him for his kind inquiry and attempted to allay any fears which might be entertained on the Pacific Coast. This assurance, also incorporated into Harrison's Letter of Acceptance, seemingly satisfied Osgoodby and ended further correspondence.[71]

When Cleveland sent his imperative message to Congress, however, Osgoodby, among others,[72] interpreted the move as an effort to pull the wool over Irish eyes. Perhaps the Californian felt that Cleveland's message was insincere and that, in reality, he was in collusion with Great Britain. Perhaps he was convinced that the

[68] Ellis P. Oberholtzer, *A History of the United States Since the Civil War*, V, 47. Republicans used this falsehood in a campaign document. See Bailey, *op. cit.*, p. 440.

[69] Nevins, *op. cit.*, pp. 412–28, absolves Cleveland from sinister political motives in drafting his message. Republican leaders of the time felt otherwise.

[70] Bailey, *op. cit.*, p. 440.

[71] George Osgoodby to Benjamin Harrison, June 28; and Benjamin Harrison to George Osgoodby, July 14, 1888, (L.C.), Vol. 34. Republicans sought from Harrison a strong statement on Chinese exclusion in his Letter of Acceptance. It should be noted that other Republicans in the Far West corresponded regularly with the General on matters political. This was not true of Osgoodby.

[72] Nevins, *op. cit.*, p. 428.

Democrats were engaged in a political stunt. At any rate, he apparently decided to try one of his own. Accordingly, on his own initiative, Osgoodby wrote directly to Sir Lionel Sackville-West, the British Minister in Washington, using the pseudonym "Charles Murchison," and representing himself as a former British subject, now a naturalized citizen of the United States.[73] An artful and confidential request for political advice, "Murchison's" epistle explained that heretofore he had always supported Cleveland and the Democrats, but was now seriously disturbed by the President's recent demand for retaliation against his native land. Was this only a temporary election trick? Once Cleveland had secured another four years in the White House, would retaliation yield to conciliation, and would renewed Anglo-American friendship and free trade again form the backbone of Presidential policy? At the end of the letter, came the bait in the trap. "As you know whether Mr. Cleveland's policy is temporary," wrote "Murchison" slyly, "I apply to you . . . for information which shall in turn be treated as entirely secret." [74]

Cleveland's biographer writes that Sackville-West "scrutinized the Murchison letter with his large, sad blue eyes, and wearily wrote an answer" [75]—one which was to undo the Democratic Presidential candidate. West's reply, dated September 13, 1888, clearly indicated that in his opinion British interests would best be served by Cleveland's re-election. In effect, therefore, a vote for Cleveland would be a vote for England. In California, Republican attorney Osgoodby was delighted. His literary trap had ensnared Cleveland, the Democratic party, and Minister West. Here indeed was grist for the Anglophobe mill. Osgoodby speedily turned the political dynamite over to Republican managers for use at the proper time.[76]

The proper time proved to be just two weeks before the national

[73] Since 1931 the complete story behind George Osgoodby's correspondence with Minister Sackville-West has been available. It is contained in a report by Osgoodby's son, Charles, in the Library of Congress, dated February 13, 1931. Bailey, *op. cit.*, p. 441, on the other hand, conjectures that Osgoodby may well have been the agent of the Republican managers from the start.

[74] Copies of the original letter may be found in the New York *Times, Herald,* and *World,* October 25, 1888. Likewise, the full correspondence between West and Osgoodby has been preserved in *The Executive Documents of the House of Representatives* (50th Cong., 2nd Sess.), I, Part II, No. 1, pp. 1667–68.

[75] Nevins, *op. cit.*, p. 406.

[76] The British Minister had impugned the good faith of Cleveland's retaliation message, and after the correspondence was made public he thrust himself even further into American politics.

election. Throughout September and October, Cleveland had enjoyed a decided political advantage, particularly in the East, as a result of his quick demand for a retaliatory law.[77] Scores of papers, including the Irish and Catholic press, announced their allegiance to Cleveland in the belief that he would take revenge against the British for America's treatment in the Canadian waterways dispute. On October 21, however, the Los Angeles *Times* unleashed the "Murchison" story.[78] Jubilation in Republican circles was instantaneous, as was political apoplexy among Irish and Anglophobe voters. The sacrificial goat had to be the British Minister. While friends of Cleveland demanded Sackville-West's immediate recall, the Democratic National Committee telegraphed Washington hotly that the Irish vote "is slipping out of our hands because of diplomatic shilly-shallying." [79] The carefully planned, perfectly timed vote-getting device had done its work. Sackville-West was handed his papers, and the Milwaukee *Sentinel* summed up Republican opinion in two crisp sentences: "Last Tuesday Mr. Cleveland gave Lord Sackville notice to quit. Next Tuesday the American people will give Mr. Cleveland notice to quit." [80]

What General Harrison himself thought of the trick can only be surmised. In any event, he was much struck by the John Bull display in the October 20th parade. Though he continued his "front porch" addresses after the West-Murchison affair had been exposed, he chose to give it no public notice. His incoming mail, however, bulged with gleeful commentaries on the political effects produced by the British diplomat's blunder. Blaine was among the first to write from New York. "Lord Sackville's letter is I think having a wonderful effect upon the Irish here and proves more at the dash of a sentence than we could by argument during the whole campaign." [81]

That very night in Madison Square Garden, before an enthusiastic crowd of Irish-Americans—all waving copies of Sackville-West's letter—Blaine flayed Cleveland the Anglophile. Russell Harrison, present at the Garden rally, forwarded to Indianapolis an eyewitness account, while steel king Andrew Carnegie, speaking for big business, wrote: "All looks bright. West's letter, I think, settles it.

[77] Nevins, *op. cit.*, pp. 428–29.
[78] Bernardo, *op. cit.*, pp. 344–45.
[79] Bailey, *op. cit.*, p. 441.
[80] November 1, 1888.
[81] James G. Blaine to Benjamin Harrison, October 25, 1888, (L.C.), Vol. 44.

Blaine, young Harrison and Quay and everyone agree. *We have it today*." [82] This bright forecast from the East was soon enhanced by a telegraphic message from San Francisco, seat of the "Murchison" strategy. The wire, delivered at Indianapolis shortly after four o'clock on October 27, elatedly informed Harrison: "California feels proud that she paved the way for your nomination and is satisfied that she has given Cleveland his *coup de grâce* by bringing out the West-Murchison correspondence and electing a Republican President." The only note of uncertainty in the long telegram was the anxious query: "How about Indiana?" [83] Tuesday, November 8, 1888, held the answer—and that was only nine days away.

---

[82] Andrew Carnegie to L. W. Abbott, October 24, 1888, Carnegie MSS, Vol. 10.
[83] M. H. DeYoung to Benjamin Harrison, October 27, 1888, telegram, (L.C.), Vol. 45.

CHAPTER XXIV

Boodle and Victory

THE FINAL FORTNIGHT of the contest in Indiana between "Beef" Cleveland and "Brains" Harrison, as young Albert J. Beveridge styled it,[1] furnished an extraordinary scene of parading pilgrims, marching bands, and shouting partisans. On June 28, hoodlums already had torn down Cleveland banners on a prominent Indianapolis thoroughfare, and two days later, after a Harrison-Morton ratification meeting in New Albany, the Democrats had got a Chinese drunk and persuaded him to hang up lanterns, explode fireworks, and shout for Harrison. Partisans had called this "the dirtiest, most contemptible, and dishonorable trick of the campaign."[2] Now it proved to be mild and harmless in comparison with both parties' desperate attempts to secure the Hoosier electoral vote. Not since Lincoln and Grant had a Presidential candidate won an easy victory in Indiana. Tilden's margin over Hayes in 1876 had been a thin 6,500 votes, and Cleveland had matched this in his 1884 victory over Blaine. In 1880, the state had given Garfield a plurality of only 7,600, and the 1888 battle, with an expected half-million voters, promised to be extremely close.

As the canvass became "hotter and hotter all the time,"[3] Republican speakers hammered at local Democratic weaknesses: the gerrymander bill of 1885, mismanagement of the state hospital for the insane, corruption in Indiana's prisons,[4] and the tally sheet for-

---

[1] Claude G. Bowers, *Beveridge and The Progressive Era,* p. 55.

[2] R. C. Buley, "The Campaign of 1888 in Indiana," *Indiana Magazine of History,* 10 (1914), 167–70.

[3] W. H. H. Miller to Sam Miller, October 3, 1888, W. H. H. Miller Letterbooks.

[4] Investigation of the Indiana hospitals had revealed several abuses under the Democratic administration. Republican stump speakers such as William D. Foulke and Albert J. Beveridge, made certain that the voters "could smell the tainted meat and see the maggots in the butter; . . . hear the blows of the brutal attendants upon the backs of the patients, etc." For the full story, see W. D. Foulke, *Fighting the Spoilsmen,* pp. 34–35.

geries of 1887.[5] The Democrats fought back; but lacking any effective defense on state and local issues, they resorted to name calling. Harrison, they said, was a machine man, whose "political existence" was "the product, the root and branch, of the worst element of Indiana machine politics." They described his actions as "by the machine, of the machine, and for the machine." In an effort to portray the General as anti-labor, the Democrats also charged that in public life Harrison was an "advocate, supporter and apologist of corporations and monopolies." [6] Behind the scenes, after conducting their own private polls, the managers for both Cleveland and Harrison predicted a Hoosier victory for their own candidates by at least 10,000 votes. Still, both state and national chairmen felt uneasy as October faded into November.

Since early fall Harrison's influential and wealthy supporters along the East Coast, especially in New York, Philadelphia, and Washington, had anxiously sought the General's own estimate of the outlook in Indiana. From their standpoint, even before the Sackville-West affair, the Cleveland-Hill split had made such a comfortable contribution that they felt sure the General could win New York by a big majority. They conceded, however, that Connecticut and New Jersey still remained doubtful. Their query was: could Harrison promise Indiana? In late September, Whitelaw Reid, acting independently of the National Committee, asked Harrison personally: "Do you need any special help in Indiana? Are the expenses of a thorough canvass and your own properly provided for?" [7] This blunt question brought from the General an equally frank confession of need: "We are doing the best we can under limitations to fulfill the promise of our Chicago representatives to take care of the state." He confessed that there were "very few Republicans in this state who are able to give very liberally to campaign uses and still a smaller number who are willing." What really troubled him, he told Reid, was the indication that the Indiana Democratic Committee "is much better supplied with funds

[5] On January 29, 1888, the United States District Court convicted two Democratic managers of election frauds and they were imprisoned. See Buley, *loc. cit.*, p. 163, and for full details see J. P. Dunn, *History of Greater Indianapolis*, I, 292–98.

[6] Buley, *loc. cit.*, p. 167.

[7] September 25, 1888, (L.C.), Vol. 42.

than our Committee." [8] Both increased Democratic activity and what he termed "unscrupulosity in Indiana" had made him uneasy. Reid undoubtedly shared this information with Elkins, who was in close touch with campaign headquarters in New York.

On October 1, 1888, Vice-Chairman Clarkson, convinced as were other party leaders that Connecticut and Indiana were crucial to the Republican cause, had informed Harrison that perhaps two of the eastern powers on the National Committee, Quay and Wanamaker, had inadvertently neglected Indiana in their efforts to secure the New York vote. Clarkson then promised Harrison that "the Executive Committee should early set aside, or determine on setting aside . . . enough means to make sure of those two states." [9] Confirming this assurance was another private note from Whitelaw Reid ridiculing the idea that Indiana could safely be left to its own resources. This time he was even more to the point: "If you people have an efficient organization by which campaign funds from the outside could still be judiciously used, I would be glad to know it." He himself pledged Harrison "a few thousand" as a personal contribution, and Clarkson followed his lead by earmarking $6,000 to help the Indiana State Committee defray expenses.[10]

Though gratified, Harrison remained uneasy. He confided to Reid that the Hoosiers were "still sailing very close to the wind," and added: "My belief is that Dem. managers are counting wholly for success upon the free use of money late in the campaign." His opposition, he charged, was "making a careful list of what they call 'floats,' " meaning "purchasable voters." [11] Undoubtedly his anxiety over this stemmed from the fear that Democrats would be able to offer a higher bribe to the "doubtful voter" than Republicans could. In fact, it seems undeniable now that workers in both parties in Indiana conducted polls which showed "where the floaters are." [12] By the middle of October, there no longer remained any

[8] September 27, 1888, *ibid.*

[9] October 1, 1888, *ibid.* Wharton Barker, as well as several United States senators, had indicated that Quay and the National Committee were concentrating on doubtful states in the East and were thereby neglecting Indiana in the matter of good speakers and campaign funds.

[10] Reid to Harrison, October 6, 1888, *ibid.*, Vol. 43.

[11] October 9, 1888, Whitelaw Reid MSS, (holograph).

[12] Matilda Gresham, *Life of Walter Q. Gresham*, II, 603–4, and Allan Nevins, *Grover Cleveland: A Study in Courage*, pp. 436–37, leave the impression that only Republicans had polled Indiana.

doubt that "the battle of the boodle" would rage on Indiana soil on Election Day, and during the hours preceding it.[13]

The history of Indiana elections showed rather clearly that, as a *Journal* editorialist pointed out, it was the "floating vote" upon which both parties had to rely for success. Whether Republican or Democrat, the rock-ribbed and buttressed voter is not disturbed by the changing tides of public opinion. Rather, said the *Journal*, it is

. . . the hundreds and thousands of voters . . . who "float" hither and thither from year to year, that the machinery and work of the contending parties are designed to influence. . . . That is what speeches are made for, papers printed for, documents issued for, polls taken for, and personal work done for, and nobody but a ninny-hammer would dream of anything else.[14]

The *Journal* spoke the truth, but not all of it. October saw strenuous efforts by both parties to lure outstanding speakers to Indiana, and after Congress adjourned Harrison himself summoned many of his Washington friends to the Hoosier stump. Also, the General goaded his state chairman, J. N. Huston, into making further strong appeals to the National Committee headquarters in New York:

. . . the Democracy are abundantly supplied with money and are using it quite lavishly and we need help. . . . we have nearly exhausted our money. . . . The enemy are importing hundreds of illegal voters and they must be watched, and I feel assured that they intend perpetrating the greatest frauds. . . . we *can certainly* carry Indiana, with help.[15]

In New York the Republican leaders understood the Hoosiers' situation well enough. Reid promised another substantial personal contribution, and Clarkson, aware of the abundance of Democratic

[13] Original charges of wholesale bribery in Indiana and elsewhere stem from rather partisan sources: Gresham, *op. cit.*, pp. 602 ff.; *Nation*, November, 1888, but especially November 22 and 29; *Sentinel*, November, December, 1888, and January, 1889; and Dunn, *op. cit.*, I, 292–309. Recent studies such as Nevins, *op. cit.*, pp. 438–39, and Eugene H. Roseboom, *History of Presidential Elections*, pp. 282–83, have accepted these stories as unquestionable. Contrary explanations have been offered by John Wanamaker, whose biographer, Herbert Adams Gibbons, *John Wanamaker*, I, 253–61, claims that "Wanamaker's defense of the large campaign fund was hard to answer." Even the legitimate expenses of a campaign of education were most costly.

[14] November 2, 1888.

[15] Huston to Elkins, October 15, 1888, Elkins MSS.

"boodle" and "their trickery in the use of it," conferred with bankers, industrial leaders, and railroad magnates in an effort to match the Democrats. Meanwhile W. H. H. Miller set off for New York to see the National Committeemen. On October 18, Chauncey Depew and Cornelius Vanderbilt paid an informal visit to Harrison at his home, news of which started the Democratic rumor that they had "left a million dollars in the state." [16] Yet Blaine himself conferred with the National Committee a week later, urging on them "the necessity of every aid to Indiana." [17]

By the end of October Harrison's correspondence breathed confidence. He advised Clarkson that "the drift is to us and has been distinctly so for a month. If we can secure an approximately fair election, I think we are safe." In this optimistic mood, the General reassured Clarkson:

I hope you will believe, that I have, at no time, felt disposed to complain. I have acted upon the theory that I was too far from the seat of war in the East to direct the movements of our forces. Grant was our greatest general, but he made a mistake in attempting to fight the battle of Nashville from City Point. Thomas, who was on the ground, knew a great deal more than he did.[18]

Prospects for Harrison's success in his home state rested, as the Indianapolis *Journal* observed, on the fact that "a large majority of legal voters" [19] were Republican. Warnings, however, against Democratic schemes involving "double-ticket frauds," the circulation of bogus ballots, and the possible disfranchisement of Negro voters, kept party workers on the alert. On the other hand, Democratic countercharges of G.O.P. chicanery filled the *Sentinel's* columns with political propaganda. This journalistic "give and take" remained fairly equal until the last day of October when behind Republican lines Indiana Democrats exploded a political bomb that could have cost General Harrison the election as well as his reputation for integrity.

On October 31, 1888, there appeared in the *Sentinel* a facsimile

16 Reported in the *Journal,* November 1, 1888.
17 Blaine to Harrison, October 25, 1888, (L.C.), Vol. 44.
18 October 27, 1888, Harrison MSS, (Indiana State Library).
19 October 29, 1888. Two days earlier Judge Gresham had been informed by D. W. Vógles: "I have little doubt about the election of Genl. Harrison, and while present indications would warrant the prediction of 10,000 maj. in Indiana, I would not be surprised at the state going for Cleveland." October 27, 1888, Gresham MSS, Vol. 37.

of the now celebrated "Blocks of Five" circular letter, dated from
New York on October 24 and bearing the apparently authentic
signature of Colonel W. W. Dudley, treasurer of the Republican
National Committee. It appeared to have been written on the
letterhead of the party's New York headquarters and to have been
destined for perusal by the Republican county leaders in Indiana.
Its message concerned "floaters" and doubtful voters, whom party
workers were to "hold" for Harrison and Hovey, thus insuring the
state a Republican plurality of 10,000. The "assistance necessary"
would come through State Chairman Huston, and the pertinent
instructions read: "Divide the floaters into blocks of five and put
a trusted man with necessary funds in charge of these five and make
him responsible that none get away and that all vote our ticket." [20]
At face value the letter seemed a clear incitement to wholesale
bribery and as such it caused tremendous consternation among
leading Republicans in Indianapolis and New York.

Press reaction followed party lines. The *Journal* immediately
attacked the letter's authenticity; its headline read: COL. DUDLEY'S
NAME FORGED. The independent *Evening News* described it editorially as "the letter of a scoundrel. We do not believe that the
Colonel wrote it; we have always regarded him as an honest man.
But if he did write it, he is a scoundrel. The letter is a plain invitation to debauch the suffrage." State Chairman Huston hurriedly
announced that "Colonel Dudley has nothing to do with the management of the Indiana campaign." In New York, Dudley, upon
seeing the newspaper facsimile, indignantly cried forgery, asserted
the innocence of his original letter, and instituted libel actions
against the three metropolitan dailies that had carried the story.[21]
Still, there remained a number of unanswered questions, and the
affair was far from settled.

If Dudley had actually written the letter, as the reproduced signature implied,[22] how had a copy fallen so soon into hostile hands?
Democrats admitted that a mail agent on the Ohio and Mississippi
Railroad (now part of the B & O system) had become curious at
the number of letters being sent to Indiana enclosed in Republican

---

[20] *Sentinel,* October 31, 1888. A facsimile (reduced one-half) has been reproduced
in Dunn, *op. cit.,* p. 299, and partial versions may be found in Gresham, *op. cit.,*
p. 604, and Nevins, *op. cit.,* p. 436.

[21] *Journal,* November 1, 3; *Sentinel,* October 31, 1888.

[22] *Journal,* November 1, 1888. Upon being interviewed, Dudley's son declared
that the signature was unlike that of his father.

National Committee envelopes. An active and loyal Democrat, the agent's suspicions got the better of him. He opened one of the letters and surmising its political importance turned it over to a leading Indiana Democrat.[23] This part of the story is probably true, for in a later memorandum, Louis T. Michener admitted that Dudley had sent identical letters to "some 90 or 100 of his friends in Indiana," including a copy for Michener's own information. The Indiana attorney general recalled:

I read it with care, found that it did no more than describe the methods of work and organization that had long been used by all parties in the state, and so I destroyed it as a letter of only passing interest, not worth preserving. I found nothing in the letter that was unusual, illegal or immoral.[24]

At the time, however, Democratic strategists had thought otherwise. They proposed to publicize the letter simultaneously in Indianapolis and New York, hoping thereby to win a decisive political advantage on the eve of the election. According to Michener, the letter was first "materially altered and enlarged so as to make it appear offensive to law and morals." It was this allegedly forged version that had now been published for the education of Hoosiers and New Yorkers.

The great uproar that greeted the letter in Indianapolis caused Harrison "much mental distress, for he and Dudley had long been intimate friends in Indianapolis and Washington." Democratic editors and orators quickly denounced Dudley and Harrison, "one for forming a hellish conspiracy and the other for his alleged intent to profit by it." [25] During the first three days of November, the *Sentinel* lashed Harrison mercilessly, enraged by the *Journal's* able

[23] Gresham, *op. cit.*, p. 605. The names of the clerk, the addressee, and the party leader were never disclosed. Also, Nevins, *op. cit.*, p. 436, gingerly states that "the letter was unquestionably authentic" and "was immediately accepted by Lucius B. Swift and other impartial Indianians." The *Sentinel,* November 3, 1888, contradicts Nevins by reporting Swift as saying: "of one thing I am convinced that the letter is a despicable forgery."

[24] "The Dudley Letter," a typed memorandum in the Michener MSS. While this explanation is quite plausible, Michener's position as a Republican party leader must be remembered, as well as the fact that he served as Dudley's law partner from 1890 to 1909.

[25] *Ibid.* Unless otherwise noted, previous quotations are culled from the above seven-page, typed memorandum, which Michener prepared in the 1920's at the request of the late Professor Albert T. Volwiler, who had planned to write a biography of Benjamin Harrison.

editorial defense of the General. The latter praised his spotless character and "the invulnerability of his career," qualities that had driven "the democratic managers to this desperate scheme." This partisan chatter the *Sentinel* termed "nauseating" to all who knew that Benjamin Harrison

. . . has for years consorted with the worst gang of political prostitutes that ever disgraced an American state; who know that he has never disavowed, repudiated, denounced, or even mildly criticized a republican rascal or a republican fraud; . . . this talk of Benjamin Harrison's spotlessness and purity is disgusting in the extreme.

Savagely pointing out that Harrison "makes long prayers in public and vaunts himself that he 'is not as other men,' " the *Sentinel* declared that "unless the General disavows and denounces William W. Dudley and his infamous program of wholesale bribery, his reputed 'spotlessness' must become a byword and a jest." [26]

Even after Michener explained personally to Harrison his belief that the "Dudley letter" was forged, the General hesitated before issuing a short public statement denying complicity. Not having seen Dudley's "true letter," his press release did no more than protect himself.[27] The Democrats still jeered, and Dudley's numerous friends felt that the General's failure to endorse the national treasurer publicly and personally amounted to a betrayal. Finally, Dudley himself, inflamed with hurt pride and overcome by sensitiveness, became decidedly bitter towards Harrison. Even after the election, though the Democrats had failed to convict him and his libel actions against the New York papers had been dropped after retractions were printed,[28] the breach between William W. Dudley and Benjamin Harrison remained.[29]

At the time, in fact, Harrison's conduct puzzled many. Yet it is understandable that, in the absence of compelling evidence, he could not immediately exonerate Dudley. He had not seen Dud-

---

[26] November 1, 2, 3, 1888.

[27] "The Dudley Letter," *loc. cit.* According to Michener, Harrison's statement appeared in "the *Journal* and other papers."

[28] *Ibid.* Michener relates that Dudley's attorneys reported that the papers concerned had offered to publish retractions if he would first dismiss the suits against them. Dudley followed their advice, whereupon each paper published a retraction consisting of a few lines in small type "buried in an obscure part of the paper where it could be found only by diligent search." Nevins, *op. cit.*, p. 437, has a different, but unsupported version.

[29] Only after the deaths of their respective wives did Dudley and Harrison finally correspond.

ley's innocent letter, and had only hearsay proof that the facsimile was a fraud. If that evidence was insufficient to clear Dudley, by the same token it was insufficient to censure him. Why, then, after the election and the inauguration, did not Harrison and Dudley get together? Michener attempted several reconciliations and found Harrison amenable. "I visited the President . . . found him as always the affectionate friend of Dudley, and he asked me to see Dudley and his wife and ask them both to visit him and Mrs. Harrison." But Dudley had friends who, according to Michener's recollections, persuaded the Colonel that the President did not really want to see him. Other friends insisted that the President ought first to vindicate him in the public print. Harrison found this impossible, and the Dudleys never came to the White House.[30]

Until election eve both parties kept the Hoosier countryside seething with rallies, picnics, processions, and the traditional barbecues. Though the Dudley affair had momentarily jarred the Republicans, the State Committee still fought fire with fire in the press and on the stump. By Saturday evening, November 3, in over twenty key areas of the state, the campaign curtain had fallen. More than 20,000 speeches had been made by prominent Republicans, and more than a million propaganda tracts had been distributed or mailed, including 300,000 lithograph pictures of Harrison and a like number of refutations of the "dollar a day lie." [31] The Republican finale came shortly after noon at Tomlinson Hall in Indianapolis on the day before election. Military bands, the marching Harrison-Morton Guards, and waves of oratory marked the occasion. The Harrison Home Glee Club, with no apologies to Stephen Foster, attempted to sum up the personalities and main issue of the campaign in one rollicking political ditty:

> Tomorrow is election day,
>   Du da, du da.
> Republicans will have their say,
>   Du da, du da day.
> The presidential nags will run
>   Du da, du da
> You bet your boots we'll have some fun,
>   Du da, du da day.

[30] "The Dudley Letter," loc. cit.
[31] Journal, November 4, 1888.

Chorus:

> We're going to work tonight
>   We're going to work all day;
> If you've any money to bet on the race
>   Don't bet on the free-trade bay.
>
> Ben Harrison is a thoroughbred,
> There are no flies upon his head,
> No clogs or heavy weights he wears,
> Protection is the flag he bears.
>
> He's a thoroughbred for a running mate,
> The fleetest in the Empire State:
> This matchless pair cannot be beat,
> And they are sure to win the heat.
>
> The free-trade scrub is inclined to kick,
> His feet are large and his neck is thick:
> He's fed on rye and British ale,
> The cockle-burrs are thick on his tail.
>
> The word is go! Around they speed,
> The thoroughbreds are away ahead;
> Behind them, blundering over the track,
> Comes free-trade scrub and British Jack.[32]

Later that same afternoon, after receiving from a Terre Haute delegation a "miniature silver-mounted plush chair, designated the 'Presidential Chair,' " [33] Harrison walked downtown to his office. Applause and cheering greeted his appearance and inspired someone to start "rolling the campaign ball" which had just arrived from Cumberland, Maryland. The great steel-ribbed sphere, weighing a thousand pounds and measuring forty-two feet in circumference and fourteen in diameter, was covered with red and white canvas. Dedicated in Cumberland, which had built a similar token for President William Henry Harrison in 1840, the sphere had been rolled through Maryland and the adjoining states, and had started towards Indiana in mid-August, stopping at principal cities in Pennsylvania, Delaware, New Jersey, New York, West Virginia, and Ohio. It was covered with dozens of campaign mottoes, arranged so as to be easily read at a distance. After some 5,000 miles of travel, the huge ball and its custodian, D. E. Brockett of Cumberland, had just reached Indianapolis. "Here it will remain," stated

---

[32] *Ibid.*, November 6, 1888.
[33] Charles Hedges (compiler), *Speeches of Benjamin Harrison*, p. 187.

Brockett, "until after the election, and then I propose rolling it to Washington." [34] On election eve he took it for a trial run down North Delaware Street to the Harrisons' home, where Carrie and the others were duly entertained by its flamboyance.

At approximately the same hour, New York City was matching and even surpassing the enthusiastic confidence that Republicans were displaying in Indianapolis. The businessmen's parade swinging along Fifth Avenue surprised even the most sanguine party leaders. Blaine wired Harrison that "the greatest political procession ever seen in New York has been passing for four hours and seems endless. Our friends are in high heart." [35]

Perhaps the day would have dragged for Harrison, waiting in Indianapolis, had it not been for the friendly letters of several National Committee members and New York workers who wrote predicting victory and joy on the morrow. Vice-Chairman James S. Clarkson, however, qualified his own prophecy by confessing that among the voters there are two quantities that "cannot be safely calculated." One, he said, was the unknown vote of "undeclared Protection Democrats" and "of Democrats disgruntled with Cleveland or their party." The other was "the silent vote of Republicans of independent income who are for Free Trade and low prices and low wages." Allied with these, wrote Clarkson, are "the influence and money of the great corporation interest, such as the Vanderbilts and Goulds and the North Pacific." [36] While numerous industrialists wanted Harrison and protection, independently wealthy railroaders and others stood to gain more by freer trade and lower payrolls.

During these final hours of great suspense only Whitelaw Reid mentioned "the Dudley business" and that was to express the hope that it had come "too late to be disastrous." [37]

Election Day was Tuesday, November 6. In the quiet of the morning a postal telegraph worker connected the Harrison home by a special wire with Republican National Committee headquarters in New York. At about 10:30 A.M. Harrison, accompanied by his son Russell, headed for Seventh Street between Delaware and Alabama where Coburn's livery stable served as the voting

[34] *Journal,* November 6, 1888.
[35] November 3, 1888, (L.C.), Vol. 45, telegram.
[36] November 2, 1888, *ibid.* This opinion serves to correct the traditional story that all vested interests favored Harrison and his party.
[37] Reid to Harrison, November 3, 1888, (L.C.), Vol. 45.

place for the third precinct of the second ward. As they drew near, a confident Republican exclaimed: "There comes the next President." The General smiled, nodded in recognition to some friends and neighbors, shook hands with one or two, then stepped inside and "presented a folded ticket that he had carried in his hand from his residence."

"Benjamin Harrison," he stated in a subdued tone with a rising inflection as his ticket, vote number 237, was deposited in the ballot-box. Shortly thereafter, Judge Byron K. Elliot and William Henry Harrison Miller voted and joined the group around Harrison. After an earnest, confidential conversation with his two friends, the General and his son "returned slowly home, the former with his eyes on the ground, saying nothing and apparently absorbed in deep thought, his son doing all the talking and gesticulating emphatically." [38] At home, after a trip to the Denison barber shop, he had another letter to read. On Saturday night, James G. Blaine had posted a letter which he had rightly calculated would reach the Republican candidate on Election Day. In it, well knowing what Harrison was enduring, he had put what moral support he could:

No man living could poll a larger Republican vote than you will receive Tuesday. I believed so before you were nominated. Every day of the campaign has confirmed my belief. Every word you have spoken has strengthened your position and you have not by commission or omission weakened yourself a tittle in any direction.

This should reach you on the morning of election day. . . . that day will be one of restlessness and I thought one more friendly assurance might agreeably engage your thoughts and your time for a few of the *slowly* moving minutes of that *dragging* period.[39]

Harrison awaited the election returns in the library of his home, where the private wire brought them in from New York in the form of bulletins. Around a large oval writing table were gathered the General, his son and son-in-law, his two law partners, and a half-dozen close friends and neighbors. As each bulletin was received, it was read aloud, "sometimes by the General, frequently by Mr. Elam or some of the other gentlemen. Mr. Russell Harrison occupied himself in assorting . . . by states." [40] During the brief intervals between bulletins, the General, "cool and self-possessed,"

[38] These details were culled from the *Sentinel*, November 7, 1888.
[39] November 4, 1888, (L.C.), Vol. 45.
[40] *Journal*, November 7, 1888.

left the library for the parlors where his wife was entertaining her feminine guests. Early returns, though scattered and few, gave the watching Republicans reassurance. About midnight most of the party left, well pleased with the reports, and at one o'clock Harrison himself retired for the night "leaving the library in the possession of his son and Mr. McKee and a few friends who remained through the night, receiving the early morning bulletins." [41]

A similar scene transpired in the White House library where President Cleveland, his wife, and a few friends kept vigil. "At midnight Secretary Whitney, crossing from the telegraph room down the second-floor corridor, announced, 'Well, it's all up.' " [42]

Although in the total popular ballot Harrison trailed Cleveland by over 90,000,[43] he had won the election by an electoral count of 233 to 168. The Republican plurality of more than 14,000 in New York, which threw 36 electoral votes into the Harrison column, proved a deciding factor. Had Cleveland carried his home state in 1888 as he had in 1884, and as he would again in 1892, he might have succeeded himself as President. Harrison, by carrying Indiana and Illinois as well as the Empire State had won a total of 73 electoral votes, which were doubled by Republican victories in Michigan, Ohio, and Pennsylvania.

Much postelection speculation centered on Cleveland's popular plurality. One estimate contended that a "slight shift in the distribution of this popular plurality" would have given Cleveland "what political wiseacres would have called a 'sweeping' victory." [44] By the same reasoning it can be argued that by adding some 2,541 votes to Harrison's slim minorities in Connecticut, Virginia, and West Virginia, he would have carried the Electoral College by 257 to 144. Such speculations, however, only serve to underscore the incontestable fact that in 1888 the popular vote was so evenly distributed that historians and statisticians have since characterized the era as "The Period of No Decision."

By early morning, Wednesday, November 7, the Harrison household found itself buried under an avalanche of telegrams, and dur-

[41] *Ibid.* It is clear that Harrison retired hopeful but uncertain, whereas the crestfallen Cleveland was convinced of his defeat by midnight.

[42] Nevins, *op. cit.,* p. 439.

[43] These and all following figures are official returns taken from W. Dean Burnham, *Presidential Ballots, 1836–1892,* pp. 141, 246–57, 887–89.

[44] Nevins, *op. cit.,* p. 439.

ing the next four days congratulatory letters arrived by the carload. Such communications overwhelmed the President-elect and more than compensated for his loss of Marion County by slightly fewer than 400 votes.[45] Amid the bushels of letters written on the day following the ballot, one contained a message and a memory especially significant to the General. Writing from his office at Fort Mason in San Francisco, Major General Oliver O. Howard conveyed the thoughts and feelings of thousands. "Dear General," the missive began,

On the tablets which hang, near the head of our bed, against the door, are the words of the day: Ask and ye shall receive, that your joy may be full. I did ask, do receive, and my joy is great. I remember you, when in your young manhood you were maneuvering your regiment near Bridgeport, Alabama. It was the first time I looked into your cheerful face. I felt stronger that you, with a noble regiment, were there. So I feel now. You have met your opponents with a cool, cheerful courage and you have already won for us a great victory. But there is more to be done. I predict for you a glorious administration at home with increased respect for our country abroad. You seem like Joshua of old who could only weaken if by any chance he forgot to consult the Lord first, before plan and before action; and who magnificently prevailed because he learned to seek first the will of Jehovah and dared to obey. Yes, it is enough for me today that General Harrison is there.[46]

When National Chairman Quay went to Indianapolis in mid-December to congratulate his chief and talk "cabinet," the Pennsylvania boss found the Hoosier still overwhelmed by victory and disposed "in true Presbyterian fashion (for he was a pious man) to believe that Providence had been on the Republican side." [47] Grasping Quay's hand, Harrison said earnestly: "Providence has given us the victory." To this explanation of how New York had been wrested from the hold of the Democrats, Quay listened politely, making no comment. Later on, disappointed by Harrison's independence in making political appointments, Quay confided to Philadelphia journalist A. K. McClure his personal sentiments. "Think of the man!" Quay exclaimed, "he ought to know that Providence hadn't a damn thing to do with it." He afterwards

[45] Buley, loc. cit., p. 185. "Harrison ran little if any ahead of the Republican State ticket. His own county went Democratic and his own precinct ran behind the Republican State ticket."

[46] November 7, 1888, (L.C.), Vol. 45.

[47] Gibbons, op. cit., I, 260.

remarked ironically that he supposed Harrison "would never know how close a number of men were compelled to approach the penitentiary to make him President." [48] Whatever truth lay behind this remark of Quay's and the Democratic charges of corruption in New York,[49] Democratic National Chairman Calvin S. Brice evidently harbored no such thoughts, at least in connection with Harrison himself. On November 9, from his Lake Erie and Western offices at 10 Wall Street, Brice heartily congratulated Harrison, adding: "You have made a great race and won the greatest prize on this earth. I do not mean the Presidency merely but the Presidency—worthy to have it and worthily won." [50]

Benjamin and Carrie Harrison were now people of destiny. As the General's college classmate, David Swing, expressed it, their victory had come "with a graceful sweep over hill and dale along the lakes and from two oceans. . . . It has come so honestly, and so full of good will toward all, so free from abuse that the campaign leaves no sting." [51] There were thousands of other letters. Typical of many was that of Republican leader Horace Porter of New York, who wrote fervently: "Every wage earner pleads more freely, every soldier of the Union holds his head a little higher and I believe Republicans everywhere stand ready to help in upholding your hands in the great work to which Providence has called you." [52] Indeed, offers of help, written and oral, overwhelmed the Harrisons and crowded their heretofore spacious home. The General, taking his own pen in hand, finally confessed to Cousin Mag:

I am worked to the verge of despair in receiving callers and trying by the aid of two stenographers and typewriters to deal with my mail. One person could not open and read the letters that come to me. I have been compelled to put them up in bales and to allow most of the ordinary letters of congratulations to go unanswered.[53]

[48] Drawing heavily from Matthew Josephson, *The Politicos, 1865-1896*, contemporary newspapers, and periodical literature, Sister Mary Lucille O'Marra, G.N.S.H., "Quay and Harrison from 1888 to 1892," pp. 13-29, summarizes the Indianapolis meeting and its aftermath.

[49] Nevins, *op. cit.*, p. 437, alleges that the final factor in Cleveland's defeat was the use of bribery in New York, and Roseboom, *op. cit.*, p. 282, suggests that in New York corruption may have affected the result.

[50] November 9, 1888, (L.C.), Vol. 46.

[51] November 12, 1888, *ibid.*

[52] *Ibid.*

[53] November 17, 1888, Messinger MSS.

From Thanksgiving Day until his departure for Washington at the end of February, President-elect Harrison was deluged with hundreds of suggestions as to whom he should choose for his official family. He was also well haunted by Hoosier applicants for federal jobs. Nevertheless, the General somehow managed to go hunting and to possess his soul in peace. He invited party leaders to submit their suggestions on patronage matters, but he kept his own counsel. For every news correspondent he had the same statement: "I am only a *listener* now and for some time to come." [54]

Carrie and Mamie escaped for a while from the confusion by going to New York on a pre-inaugural shopping tour. After their return, the General and his wife discussed and completed their plans for the journey to Washington. Having accepted the Pennsylvania Railroad's offer of a special inaugural train, they set February 25, 1889, as the date of departure. When that day dawned and the Harrisons had had breakfast, the President-elect first read aloud a chapter from the Bible, then held the usual morning prayer service in his library.[55] After that, it was time for him and Carrie to depart; the General's private secretary, E. W. Halford, has recorded that the General appeared "badly broken up. He was alone in his library for a time and full of tears when the time came to take his leave." [56]

Escorting the Harrisons to the station were Governor Hovey, Mayor Denny, General Lew Wallace, columns of G.A.R. veterans, and several thousand excited Indianapolis citizens. Thirty-two of the more prominent walked in a hollow-square formation so as to surround the President-elect's carriage with a guard of honor. As the procession moved slowly along Pennsylvania Street, the members of the Indiana legislature saluted and joined the cortege. The relatively short fifteen blocks to the depot, lined solidly with cheering admirers, took almost an hour to negotiate.

When he and Carrie finally reached the train, Harrison, not trusting his extemporaneous powers to the emotions of such an occasion, read to the crowd his moving Indianapolis farewell:

---

[54] Harrison to H. G. Davis, November 28, 1888. Elkins MSS.

[55] Elkins to Harrison, February 1, 1889, (L.C.), Vol. 64. Elkins, deeply impressed by Harrison's genuine piety, gave the story to the U. S. Press Association. See also the Elkins-owned New York *Graphic*, February 1, 1889.

[56] "Private Diary of E. W. Halford," excerpts in (L.C.) (Ac 4950 ADD. 7). According to the late Professor Volwiler, *op. cit.*, p. 3, Halford read portions of his diary to him, then burned it. Hence, the excerpts in the Harrison MSS were undoubtedly placed there by Volwiler himself.

My Good Friends and Neighbors: I cannot trust myself to put in words what I feel at this time. Every kind thought that is in your minds and every good wish that is in your hearts for me finds its responsive wish and thought in my mind and heart for each of you.

I love this city. It has been my own cherished home. Twice before I have left it to discharge public duties and returned to it with gladness, as I hope to do again. It is a city on whose streets the pompous displays of wealth are not seen. It is full of pleasant homes, and in these homes there is an unusual store of contentment.

The memory of your favor and kindness will abide with me, and my strong desire to hold your respect and confidence will strengthen me in the discharge of my new and responsible duties. Let me say farewell to all my Indiana friends. For the public honors that have come to me I am their grateful debtor. They have made the debt so large that I can never discharge it.

There is a great sense of loneliness in the discharge of high public duties. The moment of decision is one of isolation. But there is One whose help comes even into the quiet chamber of judgment, and to His wise and unfailing guidance will I look for direction and safety. My family unite with me in grateful thanks for this cordial good-bye and with me wish that these years of separation may be full of peace and happiness for each of you.[57]

On board the train at last, bound for Washington and the greatest honor within the gift of the American people, the thoughts of Carrie and Ben Harrison must have turned back to the letter he had sent her at the end of the Civil War. Protesting "a heart brimful of love," he had then written, with a soldier's fervor:

I have a good hope that by mutual help and by God's help, we may live the residue of our lives without having our heart's sunshine clouded by a single shade of mistrust or anger. I know it is possible and I would rather succeed in such an effort than to have the highest honors of earth. . . .[58]

Now, twenty-three years later, President-elect and Mrs. Harrison were still very much in love, and one of "the highest honors of earth" lay before them.

[57] Hedges, *op. cit.*, p. 191, and Halford's Diary, *loc. cit.*, entry for February 25, 1889.
[58] Harrison to his wife, May 21, 1865, (L.C.), Vol. 6. For the complete letter, see Harry J. Sievers, *Benjamin Harrison: Hoosier Warrior*, pp. 315–17.

Bibliography

Bibliography

Manuscript Sources

The primary sources for the mature years (1865–1888) in the career of Benjamin Harrison include:

1. The extensive Benjamin Harrison collection housed in the Division of Manuscripts, Library of Congress. Closed to the public and research historians alike until 1948, this is the richest font of information. Described by the Division of Manuscripts card as "Papers of Benjamin Harrison (1833–1901), lawyer, soldier, U.S. Senator, 23rd President of the U.S. Family letters and other papers covering the civil war period, a large body of papers representing the period of his service as a U.S. Senator, legal and official papers covering his post-presidential career in law, letter-books, scrap-books, etc., dated 1858–1931."
A serviceable breakdown of these materials is as follows:

183 volumes (bound) of approximately 40,000 pieces which, in the judgment of the curator of the Manuscripts Division deal primarily with Harrison's public life and activities.

55 manuscript boxes (red) judged by library authorities as not pertaining to the public and/or political aspects of Harrison's life. They contain, however, much material essential to the biographer.

58 volumes (bound) of newspaper clippings, now known as the Benjamin Harrison Scrapbook Series. Invaluable material on every phase of Harrison's private as well as his public life.

18 manuscript boxes of Tibbott transcripts. Everard F. Tibbott, once an Associated Press reporter, became Senator Harrison's secretary and remained with him through the presidential and post-presidential years.

8 manuscript boxes: "The Tibbott short hand books." Long after Harrison's death, Tibbott transcribed these thousands of letters from his own stenographic notebooks. These are the contents of the above-mentioned eighteen manuscript boxes of Tibbott transcripts.

7 manuscript boxes of "Legal material from 1851–1900."

3 manuscript boxes of Harrison and Wallace Law Firm correspondence.

80 manuscript boxes of miscellaneous materials: personal bills, checks, notes, lectures, photographs, galley proofs, invitations, guest lists, pamphlets, telegrams, memorials, etc.

2. The next largest collection of Benjamin Harrison Papers is in the private possession of James Blaine Walker and family, New York City. President Harrison's son-in-law, James Blaine Walker, and his two children, Benjamin Harrison Walker and Dr. Jane Harrison Walker, have been most courteous in placing these papers at the author's disposal.

Rich biographical material, including diaries, letters, and Harrisoniana, has helped in drawing an accurate portrait of Benjamin Harrison. Items in this collection extend from 1781 to 1935.

3. The Messinger Collection. These letters from Benjamin Harrison to "Cos. Mag," Mrs. Margaret Peltz of St. Louis, cover the period 1877–1901. They are now in the possession of Mrs. Clarence W. Messinger, Houghton, Michigan, a granddaughter of Mrs. Peltz. The author is grateful for her generosity in making copies of the letters available to him.

4. Some private and family papers are on file at the President Benjamin Harrison Memorial Home, 1230 North Delaware Street, Indianapolis, Indiana. Personal diaries and financial accounts have provided rich biographical information.

5. A select collection of Benjamin Harrison Papers is also housed in the Indiana Division of the Indiana State Library (Indianapolis).

Sundry items are scattered in the approximately fifty collections. catalogued and indexed, covering the years 1855–1901.

6. Russell B. Harrison Collection. Stored for half a century in the basement of the Terre Haute (Indiana) Savings Bank, these papers were rescued by the Vigo County Historical Society with headquarters in that city. Here, by kind permission of former Congressman William Henry Harrison, son of Colonel Russell Harrison and grandson of President Benjamin Harrison, the author researched the entire collection. These papers are now in the custody of the University of Indiana Library, Bloomington, Indiana.

7. The papers of William Henry Harrison Miller, Benjamin Harrison's law partner for a quarter of a century and his Attorney General (1889–1893), were loaned to the author. Particularly valuable were the letter books.

8. Other manuscript collections contain material pertinent to Harrison's character and place in history. They have been examined by the author with a view to forming an over-all, mature value-judgment of

Benjamin Harrison. In the Division of Manuscripts, Library of Congress, the most helpful were the papers of:

Nelson W. Aldrich, Wharton Barker, Thomas F. Bayard, Jeremiah S. Black, James G. Blaine, the Blair family, the Breckinridge family, Benjamin H. Bristow, W. P. Bynum, Howard Cale, Simon Cameron, Andrew Carnegie, William E. Chandler, Zachariah Chandler, James S. Clarkson, Grover Cleveland, Chauncey M. Depew, Don M. Dickinson, William Evarts, John W. Foster, William Dudley Foulke, James A. Garfield, Walter Q. Gresham, Eugene Hale, John Scott Harrison, Joseph R. Hawley, Eugene Gano Hay, John Hay, Horatio King, Daniel S. Lamont, Gates McCarrah Collection of Presidential Autographs, William McKinley, Daniel Manning, Manton Marble, Louis T. Michener, John T. Morgan, Justin S. Morrill, Harry S. New, Richard Olney, Matthew S. Quay, Theodore Roosevelt, Carl Schurz, John Sherman, William T. Sherman, the Short family, John C. Spooner, R. W. Thompson, John Toner, Benjamin F. Tracy, Henry Watterson, William C. Whitney, John Russell Young.

9. Other archival collections which yielded material were:

The papers of G. F. Chittenden, John Coburn, Schuyler Colfax, Lucius C. Embree, Oliver P. Morton, O. A. Sommers, Benjamin Spooner, R. S. Taylor, R. W. Thompson and W. W. Thornton—all in the Indiana State Library, Indianapolis.

The papers of John Hanna in the Indiana University Library, Bloomington, Indiana.

The papers of William H. English in the William Henry Smith Memorial Library, Indianapolis. There are 3,875 pieces relating to the affairs of English, a leading Indiana businessman, Congressman, Democrat, and historian.

The papers of George S. Bixby in the Manuscripts Division, New York State Library, Albany, New York. Letters, diaries, and scrapbooks pertaining to New York politics are prolific; also a manuscript copy of "Life and Times of David B. Hill" by George S. Bixby.

The papers of Silas W. Burt and the William T. Sherman Scrapbooks, New York Historical Society, New York City.

The papers of John Bigelow and Levi P. Morton in the Manuscripts Division, New York Public Library, New York City.

The papers of William Boyd Allison, James S. Clarkson, Grenville M. Dodge, and John A. Kasson in the Historical Memorial and Art Department of Iowa, Des Moines, Iowa.

The papers of Nils P. Haugen, Henry Demarest Lloyd, Jeremiah Rusk, Ellis Usher, and William F. Vilas in the State Historical Society of Wisconsin, Madison, Wisconsin.

The papers of Chauncey M. Depew, Yale University Library, New Haven, Connecticut.

The papers of S. B. Elkins, University of West Virginia Archives, Morgantown, West Virginia.

The papers of Joseph R. Hawley, State Library, Hartford, Connecticut.

The papers of William T. Sherman in the private possession of Miss Eleanor Sherman Fitch, New York City.

The papers of William Henry Smith, Ohio State Archaeological and Historical Society Archives, Columbus, Ohio.

The papers of John Wanamaker, Wanamaker's Department Store, Philadelphia, Pennsylvania.

The diary and papers of Bishop Francis Silas Chatard in the Cathedral Archives, Indianapolis.

The papers of James Cardinal Gibbons in the archives of the Archdiocese of Baltimore, Baltimore, Maryland.

The papers of Terence V. Powderly in the Mullen Library of The Catholic University of America, Washington, D. C.

The papers of Whitelaw Reid in the possession of the Reid Estate and stored in the Tribune Tower Building, New York City. The Division of Manuscripts, Library of Congress, recently acquired this collection.

The Harrison-Hayes Correspondence, photostated at the Rutherford B. Hayes Memorial Library, Fremont, Ohio.

Harrison items in the André deCoppet Collection housed at the Princeton University Library; likewise photostats obtained from the Pennsylvania Historical Society and the Presbyterian Historical Society, both located in Philadelphia.

Marthena Harrison Williams and William Henry Harrison Collections (privately held) yielded diary material, letters, and photographs.

The Diary of Caroline Scott Harrison and family letters in the possession of Katherine Scott Brooks, Washington, D. C.

The papers of Richard W. Thompson. Photostats furnished by the Lincoln National Life Foundation, Fort Wayne, Indiana.

10. Pertinent newspaper material is found in the following: Atlanta *Journal,* Boston *Daily Advertiser,* Boston *Herald,* Boston *Post,* Boston *Sunday Herald,* Buffalo *Evening Telegraph,* Chicago *Inter-Ocean,* Chicago *Times,* Chicago *Tribune,* Cincinnati *Commercial,* Cincinnati *Enquirer,* Cincinnati *Gazette,* Cincinnati *Times, Columbia* (S. C.) *Record,* Des Moines *Register,* Detroit *News,* Detroit *Tribune,* Evansville *Journal,* Fort Wayne *Sentinel,* Frankfort (Indiana) *Banner,* Helena (Montana) *Independent,* Huntington (Indiana) *Herald,* Independence (Missouri) *Sentinel,* Indianapolis *Daily Sentinel,* Indianapolis *Evening News,* Indianapolis *Journal,* Indianapolis *News,* Indianapolis *Sun, Iowa State Register,* Janesville (Wisconsin) *Gazette,* Kansas City *Mirror,* Kansas City *Times,* Kennebec (Maine) *Journal,* Lafayette (Indiana) *Courier,* La Porte (Indiana) *Argus,* Lebanon *Patriot,* Louisville *Courier-Journal,* Madison *Courier,* Memphis *Daily Avalanche,* Memphis *Evening Scimitar,* New Orleans *Times-Democrat,* New York *Daily Tribune,* New York *Evening Post,* New York *Mail and Express,* New York

Times, New York *World,* Norwich (Conn.) *Record,* Omaha *Bee,* Omaha *Daily Republican,* Parke County (Indiana) *Republican,* Petersburg *Press,* Philadelphia *Times,* Providence (R. I.) *Journal,* Raleigh (N. C.) *News and Observer,* Richmond (Virginia) *Dispatch,* Rochester (New York) *Morning Herald,* Springfield (Massachusetts) *Republican,* St. Louis *Post-Dispatch,* St. Paul (Minnesota) *Pioneer Press,* Syracuse *Herald,* Terre Haute *Daily and Weekly Courier,* Topeka (Kansas) *Mail,* Washington (D. C.) *Evening Star.*

In addition to a plenitude of identified newspaper clippings, which form the bulk of the fifty-eight volume Scrapbook Series in the Harrison Papers (Library of Congress), attention is called to a valuable three-volume Scrapbook Series in the Indiana State Library, the gift of Russell B. Harrison, the President's son. Its chief merit lies in the universal newspaper coverage given to the death and funeral of Benjamin Harrison in 1901. Russell Harrison had subscribed to several clipping services, and carefully preserved the unfavorable as well as favorable news and editorial comment.

Published Sources

Adams, Charles Francis. *Charles Francis Adams, 1835–1915: An Autobiography.* Boston and New York, Houghton, 1916.

Adams, Henry. *The Education of Henry Adams.* New York, Modern Library, 1931.

Alexander, DeAlva S. *Four Famous New Yorkers.* New York, Holt, 1923.

Alsberg, Henry G. (editor). *The American Guide.* New York, Hastings House, 1949.

Alumni and Former Student Catalogue of Miami University, 1809–1892. Oxford, Ohio, 1892.

American Newspaper Directory. New York, G. P. Rowell and Co., 1892.

Appleton's Annual Cyclopedia (for the years 1881 through 1888). New York, Appleton, 1881–88.

Bailey, Thomas A. *A Diplomatic History of the American People.* New York, F. S. Crofts & Co., Inc., 1946. 3d ed.

Banks, Louis A. *Religious Life of Famous Americans.* New York, Burr Printing House, 1904.

Barnard, Harry. *Rutherford B. Hayes and His America.* New York and Indianapolis, Bobbs-Merrill, 1954.

Barnhart, John D., and Carmony, Donald F. *Indiana: From Frontier to Industrial Commonwealth.* 2 vols. New York, Lewis Historical Publishing Co., 1954.

Barrett, Don C. *The Greenbacks and the Resumption of Specie Payments.* Cambridge, Mass., Harvard University Press, 1931.

Beer, Thomas. *Hanna*. New York, Knopf, 1929.

Benjamin Harrison Memorial Commission, Report of (77th Cong., 1st Sess., House Doc. No. 154). Washington, D. C., Government Printing Office, 1941.

Bernardo, C. J. "The Presidential Election of 1888." Unpublished doctoral dissertation, Washington, D. C., Georgetown University, 1949.

Biographical Directory of the American Congress, 1774–1949. Compiled by James L. Harrison. Washington, D. C., Government Printing Office, 1950.

Blaine, James G. *Twenty Years of Congress: From Lincoln to Garfield*. Norwich, Conn., The Henry Bell Publishing Co., 1884–1886.

Blaine, Walker. "Why Harrison Was Elected!" *The North American Review*, 147 (1888), 686–95.

Blake, Nelson. *William Mahone of Virginia, Soldier and Political Insurgent*. Richmond, Garrett and Massie, 1935.

Bowers, Claude G. *Beveridge and The Progressive Era*. Boston, Houghton Mifflin Co., 1932.

Boyd, James P. *Life and Public Services of Benjamin Harrison, Twenty-third President of the United States*. Philadelphia, Publishers Union, 1901.

Bridges, C. A. "The Knights of the Golden Circle: A Filibustering Fantasy," *Southwestern Historical Quarterly*, 44 (1940–41), 287–302.

Brown, Hilton U. *A Book of Memories*. Indianapolis, Butler University, 1951.

Brown, Ignatius. *History of Indianapolis from 1818 to the Present*. Published as part of *Indianapolis Directory, 1868* (*q.v. infra*).

Buley, R. C. "The Campaign of 1888 in Indiana," *Indiana Magazine of History*, 10 (1914), 162–85.

Burnett, Howard R. "The Last Pioneer Governor of Indiana—'Blue Jeans' Williams," *Indiana Magazine of History*, 22 (1926), 101–30.

Burnham, W. Dean. *Presidential Ballots, 1836–1892*. Baltimore, Johns Hopkins Press, 1955.

Carleton, William G. "The Money Question in Indiana Politics, 1865–1890," *Indiana Magazine of History*, 42 (1946), 107–50.

———. "Why Was the Democratic Party in Indiana a Radical Party, 1865–1900?" *Indiana Magazine of History*, 42 (1946), 207–28.

Carmichael, O. B. "The Campaign of 1876 in Indiana," *Indiana Magazine of History*, 9 (1913), 276–97.

Carter, Alfred G.W. *The Old Court House*. Cincinnati, P. G. Thompson, 1880.

Cary, Edward. *George William Curtis*. Boston and New York, Houghton, Mifflin and Co., 1894.

Centennial Memorial (1823–1923): First Presbyterian Church, Indianapolis, Indiana. Greenfield, Indiana, Mitchell Printing Co., 1925.

Chester, Giraud. *Embattled Maiden: The Life of Anna Dickinson.* New York, G. P. Putnam's Sons, 1951.

Chidsey, Donald Barr. *The Gentleman from New York: A Life of Roscoe Conkling.* New Haven, Yale University Press, 1935.

Clancy, Herbert J., S.J. *The Presidential Election of 1880.* Chicago, Loyola University Press, 1958.

Clarke, Grace Julian. *George W. Julian.* Indianapolis, Indiana Historical Commission, 1923.

Cleaves, Freeman. *Old Tippecanoe.* New York, Scribner's, 1939.

————. *Rock of Chickamauga: The Life of General George H. Thomas.* Norman, Okla., University of Oklahoma Press, 1948.

Clyde, Paul H. *United States Policy Toward China.* Durham, N. C., Duke University Press, 1940.

Coleman, Charles H. *The Election of 1868.* New York, Columbia University Press, 1933.

————. "The Use of the Term 'Copperhead' During the Civil War," *Mississippi Valley Historical Review,* 25 (1938), 236–64.

Colman, Edna M. *White House Gossip: From Andrew Johnson to Calvin Coolidge.* New York, Doubleday, Page and Co., 1927.

Columbia Encyclopedia, in one volume. Edited by William Bridgewater and Elizabeth J. Sherwood. New York, Columbia University Press, 1950. 2d ed.

Congressional Directory, 1881 (47th Cong., 1st Sess.). Washington, D. C., Government Printing Office, 1881.

Congressional Record, 1881–1887. Washington, D. C., Government Printing Office, 11–19 (1881–1888).

Cortissoz, Royal. *The Life of Whitelaw Reid.* New York, Charles Scribner's Sons, 1921. 2 vols.

Crandall, Andrew W. *The Early History of the Republican Party, 1854–1856.* Boston, R. G. Badger, 1930.

Crenshaw, Ollinger. "The Knights of the Golden Circle," *American Historical Review,* 47 (1941–1942), 23–50.

Crook, W. H. *Memories of the White House.* Boston, Little, 1911.

Current, R. N. *Pine Logs and Politics, A Life of Philetus Sawyer, 1816–1900.* Madison, State Historical Society of Wisconsin, 1950.

Davis, William W. "The Civil War and Reconstruction in Florida." Unpublished doctoral dissertation. New York, Columbia University, 1913.

Dearing, Mary R. *Veterans in Politics.* Baton Rouge, Louisiana State University Press, 1952.

DeSantis, Vincent P. "Benjamin Harrison and the Republican Party in the South," *Indiana Magazine of History,* 51 (1955), 279–302.

Dodge, Mary Abigail. *Biography of James G. Blaine.* Norwich, Conn., The Henry Bell Publishing Co., 1895.

Dowdey, Clifford. "The Harrisons of Berkeley Hundred," *American Heritage,* 8 (April, 1957), 58–70.

Dunn, J. P. *History of Greater Indianapolis*. Chicago, Lewis, 1910. 2 vols.

———. *Indiana and Indianians*. Chicago and New York, American Historical Society, 1919. 5 vols.

Earhart, Mary. *Frances Willard: From Prayers to Politics*. Chicago, University of Chicago Press, 1944.

Eckenrode, H. J. *Rutherford B. Hayes, Statesman of Reunion*. New York, Dodd, Mead & Co., 1930.

Edwards, Linden F. "The Anatomy Law of 1881," *The Ohio State Medical Journal*, 46–47 (1950–1951). Columbus, The Ohio State Medical Association.

Elam, Harvey W. *The Elam Family*. Xenia, Ohio, privately published, 1933.

Esarey, Logan. *A History of Indiana*. Indianapolis, B. F. Bowen, 1918. 2 vols.

Fesler, Mayo. "Secret Political Societies in the North During the War," *Indiana Magazine of History*, 14 (1918), 183–286.

Fish, Carl Russell. *The Civil Service and the Patronage*. New York, Longmans, Green & Co., 1905.

Fleming, E. McClung. *R. R. Bowker: The Militant Liberal*. Norman, Okla., University of Oklahoma Press, 1952.

Flick, Alexander C. (with Lobrano, G. S.). *Samuel Jones Tilden: A Study in Political Sagacity*. New York, Dodd, Mead & Co., 1939.

Foraker, Joseph B. *Notes of A Busy Life*. Cincinnati, Stewart and Kidd Co., 1916.

Foster, Harriet McIntire. *Mrs. Benjamin Harrison*. Indianapolis, privately published, 1908.

Foulke, William Dudley. *A Hoosier Autobiography*. New York, Oxford University Press, 1922.

———. *Fighting the Spoilsmen*. New York and London, G. P. Putnam's Sons, 1919.

———. *Life of Oliver P. Morton*. Indianapolis, Bowen-Merrill Co., 1899. 2 vols.

———. *Lucius B. Swift: American Citizen*. New York and Indianapolis, The Bobbs-Merrill Co., 1930.

Fowler, Dorothy Ganfield. *The Cabinet Politician: The Postmasters General, 1828–1909*. New York, Columbia University Press, 1943.

Furber, H. W. (editor). *Which? Protection or Free Trade*. Boston, Boston Publishing Co., 1888.

Fuess, Claude M. *Carl Schurz, Reformer*. New York, Dodd, Mead & Co., 1932.

Garis, Roy L. *Immigration Restriction*. New York, The Macmillan Co., 1927.

Gibbons, Herbert Adams. *John Wanamaker*. New York, Harper Brothers, 1926. 2 vols.

Gibson, A. M. *A Political Crime: The History of the Great Fraud*. New York, Wm. S. Gottsberger, Publisher, 1885.

Glasson, William Henry. *History of Military Pension Legislation in the United States.* New York, Columbia University Press, 1900.

Gray, Wood. *The Hidden Civil War.* New York, The Viking Press, 1942.

Grayston, Florence L. "Lambdin P. Milligan—A Knight of the Golden Circle," *Indiana Magazine of History*, 43 (1947), 379–91.

Green, James A. *William Henry Harrison: His Times.* Cincinnati, Garrett, 1941.

Gresham, Matilda. *Life of Walter Q. Gresham.* Chicago, Rand, McNally and Co., 1919. 2 vols.

Griffiths, John L., *An address by* (October 27, 1908, Indianapolis, Ind.) on the occasion of the unveiling of the statue of Benjamin Harrison; pp. 21–31 in *The Addresses* by Charles W. Fairbanks, John W. Noble, John L. Griffiths; and in *Poems* by James Whitcomb Riley. Indianapolis, Hollenbeck Press, 1909.

Guese, Lucius E. "St. Louis and the Great Whiskey Ring," *Missouri Historical Review*, 36 (1942), 160–83.

Gwynn, Stephen (editor). *The Letters and Friendships of Sir Cecil Spring Rice: A Record.* London, Constable and Co., Ltd., 1929.

Harney, Gilbert L. *The Lives of Benjamin Harrison and Levi P. Morton.* Providence, R. I., J. A. and R. A. Reid, 1888.

Harrison, Benjamin, *Reception Speeches of.* Indianapolis, Republican State Central Committee, 1888.

———. *Views of An Ex-President.* Compiled by Mary Lord Harrison. Indianapolis, Bowen-Merrill, 1901.

Harrison, John Scott. *Pioneer Life at North Bend.* Cincinnati, Robert Clarke, 1867.

Harrison, Short Review of the Public and Private Life of Gen'l Benj. (a campaign pamphlet). Indianapolis, copyrighted by C. A. Nicoli, 1888.

Haworth, Paul L. *The Hayes-Tilden Election.* New York and Indianapolis, The Bobbs-Merrill Co., 1927.

———. *Reconstruction and Union, 1865–1912.* New York, Henry Holt & Co., 1912.

Hedges, Charles (compiler). *Speeches of Benjamin Harrison.* New York, Lovell, Coryell and Co., 1892.

Hendrick, Burton J. *Life of Andrew Carnegie.* Garden City, Doubleday, Doran & Co., 1932.

Henry, R. B. *Genealogies of the Families of the Presidents.* Rutland, Vt., Tuttle, 1935.

Hepburn, A. Barton. *A History of Currency in the United States.* New York, Macmillan, 1924 (revised edition).

Hesseltine, William. *U. S. Grant.* New York, Dodd, Mead & Co., 1935.

Hiatt, Joel W. (editor). "Diary of William Owen," *Indiana Historical Society Publications*, 4 (1906), 7–134.

Hinsdale, Mary L. (editor). *Garfield-Hinsdale Letters*. Ann Arbor, University of Michigan Press, 1949.

"History of the Columbia Club," *The Columbian*, 28 (February, 1957), 3, 45.

Hoar, George F. *Autobiography of Seventy Years*. New York, Charles Scribner's Sons, 1903. 2 vols.

Holbrook, Stewart H. *The Age of the Moguls*. Garden City, Doubleday & Co., 1953.

———. *James J. Hill: A Great Life in Brief*. New York, Knopf, 1955.

Holcombe, John W., and Skinner, Hubert M. *Life and Public Services of Thomas A. Hendricks*. Indianapolis, Carlon and Hollenbeck, 1886.

Holliday, J. H. "Indianapolis and the Civil War," *Indianapolis Historical Society Publications*, 4 (1911), 525–95.

Holloway, W. R. *Indianapolis*. Indianapolis, Journal Print, 1870.

Hood, John Bell. *Advance and Retreat: Personal Experiences in the United States and Confederate Armies*. New Orleans, privately printed by Hood Orphan Memorial Fund, 1880.

Indiana, *Report of the Adjutant General, 1865–1869*. Indianapolis, Journal Print, 1870. 8 vols.

———, *Senate Journal*, 1887.

———, "Minutes Book of 70th Indiana Regiment Association: October, 1877–August, 1938," in the Benjamin Harrison Memorial Home, Indianapolis.

Indianapolis Directory, 1868. Indianapolis, Logan and Co., 1868.

Isely, Bliss. *The Presidents: Men of Faith*. Boston, W. A. Wilde Co., 1953.

Josephson, Matthew. *The Politicos, 1865–1919*. New York, Harcourt, Brace, 1938.

———. *The Robber Barons: The Great American Capitalists, 1861–1901*. New York, Harcourt, Brace & Co., 1934.

Juettner, Otto. *Daniel Drake and His Followers*. Cincinnati, Harvey Publishing Co., 1909.

Julian, George W. *Political Recollections, 1840–1872*. Chicago, Jansen, McClurg, 1884.

Keith, Charles P. *The Ancestry of Benjamin Harrison*. Philadelphia, Lippincott, 1893.

Kennedy, James H. *History of the Ohio Society of New York, 1885–1905*. New York, Grafton Press, 1906.

Kenworthy, Leonard S. *The Tall Sycamore of the Wabash: Daniel Wolsey Voorhees*. Boston, Humphries, 1936.

Klaus, S. (editor). *The Milligan Case*. New York, Knopf, 1929.

Lamar, Howard Roberts. *Dakota Territory, 1861–1889: A Study of Frontier Politics*. New Haven, Yale University Press, 1956.

Lambert, Oscar Doane. *Stephen Benton Elkins: American Foursquare*. Pittsburgh, University of Pittsburgh Press, 1955.

Lang, Louis J. (editor). *The Autobiography of Thomas Collier Platt*. New York, B. W. Dodge & Co., 1910.

Latham, Charles G., Jr. "Benjamin Harrison in the Senate, 1881–1887." Senior thesis. Princeton, N. J., Princeton University. Copy in Indiana State Library, Indianapolis.

Lewis, Lloyd. *Sherman: The Fighting Prophet.* New York, Harcourt, Brace, 1932.

Leach, Frank W. *Twenty Years with Quay.* Philadelphia, North American, 1904.

Livermore, Thomas L. *Numbers and Losses in the Civil War in America, 1861–1865.* Boston, Houghton, 1901.

Lockridge, Ross F., Jr. "The Harrisons," published as Exhibit 2, pp. 19–210 in *Report of Benjamin Harrison Memorial Commission (q.v. supra).*

Lodge, Henry Cabot. *Selections from the Correspondence of Theodore Roosevelt and Henry Cabot Lodge, 1884–1918.* New York, Charles Scribner's Sons, 1925.

Lorant, Stefan. *The Presidency.* New York, Macmillan, 1951.

McCall, Samuel W. *The Life of Thomas B. Reed.* Boston, Houghton Mifflin, 1917 *(American Statesmen,* Vol. 35).

McDonald, John. *Secrets of the Great Whiskey Ring.* Chicago, Belford, Clarke and Co., 1880.

McElroy, Robert. *Levi Parsons Morton: Banker, Diplomat and Statesman.* New York and London, G. P. Putnam's Sons, 1930.

McKee, Irving. *"Ben-Hur" Wallace.* Berkeley and Los Angeles, University of California Press, 1947.

McMurry, Donald L. "The Political Significance of the Pension Question, 1885–1897," *Mississippi Valley Historical Review,* 9 (1922), 19–36.

McPherson, Edward. *Handbook for Politics, 1882.* Washington, J. J. Chapman, 1882.

Magmer, James, S.J. "President Benjamin Harrison and the Columbian Club," *The Columbian,* 16 (1953), 16.

Marshall, Carrington T. *History of the Courts and Lawyers of Ohio.* New York, American Historical Society, Inc., 1934. 4 vols.

Marshall, John A. *American Bastille.* Philadelphia, T. W. Hartley, 1870.

Marshall, Thomas R. *Recollections of Thomas R. Marshall: A Hoosier Salad.* Indianapolis, The Bobbs-Merrill Co., 1925.

Martin, Asa E. *After the White House.* State College of Pennsylvania, Penn's Valley Publishers, Inc., 1951.

Martin, John Barlow. *Indiana: An Interpretation.* New York, Knopf, 1947.

Merriam, George S. *The Life and Times of Samuel Bowles.* New York, The Century Co., 1885. 2 vols.

Merrill, Samuel. *The Seventieth Indiana Volunteer Infantry.* Indianapolis, Bowen-Merrill, 1900.

Mississippi River Commission, Minority Report of (46th Cong., 2d Sess., Executive Document 58). Washington, D. C., Government Printing Office, 1879.

Moore, John Bassett. *International Arbitrations,* Vol. I. [n.p.] The Crane Press, 1914.

Moos, Malcolm. *The Republicans: A History of Their Party.* New York, Random House, 1956.

Morison, Elting (editor). *The Letters of Theodore Roosevelt.* Cambridge, Mass., Harvard University Press, 1951. 8 vols.

Morison, J. E., and Lane, W. B. *Life of Our President Benjamin Harrison.* Cincinnati, published for Morison and Lane, 1889.

Mott, Frank Luther. *American Journalism: A History of Newspapers in the United States Through 250 Years, 1690–1940.* New York, Macmillan Co., 1941.

Muzzey, David S. *James G. Blaine, A Political Idol of Other Days.* New York, Dodd, Mead & Co., 1934.

Myers, William Starr. *The Republican Party.* New York and London, The Century Co., 1931.

Nevins, Allan. *Grover Cleveland: A Study in Courage.* New York, Dodd, Mead & Co., 1932.

—— (editor). *Letters of Grover Cleveland.* Boston, Houghton Mifflin, 1933.

——. *Hamilton Fish: The Inner History of the Grant Administration.* New York, Dodd, Mead & Co., 1936.

——. *The Ordeal of Union.* New York, Charles Scribner's Sons, 1947. 2 vols.

"News from the Maryland Gazette," *Maryland Historical Magazine,* 17 (1922), 364–79.

Noble, John W., *An Address by,* pp. 7–18 in *The Addresses* by Charles W. Fairbanks, John W. Noble, John L. Griffiths (see Griffiths, *supra*). Indianapolis, Hollenbeck Press, 1909.

Nolan, Jeannette C. *Hoosier City, The Story of Indianapolis.* New York, Messner, 1943.

Northrop, Henry D. *The Life and Public Service of Gen. Benj. Harrison.* Philadelphia, Globe Bible Publishing Co., 1888.

Nye, Russell B. *Midwestern Progressive Politics.* East Lansing, Mich., Michigan State College Press, 1951.

Oberholtzer, Ellis P. *A History of the United States Since the Civil War.* New York, Macmillan Co., 1917–1937. 5 vols.

O'Connor, Richard. *Thomas: Rock of Chickamauga.* New York, Prentice-Hall, 1948.

Oliver, John W. *History of the Civil War Military Pensions, 1861–1885.* Madison, University of Wisconsin, 1917.

O'Marra, Sister Mary Lucille, G.N.S.H. "Quay and Harrison, 1888–1892." Unpublished master's thesis. Washington, D. C., The Catholic University of America, 1956.

Paine, Albert B. *Thomas Nast: His Period and His Pictures.* New York, Macmillan, 1904.

Palmer, Walter B. *The History of Phi Delta Theta.* Menasha, Wisc., George Banta Publishing Co., 1906.

Pearson, Charles C. *The Readjuster Movement in Virginia.* New Haven, Yale University Press, 1917.

Peck, Harry Thurston. *Twenty Years of the Republic, 1885–1905.* New York, Dodd, Mead & Co., 1907.

Perling, Joseph J. *Presidents' Sons.* New York, Odyssey Press, 1947.

Pitman, Benn (editor). *Trials for Treason in Indianapolis, 1864.* Cincinnati, 1865.

Platt, T. C. *The Autobiography of Thomas Collier Platt.* Edited by Louis J. Lang. New York, B. W. Dodge and Co., 1910.

Pollard, James E. *The Presidents and the Press.* New York, Macmillan, 1947.

Proceedings of the Republican National Convention, 1880. Reported by Eugene Davis. Chicago, The J. B. Jeffrey Printing and Publishing House, 1881.

Proceedings of the Republican National Convention, 1888. Reported by Gustavus P. English. Chicago, printed by order of the Republican National Committee, 1888.

Proceedings of the Republican State Convention, 1872. Indianapolis, Republican State Committee, 1872.

Putnam, Carleton. *Theodore Roosevelt: The Formative Years, 1858–1886.* Vol. 1. New York, Charles Scribner's Sons, 1958.

Randall, James G. *Constitutional Problems Under Lincoln.* New York, D. Appleton, 1926.

———. *Civil War and Reconstruction.* Boston, D. C. Heath & Co., 1937.

———. *Lincoln the President.* New York, Dodd, Mead & Co., 1946. 2 vols.

Ray, P. Orman. "The Milligan Case (1866)," *Dictionary of American History,* Vol. 3. New York, Scribner's, 1942. 2d ed. rev.

Rhodes, J. F. *History of the United States from the Compromise of 1850.* New York, The Macmillan Co., 1928. 9 vols.

Richardson, James D. (editor). *A Compilation of the Messages and Papers of the Presidents, 1789–1897.* Washington, 1907; New York, Bureau of National Literature, Inc., 1917. 10 vols.

Rives, F.S.J. *Congressional Globe.* Containing the debates and proceedings of the first session of the 39th Congress. Washington, D. C., Congressional Globe Office, 1866. 5 vols.

Roach, A. C. *The Cold Springs Tragedy.* Indianapolis, privately published, 1869.

Roll, Charles. *Col. Dick Thompson: The Persistent Whig.* Indianapolis, Indiana Historical Bureau, 1948.

Roseboom, Eugene H. *History of Presidential Elections.* New York, Macmillan Co., 1957.

Ross, Earl Dudley. *The Liberal Republican Movement*. New York, Henry Holt & Co., 1919.

Russo, Dorothy Ritter, and Sullivan, Thelma Lois. *Seven Authors of Crawfordsville, Indiana*. Indianapolis, Indiana Historical Society, 1952.

Sage, Leland L. *William Boyd Allison: A Study in Practical Politics*. Iowa City, State Historical Society of Iowa, 1956.

———. "The Clarksons of Indiana and Iowa," *Indiana Magazine of History*, 50 (1954), 429–46.

Sager, B. F. *The Harrison Mansion*. Vincennes, Indiana, issued by Francis Vigo Chapter, D.A.R., 1928.

Sandmeyer, Elmer Clarence. *The Anti-Chinese Movement in California*. Urbana, Ill., The University of Illinois Press, 1935.

Schurz, Carl. *The Reminiscences of Carl Schurz*. New York, The McClure Co., 1907–1908. 3 vols.

———. *Speeches, Correspondence, Political Papers*. New York, G. P. Putnam's Sons, 1913. 6 vols.

Scott, John W. *A History and Biographical Cyclopedia of Butler County, Ohio*. Cincinnati, Western Biographical Publishing Co., 1882.

Sherman, John. *Recollections of Forty Years in the House, Senate and Cabinet*. Chicago and New York, The Werner Co., 1896.

Sherman, William T. *Memoirs of General William T. Sherman*. New York, D. Appleton, 1875. 2 vols.

Sievers, Harry J. *Benjamin Harrison: Hoosier Warrior (1833–1865)*, Chicago, Henry Regnery Co., 1952.

———. "The Harrison Horror," Fort Wayne, Public Library of Fort Wayne and Allen County, 1956.

———. "A Historic Shrine," Indianapolis *Star Magazine*, October 19, 1952.

Smith, T. C. *Life of James Abram Garfield*. New Haven, Yale University Press, 1925. 2 vols.

Smith, Willard H. *Schuyler Colfax: The Changing Fortunes of a Political Idol*. Indianapolis, Indiana Historical Bureau, 1952.

Sousa, John Philip. *Marching Along*. Boston, Hale and Cushman, 1941.

Stackpole, E. J. *Behind the Scenes with a Newspaper Man*. New York, Lippincott, 1927.

Stampp, Kenneth. *Indiana Politics During the Civil War*. Indianapolis, Indiana Historical Bureau, 1949.

———. "The Milligan Case and the Election of 1864 in Indiana," *Mississippi Valley Historical Review*, 31 (1944–1945), 41–58.

Stanwood, Edward. *History of the Presidency*. Boston and New York, Houghton, Mifflin and Co., 1898.

The Statistics of the Population of the United States. Ninth Census, Vol. I, June 1, 1870. Washington, D. C., Government Printing Office, 1872.

Stealey, O. O. *130 Pen Pictures of Live Men.* New York, Publishers Printing Co., 1910.

Stephenson, Nathaniel W. *Nelson W. Aldrich: A Leader in American Politics.* New York, Charles Scribner's Sons, 1930.

Stidger, Felix F. *Treason History of the Order of the Sons of Liberty.* Chicago, privately published, 1903.

Stoddard, Henry L. *As I Knew Them: Presidents and Politics from Grant to Coolidge.* New York, Harper, 1927.

———. *Horace Greeley, Printer, Editor, Crusader.* New York, G. P. Putnam's Sons, 1946.

———. *Presidential Sweepstakes: The Story of Political Conventions and Campaigns.* Edited by Francis W. Leary. New York, G. P. Putnam's Sons, 1948.

Sulgrove, B. R. *History of Indianapolis and Marion County.* Philadelphia, L. H. Evarts and Co., 1884.

Swisher, C. B. *American Constitutional Development.* Boston, Houghton Mifflin, 1954.

Tansill, Charles Callan. *The Congressional Career of Thomas F. Bayard.* Washington, D. C., Georgetown University Press, 1946.

———. *The Foreign Policy of Thomas F. Bayard.* New York, Fordham University Press, 1940.

Tarbell, Ida. *The Tariff and Our Times.* New York, Macmillan, 1911.

Taussig, F. W. *The Tariff History of the United States.* New York, G. P. Putnam's Sons, 1923. 7th ed.

Taylor, Charles W. *The Bench and Bar in Indiana.* Indianapolis, Bench and Bar Publishing Co., 1895.

Thorndike, Rachel Sherman (editor). *The Sherman Letters.* New York, Scribner's, 1894.

Turpie, David. *Sketches of My Own Times.* Indianapolis, Bobbs, 1903

Tyner, Martha A. "Walter Q. Gresham," *Indiana Magazine of History,* 29 (1933), 297–338.

U.S. Civil Service Commission, *Fourth Annual Report, 1886–1887.* Washington, D. C., Government Printing Office, 1888.

U.S. Congress, House, *Messages and Foreign Relations, 1888.* 50th Cong., 2d Sess., 1888, House Ex. Doc. 1, pt. 1. Washington, D. C., Government Printing Office, 1888.

Van Bolt, Roger H. "The Rise of the Republican Party in Indiana," *Indiana Magazine of History,* 51 (1955), 185–220.

Volwiler, A. T. (editor). *The Correspondence Between Benjamin Harrison and James G. Blaine, 1882–1893.* Philadelphia, The American Philosophical Society, 1940.

———. "Tariff Strategy and Propaganda, 1887–1888," *American Historical Review,* 36 (1930), 76 ff.

Walker, Charles M. *Hovey and Chase.* Indianapolis, The Union Book Co., 1888.

———. *Sketch of the Life, Character and Public Services of Oliver P. Morton.* Indianapolis, Indianapolis Journal Press, 1878.

Wallace, Lew. *Life of Gen. Ben Harrison.* Philadelphia, Hubbard Bros., 1888.

Wanamaker, John. *Quayism in Pennsylvania Politics.* Philadelphia, Barse, 1898.

Warren, Charles. *The Supreme Court and the United States.* Boston, Little, Brown & Co., 1926. 2 vols.

"Wesler, Charlie, Reminiscences of," *Indiana History Bulletin,* 31 (1954), 111–12.

West, Richard S., Jr. *Admirals of the American Empire.* Indianapolis, Bobbs-Merrill, 1948.

Wheeler, Everett P. *Sixty Years of American Life, Taylor to Roosevelt, 1850–1910.* New York, E. P. Dutton & Co., 1917.

White, Horace. *Life of Lyman Trumbull.* Boston and New York, Houghton Mifflin, 1913.

White, Leonard D. *The Republican Era, 1869–1901.* New York, Macmillan, 1958.

White, William Allen. *Masks In A Pageant.* New York, Macmillan, 1928.

Williams, Charles R. *The Life of Rutherford Birchard Hayes.* Columbus, Ohio State Archaeological and Historical Society, 1928. 2 vols.

Wise, John S. *Recollections of Thirteen Presidents.* New York, Doubleday, 1906.

Woodward, C. Vann. *Origins of the New South, 1877–1913.* Baton Rouge, Louisiana State University Press, 1915.

Woodworth, Ruth. *Brochure of the History of the Harrison Home.* Indianapolis, privately printed, 1948.

World Almanac and Encyclopedia, 1894. New York, New York *World,* 1894.

World Almanac of 1949. New York, New York *World-Telegram,* 1949.

World Almanac of 1953. New York, New York *World-Telegram,* 1953.

Zimmerman, Charles. "The Origin and Rise of the Republican Party in Indiana, 1854–1860," *Indiana Magazine of History,* 13 (1917), 211–69, 349–412.

Index

Index

E

H

Habeas corpus, writ of, stays execution of Lambdin P. Milligan, 40

"Hail to the Chief," played as a salute to Harrison's nomination, 352

"Half-breeds," bury hatchet with stalwarts to support Harrison's 1888 candidacy, 382

Hale, Eugene, stumps Indiana in 1876 campaign, 116–17, n.24; impressed by Harrison's popularity, 122; desires Harrison to nominate Blaine at 1880 convention, 168; joins Harrison as freshman in the U.S. Senate, 195; aggressive leader in senatorial "School of Philosophy Club," 208

Halford, Colonel Elijah W., newspaper editor, first clerk for sub-committee on Indian Affairs, later becomes private secretary to Harrison, 275; commended by Harrison for "reliableness" and "trustworthiness," 325, n.89; strategically placed on Committee on Platform and Resolutions at 1888 convention, 332; drafts a party platform in harmony with Harrison's views, 341–42; diary entry describes Harrison on leaving Indianapolis for the inauguration, 428

Halpin, Maria, her affair with Cleveland aired during 1884 campaign, 254, n.29

Halstead, Murat, editor of Cincinnati *Commercial*, on Hayes' friendship for Harrison, 131; explores the Harrison-O. P. Morton relationship, 132–33; in 1880 preferred a Harrison-Hawley ticket, 172, n.60; alerts Harrison on clique opposing his senatorial candidacy, 186; calls Assistant Secretary of the Treasury John New "a damned fraud," 215; proofreads Harrison's campaign biography, 371; represents Harrison at Blaine's homecoming, 381; briefs Harrison on campaign trends, 390

Hampton, Wade, highly praised Harrison's first speech in Senate, 203; associated with Harrison in congressional investigation, 223, n.18

Hancock, General Winfield Scott, Democratic standard-bearer in 1880 presidential election, 173; beaten by Garfield for presidency in 1880, 182; loses Indiana by 7,600 votes, 413

Hanna, Bayless W., as Attorney General of Indiana prosecuted treasury frauds, 46–47

Hanna, John, U.S. Attorney, and Harrison's tax case, 11; associate defense counsel in Nancy Clem case, 24, n.26; his six-hour summation in second Clem trial received with silence, 28

Hanna, Mark, predicts Sherman's nomination by 1888 convention, 348

"Harmony dinner," sponsored by Depew, precedes conference and New York swing to Harrison, 345, n.60, 345–46

"Harmony meeting," 1880 political parley in New York City to unite Republicans behind Garfield, 174–75

Harrington, Henry W., Hoosier Greenback candidate for governor, 121

Harris, Addison C., joins coterie in Harrison's law office to await convention verdict, 353

Harrison, Anna, wife of President W. H. Harrison and grandmother of Benjamin, 145, 146, n.9

Harrison, Anna, sister of Benjamin Harrison, 18, n.62

Harrison, Benjamin, "the Signer," rôle in establishing State, War, and Navy Departments, Declaration of Independence and Constitution, xix; great-grandfather of Benjamin Harrison, prestige in colonial Virginia, xix, 20

Harrison, Benjamin, ancestry, xix ff., pioneer boyhood and education, xix, reads law, marries Carrie Scott (*q.v.*), his campus sweetheart, and settles in Indianapolis in 1854, xx; aligned with new Republican party, campaigns for Frémont, xx; city attorney of Indianapolis, secretary to Indiana Republican Central Committee, xx; elected Reporter of State Supreme Court, xx; commissioned second lieut. and musters 70th Ind. Vol. Inf. into Union service, xx; joins Sherman's army in battle for Atlanta, winning brigadier's star at Peach Tree Creek, xix, xxi; re-elected Supreme Court Reporter, xxi; at battle of Nashville and in the Carolinas, xx; leads the 70th in grand review in Washington, xxi; ideals as he enters an era of maturity, xix; homecoming and a hero's welcome, 4–6; physical characteristics at 32, 5; notes amazing growth in Hoosier capital, 6; new law partnership, 6–7; ambitions, happier home for wife and children, 7–8; social and church contacts, 8; economic adjustments eased by

P